Puerto Vallarta & Pacific Mexico

Ben Greensfelder
Michael Read

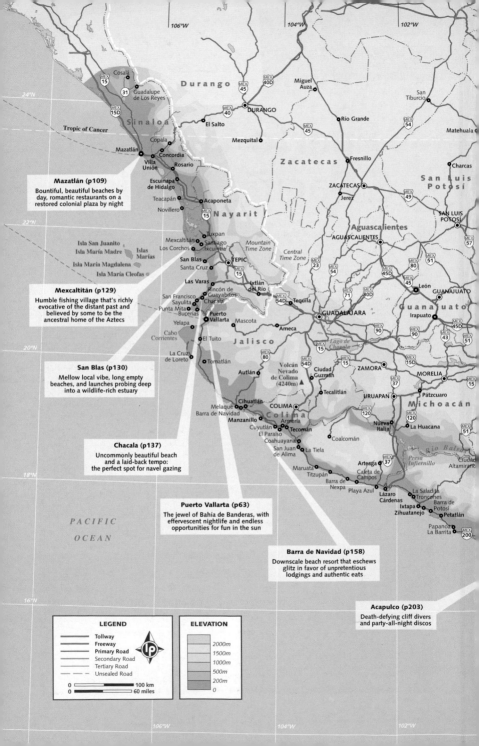

Mazatlán (p109)
Bountiful, beautiful beaches by day, romantic restaurants on a restored colonial plaza by night

Mexcaltitán (p129)
Humble fishing village that's richly evocative of the distant past and believed by some to be the ancestral home of the Aztecs

San Blas (p130)
Mellow local vibe, long empty beaches, and launches probing deep into a wildlife-rich estuary

Chacala (p137)
Uncommonly beautiful beach and a laid-back tempo: the perfect spot for navel gazing

Puerto Vallarta (p63)
The jewel of Bahía de Banderas, with effervescent nightlife and endless opportunities for fun in the sun

Barra de Navidad (p158)
Downscale beach resort that eschews glitz in favor of unpretentious lodgings and authentic eats

Acapulco (p203)
Death-defying cliff divers and party-all-night discos

LEGEND
Tollway
Freeway
Primary Road
Secondary Road
Tertiary Road
Unsealed Road

ELEVATION
2000m
1500m
1000m
500m
200m
0

0 —— 100 km
0 —— 60 miles

PACIFIC OCEAN

Oaxaca city (p224)
Fabulous art and food scenes, colonial architecture, bustling markets and first-rate handicrafts

Laguna de Manialtepec (p253)
Bird-watcher's paradise: a mangrove-lined tropical lagoon leading to the sea

Puerto Escondido (p244)
Mellow and civilized home of the Mexican Pipeline - an epic surf break

Monte Albán (p240)
Dramatically situated ruins that once held an amazing treasure trove

4

Bedazzling entertainment
lights up the night at
the Aquiles Serdán
Amphitheater,
Puerto Vallarta

ANTHONY PLUMMER

Mi Querido Pacífico

my beloved pacific

I f life is a beach, then *this* is living. Whether you live to linger undisturbed on a hidden stretch of honeyed sand or love to groove until dawn at a cosmopolitan resort-town nightclub, you'll find whatever floats your boat on Mexico's Pacific coast. This is a land of giant sunsets, mangrove-fringed lagoons, pristine bays, ramshackle fishing villages and eminently friendly folks, where sea turtles crawl ashore by the thousand on moonlit nights to lay their eggs. Just lounging around in the sand, you might look up to spot humpback whales breaching on the horizon, or a pod of dolphins surfacing just beyond the waves.

You can snorkel, surf, sail, ride horses, scuba dive, explore lagoons by boat, mountain bike along ocean cliffs and drink yourself silly (all in one day if you want). Or you can soak up the sun and read a book before indulging in the best spa treatment or full-body massage of your life. In many places you can do it all, making the central Pacific coast a great destination for families and groups of people who want to do different things on their vacation.

Spend a week in a fabulous beachfront guesthouse, where food and drink are prepared fresh daily, or embark on a harebrained road trip, bouncing down back roads to deserted beaches. You can take months exploring the coast on the cheap, roaring along the coastal highway in 2nd-class buses, or hanging onto the back of a pickup packed with locals on your way to a fishing village where they still string fishing nets by hand.

But whatever you do, don't forget your swimsuit. MICHAEL READ

A storm masses off Playa Olas Altas (p69), Puerto Vallarta

ANTHONY PLUMMER

Myths & Magic

NAME	Luz Elena Cruz
AGE	Timeless
OCCUPATION	Travel writer, *Ocho Columnas* newspaper
RESIDENCE	Guadalajara

'Almost every beach, pueblo or city along the coast offers something that separates it from the rest. The only thing they share in common is the magic that underlies this natural beauty.'

'I have the distinct fortune of knowing many of the beaches along Mexico's Pacific coast – all of which are different, each with its own special enchantment. 'Paradise' is probably the best way to describe it. Up and down the coast you'll find these unknown, deserted beaches where nature is allowed to take her course. And, well, the views are unimaginable.

'Puerto Vallarta (p63) is another story altogether, a cosmopolitan city that maintains a small-town feel. Cobblestone streets, houses with red roofs and white walls, the church and incredible art from around the world – it's all here. And it's a real treat to walk on the *malecón* (waterfront street; p75) and be able to see and touch the sculptures.

'For its part, mythic Acapulco (p203) offers some of the best sunsets around. Almost every beach, pueblo or city along the coast offers something that separates it from the rest. The only thing they have in common is the magic that underlies this natural beauty.' AS RELATED TO GREG BENCHWICK

The arches at Aquiles Serdán Amphitheater (p75) silhouetted against the dawn sky
ANTHONY PLUMMER

A Papantla Flyer (p76) cleaves the evening air, enacting an ancient ritual
ANTHONY PLUMMER

SPECTACULAR ESTUARY TRIPS

Parque Nacional Lagunas de Chacahua (p243) A birder's paradise, these lagoons along the Oaxaca coast offer glimpses of myriad avian species. Crocodiles and turtles also call this place home.

Barra de Potosí (p196) A stone's throw from the glitz and glam of Ixtapa, Barra de Potosí offers a tranquil respite and great wildlife-watching. Visitors can chat with local fishermen as they ply the waters of the mangrove-lined Laguna de Potosí.

San Blas (p130) Don't let the *jejenes* (sand flies) discourage you from visiting this cozy hamlet. With isolated beaches, good surf and bungalow-bill–style riverboat excursions, there's something for everyone.

A volleyballer takes a break on Playa de los Muertos (p69), Puerto Vallarta
ANTHONY PLUMMER

The Pacific coast is renowned for its fishing (p48) and its teeming marine life

JOHN NEUBAUER

Angelfish and filigrees of coral bejewel the waters off Isla Ixtapa (p183)

PIERCE & NEWMAN

CHARGE IT!

Top surfing picks

Bahía de Matanchén (p132) 'The world's longest wave,' according to the folks at Guinness, this roller near San Blas has taken surfers on rides longer than a mile – you might want to bring a *cerveza* (beer) out to the lineup to thoroughly enjoy this magic carpet ride.

Mexican Pipeline (p248) Lock, stock and one very big smoking barrel, this Puerto Escondido fave drops you hard and fast – a board-breaker's delight.

Playa Incognito There are so many beaches along the Pacific that it's impossible to list all the good breaks (though we give it a fair shot; see Map p49), and some undiscovered treasures certainly still exist. Take your nearest beach exit and see what lady luck turns up.

Finding Life from the Sea

NAME	Alejandro Sanchez
AGE	35
OCCUPATION	Dive master
RESIDENCE	Puerto Vallarta

'I've been diving for 22 years around the Bahía de Banderas (p74). I guess you can call it my backyard. One of the main attractions is Los Arcos (p73), an underwater national park. It's so pretty, so full of fish. In April the giant manta ray comes to these waters to mate. And there are also many colorful species of fish (p50), like the Cortez angelfish, the Mexican night sergeant, trumpet fish, eagle rays, sting rays. The waters are incredibly clear and tranquil. And the beaches are just beautiful.

'I love everything that has anything to do with this area, everything about the sea. It's my life.'

'Right now one of the most popular things around is the canopy tour (p77). Or you can take a walk along the banks of the rivers, way up. It's just gorgeous.

'The area around the Bahía de Banderas is protected by the Sierra Madre Occidental. These lovely, towering mountains are green almost year round...'

AS RELATED TO GREG BENCHWICK

Watch the sun sink below the horizon from Playa de los Muertos (p69)
ANTHONY PLUMMER

Age-Old Traditions & Modern Currents

NAME	Rámon Álvarez
AGE	31
OCCUPATION	Chef, Café des Artistes
RESIDENCE	Puerto Vallarta

'To talk about Mexican cuisine (p55) is to talk about a very great tradition. It's something for me – well, how can I say it? – 'es lo máximo,' the best. Not just because I'm Mexican, but because it is at the root of our culture – moles, salsas, *fritangas*, tortillas, *maiz*. It's really such a pleasure to be part of this. And I feel lucky knowing how to make this wide variety of Mexican specialties.

'One of the towns that forms part of Mexico's rich culture is Oaxaca (p224). Its traditions are very impressive and its cuisine is so varied. In some dishes they even use insects, something that is truly phenomenal to me.

'*La nueva cocina mexicana* (new Mexican cuisine; p58) is truly great. It's opening our doors to other countries. We should really appreciate and value this and, as Mexicans, hold our heads high in this achievement. It's worthy of praise.'

AS RELATED TO GREG BENCHWICK

Sample the mezcal at one of Oaxaca's oldest bars, La Casa del Mezcal (p236)

GREG ELMS

Food, clothes or handicrafts – Pacific coast markets (p287) sell a bit of everything
GREG ELMS

A brass band warms up for Fiesta de San Patricio (p157) in San Patricio-Melaque
MARGIE POLITZER

The tower of Puerto Vallarta's cathedral (p72) is capped by an audacious crown
ANTHONY PLUMMER

Explore the Past

NAME	Eric Van Young, PhD
AGE	60
OCCUPATION	Mexican historian at the University of California, San Diego
RESIDENCE	San Diego, California

'The scene of a lot of political and social upheaval, in some ways, the Pacific coast has been central to Mexico's history. The major indigenous civilization was the Tarascos, now known as the Purépecha (p28). A culture as highly evolved as the Aztecs, they dominated the western area of Mexico to the coast. There were other indigenous people – the Mayo and Yaqui – that were found on the coast, but their culture was far less developed.

'The initial conquest of the coast was unusually brutal. A companion of Hernán Cortés, Nuño de Guzmán, was at one point in charge of the exploration of the western coastal areas. A bit of a loose cannon, he enslaved a lot of the people and left kind of a nasty taste with the indigenous people there. The Pacific coast is romantic and remote, and in many ways it is like a paradise. Nayarit (p127) and Sonora are full of picturesque fishing villages. As you go south into Michoacán (p171) and Guerrero, it gets more and more lush and more tropical. There was a lot of slavery down there, and there are some areas that still bear a remarkably African cultural imprint even to this day.' AS RELATED TO GREG BENCHWICK

Huazolotitlán (p243), a village in Guerrero, is famous for its colorful masks

JOHN NEUBAUER

Journey back in time at the ancient Zapotec city of Monte Albán (p240) in Oaxaca

RICHARD I'ANSON

Contents

Regional Map Contents

Mazatlán p110
Nayarit p128
Puerto Vallarta p64
Jalisco, Colima & Michoacán Coasts p148
Ixtapa, Zihuatanejo & the Costa Grande p178
Acapulco & the Costa Chica p200
Oaxaca pp222-3

The Authors

MICHAEL READ
Puerto Vallarta, Mazatlán, Nayarit, Jalisco

Michael can conjugate many Spanish verbs in the present, past imperfect and, most importantly, the imperative. Having never made good on his threat to set up housekeeping south of the border, he takes every opportunity to head south from his Oakland, California, home to delve deeper into Mexico's marvelous mysteries. Having done hard time pushing pixels around for LonelyPlanet.com, in 2003 Michael succumbed to a burning case of wanderlust and hit the road as a full-time travel writer. Since then he's contributed nearly half a million words to Lonely Planet guidebooks, including *Mexico*.

My Pacific Mexico
I roll out of bed early – 9am is considered early in Puerto Vallarta – and slip down to my favorite café in the Zona Romántica, the Café San Angel (p90), for a strong coffee sweetened immoderately with Kahlua. While many visitors prefer the effervescent pleasures of town, my personal proclivities point me to a remote beach where I can ponder the horizon or gaze at my navel. I head to the pler at Playa de Los Muertos (p69) and hop on a water taxi headed to Quimixto (p107), 30 minutes away by sea. After an economical lunch of octopus *tostadas* and some sun worship on the fine beach, I enjoy an easy half-hour hike through tropical forest to an inland waterfall. Along the way I spy a meter-long iguana passing stealthily through the branches of a rubber tree. Back in Vallarta, I splurge on a well-deserved massage at Hotel Molina de Agua (p84) before sauntering back to my room for a siesta.

BEN GREENSFELDER
Ixtapa, Acapulco, Oaxaca

A native Northern Californian, Ben first saw Mexico in 1964 on a family road trip to Álamos, Sonora. Since then he's been back more than a dozen times, including six visits in the last six years for Lonely Planet projects. Each time, the marvelous country reveals more of itself, leaving Ben eager to return and explore further. He lives in Oregon with his wife of 13 years, the tireless Lonely Planet author Sandra Bao.

LONELY PLANET AUTHORS

Why is our travel information the best in the world? It's simple: our authors are independent, dedicated travelers. They don't research using just the Internet or phone, and they don't take freebies in exchange for positive coverage. They travel widely, to all the popular spots and off the beaten track. They personally visit thousands of hotels, restaurants, cafés, bars, galleries, palaces, museums and more – and they take pride in getting all the details right, and telling it how it is. For more, see the authors section on www.lonelyplanet.com.

CONTRIBUTING AUTHORS

Carolina A Miranda (The Culture) Though of South American origin, Carolina has spent numerous vacations wandering through Mexico listening to *rancheras* (classical Mexican country music), reading Octavio Paz and picking up the trade secrets to cooking a killer mole. She was the lead author on Lonely Planet's *Costa Rica* and a contributor to *Central America on a Shoestring*. She lives in New York City with her husband, Ed Tahaney.

James W Peyton (Food & Drink) James has written three books and countless magazine articles on Mexican cooking. He appears on TV, conducts cooking classes, and lectures on Mexican cuisine. He also maintains a website (www.lomexicano.com) providing information about Mexico and Mexican cooking, and consults on recipe development for the Mexican food industry. His latest book is Jim Peyton's *New Cooking from Old Mexico*.

David Goldberg MD (Health) David completed his training in internal medicine and infectious diseases at Columbia-Presbyterian Medical Center in New York City, where he has also served as voluntary faculty. He is an infectious diseases specialist in Scarsdale, New York, and the editor-in-chief of the website MDTravelHealth.com.

Getting Started

Traveling in Mexico requires little planning. You can just get on the plane or bus or into your car and go! You'll rarely have trouble finding suitable accommodation on any budget, and travel by road or plane within Mexico is easy. If you have limited time and specific goals, work out a detailed itinerary and reserve accommodations in advance. If this is your first trip to Mexico, be ready for more crowds, noise, bustle and poverty than you might be accustomed to. But don't worry – most Mexicans will be only too happy to help you feel at home in their country. Invest a little time before your trip in learning even just a few phrases of Spanish – every word you know will make your trip that little bit easier and more enjoyable.

WHEN TO GO
The tropic of Cancer cuts across Mexico just north of Mazatlán, so this stretch of coast is officially tropical. The driest months, when it may not rain at all, are from November to April. These months are also the coolest, with temperatures averaging a comfortable 26° to 29°C.

The hottest months, May to October, are also the wettest, and the hottest and wettest of all are June, July and August. Rainfall increases as you move south from Mazatlán toward Acapulco, with Acapulco receiving twice as much rain as Mazatlán. The Oaxaca coast is drier but closer in average rainfall to Acapulco than Mazatlán. May to October are also extremely humid, and it's generally more humid the further south you move.

See climate charts (p280) for more information.

The peak holiday periods are July and August, mid-December to early January, and a week either side of Easter. At these times, resorts attract big tourist crowds, room prices go up, and rooms and public transport are heavily booked, so reservations are recommended. November to April are reliably dry, warm, blissful and popular months for travel among North Americans and Europeans.

DON'T LEAVE HOME WITHOUT...

- Adequate insurance (p284)
- All the necessary paperwork if you're driving (p295)
- Waterproof sandals if you'll be boating
- Clothes to cope with Mexico's climatic variations and air-conditioned and non-air-conditioned rooms (and buses)
- Any specific toiletries you require, including contact-lens solutions and contraceptives, as these can be difficult to obtain in Mexico; also consider carrying a copy of prescriptions for any medications you will take with you – this might save you from scrutiny at customs
- A flashlight for some of those not-so-well-lit streets and stairways – and for power outages
- An inconspicuous container for money and valuables, such as a small, slim wallet or an under-the-clothes pouch or money belt (p281)
- Sun protection: a hat, sunglasses and sunscreen
- A small padlock
- A small Spanish dictionary and/or phrasebook
- A backpack for carrying it all – you can make it reasonably theft-proof with small padlocks; a light daypack, too, is useful

TOP TENS

Adventures

Adventure tourism is a burgeoning industry, with countless options for outdoor enthusiasts, including the following:

- Surfing the big Pacific waves at Puerto Escondido (p247)
- Volunteering with sea-turtle ecologists in Playa San Francisco (p143)
- Bird-watching on tropical Laguna de Manialtepec (p253)
- Boating through tropical mangroves to La Tovara (p132)
- Mountain biking in the hills overlooking Bahía de Banderas (p75)

- Sharing the seas with whales or dolphins on Bahía de Banderas (p74)
- Scuba diving in the gorgeous waters of Manzanillo (p164)
- Going after marlin, sailfish or other fierce fighters from a Zihuatanejo charter boat (p190)
- Exploring the superb hilltop ruins and tombs of Monte Albán (p240)
- Cloud-forest hiking in the gorgeous Biosphere Manantitlán (p165)

Festivals & Events

You'll really catch the Mexican mood at these events.

- Torneo Internacional de Pesca, a big-money international fishing tournament, rouses Barra de Navidad (p160) from its slumber in late January
- The commemoration of Father José María Mercado livens up San Blas (p133) on January 31 with a parade, a march by the Mexican navy and fireworks
- Carnaval (Carnival), the week leading up to Ash Wednesday, in late February or early March, is celebrated most vividly in Mazatlán (p118)
- Semana Santa (Holy Week), Palm Sunday to Easter Sunday, is particularly colorful in Puerto Vallarta (p77) and Acapulco (p211)
- The Fiesta de San Pedro Apóstol, held on June 29, celebrates the patron saint of fishing and brings a beautiful pageant to the ancient shrimping village of Mexcaltitán (p130)

- Guelaguetza, held in Oaxaca city (p230) on the first two Mondays after July 16, is a brilliant feast of Oaxacan folk dance
- The Sinaloa Fiesta de los Artes brings a series of cultural events to Mazatlán's beautiful Teatro Angela Peralta from late October through mid-November (p118)
- The Festival de los Artes, Film Festival and Gourmet Festival dominate the cultural calendar in Puerto Vallarta (p77) each year in November
- Día de Muertos (p231; Day of the Dead) is a big event in Oaxaca city, with music and dance at the main cemetery on November 2
- The festival for the Virgen de Guadalupe (p211) is celebrated by all of Mexico on December 11 to 12, but it's particularly vivid in Acapulco

The water on Mexico's Pacific coast is perfect for swimming all year long. Diving and snorkeling can be good year-round, but visibility is usually highest (except during plankton blooms) in the dry winter months. Fun surf can be reasonably expected year-round, but waves are biggest from May through to November. Deep-sea fishing, also practiced all year, has its own species-specific seasons (see p48). Bird-watchers often prefer winter visits, when birds migrate down to the coastal lagoons from North America. Whale-watching is best from January to March.

TOP TENS

Must-See Movies

Mexico has inspired Mexicans and non-Mexicans alike to make great films here.

- *The Night of the Iguana* (1964) If you've been skeptical as to whether Puerto Vallarta was ever *really* a humble fishing village, this enjoyable Elizabeth Taylor and Richard Burton romp by director John Huston will set you straight.

- *Y tu mamá también* (And Your Mother Too; 2001) Alfonso Cuarón's terrifically entertaining road movie made a star of Gael García Bernal.

- *Frida* (2002) Atmospheric Hollywood Kahlo biopic starring Salma Hayek.

- *Amores perros* (Love's a Bitch; 2000) Alejandro González Iñárritu's raw, groundbreaking movie of modern Mexico City life.

- *Traffic* (2000) Steven Soderbergh's cross-border drug movie with Michael Douglas, Catherine Zeta-Jones and Benicio del Toro; don't watch this the night before you leave for Mexico.

- *Puerto Escondido* (1992) Wry, funny travel-and-crime movie directed by Italy's Gabriele Salvatores.

- *Viva Zapata!* (1952) Marlon Brando and Anthony Quinn star in Elia Kazan's romanticized version of the revolutionary's life.

- *The Treasure of the Sierra Madre* (1948) Bogart gets gold fever in Huston's greed-stoked adventure.

- *El Mariachi* (1992) Legendary low-budget action film, shot by Robert Rodriguez in two weeks for US$7000, about a wandering musician (Carlos Gallardo) who gets mixed up in mob violence.

- *Scooby Doo and the Monster of Mexico* (2002) Scooby, Shaggy and the gang head to Mexico to prevent the ghoulish El Chupacabra from disrupting the Day of the Dead celebration.

COSTS & MONEY

On Mexico's Pacific coast, a frugal budget traveler can pay about US$20 to US$35 a day by camping or staying in budget accommodations and eating two to three meals a day in the cheapest restaurants. Add in other costs (snacks, purified water, entry to archaeological sites, long-distance buses etc), and you'll be up to US$35 to US$50 a day. If you share rooms, costs per person drop considerably.

In the midrange you can live well for US$50 to US$70 per person per day. In most places two people can easily find a clean, modern room with private bathroom and TV for US$30 to US$50.

At the top of the scale are hotels and resorts charging anywhere from US$100 to US$300, and restaurants where you pay US$30 to US$50 per person. However, you can still get a plush room for US$50 to US$75 and eat well for US$20 to US$40 per person per day.

These figures do not take into account expenses such as internal airfares or car rentals – not to mention heavy tequila consumption, disco admissions and shopping, which you should certainly budget for.

HOW MUCH?

Coco frío (fresh coconut) US$1

Internet per hour US$1-2

Corona beer US$2

Street taco US$0.50-1

Local small car rental US$50-60

TRAVEL LITERATURE

Few travel books stick solely to the subject of Pacific Mexico, but several books deal with the country as a whole and make great reading on any trip to Mexico.

Expatriate memoirist Tony Cohan rambles around Mexico to 'see how the puzzle of old and new fit together' in *Mexican Days: Journey into the Heart of Mexico* (2006). In the style of *Mexican Days* (2000), Cohan deftly travels the literary territories of history, contemporary life and old-fashioned journalism.

The Mexico Reader: History, Culture, Politics (2003) is a massive compilation of articles, essays, poetry and photographs providing an encompassing introduction to the history and culture of Mexico.

British writer Isabella Tree takes peyote with the Huicholes and meets the matriarch of Juchitán in *Sliced Iguana: Travels in Unknown Mexico* (2001), a warm, perceptive account of Mexico and its indigenous cultures.

The People's Guide to Mexico by Carl Franz (12th edition, 2002) has for 30 years been an invaluable, amusing resource for anyone on an extended trip. It doesn't attempt hotel, transport or sightseeing specifics but does provide a great all-round introduction to Mexico.

Carlos Castaneda's *Don Juan* series, which reached serious cult status in the 1970s, tells of a North American's experiences with a peyote guru in northwestern Mexico.

The 1990s saw the release of some excellent new English-language novels set in Mexico. Cormac McCarthy's *All the Pretty Horses* is the laconic, tense and poetic tale of three young latter-day cowboys riding south of the border. James Maw's *Year of the Jaguar* takes its youthful English protagonist in search of the father he has never met, from the US border to Chiapas – a book that catches the feel of Mexican travel superbly.

For information on Mexican literature, see p37.

'The 1990s saw the release of some excellent new English-language novels set in Mexico.'

INTERNET RESOURCES

Lanic (http://lanic.utexas.edu/la/mexico/) Best broad collection of Mexico links, from the University of Texas.

LonelyPlanet.com (www.lonelyplanet.com) Succinct summaries on travel in Mexico; the popular Thorn Tree bulletin board; travel news.

Lords of the Earth (www.mayalords.org) A fascinating repository of research into Mexico's ancient civilizations.

Mexican Wave (www.mexicanwave.com) 'Europe's gateway to Mexico,' a treasure trove of travel, culture and food-related material.

Mexico Connect (www.mexconnect.com) Packed with news, message and chat boards, accommodation information, articles and an endless variety of other content and links.

Mexico Tourism Board (www.visitmexico.com) Worth a peek.

Mexperience (www.mexperience.com) Full of valuable information for travel to and within Mexico.

Planeta.com (www.planeta.com) Great articles and listings for anyone interested in Mexico's ecology.

Tomzap's Pacific Coast of Mexico (www.tomzap.com) For fun, quirky and extensive information about the coasts of Jalisco, Colima and Oaxaca.

Itineraries

CLASSIC ROUTES

BUMMING AROUND
ON BAHÍA DE BANDERAS   One Week / Puerto Vallarta & Around

Spend up to three days in **Puerto Vallarta** (p63). Stroll on **Isla Río Cuale** (p72) in the morning, along **Playa de los Muertos** (p69) in the afternoon, and along the **malecón** (p75) at dusk, noting the grand **public sculptures** (p75).

Spend a day **mountain biking** (p75), **horseback riding** (p74) or **scuba diving** (p73). Or shop for **Huichol crafts** (p93) and hit the **art galleries** (p95). Sample the robust **cuisine scene** (p85) and an explosive **dance club** (p91).

Head south to **Mismaloya** (p104) for its fine beach and the stellar snor-keling around **Los Arcos** (p105), a marine park and ecological preserve. Amble into Mismaloya village for **tequila tasting** and **demonstrations** (p104), or for lunch in a **jungle restaurant** (p105).

From nearby **Boca de Tomatlán** (p106) catch a water taxi to **Yelapa** (p107) and sleep in an elegant candlelit hotel. Next morning rent a horse or hike to beaches or waterfalls.

Alternatively, head north to the understated pleasures of **Bucerías** (p97), or get back to basics in the fishing village of **La Cruz de Huanacaxtle** (p100). You might even make it to **Punta de Mita** (p102) for some **surfing action** (p102).

If you've only got a week, there's no reason to leave the sunny embrace of Puerto Vallarta's beautiful Bahía de Banderas; this trip is a mere 74km.

THE BEST OF THE PACIFIC COAST   Three Weeks / Mazatlán to Acapulco

Get your bearings in **Mazatlán** (p109), lingering only long enough to enjoy a romantic evening on Plazuela Machado. Heading south, develop a taste for idleness in the ancient fishing village of **Mexcaltitán** (p129). From **San Blas** (p130) head by boat into gorgeous mangrove wetlands or sharpen your surfing skills on Bahía de Matanchén. Why not lose a few days on the beautiful cove at **Chacala** (p137) or witness a baby-turtle release in **Playa San Francisco** (p143)?

Empty your wallet of pesos in **Puerto Vallarta** (p63), enjoying world-class dining, shopping and an all-around good time. Pause for a week of Spanish instruction in beautiful **La Manzanilla** (p153) or head to **Barra de Navidad** (p158) to relax with a book or venture by boat into the lagoon. Drop in to **Manzanillo** (p162) for some world-class scuba diving or just to enjoy the ambience of the newly gussied-up downtown waterfront.

Continue south into the wilds of Michoacán, stopping first at gorgeous **Playa Maruata** (p174), where black sea turtles come ashore nightly in season. At laid-back **Barra de Nexpa** (p174) assume the life of a surfer dude while enjoying world-class waves.

Continue your beach-happy existence in Ixtapa at tiny **Barra de Potosí** (p196), a quiet gem of a town with good scuba diving and opportunities for ecotourism. You should be wonderfully well-rested by now, and ready for the bright lights and resort-town decadence of **Acapulco** (p203).

This madcap 1409km long-haul journey appeals to never-say-die road warriors with time to spare and living to do. You'll get your fill of fun, sun and sand while getting up close and personal with the coast's most beguiling towns.

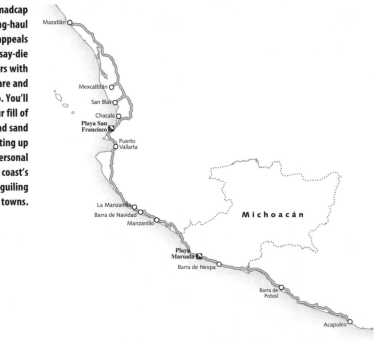

ROADS LESS TRAVELED

WANDERING AROUND OAXACA   Two or Three Weeks / Oaxaca City & Back

Before seeking out roads less traveled, spend a few days on the streets of **Oaxaca city** (p224) enjoying the cuisine, first-class museums and galleries, and exemplary handicrafts shopping. Take a day trip to the ancient Zapotec capital of **Monte Albán** (p240), one of Mexico's most impressive ancient sites.

Head south on the spectacular, winding Hwy 175, climbing high into mountainous pine forests then dropping precipitously to **Pochutla** (p254), gateway to the beach towns of **Puerto Ángel** (p255), **Mazunte** (p263) and **Zipolite** (p258). All have wonderful beaches and ample accommodation.

The westerly coastal route of Hwy 200 leads to **Puerto Escondido** (p244), where the big draws are astounding waves and, naturally, amazing surf action. Nearby, **Lagunas Los Naranjos and Palmazola** (p254) boast abundant birdlife and a local crocodile population. Bird lovers will want to go even further, to the **Laguna de Manialtepec** (p253), where roseate spoonbills are common, and to the **Parque Nacional Lagunas de Chacahua** (p243), where mangrove-fringed islands harbor numerous exotics.

Backtrack to **Bahías de Huatulco** (p265), and take your pick of beautiful beaches backed by forest. Surfers will love the right-hand point break at **Barra de la Cruz** (p273). Continue on to the sweaty, low-country **Isthmus of Tehuantepec** (p273), where Zapotec culture is strong and gringos are few. Visit the towns of **Tehuantepec** (p274) and **Juchitán** (p275) and the ancient Zapotec fortress of **Guiengola** (p275). From here, return to Oaxaca city on Hwy 190.

Oaxaca's got it all: a beautiful and artistic capital, pre-Hispanic towns and a spectacular, varied landscape. This 750km expedition gets you deep into the thick of it and out again.

TAILORED TRIPS

TURTLE TRIPPING

Mexico's Pacific coast teems with sea turtles. Start your turtle tripping in **Playa San Francisco** (p142), home to the Grupo Ecológico de la Costa Verde, which offers volunteer opportunities and releases more than 25,000 hatchlings each year. In **Cuyutlán** (p170), the Centro Tortuguero operates a thriving turtle-release program. Head into the wilds of Michoacán, where at **Playa Maruata** (p174) black turtles come ashore nightly from June to December to lay their eggs. Turtle-spotting tours on Bahía Prin-

cipal near **Puerto Escondido** (p244) often sight the elusive loggerhead turtle. Once the site of large-scale turtle slaughter, today **San Agustinillo** (p261) is known for its turtle-viewing boat trips and ecotourism ethos. In nearby **Mazunte** (p263) is the Centro Méxicano de la Tortuga, a turtle aquarium and research center. And finally, on **Bahías de Huatulco** (p265) the area's dive sites feature frequent turtle encounters.

SURFING SAFARI

With powerful waves curling into the coast's sand-rimmed bays, it's no wonder the region has attained legendary status among surfers.

South of San Blas, **Bahía de Matanchén** (p132) receives amazingly long waves in September and October, while mellow but satisfying surfing can also be had at **Playa San Francisco** (p142) and **Sayulita** (p144). On the northern tip of Bahía de Banderas, **Playa El Anclote** (p102) offers a potent point break.

Continuing south, **Playa Boca de Pascuales** (p171) is a legendary spot with aggressive barrel swells up to 5m. Deep in Michoacán are more affable – but still challenging – waves at the gorgeous **Playa La Ticla** (p173). A well-established scene in **Barra de Nexpa** (p174) celebrates point-break waves curling in from

the left, some allowing rides as long as 150m.

Further south in Ixtapa, the beaches near **Troncones** (p179) feature more than a dozen breaks. But the most famous surfing locale on the Pacific Coast is **Puerto Escondido** (p247), where you'll find waves to challenge beginners and experts alike. The biggest of these, at Zicatela, offers serious punishment to all but the most experienced surfers. You have been warned!

Snapshot

In a country where nearly 35 million live on US$2 per day, and another 35 million live on a just over US$7 per day, poverty continues to be one of Mexico's most daunting problems. By any measure, the country's political and social institutions have failed to provide upward mobility for its neediest citizens. Against this backdrop, at a time when Latin America is swinging convincingly to the left, Mexico was preparing for its July 2006 general election as this book went to press. The outcome will replace outgoing leader Vicente Fox.

The race was expected to be closely contested, with the Partido Acción Nacional (PAN; National Action Party) and its candidate, Felipe Calderón, intent on winning the presidency a second time, and the Partido de la Revolución Democrática (PRD; Party of the Democratic Revolution), now in coalition with the Partido Verde Ecologista de México (PVEM; Ecologist Green Party) and led by Mexico City mayor Andres Manuel López Obrador, equally dedicated to regaining the office it lost in the 2000 election.

With a campaign slogan of *Por el bien de todos, primero los pobres* (For the welfare of all, the poor first), the popular López Obrador had built a convincing advantage in opinion polls by proposing dramatic increases in social spending to attack pervasive poverty that he says has been exacerbated by Fox's pro-market reforms. Striking a nationalistic chord, he has signaled that he favors slowing down efforts to open the economy to foreign investors. López Obrador's opponent Felipe Calderón, in contrast, is known his for conservative business and social positions.

As you travel on Mexico's Pacific coast you may come into contact with extreme poverty, but by and large the region – and particularly its beach resorts – is fairly prosperous. Tourism, the second-largest employer in Mexico and one of the economic mainstays of the Pacific coast, keeps the local economies humming. This is particularly true in Sinaloa, Jalisco and Guerrero, home to the coast's three biggest resort towns: Mazatlán, Puerto Vallarta and Acapulco.

Most of the Pacific coast, however, relies heavily on livestock and agriculture, especially the states of Jalisco, Nayarit and Colima. Jalisco is Mexico's primary grain producer and Nayarit accounts for most of the country's tobacco production. Vegetable and tropical fruit crops are grown throughout Jalisco and Colima as well as in Michoacán, Guerrero and Oaxaca. Sinaloa's main export is shrimp.

Timber products have been a rapidly growing sector of the Pacific economy since the passage of Nafta (North American Free Trade Agreement) in 1994, which opened *ejidos* (peasant landholding cooperatives) to multinational corporations. The country's best coffee is produced in Colima and particularly in Oaxaca; in both states it forms a significant sector of the economy.

FAST FACTS

Population: 106 million

Mestizo population: 12.7 million

Type of government: federal republic

Dominant religion: Roman catholic (89%)

Dominant political parties: Institutional Revolutionary Party (PRI), the National Action Party (PAN), and the Party of the Democratic Revolution (PRD)

Literacy rate: 92% (US 99%)

GDP per person: US$9666 (as compared to US$43,555 per person in the US)

Foreign tourists entering Mexico per year: 20 million

Year that laws were enacted to protect sea turtles: 1988

Estimated number of sea-turtle eggs poached on Mexican beaches in 2005: 50,000

History

Mexico's story is always extraordinary, at times barely credible. From the awesome ancient cities to the gorgeous colonial palaces, the superb museums and the deep-rooted traditions and beliefs of the Mexicans themselves – be they the mixed-ancestry mestizos or the millions of direct indigenous descendants of the ancient civilizations – Mexico's ever-present past will never fail to enrich your journey.

FIRST AMERICANS

It's accepted that, barring a few Vikings in the north and some possible direct trans-Pacific contact with Southeast Asia, the pre-Hispanic inhabitants of the Americas arrived from Siberia. They came in several migrations between perhaps 60,000 BC and 8000 BC, during the last Ice Age, crossing land now submerged beneath the Bering Strait. The earliest human traces in Mexico date from about 20,000 BC. These first Mexicans hunted big animal herds in the grasslands of the highland valleys. When temperatures rose at the end of the Ice Age, the valleys became drier, ceasing to support such animal life and forcing the people to derive more food from plants.

Archaeologists have traced the slow beginnings of agriculture in the Tehuacán valley in Puebla state, where, soon after 6500 BC, people were planting seeds of chili and a kind of squash. Between 5000 BC and 3500 BC they started to plant mutant forms of a tiny wild maize and to grind the maize into meal. After 3500 BC, beans and a much better variety of maize enabled the Tehuacán valley people to live semipermanently in villages. Pottery appeared around 2500 BC, and some of the oldest finds in Mexico are from sites near Acapulco.

PRECLASSIC PERIOD (1500 BC–AD 250)
Olmecs

Perhaps the oldest Mesoamerican culture of dramatic scale belongs to the Olmecs, who lived near the Gulf Coast in the humid lowlands of southern Veracruz and neighboring Tabasco from 1200 BC to around 600 BC. Their civilization is famed for the awesome 'Olmec heads,' stone sculptures up to 3m high with grim, pug-nosed faces combining the features of human babies and jaguars, a mixture referred to as the 'were-jaguar,' and wearing curious helmets.

The two great Olmec centers, San Lorenzo in Veracruz and La Venta in Tabasco, were violently destroyed by marauding invaders from Oaxaca. But Olmec art and religion, and quite possibly Olmec social organization, strongly influenced later Mexican civilizations.

Pacific Mexico

Western Mexico, and the southern states of Michoacán and Guerrero, are very much shrouded in mystery. Until the 1940s the area was all but ignored by archaeologists, probably because it lacked the grand architecture, writing systems and dramatic religious deities that attracted

In addition to general information, www .mexonline.com hosts a good index of Mexican history links.

Mexico: From the Olmecs to the Aztecs by Michael D Coe gives a concise, learned and well-illustrated picture of ancient Mexico's great cultures.

TIMELINE

20,000 BC or earlier	1200 –600 BC
First humans in Mexico	Olmec civilization

researchers to the rest of Mesoamerica. Archaeological sites went unexcavated and unprotected for decades, and most were looted down the years by nonarchaeologists who sold their findings – primarily ceramics – to collectors. When study of the region's ancient past began in earnest, archaeologists faced the challenges of drawing conclusions from sites that no longer existed as left by their original inhabitants.

From Sinaloa south to the state of Guerrero, people lived in small, independent villages and chiefdoms, most, it is believed, with a distinct culture and language. Except for Guerrero, western Preclassic Mexico remained relatively isolated from the rest of Mesoamerica. The areas of present-day Nayarit, Jalisco and Colima – collectively referred to as West Mexico – have a quite distinct history. Archaeologists and art historians treat West Mexico as a unified region, which is defined by its tradition of shaft or chamber tombs, underground burial chambers at the base of shafts 2m to 16m deep. The oldest of these have been dated as far back as 1900 BC, but the most significant were probably built between 1500 BC and 800 BC. Much of what is known of the cultures of West Mexico is based on the excavation of these tombs and analysis of the clay sculptures and vessels found within, some of which can be viewed at the Museo Regional de Nayarit (p135) in Tepic.

The highly interactive website www .ancientmexico.com offers a terrific breadth of material on the art, culture and history of ancient Mesoamerica.

EARLY MONTE ALBÁN
By 300 BC settled village life, based on agriculture and hunting, had developed throughout the southern half of Mexico. Monte Albán, the hilltop center of the Zapotecs of Oaxaca, was growing into a town of perhaps 10,000. Many carvings here have hieroglyphs or dates in a dot-and-bar system, which quite possibly means that the elite of Monte Albán invented writing and the written calendar in Mexico.

CLASSIC PERIOD (AD 250–900)
Teotihuacán
The first great civilization in central Mexico emerged in a valley about 50km northeast of the center of modern Mexico City. Teotihuacán grew into a city of an estimated 125,000 people during its apogee between AD 250 and AD 600, and it controlled what was probably the biggest pre-Hispanic Mexican empire. Teotihuacán had writing and books, the dot-and-bar number system and the 260-day sacred year. The building of a magnificent planned city began around 300 BC and took some 600 years to complete.

Classic Maya
By the close of the Preclassic period, in AD 250, the Maya people of the Yucatán Peninsula and the Petén forest of Guatemala were already building stepped temple pyramids. During the Classic period, these regions produced pre-Hispanic America's most brilliant civilization, with the great cities of Tikal, in Guatemala's Petén, the most splendid of all.

Pacific Mexico
The shaft-tomb tradition that so defined Nayarit, Jalisco and Colima began to die out in the early Classic period. Objects from Teotihuacán

In 1524 Spanish conquistador Francisco Cortés de Buenaventura, a nephew of Hernán Cortés, arrived on the Jalisco–Nayarit coast. He was met by an army of 20,000 native warriors armed with bows festooned with colorful cloth banners. The bay where this occurred was thereafter known as the Bay of Flags (Bahía de Banderas).

AD 250–900	Around 1325
Classic Maya civilization flourishes	Tenochtitlán, site of present-day Mexico City, founded by the Aztecs

For a wealth of
information about the
Aztecs, including a
Nahuatl dictionary and
lessons in the language,
see www.mexica.net. The
site also contains
miscellaneous information
about Mexico's indigenous
peoples and history.

have been found in Nayarit, Jalisco, Colima and Michoacán, which suggests that Teotihuacán was probably absorbing the West Mexican cultures into its sphere. Teotihuacán was probably interested in the area for the region's precious stones and minerals.

The collapse of Teotihuacán in the 7th century was felt all throughout western Mexico and Guerrero – as it was throughout Mesoamerica – but the scattered, independent chiefdoms that characterized the coastal states continued well into the Postclassic period. The fertile coastal ecology provided plentifully for the people who hunted and farmed the coastal plains and upland valleys, and fished the coastal waters.

POSTCLASSIC PERIOD (AD 900–1521)
Aztecs

Azteca by Gary Jennings
is a sweeping historical
novel about the Spanish
conquest of Mexico,
written from a native's
point of view.

The Aztecs were the monumental Postclassic civilization. The location of their ancestral homeland is unknown, with some placing it on the island of Mexcaltitán in northern Nayarit. The Aztec capital, Tenochtitlán, was eventually founded on a lake-island in the Valle de México (site of present-day Mexico City) in the first half of the 14th century. In the mid-15th century the Aztecs formed the Triple Alliance with two other valley states and brought most of central Mexico from the Gulf Coast to the Pacific under its control. The total population of the empire's 38 provinces may have been about five million. The empire's main concern was exacting resources absent from the heartland. Jade, turquoise, cotton, paper, tobacco, rubber, lowland fruits and vegetables, cacao and precious feathers were needed for the glorification of the Aztec elite and to support the many nonproductive servants of its war-oriented state.

Tarascos

The only empire to exist in western Mexico was the Tarascos, and being fierce warriors, they were the only group to successfully resist Aztec invasions. After the Aztecs, they were the largest and most powerful empire in Mesoamerica. Called the Purépecha until the Spanish labeled them Tarascos, they ruled present-day Michoacán and parts of Jalisco, Guanajuato and Guerrero from the 12th century until the arrival of the Spanish in 1521.

Oaxaca & Guerrero

After about AD 1200 the remaining Zapotec settlements of Oaxaca, such as Mitla and Yagul, were increasingly dominated by the Mixtecs, famed metalsmiths and potters from the uplands around the Oaxaca–Puebla border. Mixtec and Zapotec cultures became entangled before much of their territory fell to the Aztecs in the 15th and 16th centuries. Around the same time, the Aztecs were establishing small strategic presences along the Guerrero coast. The Yopes, who lived around the Bahía de Acapulco, were one of the few groups who successfully resisted the expansionist Aztecs.

ENTER THE SPANISH

Almost 3000 years of civilization was shattered in just two short years, following the landing by Hernán Cortés near modern-day Veracruz on

1512	1519–21
Spanish 'discover' the Bay of Acapulco; people had already been living in the area for some 2000 years	Hernán Cortés lands near Veracruz, later captures Aztec god-king Moctezuma II and takes over Tenochtitlán

April 21, 1519. Primary sources suggest that the Aztecs were initially accommodating because, according to their calendar, the year 1519 promised the god Quetzalcóatl's return from the east. The Spaniards were well received at Gulf Coast communities that resented Aztec dominion. Cortés thus gained his first indigenous allies. After much vacillation, the Aztec god-king Moctezuma II invited Cortés to meet him, and the Spaniards were lodged in the palace of Axayácatl, Moctezuma's father. After six months in Tenochtitlán, and apparently fearing an attack, the Spaniards struck first and killed about 200 Aztec nobles trapped in a square during a festival.

William Henry Prescott's mammoth *History of the Conquest of Mexico* remains a classic, although it was published in 1843 by an author who never visited Mexico.

Cortés and his force returned to the Aztec capital only to come under fierce attack. Trapped in Axayácatl's palace, Cortés persuaded Moctezuma to try to pacify his people. According to one version of events, the king went up to the roof to address the crowds but was wounded by missiles and died soon afterward; other versions have it that the Spaniards killed him.

Following this, full-scale war broke out. After only a few major battles, 900 Spaniards and some 100,000 native allies waged a successful attack on Tenochtitlán in May 1521. By August 13, 1521, Aztec resistance had ended. The position of the conquered peoples deteriorated rapidly, not only because of harsh treatment at the hands of the colonists but also because of introduced diseases. The indigenous population fell from an estimated 25 million at the time of conquest to one million by 1605.

In 1564, Spanish ships launched from the Jalisco town of Barra de Navidad delivered the Philippines to King Philip of Spain.

From the 16th to 19th centuries, a sort of apartheid system existed in Mexico. Spanish-born colonists were a minuscule part of the population but were considered nobility in New Spain (as Mexico was then called), however humble their status in their home country. By the 18th century, criollos (people born of Spanish parents in New Spain) had acquired fortunes in mining, commerce, ranching and agriculture, and were seeking

---

INTIMATIONS OF DISASTER

In the Mesoamerican belief system, the world is poised for destruction at the end of each calendar cycle of 52 years, a passage known as 'the tying of years.' As it happened, the Spaniards arrived as one of these cycles was coming to a close. Aztec survivors of the siege on Tenochtitlán told Franciscan missionary Bernardino de Sahagún (1499–1590) of eight ominous signs that were visited on the city just prior to the arrival of the conquistadores:

- A comet appeared in the daytime sky
- A 'pillar of fire' – perhaps the same comet – appeared in the nighttime sky
- The temple of Huitzilopochtli was razed by fire
- Lightning struck the Tzonmolco temple
- The city was flooded
- Creatures with many heads but only one body walked the streets
- A weeping woman was heard singing a song of lament for the Aztecs
- A fantastic bird was caught, and when Moctezuma looked into its eyes, he saw a vision of strange men landing on the coast

---

1524	1529
Battle at Bahía de Banderas	Spanish establish the city of Oaxaca

political power commensurate with their wealth. Below the criollos were the mestizos, of mixed Spanish and indigenous ancestry, and at the bottom of the pile were the remaining indigenous people and African slaves, who had been imported by the Spaniards as early as the 1520s. (Over nearly three centuries, the slave trade brought about 200,000 Africans to the colony.) The catalyst for rebellion came in 1808 when Napoleon Bonaparte occupied most of Spain – direct Spanish control over New Spain suddenly ceased and rivalry between Spanish-born colonists and *criollos* intensified. On September 16, 1810, Miguel Hidalgo y Costilla, a criollo parish priest, issued his call to rebellion, the Grito de Dolores. In 1821 Spain agreed to Mexican independence.

MEXICAN REPUBLIC

Twenty-two years of chronic instability followed independence, during which the presidency changed hands 36 times. In 1845, the US congress voted to annex Texas, leading to the Mexican-American War (1846–48), in which US troops captured Mexico City. Under the Treaty of Guadalupe Hidalgo (1848), Mexico ceded Texas, California, Utah, Colorado and most of New Mexico and Arizona to the USA. The Maya rose up against their overlords in the late 1840s and almost succeeded in driving them off the Yucatán Peninsula. By 1862, Mexico was heavily in debt to Britain, France and Spain, who sent a joint force to Mexico to collect their debts. France decided to go one step further and colonize Mexico, sparking yet another war. In 1864, France invited the Austrian archduke, Maximilian of Habsburg, to become emperor of Mexico. His reign was bloodily ended by forces loyal to the country's former president, Benito Juárez, a Zapotec from Oaxaca.

With the slogan 'order and progress,' dictator Porfirio Díaz (ruled 1878–1911) avoided war and piloted Mexico into the industrial age. Political opposition, free elections and a free press were banned, and control was maintained by a ruthless army. Land and wealth became concentrated in the hands of a small minority.

Very early in the 20th century a liberal opposition formed, but it was forced into exile in the USA. In 1906 the most important group of exiles issued a new liberal plan for Mexico from St Louis, Missouri. Their actions precipitated strikes throughout Mexico – some violently suppressed – that led, in late 1910, to the Mexican Revolution.

FROM REVOLUTION TO REFORM

A contingent of 250,000 Mexican and Mexican-American men fought in WWII. One thousand were killed in action, 1500 received purple hearts and 17 received the congressional Medal of Honor.

The Mexican Revolution was a 10-year period of shifting allegiances between a spectrum of leaders, in which successive attempts to create stable governments were undermined by new skirmishes. The basic ideological rift was between liberal reformers and more radical leaders, such as Emiliano Zapata, who were fighting for the transfer of hacienda land to the peasants. The 10 years of violent civil war cost an estimated 1.5 to two million lives – roughly one in eight Mexicans.

After the revolution, former revolutionary leader Alvaro Obregón became president (1920–24) and steered the country toward national reconstruction. More than 1000 rural schools were built and some land was redistributed from big landowners to the peasants.

1821	1861
Mexico gains independence from Spain	Benito Juárez becomes the first indigenous Mexican president

Obregón's successor, Plutarco Elías Calles, built more schools and distributed more land. He also closed monasteries, convents and church schools, and prohibited religious processions. These measures precipitated the bloody Cristero Rebellion by Catholics, which lasted until 1929.

At the end of President Calles' term, in 1928, Obregón was elected president again but was assassinated by a Cristero. Calles reorganized his supporters to found the Partido Nacional Revolucionario (PNR; National Revolutionary Party), precursor of today's PRI (Partido Revolucionario Institucional).

Lázaro Cárdenas, former governor of Michoacán, won the presidency in 1934 with the PNR's support and stepped up the reform program. Cárdenas redistributed almost 200,000 sq km of land, mostly through the establishment of *ejidos* (peasant landholding cooperatives). The land was nearly double the amount distributed since 1920 and nearly one-third of the population received holdings.

MODERN MEXICO

The Mexican economy expanded in the two decades after WWII. By 1952 the country's population had doubled from what it was two decades earlier. Civil unrest appeared again in 1968, in the months preceding the Olympic Games in Mexico City. More than 500,000 people rallied in Mexico City's *zócalo* (main plaza) on August 27 to express their outrage with the conservative Díaz Ordaz (1964–70) administration. On October 2, with the Olympics only a few days away, a rally was organized in Tlatelolco plaza in Mexico City. The government sent in heavily armed troops and police who opened fire on the crowd, killing several hundred people.

Today, Mexico has more than 100 million citizens, with more than 20% residing in Mexico City.

The oil boom of the late 1970s increased Mexico's oil revenues and financed industrial and agricultural investments, but the oil glut in the early 1980s deflated petroleum prices and led to Mexico's worst recession in several decades. The population continued to escalate at Malthusian rates through the 1980s, while the economy made only weak progress. In 1985 an earthquake shook Mexico City and killed at least 10,000 people, causing more than US$4 billion in damage. In a climate of economic helplessness and rampant corruption, dissent grew on both the left and the right, and even within the PRI.

THE LESS THE MERRIER?

Overpopulation still looms as perhaps Mexico's greatest problem. The population in 1944 was 22 million, and by 1998 it had reached 97 million. The situation seemed hopeless in 1968 when the Vatican banned all methods of contraception. In 1970 more than 600,000 Mexican women underwent illegal operations, and 32,000 died. Government-sponsored clinics were established to offer birth-control literature, and by 1992 more than 6000 family-planning centers were established.

Mexifam is the largest nongovernment family-planning service, concentrating on the poorest areas of the country. By April 2000 it became evident that Mexifam and the government programs were working. Population growth had been reduced from 3.4% in 1970 to 1.7% in 2000 – from seven children per woman to 2.28. (Mexifam does not advocate abortion but does provide information on the morning-after pill to prevent pregnancy.)

1910–20	1930s
Almost two million people die and the economy is shattered in the Mexican Revolution	Tourists start arriving in Mazatlán and Acapulco for world-renowned sportfishing and 'exotic' beaches

Salinas, Nafta & the EZLN

The Harvard-educated Carlos Salinas de Gortari took the presidency in 1988 and set about transforming Mexico's state-dominated economy into one of private enterprise and free trade. The apex of his program was Nafta, the North American Free Trade Agreement, which came into effect on January 1, 1994. The same day a group of 2000 or so indigenous-peasant rebels calling themselves Ejército Zapatista de Liberación Nacional (EZLN; Zapatista National Liberation Army) shocked Mexico by taking over San Cristóbal de Las Casas and three other towns in the country's southernmost state, Chiapas.

After the EZLN uprising, Salinas pushed through electoral reforms against ballot-stuffing and double voting, and the 1994 presidential election was regarded as the cleanest to date. But it was hardly spotless. In March 1994 Luis Donaldo Colosio, Salinas' chosen successor as PRI presidential candidate, was assassinated in Tijuana. Colosio's replacement as PRI candidate, 43-year-old Ernesto Zedillo, won the election with 50% of the vote.

Zedillo

Within days of President Zedillo taking office in late 1994, Mexico's currency, the peso, suddenly collapsed, bringing on a rapid and deep economic recession that hit everyone hard, and the poor hardest. It led to, among other things, a big increase in crime, intensified discontent with the PRI, and large-scale Mexican emigration to the USA. Zedillo's policies pulled Mexico gradually out of recession and by the end of his term in 2000, Mexicans' purchasing power was again approaching what it had been in 1994.

Michael Meyer & William L Sherman's *The Course of Mexican History* is one of the best general accounts of Mexican history and society.

Zedillo was an uncharismatic figure, but he was perceived as more honest than his predecessors. He set his sights on democratic reform and set up a new, independent electoral apparatus that, in 1997, achieved Mexico's freest and fairest elections since 1911.

In Chiapas, Zedillo at first negotiated with the EZLN, but then in February 1995 he sent in the army to 'arrest' Subcomandante Marcos and other leaders. The rebels escaped deeper into the jungle. On-and-off negotiations eventually brought an agreement on indigenous rights in 1996, but Zedillo balked at turning the agreement into law.

The Fox Presidency

The independent electoral system set in place by Zedillo ensured that his party, the PRI, lost its 70-year grip on power in the 2000 presidential election. The winner was Vicente Fox of the right-of-center Partido Acción Nacional (PAN; National Action Party), a former state governor of Guanajuato and former chief of Coca-Cola's operations in Mexico (where more Coke per person is drunk than in any other country in the world). A 2m (6ft 6in) tall rancher with a penchant for jeans and cowboy boots, Fox entered office with the goodwill of a wide range of Mexicans who hoped a change of ruling party would bring real change in the country.

Though Fox remained personally popular and was perceived as honest and well intentioned, in the end his presidency disappointed many – largely because his party did not have a majority in Mexico's national

1960s	1994
Sleepy fishing village Puerto Vallarta emerges to become a glamorous, world-famous resort	North American Free Trade Agreement (Nafta) comes into effect

Congress and therefore could not effect many changes. Things got worse
when the PAN lost more seats to the PRI in mid-term congressional elections in 2003. Fox was thus unable to enact the reforms that he believed
key to stirring Mexico's slumbering economy, such as raising taxes or
introducing private investment into the energy sector. His government
consequently lacked money to improve education, social welfare or roads.
By the end of Fox's term of office in 2006, Mexicans' overall standard of
living was only a little higher than when he took power. Peasants and
small farmers felt the pinch of Nafta, as subsidized corn (maize) from the
USA was sold more cheaply in Mexico than was Mexican corn.

Mexicans did enjoy a certain social liberation after the PRI's grip was
prized loose. Government became more transparent, honest and accountable, and Mexicans have become more confident about expressing
their opinions and asserting their rights, aware that their rulers are now
subject to more or less fair elections. As the time to elect Fox's successor
approached, the PAN and the PRI colluded in an attempt to derail the
election favorite, Andrés Manuel López Obrador of the PRD (Partido de
la Revolución Democrática), over a legal technicality, but backed off after
an enormous Mexico City demonstration in López Obrador's favor. At
least it seemed that Fox's successor would be elected, as he was in 2000,
by a free and fair popular vote – something few Mexicans would have
believed likely 12 years before.

'Government became more transparent, honest and accountable'

2000	2003
Vicente Fox elected president, bringing to an end 70 years of power by the PRI	Relations with the US are jeopardized when Mexico refuses to support the US-led war in Iraq

The Culture
Carolina A Miranda

REGIONAL IDENTITY

It was *The Night of the Iguana* that put the Mexican Pacific coast on the world itinerary. John Huston's 1964 film adaptation of the Tennessee Williams play starred Richard Burton as a minister-cum-tour-guide leading a gaggle of American biddies down Mexico way. The local cultures were barely represented in the film, but it nonetheless managed to capture a moment when the coastline consisted of little more than a sparse string of fishing villages.

That has changed. Indigenous hamlets have ceded way to gleaming resorts and retirement communities. The hodge-podge of cultural groups that line this 2000km stretch of coast – from the Huichol in the north to the Zapotecs in the south (see p36) – mix tentatively with other segments of Mexico and the world. The northern end has a decidedly cowboy feel. Hard-working ranchers live a life centered around agriculture and livestock, entertaining themselves with rodeos and bullfights. The people of the south, more indigenous in spirit, stoically pass age-old artistic traditions from one generation to the next. In between lie pockets of settlers from all over: entrepreneurial Mexico City hoteliers who make a buck off booming Pacific tourism, former agricultural workers taken in by the growing regional service economy, and water-logged expats in search of the next good wave.

This is just another layer on the many that already existed. The coast has never had one identity, but it has always been united in its aim, which is to show tourists a good time. This is where Mexico rolls out the welcome mat to the world, where resort towns and fishing villages receive travelers with A-list hospitality and down-home taco stands. It is where the national appreciation of revelry and music are brought to hectic climax in tequila-soaked carnivals. It's the spot where Mexico comes together to have a little fun.

> Though considered inherently Mexican, the origin of the piñata is highly debated. Some attribute it to the Spanish, others to the Italians or Chinese.

> The Huichol of Jalisco and Nayarit speak a language that bears a very close resemblance to Nahuatl, the language of the ancient Aztecs.

LIFESTYLE

The tourism industry on the coast continues to attract new generations of workers from the countryside and this has put some of the country's richest people next to its poorest. The affluent inhabit lavish summer homes, gated and guarded for security, while working-class city dwellers live in multigenerational units in neighborhoods that offer few parks or open spaces. The poorest are left in hastily constructed shantytowns. In the countryside, there is a more spacious environment, with families occupying traditional houses made of wood or adobe and living on the land they cultivate.

Tourism has brought both benefit and harm. The industry keeps thousands employed along the Pacific coastline. It has brought with it a greater awareness of the need to protect vintage architecture, indigenous tradition and the natural environment. But it has also fed the drug trade and prostitution. Despite these challenges, family ties remain strong and there have been many social improvements. Gender roles, for example, continue to relax among the middle class and jobs are more accessible to women in general. A Mexican woman today will have an average of 2.28 children; in the early '70s, that average was seven. As in many Latin American countries, the overall divorce rate remains low (0.62 per 1000 people) – especially when compared with the US or the UK, which both have a rate of 4.19 per 1000 people. For gays and lesbians, the big resort towns – particularly Puerto Vallarta (see p92 and p85) – offer a well-developed and welcoming scene.

POPULATION

About three-quarters of Mexico's 106 million people currently live in cities. This represents a major shift for a country with a largely rural history. In the early part of the 20th century, only one-tenth of the population lived in cities. Much of this growth is due to a high level of internal migration: one in five Mexicans now lives in a city other than the one they were born in. As a result, heavily agricultural (and poor) states such as Oaxaca, on the southern coast, have seen thousands of young people depart to big cities in search of greater economic opportunities. Guadalajara is the largest city in Mexico's west and the second largest in the country, with a population of about five million. New housing is continually built by migrants on rural lands surrounding city centers, while local governments invest their pesos in industrial development. This rapid growth has left a strained urban infrastructure often devoid of necessary public services. But relief seems to be ahead. Though the country's population doubled between 1970 and 2000, the birth rate has slowed from 3% in the 1980s to 1.2% in 2005. On the coast, fertility rates remain low on the northern end, but swell towards the southern coast.

> Get a comprehensive calendar (in English!) of cultural events around Mexico on the handy website www .therealmexico.com.

SPORTS

The favorite sport is *fútbol* (football, aka soccer), which is less a sport than a religion. Mexico has an 18-team national division, with three of these teams based in Guadalajara: the Atlas, Tecos and Chivas. The latter team has the biggest following and, at press time, had a new, 45,000-seat stadium under construction. There are many small local leagues, so you can catch a match year-round.

Second on the list is bullfighting. A popular adage maintains that Mexicans are punctual for only two things: funerals and bullfights. *Corridas de toro* are a Sunday afternoon tradition during the October to March bullfighting season. Guadalajara, Puerto Vallarta and Acapulco are good spots to catch a *corrida*. *Charreadas* (rodeos) are also popular, particularly on the northern coast, and take place from February to November.

Baseball is another popular sport. There is a northwest Mexican league, **Liga Mexicana del Pacífico** (www.ligadelpacifico.com.mx in Spanish) and its website has information on games and locations. Increasing in visibility is the *juego de pelota* (ball game), a contemporary variant of an ancient sport. See below.

> Keep up with Guadalajara's favorite soccer team, the Chivas, at www.chivas.naranya .com/index.php (in Spanish).

THE OLD BALL GAME

It is the world's oldest team sport and was played consistently by various cultures in pre-Hispanic times. *Juego de pelota* took place on a flat court with sloping walls where players scrambled to keep a heavy rubber ball in the air by kicking it around with their hips, thighs, knees or elbows. It was volleyball meets soccer meets human sacrifice. (Some historians claim that players may have been killed after matches as an offering.) The game survives to this day – *sans* sacrifice, of course. In Michoacán, it's called *juego de pelota purépecha*, in the Mazatlán area it's known as *hulama* and in Oaxaca it is *pelota mixteca*. As a visitor, it's easiest to see a game in Oaxaca City during Guelaguetza festivities every July when the city hosts a *pelota* competition.

MULTICULTURALISM

The most significant ethnic division in Mexico is between assimilated *mestizos* (mixed-race Mexicans) and more insular full-blooded Indians who speak native languages. Mestizos make up the vast majority of the population – between 80% and 90% by some counts. Along the western coast, indigenous peoples are largely represented in one of the following ethnic groups: Zapotecs and Mixtecs in Oaxaca, Guerrero and Puebla; Purépecha in Michoacán; and the Huichol in Jalisco and Nayarit. As is happening all over the continent, the younger generations are abandoning traditional lifestyles to go work in cities, largely in service jobs. As a result, some languages and traditions are disappearing. The tourism industry, however, has had the unexpected effect of preserving some aspects of these cultures. In Teotitlán del Valle in Oaxaca, for example, travel to the region supports a local textile industry that is keeping traditional weaving techniques alive.

The most famous Zapotec in Mexican history is the venerated Benito Juárez (1806–72) from Oaxaca, who was the only full-blooded Indian to become president of Mexico.

Migration to the United States is likewise a significant issue. Almost 11 million Mexican citizens live there (with more in Canada) – where wages are, on average, six times higher. This emigration has had the consequence of turning some rural communities into virtual ghost towns. In Michoacán, for example, more than two million migrants have departed, leaving the state with a population of just over four million. The government is trying to discourage these mass migrations by supporting development and job-creation programs locally. It's a small step in the right direction. But as long as the income disparity between these neighboring countries continues to be wide, immigrants will head north.

RELIGION

Despite a rocky history in Mexico, the Catholic church (and to a larger degree, the Virgin of Guadalupe) remains the focal point of religious life for almost nine out of 10 people. But the church's grip is loosening. In 1970 more than 96% of the country identified as Roman Catholic; by the '90s that figure had slipped to 89%. Part of this is due to a growing evangelical movement comprised of, among other groups, Protestants, Seventh-Day Adventists and Mormons.

Jesús Malverde, an early-20th-century bandit from Sinaloa, is now venerated as the patron saint of drug traffickers. He has a shrine and chapel in his honor in downtown Culiacán.

Catholicism nonetheless remains a deep-seated national force. Members of the clergy were present during the early days of the Spanish conquest. By the mid-19th century the Church owned more than a quarter of all land in Mexico and controlled most schools, hospitals and charitable institutions. This led the federal government to pass a series of measures intended to clamp down on ecclesiastic power. The constitution of 1917 forbade the Church from owning property, running schools or newspapers and banned clergy from voting. After a series of anticlerical purges in the late 1930s, anti-Church sentiment eased, and in 1950 the constitutional provisions ceased to be enforced. In the early '90s, President Carlos Salinas de Gortari removed them from the constitution entirely.

Indigenous Religion

The early missionaries won over indigenous people by grafting Catholic beliefs onto pre-Hispanic ones. Today, indigenous Christianity remains a fusion of traditional Indian and Christian belief. The Huichol of Jalisco, for example, have two Christs, neither of which is as important as Nakawé, the fertility goddess. A crucial source of wisdom comes from the use of the hallucinogenic drug peyote. In Oaxaca a number of carnival celebrations are as much indigenous in content as Catholic: the Guelaguetza festival has its roots in Zapotec maize-god rituals. Customs such as witchcraft and magic still flourish. When illness strikes, indigenous communities will often seek guidance from the local *brujo* (witch doctor) or *curandero* (curer).

ARTS
Literature
A dive into Mexican literature can easily begin with Nobel Prize–winning poet and cultural critic Octavio Paz (1914–98). His most prominent work, *El laberinto de la soledad* (The Labyrinth of Solitude; 1950), is a book-length essay examining the roots of Mexican identity and culture. His poetry is also renowned. The bilingual *Collected Poems of Octavio Paz, 1957–1987* is a good start for the foreign reader. It contains his best-known verses, such as *Piedra del sol* (Sunstone).

The country is home to no small number of accomplished novelists. Foremost among them is Juan Rulfo (1918–86), who was born near Guadalajara and whose plots often unfold in the coastal state of Jalisco. His most legendary work is *Pedro Páramo*, which takes place in the turbulent period preceding the Mexican Revolution (p30). This complex yet slim novel is often cited as the precursor to magic realism.

Also significant is novelist and political commentator Carlos Fuentes (b 1928). His novel *La muerte de Artemio Cruz* (The Death of Artemio Cruz; 1962) is a metaphor on the birth of postrevolutionary Mexico. Other prominent works include *Terra nostra*, *Cambio de piel* (A Change of Skin) and *Gringo Viejo* (The Old Gringo), the latter of which is an intriguing tale about an American who joins the army of Mexican revolutionary leader Pancho Villa (c 1877–1923). Other admired works that fictionalize the Mexican Revolution are *Los de abajo* (The Underdogs) by Mariano Azuela (1873–1952) and *Como agua para chocolate* (Like Water for Chocolate) by Laura Esquivel (b 1950).

Mexico has also generated some of the continent's most lauded female writers, beginning with 17th-century Hieronymite nun and poet Sor Juana Inés de la Cruz. She produced a staggering number of plays, essays and poems, all in a baroque style. Among her most renowned works are 'Redondillas' (Quatrains) and *Primer sueño* (First Dream) – both poems. English-speakers interested in her work can pick up *A Sor Juana Anthology* by Alan S Trueblood. More contemporary feminist authors include Rosario Castellanos (1925–74), whose best-known novel *Oficio de tinieblas* (The Book of Lamentations) is the tale of an Indian rebellion; and Elena Poniatowska (b 1932), whose work *Tinisima* reimagines the life of photographer Tina Modotti (p39). Also worth a read is short-story writer Elena Garro (1920–98), author of the novellas *Primer amor* and *Busca mi esquela*, available in the English volume *First Love & Look for My Obituary*.

A new generation of writers is focused on some of the immediate issues facing Mexican society: drug trafficking, corruption and the omnipresent neighbor to the north. Élmer Mendoza (b 1949), Raúl Manriquez (b 1962), Rafa Saavedra (b 1967) and Juan José Rodríguez (b 1970) have all produced works in this vein. Unfortunately, they have yet to be translated.

NON-MEXICAN AUTHORS
Mexico has long been a muse for the voluminous travel lit produced by foreigners. Popular contemporary accounts include Tony Cohan's *On Mexican Time* and Mary Morris's *Nothing to Declare*. Of special interest to coastal travelers is *Western Mexico: A Traveller's Treasury* by Tony Burton, which contains detailed information about the region's history,

Luis Humberto Crothswaite (b 1962) is one of the few contemporary novelists available in translation. His humorous novella *La luna siempre será un amor difícil* (The Moon Will Forever Be a Distant Love) can be found on book websites such as Amazon.com.

Loads of information on Mexican museums, pre-Hispanic art and historical monuments can be found online in English and Spanish at www.mexicodesconocido.com.mx.

art and archeology. Truly worthwhile is *In Search of Captain Zero*, the engaging surf memoir by Allan Weisbacker, much of which unfolds on the Pacific coast.

The origins of the Day of the Dead celebrations go back 3000 years to Mesoamerican birth and death rituals; the dead are now honored annually on November 1–2.

Vintage accounts from the early 20th century include *Mornings in Mexico* by novelist DH Lawrence and John Steinbeck's *A Log from the Sea of Cortez*. The latter title received a tribute from contemporary American writer Andromeda Romano-Lax in 2002. She retraces the famous author's voyage in *Searching for Steinbeck's Sea of Cortez*. Also of interest are *Survivor in Mexico* by early British feminist Rebecca West and the novel *Under the Volcano* by Malcolm Lowry. A truly classic travelogue on the country is Graham Greene's *The Lawless Roads*, which covers the bitter period following the clerical purges of the '30s and served as the basis for his seminal novel *The Power and the Glory*.

Cinema & TV

From the 1930s to the late 1950s, Mexico's film industry was famously prolific, churning out 80 features a year full of dance, drama and mustachioed matinee idols in large sombreros. Since then, however, weak government funding has left the industry starved. The national film commission, Conafilm, operates on a paltry budget of a few hundred thousand dollars a year (and even that was threatened during the latest austerity measures in 2005). Filmmakers have few financial incentives – other than a 10% income-tax deduction – to create anything.

Why wade through all that baroque poetry when you can just watch the movie? *Yo la peor de todas* (I the Worst of All) is a gripping biopic on the life of 17th-century nun-poet Sor Juana Inés de la Cruz.

Despite these obstacles, Mexican cinema has managed to launch a number of award-winning films onto the global screen. The best of these is Alfonso Cuarón's *Y tu mamá también* (And Your Mother Too; 2001), which portrays a youthful road trip that is as comic and erotic as it is tragic. The film was controversial in Mexico, not only for its sexual content, but for the honest way in which it depicted the country's poverty. (Keep your eyes peeled because the Pacific coast has a starring role.) Other popular international releases have included the light romantic comedy *Sexo, pudor y lágrimas* (Sex, Shame and Tears; 1989), the Oscar-nominated dramas *Amores perros* (Love's a Bitch; 2000) and *El crimen del Padre Amaro* (The Crime of Father Amaro; 2002), and the crime caper *Nícotina* (Nicotine; 2003) – all of which are worth a watch.

The better-established TV industry balances the grit of Mexico's cinema with an endless supply of melodramatic *telenovelas* (soap operas), which are a global export. One of the more curious anecdotes in the medium's history relates to Veronica Castro. A major TV star in the 1970s, her career was faltering by the early '90s until one of her old soaps, *Los ricos también lloran* (The Rich Also Cry; 1979), was aired in Russia in 1992. The passion for the show there was tremendous. During a visit to Moscow, she was mobbed by fans, including then president Boris Yeltsin, who threw a dinner in her honor at the Kremlin.

Fine & Traditional Arts

Mexico offers an artistic feast that dates back more than two millennia. Viewers can gorge themselves on dramatic pre-Hispanic sculpture, colonial-era paintings and even cutting-edge contemporary installations.

Pre-Hispanic works are well represented throughout the country, though the best pieces are generally kept in Mexico City museums. On the Pacific coast it was the ancient Zapotec (AD 300–700) and Mixtec (AD 1200–1600) cultures that predominated artistically. Fine examples of their work are on display in Oaxaca City at the Museo Rufino Tamayo (p229) and the Museo de las Culturas (p229). Intricate funerary ceramic sculpture, created between

200 BC and AD 800 by the shaft-tomb cultures (p26) of Nayarit, Jalisco and Colima, can be found in Guadalajara at the Museo de Arqueología.

During the colonial period and after independence, Mexican art consisted largely of European-style portraiture and religious painting. The Oaxacan-born Miguel Cabrera (1695–1768) was particularly notable. He created a famous portrait of poet Sor Juana Inés de la Cruz (p37), which now resides at the Museo Nacional de Historia in Mexico City.

Out of the ashes of the revolution came the muralists. The celebrated Diego Rivera (1885–1957), David Alfaro Siqueiros (1896–1974) and José Clemente Orozco (1883–1949) were the movement's figureheads. Orozco was born in the state of Jalisco and lived for a while in Guadalajara, where his house is now open to visitors.

Other leading modern painters included Frida Kahlo (1907–54), the surrealist self-portraitist married to Diego Rivera, and Rufino Tamayo (1899–1991), who was born in Oaxaca and is known for his abstract spin on Mixtec and Zapotec art. Visitors can view the objects of Tamayo's inspiration in Oaxaca City, where a pristine collection of his pre-Hispanic figurines lies in the museum that bears his name (p229). In a class by herself is photographer Tina Modotti (1896–1942). Though born in Italy, she settled in Mexico in the early 1920s and became an accomplished photographer. A political activist and contemporary of the muralists (she appears in several of Rivera's works), Modotti reached international acclaim for her stark portraits.

A trip along the coast will reveal plenty of contemporary indigenous fine and folk art. In Nayarit and Jalisco, you'll find colorful beaded sculptures and yarn paintings by the Huichol. But it's Oaxaca City that is richest in artistic treasures: dexterously woven textiles, polished black ceramics, elaborate *alebrijes* (wood figurines), metal sculpture and contemporary fine art. The city's streets are lined with galleries catering to every taste.

> Get an up-to-date list of the plentiful art galleries and community museums in Oaxaca City at www .oaxacaoaxaca.com /galleries.htm. All listings are in English.

> For the seminal view on Frida Kahlo's life and work, read Hayden Herrera's artfully written *Frida: A Biography of Frida Kahlo*.

Architecture

The architecture of the coastline is, to some degree, unremarkable. The bigger cities – Mazatlán, Puerto Vallarta and Acapulco – didn't see real development until the late '60s and construction consisted largely of bland, modernist resorts. Any trip slightly inland, however, will turn up plenty of architectural treasures. The pre-Hispanic city of Monte Albán in Oaxaca is a glimmering example of ancient Zapotec architecture. The countryside in this region is also dotted with 16th- and 17th-century Spanish churches built in the Gothic and baroque styles. Many of these have indigenous decorative elements: wall frescoes and colorful floor tiles. The Basílica de la Soledad (p229) in Oaxaca City is a great example of an immaculate baroque building. In Guadalajara, you can knock out a few architectural styles with a single visit to the cathedral. The design techniques here consist of everything from the Churrigueresque and the baroque to the neoclassical. It's odd but educational.

Many of the older cities, such as Mazatlán, Guadalajara, Puerto Vallarta and Oaxaca City, still retain examples of Spanish colonial architecture in their older corners. Take a peek inside these adobe buildings whenever you can. They rarely look like much from the outside, but are often set around inviting, plant-filled courtyards that bring the structures to life.

Music

For many travelers, Mexican music consists of little beyond the blaring trumpets of a few tired mariachis. This is a shame. As with the country's art and literature, there is a vast terrain to be explored.

Let's start with rock. Mexico is one of the most important hubs for Latin American rock, known universally as *rock en español*. Beginning in the '80s, bands such as El Tri, Los Caifanes and Maná (the latter hailing from Guadalajara) helped make this musical form an inherently Mexican product. One of the most consistently innovative rock bands is Café Tacuba. Their box set, *Lo esencial de Café Tacuba* (2001), is a good place for an audio tour of the band's eclectic musical history.

More recent acts include the rock-rappers Molotov from Mexico City. The group has gained international acclaim with raunchy lyrics and subversive political statements. (Their drummer is, of all things, the Mexico-raised son of a US drug agent.) Seminal albums include *¿Dónde jugarán las niñas?* and *Dance and Dense Denso*. Other acts include the jazzier Plastilina Mosh, whose 1998 album *Aquamosh* was a smash hit, and Tijuana crooner Julieta Venegas, whose tender vocals provide plenty of easy listening. Her album *Sí* (2003) is worthwhile. For fans of electronica, the DJs of the Nortec Collective from Tijuana will keep you grooving with a clever synthesis of dance and traditional *norteño* (below) beats. Their album *Tijuana Sessions Vol 1* is a must-have in this genre.

MEXICAN REGIONAL MUSIC

Mexican music has its roots in *son* (sound), folk music that dates back to the early part of the 20th century and grew from a fusion of Spanish, African and indigenous sounds. These musical styles have splintered into distinct regional types.

In the dusty north, along the border, it is *norteño* that flourishes, a boot-stomping brand of polka-infused country music accompanied by boisterous accordions and *bajo sextos*, the Mexican 12-string guitar. Its roots lie in the traditional ballads – *corridos* – of the revolution. Long considered fuddy-duddy music for old-timers, the style received a boost in the 1980s when bands began singing *narcocorridos*, ballads about the

---

THE MARIACHI TRADITION

Nothing defines Mexican music better than mariachis: the groups of nattily clad itinerant musicians who wander from town to town (or restaurant to restaurant) in search of the next paid gig. Though there is some disagreement about the origins of the word, historians do agree that 'mariachi' came into existence sometime in the middle of the 19th century in the state of Jalisco, just south of Guadalajara. Mariachi bands largely comprised wandering laborers for whom music was a secondary pursuit. By default, mariachis were, for decades, the keepers of Mexican musical folklore: harvesting and archiving local sounds and lyrics as they moved around in search of agricultural work. During the revolution, in the early 20th century, they carried news, along with arsenals of new songs about battle-hardened heroes and the loves they had lost.

In addition to a singer, a traditional mariachi group consists of a couple of violins, a Spanish guitar, a *vihuela* (a small, high-pitched five-string guitar) and a *guitarrón* (an acoustic bass instrument that is held like a guitar). Modern mariachi bands typically include a trumpet or two as well. Perhaps the most legendary group in the country is the Mariachi Vargas de Tecalitlán. Founded in 1898 in the state of Jalisco by Gaspar Vargas, the group quickly achieved regional fame. They became a national sensation in the 1930s when the then president Lázaro Cárdenas hired them as the official mariachis of the Mexico City police. (Their website proclaims: 'The Mariachi Vargas was something of an oddity in the early 1930s... They showed up on time for performances and they were sober.') The group has been performing since its founding and is now in its fifth incarnation. In the process, they have inspired hundreds, if not thousands of other musicians. For information on tour dates in Mexico and abroad, log on to the Mariachi Vargas website, www.mariachivargas.com.mx.

Guadalajara is home to Mexico's most prestigious mariachi festival, held every year in September. Check out www.mariachi -jalisco.com.mx (in Spanish) for information on dates and performances.

In San Blas listen to Maná's Sueños Líquidos album. The melancholy song 'El muelle de San Blas' makes frequent reference to the town's dock.

drug trade. Their popularity is attributed to Chalino Sánchez, a raspy-voiced singer from Sinaloa who took on the drug establishment, crooning about dope deals gone bad and corrupt police officials. In 1992, at the age of 32, Sánchez was found with two bullets in his head on the side of a Sinaloa road. His death (still unresolved by the police) made him a legend and ensured that *narcocorridos* would become a permanent part of the musical pantheon. Some of the biggest, long-running *norteño* bands today include Los Tigres del Norte, Los Rieleros del Norte and Los Tucanes de Tijuana.

Banda also hails from the traditional *corrido*, but substitutes the string section with lots of brass. The sound is all oompah. One of the genre's most renowned groups is Banda El Recodo, whose members come from the port of Mazatlán. The band has been around, in one guise or another, since 1938. The music, to be honest, is an acquired taste, but El Recodo has nonetheless toured internationally – even in Japan. Other genres, such as *grupera*, combine *norteno* with Colombian *cumbia*, a tropical style of folk music from that country's Caribbean coast. Grupo Límite from Monterrey is one of the best-known bands in this arena.

Ranchera is a classical style of Mexican country music cultivated in the hills of Guadalajara. The most legendary of the country's *ranchera* singers is Vicente Fernández, who is known as 'El rey' (the King) and has taken to the stage in silver-studded regalia for more than three decades. His baritone-voiced son Alejandro is equally talented (in addition to being quite easy on the eyes). Anyone interested in reveling in the sweet agony of an achingly sung *ranchera* should listen to Alejandro's album *Que Seas Muy Feliz* (May You Be Very Happy; 1995). Pick up some tequila, drown your sorrows and let him sing your pain.

Dance

Mexico is home to hundreds of regional dances, most of which reveal a significant amount of pre-Hispanic influence. One of the most spectacular of these is the Danza de las plumas (Feather Dance), which tells the story of the Spanish conquest from a Zapotec Indian point of view. A good time to see it is during Guelaguetza (p230) in Oaxaca. In Michoacán, the Danza de los viejitos (Dance of the Little Old Men) originated as a mockery of the Spanish, whom the local Tarasco Indians thought aged very fast. The dance is generally performed around Christmas time.

If you're in the mood for vintage *rancheras*, pick up *20 Éxitos* by Lola Beltrán (1931–96). She was known as 'Lola La Grande' for singing her ballads with so much drama and emotion.

Learn about regional dancing from all over the country at www.ballet .udg.mx, the website for the Ballet Folclórico de la Universidad de Guadalajara. Its site (in Spanish) offers historical information on the roots of indigenous dance.

Environment

With biodiversity greater than any other region of Mexico, Mexico's Pacific coast provides considerable pleasure to lovers of nature. Sensualists will find a nirvana for the senses, while paradise-seekers will have plenty of territory to explore, from palm-shaded tropical shorelines and deciduous tropical-forested headlands all the way up to the cloud forests that crown the highest reaches of the Sierra Madre.

Environmental scientists, however, have reason to worry. As in other ecologically precious territories around the globe, the human impact on the environment has been enormous, and the coast has a litany of problems that threaten not only the fauna and flora but people, too.

The US Sierra Club's prestigious Chico Mendes Prize, for bravery and leadership in environmental protection, was awarded in 2005 to Felipe Arreaga and two other leaders of a peasant organization battling indiscriminate logging in the state of Guerrero. Arreaga was unable to collect the award because he was in jail on what he said was a trumped-up murder charge.

THE LAND

It's nearly 2000km by road from Mazatlán, the northernmost destination in this book, to the southeastern resort of Bahías de Huatulco in Oaxaca. Mazatlán sits about midway down a dry coastal plain that stretches south from Mexicali, on the US border, almost to Tepic, in Nayarit state. Inland from the flats stands the rugged, volcanically formed Sierra Madre Occidental, which is crossed by only two main transport routes – the Barranca del Cobre (Copper Canyon) railway, from Chihuahua to Los Mochis, and the dramatic Hwy 40 from Durango to Mazatlán.

South of Cabo Corrientes (the lip of land protruding into the Pacific near Puerto Vallarta), the Pacific lowlands narrow to just a thin strip and the mountains rise dramatically from the sea. The Sierra Madre Occidental widens near Nayarit and finishes in Jalisco, where it meets the Cordillera Neovolcánica, a volcanic range running east–west across the middle of Mexico. Known in English as the Trans-Mexican Volcanic Belt, the Cordillera Neovolcánica includes the active volcanoes Popocatépetl (5452m) and Volcán de Fuego de Colima (3960m), as well as Pico de Orizaba (5610m), the nation's highest peak.

Defending the Land of the Jaguar by Lane Simonian is the absorbing story of Mexico's long, if weak, tradition of conservation.

The main mountain range in southern Mexico is the Sierra Madre del Sur, which stretches across the states of Guerrero and Oaxaca and separates the Oaxacan coast from its capital city. As the crow flies, it's only about 160km from Puerto Ángel, the southernmost town in Oaxaca, north to Oaxaca city; but crossing the crinkled back of the Sierra takes about six hours by car.

WILDLIFE
Animals
LAND LIFE

Raccoons, armadillos, skunks, rabbits and snakes are common. One critter you'll encounter is the gecko, a harmless, tiny green lizard that loves to crawl across walls and squawk at night. Michoacán and Guerrero are home to more species of scorpions and spiders than anywhere in Mexico.

Both black and green iguanas are common along the entire coast. Both are prized for their meat and have been overhunted, especially in Guerrero and Oaxaca. Boa constrictors are sometimes spotted in lagoons.

Rarer animals – which you'll be lucky to see – include spider monkeys and the beautiful, endangered jaguar, which once inhabited much of the coast.

SEA TURTLES

The Pacific coast is among the world's chief sea-turtle breeding grounds. Of the world's eight sea-turtle species, seven are found in Mexican waters, and six of those in the Pacific. Their nesting sites are scattered along the entire coast. For information about where you have the best chances of encountering sea turtles, see p52.

Female turtles usually lay their eggs on the beaches where they were born, some swimming huge distances to do so. They come ashore at night, scoop a trough in the sand and lay 50 to 200 eggs in it. Then they cover the eggs and go back to the sea. Six to 10 weeks later, the baby turtles hatch, dig their way out and crawl to the sea at night. Only two or three of every 100 make it to adulthood. Turtle nesting seasons vary, but July to September are peak months in many places.

Playa Escobilla, just east of Puerto Escondido, is one of the world's main nesting grounds for the small olive ridley turtle, the only sea-turtle species that is not endangered. Between May and January, about 700,000 olive ridleys come ashore here in about a dozen waves – known as *arribadas* – each lasting two or three nights, often during the waning of the moon. Playa Escobilla's turtles are guarded by armed soldiers, and there is no tourist access to the beach.

The rare leatherback is the largest sea turtle – it grows up to 3m long and can weigh one ton and live 80 years. One leatherback nesting beach is Oaxaca state's Playa Mermejita, between Punta Cometa and Playa Ventanilla, near Mazunte. Another is Barra de la Cruz, east of Bahías de Huatulco.

The green turtle is a vegetarian that grazes on marine grasses. Most adults are about 1m long. For millennia, the green turtle's meat and eggs have provided protein to humans in the tropics. European exploration of the globe marked the beginning of the turtle's decline. In the 1960s, the Empacadora Baja California in Ensenada, Baja California, was canning as many as 100 tonnes of turtle soup a season.

The loggerhead turtle, weighing up to 100kg, is famous for the vast distances it crosses between its feeding grounds and nesting sites. Loggerheads born in Japan and even, it's thought, Australia, cross the Pacific to feed off Baja California. Females later return to their birthplaces – a year-long journey – to lay their eggs.

The hawksbill turtle nests along both of Mexico's coasts and can live 50 years. The coast's sixth species, the black turtle, sticks to the Pacific.

The smallest and most endangered sea turtle, the Kemp's ridley (parrot turtle), lives only in the Gulf of Mexico.

MARINE LIFE

Dolphins can be seen off the coast, as can gray, humpback and blue whales, especially from November to March, when a whale-watching trip is recommended (see p52). Early in the year, even while lying on the beach you'll probably spot whales. Sting rays and the larger Pacific manta rays can often be seen when they burst from the water with wild abandon. Tide pools harbor sea anemones, urchins, octopi, starfish, sea slugs and an array of crabs. Spend any time *under* water and you'll probably see such beauties as the Cortez angelfish, seahorses, moray eels, rays, puffers and even whale sharks. Jellyfish are abundant at the beginning of the rainy season. See p48 for information on the larger Pacific fish.

Coastal lagoons, especially in the south, once harbored thousands of crocodiles. They've now been hunted almost to extinction.

To see how one organization is helping to ensure the survival of sea turtles, visit the website of the Grupo Ecológico de la Costa Verde (www.project -tortuga.org). See also www.turtles.org for fascinating facts about turtles.

The Whale and Dolphin Conservation Society (www.wdcs.org) is the global voice for the protection of whales, dolphins and their environment. Its website includes information about how to get involved in global efforts to protect marine mammals.

PROTECTING MEXICO'S TURTLES

Despite international conservation efforts, turtle flesh and eggs continue to be eaten, and some people still believe the eggs to be aphrodisiacs. Turtle skin and shell are used to make clothing and adornments. The world's fishing boats kill many turtles by trapping and drowning them in nets. In Mexico, hunting and killing sea turtles was officially banned in 1990, but the illicit killing and egg-raiding still goes on – a clutch of eggs can be sold for more than a typical worker makes in a week.

You can visit turtle hatcheries in Cuyutlán (p170), Colima and Mazunte, Oaxaca (p263). If you want to get involved in conservation efforts, volunteer opportunities exist at the Grupo Ecológico de la Costa Verde (p142).

To help the turtles that use Mexican beaches – and most people who have seen these graceful creatures swimming at sea will want to do that – follow these rules if you find yourself at a nesting beach:

- Try to avoid nesting beaches altogether between sunset and sunrise.
- Don't approach turtles emerging from the sea, or disturb nesting turtles or hatchlings with noise or lights (lights on or even near the beach can cause hatchlings to lose their sense of direction on their journey to the water).
- Keep vehicles – even bicycles – off nesting beaches.
- Don't build sand castles or stick umbrellas into the sand.
- Never handle baby turtles or carry them to the sea – their arduous scramble is vital to their development.
- Boycott shops or stalls selling products made from sea turtles or any other endangered species.

BIRDLIFE

New legislation in Mexico bans the import and export of marine mammals for commercial purposes. The new decree should end Mexico's involvement in the international trade in dolphins, which are highly sought after for 'swim with dolphins' tourist attractions.

The lagoons and wetlands of Pacific Mexico host hundreds of species of native and migratory birds, and any break-of-dawn boat trip will send bird lovers squawking. Birds from as far north as Alaska migrate here each winter – the best season for racking up your species-spotted list. You may see parrots and parakeets, loons, grebes, frigate birds, herons, hawks, falcons, sandpipers, plovers, ibis, swifts and boobies (to name only a handful).

In Oaxaca, it's not uncommon to spot ospreys soaring above the ocean cliffs. Of course, the bird you'll see most, wherever you are, is the *zopilote* (vulture). For the best birding locations, see p52.

Plants

Saving the Gray Whale: People, Politics, and Conservation in Baja California by Serge Dedina offers a hopeful prescription for the future of conservation in Mexico.

The Sierra Madre Occidental, the Cordillera Neovolcánica and the Sierra Madre del Sur still have some big stretches of pine forest and, at lower elevations, oak forest.

Tropical forest covers much of the lowest western slopes of the Sierra Madre Occidental and the Cordillera Neovolcánica, and can also be found in the Oaxaca. These forests lose their leaves during the dry winter but are lush and verdant in the summer rainy season. Pink trumpet, cardinal sage, spider lily, *mala ratón* (literally 'rat killer') and *matapalo* (strangler fig) bloom in these forests during the rainy season. Much of this plant community, however, has disappeared as the land has been taken over by ranches and cropland.

Along the dry Pacific coastal plain, from the southern end of the Desierto Sonorense to Guerrero state, the predominant vegetation is thorny bushes and small trees, including morning glory and acacias, and savanna.

The coastal lagoons that dot the Pacific coast are home to dense mangrove forests that have thick leathery leaves and small seasonal flowers.

PARKS & RESERVES

With all the spectacular beaches and accessible lagoons, you don't have to search for a park to experience the natural elements. Fortunately, federal, state and local governments have created a handful of protected areas to preserve some of the coast's fragile ecosystems. Some are easily accessible with private transport while others require the use of local guides (who will also greatly increase your chances of spotting any wildlife).

The largest national park in this book is the Parque Nacional Volcán Nevado de Colima (21,930 hectares; p169), where you'll find two volcanoes: the extinct Volcán Nevado de Colima and the active Volcán de Fuego. The smallest national park is the 192-hectare Isla Isabel (p132), a volcanically formed island north of San Blas, Nayarit. Parque Nacional Lagunas de Chacahua (p243), in Oaxaca, protects 14,000 hectares, which incorporate two mammoth lagoons, mangroves, fishing communities and more than 13km of coastline. Created in 1998, the 119-sq-km Parque Nacional de Huatulco (p266) encompasses nine pristine bays, tropical deciduous forest, sea and shoreline.

The ancient Zapotec city of Monte Albán (p240) in Oaxaca is a protected archeological zone of 2078 hectares.

Dedicated birders should seek out the Spanish-language *Aves de México* by Roger Tory Peterson and Edward L Chalif. An alternative is *A Guide to the Birds of Mexico & Northern Central America* by Steve NG Howell and Sophie Webb.

ENVIRONMENTAL ISSUES

Mexico's environmental crises, including those of the coast, are typical of a poor country with an exploding population struggling to develop. From early in the 20th century, urban industrial growth, intensive chemical-based agriculture, and the destruction of forests for logging and to allow grazing and development were seen as paths to prosperity, and little attention was paid to their environmental effects. A growth in environmental awareness since the 1970s has managed to achieve only very limited changes.

The website for Eco Travels in Latin America (www.planeta.com) brims with information and links about Mexican flora and fauna.

Forest Depletion

Deforestation has increased considerably on the coast since the passage of Nafta in 1994, which gave international corporations access to vast *ejido* (communal) landholdings. For example, in the Sierra de Petatlán and Coyuca de Catalán regions of Guerrero's Costa Grande, 40% of its forests have been logged in less than a decade. The vast stands of white and sugar pine logged in the region (mostly by subsidiaries of Idaho-based Boise Cascade) were sold primarily in the USA. Deforestation has caused massive erosion and contributed to increased flooding, local climate changes, and oversilting of rivers.

Wetland Depletion

Mexico's rich coastal lagoons and wetlands have experienced considerable harm in recent years from shrimp farming. Shrimp farms contribute to the destruction of mangroves, permanent flooding of lagoons, the privatization of communal fishing waters, and the introduction of massive amounts of fertilizers and chemicals. The industry is booming in Sinaloa, Nayarit and Oaxaca, and receives heavy investment from the Mexican government and the World Bank. The biggest market for Mexican-farmed shrimp is the USA.

Cattle grazing also has a devastating impact on wetlands where they are drained to create pastureland. Laguna Manialtepec (p253) in Oaxaca was being reduced at an alarming rate until considerable protests from local fishing communities put a stop to it in the late 1990s.

Erosion & Water Contamination

Erosion is mainly the result of deforestation followed by cattle grazing or intensive agriculture on unsuitable terrain. In the Mixteca area of Oaxaca, around 80% of the arable land is gone.

Some rural areas and watercourses have been contaminated by excessive use of chemical pesticides and defoliants. Sewage, and industrial and agricultural wastes contaminate most Mexican rivers.

Tourism

In some places in Mexico it's hoped that ecologically sensitive tourism will benefit the environment by providing a less harmful source of income for local people. An example is Mazunte (p263), Oaxaca, a village that lived by slaughtering sea turtles until the practice was banned in 1990. Villagers then turned to slash-and-burn farming, threatening forest survival, before a low-key and successful tourism program was launched.

To see what a couple of big international conservation groups are up to in Mexico, see Conservation International (www.conservation .org) and Greenpeace (www.greenpeace.org .mx in Spanish).

In other cases, despite official lip service paid to conservation, large-scale tourism developments have destroyed fragile ecosystems. Acapulco grew at such a rate and pumped so much sewage into the Bay of Acapulco in the 1970s and 1980s that drastic measures had to be taken to reverse damage to the bay. In the case of now-developing Bahías de Huatulco, the federal government has taken steps to prevent water pollution by resorts, limited construction heights on hotels and even created a national park to preserve fragile ecosystems. But local communities have been displaced, and inland lagoons critical to the local ecosystem have been mysteriously drawn out of park boundaries (where golf courses may be drawn in).

Environmental Movement

Environmental consciousness first grew in the 1970s, initially among the middle class in Mexico City, where nobody could ignore the air pollution. Today nongovernmental action is carried out by a growing number of groups around the country, mainly small organizations working on local issues.

Joel Simon's *Endangered Mexico: An Environment on the Edge* examines Mexico's varied environmental crises with the benefit of excellent first-hand journalistic research.

Between 1999 and 2001, Guerrero's Costa Grande made continuous headlines and attracted international criticism after the military arrested and imprisoned antilogging activists Rodolfo Montiel and Teodoro Cabrera. Montiel and Cabrera started a community environmental group in 1997, which fought heavy logging of the Costa Grande. Montiel and Cabrera were imprisoned for 16 months after reportedly being tortured into confessing to trumped-up drug and weapons charges. After intense international pressure, President Fox finally ordered their release; it came a month after their original defense lawyer was assassinated in Mexico City.

Environmental campaigning today is carried out mainly by small organizations working on local issues, though some successful campaigns in recent years have rested on broader-based support, even from outside Mexico. One was the defeat in 2000 of the plan for a giant saltworks at Laguna San Ignacio in Baja California, a gray-whale breeding ground. Another was the annulment in 2001 of a large hotel project at the Caribbean turtle-nesting beach of Xcacel. Ideas for hydroelectric dams on the Río Usumacinta, along Mexico's border with Guatemala, attract broad opposition whenever they resurface, owing to their consequences for the huge watershed of what is Mexico's biggest river and for the area's many Mayan archaeological sites.

Puerto Vallarta & Pacific Mexico Outdoors

Mexico's Pacific coast is an orgy of outdoor fun. Sportfishing, diving, snorkeling, sailing, jet-skiing, water-skiing, parasailing and swimming have lured sunseekers to this spectacular shoreline for decades. But in recent years people have started to realize there's even *more* to do: kayaking, surfing, hiking, mountain biking, river rafting and wildlife viewing are becoming increasingly popular. To help plan your travels, we've compiled a brief introduction to where and how you can get active on the coast. None of these activities should distract you, however, from putting in some serious hours under the sun, flat on your back, down on the beach.

Refer to this book's destination sections for details on equipment rentals, and availability and advisability of guides.

DIVING & SNORKELING

Though it's tough to compete with the azure waters and coral reefs of the Caribbean, there are some outstanding dive sites unique to the Pacific coast – and plenty of dazzling snorkeling spots. Mazatlán, Puerto Vallarta, Barra de Navidad, Manzanillo, Zihuatanejo, Playa Manzanillo (Troncones), Faro de Bucerías, Puerto Escondido, Puerto Ángel and Bahías de Huatulco all have highly praised dive sites nearby, not to mention some first-rate outfitters who will tank you up and take you out. Operators generally charge around US$50 for a guided one-tank dive, approximately US$80 for a two-tank dive and around US$60 for a night dive.

Most dive shops offer guided snorkeling excursions, or rent snorkel equipment so you can go it alone. On beaches with good snorkeling nearby, restaurants and booths usually rent equipment, though you should check gear carefully for quality and comfort before heading out for the day. There are plenty of places to snorkel without a guide, but with a guide, you're usually taken by boat to better, hard-to-reach spots.

Many diving outfitters are affiliates of the international organizations PADI (www .padi.com) or NAUI (www.naui.org) and post their certifications in plain view. Both organizations' websites allow you to search for their affiliated dive shops in Mexico.

Each year swimmers are killed by undertow, cross-currents, whirlpools and other ocean hazards. Whenever possible seek local advice before entering the water, and keep in mind that swimming conditions can change rapidly.

SAFETY GUIDELINES FOR DIVING

Before embarking on a scuba-diving trip, carefully consider the following points to ensure you have a safe and enjoyable experience:

- Obtain a current diving certification card from a recognized scuba-diving instructional agency, either at home or from one of many in Mexico.

- Obtain reliable information about physical and environmental conditions at the dive site (eg from a reputable local dive operation).

- Be aware of local laws, regulations and etiquette about marine life and the environment.

- Make sure that you are comfortable diving and dive only at sites within your realm of experience; if available, hire a competent, professionally trained dive instructor or dive master.

- Be aware that underwater conditions vary significantly from one region, or even site, to another. Seasonal changes can significantly alter site and dive conditions. These differences influence the way divers dress for a dive and what diving techniques they use.

- Ask about the environmental characteristics that can affect your diving and how local, trained divers deal with these considerations.

SURFING

Describing all the epic surf spots on Mexico's Pacific coast would be as arduous as paddling out against a double-overhead set at Playa Zicatela – well, almost. From the 'world's longest wave' near San Blas to the screaming barrels of Puerto Escondido's 'Mexican Pipeline,' the Pacific coast is bombarded with surf. Sayulita, Barra de Navidad, Manzanillo, Playa Boca de Pascuales, Playa La Ticla, Barra de Nexpa, Playa Azul, Playa Troncones, La Saladita, Ixtapa, Playa Revolcadero, Chacahua, Barra de la Cruz – the list goes on and on.

Most beach breaks receive some sort of surf all year, but wave season is really May to October/November. Spring and fall can see excellent conditions with fewer people, while the biggest months are June, July and August, when waves can get *huge* and the sets roll like clockwork.

Shipping a surfboard to Mexico is not a problem, but most airlines charge at least US$50, and some will hit you for another US$50 on your way home – even if they told you they wouldn't; be ready.

A good board bag is advisable, but a better one doesn't necessarily guarantee fewer mishaps on the aircraft. We've talked to people who've shipped their boards in what amounted to socks and escaped ding-free, while others have blown half their vacation funds on a super-bag only to open it to the tune of a broken skeg. They're usually fine, however. You'll rarely, if ever, need a wetsuit, but a rash guard is highly recommended for protection against the sun. Bring plenty of warm-water wax, as it's tough to find south of the border. Soft racks (or some sort of packable tie-downs) are easy to carry and indispensable if you plan to do any driving or want to secure your board to a taxi. Unless you plan to surf one spot only, renting a car, or driving your own, makes everything much easier.

FISHING

Mexico's Pacific coast has world-famous billfishing (marlin, swordfish, sailfish) and outstanding light-tackle fishing year-round. Many deep-sea charters now practice catch-and-release for billfish, a practice we highly recommend because these majestic lords of the deep are being disastrously overfished.

When & Where to Fish

You can catch fish in these waters year-round, but what, how many, where and when depend on such variables as water temperature, currents, bait supply and fish migrations. In general, the biggest catches occur from April to July and October to December. Keep in mind that summer and late fall is also prime tropical storm and hurricane season.

Mazatlán (p116), 'the billfish capital of the world,' is famous for marlin, while Puerto Vallarta (p72) is known for sailfish; both offer big catches of yellowfin tuna, *dorado* (dolphinfish or mahimahi), red snapper and black sea bass. In Zihuatanejo (p190) sailfish, marlin, dorado, roosterfish and wahoo are caught most of the year, and the biggest tuna catches are in spring. In Bahías de Huatulco swordfish, sailfish and dorado are caught year-round, while marlin are caught mostly from October to May; roosterfish season is April to August.

Plenty of other light-tackle fish are caught year-round along the entire coast, including yellowtail, grouper, Spanish mackerel, sea bass, halibut and wahoo.

The Divers Alert Network (DAN; www.diversalertnetwork.org) has a comprehensive divers' health section on its website that is well worth a peek before your plunge.

The Mexican Pipeline in Puerto Escondido, Oaxaca, is one of North America's most famous waves. More a proving ground than a surf spot, it provides enthralling but dangerous surf, and is definitely not for beginners.

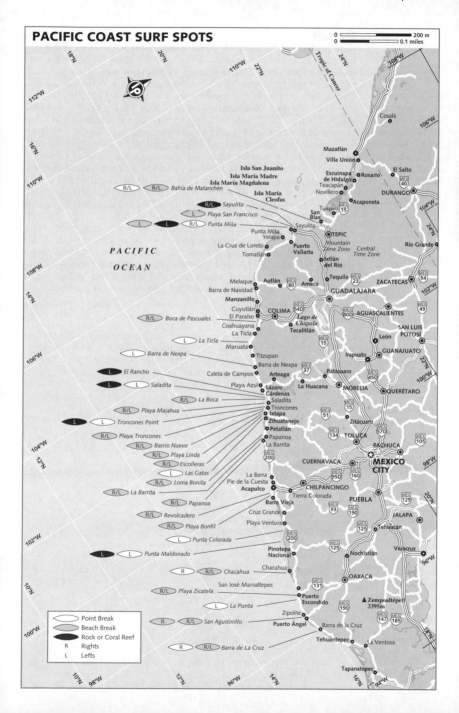

PACIFIC COAST SURF SPOTS

0 ⊨⟼⟼⟼⟼⟼ 200 m
0 ⊨⟼⟼⟼⟼⟼ 0.1 miles

PACIFIC OCEAN

Tropic of Cancer

Cosalá

Mazatlán
Villa Unión

Escuinapa
de Hidalgo
Teacapán
Novillero

El Salto

MEX 40

Rosario

DURANGO

Acaponeta

Río Grande

MEX 15

Tuxpan

San
Blas

Isla San Juanito
Isla María Madre
Isla María Magdalena
Isla María
Cleofas

R/L R/L Bahía de Matanchén

R/L Sayulita

L Playa San Francisco

L L R/L Punta Mita

Punta Mita
Yelapa

Sayulita

TEPIC

Mountain
Time Zone

Central
Time Zone

La Cruz de Loreto

Puerto
Vallarta

Tomatlán

Ixtlán
del Río

Tequila

MEX 23

ZACATECAS

MEX 54

Meleque
Barra de Navidad

Autlán

Ameca

GUADALAJARA

MEX 80

Manzanillo

Cuyutlán
El Paraíso

COLIMA

MEX 54D

Lago de
Chapala

MEX 80D

AGUASCALIENTES

MEX 49

R/L Boca de Pascuales

Coahuayana
La Ticla

Tecalitlán

SAN LUIS
POTOSÍ

L La Ticla

MEX 15

León

GUANAJUATO

Maruata

L Barra de Nexpa

Titzupan
Barra de Nexpa

Irapuato

MEX 37

Pátzcuaro

MEX 45D

MEX 100W

L El Rancho

Caleta de Campos

Arteaga

La Huacana

MORELIA

QUERÉTARO

L L Saladita

Playa Azul

Lázaro
Cárdenas
Saladita
Troncones
Ixtapa
Zihuatanejo
Petatlán
Papanoa
La Barrita

MEX 15

Zitácuaro

MEX 105

R/L La Boca

R/L Playa Majahua

TOLUCA

PACHUCA

L L Troncones Point

MEX 134

R/L Playa Troncones

R/L Barrio Nuevo

MEXICO
CITY

R/L Playa Linda

R/L Escolleras

CUERNAVACA

MEX 95D

MEX 160

L Las Gatas

R/L Loma Bonita

MEX 200

R/L La Barrita

La Barra
Pie de la Cuesta
Acapulco

CHILPANCINGO

PUEBLA

MEX 129

R/L Papanoa

Tierra Colorada

R/L Revolcadero

Barra Vieja

MEX 93

MEX 190

JALAPA

R/L Playa Bonfil

Cruz Grande

MEX 125

Tehuacán

Playa Ventura

Veracruz

MEX 125

L Punta Colorada

MEX 200

Nochixtlán

MEX 96W

L L Punta Maldonado

Pinotepa
Nacional

Chacahua

R R/L Chacahua

MEX 131

OAXACA

Zempoaltépetl
3395m

R/L Playa Zicatela

San José Manialtepec

Puerto
Escondido

MEX 190

MEX 147 MEX 185

L La Punta

Zipolite

R R/L San Agustinillo

Puerto Ángel

Barra de la Cruz

R R/L Barra de La Cruz

Tehuantepec

La Ventosa

Tapanatepec

Legend

- Point Break
- Beach Break
- Rock or Coral Reef
- R Rights
- L Lefts

Charters

Fishing charters are available in all major resort towns, and you'll find reputable local companies listed throughout this book. Always ask what's included in the rates. Fishing licenses, tackle, crew and ice are standard, but sometimes charters also include bait, cleaning and freezing, meals, drinks and tax. Live bait – usually available dockside for a few dollars – should be checked for absolute freshness. Tips for the crew are at your discretion, but US$15 to US$20 (per angler) for a successful eight hours is considered adequate. Bring along a hat, sunscreen, polarized sunglasses and Dramamine (or equivalent) whether or not you suffer from seasickness. Make sure the toilet situation is up to your standards of privacy.

Prices depend on boat type, size and season. The most comfortable is the cruiser, usually 8.6m to 14m (26ft to 42ft) in length and equipped with everything from fighting chairs (to reel in the big fish) to fish-finders and a full head (toilet). Prices range from US$250 to US$450 per boat for an eight-hour day.

The cheapest boats are *pangas*, the vessel of choice of Mexican commercial fishermen, as they put you right up close with the sea. About 6m to 8m (18ft to 24ft) long, these sturdy skiffs hold three to four people and cost between US$150 and US$200. Super-*pangas* are larger, accommodate four to six fishers comfortably and often feature toilets and a canvas top for shade. Rates start around US$300 per day per boat.

> Foreigners are barred from harvesting abalone, clams, coral, lobster, sea fans, sea shells, shrimp and turtles. Moreover, buying these items directly from fishermen is against the law.

HERE, FISHY FISHY FISH...

Who's gonna believe you if you can't even tell 'em what kind of fish you caught? This little angler's glossary should help. It will also help you communicate with Mexican guides and captains, who can usually tell you what you're most likely to catch. Keep in mind that some terms are regional. Sea bass, for instance might be called 'robalo,' 'cabrilla' or 'corvina,' depending on whom you talk to.

barracuda	*picuda*
black marlin	*marlín negro*
blue marlin	*marlín azul*
bonito	*bonito*
dolphin fish (mahimahi)	*dorado*
grouper	*garropa, mero*
halibut	*lenguado*
mullet	*lisa*
red snapper	*huachinango, pargo*
roosterfish	*pez gallo*
sailfish	*pez vela*
sea bass	*robalo, cabrilla, corvina*
shark	*tiburón*
Spanish mackerel	*sierra*
striped marlin	*marlín rayado*
swordfish	*pez espada*
tuna	*atún*
wahoo	*peto, guahu*
yellowtail	*jurel*
yellowfin tuna	*atún de aleta*

The phrase that may serve you best, however, is *'se me fue'* – 'it got away.' Then throw your hands up and say *'lo juro!'* ('I swear it!').

Depending on the season and the whims of the captain you may be able to negotiate better rates.

Licenses & Bag Limits

Anyone aboard a private vessel carrying fishing gear, both on the ocean and in estuaries, must have a Mexican fishing license whether they're fishing or not. Licenses are almost always included on charters, but you'll need your own if you choose to hire a local fisherman to take you out. In Mexico, licenses are issued by the Oficina de Pesca, which has offices in most towns. Licenses can also be obtained in the USA from the **Mexican Fisheries Department** (☎ 619-233-4324; fax 233-0344; Ste 101, 2550 Fifth Ave, San Diego, CA 92103). The cost of the license at the time of research was US$23/US$33/US$43 per week/month/year. Write, call or fax to request an application form.

The daily bag limit is 10 fish per person with no more than five of any one species. Billfish (such as marlin, sailfish and swordfish) are restricted to one per day per boat, while for dorado, tarpon, roosterfish and halibut it's two.

Surf Fishing

Surf fishing is a fun – though not always easy – way to put food in your stomach, *especially* when you're camping. No license is required when fishing from land, as many Mexicans still make their livelihood this way. You don't have to bring a pole – just find a local tackle shop (they're in any sizable fishing town, and some are listed in this book) and purchase a hand reel (a small piece of wood wrapped with fishing line) or *rollo de nylon* (spool of nylon) and some hooks, lures and weights. Some tackle shops sell live bait and *carnada* (raw bait), and it's often sold near the town pier. Shrimp and other raw baits are sold cheaply in the central markets.

Surf fishing is widely enjoyed on rocky shorelines throughout the region. With your hand reel in one hand let out some line, grab it with the other hand, swing it around your head (this takes practice) and let it go. Even if you fail horribly, it's a good way to meet local fishers who might give you a few tips.

KAYAKING, CANOEING & RAFTING

The coastal lagoons and sheltered bays of the Pacific coast are magnificent for kayaks and canoes. If you have your own boat, you'll be in heaven. If you don't, don't worry – many places rent kayaks and provide guides and transportation to boot. Parque Nacional Lagunas de Chacahua, Laguna de Manialtepec, Barra de la Cruz (near Bahías de Huatulco), La Manzanilla and Barra de Navidad are all places with brackish, bird-filled, mangrove-fringed lagoons just waiting to be paddled. Outfitters in San Blas (p131) and La Manzanilla (p153) take folks on some excellent kayaking trips. You can also rent kayaks and/or canoes and paddle off on your own at these and other places, including Bucerías, La Cruz de Huanacaxtle (both near Puerto Vallarta), Puerto Escondido and Pie de la Cuesta, near Acapulco.

White-water rafting is practiced from June to November on the Copalita and Zimatán Rivers near Bahías de Huatulco (p269); several outfitters there offer excursions.

WILDLIFE- & BIRD-WATCHING

Teeming with birdlife, lined with mangroves and sometimes even crawling with crocodiles, the coastal lagoons of Pacific Mexico are wonderful spots to see wildlife. Many of them are flanked by a small village or two

The multipurpose site Mexico Online (www .mexonline.com/tours .htm) maintains an ecotourism directory.

A Gringo's Guide to Mexican Whitewater by Tom Robey details 56 kayak, canoe and raft runs on 37 different rivers.

Avidly read by birders, Fat Birder (www.fatbirder .com) covers bird-watching worldwide and provides general information about the pursuit in Mexico.

and have docks where you can hire a local fisher to buzz you around in the cool of the morning. They'll point out birds and iguanas, crocs and turtles, maybe even a boa or two, and they'll let you fish, or stop at an island beach for a swim and a snack. See p42 for additional information on the creatures that inhabit the coast.

Sea Turtle–Watching

Seven of the world's eight sea turtle species are found in Mexican waters, and four of those make it to the Pacific shores of mainland Mexico (the others are found around Baja California and the Gulf of Mexico). Getting a glimpse of these majestic creatures is truly a highlight. There are numerous places to spy on sea turtles, but you have to know where and when to go looking. In order to protect the turtles, some beaches (most notably Playa Ventanilla) are guarded during nesting season and are off-limits to tourists. But chances of seeing the turtles at other beaches are still quite high. See the boxed text, p44, for tips on how to avoid disrupting nesting turtles if you happen to find yourself on a nesting beach.

Mexico has more species of birds than the USA and Canada combined.

Whale-Watching

Between November and March, humpback whales migrate to Pacific Mexico to mate and calve. Puerto Vallarta's Bahía de Banderas (p74) is one of their most popular stomping grounds, and a whale-watching trip from one of the city's many operators can bring you almost within kissing distance. Other great places for whale-watching (all of which have outfits offering seasonal trips out to sea) include Chacala, Rincón de Guayabitos and Bucerías, all near Puerto Vallarta. Even from the shore, it's not uncommon to see breaching whales along the entire coast during the first few months of the year.

Bird-Watching

Bird-watchers flock here year-round for the great variety of birds on offer. Even if you're not a bird-watcher, this is the perfect place to experience the rush that makes birders so fanatical. A morning float around one of

---

TOP TURTLE-WATCHING AREAS

The following coastal areas are where you're most likely to encounter sea turtles:

- **Playa San Francisco** (p143) The southern coast of Nayarit is home to Grupo Ecológico de la Costa Verde, which offers volunteer opportunities and releases more than 25,000 hatchlings each year to the sea.

- **Cuyutlán** (p170) Just south of Manzanillo, the Centro Tortuguero operates a thriving turtle-release program and a visitors' center with baby turtles on display.

- **Playa Maruata** (p174) Black turtles come ashore nightly from June to December to lay their eggs at this back-to-basics beach.

- **Puerto Escondido** (p247) Turtle-spotting tours on Bahía Principal often encounter the elusive loggerhead turtle.

- **San Agustinillo** (p262) Once the site of large-scale turtle slaughter, today this village is known for its turtle-viewing boat trips.

- **Mazunte** (p263) Home to the Centro Méxicano de la Tortuga, a turtle aquarium and research center with specimens of all seven of Mexico's marine turtle species.

- **Bahías de Huatulco** (p269) This area's terrific dive sites feature frequent close encounters with sea turtles.

the coast's many lagoons, with abundant birdlife, is an unforgettable experience. And if you do it in winter, not only will you see the native waterfowl, you'll see the North American and Alaskan species that migrate here as well. See p44 for some of the birds you might see.

The swamp forests and lagoons around San Blas are ideal for birdwatching, and there's a bird sanctuary in the nearby San Cristóbal estuary. The island of Isla Isabel, four hours from San Blas by boat, is a bird-watcher's dream. Laguna de Manialtepec in Oaxaca is another wetland bird habitat that will truly send you over the edge. There are estuary wetlands flapping with birds near La Cruz de Loreto (in Jalisco, south of Puerto Vallarta), Playa La Ticla (Michoacán) and Barra de Potosí (Guerrero). In Oaxaca, the pair of giant lagoons in Parque Nacional Lagunas de Chacahua, and the tiny lagoon of Barra de la Cruz near Bahías de Huatulco, are two other places offering plenty of chances to sneak up on birds. Inland, near Tepic (Nayarit), Laguna Santa María del Oro, an idyllic lake at 750m elevation in a 100m-deep volcanic crater, is home to some 250 species of bird, and its mountainous surroundings make a wonderful contrast to coastal ecology.

Most outfitters who offer bird-watching tours don't provide binoculars, so pack your own if this activity is on your agenda.

HIKING

Mexico's beaches make outstanding places along which to hike. The 13km beach in Parque Nacional Lagunas de Chacahua (Oaxaca); Playa Larga (near Zihuatanejo); and the endless, empty beaches of Michoacán are great for stretching the legs. Many villages on the coast have back roads or nearby trails you can explore by foot.

Some great hikes can be had inland too (if you can drag yourself away from the beach). Near Tepic, Laguna Santa María del Oro (p137) and the terrain around the extinct Volcán Ceboruco, both offer superb settings for various levels of hiking. Parque Nacional Volcán Nevado de Colima (p169), in Colima, has more good hiking. The Valles Centrales of Oaxaca are popular for guided hikes between mountain villages; they're offered by several operators based in Oaxaca city.

A Hiker's Guide to Mexico's Natural History by Jim Conrad and *Backpacking in Mexico* by Tim Burford are both must-reads for intrepid explorers planning a bipedal tour south of the border.

MOUNTAIN BIKING

Shops rent mountain bikes up and down the coast, but you're usually left to your own intuition about where to explore. Troncones, Zihuatanejo, Manzanillo, Playa Azul, San Blas, Sayulita, La Crucecita (Bahías de Huatulco) and many other coastal towns have bike rentals and are small enough places that you can navigate through town and into open terrain without the fear of being run down. You can often ride from one fishing village to another, stopping in each for a beer or a bite to eat (Troncones to La Saladita comes to mind here). Oaxaca (p230) and Puerto Vallarta (p75) have become very popular for mountain biking, and several operators listed in these chapters will take you for some beautiful rides along old mountain roads to visit tiny villages.

On the Internet, **Planeta** (www.planeta.com) has a 'Mexico Biking Guide.' See Puerto Vallarta (p75) and Oaxaca (p230) for outfitters offering some great cycling trips.

Spanish-language site Ciclismo de Montaña en México (Mountain Biking in Mexico; www .mountainbike.org.mx) is a great resource for bilingual pedalheads.

HORSEBACK RIDING

It's hard to beat a trot down the beach on a trusty Mexican horse. Horses are rented on countless beaches along the coast. Puerto Vallarta, Troncones, Zihuatanejo, Pie de la Cuesta and Bahías de Huatulco are just a few of the places where you can mount up for about US$15 to US$30 per person for a two- to three-hour guided ride. Some places will allow you to take horses on your own if you leave a small deposit and an ID. Mexican horses tend to be a bit smaller, more worn out and less inclined to run than their North American and European counterparts, but they can still be fun. Keep in mind that if a guide accompanies you, the money he or she makes is often primarily what riders tip them; around US$5 per person is usually sufficient.

Earthfoot (www.earthfoot.org/mx_pc.htm) presents small-scale, locally produced, low-impact ecotours worldwide and maintains a page dedicated to specialist guides in Pacific Mexico.

GOLF & TENNIS
Mazatlán, Puerto Vallarta, Ixtapa, Acapulco and Bahías de Huatulco all have world-class golf courses where you can swing the old irons to some spectacular views. But you'll pay a pretty price to do it: green fees run anywhere from US$60 to US$200. Carts and caddies – which are often required – can cost an additional US$30 to US$50, depending on the course.

These same resorts all have numerous tennis clubs, many of which are found in the luxury hotels. Nonhotel guests are almost always welcome to use the courts for about US$20 per hour and can rent racquets on the spot.

OTHER ACTIVITIES
Water-skiing, parasailing and banana-boat riding are widespread resort activities, especially in Acapulco, Puerto Vallarta, Zihuatanejo, Mazatlán and Bahías de Huatulco. Many of the larger resort hotels – if they're located on a bay – rent sailboats and catamarans, too. Laguna de Coyuca (p201), at Pie de la Cuesta, is famous for water-skiing and has several operators that will zip you around the lagoon. Always cast an eye over the equipment before taking off.

The two-stroke engines found on jet skis discharge as much as one third of their fuel and oil unburned into the sea and can also prove detrimental to wildlife.

Adrenaline junkies can bungee jump from a platform over sea cliffs near Puerto Vallarta (p75) or from a crane top in the middle of the hotel district in Acapulco – great for those margarita hangovers!

Food & Drink James Peyton

When the Spanish arrived in Mexico, they found a cuisine based on corn, beans, squash, chili and, along the coasts, seafood. To this they contributed beef, pork, lamb, chicken, wheat, dairy products and spices like cumin and cinnamon. While these foods combined in ways that created common threads, each area developed its own regional interpretations. To this day, the states along Mexico's Pacific coast – Sinaloa, Nayarit, Colima, Jalisco, Guerrero and Oaxaca – maintain their distinctive culinary traditions and, in each of them, talented chefs continue the process. What you find will probably bear only a passing resemblance to the items served in most Mexican restaurants outside Mexico. You will discover that Mexican cooking is far more varied and interesting than you imagined, and if you are truly interested in food, it will be one of the highlights of your trip.

STAPLES & SPECIALTIES
Seafood
For those who do not live near the coast, your visit will be an opportunity to sample seafood (mariscos) that is truly fresh. You will find fish cooked either whole (entero) or filleted (filete or fileteado). One of the most common ways of preparing both fish and shrimp is al mojo de ajo (with garlic sauce). The seafood is sautéed or grilled, then served with a sauce of garlic that is simmered in olive oil until meltingly tender. A particularly unique and delicious dish – a specialty of Sinaloa, Nayarit and Jalisco – is pescado zarandeado. Originally prepared on a wooden grill over coals, it consists of an entire specially filleted fish. The fillets are very thin and marinated with a unique combination of spices and herbs, often including garlic, mild chilies and achiote (the powdered seeds of the annato tree), and grilled. Another favorite way of using seafood is as a filling for tacos. A popular version of seafood tacos in the state of Guerrero is called pescadillos, and is made with fish, tomato, and olives, flavored with bay leaf and cinnamon. Dried seafood, often shark, is made into a hash called machaca that is popular at breakfast. All along the coast you will find seafood served al diablo. While there are infinite variations, most versions consist of seafood served with a sauce of tomato and various chilies.

In terms of preparation fish can be sautéed (empanizada or a la plancha), grilled (al carbón or a la parrilla), steamed (al vapor), smoked (ahumado), or deep fried (frito). You will also find seafood or poultry dishes prepared en escabeche (simmered in a broth with mild, fruity vinegar; onions; squash; other vegetables and exotic spices; and served at room temperature).

Mexico's Pacific coast has some of the most delicious seafood soups anywhere. They are usually made with a tomato-infused broth and can include everything from fish and squash to a medley of four or five kinds of seafood and several vegetables. Hominy may be added, creating a dish called pozole, and sometimes the fish and other seafood is ground and rolled into 'meatballs' called albondigas.

Seafood cocktails, most often of shrimp, but also made with crab, scallops, octopus, squid, oysters and scallops, are a special treat. They are often referred to as campechanas, named for the port city, Campeche, where they originated. A close cousin to the cocktails is seviche, where raw fish is marinated in lime juice; the acid in the lime 'cooks' the fish, which is then combined with spices, chilies, onions, tomatoes, cilantro and sometimes pineapple or orange juice. For these dishes, some caution is advised.

Diana Kennedy is the acknowledged doyenne of Mexican food. Her latest book, From My Mexican Kitchen: Techniques and Ingredients (2003), captures the essence of Mexico's complex food and makes it available to cooks outside the country.

For a comprehensive overview of both Mexico and its foods, visit www.mexconnect.com. Some portions of the site are free, but most require a yearly subscription of US$30.

TACO STANDS EVERYWHERE!

Looking for a cheap, quick meal on the run? Look no further than one of Mexico's ubiquitous taco stands, a godsend tailor-made for the busy budget traveler.

Amble on up to the counter and your choices are clear: *tripa* (intestine), *uba* (udder), *cabeza* (head meat) or *lengua* (tongue). Of course, the much more palatable and commonplace meat choices are *carne asada/res/bistek birria* (varieties of grilled beef) or *chorizo*. Often there will only be a few items on the menu, as different taco stands specialize in different things.

Tacos can vary in size, but are usually about three or four bites and cost around US$0.50 to US$0.75 each. Say '*con todo*' if you want extras such as beans, onion and cilantro. The tacos will be prepared to order and put on plastic plates covered in clean plastic bags (making cleanup easy but creating unfortunate trash). The best stands are bigger and offer grilled onions, complimentary salsas and radish or cucumber slices. Unless the stand has plastic chairs or is near public seating, you'll probably have to stand to munch the tacos. Pay for your meal after you eat.

And what about sanitary conditions? Well, have a peek at the stand itself: does it look clean? Is it busy? Is the food piping hot or has it been hanging loose awhile? Use your instincts – there are no guarantees, but adventurous travel is all about tasting the local fare, don't you think?

While the lime juice makes the fish opaque and firms it up, no heat is applied, so the juice does not cook the fish to the extent that all bacteria is destroyed. Therefore it should be especially fresh – sushi quality.

Meat, Poultry & More

Those who prefer meat will find a mouthwatering selection. There are many restaurants specializing in *comida norteña* (northern-style cooking) that feature char-broiled meats in various combinations – think fajitas (which are often referred to as *arrecharas*). And nearly every menu will have a selection of steaks and chops, some with beef imported from the USA, which is usually more tender, but less flavorful than the local, grass-fed offerings. Steak *tampiqueña* (Tampico-style), which includes a thin tenderloin steak served with an enchilada, quesadillas and similar *antojitos* (appetizers), as well as rice and beans, is available in myriad combinations. For poultry fans, Sinaloa has a special dish called *pollo sinaloensa*, where chicken is marinated in a perfectly balanced combination of chilies, juices and spices, and broiled over coals.

Coastal areas in Jalisco and Guerrero (especially on Thursdays) serve the *pozoles* for which those states are famous. These hominy soups are usually made with pork, but on the coast often with seafood. They are traditionally accompanied by small bowls of lime wedges, chilies, cilantro and oregano so that diners can spice up their offerings. In Guerrero you may find a breakfast dish, called *baila con tu mujer* (dance with your woman), of eggs scrambled with tomato, onion, green chilies and bits of corn tortillas. In the market of Zihuatanejo they serve special breakfast *tortas* (sandwiches) made with roast pork, pineapple, raisins, almonds, plantains, onion and potatoes.

Oaxaca is known as the 'Land of Seven Moles,' and many of these rich, complex stews of chilies, fruits, nuts and exotic spices are found on the coast. Particular favorites include *mole negro* (black mole), *colaradito* (red) and *verde* (green), named for the color of the final dish. Oaxaca also produces special tamales that are wrapped in banana leaves and filled with either *mole negro* or seafood. There, you will also find a pre-Hispanic drink called *champurrado* (hot chocolate with ground, dried corn) that is rich and delicious. The culinarily adventurous may want to try iguana, which is usually stewed, is generally tender and tastes like a combination of chicken and pork.

According to Mexican food authority Amando Farga, seviche was first called *cebiche* by Captain Vasco Núñez de Balboa after being given some by fishermen following his discovery of the Pacific Ocean in 1513. Farga speculates that the name comes from the Spanish verb *cebar*, one of whose meanings is 'to penetrate or saturate.'

The owners of www .mexgrocer.com have in-depth experience with Mexican food products and offer a large selection at reasonable prices.

Dessert

For dessert, coastal cooks take full advantage of local tropical fruits, such as *guayaba* (guava), mango, papaya and coconut. They are served fresh, in puddings, custards, various confections and ice cream. Sinaloa specializes in *pastel tres leches* (a three-milk cake made with fresh or canned evaporated cream, sweetened condensed milk and evaporated milk), which is a favorite throughout Mexico and increasingly in the USA. You may also find *tacuarines*, which are doughnut-like pastries. Acapulco cooks make special use of coconut, ginger and pineapple. They appear in both desserts and special confections called *cocadas* and *alfajores*. Jalisco is famous for a flan-like custard dessert called *jericalla*.

DRINKS
Alcoholic

You will find tequila, Mexico's national drink, everywhere, and bartenders prepare margaritas of every hue and flavor. If you wish to go native, try your tequila either neat with a bite of lime and a lick of salt, or with *sangrita* (a chaser of orange juice, grenadine, chili and sometimes tomato juice). Mamá Lucia's (p104) in Mismaloya is a great place to sample some of the country's top tequilas. Oaxaca is famous for mezcal (p237), a drink similar to tequila, but made with a different agave that is usually smoked before being distilled. Rum drinkers will find interesting light and dark varieties that are often served in a cocktail called Cuba libre (with Coca Cola and lime juice). Visitors will also find good selections of both imported and Mexican wines (whites, reds and rosés), the latter of which have improved greatly in recent years.

Nonalcoholic

Mexico has a long tradition of nonalcoholic drinks. The most popular are *tamarindo*, made with tamarind pods; *Jamaica*, made with dried hibiscus leaves; *horchata*, a combination of melon and its seeds and/or rice; and lime-ade. These delicious, fruity drinks are sold from large, keg-shaped, glass containers, often garnished with mint leaves. Be careful, however, in regard to sanitation.

You will also discover a variety of delicious and healthful smoothies and milkshakes called *licuados*, made with milk, fruits, yogurt and honey. Orange juice, nearly always freshly squeezed, is available everywhere, as

> In addition to many other items, such as corn and turkey, two of the world's most beloved edibles, chocolate and vanilla, originally came from Mexico.

> Noted chef and restaurateur Rick Bayless has a website (www .fronterakitchens.com) that is partially promotional but has a very good selection of recipes and other information on Mexican food.

WE DARE YOU

A current culinary renaissance in Mexico features pre-Hispanic foods that are often accompanied by copious amounts of tequila's fiery cousin, mezcal . One of the most popular foods is *chapulines* (chop-ooo-lean-ace), which are grasshoppers (purged of digestive matter and dried, you will be happy to hear). They come in large and small sizes, with the latter often being smoked, and are served in many ways, ranging from a taco filling to being sautéed in butter and flamed in brandy. The small, smoked variety are quite tasty and less likely to leave bits of carapace and feelers protruding from your teeth!

Jumiles are beetles, actually a type of stink bug, esteemed in central Mexico when in season in late fall and early winter. They are usually either ground with chilies, tomatoes and tomatillos to make a sauce or used as a taco filling, either toasted or live. In discussing the latter, Diana Kennedy says in *My Mexico*, 'the more fleet-footed ones have to be swept back into the mouth and firmly crunched to prevent them from escaping.' The flavor is unforgettable.

Other favorites include stewed iguana, which tastes like a cross between chicken and pork, as do armadillos, whose copious, small bones are their most irritating quality.

are juices of other fruits and vegetables. Many of these items are found in street *puestos*, or 'stalls,' and in larger, barlike establishments.

Some of the best coffee in the world is grown in Mexico, and Mexicans have a unique way of making it called *café de olla*. This 'coffee from the pot' is brewed in a special clay vessel with a raw sugar called *piloncillo* and cinnamon. *Café con leche* (coffee with milk) is also very popular. For ordinary coffee, with cream on the side, simply ask for *café con crema*. Waiters will often pour both coffee and cream at the table according to your instructions. Bottled water *(agua purificada)* and mineral water *(agua mineral)* are available everywhere.

Jim Peyton's www
.lomexicano.com is
updated quarterly and
offers regional Mexican
recipes, food-related
travel articles and a large
glossary of Mexican food
terms.

CELEBRATIONS

Feast days in Mexico are taken seriously, but resort areas are more casual in their observations. For the most part, they do not allow their traditions to interfere with the enjoyment of their visitors. However, be aware that on Christmas, New Year, Holy Week, and during the Day of the Dead, celebrated during the first two days of November, nontouristy establishments may be closed. During these times special items are often available, including *pan de muertos* (bread of the dead), made with yeast, flour, eggs, butter, nutmeg and aniseed and topped off with sprinkled or glazed sugar. Vegetarian specialties (opposite) are popular during Holy Week, and at Christmas and New Year *bacalao* (dried cod) is often served in a mild chili sauce.

WHERE TO EAT & DRINK

Where you eat will depend on your mood and budget, and the number of choices will delight you. *Palapas* are casual, thatched-roof structures found on nearly every popular beach. You will discover delicious traditional seafood cocktails and entrées at moderate to low prices.

In urban areas you will find *puestos*, street stalls that usually specialize in a single item – tacos, burritos etc. Many serve dishes passed down through generations. As always, take precautions when eating at such informal places (see above). Slightly more formal are *loncherias*, *comedores* and *taquerías*, small sit-down eateries often found in private homes in villages and at markets in towns and cities. A step up are *cafés* that serve Mexican specialties, including corn- and tortilla-based *antojitos* such as tacos and enchiladas and simple but delicious meat and seafood entrées, usually accompanied by homemade soups, steaming rice pilafs, beans and fresh vegetables.

Restaurateur and chef
Zarela Martínez has
provided the perfect
guide to the regional
cooking of Veracruz.
Zarela's *Veracruz: Mexico's
Simplest Cuisine* (2004)
is part travelogue and
filled with anecdotes and
recipes from places you
can actually visit.

Resorts and large cities offer upscale dining with local atmosphere and a mix of international foods and elegant Mexican creations. Many of their chefs practice Mexico's upscale version of fusion cooking called *nueva cocina mexicana* (new Mexican cooking), which combines regional Mexican dishes, ingredients and cooking techniques in new, aesthetically pleasing and delicious ways. Pork *vampiro* (vampire) is one such dish. It draws its inspiration from a popular Mexican drink (a *vampiro*) made with tequila, *sangrita* (a combination of orange juice, grenadine, ancho chiles or chili powder, and lime juice) and sparkling water. These ingredients are then blended and used to braise pork loin. A perfect pairing of flavors results.

To make certain your experience is positive, exercise the same caution you would when selecting any place to eat. Avoid establishments that do not appear to be busy or that seem messy or unclean. Be particularly wary of seafood served from street stalls, as their only refrigeration may be an inadequate amount of ice in a large cooler, and there may be no place for the staff to wash their hands. Remember that if it smells fishy it isn't fresh! Also, avoid mayonnaise-based sauces (which are made with egg yolks) whenever possible.

FRUIT IN A BAG

You'll see them in many parts of Mexico, in the city or on the beach: small cart vendors selling juicy slices of mango, cucumbers and jicama, or cut squares of watermelon and papaya. Each fruit or vegetable is brightly presented in a clear plastic bag or cup (with a fork or toothpick stuck on the top), tempting you to stop, drop some spare change and take a quick refreshing snack. How can you resist?

You can often also choose a mixed bag of fruit, or ask the vendor to make you a particular combination of fruits (this may up the price by a few cents, though). The price depends on the quantity of fruit in the bag and the popularity of the town with tourists. Expect to pay from US$0.60 to US$1.50, with US$1.25 as the common denominator. For an extra savory kick, have the vendor add some salt, lime juice and chili powder to your bag – this may sound a bit unconventional at first, but one taste of sweet mango with the opposing flavors of salt and chili and you might just get hooked. Plus, not many bugs can survive the double whammy of chili and lime. Hopefully your taste buds and tummy can, though.

VEGETARIANS & VEGANS

Tourist establishments have learned to cater to their patrons, including vegetarians, and visitors will find vegetarian offerings on most menus, certainly by special order. Vegetarian dishes are also on the menus of most restaurants during Lent, though not at other times.

Most waiters in the larger eateries are generally knowledgeable about what they serve and anxious to please. However, they are often not aware of the specific requirements of vegetarians, and especially vegans, and may find the concept difficult to understand – most Mexicans do without meat only because they cannot afford it, and many Mexican vegetarians eat what they do purely because they believe vegetables are healthy, rather than for ethical or philosophical reasons. So you must make your requirements very clear. Your server may believe he is bringing you a vegetarian meal when the items have been flavored with beef or chicken broth, or cooked in lard. Many Mexican soups, for instance, are vegetarian although they are often made with chicken broth or flavored with crushed bouillon. The more upscale the restaurant, the better your chances of being accommodated.

Besides being great entertainment, both the book and the film of *Like Water for Chocolate* show the importance of food in Mexico, and their use of magic realism showcases the way so many Mexicans view life.

EATING WITH KIDS

Mexicans adore children and Mexico is a child-friendly place. Most waiters will cheerfully do anything within reason to please your child, and virtually all restaurants have high chairs; just ask for a *silla para niños*. Supermarkets carry a full range of American and international brands of baby food. Stock up if you intend to visit small or remote towns.

HABITS & CUSTOMS

Coastal eating customs are less formal than in other parts of Mexico. Instead of the afternoon *comida* (meal) served in most of Mexico between 1:30pm and 4pm, lunch is usually available no later than noon, and many restaurants do not open until 6pm for dinner. It is customary for entire families to dine together, either at someone's home or at a restaurant, especially for the Sunday afternoon *comida*. If invited to someone's home for dinner, chocolates or tequila are good choices for a gift. Arriving 10 to 15 minutes late is advisable, as this is what most Mexicans do.

Mexico's attitude toward liquor is usually quite liberal, but be aware that in many communities liquor cannot be sold on election days or when the president is visiting. Also, while alcoholic beverages are usually considered a normal part of life, drinking while driving is a serious no-no!

Lots of recipes for Mexican foods can be found at http://mexicanfood .about.com.

In the margin:

Jim Peyton's *New Cooking from Old Mexico* (1999) includes a history of Mexican cooking, illustrated with traditional recipes. It also introduces Mexico's unique new contemporary cuisine, *nueva cocina mexicana*, a fusion between Mexico's traditional and regional cuisines with emphasis on elegance and presentation.

In better restaurants, tipping is expected. While 10% is considered on the low side, 15% is the norm, and 20% and is above average. Most restaurants add on Mexico's value-added tax of 15%, which is noted as IVA.

COOKING COURSES & TOURS

In Oaxaca, **Seasons of My Heart** (☎ 518-77-26; www.seasonsofmyheart.com) is operated by well-known cookbook author Susana Trilling. She also conducts culinary tours in Oaxaca and other regions of Mexico. For details of other cooking classes, see p230.

For those with particular interest in cooking and food, cookbook author and Mexico culinary expert Marilyn Tausend (www.marilyntausend.com) conducts terrific, reasonably priced culinary tours of Mexico, most of which include market tours and workshops with noted food experts and chefs.

EAT YOUR WORDS

For non-Spanish speakers, travel and dining in Mexico is no problem as English is understood almost everywhere. However, a few words in Spanish will indicate a respect for them and their culture, not to mention a willingness to risk embarrassment, and that can make a huge difference.

For further tips on pronunciation, see p310.

In the margin:

Susana Trilling has lived in Oaxaca for over 15 years and operates a fine cooking school by the same name. In *Seasons of My Heart* (1999) she introduces the reader to the fascinating food and customs of this very special area.

Useful Phrases

Are you open?
¿Está abierto?   e·*sta* a·*byer*·to
When are you open?
¿Cuando está abierto?   kwan·do e·*sta* a·*byer*·to
Are you now serving breakfast/lunch/dinner?
¿Ahora, está sirviendo desayuno/   a·o·ra e·*sta* ser·*vyen*·do de·sa·*yoo*·no/
la comida/la cena?   la ko·*mee*·da/la *se*·na
I'd like to see a menu.
Quisiera ver la carta/el menú.   kee·*sye*·ra ver la *kar*·ta/el me·*noo*
Do you have a menu in English?
¿Tienen un menú en inglés?   tye·nen oon me·*noo* en een·*gles*
Can you recommend something?
¿Puede recomendar algo?   pwe·de re·ko·men·*dar* al·*go*
I'm a vegetarian.
Soy vegetariano/a. (m/f)   soy ve·he·te·*rya*·no/a
I can't eat anything with meat or poultry products, including broth.
No puedo comer algo de carne o aves,   no *pwe*·do ko·*mer* al·*go* de *kar*·ne o *a*·ves
incluyendo caldo.   een·kloo·*yen*·do *kal*·do
I'd like mineral water/natural bottled water.
Quiero agua mineral/agua purificada.   *kye*·ro *a*·gwa mee·ne·*ral*/a·gwa poo·ree·fee·*ka*·da
Is it (chili) hot?
¿Es picoso?   es pee·*ko*·so
The check, please.
La cuenta, por favor.   la *kwen*·ta por fa·*vor*

Food Glossary
MENU DECODER

arroz mexicana	a·*ros* me·khee·*ka*·na	pilaf-style rice with a tomato base
chilaquiles	chee·la·*kee*·les	fried tortilla strips cooked with a red or green chili sauce, and sometimes meat and eggs
chiles rellenos	chee·les re·ye·nos	chilies stuffed with meat or cheese, dipped in egg batter and usually fried
empanada	em·pa·*na*·da	pastry turnover filled with meat, cheese or fruits

enchiladas	en·chee·*la*·das	corn tortillas dipped in chili sauce, wrapped around meat or poultry and garnished with cheese
ensalada	en·sa·*la*·da	salad
filete al la tampiqueña	fee·*le*·te al la tam·pee·*ke*·nya	steak, Tampico-style – a thin tenderloin, grilled and served with chili strips and onion, a quesadilla and enchilada
huevos fritos	hwe·vos *free*·tos	fried eggs
huevos rancheros	hwe·vos ran·*che*·ros	fried eggs served on a corn tortilla, topped with a sauce of tomato, chilies and onions
huevos revueltos	hwe·vos re·*vwel*·tos	scrambled eggs
nopalitos	no·pa·*lee*·tos	sautéed or grilled sliced cactus paddles
papas fritas	*pa*·pas *free*·tas	french fries
picadillo	pee·ka·*dee*·yo	a ground-beef filling that often includes fruit and nuts
quesadilla	ke·sa·*dee*·ya	cheese and other items folded inside a tortilla and fried or grilled

COOKING METHODS

a la parilla	a la pa·*ree*·ya	grilled
a la plancha	a la *plan*·cha	pan-broiled
adobada	a·do·*ba*·da	marinated with *adobo*, chili sauce
al carbón	al kar·*bon*	charbroiled
al mojo de ajo	al *mo*·kho de *a*·kho	with garlic sauce
alambre	al·*am*·bre	shish kebab
empanizado	em·pa·nee·*sa*·do	sautéed
frito	*free*·to	fried

DAIRY PRODUCTS

crema	*kre*·ma	cream
leche	*le*·che	milk
mantequilla	man·te·*kee*·ya	butter
margarina	mar·ga·*ree*·na	margarine
queso	*ke*·so	cheese

SOUPS

caldo	*kal*·do	broth or soup
pozole	pa·*so*·le	a hearty soup or thin stew of hominy, meat or seafood, vegetables and chilies
sopa	*so*·pa	soup, either 'wet' or 'dry,' as in rice and pasta

FISH & SEAFOOD

calamar	ka·la·*mar*	squid
camarones	ka·ma·*ro*·nes	shrimp
cangrejo/jaiba	kan·*gre*·kho/*khay*·ba	crab
langosta	lan·*gos*·ta	lobster
mariscos	ma·*rees*·kos	seafood
ostras/ostiones	*os*·tras/os·*tyo*·nes	oysters
pulpo	*pool*·po	octopus

MEAT & POULTRY

albóndigas	al·*bon*·dee·gas	meatballs
aves	*a*·ves	poultry
biftec	beef·*tek*	steak
brocheta	bro·*che*·ta	shish kebab

carne	*kar*·ne	meat
carne de puerco	*kar*·ne de *pwer*·ko	pork
carne de res	*kar*·ne de res	beef
carnitas	kar·*nee*·tas	pork simmered in lard
cerdo	*ser*·do	pork
chorizo	cho·*ree*·so	mexican-style bulk sausage made with chili and vinegar
chuleta	choo·*le*·ta	chop, as in pork chop
costillas de res	kos·*tee*·yas de res	beef ribs
jamón	kha·*mon*	ham
lomo	*lo*·mo	loin
lomo de cerdo	*lo*·mo de *ser*·do	pork loin
pechuga de pollo	pe·*chu*·ga de *po*·yo	chicken breast
pollo	*po*·yo	chicken
tocino	to·*see*·no	bacon

VEGETABLES, LEGUMES & GRAINS

arroz	a·*ros*	rice
calabacita	ka·la·ba·*see*·ta	squash
cebolla	se·*bo*·ya	onion
papas	*pa*·pas	potatoes
verduras	ver·*doo*·ras	vegetables

OTHER FOODS

azucar	a·soo·*kar*	sugar
pan integral	pan in·te·*gral*	wholemeal bread
pan	pan	bread
pimienta	pi·*myen*·ta	pepper
sal	sal	salt

FRUIT

coco	*ko*·ko	coconut
coctel de frutas	*kok*·tel de *fru*·tas	fruit cocktail
fresa	*fre*·sa	strawberry
piña	*pee*·nya	pineapple
platano	*pla*·ta·no	banana or plantain

DESSERTS

cajeta	ka·*khe*·ta	goat's milk and sugar boiled to a paste
helado	e·*la*·do	ice cream
nieve	*nye*·ve	sorbet
pastel	pas·*tel*	cake
postre	*pos*·tre	dessert

DRINKS

agua mineral	*a*·gwa mee·ne·*ral*	mineral water or club soda
agua purificada	*a*·gwa poo·ree·fee·*ka*·da	bottled uncarbonated water
café americano	ka·*fe* a·me·ree·*ka*·no	black coffee
café con crema/leche	ka·*fe* kon *kre*·ma/*le*·che	coffee with cream/milk
café negro	ka·*fe* *ne*·gro	black coffee
jugo de manzana	*khoo*·go de man·*sa*·na	apple juice
jugo de naranja	*khoo*·go de na·*ran*·kha	orange juice
jugo de piña	*khoo*·go de *pee*·nya	pineapple juice
té de manzanillo	te de man·sa·*nee*·ya	chamomile tea
té negro	te *ne*·gro	black tea

Puerto Vallarta

The jewel of Jalisco, Puerto Vallarta – referred to simply as 'Vallarta' by its loyal boosters – is one of Mexico's liveliest and most sophisticated resort destinations. Stretching around the sparkling blue Bahía de Banderas (Bay of Flags) and backed by lush, palm-covered mountains, you couldn't ask for a lovelier or livelier place to while away a cosmopolitan vacation. Each year millions come to laze on the dazzling sandy beaches, browse in the quaint shops, nosh in the stylish restaurants, and wander through the picturesque cobbled streets or along its beautiful seafront *malecón*. If the pretty town beaches aren't enough, you can venture out on cruises, horseback rides, dive trips and day tours – and be back in time for a late dinner and an even later outing to one of the many sizzling nightspots.

The appeal of Puerto Vallarta transcends its city limits, and everywhere you go the dazzling sea beckons. During the winter months humpback whales arrive after a long journey from arctic seas, ready for a little R&R in Mexico's warm waters. All around the bay sportfishing and diving are famously first rate, while up at Punta de Mita surfers find plenty of long, curling waves to keep them busy. Escape artists disappear into small towns such as Bucerías and La Cruz de Huanacaxtle to ease into the local rhythm.

Find yourself on a paradisiacal beach, accessible only by boat. Start with the remote coastal villages of Yelapa, Quimixto and Las Ánimas, and then set out to discover some empty beaches that you can call your own. There's no shortage of boat operators ready and waiting to take you there.

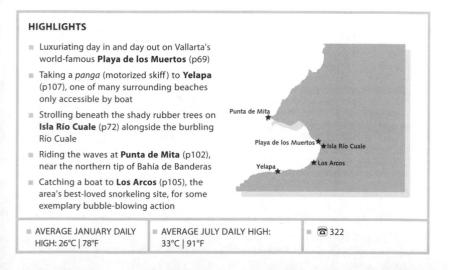

HIGHLIGHTS

- Luxuriating day in and day out on Vallarta's world-famous **Playa de los Muertos** (p69)
- Taking a *panga* (motorized skiff) to **Yelapa** (p107), one of many surrounding beaches only accessible by boat
- Strolling beneath the shady rubber trees on **Isla Río Cuale** (p72) alongside the burbling Río Cuale
- Riding the waves at **Punta de Mita** (p102), near the northern tip of Bahía de Banderas
- Catching a boat to **Los Arcos** (p105), the area's best-loved snorkeling site, for some exemplary bubble-blowing action

Punta de Mita

Playa de los Muertos ★ Isla Río Cuale

Yelapa ★ Los Arcos

- AVERAGE JANUARY DAILY HIGH: 26°C | 78°F
- AVERAGE JULY DAILY HIGH: 33°C | 91°F
- ☎ 322

HISTORY

Although indigenous peoples probably lived in this area for centuries, as they did elsewhere along the coast, the first documented settlement was in 1851, when the Sánchez family came and made their home by the mouth of the Río Cuale. Farmers and fisher folk followed, and farmers began shipping their harvests from a small port north of the Río Cuale. In 1918 the settlement was named Vallarta, in honor of Ignacio Luis Vallarta, a former governor of the state of Jalisco.

Tourists started to trickle into Puerto Vallarta back in 1954 when Mexicana airlines started a promotional campaign and initiated the first flights here, landing on a dirt airstrip in Emiliano Zapata, an area

that is now the center of Vallarta. A decade later, John Huston chose the nearby deserted cove of Mismaloya as a location for the film of Tennessee Williams' play *The Night of the Iguana*. Of his first visit, Huston later wrote 'When I first came here, almost 30 years ago, Vallarta was a fishing village of some 2000 souls. There was only one road to the outside world – and it was impassable during the rainy season. I arrived in a small plane, and we had to buzz the cattle off a field outside town before setting down.' As production on the film commenced, Hollywood paparazzi descended on the town to report on the tempestuous romance between Richard Burton and Elizabeth Taylor, and Burton's co-star,

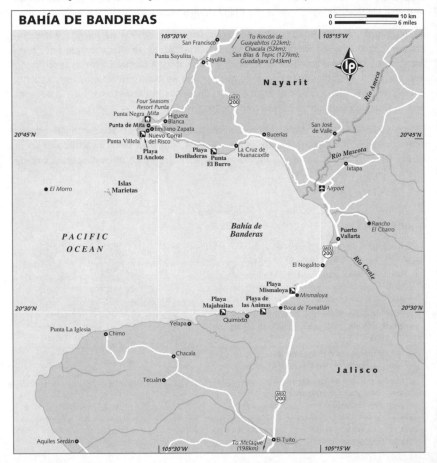

THE ART & SYMBOLOGY OF THE HUICHOL

In some of the furthest-flung and inaccessible areas of Jalisco and Nayarit, in a rugged region of about 39,000 sq km straddling the Sierra Madre Occidental, the Huichol have managed to maintain their culture through the centuries up to the present. Believed to be direct descendants of the Aztecs, there remain approximately 8000 Huichol living where they have for centuries in five autonomous mountain communities.

Huichol art reflects a belief system steeped in symbology, revealing a world where deer, scorpions, salamanders and wolves speak to shamans, arrows carry prayers, serpents bring rain and pumas carry the messages from the gods. With no written language, the Huichol document and encode their legends and spiritual knowledge in beautiful and elaborate works including yarn paintings, brightly colored beaded bowls and carvings such as puma heads and serpents. Their undeniably beautiful work is never merely decorative: each piece manifests an aspect of tradition and belief, drawn from lifelong participation in rites and ceremonies.

The hallucinogenic peyote cactus is sacred to the Huichol, who consider it a gift from the gods and use it to acquire shamanic powers or to approach enlightenment. Peyote is a prime influence on Huichol art, inspiring its vibrant color and fantastic design but also appearing as a symbol for what scholar Angela Corelis called 'the essence, the very life, sustenance, health, accomplishment, good fortune of the Huichol.'

Originally all forms of Huichol art were made as *ofrendas*, or prayer offerings to the gods. Today, some of their art is also made to sell, providing the Huichol people with a means of livelihood that encourages them to maintain and preserve their cultural and spiritual identity. In recent decades some 4000 Huichol have descended from the highlands to sell their art in cities such as Tepic, Guadalajara and Mexico City. In Puerto Vallarta fine examples are offered for sale at several locations (p93).

Visiting Huichol territory on your own is difficult, as there are no direct ground transport links or accommodations. However, Vallarta Adventures (p77) offers a half-day air tour to the remote mountain village of San Andres Coamihata, a Huichol religious and political center. The tour costs US$245 and departs from the Aerotron Aerodrome next to Puerto Vallarta international airport every Friday from December to April at 8:30am.

To learn about efforts to preserve Huichol culture or to find outlets for artwork, contact the **Centro Indigena Huichol** (☎ 457-983-7054, in the US 503-436-1376; www.huicholcenter.com; Calle Victoria 24, Huejuquilla El Alto; Jalisco 46000).

Ava Gardner, also raised more than a few eyebrows. Puerto Vallarta suddenly became world-famous, with an aura of steamy tropical romance.

This is not to say that the town had anything resembling a tourism infrastructure. Those who took advantage of Mexicana's Los Angeles–Puerto Vallarta route, inaugurated in 1962, discovered a town where cows still wandered onto the runways and where there was a notable lack of hotel beds. Moreover, during the rainy season it was often necessary for visitors to cross the swollen Río Pitillal in a canoe on the way into town. When one of the few taxis was not available, donkeys were pressed into service to carry tourists' luggage.

Guillermo Wulff, an engineer from Mexico City, fell under Vallarta's spell in the late 1950s and began building houses in what would become known as Gringo Gulch and Mismaloya. In the late 1960s, as more and more visitors came to soak up the sun and expatriates put down roots, Jalisco governor Francisco Medina Ascencio took his vision for Puerto Vallarta's emergence as a world-class destination to President Gustavo Díaz Ordaz. The president enthusiastically embraced the plan, declaring 'we will start tomorrow, hear me well, tomorrow!'

Soon the town had electric power and telephone service. Construction began on bridges and highways, banks were open for business and hotels sprouted from the sands of Playa Olas Altas. Ships began loading and offloading at the new port at El Salado – Jalisco's first – and the newly incorporated city even hosted a summit between the presidents of the United States and Mexico.

When the *peso* was devalued in 1980, causing economic hardship for Mexico at large, resort towns such as Puerto Vallarta prospered as tourists with pockets full of dollars streamed in for bargain vacations. Between 1980 and 1990 Puerto Vallarta's population doubled to reach 112,000. Through it all, the town's historic center managed to retain its vintage character, as new development was centered around the new Marina Vallarta, completed in 1993. Today, Puerto Vallarta has cemented its position on the A-list of international beach resorts, attracting nearly three million visitors per year.

ORIENTATION

Puerto Vallarta's historic center is bisected by the Río Cuale, which splits to encircle the long and narrow Isla Río Cuale. Two short road bridges, two rickety suspended bridges and a new beachside pedestrian bridge allow easy passage between the Zona Romántica to the south and the Zona Centro to the north.

North of the Río Cuale lies the more modern part of town, the Zona Centro, whose heart is the seaside Plaza Principal. The crown-topped steeple of the cathedral perches nearby. On a few long blocks paralleling the beachless *malecón* (waterfront street) are many modern boutiques, galleries, cafés, bars and restaurants, along with a few hotels. Avs Morelos and Juárez are Puerto Vallarta's two principal thoroughfares.

South of the Río Cuale is Puerto Vallarta's most picturesque district, the Zona Romántica (also called Old Town or Olas Altas), with hotels, boutiques, restaurants and bars. It has the only two beaches in the city center: Playa Olas Altas (which doesn't have 'high waves,' despite the name) and Playa de los Muertos (Beach of the Dead), which takes its strange name from a fierce fight there in the late 19th century.

North of the city is the Zona Hotelera, a strip of giant luxury hotels; Marina Vallarta, a large yachting marina (6.5km from the center); the airport (10km); the bus terminal (10.5km); and Nuevo Vallarta, a

---

PUERTO VALLARTA IN...

Two Days

Breakfast on **Isla Río Cuale** (p72), then stop in at the **Museo del Cuale** (p72) or linger beneath shady rubber trees on the Isla Río Cuale River Walk. Spread out a towel on **Playa Olas Altas** (p69) or join the happy throng on the waterfront *malecón* and enjoy the **public sculptures** (p75). Linger over dinner at one of Vallarta's splendid **restaurants** (p85) and then hit one of the raucous late-night **dance clubs** (p91).

On day two get up early (yeah, right) and continue indulging in the pleasures of the city with some **shopping** (p93) or browsing at an **art gallery** (p95). Otherwise, take your pick from the many opportunities for **outdoor adventures** (p72).

Four Days

To the two-day itinerary add an overnight trip to **Yelapa** (p107), a charming, scenic village on the southern shores of Bahía de Banderas. Luxuriate in the sand, enjoy fresh *mariscos* (seafood), or perhaps take a rejuvenating hike to a waterfall. Along the way, stop in at the seaside communities of **Quimixto** (p107) and **Las Ánimas** (p106) for more snorkeling, hiking or beach bumming. All three towns are accessible only by boat.

One Week

Add on a day enjoying Puerto Vallarta's epic landscapes from the perspective of a **mountain bike** (p75) or a **riding saddle** (p74). Explore underwater at one of the area's great **diving** and **snorkeling sites** (p73) or test your skills while enjoying some world-class **sportfishing** (p72).

Take a day or two to enjoy one or more of the small waterfront communities north of town. Find new ways to relax in **Bucerías** (p97) with its less-crowded beaches or in **La Cruz de Huanacaxtle** (p100), a simple fishing village. Alternatively, learn or practice the art of surfing at **Playa El Anclote** (p102).

PUERTO VALLARTA & AROUND

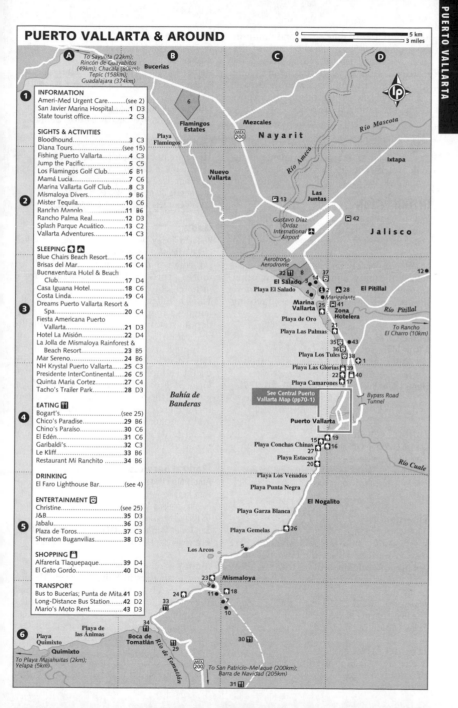

INFORMATION
Ameri-Med Urgent Care..........(see 2)
San Javier Marina Hospital........**1** D3
State tourist office.....................**2** C3

SIGHTS & ACTIVITIES
Bloodhound.............................**3** C3
Diana Tours...........................(see 15)
Fishing Puerto Vallarta.............**4** C3
Jump the Pacific.......................**5** C5
Los Flamingos Golf Club...........**6** B1
Mamá Lucia.............................**7** C6
Marina Vallarta Golf Club.........**8** C3
Mismaloya Divers.....................**9** B6
Mister Tequila.........................**10** C6
Rancho Manolo........................**11** B6
Rancho Palma Real...................**12** D3
Splash Parque Acuático............**13** C2
Vallarta Adventures..................**14** C3

SLEEPING 🏠 🏕
Blue Chairs Beach Resort..........**15** C4
Brisas del Mar..........................**16** C4
Buenaventura Hotel & Beach
  Club...................................**17** D4
Casa Iguana Hotel...................**18** C6
Costa Linda.............................**19** C4
Dreams Puerto Vallarta Resort &
  Spa....................................**20** C4
Fiesta Americana Puerto
  Vallarta...............................**21** D3
Hotel La Misión.......................**22** D4
La Jolla de Mismaloya Rainforest &
  Beach Resort.......................**23** B5
Mar Sereno.............................**24** B6
NH Krystal Puerto Vallarta........**25** C5
Presidente InterContinental.......**26** C5
Quinta Maria Cortez.................**27** C4
Tacho's Trailer Park..................**28** D3

EATING 🍴
Bogart's.................................(see 25)
Chico's Paradise.......................**29** B6
Chino's Paraíso.........................**30** C6
El Edén...................................**31** C6
Garibaldi's...............................**32** C3
Le Kliff...................................**33** B6
Restaurant Mi Ranchito **34** B6

DRINKING
El Faro Lighthouse Bar..............(see 4)

ENTERTAINMENT 🎭
Christine................................(see 25)
J&B..**35** D3
Jabalu...................................**36** D3
Plaza de Toros........................**37** C3
Sheraton Buganvilias................**38** D3

SHOPPING 🛍
Alfarería Tlaquepaque..............**39** D4
El Gato Gordo........................**40** D4

TRANSPORT
Bus to Bucerías; Punta de Mita.**41** D3
Long-Distance Bus Station........**42** D2
Mario's Moto Rent...................**43** D3

new resort area of hotel and condominium development (15km). To the south of the city, in a more natural setting than Zona Hotelera, are more large resorts and some of the most beautiful beaches in the area.

For details on getting to/from the airport or the bus station, see p96.

Maps

Guía Roji publishes a detailed *Ciudad de Puerto Vallarta* map; it's available from major Internet booksellers. Tourist maps are available at the tourist office (opposite).

INFORMATION

Puerto Vallarta is in Jalisco state, one hour ahead of nearby Nayarit, so set your watches forward an hour. Also note that any opening hours or days listed in this chapter, especially for restaurants or shops, reflect the busy winter season; in other seasons, hours and days tend to be more limited, with some businesses even closing down altogether.

Bookstores

A Page in the Sun Bookshop-Café (Map pp70-1; ☎ 222-36-08; cnr Olas Altas & Diéguez) Buys and sells used English-language books, and serves great coffee.
Libros Libros Books Books (Map pp70-1; ☎ 222-71-05; 31 de Octubre 127) Has a fair selection of magazines and books, including Lonely Planet guides, in English.

Cultural Centers

Centro Cultural Río Cuale (☎ 223-00-95; Isla Río Cuale; ☺ 10am-2pm & 4-7pm Mon-Sat) Beautifully situated on Isla Río Cuale, offering graphic and fine arts courses. A schedule of courses open to the general public is posted by the office.

Emergency

The tourist police corps, dressed in white safari outfits with matching helmets, are easy to spot. You'll see the bilingual officers buzzing proudly around town in shiny ATVs (all-terrain vehicles) and on foot along the *malecón*.
Ambulance (☎ 222-15-33)
Fire Department (☎ 223-94-76)
Police (☎ 060, 223-25-00)

Internet Access

There are so many Internet places they are practically a plague, especially in the Zona Romántica.

PVC@fe.com (Map pp70-1; Olas Altas 250; per hr US$3; ☺ 7am-1am) Wireless access, fast machines, good coffee and cheap Internet calls.
Storba's Caffe (Map pp70-1; east of Plaza Principal, 2nd fl; per hr US$2; ☺ 9am-10pm) Fast, relaxed and central but hot.
Vallart@Millenium (Map pp70-1; Madero 370; per hr US$2; ☺ 9am-10:30pm) Also fast but considerably cooler.

Laundry

There are many laundries around town, all of which are closed on Sunday and charge less than US$4 per load.
Lavandería Blanquita (Map pp70-1; Madero 407A)
Lavandería Elsa (Map pp70-1; Olas Altas 385)

Media

Vallarta Today (www.vallartatoday.com) and **Vallarta Tribune** (www.vallartatribune.com) are free, informative daily papers conceived for tourists; you'll find them throughout town in hotel lobbies and at restaurants. *Puerto Vallarta Lifestyles* is a quarterly English-language magazine with good maps, in-depth restaurant reviews, a complete real-estate section and information on shopping, art galleries, activities and tours. *Bay Vallarta* is a free monthly guide with useful culture and shopping listings. *Vallarta Map & Dining Guide* is the official guide for the local restaurant association, including a lengthy directory of restaurants and plenty of maps. *Gay Guide Vallarta* is an up-to-date, definitive guide to gay businesses and events.

Medical Services

Ameri-Med Urgent Care (Map p67; ☎ 226-20-80; Plaza Neptuno, Marina Vallarta) A modern American-style hospital charging American-style fees. They advertise that US medical insurance is accepted.
San Javier Marina Hospital (Map p67; ☎ 226-10-10; Av Ascencio 2760) Vallarta's best-equipped hospital.

Money

Most businesses in Vallarta accept US dollars as readily as they accept pesos, though the rate of exchange they give is usually less favorable than at banks. Several banks can be found around Plaza Principal, but they often have long queues. Most of the banks also have ATMs.

Vallarta has many *casas de cambio* (exchange houses); it may pay to shop around, since rates differ. Though their rates are less favorable than the banks, the difference may be slight, and the longer opening hours and faster service may make using them worthwhile. Most are open around 9am to 7pm daily, sometimes with a 2pm to 4pm lunch break. Look for them on Insurgentes, Vallarta, the *malecón* and many other streets.

American Express (AmEx; Map pp70–1; ☎ 223-29-55; cnr Morelos & Abasolo; ◷ 9am-6pm Mon-Fri, 9am-1pm Sat) Also near the center.

Banamex (Map pp70–1; cnr Zaragoza & Juárez; ◷ 9am-5pm Mon-Fri, 9am-2pm Sat) On the south side of the plaza (Western Union is also situated here).

Post

Main post office (Map pp70–1; Mlna 188) Send your postcards home from here.

Telephone

Vallarta has many *casetas telefónicas* (public telephone call stations), including one on Plaza Lázaro Cárdenas and another at Cárdenas 267. Public card phones are plentiful everywhere in town. Calling Canada or the USA isn't cheap – expect to pay at least US$1 per minute.

Telecomm (Map pp70–1; Hidalgo 582; ◷ 8am-7pm Mon-Fri, 9am-noon Sat & Sun) Offers fax as well as phone service.

Tourist Information

Sponsored by the visitors bureau and tourist board, www.puertovallarta.net provides a wealth of information regarding lodging, activities and attractions.

Municipal tourist office (Map pp70–1; ☎ 223-25-00 ext 230; Juárez s/n, in Municipal bldg; ◷ 8am-4pm Mon-Fri) Vallarta's busy but competent office, at the northeast corner of Plaza Principal, has free maps, multilingual tourist literature and bilingual staff.

State tourist office (Map pp70–1; Dirección de Turismo del Estado de Jalisco; ☎ 221-26-76, 221-26-80; Plaza Marina, Local 144 & 146; ◷ 9am-5pm Mon-Fri) In Marina Vallarta, this is the place to go for information about attractions throughout the state of Jalisco.

DANGERS & ANNOYANCES

Puerto Vallarta has an extraordinarily low crime rate, but police occasionally stop and frisk locals and tourists, checking for drugs.

Expect to be approached by the omnipresent touts who are intent on reeling in potential buyers to timeshare presentations. If you choose to attend a presentation – perhaps swayed by the promise of a free meal, tour or cruise – be prepared to fend off the 'hard

sell.' And if you're tempted to buy, make absolutely sure you know what you're getting yourself into, lest you be paying off your vacation years into the future.

SIGHTS

Puerto Vallarta has amazing natural scenery and a growing number of cultural attractions. Beaches remain Vallarta's main draw, and many visitors have no desire to leave the warm sand. Restless souls need not go far to find activities such as swimming with dolphins, bungee jumping, mountain biking and whale-watching. Snorkeling, scuba diving, deep-sea fishing, water-skiing, windsurfing, sailing, parasailing, and riding the 'banana' can be arranged on the beaches in front of any of the large hotels or by making arrangements with the tourist office.

Beaches

Only two beaches, **Playa Olas Altas** and **Playa de los Muertos** are handy to the city center; they're both south of the Río Cuale.

The most significant of the two is Playa de los Muertos, a mile-long stretch of yellow sand dotted by *palapa* (thatched-roof) restaurants and beachfront hotels. The surf is gentle and there's rarely an undertow, making for good swimming and family-friendly conditions. From the recently constructed pier at the terminus of Francisca Rodriguez, water taxis depart for destinations including Yelapa, Quimixto and Los Arcos islands. According to local legend, the Beach of the Dead was named for a grisly battle fought here over a century ago between smugglers working in the gold and silver mines of the Río Cuale and the natives who tried to take their stolen booty from them. When the fight was over, or so the story goes, the beach was strewn with bodies (much as it is today!).

Trendy gay men head to the section of beach called **Blue Chairs**, at the southern end of Playa de los Muertos (there are blue, green and yellow chairs here). For a more isolated gay beach, see p74.

North of town, the shoreline curves to the west all the way to Punta de Mita, many miles away. Beaches along the way include **Playa Camarones**, **Playa Las Glorias**, **Playa Los Tules**, **Playa Las Palmas** and **Playa de Oro**. Further north, at Marina Vallarta, is **Playa El**

CENTRAL PUERTO VALLARTA

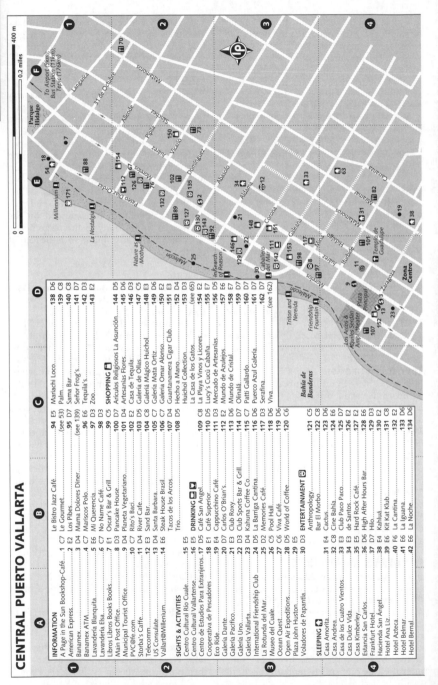

INFORMATION
A Page in the Sun Bookshop-Café.....1 C7
American Express.....2 E2
Banamex.....3 D4
Banamex ATM.....4 C7
Lavandería Blanquita.....5 E6
Lavandería Elsa.....6 C7
Libros Libros Books Books.....7 E1
Main Post Office.....8 D3
Municipal Tourist Office.....9 D4
PVC@fe.com.....10 C7
Storba's Caffe.....11 D4
Telecomm.....12 E3
US Consulate.....13 D4
Vallart@Millenium.....14 E6

SIGHTS & ACTIVITIES
Centro Cultural Río Cuale.....15 E5
Centro Cultural Vallartense.....16 E5
Centro de Estudios Para Extranjeros..17 D5
Cooperativa de Pescadores.....18 E1
Eco Ride.....19 E4
Galería Dante.....20 D7
Galería Pacífico.....21 E3
Galería Uno.....22 D3
Galería Vallarta.....23 D4
International Friendship Club.....24 D5
La Rotunda del Mar.....25 C6
Museo del Cuale.....26 C5
Ocean Quest.....27 C6
Open Air Expeditions.....28 D5
Plaza John Huston.....29 E5
Voladores de Papantla.....30 D3

SLEEPING
Casa Amorita.....31 E4
Casa Andrea.....32 C8
Casa de los Cuatro Vientos.....33 E3
Casa Dulce Vida.....34 E3
Casa Kimberley.....35 E5
Estancia San Carlos.....36 D6
Frankfurt Hotel.....37 D7
Hacienda San Angel.....38 E4
Hotel Ana Liz.....39 F6
Hotel Azteca.....40 F6
Hotel Belmar.....41 E6
Hotel Bernal.....42 E6

Le Bistro Jazz Café.....94 E5
Le Gourmet.....(see 53)
Los Pibes.....95 D7
Mama Dolores Diner.....(see 139)
Mariscos Polo.....96 E6
Mi Querencia.....97 D3
No Name Café.....98 D3
Oscar's Bar & Grill.....99 C5
Pancake House.....100 D7
Planeta Vegetariano.....101 D4
Rito's Baci.....102 E2
River Café.....103 D5
Sand Bar.....104 C8
Santa Barbara.....105 C7
Steak House Brasil.....106 C7
Tacos de los Arcos.....107 D4
Trio.....108 D3

DRINKING
Café San Angel.....109 C8
Café Superior.....110 E1
Cappuchino Café.....111 D3
Carlos O'Brian's.....112 E2
Club Roxy.....113 D6
Club Sports Bar & Grill.....114 D7
Kahuna Coffee Co.....115 C7
La Barriga Cantina.....116 D6
Memories Café.....117 D3
Pool Hall.....118 D6
Viva Café.....119 D6
World of Coffee.....120 C6

ENTERTAINMENT
Anthropology.....121 C5
Bar El Morbo.....122 C8
Cactus.....123 D6
Cine Bahía.....124 E6
Club Paco Paco.....125 D7
de Santos.....126 E2
Hard Rock Café.....127 E2
High After Hours Bar.....128 E6
Hilo.....129 D3
Kahlúa.....130 E2
Kit Kat Klub.....131 C8
La Cantina.....132 E2
La Iguana.....133 D6
La Noche.....134 D6

Mariachi Loco.....138 D6
Palm.....139 C8
Sama Bar.....140 C8
Señor Frog's.....141 D7
Tequila's.....142 D3
Zoo.....143 E2

SHOPPING
Artículos Religiosos La Asunción....144 D5
Artesanías Flores.....145 D6
Casa de Tequila.....146 D3
Galería de Ollas.....147 C5
Galería Mágico Huichol.....148 D6
Galería Mata Ortiz.....149 D6
Galería Omar Alonso.....150 D2
Guantanamera Cigar Club.....151 D4
Hecho a Mano.....152 D4
Huichol Collection.....153 D3
La Casa de los Gatos.....(see 65)
La Playa Vinos y Licores.....154 E2
Lucy's Cucú Cabaña.....155 E7
Mercado de Artesanías.....156 D5
Mundo de Azulejos.....157 E2
Mundo de Cristal.....158 E7
Olinalá.....159 D7
Patti Gallardo.....160 D7
Puerco Azul Galería.....161 D6
Serafina.....162 D7
Viva.....(see 162)

Triton and Nereida
Friendship Fountain
Bahía de Banderas
Los Arcos & Aquiles Serdán Amphitheater
Templo de Guadalupe
Zona Centro
Plaza Principal
Parque Hidalgo
To Airport (9km); Bus Station (11km); Tepic (176km)

0   0.2 miles
0   400 m

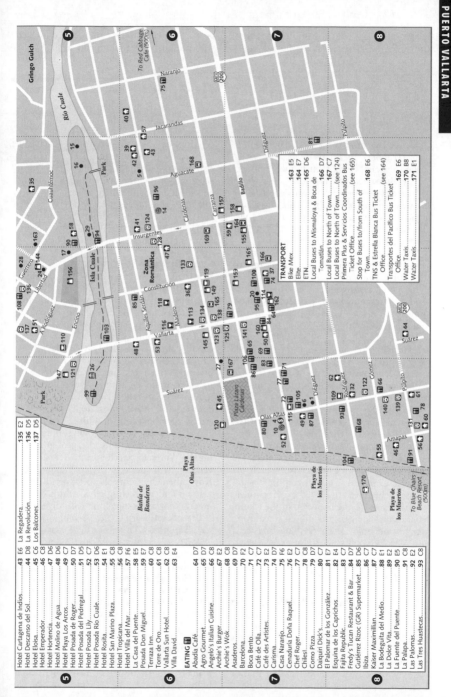

Salado. Nuevo Vallarta also has beaches and there are others, less developed, right around the bay to Punta de Mita.

For beaches further north or south of town, see North of Puerto Vallarta (p97) and South of Puerto Vallarta (p103).

Isla Río Cuale

This small island at the mouth of the Rio Cuale is a charming place shaded by old *hule de oro* (rubber) trees. This is where the city's earliest residents built their humble homes.

The **Museo del Cuale** (Map pp70-1; Paseo Isla Río Cuale s/n; admission free; ⏰ 10am-7pm Mon-Sat), near the western end of Isla Río Cuale, has a collection of beautiful pottery, grinding stones, clay figurines and other ancient objects. Text panels are in Spanish and English.

Upstream you'll notice two rickety cable **suspension bridges** connecting the island to the Zona Romántica. As you pass over them, you'll need your sea legs: the bridges tend to buck and sway, particularly when some little rascal starts to shake it just as you reach the center.

You'll find it hard to resist the **Mercado de Artesanías** (p93), on the adjacent riverbank as you progress up the island. Further on is **Plaza John Huston**, where a stoic bronze sculpture of the film icon sitting in his director's chair holds court.

Continuing up the island, pay a visit to the gallery at **Centro Cultural Vallartense**, a small volunteer-run arts center offering classes and small exhibitions by local talent. Nearby is the new **Centro Cultural Río Cuale** (⏰ 10am-2pm & 4-7pm Mon-Sat), which offers classes in fine arts and graphic design. Course schedules are posted by the office.

Just beyond is the rocky tip of the island, where you can gaze up the clear running stream and enjoy the refreshing breeze. If you're lucky, you'll catch a glimpse of a slow-moving iguana slinking through the trees.

Cathedral

On Hidalgo, one block from Plaza Principal, stands **La Paroquia de Nuestra Señora de Guadalupe**, named for Mexico's favorite – and the city's patron – saint. The simple brick architecture might seem austere were it not for the audacious crown that sprouts like a jaunty mushroom from the tower. Interestingly, the crown is modeled after that of Empress Carlota, the 19th-century Belgian-born royal who briefly administered Mexico with her husband, Maximilian, at the behest of Napoleon III. The cathedral's doors are unlocked from 9am to 5pm.

ACTIVITIES

Puerto Vallarta is simply chock-full of activities. Head toward the sea for diving, snorkeling, windsurfing, fishing and sailing. (Most activities can be arranged on the beaches in front of any of the large hotels.) Parasailing is also very popular, but there have been some accidents in the past and the activity should be considered potentially hazardous. Turn inland to ride horses, play golf or drive off-road. For the sedate, wildlife-watching boat tours and scenic cruises are a good option; some include meals and plenty of drinks.

Scuba Diving & Snorkeling

Below the warm, tranquil waters of Bahía de Banderas is a world of stingrays, tropical fish and garishly colored corals. The most spectacular spots for diving and snorkeling are **Los Arcos** (opposite), the rocky islands in the bay just south of town (now a protected ecological zone), and **Las Islas Marietas** (opposite) at the entrance to the bay, surrounded by impressive reefs, underwater caves, tunnels and walls. Dolphins, whales and giant manta rays are often sighted between December and April. Most folks get to Los Arcos via a boat tour or a hired skiff.

Vallarta has several diving operators. Most dives include transport, gear and light meals. Water is clearest from May to November, with peak clarity in October and November. Operators also offer certification courses and snorkeling trips (which usually means snorkelers tag along with divers).

Ocean Quest (Map pp70-1; ☎ 223-41-03; www.mexico scuba.com; Cárdenas 230; snorkeling US$25, 2-tank dive trip US$65-115, PADI open-water certification US$280) is well regarded for its small-group excursions to both well- and lesser-known sites. English and German are spoken.

Vallarta Adventures (snorkeling/2-tank dive trip US$25/99, PADI open-water certification US$370) has 'gold-palm' instructors and acclaimed service (p77).

Sportfishing

Deep-sea fishing is popular all year, with a major international sailfish tournament held every November. Prime catches are

TOP FIVE DIVING SITES

Any Puerto Vallarta diving provider worth its salt offers trips to the following roundly celebrated diving sites.

El Morro

Just beyond the northernmost waters of the bay, 42km north of Puerto Vallarta, this secluded dive site offers thrills to advance divers. Humpback whales, sailfish, dolphins and even the occasional whale shark are spotted here. Equally grand is the underwater landscape, characterized by a good collection of pinnacles and caves.

Las Islas Marietas

These beautiful islands, nearly 34km from Puerto Vallarta on the north side of the bay, are a diver's dream. Underwater caves and coral reefs shelter great hordes of tropical fish, and whale, dolphin and giant manta-ray sightings are common. Invariably, divers are monitored by personable blue-footed boobies watching from the rocks. Between dives, the divers stretch out on Playa del Amor and count their blessings.

Los Arcos

Far and away the most popular diving destination in Bahía de Banderas and a protected National Underwater Park, Los Arcos (Map p67) is a picturesque spot that features gnarly granite rock formations rising from the sea. Near the largest of the arches you'll enjoy good visibility and depths ranging from 8m to 20m. Follow the shelf to the edge and hover over the abyss of Devil's Canyon, which drops off to a jaw-dropping 600m.

Playa Majahuitas

At the southern end of the bay and accessible only by boat is the hidden cove of Majahuitas. In between dives divers disembark and linger on the beach at Quimixto over lunch. Back in the water, divers commonly spot eels darting in and out of black coral, manta rays, dolphins and any number of brightly colored tropical fish.

Chimo

You're not likely to have to mingle with those pesky snorkelers at the dive sites near this small fishing village, which lies 42km from Puerto Vallarta on the bay's southern coast. Giant manta rays are plentiful during the winter months, and great swarms of tropical fish are a sure bet all year long. Its most unique feature, however, is the amazing pinnacles rising from a wide underwater plateau called Torrecillas.

---

sailfish, marlin, tuna, red snapper and sea bass. Fishing trips can be arranged dockside at Marina Vallarta or at the cooperative on the *malecón*. Moreover, *pangas* can be hired on the beach in front of several major hotels, including Hotel Playa Los Arcos on Playa de Los Muertos and NH Krystal on Playa de Oro. The going rate is US$25 to US$30 per hour for trips of two to three hours. Equipment and bait is included, but you may have to negotiate for cold drinks!

Cooperativa de Pescadores (Map pp70-1; ☎ 222-12-02; fishing charters for 1-8 people from US$90; ☺ 7am-10pm Mon-Sat) This cooperative, with an office on the *malecón*, adjacent to the Hotel Rosita,

acts as an agent for a long list of sportfishing boats. During the low season try your luck at fishing for a discount.

Fishing Puerto Vallarta (Map pp70-1; ☎ 224-72-50; www.fishingpuertovallarta.4t.com; Marina Vallarta) Trawl from the *Carolina*, a 30ft sportfisher. Prices are US$100 per person or US$350 for the whole boat for up to four customers. Gear and hotel pickup is included.

See p96 for information on hiring private yachts or *pangas*.

Cruises

A host of daytime, sunset and evening cruises are available in Vallarta. The most popular ones are the cruises to Yelapa and Las Ánimas beaches; others go to Las Islas Marietas, further out. Prices start at US$45 for sunset cruises and beach trips. Longer trips lasting four to six hours, with meals and bottomless cocktails, will set you back US$80 to US$100. To pick the right cruise, ask your fellow travelers or inquire at the tourist office.

The **Marigalante** (☎ 223-03-09; www.marigalante.com.mx) is a reproduction Spanish galleon that does daytime cruises from 9am to 5pm (US$65) and an evening cruise from 6pm to 11pm (US$70) that culminates in a mock pirate attack on the *malecón*. It departs from the Terminal Maritima, off Blvd Francisco Ascencio, opposite Sam's Club.

On Thursday **Diana Tours** (☎ 222-15-10; www.bluechairs.com/cruisepay.htm) offers an all-day gay and lesbian cruise, with plenty of food, drink and snorkeling (US$75).

Bloodhound (☎ 01-322-222-22-85; tours adult/child US$50/25) is a graceful 30m (98ft) replica of a 1874 British yacht. It runs four-hour whale-watching cruises on Fridays at 9am from mid-December to mid-March, and at other times visits Las Islas Marietas for snorkeling. Tours depart from the Hotel Westin Regina in Marina Vallarta.

If you just want to visit the beaches, a cheaper way to get there is by water taxi (p96).

Dolphin- & Whale-Watching

A frequent, year-round visitor to Bahía de Banderas, the Pacific bottlenose dolphin is often seen leaping out of the water or gliding along the bows of the boats. Humpback whales also visit from late November to March to bear their calves (see below).

Whale-watching trips operate from December to March, when humpback whales are in the bay mating, bearing young and caring for new calves. Open Air Expeditions is a popular operator; Vallarta Adventures (p77) also does whale-watching trips. Both kids and adults can enjoy close encounters with Pacific bottlenose dolphins at Vallarta Adventures Dolphin Adventure (see Puerto Vallarta for Children, p76).

Horseback Riding

Explore Vallarta's jungly mountains from the privileged perspective of horseback. Most stables charge around US$15 per hour or US$100 for a full-day excursion. For a short ride suitable for children, there are sometimes horses for rent around Playa Olas Altas, near the western end of Carranza.

Rancho El Charro (Map p64; ☎ 224-01-14; www.ranchoelcharro.com; rides US$47-100) Recommended for their healthy horses and scenic three-to eight-hour trots into the Sierra Madres. Several rides are conceived for kids. Setting them apart from competitors are their multi-day tours, including the tempting Overnight Lost in the Jungle Ride (US$350).

Rancho Palma Real (Map p67; ☎ 221-12-36; www.ranchopalmareal.com; Carretera Vallarta; rides from US$62) In the village of Las Palmas, 40 minutes by car northeast of Puerto Vallarta, this ranch offers two off-the-beaten-track routes and a popular excursion to El Salto, a lovely jungle waterfall. Its office is on Carretera Vallarta, about five minutes north of the airport.

For a short ride, suitable for children, there are sometimes horses for rent around Playa Olas Altas, near the western end of Carranza.

BAHÍA DE BANDERAS

Measuring 42km from north to south and one of the largest bays in the world, the Bay of Flags was supposedly formed by an extinct volcano slowly sinking into the ocean. It now has a depth of some 1800m and is home to an impressive variety of marine life.

Like many people reading this book, humpback whales come here to mate during the winter months. They leave their feeding grounds in Alaskan waters and show up in Mexico from around November to the end of March. Once they arrive, they form courtship groups, mate, or bear the calves that were conceived the year before. Although the mating rituals of humpbacks remain a mystery, they are thought to be promiscuous breeders. By the end of March, the whales' attention turns to the long journey back to their feeding grounds up north.

With the humpbacks gone, the giant manta rays take their turn. During the month of April you may catch sight of their antics as they jump above the water's surface, flashing their 4m-wide wings in acrobatic displays that you can sometimes see from boats or even from the shore.

Golf & Tennis

In recent years Vallarta's acquired four new golf courses. Most acclaimed is the Jack Nicklaus–designed **Four Seasons Punta Mita** (Map p64; ☎ 291-60-00; Four Seasons Resort Punta Mita; green fees/club rentals US$260/60), where golfers are blissfully distracted from the challenging course by sweeping ocean vistas. One hole is on a natural island and requires the use of an amphibious golf cart.

There are also other courses:

Marina Vallarta Golf Club (Map p67; ☎ 221-00-73; Paseo de la Marina s/n; green fees US$136) An exclusive 18-hole, par-74 course just north of Marina Vallarta.

Los Flamingos Golf Club (Map p67; ☎ 298-06-06; Hwy 200 s/n; green fees US$95) Recently renovated, 13km north of town.

Most of the large luxury hotels have tennis courts and charge between US$15 to US$20 to smash the ball around. Call in advance to reserve a court. The following welcome nonguests for tennis:

NH Krystal Puerto Vallarta (Map p67; ☎ 224-02-02; Av Las Garzas s/n, Zona Hotelera)

Fiesta Americana (Map p67; ☎ 224-20-10; Paseo de las Palmas s/n, Zona Hotelera)

Mountain Biking

Surrounded by the mountains, jungle and sea, Vallarta offers some truly thrilling mountain biking.

The adventure-loving **Eco Ride** (Map pp70-1; ☎ 222-79-12; www.ecoridemex.com; Miramar 382; tours US$45-175) offers guided cycling tours suited for beginners and badasses alike. All are one-day rides. The most challenging is a 50km hair-raising expedition from El Tuito, a small town at 1100m, through Chacala and down to the beach in Yelapa. The views are stunning along the way. Other tours include an easy trip to Vallejo, a typical local village, and a technical ride to El Salto waterfall.

Bike Mex (☎ 223-16-80; Guerrero 361; ✆ 8am-8pm Mon-Sat) runs quite a few hiking and mountain-bike tours using experienced bilingual guides, tailored to your level of fitness and experience. Mountain bike rentals are available for US$33 per day.

Bungee Jumping

The good folks at the **Jump the Pacific** (Map p67; ☎ 228-06-70; www.vallarta-action.com; ✆ 10am-6pm) bungee jump promise that 'if the cord breaks your next jump is free.' From a platform jutting out over the sea cliffs, it's a 40m plunge. It's 9km southwest of Puerto Vallarta on the road to Mismaloya.

WALKING TOUR

It's Saturday evening at dusk on Puerto Vallarta's *malecón*, the broad seawall boardwalk that stretches the length of downtown Vallarta. You and your companion – like nearly everyone else, it seems – have joined the cheerful throng for one of this town's most popular traditions: the twilight promenade.

This walking tour focuses on one of Puerto Vallarta's most beguiling assets: its collection of bronze public sculptures. Begin at the south end of the beachfront boulevard at the **Aquiles Serdán Amphitheater** and **Los Arcos** (the Arches); here you'll find frothy live entertainment, including clown and pantomime shows, folkloric dance and live music.

WALK FACTS

Distance 740m
Duration one hour

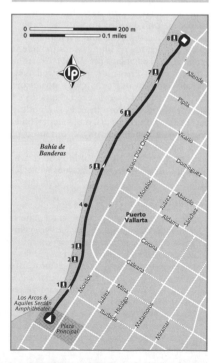

Just north are the three leaping dolphins known as the **Friendship Fountain (1)** by California artist James 'Bud' Bottoms. It was installed in 1987 as a gift to Vallarta from sister city Santa Barbara.

Every seaside city on Mexico's Pacific coast has at least one mermaid statue, but few are as lovely as Italian artist Carlos Espino's **Triton and Nereida (2)**, depicting two wistful lovers reaching for each other. Triton, son of Neptune, and his sea nymph mate Nereida, took their place on the *malecón* in 1990.

Vallarta's most recognizable statue is Rafael Zamarripa's **Caballero del Mar (3;** the Seahorse), featuring a naked boy riding bareback on a 3m-tall seahorse. The original sculpture, once located at the end of Playa de los Muertos, was tossed into the drink by Hurricane Kenna, and was so missed that Zamarripa was quickly commissioned to create a new one.

With the installation of Guadalajara artist Sergio Bustamente's **In Search of Reason (4)** in 1990, *malecón* statuary took a sharp left turn into surrealism. Two pillow-headed children climb a ladder leading to nowhere, as their robed mother directs them from the sidewalk. Passersby are irresistibly drawn to follow the puff-headed imps up the rungs.

Similarly interactive and even more bizarre is Alejandro Colunga's transcendent installation **La Rotunda del Mar (5)**. Six mutant alien sea creatures with clawed feet, serrated spines and prodigious posteriors take the shape of high-backed chairs; to sit on one of these bizarre thrones is an oddly mystical – or perhaps just odd – experience. Nearby is a bench seemingly composed of eyes, ears and feet.

Representing the cycle of life and death, Tapatio Adrian Reynoso's **Nature as Mother (6)** offers a spiraling wave on a snail for your reflection. Further on is Ramiz Barquet's well-loved **La Nostalgia (7)**, a romantic bronze rendering of the artist and his wife.

The walking tour concludes at one of Vallarta's most audacious sculptures, Mathis Lídice's **Millennium (8)**, adjacent to the Hotel Rosita. Depicting a host of mythic figures emerging from a wave and crowned by a buxom nude offering a dove to the sky, the whole thing looks like it's about to topple into the sea.

COURSES

Centro de Estudios Para Extranjeros (CEPE; Map pp70-1; ☎ 223-20-82; www.cepe.udg.mx; Libertad 105-1) Courses range from US$93 for a week of basic tourist Spanish to US$431 for a month of university credit courses. Private instruction costs US$21 per hour. The center, associated with the Universidad de Guadalajara, provides lodging for US$23 to US$49 per night and also arranges homestays with local families. Two 'content courses' are also offered both in English and Spanish: one focuses on Mexican culture from an anthropological standpoint, the other on modern Mexican history.

PUERTO VALLARTA FOR CHILDREN

Dolphins seem to like kids almost as much as kids like dolphins. At **Vallarta Adventures Dolphin Adventure** (Map p67; ☎ 297-12-12; www.vallarta-adventures.com/dolphins; Av Las Palmas 39, Nuevo Vallarta), you and your kids can experience thrilling close encounters with Pacific bottlenose dolphins in either a lagoon or special pool, ranging in price from US$60 to US$250. A new offering is the Dolphin Kids program for tots aged four to eight, where

---

AERIALISTS OF THE GODS

Bringing considerable excitement to the *malecón* on Saturday and Sunday evenings, the **Voladores de Papantla** (Papantla Flyers) enact a pre-Hispanic religious ritual wherein four men attached by ropes swing upside down with open arms from a 18m pole. A fifth man balanced at the pole's zenith plays a hand-carved flute to represent the songs of birds, or beats a *tambor* (drum) to evoke the voice of God. The ritual is tied to an ancient Totonaca legend in which the gods commanded 'You shall dance. We will watch.'

The four men signify the four cardinal points, and the pole represents the fertility goddess Tlazoleotl. Each of the four *voladores* flies 13 times around the pole for a total of 52 revolutions, evoking the 52 years of the Mayan calendar's solar cycle. Thus, the ritual is performed as a spiritual gift to the gods so that a new sun can be born.

The Voladores de Papantla perform every Saturday and Sunday night at 6pm, 6:30pm, 8pm, 8:30pm, 9pm and 10pm.

participants enjoy a thrilling, educational encounter with dolphin babies and their proud mothers.

Kids will also enjoy **Splash Parque Acuático** (Map p67; ☎ 297-07-08; Hwy 200, Km 155; admission US$9), which has 12 water slides, a lazy river swimming pool and a daily dolphin show.

TOURS

International Friendship Club (Map pp70-1; ☎ 222-54-66; www.pvmexico.com; Libertad 105; ☯ office 9:30am-1:30pm Mon-Fri) offers US$30, 2½-hour tours that take you inside some of Vallarta's most luxurious private homes. They are given only in winter and start at 11am Wednesday and Thursday at the Hotel Posada Río Cuale.

Casa Kimberley (Map pp70-1; ☎ 222-13-36; www.casakimberley.com; Zaragoza 445; tours US$7.50; ☯ 9am-6pm), the house that Richard Burton bought for Elizabeth Taylor in the 1960s, has been left virtually untouched since an American family bought it in 1990. Guided tours are informal, and if you fall in love with the place and the host family, you can spend the night.

Several tour companies specialize in nature and the outdoors.

Vallarta Adventures (Map p67; ☎ 297-12-12, in the US 866-256-2739; www.vallarta-adventures.com; Av Las Palmas 39, Marina Vallarta) offers canopy adventures (child/adult US$55/US$77), wild dolphins and snorkeling (US$66) and romantic dinner shows on a private beach (US$82). In their four-hour canopy tour, thrill seekers can whoosh from tree to tree on zip lines strung high above the forest floor, among hanging wild orchids, native birds and reptiles.

Canopy Tours de los Veranos (☎ 223-05-04; www.canopytours-vallarta.com; cnr Insurgentes & Diéguez; tour adult/child US$79/58; ☯ 9am-2pm hourly) offers an extensive zip-line course on an ecopark near Mismaloya.

Open Air Expeditions (Map pp70-1; ☎ 222-33-10; www.vallartawhales.com; Guerrero 339) offers in-season whale-watching (US$75), bird-watching (US$60 to US$80), hiking (US$60) and customized tours, including snorkeling, jungle hiking and bird-watching.

FESTIVALS & EVENTS

Semana Santa (Holy Week) is the busiest holiday of the year in Puerto Vallarta. Hotels fill up and hundreds (or thousands) of excess visitors camp out on the beaches and party. It's a wild time.

Fiestas de Mayo, a city-wide fair with cultural and sporting events, music concerts, carnival rides and art exhibits, is held throughout May.

In September, Puerto Vallarta stages several events commemorating **Mexican independence**. On **Charro Day** (September 14), Mexican horsemen and women ride with great élan through the streets wearing traditional *charro* (cowboy) attire. In the evening at various *charro* rings, there are bullfights, calf-roping and other spectacles. The lively **Independence Eve** celebration takes place on the 15th. From a balcony at City Hall, the mayor oversees the lighting of the flame of independence and then leads a parade through town. At 11pm the central plaza fills with revelers belting out the traditional *grito* (shout; *¡Viva México!*), followed by an impressive fireworks display over the bay. The next day, a national holiday, sees more colorful parades and festivities in the streets.

November is a busy month for the local cultural calendar, with the city-wide **Festival de las Artes**, featuring a month-long series of gallery exhibitions and beachside theatre performances. Gourmets come from far and wide to celebrate the annual 10-day **Puerto Vallarta Gourmet Festival** (www.festivalgourmet.com), held mid-month. Showcasing the talents of local chefs and guest chefs from around the world, the festival features gourmet cooking classes, wine tastings and other delicious events. Also mid-month is the **Puerto Vallarta Film Festival** (www.puertovallartafilm.com).

Día de Santa Cecilia (November 22) honors the patron saint of mariachis, with all the city's mariachis forming a musical procession to the cathedral in the early evening. They come playing and singing, enter the church and sing homage to their saint, then go out into the plaza and continue to play. During the entire day one or another group of mariachis stays in the church making music.

Held each year in mid-November, the **Torneo Internacional de Pez Vela y Marlin** (Sailfish & Marlin International Tournament; www.fishvallarta.com) held its 50th anniversary in 2005; dates vary according to the phase of the moon, which must be right for fishing.

All Mexico celebrates December 12 as the day of the country's patron saint, the **Virgen de Guadalupe**. In Puerto Vallarta the celebrations are more drawn out, with pilgrimages and processions to the cathedral day and night from December 1 until the big bash on the 12th.

SLEEPING

Vallarta has a good selection of accommodation for every price bracket. Budget travelers are well accommodated in a number of atmospheric small hotels. Midrange hotels represent a considerable step up from the budget options in price, comfort and ambience, but still offer a good value. The top end is largely dominated by five-star and Grand Tourism hotels, which have hundreds of rooms and mainly cater to package tours. These are best reserved through a travel agent or on the Internet as rates are considerably lower than the 'walk-in' rates quoted in this book. The true gems at the top end are Puerto Vallarta's good selection of special, small and stylish places, which provide a good alternative for those looking for something more intimate.

Prices here reflect the mid-December to mid-April high season; low-season rates can fall 20% to 50%. For accommodation at Vallarta's busiest times – during Semana Santa or at Christmas and New Year's – reserve in advance, and be prepared to pay 20% to 40% more than the prices listed here. The most expensive hotels will most likely tack on almost 18% in taxes, so ask beforehand if these are included. Many budget and some midrange establishments only charge the IVA and ISH taxes if you require a receipt. And remember, if you plan on staying a week or more, negotiate for a better rate; monthly rates can cut your rent by half.

South of the Río Cuale
BUDGET
South of the Río Cuale on Calle Madero are clustered many of Vallarta's most economical hotels, running the gamut from gloomy to good. They are a bit far from the action, but the prices are right.

Hotel Hortencia (Map pp70-1; ☎ 222-24-84; www .hotelhortencia.com; Madero 336; s US$23-35, d US$28-40, tr US$33-45, q US$38-50; 🔀) Perhaps Puerto Vallarta's most agreeable budget accommodations, this family-run hotel offers 20 very good and clean rooms on three floors set around a plain, open courtyard. For a place with few frills, you'll notice right away that the few on offer are thoughtfully presented

and of high quality. Each room has a tiled desk with desk lamp, large mirrors, refrigerator, cable TV and fan; they're bright and welcoming with appealing tile work, quality furnishings and up-to-date bathrooms. The front rooms have balconies but suffer from a fair amount of street noise; if you crave quiet take one of the inside rooms. The more expensive rooms have air-con, and one on offer features a kitchen. In the small lobby, you'll usually find most of the family sitting around waiting to welcome you.

Hotel Posada Lily (Map pp70-1; ☎ 222-00-32; Badillo 109; s US$30-35, d US$50-55) So you've come to town with limited funds, and you want to reserve these for two-for-one margaritas at dusk. You could choose to slumber in one of the very cheap guesthouses several blocks from the beach or you could spend a few pesos more and take up residence at this amazingly priced option just off the beach. It's a no-brainer. Sure, it's plain, but the 18 rooms are clean and pleasant with fridge, TV and good light. The larger rooms have three beds – bring your friends! – and there are small balconies overlooking the street. The simple, hand-painted decorations and chintzy paintings are icing on the cake. Just don't ask for room service.

Hotel Belmar (Map pp70-1; ☎ 223-18-72; www.bel marvallarta.com; Insurgentes 161; s/d/tr US$36/46/61, with air-con add US$6; 🔀) One of the choicest budget places in town, this colorful hotel near the Río Cuale offers clean and comfy rooms with few frills but plenty of personality. The Belmar has long served budget-minded travelers with rooms providing simple comfort. They have tiled floors, wee TVs, ceiling fans and miniature bathrooms; they are a bit small but cozy in their austerity. Snag one with a balcony or, better yet, one of the corner units to take advantage of cross-ventilation. Well-chosen art and simple decor add a small flourish. The brightly painted lobby devotes considerable wall space to extravagant original works of art, and the owners will gladly act as your emissaries to Puerto Vallarta's thriving art scene.

Hotel Villa del Mar (Map pp70-1; ☎ 222-07-85; www .hvilladelmar.com; Madero 440; s US$20-27, d US$28-32, tr US$33-37) This one-of-a-kind budget place resembling a brick fortress came into its own in the 1970s and hasn't changed much since. Along the way someone applied an awful lot of paint that is not quite orange and not quite pink. The owners keep the hotel spick-and-span ('cleanness' it says on the business card) and the air is heavy with disinfectant. The cheapest rooms are tiny and dour with little light; you're much better off dropping the couple of extra bucks for one with a terrace. On the roof are two desirable apartments (per week US$400) with kitchenettes, a moon deck and many nooks and crannies good for relaxing with a book.

Hotel Azteca (Map pp70-1; ☎ 222-27-50; Madero 473; s US$27-32, d US$32-37, tr US$37, apt US$47) This graceful old-timer offers decent, good-value rooms surrounding an intimate shady palm-potted courtyard. Most of the rooms, unfortunately, are rather dark (though street-facing rooms are lighter), but on the bright side this serves to keep down the temperature. Some have kitchens, dining tables and desks. All have fans and are very clean with old tile floors and small bathrooms. On the roof are a few simple chairs and tables, affording tremendous views over the town and into the mountains. Also on the roof is a small and bright apartment with a kitchen and two beds, offering privacy.

Hotel Cartagena de Indios (Map pp70-1; ☎ 222-69-14; hotelcartagenapv@yahoo.com.mx; Madero 428; s US$20-23, d US$25-28, tr US$30-34) Basic but decent, this hotel's street-facing balcony rooms are brighter and more pleasant. Singles are tiny, however. The more expensive rooms include TV.

Posada Don Miguel (Map pp70-1; ☎ 222-45-40; hpdm322@prodigy.net.mx; Insurgentes 322; s/d US$20/30; 🅿 🛍) This place has rooms so large you can do three cartwheels down their length. They'd be better if stocked with more furniture, but remain a good deal. Kitchenettes,

air-con and TV are available for extra, and it's clean. Have a splash in the small pool.

Other recommendations:

Hotel Bernal (Map pp70-1; ☎ 222-36-05; Madero 423; s/d US$16/21) An old standby with dark, basic, cleanish rooms around a courtyard.

Hotel Ana Liz (Map pp70-1; ☎ 222-17-57; Madero 429; s/d US$15/18) Acceptable, inexpensive.

MIDRANGE

Terraza Inn (Map pp70-1; ☎ 223-54-31; www.terrazainn .com; 299 Amapas; r US$70-80) Nestled on terraces opposite Playa de los Muertos, this little gem has a class and style all its own, providing a welcome change from the homogenous beach hotels. With only 10 units, the owners have devoted themselves to making each unique, comfortable and attractive. With stained-glass windows in the showers, romantic hand-carved furniture, and comfortable chaise longues on the balconies, the individually named rooms have interesting architectural features, such as arched doorways, columns and brick ceilings with exposed timbers. Each unit comes with a double bed, a daybed, a TV and a small kitchen with fridge.

Hotel Eloisa (Map pp70-1; ☎ 222-64-65; www.hotel eloisa.com; 179 Cárdenas; s US$64-83, d US$76-90, tr US$82-96, ste US$148; 🅿 🛍) With a great location just off the beach, this recently renovated hotel, with 70 rooms and eight thoughtfully designed suites, has an understated charm. For the price, it's one of the best values in town. The standard rooms are pleasingly decorated with rustic furniture, tiled floors and two double beds with floral-print spreads. The suites have eye-catching tiled bathrooms and kitchens and bright sitting areas, good

---

AUTHOR'S CHOICE

Hotel Emperador (Map pp70-1; ☎ 222-1767; www.hotelemperadorpv.com; 114 Amapas; d US$55-80, ste US$89-200; 🅿 💻 🛍) This up-to-date beach hotel on Playa de los Muertos gives a lot of bang for the buck with thoughtfully designed rooms and suites, many with incomparable views of the coast. The fresh oceanfront rooms celebrate the sea with large balconies complete with dining tables and kitchenettes for preparing and eating food alfresco. Each tiled unit is furnished with a fridge, king-sized bed and sleeper couch as well as air-con, cable TV and in-room phones. Well-chosen decor gives each unit a patina of warmth and grace. The hotel overlooks an ideal swimming beach, where mariachi bands stroll about looking for business and drum circles coalesce in the sweaty heat of the afternoon. The beach is appointed with several shady palm-roofed *palapas* (where you can try to hide from the jewelry touts). There's also an excellent beach-level restaurant and bar, the Lazy Lizard, where you may find yourself whiling away the afternoon counting empty margarita glasses.

for entertaining. Some feature terrific sea views and furnished balconies. The bedrooms have large mirrors, plenty of closet space and shuttered blinds that open up to the main area. White canvas blinds over the windows emit a pleasant diffused light. Up on the roof, there's a small pool, plenty of room for luxurious sunbathing, and gratifying views over the town and to the cathedral in the distance.

Vallarta Sun Hotel (Map pp70-1; ☎ 22-31-523; vallartasun@usa.net; Rodríguez 169; d US$55-65; P 🖾 🖾) Only a short walk from one of the town's most glorious stretches of sandy beach, it overlooks a quiet cobbled street on the southern fringes of the Zona Romántica. The hillside location catches the ocean breezes, providing a measure of relief on scorching hot days. Each of the 21 units is done up with Mexican flourishes, including mission-style cathedral ceilings, tiled floors, rustic wood furniture and hand-carved headboards. They are spiffy and attractive, with air-con, fridges, two beds, desks and multiple mirrors. Six open up to an attractive pool, while the brighter upstairs units have balconies, several offering terrific sea views. There's secure covered parking, and frequent promotions bring the price down. At time of research, a third night was free, and children under the age of 10 could stay at the hotel free of charge.

Hotel Posada Río Cuale (Map pp70-1; ☎ 222-04-50; riocuale@pvnet.com.mx; Serdán 242; d/tr US$65/80; 🖾 🖾) Well located and appointed, this hotel offers colonial-style rooms with air-con and cable TV. The grounds are leafy and pleasant, and if you crave salt water rather than the chlorinated type, the beach is only two blocks away. The rooms are tasteful if a bit dark; avoid the ones facing noisy Av Vallarta. A big bonus is Le Gourmet, a pleasant, dependable restaurant serving generous, well-priced breakfast platters with whimsical names like 'This Is Your Brain in Mexico' (spicy scrambled eggs). At dinner, regional specialties and seafood rule the menu: try the lobster simmered in orange liqueur. A godsend in the summer heat, the pool is centrally located and convenient to the bar. Fortunately, the peeing boy (fountain) is well away from the pool area.

Frankfurt Hotel (Map pp70-1; ☎ 222-34-03; www.hotelfrankfurt.com; Badillo 300; r US$30, bungalow US$41, apt US$41-60) Despite a name that evokes the Old World, this bohemian playground could only exist in Puerto Vallarta. Set in a large garden with squawking parrots, the Frankfurt is an urban tropical haven. The German owner and his Mexican wife run this place to their own standards (fortunately, they're good ones). The prodigious foliage attracts wild parrots who come to mock their brethren locked in cages. On offer are a total of 20 units, each distinct and with loads of personality. The simple rooms are dated but immaculately kept, facing a large, jungly open area affording glorious shade. The bungalows stay cool on hot days and feature large porches, couches, TVs, fridges and sitting areas. The nine apartments, some quite large and with two bedrooms, have kitchenettes and cable TV. There's also space for six trailers with hook-ups, available for a scant US$15 per day. There's no air-con, but the shady forest canopy keeps the rooms fairly comfortable.

Hotel Posada de Roger (Map pp70-1; ☎ 222-08-36; www.posadaroger.com; Badillo 237; s/d/tr/q US$50/60/70/80; 🖾) This four-story guesthouse comes with some good foreigner hangout spots, such as a 2nd-floor pool and plant-filled courtyards. Maze-like outside hallways surround clean rooms with TV, dark wood furniture and – if you're lucky – a balcony. This was one of the first backpacker haunts in town, and folks still talk about the lascivious free spirits that used this place as their hive in the 1970s. The large and shady courtyard with its dripping fountain is a perfect place to escape the heat and compare travel tales with other travelers. On the 2nd floor, the motif of repose is extended with a small pool and plenty of chaise longues. Alas, the rooms are a bit musty and ill-equipped for basic security, but they're pleasant enough, with phones, ancient air-conditioners, well-worn furniture, diminutive TVs and creaky ceiling fans. The bathrooms sport large tiled showers big enough for three free spirits. For brightness and cross-ventilation, choose the rooms overlooking the street.

Estancia San Carlos (Map pp70-1; ☎ 222-54-84; Constitución 210; d/q US$64/110; P 🖾 🖾) With spacious and appealing fully equipped apartments with plenty of thoughtful touches, this old-timer provides exceptional value in the heart of the Zona Romántica. Some folks stay here for months. The two-room apartments on offer are large and pleasant with plenty of personality. Each has tiled floors, air-con, TV, sparsely equipped kitchens and (sometimes) private balconies. Sweetening the deal are comfortable king-sized beds, dining areas and bathrooms decked out with inviting hand-painted tiles. Kids go nuts in the small courtyard swimming pool, which is embellished with the double cascades of a roaring waterfall. A secure, covered parking lot serves those arriving under their own steam. The accommodating proprietor lives on the property and runs the place with considerable panache.

Torre de Oro (Map pp70-1; ☎ 222-44-88; 132 Púlpito; r US$79, ste US$99-130; 🔀 🏊) This old resort with 31 rooms and 12 suites is popular with families for its proximity to the beach and cheerful service. The rooms, with dark-red curtains and jungle-print couches, seem to have been appointed by a gentleman bachelor. Each is decorated with original paintings, but these seem to have been completed on a tight deadline and range from laughable to offensively bad. But the rooms are clean, don't smell bad, and overall provide fair value. If you opt for a standard room, take one of the corner units for superior light and a cross breeze. The suites have kitchens, a master bedroom and two daybeds. All rooms have either ocean or mountain views. An all-inclusive plan also is available.

TOP END

Casa Andrea (Map pp70-1; ☎ 222-12-13; www.casa-andrea.com; Rodríguez 174; per week 1-/2-bedroom US$450/800; 🔀 🏊) This gorgeous retreat rewards the handful of folks savvy enough to make their winter reservations here. What greets them are 10 beautifully decorated apartments on spacious grounds with flowery garden patios and a pool. Each apartment has a pleasant garden view, and is decorated with original paintings and native crafts, with king- or queen-sized beds and well-equipped modern kitchens. Some may like the fact that the apartments lack TVs, but if this comes as a shock you'll find a large-screen model downstairs in the well-stocked lending library. Other amenities include laundry facilities, a small gym and a recently added Internet room. No children under five.

Hotel Tropicana (Map pp70-1; ☎ 222-09-12; www.htropicanapv.com; 214 Amapas; d US$82-98, ste US$132;

🔀 🖥 🏊) On one of the quieter streets of beachfront Vallarta, this venerable 160-room beach hotel is a multilevel affair sporting views of swaying palms and the ocean extending to the horizon. When stepping into the impressive three-story lobby, with its marble floors and immense wrought-iron chandelier tethered from a brick dome, even the most jaded traveler may be moved to emit a low whistle of appreciation. The ground level is immaculately landscaped with brick terraces, a large fountain, open-air bars and a splendid pool. The standard rooms are appealing, with cooling white-brick walls, attractive carved headboards, hand-painted woodwork and rustic furniture. The balconies offer privileged views of the hotel terrace and the beach, revealing the overall quality of the property. The superior rooms are larger, with extra closet space, but have the same amenities as the standard rooms and are not really worth the extra expense.

Hotel Playa Los Arcos (Map pp70-1; ☎ 222-05-83, in the US 800-648-2403; www.playalosarcos.com; 380 Olas Altas; d US$116-140, ste US$166; 🔀 🏊) For a large beach hotel, this place gets it right. The recent renovations have given the property a streamlined colonial elegance. With its thoughtfully appointed rooms, giant pool and beachfront position, you'll find little to object to…that is, as long as you like kids. Families and honeymooners have made the place one of Vallarta's most popular hotels. Rooms and suites are divided between three buildings, one smack dab on the beach and two more on the other side of Calle Olas Altas. All of the rooms are spacious and bright, with air-con, phone, cable TV, hair dryers, room safes and other amenities that you would expect at this price level. The suites include fully equipped kitchens with dining tables. The beach is Vallarta's best, with plenty of lounge chairs and shade structures. Kids stay free, there's a gratis parking service, and an all-inclusive plan is available.

Hotel San Marino Plaza (Map pp70-1; ☎ 222-30-50; www.hotelsanmarino.com; Rodolfo Gómez 111; high season all-inclusive s/d/tr US$123/153/214; 🅿 🔀 🖥 🏊) Built in a 1960s-era cram-'em-in style pioneered in Acapulco, it's not the most attractive hotel in town, but it's right on the beach and kids seem to love it. The pool is where you'll find all the action; it's surrounded on three sides by blindingly white eight-story blocks of rooms with balconies. Standard rooms have all the expected amenities but smell a tad musty. Oceanfront rooms are sizable, with large balconies and amazing views over the beach and down the coast. There's a pleasant breezy restaurant fronting a second pool; meals are served buffet style. Activities offered include beach volleyball, aqua aerobics and handcrafts.

South of the City Centre
MIDRANGE

Quinta Maria Cortez (Map p67; ☎ 221-53-17; www .quinta-maria.com; Calle Sagitario 132; ste US$117-280 incl breakfast; 🍴 🛋) Just south of town off Hwy 200, this is perhaps the most atmospheric and sophisticated place to stay near Vallarta. The seven spacious and romantic suites, all different sizes, are furnished with a distinct style the proprietor calls 'Mexiterranean.' Most come with kitchen, fireplace and sea views, and breakfast is served in a terraced, *palapa*-covered common space. The suites are equipped for comfort and convenience, with direct-dial phones, fluffy towels and bathrobes, fancy soaps and shampoos and in-room safes. Definitely reserve in advance.

Costa Linda (Map p67; ☎ 223-0553; costalinda hotel@hotmail.com; Hwy 200, Km 1.5, Playa Conchas Chinas; apt/penthouse US$60/90; 🛋) The grounds are a little unkempt and in need of an update, but the capacious units and deep discounts for longer stays make this place a good value for budget travelers. The 23 apartments with kitchens are well kept if a bit musty. The two penthouse units are large and attractive, with timbered cathedral ceilings, sleeping lofts and balconies; one comes with air-con. It also has a small pool and, in the courtyard, a mammoth 300-year-old rubber tree with a palm grafted to the trunk. Perched on the southern edge of town on Hwy 200, it's not an easy matter to walk down to the beach, but the Mismaloya bus passes often.

Brisas del Mar (☎ 222-18-00; www.brisasvallarta .com; 10 Abedul; apt US$90-100; 🍴 🖥 🛋) With perhaps the best views in town, this comfortable small hotel is a quiet, get-away-from-it-all haven, ideal for couples and larger groups alike. Choose an upper-level apartment to take full advantage of the views. Each unit is gussied up in warm earth tones and original paintings. The kitchens – fitted with modern appliances

including microwave, blender, toaster and coffeemaker – open themselves to the balcony. On the top level is a huge penthouse with two bedrooms and baths, and plenty of space in the main living area to park the kids. It's a swanky affair with shiny blue-tile floors, cathedral ceilings and a roomy balcony with shaded patio tables. Internet access is provided to guests for a pittance. A steep stairway descends down to Amapas and beach access, but an afternoon by the pool is almost as good.

TOP END

Presidente InterContinental (Map p67; ☎ 228-01-91; www.intercontinental.com/puertovallarta; Hwy 200, Km 8.5; d US$431-466, ste US$781-1947; 🅿 🍴 🖥 🛋) This luxurious five-star behemoth pampers its guests with rejuvenating luxury. There's a spectacular view from the lobby, but you'll likely spend more time on the fine, yellow- sand beach. With 120 chic suites feature timbered ceilings, huge bathrooms with separate tub and shower, spacious dressing and sitting areas, and balconies. Each room also is equipped with DVD and CD players, and is stocked with all-natural, ooh-la-la French beauty products. If you really want to put on the ritz, you can take advantage of a full-service spa or the international water and pillow menus. Two good restaurants feature healthy low-calorie fare. Recreational activities include kayaking, yoga and grass-court tennis, and, as to be expected, the pool is divine.

Dreams Puerto Vallarta Resort & Spa (Map p67; ☎ 221-50-00, in the US 866-237-3267; www.dreams resorts.com; Hwy 200, Km 3.5; all-inclusive d US$298-333, ste US$598-1500; 🅿 ✖ 🍴 🖥 🛋) Formerly the Camino Real, this storied luxury property recently emerged from a splendid makeover. Sitting pretty before a jungle backdrop and with one of Vallarta's most beautiful beaches, the hotel offers a sense of luxury and privacy.

North of the Río Cuale
BUDGET

Hotel Posada del Pedregal (Map pp70-1; ☎ 222-06-04; Rodríguez 267; s/d US$40/50, ste US$70-120; ✖) On a busy mercantile street with a mixture of tourist and local shops, this budget option offers simple rooms overlooking an old courtyard. It's a basic but pleasant hotel with 21 rooms, only a stone's throw from the handicrafts market and the picturesque Río Cuale. On offer are street-front studio suites sporting small kitchens and a balcony, and small but bright standard rooms. All units come with fridges, tile floors and attractive, up-to-date bathrooms. Each is individually named and has a distinct, understated personality. The best, Cisne, is also the most expensive and the only one with air-con. At last visit the place was heavy with the aroma of pesticide; hopefully, when you arrive, this will be replaced by a lack of pests!

MIDRANGE

La Casa del Puente (Map pp70-1; ☎ 222-07-49; www
.casadelpuente.com, Libertad s/n; r/apt US$60/86) This guesthouse is unique in that it has only one room and two apartments, all so large, comfortable and wonderfully decorated that they feel like small houses. Tucked in behind the restaurant La Fuente del Puente, overlooking the Río Cuale, it's in a charming location. Once you pass through the gate you'll feel like you're deep in the jungle. Huge trees filled with winging birds and the occasional iguana spread their limbs to shade the house as the river passes by below. Owned by the grandniece of American naturalist John Muir, all three units are beautifully appointed, with period antiques and tasteful bric-a-brac. The apartments come complete with cozy Mexican-style kitchens, and the friendly resident caretaker is on hand to make sure you feel at home. You'll want to reserve well in advance.

Casa Dulce Vida (Map pp70-1; ☎ 222-10-08; www
.dulcevida.com; Aldama 295; ste US$80-180; 🏊 🐾) With the look and feel of an Italian villa, this collection of seven spacious suites with modern kitchens and private entrances offers graceful accommodations and delicious privacy. Most have private terraces and gratifying views of Bahía de Banderas. Back in the 1950s, this part of Vallarta was favored by the many cultural luminaries who came here from 'el norte' to familiarize themselves with the pleasures of genteel Mexican repose. Noted American painter Edith Hoyt was a frequent guest, leaving behind several paintings that are on display to this day. The tastefully appointed suites boast airy rooms with 14ft ceilings and plentiful windows, with sunny living areas and extra beds for groups. The largest and most splendid of them has three

bedrooms. Even when the place is fully booked it retains a quiet and intimate atmosphere. There's a well-situated pool and manicured tropical gardens.

Casa de los Cuatro Vientos (Map pp70-1; ☎ 222-
01-61; www.cuatrovientos.com; Matamoros 520; r/ste US$60/69; 🐾) Thriving in its hilly residential location, this guesthouse harbors peaceful, friendly rooms above a garden patio. The upper ones have partial views. Though not large, the rooms are rather cozy, with white-brick walls, hand-painted trim and gleaming red-tile floors. Each has a double bed and is cooled by a fan and salty breezes. The corner rooms are preferable for natural light and cross-ventilation. Quality furnishings, ranging from hand-carved Mexicana to retro pieces from the 1950s, add style and class. Elsewhere, the decorations reflect the proclivities of the owner, with plenty of theater posters and Puerto Vallarta memorabilia. For those wanting more space, there's a two-room suite with a large bedroom and two daybeds. The rooftop bar is an attraction unto itself, affording terrific views of the cathedral and the entire bay.

Hotel Rosita (Map pp70-1; ☎ 222-10-33; www.hotel
rosita.com; Paseo Díaz Ordaz 901; d/tr US$68/77; 🐾 🏊) The Rosita is not the most up-to-date place in town, but therein lies its charm. While some other Vallarta hotels have been renovated into indistinguishable, mind-numbing homogeneity, this old place looks like it hasn't changed a whit since opening in 1948. (On the other hand, the word 'charm' can hardly be applied to corroded shower fixtures.) The rooms are no-nonsense but clean, painted in warm colors and filled with worn furniture that's seen better days and lots of them. Cheaper street-side rooms are noisy and a bit outdated, but there are more pleasant rooms on offer upstairs. The terrace has a ho-hum pool – it would be a nice place to look out to sea if it weren't for the chain-link fence blocking the view.

TOP END

Hacienda San Angel (Map pp70-1; ☎ 222-26-92; www
.haciendasanangel.com; Miramar 336; d US$250-475; 🅿 🐾 🏊) This, the most noteworthy of Puerto Vallarta's recently opened hotels, elicits *oohs* and *ahs* from most guests, but for others the eye candy comes off as just a bit too sweet. Enough with the soothing dripping fountains already! Every nook and

cranny of the place is crammed with colonial flourish, from domed porticos and old mission antiques to statues of angels playing guitars and even saxophones. The details are so solicitously conceived that you almost feel manipulated into a state of restive bliss. But after a while, even the most jaded grump may be won over by the thoughtful attentions of the staff and the culinary magic practiced in the oh-so-colonial kitchen. The nine suites are individually decorated and undeniably luxurious, and each of the two pools affords tremendous views of the cathedral or Bahía de Banderas. There's also a daily cocktail hour and breakfast brought to your door each morning. Who could complain?

Hotel Molino de Agua (Map pp70-1; ☎ 222-19-07; www.molinodeagua.com; Vallarta 130; cabin all-inclusive per person s/d US$113/88, cabin noninclusive d/r US$101/113, ste US$175-225; ✦ ☎) With its central location, this hotel lets you get away from it all without really *being* away from it all. This lush 0.8-hectare property at the mouth of the Río Cuale offers a tranquil retreat right in the heart of town. Small but cute cabanas are set in a beautiful jungle environment; there are also well-appointed rooms and suites with ocean views. All come with air-con and small terrace, and there are bars, pools, whirlpool baths and two restaurants. Once you go through the gates, the hullabaloo of town quickly recedes as you pass into an exceedingly attractive jungle garden. Shady walkways lead past two splendid swimming pools and through abundant greenery. Two gigantic *hule de oro* (rubber) trees spread their limbs like outstretched arms, providing a shady embrace. The brick cabanas are simple rustic-chic and have no phones or TVs to disturb your reverie. The popular and simply elegant beachfront rooms and suites afford more privacy. At US$30 for a 75-minute rubdown, the therapeutic massages on offer are a great bargain; you might also want to reward yourself with a sea-salt or fruit-sugar body scrub.

Casa Kimberley (Map pp70-1; ☎ 222-13-36; www.casakimberley.com; Zaragoza 445; d US$110; ☎) When Elizabeth Taylor and Richard Burton took up residence in town during the 1960s, it sealed Vallarta's reputation as a swanky playground. The two adjacent houses at Casa Kimberly, connected by a pink 'love bridge,' were where the famously tempestuous romance played out. Burton bought the first house

as a birthday gift for his paramour in 1962 and, soon after, built the second mansion for himself. The three suites still retain the allure of a cocktail-era love nest. Burton himself put much loving attention into the design of the bar, over which figures of various Catholic saints cast a wary eye. It's kept fully stocked as a tribute to its creator, who some remember as the patron saint of the tipple. Full breakfast is included.

Casa Amorita (Map pp70-1; ☎ 222-49-26; www.casaamorita.com; Iturbide 309; r US$135; ☎) Located on a quiet street with no souvenir shops or other trappings of tourism, this romantic getaway is one of Vallarta's most unique and luxurious accommodations. Some may find it a wee bit precious, but others will swoon. With just four rooms and a capacity of only eight guests, you can be assured that you will be treated to lavish hospitality. The two 2nd-floor rooms catch the sea breezes; one opens up to a mammoth mango tree while the other affords expansive views (it's said you can spy passing whales from your bed in wintertime). The beds are very comfortable, with imported German mattresses and down comforters and pillows. Complimentary breakfasts are fresh, hearty and healthy. There's also a shady rooftop bar with privileged views of the town, and a friendly rottweiler named Maya.

North of the City Centre
BUDGET
Tacho's Trailer Park (Map p67; ☎ 224-21-63; Camino Nuevo al Pitillal s/n; tent or RV sites US$20; ☎) This large and agreeable RV park offers grassy spots and plenty of shady trees. To find it, turn east at Sam's Club on Hwy 200; Tacho's is approximately 1km on the left.

MIDRANGE
Hotel La Misión (Map p67; ☎ 222-71-04; Av México 1367; s/d/ste US$45/57/69; ✦ ☎) A tad removed from the party-all-the-time ruckus of the Zona Romántica, this cheerful hotel favored by Mexican travelers gives a lot of bang for your buck. An excellent restaurant serving economical fare closes the deal. The lobby and adjoining restaurant are quaint in just the right way. On arrival, you'll be tempted to drop your bags and head straight for a table in the eminently appealing dining room, which comprises the entire first floor of the hotel. Here they serve

tremendous Mexican breakfasts and fresh seafood favorites throughout the day. Upstairs, the rooms are painted in bright pastels and appointed with modest colonial decor and whimsical artworks. The more expensive apartments, ideal for families, feature fully equipped kitchens and glass-topped dining tables. Head to the roof for sun worship, where you'll enjoy the views while soaking in an impossibly tiny pool.

TOP END

Buenaventura Hotel & Beach Club (Map p67; ☎ 226-70-00; www.hotelbuenaventura.com.mx; Av México 1301; s/d/tr US$157/180/203; 🏖 🖳 🖭) This high-quality beach hotel offers appealing rooms and impressive hacienda-style architecture. The tile-floored rooms and suites have bright stucco walls with either two double beds or one king. Superior rooms up the ante with whirlpool baths, balconies and ocean views; suites add a kitchenette and living area. Whimsical 'magical realist' art abounds, and two large pools and plenty of lush greenery are used to positive effect. The two restaurants and a snack bar serve up exemplary fare. And then there's the beach: it's not the biggest in town, but the waters

are gentle and you can enjoy a measure of privacy. All-inclusive plans are available.

Fiesta Americana Puerto Vallarta (Map p67; ☎ 224-20-10; www.fiestaamericana.com; Francisco Medina Ascencio, Km 2.5; d US$180; 🅿 🏖 🖳 🖭) This hotel is one of the nicest in the Zona Hotelera, with a stunning lobby ringed by an artificial stream and sitting pretty under a giant *palapa* roof said to be the largest in the world. The wide and wonderful yellow-sand beach is one of Vallarta's loveliest, with limpid waters ideal for swimming. The nine-story terracotta high-rise houses 291 rooms looking over the pool and out to sea. The tile-floored rooms have private balconies and deluxe amenities; they're quietly elegant, with marble trim and wicker furniture. The massive pool is enhanced by a huge fountain and beguiling swim-up bar, and the afternoon water-volleyball games create quite a stir. Three restaurants and a lobby bar with nightly live music help ensure that most guests never leave the property.

EATING

Foodies are pampered in Puerto Vallarta. A goodly number of noteworthy chefs from abroad have put down roots, offering

---

GAY & LESBIAN RESORTS & INNS

Come on 'out' – the rainbow flag flies high over Puerto Vallarta. The **Gay Guide Vallarta** (www .gayguidevallarta.com) booklet has tons of information and a helpful map for finding gay-friendly businesses. Useful websites include www.discoveryvallarta.com and www.doinitright.com.

   Blue Chairs Beach Resort (Map p67; ☎ 222-50-40; www.bluechairs.com; Almendro 4; d US$69-109, apt US$79-129; 🏖 🖭) Overlooking one of Mexico's most famous gay beaches, this resort is a good place to let it all hang out (although officially the beach has a 'no nudity' policy). Amenities are conducive to socializing: there are bars and restaurants on the beach and roof, with a pool on the roof as well. The rooftop bar is particularly raucous, with nightly live entertainment. The breezy and attractive rooms have cable TV and air-con; apartments have kitchenettes. The resort also offers a full menu of tours, excursions, massage and spa services, and scuba-diving instruction and trips.

   Hotel Descanso del Sol (Map pp70-1; ☎ 222-52-29; www.descansodelsol.com; Suárez 583; s/d US$90/110, ste US$120-140; 🏖 🖭) This hotel on the hill is a well-established enclave. Don't be surprised to find 20 men crammed into the hot tub at dusk. Standard rooms are chintzy, but the suites are much better, with full kitchen and plenty of natural light. Some of the fixtures could use an update, but most guests don't quibble and spend most of their time on the roof enjoying the breathtaking panoramic views.

   Paco's Paradise (Map p67; ☎ 227-21-89; www.pacopaco.com; dm US$20, ste US$65-75; 🌙 closed Mon & Tue) Accessible by boat only, this rustic (electricity-free) getaway on 11 hectares of wilderness with a private beach is quite a deal. Groups leave from Club Paco Paco (p92) at 11am.

   Villa David (Map pp70-1; ☎ 223-03-15; www.villadavidpv.com; Galeana 348; r/ste with full breakfast US$93/119; 🏖 🖭) This low-key, unique and totally gay villa is a wonderful alternative to more crowded places near Playa Olas Altas. Rooms are spacious with colonial-style decor. Views from the rooftop are extraordinary. Reservations are essential.

competing menus of tremendous breadth and variety. Naturally, there are numerous economical, family-run eateries serving mouthwatering traditional Mexican fare, and the taco stands lining the streets of the Zona Romántica make quick meals a delicious proposition.

Just north of the river, the Mercado de Artesanías has simple and cheap stalls upstairs serving typical Mexican market foods. For more tourist-oriented fare, head toward Paseo Díaz Ordaz, the street fronting the *malecón*: it's thick with restaurants and bars. Many have upstairs terraces offering fine views of the bay.

South of the Río Cuale

BUDGET

If you're watching your budget, look for taco stands that sprout in the Zona Romántica early in the evenings – they serve some of the best and cheapest food in town. For inexpensive seafood stands, try the corner of Serdán and Constitución. There are also a few small, economical, family-run restaurants along Madero. Women sell delicious *tamales* and *flan* along Insurgentes at dusk.

The following restaurants are all south of the Río Cuale.

Pancake House (Map pp70-1; ☎ 222-62-72; Badillo 289; mains US$3-5; ☼ 8am-2pm) You may have to wait in line here because the amazing array of pancakes and other breakfast goodies have made this place more than popular. The food is good in a diner kind of way, but coffee fans should skip the free refills and buy themselves an espresso.

Las Tres Huastecas (Map pp70-1; ☎ 222-30-17; Olas Altas & Rodríguez; mains US$3-7; ☼ 7am-7pm) This is the place for delicious Mexican favorites in a homey atmosphere at local prices. The charming owner, a poet calling himself 'El Querreque,' recites verse as readily as he does the house specialties.

Fredy's Tucan Restaurant & Bar (Map pp70-1; ☎ 223-07-78; cnr Badillo & Vallarta; mains US$3-6; ☼ 8am-2am; ☒) This spick-and-span eatery is a foreigner magnet for breakfast specials like pancakes, waffles and omelets. If you're really hungry, go for the *campesino* breakfast, with a big portion of tender skirt steak and *chilaquiles* (fried tortilla chips with sauce and scrambled eggs). It also serves lunch, dinner, snacks and drinks, and at night this place turns into a bar. The food

is fine, though the coffee has garnered some criticism (try it and let us know).

Chiles! (Map pp70-1; ☎ 223-03-73; Púlpito 122; mains US$5-8; ☼ 11am-6pm Mon-Sat Nov-May) Chiles! grills up good-sized servings of burgers, hotdogs, roasted chicken and veggie burgers. Get a side of potato salad, coleslaw or chili with beans and head to the beach to digest it all.

Como Pizza (Map pp70-1; ☎ 222-32-72; Vallarta 279; pizza US$5-9; ☼ noon-4am Tue-Sun) This place belts out live tunes Friday and Saturday nights, which go well with the brick-oven, wood-fired pizza. The feel is upscale and open, the location is ground zero for hoppin' bars, and there's a pool table.

Santa Barbara (Map pp70-1; ☎ 223-20-48; Olas Altas 351; mains US$7-9) Attracts gringos like gringos attract sunburn. A comfort menu of burgers, sandwiches, pizzas, seafood and margaritas help ease the hunger pangs after a day of sunning, and the 2nd floor is gorgeous. Plus, there's bingo twice a week.

MIDRANGE

The following restaurants are found in the Zona Romántica.

Boca Bento (Map pp70-1; ☎ 222-91-08; Badillo 180; mains US$7-13; ☼ 6-11pm) This new, cosmopolitan place strikes the right balance with its 'Latina Asiatica cuisine.' Gorge on dishes like chipotle (dried, smoked jalapeño) honey-glazed ribs (US$19) in an urbane environment.

Mariscos Polo (Map pp70-1; ☎ 222-03-64; Madero 362; mains US$6-13; ☼ noon-10pm) This breezy, comfortable eatery deep in the Zona Romántica serves seafood and salads in a warm, music-filled environment. Start with a smoked marlin taco (US$1) and finish the job with a roasted shrimp skewer (US$14) or octopus burrito (US$6). Mmm!

Kaiser Maximillian (Map pp70-1; ☎ 222-50-58; Olas Altas 380B; mains US$7-18; 🕑 8am-midnight Mon-Sat; 🎇) Get your well-prepared Wiener schnitzel (US$16) or fresh *roter Rubensalat* (beet salad) at this upscale Austrian restaurant. There's also good coffee, desserts, snacks and meals, all with an Austrian flavor. It's popular for evening drinks.

Angelo's Italian Cuisine (Map pp70-1; ☎ 223-20-88; Gomez 158; mains US$8-22; 🕑 4-10:30pm; 🎇) The red wine flows and the wait staff is jovial. Enjoy certified Angus steaks and well-prepared, straightforward Italian fare, served either on a spacious sidewalk patio or in a romantic, air-conditioned dining room.

Le Gourmet (Map pp70-1; ☎ 222-04-50; Serdán 242; mains US$8-18; 🕑 7am-9pm) At Hotel Posada Río Cuale, this pleasant restaurant serves generous, well-priced breakfast platters with whimsical names like 'This Is Your Brain in Mexico' (spicy scrambled eggs). At dinner, regional specialties and seafood rule the menu; try the lobster simmered in orange liqueur.

Café de Olla (Map pp70-1; ☎ 223-16-26; Badillo 168A; mains US$6-18; 🕑 9am-11pm Wed-Mon) This small, busy and very pleasant tourist-oriented restaurant serves great traditional Mexican food at good prices.

Archie's Wok (Map pp70-1; ☎ 222-04-11; Rodríguez 130; mains US$9-18; 🕑 2-11pm Mon-Sat) The setting here is elegant but urban. The menu changes but it's always Asian fusion cuisine, with savory fish in rich tropical sauces as the highlight. There's live music Thursday through Sunday.

Abadía Café (Map pp70-1; ☎ 222-67-20; Badillo 252; mains US$12-22; 🕑 6-11pm, closed Tue; 🎇) This super-stylish, air-conditioned café has a varied menu of well-prepared, pricey, but unique dishes such as the house favorite, duckling breast in Chiapas coffee sauce.

Carisma (Map pp70-1; ☎ 222-49-59; Badillo 284; mains US$10-19; 🕑 5pm-midnight) Carisma posts its menu at the doors, but beware: one innocent peek and the eager waiters practically reel you in. Luckily, the food is good: savor rustic octopus, hot garlic crab or rib-eye steak. Pizzas and pastas are also available, as are mixed drinks and something called 'sexy coffee.'

Sand Bar (Map pp70-1; ☎ 222-08-94; Rodriguez at Playa de los Muertos; mains US$8-18; 🕑 7am-11pm) This place serves salads, seafood, ribs, burgers, tacos and frogs' legs. The real reason you're here, however, is to eat on the beach under a shady *palapa*.

Asaderos (Map pp70-1; ☎ 044-342-957-90; Badillo 223; buffet US$10; 🕑 2-11pm Sun-Tue) Asaderos grills up plenty of barbecued chicken, steak, ribs and Mexican sausage for the popular all-you-can-eat package. Salad and bread are included, but the drinks tack onto the restaurants' profits. The sidewalk or *palapa* seating is pleasant, and there's live music. Add tax to the rates.

Fajita Republic (Map pp70-1; ☎ 222-31-31; cnr Badillo & Suárez; mains US$9-18; 🕑 5pm-midnight) With pleasant open-air dining on a leafy, atmospheric patio, this popular fajita factory grills up generous portions of shrimp, vegetables, steak and chicken with plenty of guacamole. Wash it all down with a pitcher of mango margaritas.

TOP END

In the heart of the Zona Romántica are a good mix of upscale restaurants, including a couple of notable recent arrivals.

Casa Naranjo (Map pp70-1; ☎ 222-35-18; Naranjo 263; mains US$7-19; 🕑 6-11pm) This chic newcomer has an unabashed predilection for the color orange and a dining room that wraps around the exposed kitchen. On the menu is delicious, fussed-over fare like saffron mussels, ginger-grilled scallops and invigorating cold soups.

La Palapa (Map pp70-1; ☎ 222-52-25; Púlpito 103; mains US$7-48; 🕑 8am-1pm & 6-11pm) This is elegant beach dining at its best. Chilean sea bass with blonde miso and pickled ginger is just one example of the delicacies on the menu. Tables are positioned to take full advantage of the sea views, making it a particularly marvelous spot at sunset or for breakfast.

Red Cabbage Café (☎ 223-04-11; Rivera del Río 204A; mains US$8-20; 🕑 5-10:30pm; 🎇 ✖) Though the atmosphere is casual, with fabulous eclectic and bohemian artwork, the food is serious Mexican *alta cocina* (haute cuisine). This is the only nonsmoking restaurant in town. Try the subtle mole or hearty vegetarian dishes. To get there from the Zona Romántica, begin at Insurgentes and then follow Cárdenas east five long blocks. Take a right turn before the green bridge and go approximately one more block. It's about a 10-minute walk. Reservations are recommended.

Ibiza (Map pp70-1; ☎ 222-63-53; Suárez 321; mains US$11-20; ☯ 5-11pm) Paella, Sicilian chicken and gazpacho are among the repertoire of dishes at Ibiza. The atmosphere is airy and open, and there's live jazz Wednesday to Friday nights at 7:30pm.

Los Pibes (Map pp70-1; ☎ 223-20-44; Badillo 261; mains US$9-24; ☯ 5-11pm Mon-Sat) Proudly serves Sterling Silver meat from the USA (which one assumes is an asset). Steaks are grilled Argentine-style; try the *bife de chorizo* (sirloin), which is the most basic cut in Argentina. There's another branch up north at the yacht harbor in Marina Vallarta.

Chef Roger (Map pp70-1; ☎ 222-59-00; Badillo 180; mains US$13-25; ☯ 6:30-11pm Mon-Sat) You'll need to arrive here in fancy threads, and with reservations (crucial on weekends). Only then can you enjoy the romantic outdoor fountain seating and fabulous meals like carpaccio of ostrich with pesto and parmesan cheese. Expect elegance and bring a fat wallet.

Daiquiri Dick's (Map pp70-1; ☎ 222-05-66; Olas Altas 314; mains US$7-21; ☯ 9am-10:30pm) An elegant dining establishment, despite its name. Nibble roast duck with scalloped sweet potatoes, bite into the sesame-encrusted tuna or wrestle with lobster tacos. Southwest colors, soft music and a beautiful view help it all go down easy.

Steak House Brasil (Map pp70-1; ☎ 222-29-09; Carranza 210; women/men US$14/17; ☯ 2pm-midnight; ☒) Carnivores rejoice! Here the meat-hungry masses devour gut-busting portions of sirloin, filet mignon, ribs and turkey. One price gets you all you can eat, including a choice of three salads, soup, veggies and corny live music.

El Palomar de los González (Map pp70-1; ☎ 222-07-95; Aguacate 425; mains US$10-20; ☒) The superb view over the city and bay is a big draw at this hillside restaurant, especially at sunset. Jumbo shrimp and fillet steak are specialties. It's a steep climb up here, so get a taxi or work up an appetite.

North of the Río Cuale
BUDGET
The Mercado de Artesanías, just north of the river, has simple stalls upstairs serving typical Mexican market foods. You'll find the following eateries north of the Río Cuale in El Centro.

Esquina de los Caprichos (Map pp70-1; ☎ 222-09-11; cnr Miramar & Iturbide; tapas under US$4; ☯ noon-10pm Mon-Sat) This Spanish-Mexican tapas hole-in-the-wall serves delicious garlic-heavy gazpacho, buttery grilled scallops and much more. Though in a small, stark setting, it's entertaining and popular.

Cenaduría Doña Raquel (Map pp70-1; ☎ 222-30-25; Vicario 131; mains US$3-5; ☯ 6-11:30pm Mon & Wed-Fri, 2-11pm Sat & Sun) You can smell the richness of the traditional Mexican basics served in this local haven from a block away. Friendly atmosphere and friendly prices.

Planeta Vegetariano (Map pp70-1; ☎ 222-3073; Iturbide 270; buffet US$3.50-6; ☯ 8am-10pm) Serves up all-you-can-eat quality buffets at every meal, and they are a vegetarian's dream. Just come: you won't be disappointed. All around are wonderfully painted murals, and the hilly pedestrian street outside is a peaceful backdrop.

Tacos de los Arcos (Map pp70-1; Zaragoza 120; tacos US$1; ☯ noon-midnight) In a class by itself, Tacos de los Arcos is simple but indulgent, with all the fixings. Look for the 'Hooters' sign and follow it down.

Archie's Burger (Map pp70-1; ☎ 222-43-83; cnr Morelos & Pipila; mains less than US$5; ☯ noon-1am Tue-Sun) At this tiny shack of a place budding surfers can catch some burgers, hotdogs, fries, surfer videos and reggae music. Don't bring your surfboard: there isn't much room.

MIDRANGE
Barcelona (Map pp70-1; ☎ 222-05-10; cnr Matamoros & 31 de Octubre; tapas US$3.50-7; ☯ noon-11:30pm Mon-Sat, 5:30-11:30pm Sun) Requires a walk up a hill and some stairs, but the grand view and excellent tapas are worth it. Lamb, duck and vegetarian dishes are also served. Try to get a table on the patio up top, and by all means order a sangria!

Las Palomas (Map pp70-1; ☎ 222-36-75; cnr Paseo Díaz Ordaz & Aldama; mains US$9-28; ☯ 8am-11pm) Looking over the *malecón* from its comfortable perch, Las Palomas is a popular place for people-watching. The menu lists seafood, chicken crepes and authentic Mexican specialties, and the decor is smart and festive. Soft music serenades loud and happy gringo voices – perhaps they scored a 'free margarita' coupon?

La Dolce Vita (Map pp70-1; ☎ 222-38-52; Paseo Díaz Ordaz 674; mains US$7-10; ☯ noon-2am; ☒) This is a cheerful, often crowded spot for wood-fired pizzas and people-watching. On Friday night there's handmade gnocchi. Live jazz plays Thursday to Sunday for the crowded floor.

No Name Café (Map pp70-1; ☎ 223-25-08; cnr Morelos & Mina; mains US$5-20; ❤ 8am-1am; ❈) Serving all-American favorites, this restaurant and sports bar has 31 (count 'em) TV sets. Obviously, a good place to catch your choice of game. It claims to serve the best ribs in Mexico: you be the judge. Phone for free delivery.

Mi Querencia (Map pp70-1; ☎ 222-20-30; Morelos 426; mains US$6-18; ❤ 8am-2am) Seviche – the marinated seafood and lime dish that makes an appearance on nearly every Pacific coast menu – gets gussied up here with variations featuring coriander, pineapple, beet juice and oranges. Similar liberties are taken with the shrimp dishes.

La Bodeguita del Medio (Map pp70-1; ☎ 223-15-85; Paseo Díaz Ordaz 858; mains US$7-15; ❤ 11am-2:30am) Test the authenticity of this Cuban joint by trying the Cuban paella or gazpacho with a Caribbean twist. A retractable roof and 2nd-floor balcony make for an open feel and good views over the *malecón*. There's live music all day (if you're lucky).

Rito's Baci (Map pp70-1; ☎ 222-64-48; Domínguez 183; mains US$7-17; ❤ 1-11pm) This place stands proud in cozy spaces filled with foreign patrons sampling delicious Italian cuisine. Moody music and small front tables make it better for romantic liaisons than large rowdy groups.

La Fuente del Puente (Map pp70-1; ☎ 221-11-41; Insurgentes 107; mains US$5-11; ❤ 8am-11pm) Perched over the Río Cuale at the bridge, this delightfully situated café serves traditional regional specialties from all corners of Mexico. It's particularly charming for breakfast in the morning, when the birds along the river turn up the volume and iguanas pass noiselessly in the trees overhead.

TOP END

Trio (Map pp70-1; ☎ 222-42-28; Guerrero 264; mains US$14-26; ❤ 6pm-midnight; ❈) The two European chefs put a lot of passion into the seasonal menu at this elegant restaurant-bar-bistro. Mexican and Mediterranean flavors blend beautifully in dishes like lamb ravioli, chili-roasted snapper or Lebanese salad. The rooftop bar area is choice for an after-dinner libation.

Café des Artistes (Map pp70-1; ☎ 222-32-28; Sánchez 740; mains US$18-29; ❤ 6-11:30pm; ❈) This cosmopolitan restaurant has a romantic ambience to match its exquisite French cuisine. It's not so elegant that 'happy birthday' songs aren't belted out every night, though. Local seafood is featured in many of the dishes, with adventurous dishes like 'soft shell crab and beef tongue fantasy.' Reservations are recommended.

North of Puerto Vallarta
TOP END
North of town, the top-end hotels in the Zona Hotelera and Marina Vallarta all have top-end restaurants. Recommended places:

Bogart's (Map p67; ☎ 224-02-02; Av Las Garzas s/n; mains US$7-14; ❤ 8am-midnight) At NH Krystal Puerto Vallarta (p92); gourmet international cuisine.

Garibaldi's (Map p67; ☎ 226-11-50; Paseo de la Marina Sur 105; mains US$6-16; ❤ 8am-midnight) At Westin Regina Resort; fine seafood in a beachfront setting.

Isla Río Cuale
TOP END
The riverside setting of the three restaurants on the island makes for a romantic and relaxing dining experience.

Le Bistro Jazz Café (Map pp70-1; ☎ 222-02-83; Isla Río Cuale 16A; mains US$10-30; ❤ 9am-midnight Mon-Sat; ❈) Overlooking the river, this swanky spot is good for a martini but even better for its scrumptious cuisine, pleasant jazz recordings and beautiful tropical scenery. The menu is replete with gourmet fare like mahimahi, shrimp Portuguese and 'lobster of desire.' For breakfast there are savory crepes and eggs Benedict.

River Cafe (Map pp70-1; ☎ 223-07-88; Isla Río Cuale 4; mains US$10-22; ❤ 9am-midnight; ❈) Imaginative seafood dishes are a highlight of this well-regarded and delightfully situated restaurant. Try shrimp with pecans and orange sauce, or the delectable shellfish salad. There's live jazz in the evenings Thursday through Sunday.

Oscar's Bar & Grill (Map pp70-1; ☎ 223-07-89; Isla Rio Cuale 1; mains US$10-21; ❤ 11am-11pm) On the peaceful seaward tip of Isla Río Cuale, this restaurant is a fine choice for a romantic meal. Enjoy dishes like vegetable crepes with corn and *poblano* peppers (US$13) or superfresh mahimahi fillet baked in basil and parmesan (US$21).

Self-Catering

Cater your own picnic and save some pesos.

Gutiérrez Rizoc (GR; Map pp70-1; cnr Constitución & Serdán; ⏰ 6:30am-11pm) A well-stocked, air-con supermarket; OK for self-catering or a small indulgence.

Agro Gourmet (Map pp70-1; ☎ 222-53-57; Badillo 222; ⏰ 9am-6pm Mon-Fri, 9am-3pm Sat) This small health-food store sells seasonal veggies, whole-wheat bread, grains and spices.

DRINKING

Not surprisingly for a city where lounging around is one of the preferred activities, Vallarta has many choice spots for sipping a strong coffee or tipping a tipple. Coffee shops open early and close late, and most bars keep 'em coming well after midnight.

Coffee Shops

There are plenty of places in Vallarta to satisfy those java cravings and keep your energy levels buzzing.

Café San Angel (Map pp70-1; ☎ 223-21-60; Olas Altas 449) Start your day in this artsy, relaxed café with sidewalk tables filled with gringos sitting pretty, sipping their black coffee and nibbling on snacks and sweets. Try coffees laced with whiskey, tequila or Kahlua (US$3.50).

Kahuna Coffee Co (Map pp70-1; ☎ 222-16-93; Badillo 162; bagels US$1.50-3, coffee US$1-3) Great for when you're jonesin' for a jalapeño bagel with horseradish cream cheese. This tiny, Canadian-run coffee joint sells other bagel flavors like garlic and bialy, spreadable on top with blackberry, nuts and raisins or veggie cream cheeses. Lox sandwiches are available, and it's also got good java, including frozen versions.

Café Superior (Map pp70-1; ☎ 222-44-23; Encino 55; mains US$3-5.50, coffee US$1-2.50; ⏰ 8am-8pm Tue-Sat, 8am-4pm Sun-Mon) Brews up some great (albeit pricey) stuff, and is efficiently run by a Seattle native. Also on order are tuna salad, nachos, veggie sandwiches, milkshakes and Western-style breakfasts. The corner-store ambience is intimate and casual, with plenty of open doors for street-watching.

World of Coffee (Map pp70-1; cnr Cárdenas & Olas Altas; coffee US$1-3) Here you can have your carrot cake and eat it, too – with an iced latte, even. It's not atmospheric, but there is pleasant, covered sidewalk seating and it's across from a park. Avoid the pricey Internet service.

Viva Café (Map pp70-1; Cárdenas 292) Perks and bubbles its java among small tables and artsy clutter. Order your usual fancy coffees; packaged grounds are also available for purchase.

Cappucchino Café (Map pp70-1; Galeana 104; coffee up to US$5) Steams up lattes, mochas and espresso from its 2nd-story open loft. There's a great view of the little seahorse boy statue and some nice-looking desserts.

Bars

It's easy to become inebriated in Puerto Vallarta, where two-for-one happy hours are as reliable as the sunset and the margarita glasses look like oversized snifters. The following bars are preferred watering holes.

La Barriga Cantina (Map pp70-1; Madero 259) This is the perfect bar, in a self-proclaimed 'spicy little neighborhood.' Attracting both gringos and locals, this cozy and friendly place has free pool and a well-curated jukebox.

La Bodeguita del Medio (Map pp70-1; ☎ 223-15-85; Paseo Díaz Ordaz 858) This graffiti-covered Cuban joint has live music, stiff mojitos and good views over the *malecón*.

El Faro Lighthouse Bar (Map pp70-1; ☎ 221-05-41; Royal Pacific Yacht Club, Marina Vallarta; ⏰ 5pm-2am) Not too many lighthouses serve cocktails, but this one sure does. Panoramic views of the bay in the moonlight are a surefire prelude to a kiss.

Club Roxy (Map pp70-1; Vallarta 217) This club has a dark, crowded atmosphere while music (Santana, say) fills the air. Middle-aged and sometimes skimpily clad rockers sway and smooch in the deepest corners or in plain sight. The live music is pretty good.

Club Sports Bar & Grill (Map pp70-1; ☎ 222-02-56; Badillo 286) Ice hockey dominates on the screens, while at the bar aging hippies share space with purple-haired ladies. It's friendly, modern, casual and bright.

Pool hall (Map pp70-1; Madero 279) This is *not* the kind of place where you'll find Tom Cruise types twirling their cues and kicking shit. It's large, full of tables and downright seedy. Get drunk and challenge the locals (all male) to a game.

Other possibilities:

Memories Café (Map pp70-1; Mina & Juárez; ⏰ 7pm-midnight) Conversation is king at this down-to-earth, low-key spot.

Carlos O'Brian's (Map pp70-1; ☎ 222-14-44; Paseo Díaz Ordaz 786) A favorite drinking hole for rabble-rousing gringos.

ENTERTAINMENT

Dancing and drinking are Puerto Vallarta's main forms of night-time entertainment. In the evenings many people stroll down the *malecón*, where some wonderfully creative 'Dr Seuss-on-acid' sculpture has been placed. Also lining the *malecón* are plenty of romantic open-air restaurants and heaps of riotous bars. Entertainment is often on tap in the amphitheater by the sea (opposite Plaza Principal), and the softly lit Isla Río Cuale is a quiet haven for a romantic, early evening promenade.

Clubs & Discos

Along the *malecón* are a bunch of places where teen and 20-something (or even older) tourists get trashed and dance on tables. On a good night, they might stay open to about 5am. You can see from the street which one has the most action. Usually there's no cover charge, but drinks are on the expensive side, except during the 'happy hours,' which can be any time from 8pm to 11pm.

de Santos (Map pp70-1; ☎ 223-30-52; Morelos 771; weekend cover US$10; ☿ Wed-Sun; ☒) Vallarta's choicest nightspot commands the most artful DJs and an open-air rooftop bar furnished with oversized beds. On the dance floor the music is frenetic, but there's also a mellow chill lounge.

Zoo (Map pp70-1; ☎ 222-49-45; Paseo Díaz Ordaz 638; weekend cover US$11; ☒) Sports an animal scene, and I'm not just talking about the decor. Grilled windows resemble cages, so if you're up for a wild time step inside – carefully. You may be greeted with all-the-margaritas-you-can-drink hour. Ignore the gorilla at the door; he's a brute.

Hilo (Map pp70-1; ☎ 223-53-61; Paseo Díaz Ordaz 588; weekend cover US$7-10; ☒) A cool space well-designed for getting a groove on, with epic statues of revolutionary heroes.

Hard Rock Café (Map pp70-1; ☎ 222-55-32; Paseo Díaz Ordaz 652; ☿ 11am-2am) In the same area, but gets an older, more sedate, T-shirt-collecting crowd. Spin to live music every night but Monday.

Kahlúa (Map pp70-1; ☎ 222-24-86; cnr Paseo Díaz Ordaz & Abasolo) Blares loud disco beats from its huge windows. Inside, gringos check each other out and look for dates, while reaping the rewards of a constant happy hour.

La Regadera (Map pp70-1; ☎ 222-39-76; Morelos 664) Dark, smoky and popular with young local drinkers and dancers. Come for a visit if you want to hear Mexicans singing loudly and badly.

La Cantina (Map pp70-1; ☎ 222-17-34; Morelos 700) Also attracts the young, hip and uninhibited, sitting daintily on barstools. Again, it's a mostly Mexican crowd.

La Revolución (Map pp70-1; ☎ 222-06-06; Matamoros 235) A cool and casual local joint attracting a good mix of gringos and Mexicans. It's one of the oldest bars in Vallarta: Liz Taylor and Richard Burton hung out here. Wednesday night there's live music, but other times there's open mike – pick up the sax and join in.

South of the Río Cuale, a wider variety of nightspots cater to a more diverse clientele, and drink prices are generally lower than on the *malecón* scene.

High After Hours Bar (Map pp70-1; Cardenas 329; cover US$10) This hipster haven features oxygen-huffing and dance floor action 'till the sun comes to dance.'

Señor Frog's (Map pp70-1; ☎ 222-51-71; cnr Vallarta & Carranza; admission US$9-11; ☿ 11am-4am) Employs waiters eager to recruit female patrons, and has a sign that prominently declares 'Topless women = free drinks; topless men = no service.' Nightly shows include wet T-shirt, bikini and wet boxer. You can guess what kind of place this is. There's no admission charge if you're having dinner. If you don't have time to get alcohol poisoning here, there are other locations in Mazatlán, Ixtapa and Acapulco.

Cactus (Map pp70-1; ☎ 222-03-91; Vallarta 399; men/women US$24/14) A modern disco that plays host to a bikini or wet T-shirt contest some nights. The cover charge (though sometimes estrogen is so needed it gets in free) includes an open bar – which does nothing to promote responsible drinking. Isn't it great?

North of the city, some of the large resort hotels have bars and nightclubs, but they're usually low energy, high-priced affairs. They're busier at holiday times, when well-dressed Mexicans strut their stuff. To cut the cost of the cover charge, look for discount coupons in tourist pamphlets.

Christine (Map p67; ☎ 224-69-90; ☿ 10pm-5am) At the NH Krystal Puerto Vallarta (p92), this flashy dance club is occasionally explosive, with cutting-edge sound and lighting systems. Cover charges (free to US$10 to US$25) fluctuate depending on your gender

GAY & LESBIAN CLUBS & NIGHTSPOTS

Puerto Vallarta has a formidable selection of gay bars, nightclubs and restaurants. Blue Chairs is the most popular, visible gay beach bar, with droves of gay couples enjoying the ubiquitous sun rays and cool drinks. It's at the southern end of Playa de los Muertos.

Club Paco Paco (Map pp70-1; ☎ 222-18-99; www.pacopaco.com; Vallarta 278) With a disco and cantina, this venerable institution is most famous for its transvestite revues (cover US$6; midnight and 3am Thursday to Sunday).

Los Balcones (Map pp70-1; ☎ 222-46-71; Juárez 182; cover US$2-4, before 10pm free) One of the oldest gay haunts in town, this place has little upstairs balconies where trendy hipsters like to be seen. Great cozy spaces and colorful walls accompany DJ music and nightly strippers.

Anthropology (Map pp70-1; Morelos 101; cover US$6) Exotic snake and Maya themes seduce the punters. Hot male bodies are on display for one another, and if you're lucky salsa beats will be on tap. If you're not so lucky, you'll get heavy techno thump. Check out the dark, more intimate rooftop patio.

The Palm (Map pp70-1; Olas Altas 508; cover US$4, before 9pm free) A different show is held every night, including comedy, jazz, pop Latin music or guest performers. Spinning lights, snazzy colors and palm decor make it all seem like a dream. As one of the gay owners says: 'No one has to be lonely here.'

Depending on the alignment of the stars, the following gay bars are mostly mellow. **Kit Kat Klub** (Map pp70-1; ☎ 223-00-93; Púlpito 120; 🅧) is an ultra-hip dinner-show spot with wicked martinis. **La Noche** (Map pp70-1; 257 Cardenas; 🕒 4pm-2am) is well loved for its convivial atmosphere and buff bar tenders. **Sama Bar** (Map pp70-1; ☎ 223-31-82; 510 Olas Altas; 🕒 5pm-2am) is a likable small place with big martinis. **Bar El Morbo** (Map pp70-1; ☎ 223-43-47; Olas Altas 463) glows in the dark, literally. Plus there's a free Jacuzzi on the roof (open Friday to Monday nights; bring your speedos, or don't).

and the night. Sometimes an open bar is included. Terraced levels, spinning spotlights and hip hop music delight well-dressed dancers downing overpriced and weak drinks. Still, it's flashy, modern and lively.

Jabalu (Map p67; ☎ 223-40-99; Francisco Ascencio 1735; 🕒 10pm-3am Sun-Thu, 10am-5am Fri-Sat) Just north of the Sheraton Buganvilias, this place stirs up some passionate salsa and merengue for a varied crowd. Balloons and colored lights add to the mix, although it's not cutting-edge cool. Cover vary, but run around US$9 on weekends.

J&B (Map p67; ☎ 224-46-16; Francisco Ascencio, Km 2.5; admission Wed-Sun US$9, Mon-Tue free; 🕒 10pm-6am) Swings with salsa, cumbia and merengue, mostly. The live stuff starts at 12:30am Wednesday to Sunday, and a somewhat tacky tropical theme encourages casual dress. The crowd runs into 40-somethings.

Mariachis

Two places present regular traditional Mexican music performed by mariachis. One attracts mostly tourists; the other is mainly for Mexicans.

Tequila's (Map pp70-1; ☎ 222-57-25; Galeana 104; 🅧) The 2nd-story location on the *malecón* makes for an excellent backdrop to the live mariachi music every night (except Monday), starting at around 7:30pm or 8pm. Try one of the many versions of tequila.

Mariachi Loco (Map pp70-1; ☎ 223-22-05; cnr Cárdenas & Vallarta; cover US$3; 🕒 shows 6:30 & 10.30pm; 🅧) Usually attracting an exuberant all-Mexican crowd, this restaurant-bar presents an entertaining (if slightly amateur) show of music, comedy and mariachi every night. It's a great bit of local color, but you'll need good Spanish to get the jokes.

Fiestas Mexicanas

These fun folkloric shows give tourists a crash course in not-very-contemporary Mexican culture.

La Iguana (Map pp70-1; ☎ 222-01-05; Cárdenas 311; admission US$50; 🕒 7-11pm Thu & Sun; 🅧) Said to be the original of this much-copied tourist entertainment. The deal here includes a Mexican buffet, open bar, live music, folkloric dances, mariachis, cowboy rope tricks, bloodless cockfights and a piñata.

Some of the big resort hotels also do Fiesta Mexicana nights, including the **NH Krystal Puerto Vallarta** (Map p67; ☎ 224-02-02 ext 2091; Las Garzas s/n; admission US$48; 🕒 shows Tue &

Sat 7pm; ⊠). It's considered one of the best Fiestas Mexicanas, though it's not cheap. Add fireworks to the above.

Sheraton Buganvilias (Map p67; ☎ 226-04-04; Francisco Ascencio 999) is another big-name hotel that offers up a decent Mexican Fiesta night (held on Thursdays).

Cinemas

Cine Bahía (Map pp70-1; ☎ 222-17-17; cnr Insurgentes & Madero; admission US$3.80; ⊠) For a less frenetic evening out, catch a movie in air-con comfort at Cine Bahía. Recent releases are often shown in English with Spanish subtitles.

Bullfights

Bullfights (☎ 224-11-75; admission US$14-28; ⊠ 5pm Wed Nov-May) These are held in Plaza del Toro (Map pp70-1) opposite the marina. Any travel agency or luxury hotel worth its salt will have information or sell tickets.

SHOPPING

Shops and boutiques in Puerto Vallarta sell fashion clothing, beachwear and just about every type of handicraft made in Mexico, but prices are high, reflecting the richness of the area.

Markets

There are a few markets concentrating on craft stalls, and these are the places to go for cheaper prices and some hard bargaining.

Mercado de Artesanías (Map pp70-1; ☎ 223-09-25; A Rodríguez 260) A maze of more than 150 craft stalls, this market offers touristy T-shirts, Taxco silver jewelry, *sarapes* (cloaks) and *huaraches* (leather sandals), wool wall-hangings, painted pottery and blown glass, among many other things. Tons of other shops line Agustín Rodríguez, facing the market. Bargain like your life depended on it: walk away and prices plummet.

The most atmospheric handicraft district, however, is the shady and tropical strip on Isla Río Cuale, where stands sell crafts daily for comparable prices.

Shops & Boutiques

Olinalá (Map pp70-1; ☎ 222-49-95; Cardenas 274) This excellent gallery displays authentic Mexican dance masks, folk art, rural antiques, fine guitars and contemporary paintings.

Serafina (Map pp70-1; ☎ 223-45-94; Badillo 260) A bit funky, with a good and crowded selection

of pottery virgins, clothing, bags (leather, cloth, plastic) and jewelry.

Patti Gallardo (Map pp70-1; ☎ 222-57-12; Badillo 250) A great place for handmade and unique 'eclectic art' (though not necessarily Mexican) made mostly by women: jewelry, sculpture, picture frames, knick-knacks and more. It's not cheap.

Puerco Azul Galería (Map pp70-1; ☎ 222-86-47; Constitución 325) This beguiling, well-curated shop tempts with a treasure trove of movie posters, quirky original art, 'kitsch mexicana' and delightful curios.

Viva (Map pp70-1; ☎ 222-40-78; Badillo 274) The type of establishment that exclaims 'Welcome to Viva!' as you walk in. The stuff's fabulous, of course: funky sunglasses, stylish espadrilles and excellent straw hats and beach bags. Creative and original jewelry's the specialty, though, with over 450 international designers represented. There's a considerate sofa for the hubbies.

El Gato Gordo (Map p67; ☎ 223-03-00; Av de México 1083) This is Vallarta's best source for *lucha libre* (Mexican wrestling) masks; also boasts a small but choice selection of Cuban cigars.

La Casa de los Gatos (Map pp70-1; ☎ 222-30-76; Badillo 220) This casual place carries a variety of fairly priced and eccentric stuff, including some Huichol beadwork.

Huichol Crafts

Puerto Vallarta is a prime place to shop for indigenous Huichol beadwork, thread paintings (made by pressing thread into a wax-covered board) and jewelry. The best selection can be found at **Artesanías Flores** (Map pp70-1; ☎ 223-07-73; Cardenas 282), **Huichol Collection** (Map pp70-1; ☎ 223-21-41; Morelos 490) and **Galería Mágico Huichol** (Map pp70-1; ☎ 222-30-77; Corona 179).

Home Decor

Alfarería Tlaquepaque (Map p67; ☎ 223-21-21; Av de México 1100) This large showroom has been in business for decades, offering the best prices and selection of baked earthenware, blown glass and ceramics.

Mundo de Cristal (Map pp70-1; ☎ 222-41-57; Insurgentes 333) Stocks an incredible selection of hand-blown glass.

Lucy's Cucú Cabaña (Map pp70-1; Badillo 295) Lucy's stocks some fine, fun crafts from all over the country – Oaxacan wood animals, papier-mâché masks and recycled metal

BULLFIGHTING ON MEXICO'S PACIFIC COAST

When considering an afternoon at a bullring, one thing to keep in mind is that all *corridas del toro* (bullfights) and all *plazas del toro* (bullrings) are not alike. Mexico's Pacific Coast is considered a region without much local enthusiasm for bullfighting, and bullfights performed here are largely motivated by the tourist dollar.

Puerta Vallarta has the largest and newest plaza along the coast – it's a smaller version of the famous Plaza del Toro in Mexico City. Bullfighting happens on Wednesday afternoons, timed with the arrival of cruise ships. In Latin America, the bullfighting season is December through April (during the summer and fall the bullfighters go to Spain). The best bullfights tend to happen during a town's fiesta, but bullfights are never guaranteed to be 'good' – even the best bullfighters have bad days, and the best bullfighters rarely perform at plazas along the Pacific Coast.

The bullfights you are most likely to see in Puerto Vallarta are real bullfights with real bulls, but technically you are more likely to see a *novillada* (novice bullfight) with *novilleros* (novice bullfighters) fighting *novillos* (younger bulls, between three and four years old). *Novilleros* are professional bullfighters, but they are less experienced than *matadors de toros* (experienced bullfighters who have passed a ceremony called an *alternativa* that allows them to fight fully grown *toros* of at least four years).

Otherwise, the bullfights you are likely to see here are much the same as bullfights anywhere. The bullfighters enter the bullring in a formal procession, each followed by his assistants. A bullfighter will normally fight two bulls in one afternoon; in Vallarta there are typically two bullfighters and four bulls. Bullfight fans will appreciate how the bullfighter builds a series of passes with the bright magenta cape, then later with the smaller red cape. The bull is almost always killed at the end of the bullfight, and the bullfighter is expected to kill the animal quickly, though that doesn't always happen. There is always blood, and it isn't pretty.

Bullfighting was first imported to Mexico with the conquistadors in 1562; the first bullfight in Mexico was in honor of the return visit of Hernando Cortés. Though its popularity is declining, bullfighting is an inextricable part of Mexican culture, and the best Mexican bullfighters are highly respected in all bullfighting countries. So, for a break from the beaches and nightlife, you can't find something more dramatic and memorable than an afternoon at the bullring. You will not be disappointed by the pageantry and grace of the bullfighters or by the awesome power of the bulls – incredibly agile and dangerous animals that live a life as pampered as a thoroughbred horse until their day in the ring. It is something to experience and, the closer your seats, the more you will see. If you are a bit squeamish, however, it is best to get the cheaper seats in the mid-range *tendidos*: the more expensive *barrera* seats (front rows) are often a bit too close to the blood-letting for first timers.

Bullrings along the Pacific Coast (you'll also find them in Mazatlán and Acapulco) rarely sell out, so you can purchase a cheaper ticket and discreetly scoot closer if you want a better look. Tickets are sold for the shady *(sombra)* or sunny side *(sol)*. The shady side is more comfortable and closer to the action. You can usually get tickets at the plaza before the bullfight. Come early and enjoy the ambience; look around for the Patio de Caballos and sneak a peak at the snazzily dressed bullfighters before they enter the ring.

If you want your first bullfight to be a good one, you might want to consider attending in a different part of Mexico – some of the best rings are in Mexico City, Aguas Calientes, Queterero and Zacatecas.

arts – among a lot of other things. The owners started an animal rescue program in Vallarta.

Mundo de Azulejos (Map pp70-1; ☎ 222-26-75; Carranza 374) This place has to have the best selection of artistic tiles in Vallarta. They're not cheap, but they'll custom-make whatever you can think up.

Artículos Religiosos La Asunción (Map pp70-1; ☎ 222-31-86; Libertad 319) This is the place to come for all sorts of religious paraphernalia. Check out the calendars (US$1) – they make great souvenirs.

Hecho a Mano (Map pp70-1; ☎ 223-28-19; Zaragoza 160) Lots of furniture and home decor is on offer here, all made in Mexico and fabulous.

Tequila & Cigars

Casa de Tequila (Map pp70–1; ☎ 222-20-00; Morelos 589) This place pours high-quality tequila shots…for free. They also sell the stuff, so they don't appreciate moochers. It's a good place for information on the national drink, if you're curious.

    La Playa Vinos y Licores (Map pp70–1; ☎ 223-18-18) Here's a good place to buy the two bottles of tequila you're allowed to take back into the USA. They also have a branch at Olas Altas 246 and Gomez 138.

    Guantanamera Cigar Club (Map pp70–1; ☎ 223-35-07; Corona 186B) This is the place to have your Cubanos rolled.

Art Galleries

Puerto Vallarta has more than its fair share of contemporary fine art galleries. The following are some of the best known for their consistent quality and selection:

Galería Dante (☎ 222-24-77; www.galleriadante.com; Badillo 269) Paintings and contemporary sculpture.

Galería Mata Ortiz (Map pp70–1; ☎ 222-74-07; Cárdenas 268A) Very small but fine collection of pottery.

Galería de Ollas (Map pp70–1; ☎ 223-10-45; Morelos 101) Displays more beautiful pottery, much of it intricately painted. Bring your wallet.

Galería Omar Alonso (Map pp70–1; ☎ 222-55-87; Vicario 249) Mostly antique and contemporary photography.

Galería Pacífico (☎ 222-19-82; Aldama 174) Open since 1987, with an emphasis on local painters.

Galería Uno (☎ 222-09-08; Morelos 561) Mexican fine art in all mediums since 1971.

Galería Vallarta (☎ 222-01-90; Juárez 263) Paintings by Mexico's most collected painters.

GETTING THERE & AWAY
Air

Puerto Vallarta's **Gustavo Díaz Ordaz International Airport** (PVR; Map p67), on Hwy 200 about 10km north of the city, is served by several national and international airlines. Inside are many duty-free shops, exchange houses (including AmEx; good rates) and car-rental stalls (again, better rates than in town). There are also some very expensive bars, restaurants and souvenir shops; bring a small bottle of water to save yourself a couple of thirsty bucks.

Aeroméxico (☎ 224-27-77) Service to Los Angeles, San Diego, Guadalajara, La Paz, León, Mexico City, Morelia and Tijuana.

Alaska Airlines (☎ 221-13-50, in the US 800-426-0333) Direct service to Los Angeles, San Francisco and Seattle.

America West (☎ 221-13-33, in the US 800-263-2597) Direct service to Las Vegas, Los Angeles, Phoenix and San Diego.

American Airlines (☎ 221-17-99; in the US 800-433-7300) Direct service to Austin, Chicago, Dallas, Mexico City and St Louis.

Continental (☎ 221-10-25, in the US 800-231-0856) Direct service to Houston and Newark.

Frontier (☎ in the US 800-432-1359) Direct service to Denver and Kansas City.

Mexicana (☎ 224-89-00, in the US 800-531-7921) Direct service to Chicago, Guadalajara, Los Angeles and Mexico City.

Ted (☎ in the US 800-225-5833) United's budget carrier offers direct service to Denver and San Francisco.

Bus

Vallarta's long-distance bus station (Map p67) is just off Hwy 200, about 10km north of the city center and 2km north of the airport.

    Most intercity bus lines have offices south of the Río Cuale, where you can buy tickets without having to make a trip to the station. They include Elite, TNS and Estrella Blanca, on the corner of Badillo and Insurgentes (Map pp70–1); ETN, Primera Plus and Servicios Coordinados, at Cárdenas 268; and Transportes del Pacífico, at Insurgentes 282 (Map pp70–1).

    Daily departures from the main terminal include the following:

Barra de Navidad (US$17, 3½hr, 4 1st-class; US$13, 4hr, 5 2nd-class) Same buses as to Manzanillo.

Guadalajara (US$32-39, 5½hr, 36 1st-class)

Manzanillo (US$20, 5hr, 3 1st-class)

Mazatlán (US$27-29, 8hr, 7 1st-class) You can also take a bus to Tepic, where buses depart frequently for Mazatlán.

Mexico City (US$69-71, 14hr, 8 1st-class; US$95, 13hr, 1 deluxe) To Terminal Norte.

Rincón de Guayabitos (US$6, 1½hr) Same buses as to Tepic.

San Blas (US$10, 3½hr, 2nd-class 3pm) Or take a bus to Tepic for transfer.

San Patricio-Melaque (US$13, 3½hr, 4 1st-class; US$10, 4hr, 4 2nd-class) Same buses as to Manzanillo.

Sayulita (US$2, 1hr, 10 2nd-class)

Tepic (US$12, 3½hr, frequent 1st- and 2nd-class)

Car & Motorcycle

Starting at about US$60 per day, car rentals are pricey during high season, but deep discounts are offered during other times, particularly if you book online.

    Due to immediate competition, showing up in person at the airport car-rental counters can result in the best deals (watch out for those tricky downtown timeshares posing as rental-car companies). Negotiating is always a possibility.

Check with your credit card company back home to see if car insurance for a rental abroad is covered (to be covered, you must use that credit card to pay for the rental); sometimes the coverage is limited to rentals of less than two weeks. Paying cash is often cheaper, and you won't be forced to use the rental companies' self-favored rate of exchange (check the fine print on the contract). For more information about renting cars in Mexico, see p300.

The following car-rental agencies are at the airport:

Avis (☎ 221-16-57)
Budget (☎ 221-17-30)
Dollar (☎ 221-10-01)
Hertz (☎ 221-14-73)
National (☎ 221-12-26)

Mario's Moto Rent (Map p67; ☎ 229-81-42; Av Ascencio 998), opposite the Sheraton Buganvilias hotel, rents out trail bikes (US$15 per hour) and scooters (US$12 per hour).

GETTING AROUND
To/From the Airport

The cheapest way to get to/from the airport is on a local bus for US$0.40. 'Aeropuerto,' 'Juntas' and 'Ixtapa' buses from town all stop right at the airport entrance; 'Centro' and 'Olas Altas' buses go into town from beside the airport entrance. A taxi from the city center costs around US$6.

From the airport to town, fixed taxi stands inside the airport ask different prices depending on where you want to go: they charge approximately US$10/US$14/US$18 to Marina Vallarta/Centro/Zona Romántica (also called Old Town or Olas Altas). But go outside the airport (you may need to cross the blue and orange pedestrian bridge) and passing taxis charge around US$8/US$12/US$16 for the same destinations.

Bicycle

If you're after a two-wheeled buzz, **Bike Mex** (Map pp70-1; ☎ 223-16-80; Guerrero 361) and **Eco Ride** (Map pp70-1; ☎ 222-79-12; Miramar 382) rent mountain bikes for guided or self-guided tours starting at US$25 per day. See p75 for more information.

Boat & Water Taxi

In addition to taxis on land, Vallarta also has water taxis to beautiful beaches on the southern side of the bay that are accessible only by boat.

Water taxis departing from the pier at Playa de los Muertos head south around the bay, making stops at Playa Las Ánimas (25 minutes), Quimixto (30 minutes) and Yelapa (45 minutes); the round-trip fare is US$20 for any destination. Boats depart at 9:30am, 10:30am, 11am, noon, 4pm, 4:30pm and 5pm.

A water taxi also goes to Yelapa from the beach just south of Hotel Rosita, on the northern end of the *malecón*, departing at 11:30am Monday to Saturday (US$14 one way, 30 minutes).

If you buy a return ticket from any particular water taxi, you have to return with the same boat at the time the boat operator has set to return. If you buy just a one-way ticket, you can take any boat back with any boatman, though if you go to more isolated places you should probably buy a return ticket so someone knows to come back for you.

Cheaper water taxis *(pangas)* to the same places depart from Boca de Tomatlán (p106), south of town, which is easily reached by local bus.

Private yachts and *lanchas* can be hired from the south side of the Playa de los Muertos pier. Expect to pay anywhere between US$75 and US$150 per day. They'll take you to any secluded beach around the bay, and many have gear aboard for snorkeling and fishing. *Lanchas* can also be hired privately at Mismaloya and Boca de Tomatlán, but they are expensive.

Bus

Local buses that are marked 'Ixtapa' and 'Juntas' go to the bus station; 'Centro' and 'Olas Altas' buses run into town from beside the long-distance bus station parking lot. A taxi between the center and the bus station costs US$5 to US$8.

Local buses operate every five minutes from 5am to 11pm, on most routes and cost US$0.40. Plaza Lázaro Cárdenas at Playa Olas Altas is a major departure hub. Northbound local bus routes also stop in front of the Cine Bahía, on Insurgentes near the corner of Madero.

Northbound buses marked 'Hoteles,' 'Aeropuerto,' 'Ixtapa,' 'Pitillal' and 'Juntas' pass through the city heading north to the airport, the Zona Hotelera and Marina Vallarta; the 'Hoteles,' 'Pitillal' and 'Ixtapa' routes can take you to any of the large hotels north of the city.

Southbound 'Boca de Tomatlán' buses pass along the southern coastal highway through Mismaloya (US$0.50, 20 minutes) to Boca de Tomatlán (US$0.75, 30 minutes). They depart from Constitución near the corner of Badillo every 15 minutes from 6am to 11pm.

Taxi

Cab prices are regulated by zones; the cost for a ride is determined by how many zones you cross. A typical trip from downtown to the Zona Hotelera costs US$4 to US$7; fare to Mismaloya is about US$10. Always determine the price of the ride before you get in.

AROUND PUERTO VALLARTA

The appeal of Puerto Vallarta is not limited to its city limits; all around Bahía de Banderas are many beautiful beaches, some with small towns catering to visiting tourists. Many of these destinations are interesting enough to be worth a visit, and each can be seen in a day or less.

NORTH OF PUERTO VALLARTA

North of town, in the Zona Hotelera, are the sandy stretches of Camarones, Las Glorias, Los Tules, Las Palmas, Playa de Oro and, past the Marina, El Salado. Nuevo Vallarta, an expansive land of all-inclusive behemoth beach hotels, is just past here. And beyond that, up toward the roof of the bay, are the day-trip destinations of Bucerías, La Cruz de Huanacaxtle and Playa El Anclote (at Punta de Mita), with more beaches dotted between.

Remember that as you travel from Jalisco state to Nayarit state (the border is between Marina Vallarta and Nuevo Vallarta) you need to set your watch back an hour. Any business hours listed in the following towns reflect winter high-season hours; in summer, hours and days are often cut back, but hotel prices go down as well.

Bucerías

☎ 329 / pop 8800

From the freeway, Bucerías looks like another road-straddling town you'd just as soon zoom by on your way to somewhere else. But turn toward the sea and you'll find a restful, traditional town that warrants an unloading of baggage and a day or two of repose. More than a few visitors have found the place so much to their liking that they've stuck around and put down roots, resulting in a smattering of smart restaurants and a choice of quality lodging. The main draw, naturally, is the expansively long, beautiful and surfable beach, which fronts cobblestone and bougainvillea-lined streets. There are several *palapa* restaurants serving seafood cooked the local way, and outdoor touristy shopping stalls not far away. From December to March you can go on whale-watching trips. All this, along with a less-harried feel than Puerto Vallarta, makes for a worthy day trip – and there's a rewarding variety of places to stay if you decide to stretch your visit a bit longer.

The big local celebration, **Fiesta de la Virgen de la Paz**, is held each year in mid-January to honor the town's patron saint, Nuestra Señora de la Paz. Local boatmen deck their launches out with palm fronds, paper streamers, flowers and balloons in anticipation of a blessing from the priest.

Bucerías consists of just a few very long blocks paralleling the beach and Hwy 200. It's a four-stoplight town. The **post office** (cnr González & Héroes de Nacozari) faces the highway. Internet service is available at Sandrina's restaurant for US$2 per 30 minutes (or free, if you purchase breakfast or lunch). There's an ATM on the western edge of the highway near the corner of Guerrero.

ACTIVITIES

Coral Reef Surf Shop (☎ 298-02-61; surf-mexico.com /sites/coralreef; Héroes de Nacozari & Melgar; 9am-7pm Mon-Sat) is a full-service shop that rents longboards (US$19 per day) and boogie boards (US$8 per day). Long- and short-boards are for sale; after you've broken them in you can bring them back for repairs. Surf lessons and guides/boats for both local and long-distance trips are also offered, as are whale-watching tours in season.

BUCERÍAS

EATING 🍴
Aduato's Beach Club........................**10** A2
Claudio's Meson Bay.......................**11** A2
Dugarel Plays.................................**12** A2
Karen's Place.................................**13** C3
La Cocina De Jorge.........................**14** D3
Mark's Bar & Grill............................**15** C3
Roga's Restaurant & Bar..................**16** B3
Roots Vegetarian Restaurant
   & Juice Bar.................................**17** C2
Sandrina's....................................**18** C3

DRINKING 🍷
Gecko Pub.....................................**19** C2

PACIFIC
OCEAN

INFORMATION
ATM...**1** B1
Post Office.......................................**2** C2

SLEEPING 🛏
Bungalows Unelma............................**3** D3
Bungalows Vista de Oro......................**4** B1
Casa Tranquila................................**5** C2
Hotel Palmeras...............................**6** C3
Olas Altas Hotel..............................**7** B2
Posada Don Arthur...........................**8** B2
Suites Costa Dorada.........................**9** C3

SLEEPING

Bucerías has only a few truly budget options, and only a few more places priced
in the midrange. However, if your budget
allows a night's sleep in the US$100 range,
you can choose from a diverse selection of
quality digs.

Prices quoted are for high season; you'll
pay considerably less in the heat of the
summer. Most hoteliers are amenable to
bargaining, particularly if you plan to stick
around for more than a few days.

For longer-term villa rentals, try websites such as www.sunworx.com or www.las
-palmas-travel.com.

Budget

Bungalows Vista de Oro (☎ 298-03-90; cnr Flores
Magnón & Bravo; d/q US$20/28; 🏊) Terraced up a
hillside, this friendly, funky-flavored, and
pink-themed place is a block east of the
highway on the inland side of town (look
for the red pagoda and cross the highway).
The big, fan-cooled bungalows are good
but basic and work well for large, unfussy
groups. There's also a two-story pool slide.

Olas Altas Hotel (☎ 298-04-07; cnr Héroes de Nacozari & Cuauhtémoc; s US$25-28, d US$35-38; 🏊) This
bright-green hotel on the main drag has
good, clean, modern and large rooms. The
more expensive rooms in each category include air-con and TV.

Bucerías Trailer Park (☎ 298-02-65; PO Box 148,
Bucerías, Nayarit 63732; sites day/month US$25/500; 🏊)
Elizabeth Taylor once counted this property
among her collection of vacation homes.
The 48 pleasant sites, about 1km from the
town center, have full hookups and good
drinking water. There's a boat ramp nearby
and a pleasant restaurant in the living room
of the lovely house.

Midrange

Casa Tranquila (☎ 298-17-67; www.casatranquila
-bucerias.com; Morelos 7A; d US$45-55; 🏊 🐶) *Tran-
quila* is the operative word at this breezy,
casual hideaway run by Patricia Mendez and
Joann Quickstad, an affable iced-tea-loving
couple who put down roots in Bucerías
in 2001 and decided to stick around. The
five one-bedroom units are cozy and individually decorated. Each comes with a

well-equipped kitchen and feels like home right away. On site is a bookstore and coffee shop, and Joann offers therapeutic massage (US$45 per hour). The proprietors proudly put forth that they 'make all kinds of deals.'

Hotel Palmeras (☎ 298-12-88; www.hotelpalmeras .com; Cárdenas 35; r US$36-64; 🆒 ✖ 🔛 🖳) In proximity to some of the town's best restaurants, this well-run hotel provides nine smoke-free one- and two-bedroom kitchenette apartments, all well appointed and modern. The hotel has wireless Internet, a leafy patio and an extra-large pool. Discounts are offered for longer stays.

Posada Don Arthur (☎ 298-09-95; texmexnay@ hotmail.com; Av del Pacífico 6; d/q US$35/48; ✖) The manager initially seems a tad gruff, but once you get to know him you'll find that he's merely discriminating. The location is central and the six rooms are large and OK for this budget, with kitchens, air-con and cable TV. At last visit, work was moving forward on a café. It's good for longer stays, as there's a fair-sized apartment with kitchen suitable for a cozy couple or four good friends (US$750 per month).

Top End

Bungalows Unelma (☎ 298-00-80; unelma@prodigy .net.mx; Cárdenas 51; d US$105; ✖) This unique, tropical hideaway offers a little slice of paradise with its two beachside bungalows surrounded by lush, manicured gardens. Each has an outdoor living room and kitchenette. A manicured lawn leads to the beautiful beach with a private sunbathing area and comfortable deck chairs. The bungalows are very private and secured day and night from both the street and the beach. Kitchens are fully stocked and one unit comes with air-con. Boogie boards, sea kayaks and hammocks are part of the deal.

Suites Costa Dorada (☎ 298-21-00, in Guadalajara for reservations 333-825-86-16; www.scostadorada.com; ste US$128-307; 🆒 ✖) This six-story hotel looks big in this small town. The huge suites with kitchens and ocean-view terraces comfortably contain the whole family.

Bungalows Arroyo (☎ 298-02-88; bungalows arroyo@hotmail.com; Cárdenas 500; bungalows US$100-120; 🅿 ✖ ✖ 🖳 🖳) This popular home-away-from-home five blocks east of the Hotel Palmeras offers 15 two-bedroom apartment-style units half a block from the beach. The comfortable units, arranged around a palm-shaded swimming pool, sport king-sized beds, balcony, kitchen and living and dining areas. They fill up quick in the winter, so book early.

At the northern end of town is a quiet subdivision called Playas de Huanacaxtle; here you'll find a series of cul-de-sacs lined with vacation homes and a few upscale accommodations.

Condo-Hotel Vista Vallarta (☎ 298-03-61; vista vallarta@prodigy.net Av de los Picos s/n, Playas de Huanacaxtle; ste US$98; ✖ 🖳) This three-story stucco hotel enjoys a healthy rate of return clientele for its bright, well-appointed apartments arranged around a shady beachside pool. The spacious two-bedroom suites include dining rooms, kitchenettes and ocean-view balconies. The place empties out in the summer, when the proprietors are apt to make a deal on the price.

Bungalows Princess (☎ 298-01-00; bungalows princess@prodigy.net.mx; Retorno Destiladeras, Playas de Huanacaxtle; bungalow US$90-130; ✖ 🖳) The two-story beachfront bungalows on offer here have kitchens and provide plenty of space and privacy suited to families and small groups. Also on offer are more economical suites. All units have phones and satellite TV.

Bungalows Los Picos (☎ 298-04-70; www.lospicos .com.mx; Av Los Picos & Retorno Pontoques, Playas de Huanacaxtle; 2-/3-bedroom bungalow US$100/120, ste/studio US$80/35; 🅿 ✖ 🖳) This beachfront complex delivers the goods with excellent large bungalows ideal for groups of four to eight. The largest of the bunch enjoy sweeping ocean views and have pleasant eating and living areas. All units have cable TV, but only some have air-con. Two pools and ample garden areas make this an ideal place to hole up for a while and practice the art of relaxation.

EATING & DRINKING

Many of Bucerías eateries are operated by expats, and the competition makes for some very high-quality Western food.

Karen's Place (☎ 298-14-99; mains US$9-18, breakfast US$4-5; 🕙 9am-9pm Tue-Sat, 9am-3pm Sun) Near Juárez at the beach, Karen's spins up thirst-quenching cocktails to go along with their sushi, mahimahi and coconut shrimp. Salads and sandwiches are also fixed up. Western-style breakfasts start the day, live music is staged on Tuesday and Thursday nights in season, and a popular champagne

Sunday brunch ends the week. Enjoy the view from the terraced dining area.

Marks Bar & Grill (☎ 298-03-03; Cárdenas 56; mains US$9-20; ☺ noon-10:30pm) Foodhounds are known to make a special trip to Bucerías just to eat here, and it's not hard to see why. It's the most elegant restaurant in town, with a welcoming and breezy dining room where you can enjoy a nice cocktail before tucking into that Black Angus New York steak, ricotta ravioli with goat's cheese or lentil-crusted flounder over mashed potatoes. The bar is haunted by expats comparing notes or watching the game.

Roots Vegetarian Restaurant & Juice Bar (☎ 298-25-04; Cárdenas 40; mains US$4-8; ☺ noon-midnight) Vegetarians take refuge in this recently opened eatery. The fresh and vibrant cuisine is best washed down by the fresh-squeezed fruit juices and exotic smoothies.

Roga's Restaurant & Bar (☎ 298-15-65; Bravo s/n; mains US$10-17; ☺ 2-10pm Mon-Sat) This swanky spot perched on a cliff overlooking the town is a tequila lover's dream. They keep a cellar stocked with the stuff, and offer good deals on the Corralejo brand and a rare agave distillate called *raicilla* (which may induce a slightly psychedelic state). The menu is grounded in seafood dishes like tequila shrimp and barbecued oyster fajitas. To get there you can slog up Calderón or take the elevator from the highway.

Sandrina's (☎ 298-02-73; Cárdenas 33; mains US$4-11; ☺ 10am-10pm Wed-Mon) Has a great backyard patio where you can savor Mediterranean chicken, Greek or Caesar salads, hummus, lasagne and souvlaki. They also bake some great stuff: try the Kahlua flan or chocolate cream-cheese brownies. This place is all-gringo – there's even Internet service, free for customers.

Aduato's Beach Club (☎ 298-04-06; Av del Pacífico s/n; ☺ noon-10pm) Your host Aduato Ramos, a garrulous and welcoming soul, invariably greets newcomers as if they were family. He'll be happy to show you old newspaper clippings, revealing him to have once been director John Huston's house boy. Give him a wink and ask for a shot of his special *raicilla*. The menu, like so many others round here, is filled with seafood dishes such as octopus burritos and red snapper drenched in garlic butter.

Dugarel Plays (☎ 298-17-57; Av del Pacífico s/n; mains US$8-20; ☺ 10am-10pm) Overlooking the beach, this old-school place sits on a rickety-looking wooden terrace with great sea views. You'd do well to go for the giant prawns, lobster or red snapper. The bartender is kept busy whipping up margaritas; two-for-one drink specials are doled out between 4pm and 6pm.

Claudio's Meson Bay (☎ 298-16-34; Av del Pacífico; mains US$5-18; ☺ 11am-11pm) All-you-can-eat salad bars are few and far between, but at this beachside *palapa* they also set out an endless supply of shrimp and fish on Monday, barbecue on Wednesday and Mexican favorites and margaritas on Friday night.

La Cocina de Jorge (☎ 298-06-13; Abasolo 5; breakfast US$2.50-4.50; ☺ 9am-noon Tue-Sun) This is the place for a filling and economical Mexican breakfast. The menu has the usual suspects and one puzzling but delicious standout: *juevos divorciados*, drenched in red and green salsa.

Pie in the Sky (☎ 298-08-38; Héroes de Nacozari 202; ☺ 8am-10pm) On the highway at the first stoplight coming into town from Puerto Vallarta. The *besos* (brownies, US$3), chocolate mousse and decadent cakes (slice/whole US$3/24) are so good that you'll want to spend a small fortune on goodies to go. Breakfast and gourmet coffees are also served.

Gecko Pub (☎ 298-18-61; Morelos; ☺ 1pm-2am) This small bar near Cárdenas nurses some barstools and a few tables. There's darts, pool and a jukebox. Drinks are two-for-one on some nights, and ladies drink free on Wednesday and Thursday nights.

GETTING THERE & AWAY

There are buses every 15 minutes from Puerto Vallarta, leaving from across from the Sheraton Buganvilias hotel in the Zona Hotelera. The trip takes 30 minutes and costs US$2; in Bucerías, get off at the second stoplight and walk inland to the plaza (unless you're only going to Bucerías for brownies at Pie in the Sky; in this case, get off at the first stoplight).

La Cruz de Huanacaxtle
☎ 329 / pop 2300

Travelers are just starting to catch on to the traditional little Mexican fishing town of La Cruz de Huanacaxtle. Fidgety sorts may find the pace of life here underwhelming, but those who enjoy simple pleasures might fall under its spell. Get to know the locals or hear the interesting stories of the expats who've made this home. Hold court in the pretty plaza, conjugating verbs beneath a shady tree, or watch a fisherman skillfully throwing his net out from the shore.

Local lore puts forth that the town earned its name when the body of an indigenous woman was buried at the base of a giant *huanacaxtle* tree. In tribute a large cross, 2m by 1m, was carved into the trunk of the tree.

The town puts on its best face during its lively annual fiesta in early May, when the church bells toll for patron saint Santa Cruz, the streets fill with food stands and games, and there's a big fireworks show over the bay.

La Cruz supports a growing selection of cosmopolitan restaurants and a pleasant yacht harbor area where many gringos anchor for free. Fishermen sell their catch at the dockside every morning, and there's a village market on Wednesday from 9am to 1pm. Traffic is rare but tourism is starting to pick up – enjoy it while you can.

ACTIVITIES

Acción Tropical (☎ 329-295-50-87; www.acciontropical .com; Langosta 3; ☼ 9am-2pm & 4-8pm) is a friendly operation that rents surfboards (US$25 per day) and kayaks (US$13 per hour); offers surfing lessons (two hours, US$75) and surfing trips (from US$75); and also offers snorkeling excursions to Las Islas Marietas (up to eight people US$117). Whale-watching, boating and fishing trips are also available. Another branch is at Punta de Mita.

Sportfishing, whale-watching and boat trips are also offered by seasoned professional **Captain Fidel Ramirez** (☎ 295-50-55; columbia fishing@hotmail.com; Coral 18; per hr US$30).

SLEEPING

La Cruz's accommodation scene is dominated by long-term villa rentals, with only a few traditional hotels.

La Cruz Inn (☎ 295-5849, in the US 707-961-0636; www.lacruzinn.com; r/apt US$100/125; ☼ ☼ ☼) A charming and exceedingly peaceful accommodation situated next to the church just off the plaza. On offer are four tastefully furnished apartments with open-air kitchens and sitting areas. There's an economical room for rent and an attractive small pool and leafy patio area. Kayaks and bicycles are also available.

Bungalows Sukasa (☎ 214-47-04; Coral 25; s/d/tr US$25/36/56; ☼) This small hotel in the heart of town offers eight well-priced and decent rooms with kitchens. There's a small pool in the grassy courtyard.

Villa Bella Bed & Breakfast Inn (☎ 295-51-61, in the US 877-513₋1662; www.villabella-lacruz.com; r US$80, ste US$140-228; ☼ ☼) Perched on top of a hill with a sweeping view of Bahía de Banderas and the Sierra Madres, this upscale retreat offers somewhat over-decorated rooms that are nonetheless bright and comfortable. Some find the panoramic lap pool and sumptuous breakfasts seductive. Spanish classes (US$25/ US$120 per hour/week) and airport transportation are offered by arrangement.

EATING & DRINKING

Like its neighbor Bucerías, La Cruz supports several stylish expat-run restaurants in addition to typical Mexican eateries. On Saturday and Sunday nights near the plaza, family-run taco stands are set up serving delicious corn tortillas and all the fixings, and the whole town turns out to mingle.

Café Galería Arte Huichol (☎ 295-50-71; www .hikuri.com; Coral 66; breakfast US$3-5; ☼ 8am-5pm Mon-Sat) Situated in a very peaceful courtyard with a gurgling fountain and shady trees, this a great, easygoing hangout – and more than just a café. Wayland and Aruna are Brits with a one-of-a-kind story of designing and building their own boat (with money made by selling tacos on the streets of London), having a baby, then sailing around Central America for 10 years before finally settling in at La Cruz de Huanacaxtle. Here they established a T-shirt printing shop, carpentry workshop, Huichol crafts-center store and café. Wayland also started a project of building and distributing spinning wheels for the Huichol locals to weave more efficiently. You can see Huichol sandals being made, and a sale percentage of the Huichol-designed T-shirts sold are donated to Huichol projects in Mexico. If that isn't enough to make you feel all fuzzy inside, try the delicious breakfasts (waffles, pastries and the like), salads, sandwiches, iced lattes or lemonades.

Philo's (☎ 295-50-68; Delfín 15; mains US$4-12; ☼ 10am-1am Tue-Sun; ☼) Philo's is a little bit of everything – restaurant, bar, music studio and cultural center. Here's the line-up: Monday is Monday night football, Tuesday is jam-session night, Wednesday there's free pool, Thursday is open mike, on Friday and Saturday live music rocks, and on

Sunday there's more football. Burgers and grilled sandwiches run less than US$6, and yoga, foreign-language and guitar classes are also offered.

Caledonia (☎ 329-295-50-21; Marlin 8; mains US$7-17; ☺ 5-11pm) This elegant Scottish-run restaurant has plenty of international wines and some beautiful outdoor seating. Savor seafood cannelloni, chicken cacciatore or the half-rack of pork ribs (all around US$10). It offers pizza and bar drinks, too.

Black Forest (☎ 295-52-03; Marlin 16; mains US$6-12; ☺ 5-10pm Sun-Fri) This romantic, cosmopolitan restaurant has become well known throughout the Vallarta area for Chef Winfried Küffner's delicious schnitzel, fried veal sausage and Hungarian goulash, not to mention his long list of mouthwatering desserts. There's live music on Friday nights.

Restaurante La Glorieta de Enrique (☎ 278-32-92; Coral 26; breakfast US$3; ☺ 8am-7pm) A simple *palapa* restaurant on the roundabout, this local haunt is a fine place to while away a long morning over coffee and a paperback.

Brittania Bar (Coral 68; ☺ 6pm-midnight Tue-Sun) With the look of a wannabe medieval castle, this watering hole and social hall is the only place in town to draw a cool Guinness.

GETTING THERE & AWAY

It's easy to reach La Cruz de Huanacaxtle: simply hop on a north-pointing Punta de Mita bus anywhere along Puerto Vallarta's Zona Hotelera (US$2, every 15 minutes).

Punta de Mita, Playa El Anclote & Around

☎ 329 / pop 500

Almost at the very northern tip of Bahía de Banderas is the Punta de Mita peninsula. Here lie some creamy strands of beaches, including Playa El Anclote, which is popular with surfers and boogie boarders. Ubiquitous seafood *palapa* restaurants on the beach offer great views of the bay and a distant Puerto Vallarta. Not a bad deal for those who also come to enjoy the beach, go on boat trips or try their balance in the surf.

Playa El Anclote is in the village of Nuevo Corral del Risco. To get there, head downhill from the main road; at the T-junction at the bottom is the beachside road Av Anclote, where most of the local businesses operate. Occupying higher ground just to the east is its sister village Emiliano Zapata,

where many of the region's accommodations are to be had.

You can log on to the Internet at Riki's Café in Nuevo Corral del Risco.

ACTIVITIES

Playa El Anclote is justifiably famous for surfing. **Acción Tropical** (☎ 291-66-33; Anclote; Nuevo Corral del Risco), where local surfing honcho Eduardo del Valle Ochoa provides his considerable expertise from a shady spot across from the *palapa* restaurants on the beach road. Here you can book surfing lessons (two hours, US$75) and boat trips in the bay, including snorkeling, sportfishing (three hours, US$110) and whale-watching in season. You can also rents kayaks and surfboards.

Surfing is also the primary concern of **Tranquilo Surf Adventures** (☎ 291-64-75; www .tranquilosurf.com; Pez Vela 130, Nuevo Corral del Risco), a small company promoting low-impact surfing. From November through April they operate a surf school catering to individuals and small groups in pursuit of 'a liquid foundation to surfing.' During the summer months the business shifts to surfing safari adventures to secluded corners of southern Mexico, led by Josué Villegas, a home-grown surf legend.

Formerly a fishing cooperative, **Caseta Cooperativa Corral de Riscos Servicios Turisticos** (☎ 291-62-98; Anclote 17; ☺ 9am-4pm Mon-Sat) offers sightseeing and snorkeling tours to Las Islas Marietas, an hour offshore; fishing trips ($40 per hour); whale-watching (December to March); and surf instruction.

SLEEPING & EATING

Huerta de la Paz (☎ 291-63-37; www.huertalapaz .com; Carretera Higuera Blanca, Km 4; cabana US$55-125) This self-styled 'ethnobotanical permaculture ranch' strongly appeals to those who enjoy an environment that promotes the values of meditation and mindfulness. Sitting pretty in its jungly garden setting, it offers four fan-cooled thatch-roofed units with tasteful decor and organic vegetarian meals (breakfast is included). Yoga classes and massage are also offered. To get there, take the turnoff for Higuera Blanca from the main road and follow the signs; it's before the turnoff for Playa Punta de Mita.

Hotel Coco's (☎ 291-63-75; cocosmita@yahoo.com; Av de las Pangas s/n, Nuevo Corral del Risco; d US$20)

Loved by surfers for its economical rates and air of insouciance, this cheerful accommodation with eight clean rooms is Playa El Anclote's best bargain. It's on the main road into town.

Meson de Mita Bungalows (☎ 291-63-63; meson demita@yahoo.com; Anclote 200; r US$50-80; 🖳 🖳) With a big *palapa* restaurant and a privileged location right on Playa El Anclote, this hotel was under construction at last visit but was already revealing its promise. The rooms are clean and have daybeds and satellite TV. The largest sleeps six.

Punta Mita Hotel (☎ 291-62-69; Zapata 5, Emiliano Zapata; d with/without kitchen US$35/45; 🖳) It's simple and clean, with nondescript ocean views and a small pool. Some rooms have kitchenettes. You'll find it on the dusty road fronting the beach, south of the T-junction.

Casa Contenta (☎ 294-64-14; www.puntamita -beach.com; Montaño 40, Emiliano Zapata; r US$55) At the home of friendly former Californian Susan Ingle, this is a single studio suite with an expansive deck and tremendous views of the bay. Painted in bright colors and filled with thoughtful touches, it's exuberantly pleasant, with a queen-sized bed, large bathroom and open-air kitchen.

Casa Las Palmas (☎ 291-63-04; elas_palmas72@ hotmail.com; Francisco Madero s/n, Emiliano Zapata; 1-bedroom apt US$60-70, 2-bedroom apt US$90; 🖳 🖳 🖳) Immaculate and welcoming, this well-run operation in Emiliano Zapata offers five large brick and stucco apartments in a garden setting. Guests enjoy access to a large swimming pool, Jacuzzi, barbecue grill,

kayaks, snorkeling gear and surfcasting poles. With wireless Internet, satellite TV, DVD players, large book-lending library and even a telescope for whale-watching, you just may decide to extend your vacation.

Riki's Café (☎ 291-62-72; Av Las Pangas s/n, Nuevo Corral del Risco; mains US$4-6; 🕙 8:30am-6pm Tue-Sun) A small café and meeting place, this friendly establishment serves simple food and offers Internet access. This is all just a front, however, for German transplant Riki's true passion: therapeutic massage (60/90 minutes US$55/US$85).

El Dorado (☎ 291-62-96; Anclote s/n, Nuevo Corral del Risco; 🕙 11am-sunset) Overlooking Playa El Anclote, this is the oldest restaurant in town, meaning that it enjoys first pick from the fishermen's daily catch.

GETTING THERE & AWAY
To get to Playa El Anclote, simply take any Punta de Mita bus roaming north on the Zona Hotelera (US$2, every 15 minutes) and get off at Nuevo Corral del Risco, the town above Playa El Anclote.

SOUTH OF PUERTO VALLARTA
South of town, off scenic Hwy 200, are the beaches of Conchas Chinas, Estacas, Los Venados, Punta Negra, Garza Blanca and Gemelas. Above this lovely shoreline (and blessed with stunning sea views) perch upscale hotels, timeshare condos, and villas owned by the very rich and very lucky.

Near these beaches and also located further south are the hamlets of **El Nogalito**,

---

DETOUR: GUADALAJARA

There's nothing wrong, of course, with spending your entire vacation with your toes buried in the sand, but if you want to get a better sense of what makes Mexico tick then a visit to exciting and gracious Guadalajara might be in order. The home of mariachi music, tequila, *charreadas* (rodeos) and the Mexican hat dance, a couple of days in Mexico's second-largest city provides an engrossing and entertaining education. Despite its size, Guadalajara is not an overwhelming city. Its pedestrian lanes, walkable streets and handy public-transport system make getting around easy. Short-term visitors spend most of their time basking in the ambience of the Centro Histórico, with its many leafy plazas, 400-year-old cathedral and stunning murals by José Clemente Orozco. Equally absorbing are the nearby towns of Zapopan for its 18th-century basilica and thriving nightlife scene; Tlaquepaque for its peerless shopping opportunities; and Tonalá for its busy street market.

Guadalajara is 374km from Puerto Vallarta (six hours by car or bus). If driving, head north from town on Hwy 200 to its end at Chapatilla, then south on Hwy 15. Frequent 1st-class buses leave throughout the day from the long-distance bus terminal (US$29 to US$32). Direct air service from Puerto Vallarta to Guadalajara is provided by Mexicana and Aeroméxico.

Playa Mismaloya, Boca de Tomatlán, Las Ánimas, Quimixto and Yelapa – these last three are reachable only by boat. There are also quite a few upscale restaurants, both near the highway and further inland, which for some folks are a worthy destination in themselves.

El Nogalito

This small inland riverside community, about 5km south of Puerto Vallarta and 1km inland, offers a lush tropical setting for repose and good opportunities for exploration. Hang out here, enjoy the beautiful river and surrounding jungle, and take a one-hour hike up the Río El Nogalito to some gorgeous, unnamed and rarely visited cascades. Despite its proximity to Hwy 200, tourism has not taken a serious foothold, so don't expect too many services.

Contacto Natural Health Spa and Resort (☎ 221-54-19; www.contactonatural.com; Naranjo 123; all-inclusive US$100-140; 🏊) is a restful retreat for the body and senses. Here you can truly relax in quiet, wooded surroundings and be rejuvenated by a long menu of body therapies and massage. The all-inclusive rate includes vegetarian meals and four therapies per day. The 12 rooms are rustic but comfortable. The resident duo of a great dane and a chihuahua will keep you company as you walk along the beautiful Arroyo Nogalito.

For a good, atmospheric meal, spend an afternoon luxuriating at the jungle ranch **El Nogalito** (☎ 221-52-25; mains US$8-20; 🕐 noon-5:30pm). The property is awash in the sound of the river burbling by and surrounded by abundant vegetation, giving joy to bird watchers. The menu offers a good selection of international dishes in addition to several local delicacies, including coal-grilled shrimp and snapper *zarandeado*, cooked whole with spices and vegetables.

Mismaloya

The small but attractive and busy cove beach of Mismaloya, about 12km south of Puerto Vallarta, was the location for the 1963 Elizabeth Taylor/Richard Burton flick *The Night of the Iguana*. It's now dominated by the 303-room La Jolla de Mismaloya hotel (opposite), and the buildings used in the film (look toward the south side of the cove) live on as seafood restaurants. There are also plenty of tourist shopping stalls and

people enjoying many water activities – not quite the scene for those seeking enlightenment, at least in the traditional vein. To reach Mismaloya Beach take the coastal bus (see p96) and get dropped off right after the La Jolla de Mismaloya.

From Mismaloya you can head inland along a riverside dirt road to a couple of rustic yet upscale restaurants notable for their lush outdoor locations and for being able to function without electricity or telephone. Horses can be hired at Mismaloya for the ride up. Take insect repellent.

SIGHTS

Rising from the sea, offshore to the north beyond the cove, are the intriguing rocky islands known as **Los Arcos** (p73), a protected marine park and ecological preserve. It's one of the best snorkeling spots in the Puerto Vallarta area.

Mamá Lucia (☎ 296-51-89; 5 de Mayo s/n; 🕐 10am-5pm) If you've ever wondered why the best tequila simply must be '100% pure agave,' you'll see, smell and taste the reason at this boutique distillery and demonstration farm. Drop by and get up close and personal with some lovely blue-agave specimens planted in neat rows. A guide explains how, after a long life of repose lasting eight to 10 years, the agave plant has its heart (piña) carved out by harvesters called *jimadors*. Resembling a wooden pineapple, it's then halved or quartered and roasted in an adobe oven for 24 to 36 hours. Next comes the satisfying moment everyone's been waiting for: the piña is crushed to release the sweet (and so hard to come by) agave nectar. You'll want to spread it on toast. But no, instead it's distilled twice in a large round kettle called a pot still for a total of about six hours, and then aged in sweet old bourbon barrels. The demonstration is free, but of course the good people at Mamá Lucia would love it if you'd take some of their delicious product home with you. Choose a delicate *añejo* or perhaps an almond-flavored agave liqueur.

Mister Tequila (Map p67; ☎ 228-05-34; 5 de Mayo s/n; 🕐 9am-5pm Mon-Sat, 9am-2:30pm Sun) Next door to Mamá Lucia is this veritable tequila superstore, with an incredible selection of boutique tequilas from all corners of Jalisco and Nayarit. Be careful, the free tastings can quickly get out of hand.

ACTIVITIES

Mismaloya Divers (Map p67; ☎ 228-00-20) On the dirt road leading to the beach you'll find this tourism provider offering three- to four-hour tours to Los Arcos, Las Animas, and Quimixto (up to 10 people US$150), and in-season whale-watching tours (US$35 per hour). True to their name they also offer diving trips (one-/two-tank dive US$65/US$85) and rent snorkeling gear (US$15 per day).

Rancho Manolo (Map p67; ☎ 228-00-18; horseback rides US$15-20) Located beneath the Mismaloya bridge, on the opposite side from the resort, this cheerful operation keeps 25 horses and ponies fat and happy. Their two most popular tours are jaunts through an exuberant jungle landscape to Chino's Paradise restaurant (1½ hours, US$15) and to another remote jungle restaurant, El Edén (three hours, US$20). Double saddles are available for kids.

From Playa Mismaloya, launches can be hired for snorkeling tours or passage to the nearby islands. At last visit, the going rate was US$35 per hour, or US$150 for a full day for up to eight persons.

SLEEPING

Casa Iguana Hotel (Map p67; ☎ 228-01-86; www.casa iguanahotel.com; Av 5 de Mayo 455, Mismaloya; ste US$85-250; P ⊠ ⬜ ⬜) Providing a welcome alternative to the nearby mega-resort, this excellent mid-sized hotel on land carved from the jungles of Mismaloya offers eminently pleasant and well-appointed suites, perfect for families and those who eschew ostentatious hullabaloo. The place is well run, with a feeling of style and substance throughout. If you're traveling with kids, the two-bedroom suites (and humongous TVs in the living room) offer the possibility for mom and dad to get some privacy behind closed doors. Each of the 53 units is painted in warm hues of orange and yellow, with good-natured art and rattan furniture. Well-equipped kitchens and large dining tables make home-cooked meals a pleasure. Another option for meals is the pleasant open-air restaurant, La Cocina. The compact grounds are lushly gardened with a fish pond and large elevated hot tub. Extras include well-priced massage, a laundry facility and Internet café.

Mar Sereno (Map p67; ☎ 228-08-79; www.mar sereno.com; Hwy 200, Km 15; r US$50, ste US$70-80;

P ⊠ ⬜ ⬜) Offering quite a bargain, this 11-story hotel is often underbooked and therefore quite peaceful. You might even get a whole floor to yourself! The rooms and overall appearance are quite appealing, and the panoramic views from the lobby restaurant undeniably seductive. There's no beach to speak of, but there is a saltwater bathing area carved out of the rocks below. You'll find it between Mismaloya and Boca de Tomatlán.

La Jolla de Mismaloya (Map p67; ☎ 226-06-60; www.lajollademismaloya.com; Hwy 200, Km 11.5; ste US$240-1360; P ⊠ ⊠ ⬜ ⬜) Carved out of the jungle in Mismaloya, this big resort tries mightily to be sumptuously luxuriant while maintaining its eco-chic credentials at the same time. The suites feature marble floors and over-the-top floral-print bedspreads, with balconies looking out over the expansive courtyard, four impressive pools and scores of coconut palms. Activities include snorkeling, scuba, mountain biking and horseback riding excursions, and there's also a full-service spa.

EATING

Chino's Paraíso (Map p67; mains US$11-21; ☒ 10am-6pm) Located where relaxing tiers of *palapa*-covered tables decorate rocky ledges on both sides of a river (cross a footbridge), this place is about 2.8km south of Mismaloya. There's a swimming hole too – bring your swimsuit and towel. Seafood and meats are on the menu, but try to avoid being here between 1pm and 3pm, when hungry tour groups arrive for lunch. Look for iguanas – they'll be checking you out.

El Edén (Map p67; mains US$10-18; ☒ 11am-5pm) This place is worth it if you've hired a horse or taxi, or have wheels; only serious hikers will enjoy the long and dusty walk up (5.5km further upriver from Chino's, and about 7km total from Mismaloya and the highway). The trip rewards you with another pleasant restaurant overlooking the same river. It's still airy but more closed in than Chino's. There are hikes and waterfalls in the area. Also, note the helicopter skeleton lying near the stairs; it was used in Arnold's flick *Predator*.

Back on the highway, going south toward Boca de Tomatlán, is yet another noteworthy restaurant, at least for those with fat wallets.

Le Kliff (Map p67; ☎ 224-09-75; Carretera 200, Km 17.5; mains US$10-28; ☯ noon-11pm) Le Kliff brags about being the best whale-watching spot in Vallarta…and that may be right. Its dramatic cliff-hanging location south of town is matched by a super seafood menu – try the tequila jumbo shrimp (US$28) or go all the way with the seafood carousel, a lobster-shrimp-fish combination (US$86 for two).

GETTING THERE & AWAY
Grab a cab, drive or hop on a 'Mismaloya' or 'Boca' bus (US$1.50); they leave Puerto Vallarta from the corner of Constitución and Badillo.

Boca de Tomatlán
About 4km past Mismaloya, Boca de Tomatlán is a peaceful, less commercialized seaside village in a small cove where the Río de Tomatlán meets the sea – a jungly place with quiet water, a nice beach and several small restaurants.

On the beach, **Restaurant Mi Ranchito** (☎ 228-07-07; mains US$4-16; ☯ 8am-6pm) provides a pleasant spot to eat while you wait for your boat. They sell the much-loved local specialty *pescado zarandeado* (a charcoal-broiled fish stuffed with onion, tomatoes, peppers and spices) by the kilogram for US$16.

There are no hotels in the village, but if you wish to loiter you may as well do it in style at **Casa Tango** (☎ 224-73-98; www.tangorentals .com; house US$120/550), an attractive two-bedroom bayfront house surrounded by dense jungle and sleeping four. It's owned by a friendly Argentine and his Scottish partner, who also offer a good selection of other vacation rentals in the area and orchestrate personalized tours.

AUTHOR'S CHOICE

Majahuitas (☎ 800-508-7923; www.mexico boutiquehotels.com/majahuitas; Playa Majahuitas; casita US$375) Peaceful, primitive and elegantly luxurious, this electricity-free, phoneless getaway is about as far from 'regular' life as you can get. There are only eight, open-air casitas on this secluded white-sand beach, making it extremely romantic. Playa Majahuitas is only reachable by boat from Boca de Tomatlán, so you'll need to make reservations.

The highway swings inland from Boca, and you can follow it 5km to the pricey restaurant **Chico's Paradise** (Map p67; ☎ 223-60-55; Hwy 200, Km 20; mains US$9-24; ☯ 10am-6pm), which perches above the Río de Tomatlán. Dining areas under rustic *palapas* look down to idyllic swimming holes and small waterfalls, and you can sunbathe on large boulders while enjoying the lush jungle backdrop. The menu, predictably, speaks of seafood and Mexican dishes.

GETTING THERE & AWAY
Take a bus marked 'Boca' (US$1.50) from the corner of Constitución and Badillo in Puerto Vallarta.

Pangas carrying up to eight passengers depart from the beach here to Las Ánimas, Quimixto and Yelapa.

Las Ánimas, Quimixto & Yelapa
A stay in Puerto Vallarta without an excursion to the paradisiacal tropical havens of Las Ánimas, Quimixto or Yelapa would be a serious oversight. Beyond the reach of roads, they are accessible only by boat – getting there is half the fun. Along the coastline verdant mountains rise from the sea and deserted beaches and picturesque coves beckon. Only Yelapa provides the opportunity to spend the night.

Wear your waterproof sandals, as landings are often wet, and by all means carry insect repellent just in case the mosquitoes are in the mood to swarm.

Water taxis carrying up to eight passengers depart from Boca de Tomatlán hourly from 9am to 11am and 1pm to 4pm to Playa Las Ánimas (US$5.50, 25 minutes), Quimixto (US$6.50, 35 minutes) and Yelapa (US$10, 45 minutes). They also leave from Puerto Vallarta (p96).

PLAYA DE LAS ÁNIMAS
Beach of the Spirits, a 20-minute ride by boat from Boca de Tomatlán, is a lovely stretch of sugary sand fronting a small fishing village. An afternoon spent here provides the most delicious sort of escapism. Your culinary needs will be simply but marvelously met by the good selection of *palapa* restaurants offering ultrafresh seafood such as shrimp empanadas or whole fried red snapper. Dessert is provided by the pie ladies who wander the beach with coconut

or lemon meringue pies for sale. Should you decide to pry yourself from the sands and ease into the water you'll discover some superlative snorkeling opportunities along the rocky shoreline at the far end of the beach. Or you may wish to shake the sand off with a hike through the rain forest to Quimixto, via an adventurous coast trail, in about an hour.

When you get dropped off, let the boatman know what time you'd like to be picked up. But if he doesn't show up, there are always fishermen on hand ready to transport you for a slight markup in price.

QUIMIXTO

A 30-minute boat ride from Boca, the equally lovely Quimixto has a sandy beach lined with seafood restaurants against a jungle backdrop. Just east, past a rocky point, is a pretty and deserted little beach. Lounge on the beach and gorge on *mariscos*, but don't leave without making the undemanding half-hour inland hike to a beautiful waterfall and swimming hole. The hike requires four to five shallow river crossings (wear waterproof sandals). Alternatively – and by doing so you'll be supporting local families whose livelihood depends on it – you can hire a horse to take you up for US$10. At the falls, two rustic restaurants sell somewhat pricey refreshments. To avoid crowds, make the trip as early in the day as possible.

Further on along the same trail, perhaps another 40 minutes by foot, is yet another waterfall that you are likely to have all to yourself. Along the way you'll enjoy beautiful vistas and ever-changing scenery as you pass through the lush vegetation along the river.

YELAPA

Furthest from town, Yelapa is one of Vallarta's most popular boating destinations, and home to a sizable colony of foreign residents in addition to 100 or so Mexican families. Its picturesque beach cove with turquoise-colored waters is crowded with restaurants, tourists and parasailers during the day but empties out when the boats leave in the late afternoon. There are plenty of horses for rent and hikes to beaches and waterfalls (head upriver), but just a walk around the funky little town, most of which overlooks the cove, is pleasant.

There are now payphones scattered throughout the village and even a couple of Internet cafés. An up-to-date compendium of information about Yelapa can be accessed at www.yelapa.info.

Sleeping

There are quite a few places to stay here, particularly if you're willing to book for three or more days. You can usually find a place to stay by merely inquiring on the beach or visiting the Palapa in Yelapa office at the southern end of the beach. Prices can rise if you miss that last boat. During the peak season it's safest to reserve in advance.

Hotel Lagunita (☎ 209-50-56; www.hotel-lagunita .com; d US$80-125; 🏊) The nicest midrange place in Yelapa, this hotel offers rustic-chic cabanas with one or two double beds, private bathrooms with hot water, electricity and fan. The 32 units are breezy and welcoming, painted in strong colors with plenty of local flair. There's also a pleasant restaurant bar, a well-kept pool, therapeutic massage and the occasional yoga class. Prices drop precipitously during the low season.

Verana (☎ 222-23-60, in the US 800-677-5156; www .verana.com; d villa US$200-450; ✖ 🏊) Perched on a hillside with magnificent views of the mountains and sea, this getaway offers six beautifully designed bungalows that *Architectural Digest* magazine saw fit to swoon over. Each has been lovingly appointed and creatively designed by a former film-production designer and his partner, a prop stylist. It has a full-service spa and a much-ballyhooed chef to help you achieve the restive state of bliss that you paid good money for. There's a five-day minimum for reservations, and a mandatory food plan (US$95) providing breakfast and dinner.

La Joya de Yelapa (☎ 209-51-40; www.bungalows yelapa.com; d per day US$60-75, per week US$450) Located behind Marlin Restaurant near the stable, this is a basic option offering exceptionally private fan-cooled pine cabins with earthen floors, two double beds, hot water and coffeemakers.

Casa Milagros (☎ 329-298-14-70; s/d US$35/45) Way up in town, up the alleyway toward the mouth of the bay, is this friendly, modern spot with 10 simple rooms. The views from the terraces are unbelievable, but you'll have to climb 178 stairs just to reach the place.

Blue Moon Hotel (☎ 209-50-62; javier_rodriguez@ yahoo.com; r US$40-50) Right on the beach, this simple hotel offers a good selection of rooms with comfortable beds and hot water. Inquire at Chico's restaurant.

Apartamentos La Barca (☎ 209-50-73; per night/ week US$20/140) Budget accommodations can be had at this Spartan option by the Río Tuito, which offers a rustic open-air apartment sleeping up to six with hot water and a utility kitchen. Your host, Valentín, can often be found on the beach.

Eating

Yelapa supports some 20 restaurants catering both to locals and visitors. The atmosphere in all of the restaurants is decidedly casual.

Chico's (☎ 209-50-62; mains US$5-10; ☺ lunch) This old favorite was among the first to open for business on the beach and has been setting the standard ever since. You'll do well to order a steaming plate of giant shrimp served with the requisite garlic, butter and spices, or fresh red snapper or dorado with handmade tortillas.

Vortex Café (mains US$3-8; ☺ breakfast & lunch) This friendly eatery serves delicious international breakfasts and lunches, including espresso, bagels, baked goods, seafood, and pizzas baked in a wood-fired oven. It frequently remains open in the evenings, with live music. A few recently added terminals provide Internet access.

As in Quimixto, pie ladies ply the beach with stacks of pies balanced on their heads. You can purchase by the slice or by the pie, and they'll even bake to order.

Getting There & Away

Most visitors arrive via water taxi from either Puerto Vallarta (p96) or Boca de Tomatlán (p106).

From 8:30am to 5pm, water taxis depart for Puerto Vallarta and Boca de Tomatlán

from the small pier next to the Yacht Club and from the beach. Before departing they cruise slowly down the beach to pick up anybody that is waiting.

El Tuito

After passing Boca de Tomatlán, Hwy 200 curves inland and climbs through high pine forests. Then, about 45km south of Puerto Vallarta, it reaches the small, traditional pueblo of El Tuito, which stretches east about 2km. While not incredibly impressive from the highway, it's a pleasant spot if you want to explore a completely untouristy, practically traffic-free and very Mexican place. It's also distinct in that the church is behind the cute plaza and not on it. Be prepared for curious stares, as not many gringos stop here.

There's a unique restaurant nearby, about 2km south past El Tuito and just off the highway. Look for signs leading to **Rancho Altamira** (☎ 322-269-00-35; Km 167; ☺ 11am-7pm). The open but covered restaurant sits on a lofty knoll overlooking green brushy hills, some agave fields and a pond full of ducks and geese. Deer, peacocks and ostriches (that's right) scamper around in the distance, and from your aerie a gentle breeze caresses you while you wolf down the very generous portions of meat and seafood dishes (US$7 to US$22). Afterwards, cocktails and tequila shots will wriggle and twitch your whiskers (if you happen to have any). The restaurant offers fishing and horseback tours (US$12 per hour) as well.

If you need to spend the night, back in town and on the highway there's the decent, modern **Hotel Real de Valle** (☎ 269-00-11; r US$30-45, ste US$55; ☺ ☎), with rooms arranged around a shady garden and an astonishing airbrushed mural in the lobby. El Tuito is easily reached via long-distance buses heading south from Puerto Vallarta.

Mazatlán

Warm and beachy Mazatlán is just a hair's breadth south of the tropic of Cancer in Sinaloa state. This is the Meh-*hee*-co you come to when all you want to do is lie back on the sand, tip that sombrero way down over your chin and let the rest of you soak up the coastal rays.

Striking for its many personalities, Mazatlán reveals itself through its gritty port, its romantic historic center and its thriving tourist playground, the Zona Dorada (Golden Zone). One of Mexico's glitzy prototypical resort towns of the mid-20th century, the city remains a prime destination for a hassle-free, fun-in-the-sun vacation, catering to visitors with an abundance of cheap knick-knack stores, taxis, oversized mega-resorts and gringo-friendly restaurants.

But there's more to discover in Old Mazatlán, which in recent years has been revitalized by a flowering cultural scene. Here you'll find a beguiling mixture of cosmopolitan restaurants, bars and art galleries against a backdrop of well-preserved colonial edifices and cobbled streets. Catch a performance at the wonderful, refurbished Teatro Ángela Peralta and then a late-night bite at the atmospheric Plazuela Machado and you may decide to stick around for an extra day to go apartment hunting.

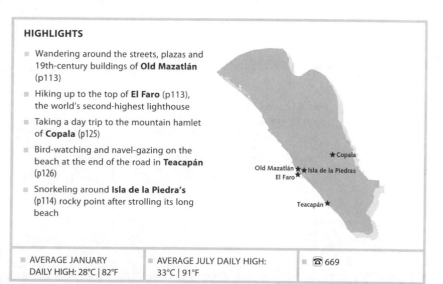

HIGHLIGHTS

- Wandering around the streets, plazas and 19th-century buildings of **Old Mazatlán** (p113)

- Hiking up to the top of **El Faro** (p113), the world's second-highest lighthouse

- Taking a day trip to the mountain hamlet of **Copala** (p125)

- Bird-watching and navel-gazing on the beach at the end of the road in **Teacapán** (p126)

- Snorkeling around **Isla de la Piedra's** (p114) rocky point after strolling its long beach

★ Copala

Old Mazatlán ★★ Isla de la Piedras
El Faro ★

Teacapán ★

| ■ AVERAGE JANUARY DAILY HIGH: 28°C \| 82°F | ■ AVERAGE JULY DAILY HIGH: 33°C \| 91°F | ■ ☎ 669 |

History

In pre-Hispanic times Mazatlán (which means 'place of deer' in Nahuatl) was populated by the Totorames, who lived by hunting, gathering, fishing and agriculture. On Easter Sunday in 1531, a group of 25 Spaniards led by Nuño de Guzmán officially founded a settlement here, but almost three centuries elapsed before a permanent colony was established in the early 1820s. The port was blockaded by US forces in 1847, and by the French in 1864, but Mazatlán remained little more than a fishing village for the next 80 years. 'Old' Mazatlán, the traditional town center, dates from the 19th century. Tourists started coming in the 1930s, mainly for fishing and hunting, and some hotels appeared along Playa Olas Altas, Mazatlán's first tourist beach, in the 1950s. From the 1970s onward, a long strip of modern hotels and tourist facilities had spread north along the coast.

Orientation

Old Mazatlán, the city center, is near the southern end of a peninsula, bounded by the Pacific Ocean on the west and the Bahía Dársena channel on the east. The center of the 'old' city is the cathedral, on Plaza Principal, surrounded by a rectangular street grid. At the southern tip of the peninsula, El Faro (the Lighthouse) stands on a rocky prominence, overlooking Mazatlán's sportfishing fleet and La Paz ferry terminal.

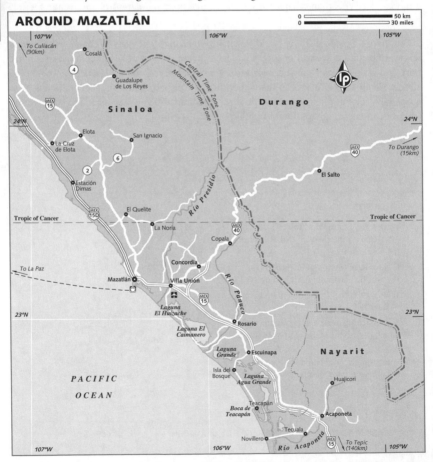

AROUND MAZATLÁN

There is a bus-covered, beachside boulevard (which changes names frequently) running along the Pacific side of the peninsula from Playa Olas Altas, around some rocky outcrops, and north around the wide arc of Playa Norte to the Zona Dorada, a concentration of hotels, bars and businesses catering mainly to package tourists. Further north there are more hotels, a marina and some timeshare condominium developments.

East of the Mazatlán peninsula, Isla de la Piedra is a short boat ride from town, though it's not really an island any more – landfill from the airport construction has joined it to the mainland. The wide, sandy beach here is lined with open-sided, *palapa* (palm-thatch–roofed) restaurants.

MAPS

Guía Roji publishes a detailed *Ciudad de Mazatlán* map that's available from major Internet booksellers. Basic tourist maps are available at the tourist office.

Information

Opening hours reflect winter schedules; summer hours may be more limited.

BOOKSTORES

Mazatlán Book & Coffee Company (Map p115; ☎ 916-78-99; Camarón Sábalo s/n; ☟ 9am-7pm Mon-Sat) Across from Hotel Costa de Oro, with used books in English for sale or barter.

Sanborn's (Map p112; ☎ 992-01-91; La Gran Plaza; ☟ 7:30am-1am) Spanish-language books, maps and guidebooks.

EMERGENCY

Ambulance (☎ 986-79-11)
Fire Department (☎ 981-27-69)
Police (☎ 060)

INTERNET ACCESS

Internet cafés are plentiful in Old Mazatlán and all charge about US$1 per hour; places in the Zona Dorada charge as much as US$2.75. Many private telephone offices also offer Internet service. All places listed here have air-con.

Cyber Café Mazatlán (Map p115; Camarón Sábalo 204; per hr US$2.50 ☟ 10am-10pm) Pricey but fast, hip and convenient.

Oldtown@ccess (Map p114; Constitución 519; per hr US$1; ☟ 9am-1am) With a bohemian flavor, at Altazor Ars Café on Plazuela Machado.

Italian Coffee Company (Map p112; Av del Mar 1020; ☟ 7am-10pm Mon-Sat, 10am-10pm Sun) Free wireless access and good java.

LAUNDRY

Lavandería La Blanca (Map p115; Camarón Sábalo 357; per 3kg US$5)
Lavamar (Map p115; Playa Gaviotas 214; per kg US$5)

MEDIA

Most hotels have city maps, restaurant and activity advertisements, and free English-language newspapers such as *Pacific Pearl* (www.pacificpearl.com) and *Mazatlán Interactivo* (www.mazatlaninteractivo.com). In Old Mazatlán pick up the free bilingual *Viejo Mazatlán*, which is the best source of information about the cultural life around town.

MEDICAL SERVICES

There are several clinics on Camarón Sábalo, in the Zona Dorada, that cater to gringos who come down with a case of indigestion or worse.

Clínica Balboa (Map p115; ☎ 916-79-33; Camarón Sábalo 4480; ☟ 24hr) English is spoken at this well-regarded walk-in medical clinic.

MONEY

Banks, most with ATMs, and *casas de cambio* are plentiful in both old and new Mazatlán. There are Bancomer and Banamex branches near Plaza Principal (Map p114) and a **Banamex** (Map p115; Camarón Sábalo) in the Zona Dorada. **American Express** (Map p115; Centro Comercial Balboa, Camarón Sábalo s/n) is in the Zona Dorada.

POST

Main post office (Map p114; Juárez s/n) On the east side of Plaza Principal.

TELEPHONE

Computel (Map p114; Serdán 1516; ☟ 7am-9pm) Telephone, fax and limited Internet services, and friendly, helpful staff.

Telecomm (Map p114; Juárez s/n; ☟ 8am-7pm Mon-Fri, 9am-1pm Sat) Next to the post office, with quiet pay phones in private cabins, fax and Internet service.

TOURIST INFORMATION

Coordinación General de Turismo (Map p114; ☎ 981-88-86/87; Carnaval 1317; www.sinaloa-travel.com in Spanish; ☟ 9am-5pm Mon-Fri) Helpful staff with information about hotel deals as well as what to see and do in Mazatlán and Sinaloa state.

MAZATLÁN

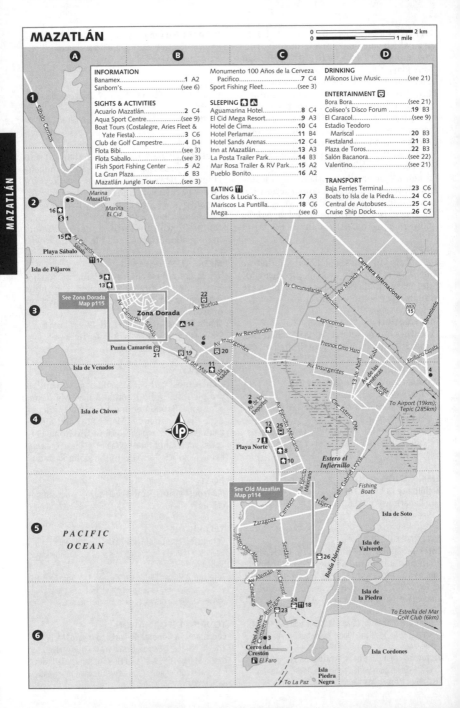

Sights

OLD MAZATLÁN

Old Mazatlán is a forward-thinking place rooted firmly in the past. It's the cultural heart of the city with well-curated museums, contemporary galleries, colonial architecture and historic monuments. At its center is the soaring 19th-century **cathedral** (Map p114; cnr Juárez & 21 de Marzo) with its high, yellow twin towers and a dramatic interior. Built from 1875 to 1890, it faces the shady, peaceful **Plaza Principal**.

A short walk southwest will bring you to the tree-lined **Plazuela Machado** (Map p114; cnr Carnaval & Constitución). The plaza and surrounding streets are abuzz with art galleries, cafés and restaurants. Here is the heart of Mazatlán's cultural flowering and the continuing focus of the city's admirable restoration efforts. The center of attention is the **Teatro Ángela Peralta** (Map p114; ☎ 982-44-46; www.teatroangelaperalta.com in Spanish; Carnaval 47), half a block south of the plaza. The theater was built in 1860, and reopened in 1992 after a five-year restoration project. Cultural events of all kinds are presented here (see p122), and the opulent interior is open for viewing most days. It's surrounded by historic buildings and attractive sidewalk cafés, restaurants and bars.

At the southern end of the peninsula, a particularly prominent rocky outcrop provides the base for **El Faro** (Map p112), 135m above sea level and supposedly the second-highest lighthouse in the world (after the one in Gibraltar). You can climb up there for a spectacular view of the city and coast. The hill, called Cerro del Crestón, was once an island, but a causeway built in the 1930s now joins it to the mainland. Mazatlán's sportfishing fleet, the ferry to La Paz and some tourist boats (see p117) dock in the marina on the east side of the causeway.

MUSEUMS

The **Museo Arqueológico** (Map p114; ☎ 981-14-55; Sixto Osuna 76; admission US$2.50; ☺ 10am-6pm Mon-Sat, 10am-3pm Sun) is an interesting little archaeological museum with a small permanent collection of artifacts from around Sinaloa state, a selection of historical photos of Mazatlán, and changing thematic exhibitions. Some signs are in English. Opposite, the small **Museo de Arte** (Map p114; ☎ 985-35-02; cnr Sixto Osuna & Carranza; admission free; ☺ 10am-2pm &

4-7pm Tue-Sun) has permanent and changing exhibits by Mexican artists (all signs are in Spanish).

Also worth a peek is the **Machado Museo Casa** (Map p114; Constitución 79; adult/student US$2/1; ☺ 9am-6pm), a beautifully restored 19th-century house filled with a collection of French and Austrian furniture, clothing and other antiques. Some exhibits have signs in English.

BEACHES & ZONA DORADA

With over 16km of beaches, it's easy to find a stretch of sand to call your own in Mazatlán. The following beaches are listed in geographic order, from south to north.

In Old Mazatlán, the crescent-shaped **Playa Olas Altas** (Map p114) is where tourism first flourished in the 1950s. The pebbly beach is not ideal for swimming but it's a grand place to watch the sun drop into the sea or soak up some regional history. Signs on the faded '50s hotels facing along the seafront road, Paseo Olas Altas, commemorate some of the area's first visitors, such as writer Jack Kerouac and photographers Tina Modotti (p39) and Edward Weston.

Flanked by a broad *malecón* (waterfront street) popular with joggers and strollers, the golden sands of **Playa Norte** (Map p112) begin just north of Old Mazatlán and arc toward **Punta Camarón** (Map p112), a rocky point dominated by the conspicuous castle-like Fiesta Land nightclub complex. The traffic circle here marks the southern end of the **Zona Dorada**, an unabashedly touristy precinct of hotels, restaurants, bars and souvenir shops.

The most luxurious hotels face the fine, uncrowded beaches of **Playa Las Gaviotas** (Map p115) and **Playa Sábalo** (Map p112), which extends north of the Zona Dorada. Sheltered by picturesque islands, here the waters are generally calm and ideal for swimming and water sports; on offer are sailing excursions, water-skiing, banana-boat rides and parasailing. To reach these beaches from downtown, just hop on a 'Sábalo-Centro' bus; these originate at the market on Juárez and travel along Av del Mar.

Further north, past the ever-evolving Marina Mazatlán, are the undeveloped, serene beaches of **Playa Brujas** (Witches' Beach) and **Playa Cerritos**. Both sport a few excellent seafood restaurants and are well

MAZATLÁN

MAZATLÁN

OLD MAZATLÁN

0 — 400 m
0 — 0.2 miles

INFORMATION
Banamex.................................1 C3
Bancomer..............................2 C3
Computel...............................3 B4
Coordinación General de
Turismo.................................4 C4
Main Post Office....................5 C3
Oldtown@ccess...............(see 24)
Telecomm..............................6 C3

SIGHTS & ACTIVITIES
Carpe Olivera.........................7 B4
Cathedral...............................8 C3
Centro de Idiomas.................9 B4
Cliff Divers............................10 A3
Machado Museo Casa..........11 B4
Monumento a la Continuidad de la
Vida.....................................12 A3
Monumento al Pescador......13 C1
Monumento al Venado........14 B4
Museo Arqueológico............15 B4
Museo de Arte.....................16 B4
Observation Deck.................17 A3
Saltwater Pool..................(see 7)

SLEEPING
Hotel Belmar........................18 B4
Hotel Central........................19 B4
Hotel del Río........................20 C2
Hotel La Siesta.....................21 B4
Hotel México........................22 C1
Royal Dutch B&B.................23 C4

EATING
Altazor Ars Café...................24 C4
Ambrosia..............................25 B4
Beach Burger...................(see 24)
Café Pacifico....................(see 28)
Cenaduria El Túnel..............26 C4
La Copa de Leche................27 B4
La Tramoya..........................28 B4
Mariscos El Camichín..........29 B2
Marza Pack..........................30 C3
Pedro y Lola........................31 C4
Puerto Viejo.........................32 B4
Restaurant Los Pelícanos.....33 B2

DRINKING
Edgar's Bar..........................34 C4
La Tertulia...........................35 B4
Vitrola's Bar.........................36 B3

ENTERTAINMENT
Teatro Ángela Peralta...........37 C4

SHOPPING
Centro Mercado...................38 C3

PACIFIC OCEAN

Playa Norte

To Zona Dorada
(3.5km)

Parque
Martiniano
Carvajal

*Bahía de
Olas Atlas*

Playa Olas Altas

To Best Western
Hotel Posada
Freeman (150m)

Cerro de
la Nevería

La Mazatleca

To Bus
Terminal
(1.5km)

Parque
Zaragoza

Palacio
Municipal

Plaza
Principal

Plaza
Hidalgo

Plazuela
Machado

To Baja Ferries
Terminal (1km)

loved by surfers. To get there by bus, catch a 'Cerritos Juárez' bus from the Fiestaland complex or from along Camarón Sábalo in the Zona Dorada.

ISLANDS

Those three photogenic land masses jutting from the sea are Mazatlán's signature islands. **Isla de Chivos** (Island of Goats; Map p112) is on the left, and **Isla de Pájaros** (Island of Birds; Map p112) is on the right. The most visited is the one in the middle, **Isla de Venados** (Deer Island; Map p112). Designated a natural reserve for the protection of native flora and fauna, its secluded beaches are wonderful for a day trip and its limpid waters ideal for snorkeling.

A five-hour excursion to Isla de Venados leaves from the marina at **El Cid Mega Resort** (Map p112; ☎ 913-33-33, ext 3341; www.elcid.com; Camarón Sábalo s/n; ☯ 9:30am Tue-Sat). The trip costs US$42 per person, lasts five hours and includes a banana-boat ride, snorkel equipment, a bilingual guide, kayak access, lunch and drinks. Alternatively, from the beach at El Cid catch a ride to the island on an amphibious vehicle (per person US$8; ☯ 10am, noon & 2pm).

Isla de la Piedra

Escape artists love Stone Island for its beautiful, long, sandy beach bordered by coconut groves, and anyone with an appetite sings the praises of the simple *palapa* restaurants. Surfers come for the waves, and on Sunday afternoons and holidays the restaurants draw Mexican families for music and dancing, and an infectious party vibe takes over. At other times the beach is nearly empty. It is possible to camp here, too.

To get there, take a small boat from the Playa Sur embarcadero near the Baja Ferries terminal (US$1 round-trip; ☺ every 10min 7am-6pm). You'll be dropped off at a jetty a short walk from the Isla de la Piedra beach. 'Playa Sur' buses leave for the boat dock from the north side of the Plaza Principal.

Activities
SURFING

With a season lasting from late March through November, Mazatlán sports several noteworthy surfing sites and a couple of great surf shops to boot. The most famous waves include two that break near downtown. Off **Punta Camarón** is a dependable right-hander, and north of the old fort is a famous lefty known as the **Cannon**. Off **Isla de la Piedra** (Map p112) you'll find a beach break with perfect peaks, but unless there's a decent swell you're better off grabbing a beer and watching from the beach. Rolling in at **Playa Brujas** each morning is a big left that you can set your watch to.

The longest-established surf shop in town is **Mazatlán Surf Center** (Map p115; ☎ 913-18-21; www.mazatlansurfcenter.com; Camarón Sábalo 500-4; board rentals per day/week US$20/70, lessons US$35; ☺ 10am-9pm Mon-Sat, 1-9pm Sun), known for its

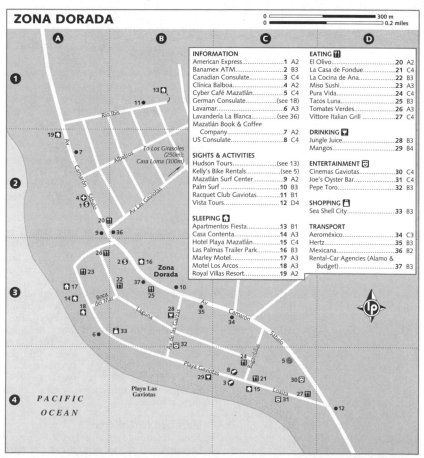

ZONA DORADA

0 .... 300 m
0 .... 0.2 miles

INFORMATION		EATING 🍴	
American Express...................**1** A2		El Olivo.................................**20** A2	
Banamex ATM.........................**2** B3		La Casa de Fondue................**21** C4	
Canadian Consulate................**3** C4		La Cocina de Ana...................**22** B3	
Clínica Balboa.........................**4** A2		Miso Sushi............................**23** A3	
Cyber Café Mazatlán...............**5** C4		Pura Vida..............................**24** C4	
German Consulate................(see 18)		Tacos Luna............................**25** B3	
Lavamar.................................**6** A3		Tomates Verdes.....................**26** A3	
Lavandería La Blanca............(see 36)		Vittore Italian Grill **27** C4	
Mazatlán Book & Coffee			
Company............................**7** A2		DRINKING 🍷	
US Consulate..........................**8** C4		Jungle Juice..........................**28** B3	
		Mangos................................**29** B4	
SIGHTS & ACTIVITIES			
Hudson Tours.....................(see 13)		ENTERTAINMENT 🎭	
Kelly's Bike Rentals...............(see 5)		Cinemas Gaviotas.................**30** C4	
Mazatlán Surf Center **9** A2		Joe's Oyster Bar....................**31** C4	
Palm Surf.............................**10** B3		Pepe Toro............................**32** B3	
Racquet Club Gaviotas..........**11** B1			
Vista Tours...........................**12** D4		SHOPPING 🛍	
		Sea Shell City........................**33** B3	
SLEEPING 🛏			
Apartmentos Fiesta...............**13** B1		TRANSPORT	
Casa Contenta......................**14** A3		Aeroméxico..........................**34** C3	
Hotel Playa Mazatlán............**15** C4		Hertz....................................**35** B3	
Las Palmas Trailer Park..........**16** B3		Mexicana..............................**36** B2	
Marley Motel........................**17** A3		Rental-Car Agencies (Alamo &	
Motel Los Arcos....................**18** A3		Budget)..............................**37** B3	
Royal Villas Resort.................**19** A2			

PACIFIC OCEAN

popular surfing lessons and expert advice. **Palm Surf** (Map p115; ☎ 914-06-87; www.palmsurf shop.com.mx; Camarón Sábalo 333; board rentals per day US$25, lessons US$35; ☼ 9:30am-8pm Mon-Sat) is also a contender, with plenty of boards for rent and surf excursions to far-flung spots like Patolé, Celestinos and Mármol.

OTHER WATER SPORTS

The **Aqua Sport Center** (Map p112; ☎ 913-04-51; El Cid Mega Resort) is the place to go for water sports, including scuba diving (US$60 for a one-tank dive); snorkeling rentals (US$8 per day); jet-skiing (US$54 per half hour); para-sailing (US$30); and kayak rentals (US$15 to US$25 per hour). Water-sports equipment can also be hired on the beaches in front of most of the other large beachfront hotels.

HORSEBACK RIDING

If you love to canter on the beach, or dream of doing so, your best bet is with **Ginger's Bi-Lingual Horses** (Map p112; ☎ 988-12-54; Playa Brujas; per hr US$25; ☼ 10am-4pm Mon-Sat). Unlike at some other Mexican stables, here the horses are healthy, happy and eager to stretch their legs on the trails leading through coconut plantations on to the open beach. Longer rides into the hills are possible. Take a 'Cerritos Juárez' bus from Zona Dorada, or a taxi to Playa Brujas.

Short rides can also be arranged on Isla de la Piedra at Restaurant Puesta de Sol (US$5), but the horses here are lackluster compared to Ginger's pampered mounts.

SPORTFISHING

With an excellent location at the confluence of the Sea of Cortez and the Pacific Ocean, Mazatlán is world famous for its sport-fishing – especially for marlin, swordfish, sailfish, tuna and *dorado* (dolphinfish). It can be an expensive activity (US$400 to US$450 for a day in an 11m cruiser with four people fishing), though small-game fishing from a 7m *super panga* boat is less expensive (US$200 to US$240 with up to six people fishing). All operators should offer tag-and-release options. For the winter high season, make fishing reservations far in advance.

Boats leave from the El Cid Resort marina and from Marina Mazatlán, but the best prices are offered by the operators based on the peninsula on Calz Camarena.

Aries Fleet (Map p112; ☎ 916-34-68; www.elcid.com; El Cid Marina)
Flota Bibi (Map p112; ☎ 981-36-40; www.bibifleet.com; Calz Camarena s/n)
Flota Saballo (Map p112; ☎ 981-27-61; Calz Camarena s/n)
Flota Neptuno (Map p112; ☎ 982-45-65; Calz Camarena s/n)
Star Fleet (Map p112; ☎ 982-26-65; www.starfleet .com.mx; Calz Camarena s/n)

Freshwater large-mouth bass fishing is also caching on, particularly at scenic Lake El Salto, one hour north of town. **iFish Sport Fishing Center** (Map p112; ☎ 913-16-21; www.ifishmexico .com; Camarón Sábalo 1504) runs day trips (per person US$278) and houses fisher folk in a comfortable lodge (three nights all-inclusive per person costs US$1074). Prices include transport, equipment and all meals.

GOLF & TENNIS

There's golf at the **Club de Golf Campestre** (Map p112; ☎ 980-15-70; www.estrelladelmar.com; Hwy 15; green fees 9/18 holes US$18/25), east of town; the **Estrella del Mar Golf Club** (Map p112; ☎ 982-33-00; Isla de la Piedra; green fees US$110), south of the airport by the coast; and **El Cid Mega Resort** (Map p112; ☎ 913-33-33; Camarón Sábalo s/n; 9/18 holes US$60/75), north of the Zona Dorada.

Play tennis at the **Racquet Club Gaviotas** (Map p115; ☎ 913-59-39; cnr Río Ibis & Bravo; per hr U$12) in the Zona Dorada, at El Cid resort and at most of the large hotels north of the center.

Courses

Centro de Idiomas (Map p114; ☎ 985-56-06; Aurora 203; www.spanishlink.org; 2/4hr classes per week US$142/170) offers Spanish courses from Monday to Friday with a maximum of six students per class. The curriculum is best suited to beginning or intermediate students. You can begin any Monday and study for as many weeks as you like; registration is every Saturday morning from 9am to noon. Discounts are given on the fourth week. The school also facilitates volunteer work within the community. Homestays (shared/private room US$155/US$170 per week) can be arranged with a Mexican family and include three meals a day.

Mazatlán for Children

Kids love this town, if only for the many opportunities to get wet. One of the most economical and enjoyable places to accomplish this is at the delightful, all-natural **saltwater pool** (Map p114) below the Carpe Olivera statue on Paseo Olas Altas. Here kids and adults splash around as waves crash over the pool's seaward edge. There are bathrooms and changing rooms (US$0.30).

Splashing around is also the featured activity at **MazAgua** (Map p112; ☎ 988-00-41; Entronque Habal-Cerritos s/n; admission US$8.50; ☽ 10am-6pm Mar-Dec), where kids can go hog wild with water toboggans, a wave pool and other amusements. The 'Cerritos-Juárez' bus takes you there from anywhere along the coastal road.

Acuario Mazatlán (Map p112; ☎ 981-78-15; www .acuariomazatlan.gob.mx; Av de los Deportes 111; adult/ child US$5/3; ☽ 9:30am-6pm), a block inland from Playa Norte, has 52 tanks with 250 species of freshwater and saltwater fish and other creatures. Sea-lion, diving and bird shows are presented four times daily.

Quirky Mazatlán

Puerto Vallarta has its high-art sculptures, and Manzanillo its epic Swordfish Memorial. But Mazatlán's audacious collection of kitsch statuary is in a category of its own.

At the waterfront on the western edge of the historic center you'll find several of the town's seafront monuments. At the north end of Playa Olas Altas is **Carpe Olivera** (Map p114), a statue of a buxom mermaid in pike position, drawing passersby irresistibly down the stairs to the rocks below and a saltwater dipping pool (see opposite). Nearby is the small **Monumento al Venado** (Monument to the Deer; Map p114) – a tribute to the city's Nahuatl name – depicting a rather forlorn-looking deer on a pedestal in the middle of the street. Further north is the kitsch masterpiece **Monumento a la Continuidad de la Vida** (Monument to the Continuity of Life; Map p114), featuring a nude, gesticulating couple with big hair and nine leaping, rusty dolphins.

From a nearby platform **cliff divers** (*clavadistas*; Map p114) cast their bodies into the ocean swells below for your enjoyment. Tip accordingly. They usually perform around lunchtime and in the late afternoon, but they won't risk their necks until a crowd has been assembled. Also here is an unnamed **observation deck** (Map p114) perched atop a stony precipice. You won't want your

kids going anywhere near it. It takes considerable nerve to scale the arching brick stairway – there's no rail and a long drop to open sea on either side – but it's even more unsettling going back down.

Overlooking the southern end of Playa Norte is the **Monumento al Pescador** (Monument to the Fisherman; Map p114). This bully pigeon perch, commissioned in 1958, depicts a nude fisherman with Tin Tin hair and enormous feet. You can tell he's a fisherman, as he's clutching a net (although it looks more like a beach towel). To his side is a tawdry muse splayed on a swoosh, looking more like Miss September than a fisherman's friend.

Elsewhere are statues of a dapper chap on a motorcycle, a mermaid getting directions from a cherub, a leaky copper beer tank commemorating the first century of Pacífico beer, and a memorial to local songbird Lola Beltrán. Take a walk – you can't miss 'em.

Tours

BICYCLE TOURS

Kelly's Bike Rentals (Map p115; ☎ 914-11-87; www .kellys-bikes.com; Camarón Sábalo 204; tours US$28, mountain bike rental per day US$15; ☽ 10am-2pm & 4:30-8pm Mon-Sat) leads wild and woolly four- to six-hour mountain-bike tours into the hills, over dirt roads and challenging single-track trails. They also offers custom trips on some of Sinaloa's most scenic paved routes.

BOAT TOURS

In addition to trips to **Isla de Venados** (see Islands, p114), several boats do 2½-hour sightseeing tours, mostly leaving from the docks off Calz Camarena, near El Faro, at 11am (US$15 including hotel transfers). Two-hour sunset cruises, sometimes called 'booze cruises,' include hors d'oeuvres and the requisite booze (US$15 to US$25, depending on your thirst). To find out what's going on, look for flyers around town, talk to a tour agent or call the operators of boats such as **Costalegre** (Map p112; ☎ 982-31-30; Calz Camarena s/n) and **Yate Fiesta** (Map p112; ☎ 981-71-54; Calz Camarena s/n).

LAND TOURS

Several companies offer a variety of tours in and around Mazatlán. Prices are about the same from company to company for the same tours: US$20 for a three-hour city tour, US$38 to US$48 for a colonial tour to the foothill towns of Concordia and Copala, and US$35 for a tequila factory tour that includes the village of La Noria. If you make reservations, either by calling or having a travel agent book for you ahead of time, they will pick you up from your hotel. Paying in pesos yields a better deal. Recommended agencies:

Hudson Tours (Map p115; ☎ 913-17-64; www.hudson tours.com; Río Ibis 502, Apartamentos Fiesta) Smaller, more personalized tours that include shopping and spearfishing.

Marlin Tours (Map p112; ☎ 913-53-01; www.toursin mazatlan.com; Camarón Sábalo 1504) Friendly and long-standing, with tours to Copala, Concordia and Rosario.

Vista Tours (Map p115; ☎ 986-83-83; www.vistatours .com.mx; Camarón Sábalo 51) Bigger range to choose from, including Cosalá and the San Ignacio Missions.

Mazatlán Jungle Tour (Map p112; ☎ 914-14-44; Calz Camarena s/n) Offers a jungle tour by boat into the mangrove swamps of Isla de la Piedra (US$45).

Festivals & Events

Mazatlán has one of Mexico's most flamboyant **Carnaval** celebrations. For the week leading up to Ash Wednesday (the Wednesday 40 days before Easter), the town goes on a nonstop partying spree. People from around Mexico (and beyond) pour in for music, dancing and general revelry. Be sure to reserve a hotel room in advance. The party ends abruptly on the morning of **Ash Wednesday**, when Roman Catholics go to church to receive ash marks on their foreheads for the first day of Lent.

A **torneo de pesca** (fishing tournament) for sailfish, marlin and *dorado* is held in mid-May and mid-November. Golf tournaments and various cultural festivals are held throughout the year; the tourist office has details.

The **Sinaloa Fiesta de los Artes**, featuring local talent and troupes traveling from afar, is staged at the Teatro Angela Peralta and other local venues from late October through mid-November.

On December 12 the day of the **Virgen de Guadalupe** is celebrated at the cathedral. Children come in colorful costumes.

Sleeping

Visitors have a choice of a luxury package-tour resort, old-style Mexican ambience, or the very basic beach-bum option. The most luxurious hotels front the beaches

north of the Zona Dorada, where the mid-range hotels rule. Most budget options are south of the Zona Dorada and in the center overlooking Playa Olas Altas. The following prices are for high season; lower rates may be available from May through October, or for longer stays. At peak periods, however, prices can rise by as much as 40%.

During nonholiday periods, there are some good deals among the more expensive places along Playa Norte and the Zona Dorada.

BUDGET

Hotel Central (Map p114; ☎ 982-18-66; Domínguez 2; s/d US$20/23; 🔀) Making up in creature comforts what it lacks in architectural charm, the Hotel Central is a well-kept, well-run place in the heart of Old Mazatlán. Enthusiastically air-conditioned, it's popular with Mexican business travelers.

Hotel Perlamar (Map p112; ☎ 985-33-66; cnr Av del Mar & Isla Asada; r US$18-20, with air-con & TV US$25; P 🔀) Off the main drag near Playa Norte, this little lemon-yellow hotel is cheaply built and cheaply priced. Rooms are perfectly respectable, tidy and clean, albeit crowded.

Hotel del Río (Map p114; ☎ 982-44-30; Juárez 2410; d/q US$25/50; P 🔀) This tidy hotel close to the beach in a working-class neighborhood is a long-time traveler favorite. Limited English is spoken and cable TV is available for US$2 more per day.

Hotel México (Map p114; ☎ 981-38-06; México 201; s/d US$10/15) With colorful tiled floors, dusty curtains and rustic bathrooms, this family-run cheapie still has some colonial charm. Just a block from the beach, it's a good deal.

Hotel Belmar (Map p114; ☎ 985-11-12/13; Paseo Olas Altas 166 Sur; r interior/sea view US$26/33; P 🔀 🔀) Some people love the retro appeal of this totally faded 1960s classic, with its labyrinthine hallways and striking ocean views from private balconies, but others can't look past the rough edges. The pool is permanently murky and other maintenance has clearly been deferred.

Restaurants that may have *very* basic rooms for rent (US$6 to US$12 per night) include Casa Zen, Elvira, Florencio's and Doña Chavela. Tent camping is possible under the *palapas* on Isla de Piedra; English-speaking Victor or Chris at Victor's *palapa* restaurant can advise about security. You'll find it front and center on the beach.

The trailer parks are near the beaches toward the north end of the town, though most of them are not especially attractive for tent camping. The following places offer weekly and monthly discounts.

Mar Rosa Trailer & RV Park (Map p112; ☎ 913-61-87; mar_rosa@mzt.megared.net.mx; Camarón Sábalo 702; tent/trailer US$15/30) Lacks sufficient shade but the location is hard to beat.

La Posta Trailer Park (Map p112; ☎ 983-53-10; Buelna 7; sites US$18; ☐ ☒) This place offers more services (broadband Internet, coin-op laundry and a covered party area) than comfort.

Las Palmas Trailer Park (Map p115; ☎ 913-53-11; Camarón Sábalo 333; sites US$16) Tucked between a couple of high-rises, Las Palmas is semishaded.

MIDRANGE

Not every room in a midrange hotel has air-con, so be sure to ask for it if you want it. The rooms and apartments in this price bracket are a great deal for families.

Best Western Hotel Posada Freeman (Map p114; ☎ 985-60-60, in the US 866-638-8806; http://book .bestwestern.com/bestwestern; Paseo Olas Altas 79; r US$75-95, ste US$120; ☐ ☒ ☒ ☐ ☒) Towering over Old Mazatlán's waterfront, this recently reborn hotel (originally built in 1949) offers character, comfort and grand ocean views. A free daily breakfast buffet, the 'Sky Room' bar and a winning rooftop pool make it an exceptional value. Add tax to rates.

Apartamentos Fiesta (Map p115; www.mazatlan apartments.com; Río Ibis 502; studio/1-/2-bedroom US$32/ 46/60; ☐ ☒ ☒) This place has 12 apartments, all different in size and layout. All have kitchens and pleasing decor and are

AUTHOR'S CHOICE

Royal Dutch B&B (Map p114; ☎ 981-43-96; www.royaldutchcasadesantamaria.com; Constitución 627; d with/without breakfast US$75/45; ☒) Near Plazuela Machado, this cozy inn is a true treasure in a world of impersonal hotels. Inhabited by the same family for four generations, the 18th-century house retains many original windows and ceilings. Choose from three lovingly and tastefully decorated rooms offered by Alicia and Wim, a welcoming Mexican-Dutch couple. Prices include a sumptuous full European breakfast and 5pm tea time.

peacefully located in or near the leafy garden area. English is spoken.

Motel Los Arcos (Map p115; ☎ 913-50-66; www.motel losarcos.com; Playa Gaviotas 214; s/d US$85/95, ste US$105-120; ☐ ☒ ☒) This attractive hotel features good-value suites with kitchenettes and commanding sea views. They're very comfortable, spacious and clean, and the beach is right there.

Los Girasoles (Map p115; ☎ 913-52-88; fax 913-06-86; Gaviotas 709; apt US$60-69; ☐ ☒) In a pleasant residential area, these comfortable, spacious and sparkling-clean apartments share a well-tended pool and are worth the somewhat inconvenient location.

Marley Motel (Map p115; ☎ 913-55-33; motmarley@ mzt.megared.net.mx; Playa Gaviotas 226; 1/2 beds US$75/ 93; ☒ ☒ ☐) This small motel offers pleasant seafront apartments with well-equipped kitchens and – best of all – privileged beach access.

Hotel La Siesta (Map p114; ☎ 981-26-40, 800-711-52-29; www.lasiesta.com.mx in Spanish; Paseo Olas Altas 11 Sur; r US$35, with view US$47; ☐ ☒) La Siesta has a lush courtyard of overgrown plants and creaking stairways covered by worn Astro-Turf. All 51 spacious and tidy rooms have cable TV and a touch of character. Sunset on a private balcony facing the sea is worth the extra bucks.

Hotel Sands Arenas (Map p112; ☎ 982-00-00; www.sandsarenas.com in Spanish; Av del Mar 1910; d/tr US$75/82; ☐ ☒ ☒) If your kids are impressed by swimming pools with a spiraling water slide, they may find happiness here. Rooms are spotless, modern and large and come with satellite TV and refrigerator. Best of all, the beds are firm.

Hotel de Cima (Map p112; ☎ 985-74-00, 800-696-06-00; Av del Mar 48; r from US$34; ☐ ☒ ☒) The paint is peeling in most of the rooms at this wannabe fancy hotel. It's clean and has a tunnel to the beach, but it's only a tiny step up from the budget options. Don't pay a peso more than the semipermanent promotional rate.

Aguamarina Hotel (Map p112; ☎ 981-70-80; www.aguamarina.com; Av del Mar 110; r/ste US$94/128; ☐ ☒ ☒ ☒) This hotel satisfies most picky tourists with very clean, spacious abodes. The rooms aren't fancy but the service is top notch and the pool provides a nice place to sunbathe (in spite of the fact that it fronts busy Av del Mar). Prices drop precipitously during low season.

MAZATLÁN

TOP END

Rooms at Mazatlán's top-end hotels can be reserved quite economically as part of a holiday package – see your travel agent or poke around online.

Hotel Playa Mazatlán (Map p115; ☎ 989-05-55; www.playamazatlan.com.mx; Playa Gaviotas 202; garden view US$95, ocean view US$106-120, ste US$136-196; 🌊 🏊) Run with crisp efficiency, this establishment's 425 well-appointed rooms are popular with organizers of packaged vacations. It's generic but serviceable, and the pools, common areas and sea views are terrific.

Royal Villas Resort (Map p115; ☎ 916-61-61, 800-696-70-00; www.royalvillas.com.mx; Camarón Sábalo 500; ste US$95-$450; 🅿 🌊 🏊 🖥 🌊) The Royal Villas pyramid is better looking on the inside with fabulous rooms that sleep at least four. They all have kitchens and dining rooms, balconies and comfortable set-up. The large terraced sea-view balconies are simply stunning.

Hotel Faro Mazatlán (Map p112; ☎ 913-11-11; Punta de Sábalo s/n; r US$110-195, ste US$220; 🅿 🌊 🏊 🖥 🌊) All gussied up following a recent renovation, this appealing luxury hotel at Marina Mazatlán offers peace and tranquility on a dramatic clifftop setting. There's protected swimming in the cove below, two tennis courts, a gym and a heated pool. The rooms are pleasantly bright and welcoming, with full bathrooms and firm mattresses. An all-inclusive plan is available starting at US$95 per person.

Pueblo Bonito (Map p112; ☎ 914-37-00; www.pueblobonito.com; Camarón Sábalo 2121; ste US$135-265; 🅿 🌊 🏊 🖥 🌊) Overlooking a nearly private stretch of sandy beach, this upscale hotel has an elegant colonial facade, a fantastic pool and all the facilities you'd expect at the top end. Add tax to rates.

Inn at Mazatlán (Map p112; ☎ 913-55-00; www.innatmaz.com; Camarón Sábalo 6291; r US$105-125, ste US$150-240, penthouse US$700; 🌊 🌊 🏊 🌊) The 208 bright, cheerful rooms and suites – all with ocean views, private balconies or terraces and decked out with amenities – are agreeable for longer stays. The pricey three-bedroom, eight-person penthouse makes for royal digs if you're traveling with a group. It's right on the beach. Add tax to rates.

Casa Contenta (Map p115; ☎ 913-49-76; www.casacontenta.com.mx; Playa Gaviotas 224; apt/house US$94/222; 🅿 🏊 🌊) Casa Contenta has just a few intimate apartments, some with partial ocean views. There's a tiny pool and the intimate grounds are nicely tended. An oceanfront six- to eight-person house is also available.

El Cid Mega Resort (Map p112; ☎ 913-33-33; www.elcid.com.mx; Camarón Sábalo s/n; r US$160, ste US$200-530; 🅿 🌊 🏊 🖥 🌊) Decked out in 1980s-style luxury, this 1068-room, 2.9 sq km minicity has it all – seven pools, several dive shops, restaurants, travel agencies, kids' areas, gyms and more. If you want to get away from it all and keep your vacation easy but entertaining, this is the place. It's best to reserve ahead of time to get the best deal – discounts are abundant.

Eating

With all those fishing and shrimping boats heading out to sea every morning, it's no wonder that Mazatlán is famous for fresh seafood. If you love shrimp, you'll be in heaven, but also try *pescado zarandeado*, a delicious charcoal-broiled fish stuffed with onion, tomatoes, peppers and spices. A whole kilo, feeding two people well, usually costs around US$10.

The restaurants in the Zona Dorada cater mainly to the tourist trade. For something better, head to the heart of Old Mazatlán and Plazuela Machado, a delightful space with old Mexican tropical ambience. It's sublime in the evening when music plays, kids frolic, the plaza is softly lit and cool drinks, snacks and meals at outdoor tables help create a very romantic atmosphere.

The most centrally located supermarket is **Marza Pack** (Map p114; Serdán & Flores), but for serious larder replenishment head to the **Mega** (Map p112; La Gran Plaza) superstore.

OLD MAZATLÁN & AROUND
Budget

Beach Burger (Map p114; ☎ 981-43-56; Constitución 513; burgers US$2-4; 🕙 noon-midnight) This southern California–style burger joint is not really on the beach, but on a beautiful night at one of the sidewalk tables you shan't care a whit. The big burgers really stick to the ribs (and they've got those too).

Cenaduría El Túnel (Map p114; Carnaval 1207; mains US$2-5; 🕙 noon-midnight) This atmospheric cheapie has been serving local favorites such as *pozole* (a hearty soup) and smoked marlin enchiladas in a long, narrow dining room for over 50 years.

AUTHOR'S CHOICE

Ambrosia (Map p114; ☎ 985-03-33; Sixto Osuna 26; mains US$4-8; ⏰ 11am-11pm; 🍴) Never want to see another cheese enchilada? Can't remember what you ever saw in that shrimp? This simple vegetarian mecca has one of the largest and most creative menus in town. Choose from many inventive dishes made with wheat gluten or tofu, or treat yourself to something really special, like *nopales rellenos* (cactus stuffed with goat's cheese and covered with a pumpkin sauce). Delicious, crunchy salads, a good wine selection and superb coffee round out the diverse menu. The lunch special (US$7, available from noon to 4pm Monday to Friday) promises a big, nutritious meal at a bargain.

Midrange

Altazor Ars Café (Map p114; ☎ 981-55-59; Constitución 519; mains US$6-8) This popular, romantically lit cultural spot has great light fare all day: bagels, pancakes and marlin ranchero (cooked with tomatoes, chilies and onion) for breakfast, baguette sandwiches and salads for lunch, and generous seafood cocktails and pasta dishes for dinner. There's live music nightly and movies are screened on Wednesday night.

Pedro y Lola (Map p114; ☎ 982-25-89; Carnaval 1303; mains US$7-12; ⏰ 10am-2am) Named after beloved Mexican singers Pedro Infante and Lola Beltrán, this popular sidewalk restaurant-bar serves seafood, burgers and toned-down Mexican favorites. It's good for big groups or romantic couples. Beware: menu prices do not include tax.

Café Pacífico (Map p114; ☎ 981-39-72; Constitución 501; mains US$4-9; ⏰ 10am-2am; 🍴) A bar, café or restaurant, depending on your needs, the Pacífico has been a mainstay on Plazuela Machado for years, thanks to its solid food, stiff drinks and friendly service.

La Tramoya (Map p114; ☎ 985-50-33; Constitución 509; mains US$6-15; ⏰ 11am-2am) Here hearty Mexican meat dishes are set out on spacious sidewalk tables. Feeling adventurous? Try the *carne azteca*, a steak stuffed with *huitlacoche* (corn truffle, a fungus that grows on maize) served on a bed of nopales cactus.

Around the seafront, along Paseo Claussen and Paseo Olas Altas, assorted restaurant-bars specialize in seafood and cold drinks. Most have outdoor tables or open-sided seating areas.

La Copa de Leche (Map p114; ☎ 982-57-53; Paseo Olas Altas 122; mains US$6-16) Harking back to a bygone Mazatlán, this old-timer on the waterfront is prized by the local gentry for its authentic menu, which is considerably more interesting than the restaurant's name ('the Cup of Milk') suggests. You'd do well to try the hearty *sopa de mariscos* (soup with squid, shrimp, fish and a wedge of lime).

Mariscos El Camichín (Map p114; ☎ 985-01-97; Paseo Claussen 97; mains US$6-12; ⏰ 11am-10pm) Facing Playa Norte, this popular patio restaurant serves delicious seafood and *pescado zarandeado* under a cool *palapa* roof. Suave elderly mariachis are known to play in the back room.

Restaurant Los Pelícanos (Map p114; ☎ 982-43-45; cnr Paseo Claussen & Uribe; mains US$4-7; ⏰ 10am-6pm) Basic, fresh and cheap, this small open-air thatched-roof place makes some of the tastiest seviche in Mazatlán. Sea views and breezes make it a grand spot for a sunset beverage.

Puerto Viejo (Map p114; ☎ 982-18-86; Paseo Olas Altas 25; mains US$3-7; ⏰ 11am-11pm Sun-Thu, 11am-1am Fri & Sat) This super casual, inexpensive seafood restaurant and watering hole is popular with locals and expats, especially at sunset and in the evening, when the sea breeze comes through the open sides.

Mariscos La Puntilla (Map p112; ☎ 982-88-77; Flota Playa Sur s/n; mains US$6-13; ⏰ 8am-7pm) Popular with Mexican families for the weekend breakfast buffet (US$8 to US$13), this open-air eatery has a relaxed atmosphere and fantastic *pescado zarandeado*. It's near the Isla de la Piedra ferries, on a small point with a view across the water.

ZONA DORADA & AROUND
Budget

Tomates Verdes (Map p115; ☎ 913-21-36; Laguna 42; mains US$3-5 ⏰ 9am-5pm Mon-Sat) This cozy and unpretentious lunch spot serves flavorful soups such as *nopales con chipotle* (spicy cactus). Also try *pechuga rellena* (stuffed chicken breast).

La Cocina de Ana (Map p115; ☎ 916-31-19; Laguna 49; mains US$3-7; ⏰ noon-4pm Mon-Sat) Ana offers buffet lunch fare such as meatball soup, chili con carne and paella in a small and homey dining area. It's a good antidote to all that fancy tourist junk food.

Pura Vida (Map p115; ☎ 916-58-15; cnr Bugambilias & Laguna; fresh juice US$2-3, snacks US$3-6; ☑ 8am-10:30pm) This healthy mecca squeezes out fresh juices and serves vegetarian fare ranging from buckwheat pancakes and veggie omelets to whole-wheat pizzas and garden burgers. Equipped souls can log on via the wireless network.

Tacos Luna (Map p115; Camarón Sábalo 400 block; tacos US$1; ☑ noon-midnight) This oversized taco stand is the place to chow down local-style.

Midrange

La Casa de Fondue (Map p115; ☎ 913-29-59; Playa Gaviotas 63; mains US$8-12; ☑ 1pm-midnight) If you've been hankering to dip raw meat into hot oil – admit it – this recent arrival makes it possible. In addition to classic dishes such as Roquefort and chocolate fondue, they also serve a Mexican variation made from cheese, tequila and cilantro.

Carlos & Lucia's (Map p112; ☎ 913-56-77; Camarón Sábalo s/n; mains US$8-18; ☑ 8am-11pm Tue-Sun) For something different, try this cheerful Cuban-flavored joint with exemplary *mojitos* and toothsome dishes like *picadillo*, a spaghetti dish with island seasoning, raisins and plenty of garlic.

Miso Sushi (Map p115; ☎ 913-02-99; Las Gaviotas 17; sushi rolls US$3-10; ☑ 1-11pm) Mazatlán has several sushi restaurants, but none as cosmopolitan as this trendy newcomer. It's recommended for its stylish urban decor, good music and superfresh, well-presented fare.

El Olivo (Map p115; ☎ 916-30-23; Las Gaviotas 205; mains US$ 2-10; ☒) This upscale café and deli serves gourmet sandwiches, strong coffee, crêpes, incredible salads, omelets and plenty of vegetarian options.

Top End

Casa Loma (Map p115; ☎ 913-53-98; Las Gaviotas 104; mains US$8-17; ☑ 1:30-10:30pm; ☒) Its devoted clientele ranks this secluded restaurant as one of the very best in Mazatlán. Escape the tourist scene and enjoy a sophisticated and high-quality meal in a homey atmosphere.

Vittore Italian Grill (Map p115; ☎ 986-24-24; Playa Gaviotas 100; mains US$8-22; ☑ noon-midnight) This popular spot is a fine choice for an elegant night out. The service is rather formal and the menu heavy on delicious calorie-rich pasta dishes.

Drinking

Edgar's Bar (Map p114; ☎ 982-72-18; cnr Serdán & Escobedo; ☑ 9am-midnight) For a taste of Old Mazatlán, grab a pint or two at this crusty old bar, a mainstay since 1949. The fan in the corner seems better suited to an airplane hangar, but it really does the trick on a hot day. The bar is adorned with original photographs, has a jukebox, and, according to the sign on the door, welcomes women.

La Tertulia (Map p114; ☎ 983-16-44; Constitución 1406; ☑ closed Sun) This hip and lively spot is decorated exclusively with bullfighting posters and the stuffed heads of vanquished *toros* (bulls).

The following watering holes are ideal for heavy partying and youthful exploits:

Chief Geronimo's (Map p112; ☎ 984-24-77; Av del Mar s/n) Popular with college students for its generous drink specials (and shrimp served by the kilo).

Mangos (Map p115; ☎ 916-00-44; Playa Gaviotas 404) Dancing and drinking in a tropical-themed atmosphere. Gets wild on weekends.

Jungle Juice (Map p115; ☎ 913-33-15; Av de las Garzas 101) A cantina-style place with exotic fruit drinks and a breezy nook upstairs.

Entertainment

Mazatlán has more to offer than fun in the sun. Choose from a range of nightspots, from pulsing discos to thriving gay venues, or take in some culture at the restored Ángela Peralta theater. For a real Mazatlán experience, head to the beach at Isla de la Piedra on Sunday afternoon for live music and dancing at one or more of the *palapa* restaurants, where you'll engage in some hard drinking and hot dancing with a local crowd.

Entertainment listings can be found in the tourist papers *Pacific Pearl* or *Viejo Mazatlán*, available in hotel lobbies around town.

THEATER

Teatro Ángela Peralta (Map p114; ☎ 982-44-46; www.teatroangelaperalta.com in Spanish; Carnaval 47) A night at the Peralta is a must if you want to feel the pulse of Mazatlán's burgeoning culture scene. The lovingly restored 19th-century theater, saved from dereliction and reopened in 1992, has an intimate auditorium with three narrow, stacked balconies. Events of all kinds – movies, concerts, opera, theater and more – are presented. A kiosk on the walkway out front announces current and upcoming events here and at other venues around town. The schedule is most interesting during the annual Sinaloa Fiesta de los Artes (p118).

NIGHTCLUBS

Fiestaland (Map p115; ☎ 984-16-66; Av del Mar s/n) That ostentatious white castle on Punta Camarón, at the southern end of the Zona Dorada, is home to two of Mazatlán's most popular nightspots. The scene starts percolating around 9pm, boiling over after midnight. Valentino (cover US$6 to US$8) draws well-dressed Mexican and foreign tourists to three throbbing dance floors. If the DJ offends, you can escape to Bora Bora (cover US$6), popular for its sand volleyball court, swimming pool, beachside dance floor and lax policy on bar-top dancing.

Joe's Oyster Bar (Map p115; ☎ 983-53-33; Loaiza 100; cover US$5) Just 500m north of Fiestaland, behind Hotel Los Sábalos, this popular spot is fine for a quiet drink until early evening, but it goes ballistic after 11pm when it's packed with college kids dancing on tables, chairs and each other.

El Caracol (Map p112; ☎ 913-33-33; in El Cid Mega Resort, Camarón Sábalo s/n; ☺ closed Mon; ☒) This after-hours favorite attracts a smartly dressed crowd for techno, hip hop, salsa and *cumbia* (Colombian folk music). On select Saturday nights, they stage a messy event called a 'foam party.'

LIVE MUSIC

If you get a chance, try to hear a rousing traditional *banda sinaloense* – a boisterous brass band unique to the state of Sinaloa and especially associated with Mazatlán. Watch for announcements posted around town or broadcast from slow-moving cars with speakers mounted on top. Venues to try:

Coliseo's Disco Forum (Map p112; Av del Mar 406; admission US$6-12; ☒) Big shows at least once a month.

Mikono's Live Music (Map p112; ☎ 984-16-66; Fiestaland, Av del Mar s/n; admission US$6-12; ☒)

SPORTS

Bullfights & Rodeos

Plaza de Toros (Map p112; Buelna) Just inland from the Zona Dorada traffic circle, the bullring hosts *corridas de toros* on Sundays at 4pm from mid-December to Easter; the 'Sábalo-Cocos' bus will drop you there. Tickets for bullfights are available from travel agencies, major hotels, the Bora Bora shop beside Valentino disco (in Fiestaland) and the **Salón Bacanora** (☎ 986-91-55), beside Plaza de Toros.

Charreadas (rodeos) are infrequently held at the Plaza de Toros. Tickets cost about US$4.50 and are available through local travel agents and hotel concierge desks.

Baseball

Mazatlán's baseball team, **Los Venados** (www.venadosdemazatlan.com) makes its home at the large and modern Estadio Teodoro Mariscal (Map p112); the season starts in early October and continues through March. The box office opens at 10am on game days (US$1 to US$9.50 admission).

GAY & LESBIAN MAZATLÁN

Mazatlán's gay scene isn't nearly as effervescent as that in Puerto Vallarta (p92) or Guadalajara, but as long as your expectations are kept in check a reasonably good time is possible.

Forget cruising in Plaza Principal: you'll do much better operating from one of the sidewalk tables at the restaurants lining gorgeous Plazuela Machado. The beach scene is equally low-key. There's no 'official' gay beach, but extra privacy can be enjoyed at some of the secluded beaches on the islands that line the coast. One reader writes to recommend **Isla de las Chivas**, a tiny island near Isla de la Piedra. You should have no problem negotiating passage via a launch operating from the Playa Sur embarcadero, near the ferry terminal.

Bar action is primarily limited to two spots. In the Zona Dorado, **Pepe Toro** (Map p115; ☎ 914-41-76; www.pepetoro.com; Av de las Garzas 18; ☺ Thu-Sun; ☒) is a colorful and lively club attracting a fun-loving mixed crowd. On Saturday night there's a transvestite strip show at 1am. Staff also spin a good mix of danceable grooves. For something more elegant, try **Vitrola's Bar** (Map p114; www.vitrolasbar.com; Frias 1608; ☺ 5pm-1am Tue-Sun), a new gay bar in a beautifully restored building decorated with antiques. It's romantically lit, the bar is brass-edged and overall it's more button down than mesh muscle shirt.

FIESTA MEXICANAS

The Fiesta Mexicana is a corny spectacle providing a reductive view of Mexican culture, but it's all in good fun. For three hours, guests are treated to a floor show of folkloric dance and music, a generous buffet dinner and an open bar. Several of the largest luxury hotels stage these extravaganzas, but the hands-down favorite is the one at **Hotel Playa Mazatlán** (Map p115; ☎ 913-44-44; Playa Gaviotas 202; admission US$26; ☒ 7pm Tue, Thu & Sat; ☒). Call the hotel for reservations or reserve at a travel agency.

CINEMAS

Cinemas Gaviotas (Map p115; ☎ 983-75-45; Camarón Sábalo 218; admission US$4, Wed US$2; ☒) Six screens here show recent releases, including some in English.

Shopping

Most of your tourist shopping needs will be met in the Zona Dorada, where plenty of clothes, pottery, jewelry and craft stores are located. Wander along Loaiza and you're sure to find something to bring home.

Sea Shell City (Map p115; ☎ 913-13-01; Loaiza 407; ☒ 9am-7pm) Packed with an unbelievable assortment of you know what. For something less common, try the shopping complex at Hotel Playa Mazatlán where several high-end shops sell fine crafts including masks from Guerrero, tinware from Oaxaca, and Talavera pottery.

Tianguis de Juárez (Juárez Flea Market; Map p112) Come here for local flavor. Hop on a bus heading east to the, which is held every Sunday starting at 5am; the ride takes 20 minutes. You can't buy snake oil, but you can come close – snakeskins, bootleg CDs, used clothes, housewares, tools, hamsters, taco stands and other Mexican treats are for sale.

Centro Mercado (Map p114; cnr Ocampo & Serdán) Here in Old Mazatlán you can enjoy a classic Mexican market experience, complete with vegetable stands, spice dealers, food stalls and shops selling bargain-priced crafts. In the streets surrounding Plazuela Machado, a growing selection of galleries and boutiques give joy to browsers.

Getting There & Away

AIR

Rafael Buelna International Airport (MZT; Map p112; ☎ 928-04-38), 27km southeast of the Zona Dorada, is served by the following carriers.

Aero California (☎ 913-20-42; airport) Direct service to Los Angeles and Tijuana.
Aeroméxico (Map p115; ☎ 982-34-44; Camarón Sábalo 310) Service to Atlanta, Los Angeles, Phoenix and Tucson, via Mexico City. Direct service to La Paz, Guadalajara and Mexico City.
Alaska Airlines (☎ 913-20-42; airport) Direct service to Los Angeles, San Francisco and Seattle.
America West (☎ 981-11-84; airport) Direct service to Los Angeles and Phoenix.
Mexicana (Map p115; ☎ 982-77-22; Camarón Sábalo, near Las Gaviotas) Service to Chicago, Denver, Los Angeles, Miami and San Antonio, via Mexico City. Direct service to Guadalajara and Mexico City.

BOAT

Baja Ferries (Map p112; ☎ 984-04-71; www.bajaferries.com; adult/child aged 3-11 US$75/38; ☒ ticket office 8am-4pm Mon-Sat, 9am-1pm Sun) operates ferries between Mazatlán and La Paz in Baja California Sur (to the port of Pichilingue, 23km from La Paz). The 15-hour ferry to Pichilingue departs at 4pm (you should be there with ticket in hand at 3pm) on Monday, Wednesday and Friday from the terminal at the southern end of town (off Av Barragan, near the Playa Sur embarcadero). Tickets are sold from two days in advance until the morning of departure. Passage for vehicles (US$120/US$200/US$570 for a motorcycle/car/trailer up to 9m) and cabins (US$25 to US$75) is available.

BUS

The **Central de Autobuses** (main bus station; Map p112; Av de los Deportes, off Ejército Méxicano) is three blocks inland from the northern end of Playa Norte. It's a full service station with a tourist module, phone offices, authorized taxi stands and left-luggage service. All bus lines operate from separate halls in the main terminal. Local buses to small towns nearby (eg Copala, Rosario) operate from a smaller terminal, behind the main terminal. There are several daily long-distance services:
Culiacan (US$13, 2½hr, 24 1st-class)
Durango (US$39, 7hr, 6 1st-class)
Guadalajara (US$31, 9hr, 16 2nd-class; US$35-45, 8hr, 9 1st-class)
Manzanillo (US$56, 12hr, 1 1st-class)
Mexico City (US$16, 18hr, 13 2nd-class; US$81-95, 8hr, 12 1st-class) To Terminal Norte.
Monterrey (US$86, 16hr, 3 1st-class)
Puerto Vallarta (US$33, 7hr, 1 1st-class) Or take a bus to Tepic, where buses depart frequently for Puerto Vallarta.

Tepic (US$15, 4½hr, 16 1st-class)
Tijuana (US$76, 28hr, 16 2nd-class; US$88, 26hr, 3 1st-class)

To get to San Blas (290km), go first to Tepic then get a bus from there.

Getting Around

TO/FROM THE AIRPORT
Colectivo (shared) vans and a bus operate from the airport to town, but not from town to the airport. Taxis are about US$20 to US$25.

BUS
Local buses run daily from 6am to 10:30pm. A trip on the regular white buses costs US$0.45, while Urban Plus air-con green buses cost US$0.80. A useful route for visitors is the Sábalo–Centro, which travels from the Centro Mercado (Map p114) in the center to Playa Norte via Juárez, then north on Av del Mar to the Zona Dorada and further north on Camarón Sábalo. Another is Playa Sur, which travels south along Ejército Méxicano near the bus station and through the city center, passing the market, then to the ferry terminal and El Faro.

To get into the center of Mazatlán from the bus terminal, go to Ejército Méxicano and catch any bus going south (to your right if the bus terminal is behind you). Alternatively, you can walk 500m from the bus station to the beach and take a 'Sábalo–Centro' bus heading south (left) to the center.

BICYCLE
Kelly's Bike Rentals (Map p115; ☎ 914-11-87; Camarón Sábalo 204; ☒ 10am-2pm & 4:30-8pm Mon- Sat) rents out mountain bikes for US$3.50/US$17 per hour/day.

CAR & MOTORCYCLE
Shop around for the best rates, which begin at US$60 per day during the high season. There are several rental agencies in town:
Alamo (Map p115; ☎ 913-10-10; Camarón Sábalo 410)
Budget (Map p115; ☎ 913-20-00; Camarón Sábalo 402)
Hertz (Map p115; ☎ 913-60-60; Camarón Sábalo 314)

Various companies on Camarón Sábalo in the Zona Dorada rent out motor scooters – you'll see the bikes lined up beside the road. Prices are somewhat negotiable, ranging from US$12 per hour to US$50 per day.

You need a driver's license to hire one; a car license from any country will do.

PULMONÍA & TAXI
Mazatlán has a special type of taxi called a *pulmonía*, a small open-air vehicle similar to a golf cart – usually a modified VW. There are also regular red-and-white taxis and green-and-white taxis called 'ecotaxis' that have rates from US$2.50 to US$5 for trips around town. *Pulmonías* can be slightly cheaper (or much more expensive) depending on your bargaining skills, time of day and whether there is a cruise ship in port or not.

AROUND MAZATLÁN

Several small, picturesque colonial towns in the Sierra Madre foothills make pleasant day trips from Mazatlán. Note that if you visit on a Sunday, many things will be shut down.

Getting There & Away
Buses to all these places depart from the small bus terminal at the rear of the main bus station in Mazatlán.
Concordia (US$2, 1½hr, every 15min 6am-6pm)
Copala (US$3, 2hr, 3 1st-class)
Cosalá (US$9, 3hr, 2 2nd-class)
Rosario (US$3, 1½hr, hourly 6am-6pm) Take an 'Escuinapa' bus, or any heading south on Hwy 15.

Tours to these spots are available as well (see p117).

CONCORDIA
Founded in 1565, Concordia has an 18th-century church with a baroque facade, elaborately decorated columns, a daily market around it, and hot mineral springs nearby. The village is known for its manufacture of high-quality pottery and hand-carved furniture. It's about a 45-minute drive east of Mazatlán; head southeast on Hwy 15 for 20km to Villa Unión, turn inland on Hwy 40 (the highway to Durango) and go another 20km.

COPALA
Also founded in 1565, the charming little town of Copala, 25km past Concordia on Hwy 40, was one of Mexico's first mining

---

DETOUR: TEACAPÁN

Travelers grown weary of the bright lights of the city are increasingly drawn to this tiny fishing village at the tip of an isolated peninsula, 126km to the south of Mazatlán at the border of Nayarit and Sinaloa. Surrounded by a rich mangrove ecosystem and in close proximity to several pristine beaches, Teacapán is prime territory for escape artists and nature buffs.

The surrounding estuaries are replete with egrets, ducks and herons. Boating excursions into the mangrove swamps can be arranged with local fishermen at Boca de Teacapán, the natural marina. Local guide Mariano Azuela (☎ 954-53-86) offers trips to **Isla de Pajaros** (Map p112), an epic bird-watching spot, and to local archaeological sites. Nearby beaches include La Tambora, with a smattering of *palapa* restaurants and camping opportunities, and the even more secluded spots Las Cabras, Las Lupitas and Los Angeles.

Villas Maria Fernanda (☎ 954-53-93; www.villasmariafernanda.com; r/ste/house US$36-48/65/160; 🞫 🞰) is an attractive small resort offering spacious, comfortable rooms, suites with kitchens and a house for up to 10 people. Kids love the cheerful pool with water slide.

Restaurant & Bungalows Señor Wayne (☎ 954-56-95; r/cabaña US$20/30; 🞫), an immaculate family-run operation, has seven clean rooms and two economical *palapa*-roofed cabanas. Also on the premises is Teacapán's best restaurant (mains US$6 to US$12, restaurant open 8am to 8pm), serving big breakfasts, steaks and seafood.

To get there from Mazatlán's 2nd-class bus terminal (adjacent to the Central de Autobuses), catch one of the frequent buses to Escuinapa (US$4, 2½ hours) and transfer there for Teacapán (US$3, one hour).

---

towns. It has a colonial church (1748), red-tiled houses and a tiny museum, and local urchins sell donkey rides while pigs and chickens roam the cobbled streets. There are a couple of hotels; try the quaint **Copala Butter Company** (☎ 985-42-25; r US$30) if you decide to spend the night, though you can visit both Concordia and Copala in a day – even on public transport. Take an *auriga* (transport pickup), between the two towns (US$2, 30 minutes).

ROSARIO

Another colonial mining town, Rosario (65km southeast of Mazatlán on Hwy 15) was founded in 1655. Its most famous feature is the gold-leaf altar in its church Nuestra Señora del Rosario.

COSALÁ

In the mountains north of Mazatlán, Cosalá is a beautiful colonial mining village dating from 1550. It features a 17th-century church, an even older chapel, a historical and mining museum in a colonial mansion on the leafy plaza, and four hotels. Attractions nearby include **Vado Hondo,** a *balneario* (bathing resort) with a large natural swimming pool and three waterfalls, 15km from town; **La Gruta México**, a large cave 18km from town; and the **Presa El Comedero** reservoir, 20km from town, with hired rowboats for fishing.

To get to Cosalá, head northwest on Hwy 15 for 113km to the turnoff (opposite the turnoff for La Cruz de Elota on the coast) and then go about 45km up into the mountains. If taking the direct bus, consider staying the night, since bus schedules are such that you only get one hour in town before needing to head back the same day (but check and make sure this is still the case). The more adventurous can always visit Cosalá in one day by taking any bus heading to the coast highway, then another back to Mazatlán.

Nayarit

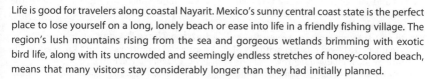

Life is good for travelers along coastal Nayarit. Mexico's sunny central coast state is the perfect place to lose yourself on a long, lonely beach or ease into life in a friendly fishing village. The region's lush mountains rising from the sea and gorgeous wetlands brimming with exotic bird life, along with its uncrowded and seemingly endless stretches of honey-colored beach, means that many visitors stay considerably longer than they had initially planned.

If it's action and adventure you're after, you'll find it in San Blas, where small boats leave daily for the inner reaches of an extensive jungle estuary. Or perhaps you seek to test yourself on the long swells curling into Bahía de Matanchén. Snorkelers find underwater satisfaction at Isla Islote, the humpback island rising from the sea near Rincón de Guayabitos. Hikers and birdwatchers get what they came for in the exceptionally scenic coastal town of Chacala.

It's also a region awash in history and culture. In Mexcaltitán, believed by many to be the mythical Aztlán, you can learn about the peregrinations of Aztec people prior to the founding of Tenochtitlán (modern Mexico City), and imagine what life was like in ancient Mexico. The capital of Nayarit, inland Tepic, is an unpretentious city with a number of museums and a pleasant center where the Huichol – one of a few indigenous peoples in Nayarit – live.

Public transportation is straightforward, getting you to most destinations without much hassle. In several small beach resorts, featuring wholesome family-run restaurants and hotels, you can enjoy a beach vacation free of the ostentatious hullabaloo of the major resort centers. All in all, Nayarit is pretty neat.

NAYARIT

HIGHLIGHTS

- Boating along mangrove jungles and spotting sunning birds and crocodiles from **San Blas** (p132)
- Sampling the *tamales camarón* (shrimp tamales) in the ancient shrimp-fishing village of **Mexcaltitán** (p130)
- Watching turtle hatchlings enter the sea for the first time in **Playa San Francisco** (p143)
- Beach-bumming and sharpening your surfing skills in **Sayulita** (p144)
- Languishing on one of the region's loveliest beaches in **Chacala** (p137)

Mexcaltitán ★
San Blas ★
★ Chacala
Playa San Francisco ★
★ Sayulita

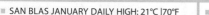

SAN BLAS JANUARY DAILY HIGH: 21°C |70°F   SAN BLAS JULY DAILY HIGH: 30°C | 86°F

SANTIAGO IXCUINTLA

☎ 323 / pop 18,000

Despite its charming plaza and impressive gazebo held aloft by eight busty iron muses, Santiago Ixcuintla, sitting inland about 230km southeast of Mazatlán, is mainly of interest as the jumping-off point for the historic island village of Mexcaltitán de Uribe (usually referred to as Mexcaltitán).

The **tourist office** (☎ 235-05-95; ☼ 9am-3pm Mon-Fri) and Internet services are on the *zócalo* (main plaza), while banks with ATMs and money exchange are nearby.

Centro Huichol (☎ 235-11-71; Calle 20 de Noviembre 452 & Constitución; ☼ 10am-7pm Mon-Sat) is a handicrafts center where indigenous Huichol make their distinctive arts and crafts; you'll find it 10 blocks northeast of the city center on the road to Mexcaltitán. Opening hours are erratic, so if the door is shuttered, give it a vigorous knocking and someone usually will open it. There's a *mariscos* (seafood) restaurant next door, making for a pleasant lunch stop on the way to Mexcaltitán.

A couple of hotels are near the market. The only one providing a measure of decency is **Hotel Casino Plaza** (☎ 235-08-50; Ocampo 40; s/d/tr US$26/30/34; P ✷), which has dark, modern rooms with TV. The hotel's surprisingly good Los Vitrales restaurant (with mains costing US$3 to US$8) serves local specialties in a modern, air-conditioned space. There's a market with cheap food stalls two blocks north of the *zócalo*.

Getting There & Away

Santiago Ixcuintla is about 8km west of the Hwy 15 *crucero* (turnoff).

Buses from Tepic (US$3, 1½hr, Elite) leave frequently for Santiago Ixcuintla. You can take a Tepic, Guadalajara or San Blas bus and be let off at Las Peñas, a highway town about 10km before the Santiago Ixcuintla *crucero*; from here there are frequent buses (US$1.50), *taxis colectivos* (shared taxis; US$1.75) or taxis (US$9). Avoid going all the way to the *crucero* and waiting there for a bus to take you in; at night it's not a safe place to hang around.

Three bus lines operate in town, each within a block of each other and about two

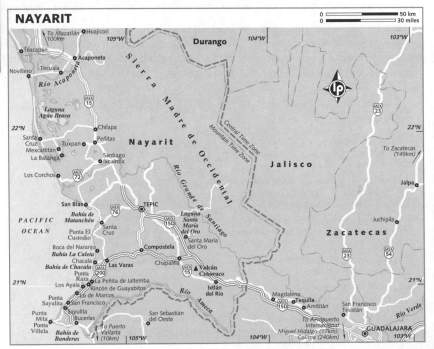

NAYARIT

AZTEC LAUNCH PAD?

A visit to ancient Mexcaltitán is undeniably evocative of the distant past. But was it really once Aztlán, the mythical ancestral homeland of the Aztecs?

The local version of the town's origins contends that the Aztecs left here around 1091 to begin the generations-long migration that eventually led them to Tenochtitlán (modern Mexico City) around 1325. Proponents point to the striking similarities between the cruciform design of Mexcaltitán's streets to the urban layout of early Tenochtitlán. Also cited is a pre-Hispanic bas-relief in stone found in the area – now on display in the Museo Regional de Nayarit (p135) in Tepic – depicting a heron clutching a snake, an allusion to the sign the Aztecs hoped to find in the promised land. And then there are the chronicles of reports by Aztecs to Spanish missionaries, including one in which it was related that the ancestors 'lived in that beautiful happy place they called Aztlán, where they were surrounded by all kinds of ducks, herons, marine crows and water hens.' Indeed, the name Aztlán means 'place of egrets' – and there are certainly plenty of those milling about.

But not everyone's so sure. Competing theories place Aztlán in the Four Corners area of the United States, in Wisconsin and even Alaska. No serious archaeological study has ever been undertaken in Mexcaltitán according to Jesus Jauregui, an expert based in western Mexico at the Instituto Nacional de Antropología y Historia. 'Aztlán is a mythical place, not a historical one.'

Local opinion goes both ways. One fisherman who had considered the facts as displayed at the town's museum wasn't buying it. 'Why would anyone leave?' he asked.

blocks west of the *zócalo* near the intersection of Avs Zaragoza and 20 de Noviembre. Various long-distance buses leave daily from Santiago:

Mazatlán (US$15, 4hr, 5 Rapido del Sur & 1 Pacífico)
Guadalajara (US$18, 5hr, 5 Norte de Sonora)
Puerto Vallarta (US$14, 4½hr, 3 Norte de Sonora)
San Blas (US$3.50, 1½hr, 3 Norte de Sonora)
Tepic (US$3, 1½hr, 32 Norte de Sonora)

Combis (minibuses) from Santiago Ixcuintla to La Batanga (the departure point for boats to Mexcaltitán) depart from the Terminal de Taxis Foráneos, on Juárez at Hidalgo, three blocks north of the market, at 7am, 10am, noon and 3pm. The trip costs US$1.80. Transportes del Pacífico also runs a 2nd-class bus to La Batanga daily at 4pm (US$1.50, one hour, 37km).

MEXCALTITÁN

☎ 319 / pop 2000

Carrying on much as it always has, this small, safe and friendly shrimp-fishing hamlet has an intriguing history that stirs the imagination. Visitors arrive at the ancient island village via a 15-minute *lancha* (fast, open, outboard boat) ride through mangrove channels full of fish, shrimp and the birds that eat them. A tremendous quantity of *camarones* (shrimp) is gathered on the island each day to be tallied and distributed; you'll

see it everywhere spread out on the sidewalk, gathered in buckets or sold in tamales from a wheelbarrow.

Tourism has scarcely touched Mexcaltitán, though it does have pleasant waterside restaurants and a small museum. Sometimes referred to as the 'Venice of Mexico,' it is surrounded completely by the Laguna Grande de Mexcaltitán, and the dirt streets are sometimes covered with water after heavy rains. All travel is then done in canoes. These days, however, dikes far upstream in Durango state control water flow and flooding is rare.

Many believe the island to be the site of the mythical Aztlán (meaning 'place of egrets'), the original homeland of the Aztec people. Some academics, however, are skeptical of this story, and there has never been a serious archaeological study of the town. Being here is considerably more fun if you believe the story.

At dusk the streets fill with children and by 8pm it's as if they own the place. In the plaza a sound system blares from the periphery as teenagers dance to Mexican hip-hop and Eminem. Elsewhere, women play *lotería*, a game remotely resembling bingo.

Orientation & Information

Mexcaltitán is delightfully free of cars, filled instead with bicycles and handcarts. The main street rings the center of the island, which is a small oval, about 350m from east to west, 400m from north to south. The central *zócalo* has a church on its east side, and the museum on its north side. The hotel is a block behind the museum.

All the telephones on the island go through one operator; look for the *'larga distancia'* (long distance) sign one block west of the *zócalo*. From outside the island, phone the **switchboard** (☎ 232-02-11) and ask for the extension you want.

Sights & Activities

The **Museo Aztlán del Origen** (admission US$0.50; ⏰ 9am-2pm & 4-7pm), on the northern side of the plaza, is small but enchanting. Among the exhibits are many interesting ancient objects and a reproduction of a fascinating long scroll, the Códice Ruturini, telling the story of the peregrinations of the Aztec people, with notes in Spanish. Rendered in a vaguely cartoonish style, the scroll reminds one of an outtake from *The Simpsons*.

You can arrange for **boat trips** (about US$5 per hour) on the lagoon for bird-watching, fishing and sightseeing – every family has one or more boats.

Festivals & Events

Semana Santa (Holy Week) is celebrated in a big way here. On Good Friday everyone takes to the streets and the normally placid town comes to life. After a life-size crucifix is carried through the streets, sound systems are fired up and the central plaza becomes party central until dawn. For the **Fiesta de San Pedro Apóstol**, celebrating the patron saint of fishing and held on June 29, statues of Sts Peter and Paul are taken out into the lagoon in decorated *lanchas* for the blessing of the waters. Festivities start around June 20, leading up to the big day.

Sleeping & Eating

Hotel Ruta Azteca (☎ 232-02-11, ext 128; Venecia 5; s/d/tr US$15/20/30) The best, worst and only hotel in town. Rooms are simple and marginally clean; insist on one in the back with a view of the lagoon.

The *tamales camarón* (US0.$50) sold from a wheelbarrow on the streets in the morning are a local culinary highlight. On the east shore, accessible by a rickety wooden walkway, **Restaurant Alberca** (mains US$4-6; ⏰ 7am-6pm) has a great lagoon view

and a menu completely devoted to shrimp. Don't leave town without trying local specialty *albóndigas de camarón*, battered and fried shrimp balls served in a savory broth.

Getting There & Away

From Santiago Ixcuintla (p128), take a *combi* or bus to La Batanga, a small wharf from which small boats depart for Mexcaltitán. The arrival and departure times of the *lanchas colectivas* are coordinated with the bus schedule. The boat journey takes 15 minutes and costs US$0.80 per person. If you miss the *lancha colectiva,* you can hire a private one for US$5 between 8am and 7pm.

SAN BLAS

☎ 323 / pop 9000

The tranquil fishing village of San Blas, 70km northwest of Tepic, was an important Spanish port from the late 16th to the 19th centuries. The Spanish built a fortress here to protect their *naos* (trading galleons) from marauding British and French pirates. Later, Romantic poet Longfellow saw fit to honor the town and its bells in a long poem, completed just days before he keeled over. Visitors come to enjoy isolated beaches, fine surfing, abundant birdlife and tropical jungle reached by riverboats. A smattering of lively bars and restaurants and an amiable beach scene add to the mix, making for an enjoyable stay.

The bad news: at dusk there's a pernicious proliferation of *jejenes* (sand flies), tiny gnatlike insects with huge appetites for human flesh. Carry insect repellent and check the screens in your hotel room. (If you find these warnings exaggerated, count yourself lucky.)

Orientation

San Blas sits on a tongue of land situated between Estuario El Pozo and Estuario San Cristóbal, with Playa El Borrego on the Pacific Ocean on the southern side. A 36km paved road connects San Blas with Hwy 15, the Tepic–Mazatlán road. This road goes through town as Juárez, the town's main east–west street. At the small *zócalo* it crosses Batallón de San Blas (Batallón for short), the main north–south street, which heads south to the beach.

Information

Banamex (Juárez s/n) Has an ATM.

Alfa y Omega (Canalizo 194; per hr US$1; ☉ 9am-11pm Mon-Sat, noon-11pm Sun) Speedy Internet access.

Health Clinic (☎ 285-0232; ☉ 9am-4pm Mon-Sat).

Post office (cnr Sonora & Echeverría)

Caseta Telefónica (☎ 285-12-05; Canalizo 5; ☉ 9am-9pm)

Tourist office (☎ 285-00-05, 285-03-81; Casa de Gobierno; ☉ 9am-3pm Mon-Fri) On the east side of the *zócalo*, this basic tourist office has a few maps and brochures about the area and the state of Nayarit.

Sights & Activities

Although the beaches dominate here, everyone loves the boat tours through the estuaries where birds and wildlife abound.

From December to May, **Diving Beyond Adventures** (☎ 285-12-81, in the US 415-331-7925; www.divingbeyond.com; Juárez 187b) organizes and leads affordable adventure experiences, including diving, kayaking, hiking, birdwatching, whale-watching, jungle boat tours, and visiting historical sites. It uses local guides and practices sound low-impact environmental tours. Its signature – and most expensive – trip is a three-day diving, fishing and camping extravaganza to Isla Isabel. It costs US$715 per boat for up to four guests, and an additional US$30 per tank for diving (arrive with proof of diving certification if you plan to scuba dive). It also rents kayaks (US$20 for four hours).

BOAT TRIPS

A boat trip through the jungle to the fresh-water spring of **La Tovara** is a real San Blas highlight. Small boats (maximum 13 passengers) depart from the embarcadero. Boats go up Estuario San Cristóbal to the spring, passing thick jungle vegetation and mangroves rife with exotic birds. The limpid waters of Tovara are gorgeous to behold, but resist taking a dip and instead gaze at the scene from the adjacent restaurant: a swimmer was attacked by a crocodile here in early 2006.

For a few dollars more, you can extend the trip from La Tovara to the **Cocodrilario** (crocodile nursery), where reptiles are reared in captivity for later release in the wild. For a group of up to four people, it costs US$32 to go to La Tovara (3½ hours) and US$40 to the Cocodrilario (four hours); it costs US$8 to US$10 for each extra person. Shorter boat trips to La Tovara can be made from near Matanchén village, further up the river; they take an hour less and are a few dollars cheaper.

The mangrove ecosystem surrounding San Blas is a sanctuary for 300 species of birds – you don't have to be a birder to get a thrill from an encounter with the flamingo-like roseate spoonbill. A five-hour bird-watching trip up the Estuario San Cristóbal to the **Santuario de Aves** (Bird Sanctuary) can be arranged at La Tovara embarcadero by the bridge; the cost is US$60 for up to four people.

Other boat trips depart from a landing on Estuario El Pozo. They include a trip to **Piedra Blanca** (two hours, US$40) to visit a statue of the Virgin; to the **Isla del Rey** peninsula, just across from San Blas (US$1); and to **Playa del Rey**, a 20km beach on the other side of Isla del Rey. From here you can also hire boatmen to take you on bird-watching excursions for about US$15 per hour.

Boatmen also offer fishing and sightseeing trips from small boats docked on Campeche on the edge of the estuary. The going rate is US$25 per hour for groups of up to eight people.

You can make an interesting trip further afield to **Isla Isabel**, also called Isla María Isabelita, three hours northwest of San Blas by boat; trips cost US$260 for up to five people. Permission from the port captain is required to visit the island, and a couple of days is needed to take it in. Designated a national park, the island is a bird-watcher's paradise, with colonies of many species and a volcanic crater lake. There are no facilities, so you need to be prepared for self-sufficient camping. For trips to Isla Isabel, ask at the boat landing on Estuario El Pozo or, for an inclusive tour, consult with Diving Beyond Adventures.

BEACHES

The beach closest to town is **Playa El Borrego**, at the end of Azueta. Broad waves roll in with bravado. Stoner's (below) rents out surf-boards, boogie boards and bikes. Swimming can be treacherous in some conditions – beware of rip currents and heed locals' warnings.

The best beaches are southeast of town around Bahía de Matanchén, starting with **Playa Las Islitas**, 7km from San Blas. To get there, take the road toward Hwy 15, and turn off to the right after about 4km. This paved road goes east past the village of Matanchén, where a dirt road goes south to Playa Las Islitas. The road continues on to follow 8km of wonderfully isolated beach. Further on, **Playa Los Cocos** and **Playa Miramar**, also popular for surfing, have *palapas* (thatched-roof shelters) under which you can lounge and drink fresh coconut milk.

SURFING

With many beach and point breaks, San Blas is the place where many beginner and intermediate surfers choose to hone their skills. The season starts in May, but the waves are fairly mellow until September and October when the south swell brings amazingly long waves curling into **Bahía de Matanchén**. Surf spots include El Borrego, Second Jetty, La Puntilla, Stoner's, Las Islitas and El Mosco.

At Playa El Borrego, **Stoner's Surf Camp** (☎ 285-0444; www.stonerssurfcamp.com; surfboard/boogie-board rental per hr US$3/2, per day US$10/8, lessons per hr US$15) is the nexus of the scene. National long-board champion 'Pompis' Cano gives lessons and holds court under the *palapa*. There are also four rustic cabins (US$10 to US$15), space to camp (US$3) and tent rentals (US$2).

CERRO DE LA CONTADURÍA

Just west of the bridge over Estuario San Cristóbal, the road passes the Cerro de la

Contaduría. Climb up the hill and see the ruins of the 18th-century Spanish **La Contaduría Fort** and **Templo de la Virgen del Rosario** (admission US$0.70); there's a fine view from the top.

Festivals & Events

Every year on January 31 the anniversary of the death of **Father José María Mercado** is commemorated with a parade, a march by the Mexican navy and fireworks in the *zócalo*. Mercado lived in San Blas in the early 19th century and helped Miguel Hidalgo y Costilla (p30) with the independence movement by sending him a set of old Spanish cannons from the village.

On February 3 festivities for **San Blas**, the town's patron saint, are an extension of those begun on January 31, with traditional dance and musical performances.

Sleeping

San Blas has plenty of economical guesthouses and one noteworthy fine hotel. In local parlance, a 'bungalow' sleeps more than two and includes a kitchen.

BUDGET

Hotel Ranchero (☎ 285-08-92; Batallón 102; r with/ without bathroom US$15/10) Basic and friendly, this popular place has eight rooms and a communal kitchen for guests.

Motel Morelos (Batallón 108; r US$15-20) Morelos is stark but homey, with rooms around a central courtyard. An old pelican has made the place home for over a decade, ever since the proprietors nursed him back to health following an injury. He's cute but decidedly not cuddly.

Hotel Bucanero (☎ 285-01-01; Juárez 75; s/d/ tr US$15/25/35; **P** **&**) This hotel has seen better days, but it still sparkles with old, salty character. The dark, rough-around-the-edges rooms are set around a big leafy courtyard. There's a lively weekend disco next door.

Tent campers should be prepared for the swarms of insects, especially at sunset. There are a couple of options:

Trailer Park Los Cocos (☎ 285-00-55; Azueta s/n; tent/RV sites US$8/13) Pleasant and grassy with just enough trees.

Playa Amor Campground (Playa Los Cocos; tent/RV sites US$8/14) A 15-minute drive east of town. It's attractive and on the beachfront, with sunset views and few mosquitoes.

MIDRANGE & TOP END

Hotel Hacienda Flamingos (☎ 285-09-30; www .sanblas.com.mx; Juárez 105; s/d US$68/85, ste US$76-105; **&** **&**) This superbly restored colonial gem provides the classiest accommodations in town. All of the spacious rooms around the quaint courtyard have been tastefully modernized with coffeemakers and TVs. The swimming pool is surrounded by a pleasant, green garden.

Casa Roxanna Bungalows (☎ 285-05-73; El Rey 1; www.casaroxanna.com; bungalows US$50-60; **&** **&**) This elegant, gay-friendly haven offers five capacious bungalows and a long pool on spacious manicured grounds. English is spoken and discounts are offered for longer stays.

Bungalows Conny (☎ 285-09-86; www.bungalows conny.com; Chiapas 26; r US$35, bungalow US$45-50; **&** **&**) In a quiet part of a quiet town, this new place with only four units rests easy with modern rooms and bungalows. The largest is fresh and feels like a small apartment, with a separate bedroom and large kitchen.

Hotel Garza Canela (☎ 285-01-12; www.garza canela.com; Paredes 106 Sur; s/d US$94/120, ste US$134-164; **P** **&** **&**) Modern, professional and comfortable, the Garza Canela is a reliable top-end choice. Standard rooms are spacious and decorated in colonial style, while the suites are enormous and contemporary, with frosted glass and marble floors. It's also home to Restaurant El Delfín, the best restaurant and gift shop in town.

Hotel Posada del Rey (☎ 285-01-23; www.sanblas mexico.com/posadadelrey; Campeche 10; d/tr/ste US$35/ 40/45; **&** **&** **&**) This family-run business with a low-key but friendly atmosphere has clean, modern rooms surrounding a cozy courtyard with a swimming pool. It has a small bar and restaurant in the high season.

Eating

San Blas is a casual town with casual restaurants, all serving fresh seafood. On the beach, *palapa* restaurants are notable for delicious fish cooked in the *campechano* style, with tomatoes, onion, octopus, shrimp and oyster. The cheapest eats can be found at the local *mercado* (market) on Sonora and Batallón.

Restaurant El Delfín (☎ 285-01-12; Paredes 106 Sur; mains US$9-18; **&**) At Hotel Garza Canela, this restaurant is the best choice for fine dining, serving an impressive array of rich, gourmet dishes such as anise-accented fish or cumin-peppered shrimp. Desserts are magnificent and the international wines reasonably priced.

Restaurant La Isla (☎ 285-04-07; cnr Paredes & Mercado; mains US$5-8; ☒ 2-9pm Tue-Sun; ☒) La Isla grills near-perfect seafood, but it's also worth coming in just to check out the over-done seashell decor – it's so tacky it's cool.

La Familia (☎ 285-02-58; Batallón 16; mains US$4-8) Decorated in a bottom-of-the-sea spirit, this family restaurant asks moderate prices for delicious seafood and Mexican dishes.

Wala Wala (☎ 285-08-63; Juárez 94; mains $6-15; ☒ closed Sun) This cheerfully decorated restaurant serves inexpensive, tasty, home-style meals. It's mostly basic Mexican and pasta with a few specialties such as lobster and *pollo con naranja* (chicken with orange).

If you're looking to eat where the waves crash, head to Playa El Borrego, where *palapas* line the beach. **Caballito del Mar** (☎ 285-04-07; Playa El Borrego; mains US$8-15) cooks up remarkably sophisticated seafood dishes and *pescado zarandeado* (filleted fish marinated with spices and herbs and grilled). At Stoner's Surf Camp, **Playa Azul** (☎ 285-04-44; Playa El Borrego; mains US$3.50-5.50) is a traveler hangout with good music, lots of hammocks and well-prepared fare (including vegetarian).

Drinking & Entertainment

The nightlife in San Blas is unexciting but pleasant enough, with a good selection of low-key watering holes to choose from. Most open up at dusk and close late, which means midnight in this town.

San Blas Social Club (cnr Juárez & Canalizo) Jazz records line the wall; pick one out and the gentleman bartender will slap it on. There's live music Friday and Saturday, movies every Wednesday, and good strong coffee every morning.

Mike's Place (Juárez 36) This lively bar primes the dance floor with a good mix of blues and rock music. There's live music Friday to Sunday.

El Cocodrilo (Juárez 6) This old favorite still attracts gringos in the evening, using well-priced cocktails as bait.

Australia Bar (Juárez 34) The long bar of this upstairs pool room is dotted with cool youths and grungy foreigners throwing drinks back.

Getting There & Around

The little **bus station** (cnr Sinaloa & Canalizo) is served by Norte de Sonora and Estrella Blanca 2nd-class buses. For many destinations to the south and east, it may be quicker to go to Tepic first. For Mazatlán, transfer in Tepic. There are daily departures to various destinations:

Guadalajara (US$18, 5hr, 1 1st-class, 7am)
Puerto Vallarta (US$11, 3½hr, 4 1st-class)
Santiago Ixcuintla (US$3.50, 1hr, frequent 2nd-class)
Tepic (US$4.25, 1hr, 2nd-class hourly 6am-8pm)

Second-class buses also depart from the corner of Sinaloa and Paredes several times a day, serving all the villages and beaches on Bahía de Matanchén.

Taxis line up along the southern edge of the *zócalo* and will take you around town and to nearby beaches – a good option with two or more people. A trip to Playa El Borrego will set you back US$4. Rent bicycles from **Wala Wala** (☎ 285-08-63; Juárez 94; per hr/day US$1.50/5) or **Stoner's Surf Camp** (☎ 285-0444; per day US$6).

TEPIC

☎ 311 / pop 266,000 / elevation 920m

Founded by the nephew of Hernán Cortés in 1524, Tepic is an old city even by Mexican standards. Today the capital of Nayarit is a forward-thinking, predominantly middle-class place, retaining few vestiges of its distant past. Many travelers pass through the outskirts of town without looking back, but those that take a day to nose around may come to appreciate the provincial hustle and bustle playing out on its narrow streets. Indigenous Huichol are often seen here, wearing their colorful traditional clothing, and Huichol artwork is sold on the street and in several shops. Adding interest are an imposing neo-Gothic cathedral and several interesting museums.

Orientation

Plaza Principal, with the large cathedral at the eastern end, is the heart of the city. Av México, the city's main street, runs south from the cathedral to Plaza Constituyentes, past banks, restaurants, the state museum and other places of interest. The bus station is on the southeastern side of the city, about 2km from Plaza Principal, with plenty of buses serving the center. Peripheral roads

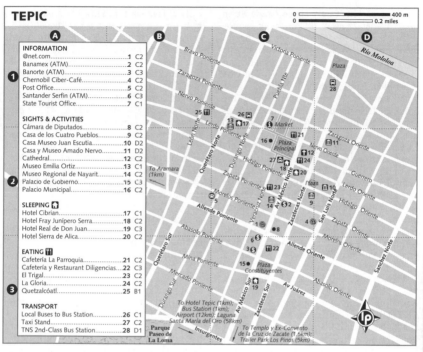

TEPIC

INFORMATION
@net.com	**1** C2
Banamex (ATM)	**2** C2
Banorte (ATM)	**3** C3
Chernobil Ciber-Café	**4** C2
Post Office	**5** C2
Santander Serfin (ATM)	**6** C3
State Tourist Office	**7** C1

SIGHTS & ACTIVITIES
Cámara de Diputados	**8** C2
Casa de los Cuatro Pueblos	**9** C2
Casa Museo Juan Escutia	**10** D2
Casa y Museo Amado Nervo	**11** D2
Cathedral	**12** C2
Museo Emilia Ortiz	**13** C1
Museo Regional de Nayarit	**14** C2
Palacio de Gobierno	**15** C2
Palacio Municipal	**16** C2

SLEEPING
Hotel Cibrian	**17** C1
Hotel Fray Junípero Serra	**18** C2
Hotel Real de Don Juan	**19** C3
Hotel Sierra de Alica	**20** C2

EATING
Cafetería La Parroquia	**21** C2
Cafetería y Restaurant Diligencias	**22** C3
El Trigal	**23** C2
La Gloria	**24** C2
Quetzalcóatl	**25** B1

TRANSPORT
Local Buses to Bus Station	**26** C1
Taxi Stand	**27** C2
TNS 2nd-Class Bus Station	**28** D1

allow traffic to pass through Tepic without entering the city center.

Information

The **state tourist office** (☎ 216-56-61, 212-80-36; www.turismonayarit.gob.mx; cnr Puebla Nte & Nervo Pte; ☻ 8am-8pm) is a great resource with free maps and extensive information about Tepic and the state of Nayarit.

Banks (with ATMs) and *casas de cambio* line Av México Nte between the two plazas; you'll find the post office at the corner of Durango Sur and Morelos.

Access the Internet at **Chernobil Ciber-Café** (☎ 217-69-22; San Luis Potosí Nte 46; per hr US$1) or **@net.com** (Av México Sur s/n, Plaza Milenio; per hr US$1).

Sights

The large **cathedral** on Plaza Principal was dedicated in 1750; the neo-Gothic towers were completed in 1885. On the other side of the plaza from the cathedral is the **Palacio Municipal** (city hall), where you'll often find Huichol selling handicrafts at very good prices under the arches. On Av México Nte, south of the plaza, look inside the Nayarit

state government buildings –Palacio de Gobierno and the Cámara de Diputados – to see some impressive and colorful **murals**.

The 18th-century **Templo y Ex-Convento de la Cruz de Zacate** (cnr Calz del Ejército & Av México; ☻ 9am-4:30pm Mon-Fri) is about 2km south of the cathedral. It was here in 1767 that Father Junípero Serra organized his expedition that established the chain of Spanish missions in the Californias; you can visit the room where he stayed, but there's not much else to see.

MUSEUMS

Housed in a palatial 18th-century residence with a lovely courtyard, **Museo Regional de Nayarit** (☎ 212-19-00; Av México 91 Nte; admission US$3; ☻ 9am-6pm Mon-Fri, 9am-3pm Sat) concerns itself primarily with pre-Hispanic objects, including ancient pottery and tomb artifacts, as well as art and exhibits that shed light on Huichol art and cosmology. Considerably less interesting are the examples of colonial painting on display.

A couple of interesting museums are housed in impressive restored colonial residences. The **Casa y Museo Amado Nervo** (☎ 212-29-16; Zacatecas 284 Nte; admission free; ⊗ 9am-2pm Mon-Fri, 10am-2pm Sat) celebrates the life of poet Amado Nervo, born in this house in 1870. The collection is slight, but the house itself is lovely to behold. The **Casa Museo Juan Escutia** (☎ 212-33-90; Hidalgo 71 Ote; admission free; ⊗ 9am-2pm & 4-7pm Mon-Fri) was the home of Juan Escutia, one of Mexico's illustrious Niños Héroes (child heroes), who died in 1847 at age 17 defending Mexico City's Castillo de Chapultepec from US forces during the Mexican-American War. It's simply furnished and evocative of early 19th-century Mexico.

The **Museo de los Cuatro Pueblos** (☎ 212-17-05; Hidalgo 60 Ote; admission free; ⊗ 9am-2pm & 4-7pm Mon-Thu, 9am-1pm Fri & Sat) displays contemporary popular arts of the Nayarit's Huichol, Cora, Nahua and Tepehuano peoples, including clothing, yarn art, weaving, musical instruments, ceramics and beadwork.

Aramara (☎ 216-42-46; Allende 329 Pte; admission free; ⊗ 9am-2pm & 4-7pm Mon-Sat, 10am-3pm Sun) is a small museum of visual arts about 1.5km west of the town center. The **Museo Emilia Ortiz** (☎ 212-26-52; Lerdo 192 Pte; admission free; ⊗ 9am-7pm Mon-Sat) honors the Mexican-school painter Emilia Ortiz (1917–96) and her work.

Sleeping

In its historic center Tepic rewards travelers with a good selection of comfortable, independent hotels that won't break the bank.

Hotel Sierra de Alica (☎ 212-03-22; Av México 180 Nte; s/d US$44/57; P ⊗) An old hotel that's kept its standards intact, this midrange favorite has 60 bright, spacious rooms with satellite TV and phones. It's so close to Plaza Principal you can hear the cathedral bells ring.

Hotel Real de Don Juan (☎ /fax 216-18-88; Av México 105 Sur; r/ste US$73/105) Though it looks old and has some character, this hotel is thoroughly modern. The 48 rooms are done up in appealing pastel colors, with luxurious king-size beds and marble-accented bathrooms. A good restaurant and classy bar dominate the 1st floor.

Hotel Cibrian (☎ 212-86-98; Nervo 163 Pte; s/d US$20/25; P) This central hotel provides an excellent value with its clean, bright rooms with TV, telephone and enclosed parking. Rooms overlooking the busy street can get noisy. There's also a good, economical restaurant.

Hotel Fray Junípero Serra (☎ 212-25-25; www .frayjunipero.com.mx in Spanish; Lerdo 23 Pte; s/d US$61/67, ste US$80-154; P ⊗ 🖳) Rooms in this modern hotel are tastefully appointed and come with deluxe amenities, including wireless Internet and satellite TV; some have a view over the plaza.

Hotel Tepic (☎ 213-17-77; fax 210-05-45; Dr Martinez 438 Ote; s US$15-18, d US$23-28; ⊗) Weary travelers get some much-needed shut-eye at this good, modern hotel next to the bus station.

Trailer Park Los Pinos (☎ 210-27-28; Blvd Tepic-Xalisco 150; RV/tent sites US$15/4) About 5km south of town, this spacious park offers 24 trailer spaces with full hookups and wireless Internet. The leafy, grassy grounds make tent camping a pleasure.

Eating & Drinking

In contrast to most Mexican cities, Tepic has a good selection of vegetarian restaurants but, in keeping with the region, their local specialties are all shrimp-based.

El Trigal (☎ 216-40-04; Veracruz 112 Nte; mains under US$3; ⊗ 8:30am-9pm Mon-Fri, 8.30am-7pm Sat & Sun) This inexpensive vegetarian restaurant has tables in an attractive courtyard. Offerings include whole-wheat quesadillas, veggie burgers and an excellent *menú del día* (lunch special).

La Gloria (☎ 217-04-22; cnr Lerdo Ote & Av México Nte; mains US$5-16; ⊗ 7:30am-11pm) With live music and tables on a balcony overlooking Plaza Principal, La Gloria is an especially enjoyable place for an evening meal. The menu, firmly rooted in shrimp and fish, is a little more adventurous than the average.

Quetzalcóatl (☎ 212-99-66; León 224 Nte; mains under US$4; ⊗ closed Sun) A friendly, inexpensive vegetarian restaurant with a pretty courtyard, relaxing music and tasteful decor.

Cafetería y Restaurant Diligencias (☎ 212-15-35; Av México 29 Sur; mains US$2-4; ⊗ breakfast, lunch & dinner) Popular with locals for its *comida corrida* (set-price lunch and dinner menu), Diligencias serves up quality coffee, snacks and full meals all day long in a vintage dining hall.

Cafetería La Parroquia (Nervo 18 Ote; snacks US$1-3.50) On the northern side of the plaza, upstairs under the arches, this place is very pleasant for breakfasts, drinks and inexpensive light meals. They also do good coffee.

Getting There & Away

AIR
Tepic's **airport** (TPQ; ☎ 214-18-50) is in Pantanal, 12km (or a 20-minute drive) from Tepic, going toward Guadalajara. **Aero California** (☎ 214-23-20; Airport) and **Aeroméxico** (☎ 213-90-47; Airport) offer direct flights to Mexico City and Tijuana, with connections to other centers.

BUS
The bus station is on the southeastern outskirts of town; local buses marked 'Central' and 'Centro' make frequent trips between the bus station and the city center; local buses depart from the corner of Nervo Pte and Durango Nte. The bus station has a cafeteria, left-luggage office, shops, post office, tourist information, card phones, a Telecomm office and an ATM.

The main bus companies are Elite, Estrella Blanca (EB), Ómnibus de México (OB; all 1st-class), and Transportes del Pacífico (TP; 1st- and 2nd-class). There are daily departures to various destinations:

Guadalajara Elite (US$20, 3½hr, frequent 1st-class); Futura (US$17, 3½hr, frequent 2nd-class)
Mazatlán Elite (US$20, 4½, hourly 1st-class; US$15, 4½, hourly 2nd-class)
Mexico City OB (US$57, 10hr, hourly 1st-class); Elite & EB (US$50, 11hr, hourly 2nd-class) To Terminal Norte.
Puerto Vallarta TP (US$15, 3½hr, 1st-class 9pm; US$12, 3½hr, hourly 2nd-class 1am-10pm)

TNS (Transportes Norte de Sonora) operates a small terminal north of the cathedral near the Río Mololoa with 2nd-class service to San Blas (US$4.25, one hour, hourly from 5am to 7pm) and Santiago Ixcuintla (US$3, 1½ hours, half-hourly from 6am to 7pm).

Getting Around
Local buses operate from around 6am to 9pm (US$0.30). *Combis* operate along Av México from 6am to midnight (US$0.30). There are also plenty of taxis, and a taxi stand on the south side of Plaza Principal.

AROUND TEPIC
Laguna Santa María del Oro
Surrounded by steep, forested mountains, idyllic Laguna Santa María del Oro (elevation 730m) fills a volcanic crater 2km around and thought to be over 100m deep. The clear, clean water takes on colors ranging from turquoise to slate. It's a great pleasure to walk around the lake and into the surrounding mountains, spotting numerous birds (some 250 species) and butterflies along the way. You can also climb to an abandoned gold mine, cycle, swim, row on the lake, kayak, or fish for black bass and perch. A few small restaurants serve fresh lake fish.

Koala Bungalows & RV Park (☎ 311-264-36-98; koala@nayarit.com; Santa Maria del Oro; per person tent/r/ bungalow US$5/30/43, cabin US$57-71) is an attractive, peaceful park with a restaurant, campsites and well-maintained bungalows in several sizes. It's owned and operated by a friendly Englishman, who's an excellent source of information about the lake.

To get there, take the Santa María del Oro turnoff about 40km from Tepic along the Guadalajara road; from the turnoff it's about 10km to Santa María del Oro, then another 8km from the village to the lake. Buses to the lake depart from in front of the bus station in Tepic three times daily (US$3, one hour).

Volcán Ceboruco
This extinct volcano, with a number of old craters, interesting plants and volcanic forms, has several short, interesting walks at the top. Theirs is plenty of vegetation growing on the slopes, and the 15km cobbled road up the volcano passes lava fields and fumaroles (steam vents). The road begins at the village of Jala, 7km off Hwy 15D, between Tepic and Guadalajara; the *crucero* is 76km from Tepic, 12km before you reach Ixtlán del Río. There's no public transportation, so you'll need your own wheels.

Ixtlán del Río
The small town of Ixtlán del Río, about 1½ hours (88km) south of Tepic along Hwy 15D, is unremarkable in itself, but fans of controversial author Carlos Castaneda will remember that this is where Don Juan took Carlos in the book *Journey to Ixtlán*. Outside Ixtlán, the **Los Toriles** archaeological site has an impressive round stone temple, the **Templo a Quetzalcóatl** (⏰ 9am-5pm). Any bus between Tepic and Guadalajara will drop you at Ixtlán.

CHACALA
☎ 327 / pop 400
The tiny coastal fishing village of Chacala, 96km north of Puerto Vallarta and 10km west of Hwy 200 and Las Varas, sits pretty

along an amazingly beautiful little cove on Bahía Chacala backed by verdant slopes and edged by rugged black rocks at either end. The horizon is perfectly framed by the embrace of the cove, and the sound of the waves is gently mesmerizing. With more and more visitors coming each year, the town is changing, albeit slowly, but for now it remains a great place to unwind and send your regards to the horizon.

Chacala has just one main, sandy thoroughfare and a few cobbled side streets. Camping is possible at several of the beachside *palapa* restaurants, but there are also some unique accommodations to choose from.

Activities

Hereabouts, the sea provides most of the action. The waters of **Bahía Chacala** are calm and clear most days, allowing for relaxing water sports and exemplary snorkeling (bring your own gear, as you won't find it for rent in town). Local *panga* (motorized skiff) captains, easily encountered on the beach, are available to ferry you to favorite spots like **Bahía La Caleta**, 15 minutes north by boat. Here surfers rejoice to find a fine left-breaking point break.

You can also hike through the jungle to **Playa La Caleta**, about 1½ hours to the north; it's a challenging but rewarding slog with a happy ending on a deserted beach known for its big waves. Along the way you're likely to see a great variety of bird life, including exotics such as the West Mexican chachalaca or the Pacific slope flycatcher. You can arrange to have a *panga* pick you up on the beach for transport back to Chacala.

At Casa Pacífica (right), you can inquire about local guides and pick up copies of hand-drawn hiking maps and a brochure called *Birds of Chacala*.

Sleeping & Eating

Restaurant Laguna Encantada (☎ 272-03-08; camping free) If you're a camper, consider asking for a beach space outside this place, toward the north end. It's free, as long as you support the restaurant by eating there a few times.

Restaurant El Delfín (☎ 272-10-67; camping sites US$5) Campers also have it good here on a large grassy area under neat rows of palm trees. The casual open-air restaurant serves

basic fare. You'll find it toward the south end of the beach.

On or near the beach, decent spots to lay your head include **Posada Familia** (☎ 219-40-15; r US$40-50; ☒), **Restaurant Tres Hermanos** (☎ 272-10-67; r US$30) and **Posada Sarahi** (☎ 219-40-12; r US$30-45).

Folks interested in getting to know some locals should check out **Techos de México** (☎ 275-02-82; www.playachacala.com/techos.htm; r US$18-40), a series of seven homes with room for up to four people. Rooms are updated but basic and are separate from the host home. Some come with a kitchen.

Casa Pacífica B&B (☎ 219-40-67; www.casapacifica chacala.com; d US$60-70 incl breakfast) At this relaxing midrange option, three large, beautiful suites come with queen-size beds and a kitchen. Owner Susana Escobido is exceptionally knowledgeable about the area and manages eight other vacation rentals in Chacala (US$35 to US$100 per night).

Mar de Jade (☎ 219-40-60; www.mardejade.com; Playa Chacala s/n; s/d US$138/220, s ste US$165-188, d ste US$244-275; ☒) Considerably more than just a hotel, this lovely workshop center, spa, Spanish school and organic farm offers a relaxing atmosphere in the company of some very interesting people. Three healthy meals are included and mealtime is something of a thought exchange. Yoga and meditation are typical morning activities.

Majahua (☎ 219-40-54; www.majahua.com; Playa Chacala s/n; r US$129-194, ste US$355, all incl breakfast) Super chic and tucked away in the unspoiled jungle overlooking the edge of the cove, this earthy ecolodge offers five beautifully designed rooms, a fantastic outdoor restaurant and spa services. It's a five-minute walk from the parking area, just up the road from Mar de Jade.

You can grab a meal or snack at any of the dozen-plus *palapa* restaurants on the beach. For super-fresh seafood, head to the dock early in the morning and buy your own fish; some restaurants will cook it up for free (or for a small fee), as long as you buy side dishes and drinks there too.

La Brisa (☎ 291-40-15; mains US$5-12; ☒ 8am-10pm) The best of the beach restaurants, La Brisa does good morning coffee and seafood prepared the local way. If you've a hankering for something decadent, go for the *camarones* Costa Azul, shrimp stuffed with ham, tuna and cheese.

Mauna Kea Café (☎ 219-40-67; breakfast US$5-6; ☺ 8-10am Mon-Sat) A tiny, unconventional and casual rooftop café at Casa Pacífica, Mauna Kea serves up full, hearty breakfasts, good coffee and Hawaiian-style waffles.

Getting There & Away

To reach Chacala, get off the bus at Las Varas (any 2nd-class bus will stop here, as will most – but not all – 1st-class buses) and take a *taxi colectivo* (shared taxi) to Chacala (US$2, 15 minutes). A private taxi sets you back US$10 to US$15.

AROUND CHACALA

Hidden in the mountains up a rough dirt road is **Jamurca** (admission US$1.50; ☺ 9am-5pm Thu-Tue). At these rustic hot springs, it is said, the Huichol *marakames* (shamans) once took ritual baths to purify their bodies and souls. You can do the same in three concrete pools. Bring a picnic lunch to enjoy in the garden as iguanas look on. You'll need your own wheels to get there; on Hwy 200 look for the swimmer pictograph 2km north of Las Varas at a town called Las Cuatas, then head south about 4km on the rutted road.

RINCÓN DE GUAYABITOS

☎ 327 / pop 3000

On the coast about 60km north of Puerto Vallarta, Rincón de Guayabitos ('Guayabitos' for short) is a tailor-made beach-resort town catering to Mexican vacationers and winter visitors from Canada and other cold places. It's nothing fancy and shows its weathered age, but its appeal lies in its slow, uncomplicated pace and relative lack of gringos. As you lie on the beach wiggling your toes in the sand, vendors pass by selling fish roasted on a stick and cool, fresh coconuts. Guayabitos gets overrun during Semana Santa, Christmas, and the July and August school holidays. Weekends are busy, but the beautiful beach is practically empty the rest of the week.

Orientation & Information

Rincón de Guayabitos is on the coast just west of Hwy 200. At the north entrance to town, a high-water tower emulates an elongated mushroom. Turn into town here and soon you'll be on Guayabitos' main street, Av del Sol Nuevo. It's lined with shops,

restaurants and hotels. More restaurants and hotels sit along the beach, one block over – they're reached by side streets, as there's no road along the waterfront.

The nearest bank is in La Peñita de Jaltemba, 3km north of Guayabitos, but there's an ATM at **Villas Buena Vida** (☎ 274-02-31; Retorno Laureles s/n).

EquiNoxio Internet (Av del Sol Nuevo s/n; per hr US$3.50) The only place to log on, with plug-ins for laptops.

Delegación de Turismo (☎ /fax 274-06-93; Av del Sol Nuevo s/n; ☺ 9am-2pm & 4-6pm Mon-Sat, 9am-2pm Sun) Near the water tower; provides information on the local area and the state of Nayarit.

Post office (☺ 8am-2pm Mon-Fri) Behind the *zócalo*, near the tourist office.

Sights & Activities

From the beach you can take a *panga* or a glass-bottom boat (up to five people US$35/US$25) out to the gorgeous snorkeling nirvana **Isla Islote** (a few kilometers offshore), where you can rent snorkeling gear and eat in a simple restaurant.

North of Guayabitos, **Boca del Naranjo** beckons, with wild waves crashing onto the beach and mangroves ideal for kayaking and bird-watching. To get there, drive 6km north from the turnoff to Chacala on Hwy 200 and take the signed left to the village of La Lima de Abajo and continue a short distance further to the beach.

For something different, climb the 224 steps to **Cerro de la Santa Cruz** (Hill of the Holy Cross), known locally as La Cruz. From here you'll enjoy fantastic views of Bahía de Jaltemba and of the handsome green scarp of the Sierra Madres to the west. Pilgrims make the climb en masse at Easter, but the rest of the year you're likely to have the lookout to yourself. You'll find the path at the southern terminus of Av del Sol Nuevo.

Boat operators offer whale-watching trips from November to March. If you want to test out a different beach, try Playa Los Ayala (p141), about 2km south of Guayabitos.

Sleeping

Most of Guayabitos' accommodations are midrange bungalows with kitchens, pitched at families. Single travelers will have a harder time finding cheap rooms. The following prices are for the winter high season, though the high-priced months can vary

from one establishment to another. Staying a while? Negotiate discounts.

Posada Jaltemba (☎ 274-01-65; cnr Av del Sol Nuevo & Retorno Laureles; d/q US$30/60, bungalows US$40-85; P ☒ ☎) A good deal. The attractive, vine-covered stucco-and-brick buildings shine with charming rustic touches and tropical plants. Rooms fit right into this mold.

Hotel Posada la Misión (☎ 274-03-57; posadala mision@prodigy.net.mx; Retorno Tabachines 6; d/tr US$72/78, bungalows US$80-128; P ☒ ☎) This hotel has a colonial theme going, with beautiful tiles lining open halls in front, great sea views out back and a pretty, amoeba-shaped pool in the middle. Rooms are nice and quaint, and bungalows have balconies.

Villas Buena Vida (☎ 274-02-31; www.villas buenavida.com; Retorno Laureles s/n; r US$64, ste US$91-119; P ☒ ☎) With its beachfront swimming pool and balconies overlooking the ocean, this luxurious hotel is a great place to splash out. Villas sleep one to four people; suites sleep five to six people. The hotel also presents its guests with sportfishing, snorkeling, biking and horseback-riding opportunities.

Hotel Guayabitos (☎ 274-09-20; Av del Sol Nuevo 17; d/q US$32/45, bungalows US$50-70; P ☒ ☎) This new hotel has a large pool, secure parking and comfortable rooms with kitchenettes. Its air-conditioned restaurant offers hearty local dishes like *camarones del diablo*, an exuberantly spiced shrimp dish (US$9). Mains cost US$4 to US$11, and the restaurant is open from 8am to 10pm.

Posada Real (☎ 274-07-07; cnr Av del Sol Nuevo & Huanacaxtle; d/q US$45/65, bungalows d/q US$50/70; P ☒ ☎) Possessing the town's most audacious paint job, this cheerful hotel has decent rooms and a good restaurant. The bungalows come with kitchens. The hot tub is big enough for you and all your friends.

Other options:

Paraíso del Pescador Trailer Park & Bungalows (☎ 274-00-14; paraisodelpescador@hotmail.com; Retorno Ceibas; tent & RV sites US$21, r US$55, ste US$110, 4-/8-person bungalows US$65/165) Stark and basic, but right on the beach.

Bungalows y Hotel Pancho Villa (☎ 324-02-46; Av del Sol Nuevo s/n; s/d US$20/25, bungalows US$52-75; ☎) Has small, musty rooms and bungalows in motel-like digs, but they don't cost an arm or a leg. At least there's a pool.

Eating

On the main drag you'll find many economical spots to grab a bite; local tastes tend to gravitate toward *pollo asado* (grilled chicken) and fried fish, along with plenty of shrimp dishes.

El Campanario (☎ 274-03-57; Retorno Tabachines 6; mains US$5-9; ☻ 7am-10pm) This place serves up good fish, burgers, enchiladas and omelets, among other menu items. Nibble on them in airy, casual and intimate surroundings, beautifully tiled and set with hanging ceramic parrots. It's at the Hotel Posada la Misión.

Beto's (☎ 274-05-75; Av del Sol Nuevo s/n; mains US$3-10; ☻ 7am-9pm) Beto's is popular with large families for its simple, no-nonsense Mexican menu. Seafood, *pozole* (a hearty soup of hominy, meat or seafood, vegetables and chilies) and other treats keep everyone happy.

Arthur's 'Los Super' Tacos (Av del Sol Nuevo s/n; tacos US$.80; ☻ 5-11pm) This is the best place in town for a really cheap meal; It makes its own tortillas and salsas.

Roberto's (Retorno Jacarandas; mains US$6-12; ☻ 8am-6pm Wed-Mon) Serving up seafood and meats in a casual, covered patio, this place caters to the breakfast and lunchtime sand-covered crowd. Look for it on the beach; Roberto's also does breakfast.

George & Gary's (☎ 274-04-00; Av del Sol Nuevo s/n; mains under US$5; ☻ 7am-9:30pm) G&G's grills up burgers, tosses chef salads and percolates fancy coffees – that's about the extent of its lunch menu. It's also popular with gringos for the breakfast waffles (US$3.50). There's a book exchange here, too.

La Piña Loca (☎ 274-11-81; Retorno Tabachines 7; mains US$4-16; ☻ 7am-10pm) This place sits cute and homey, colorful and small. It's totally open and airy, serving breakfast, lunch and dinner from a Mexican menu.

Rincón Méxicano (☎ 274-06-63; cnr Cedros & Retorno Laureles; mains US$6-11; ☻ closed Wed) Attached to the beachfront Hotel Estancia San Carlos, this restaurant has a lunch and dinner menu with barbecue ribs, interesting beef dishes and imaginative meals such as shrimp in mango and red-wine sauce.

Getting There & Away

Rincón de Guayabitos doesn't have a bus terminal. Second-class buses coming from Puerto Vallarta (US$5.50, 1½ hours, 72km) or Tepic (US$6, two hours, 83km) may drop you on the highway at Rincón de Guayabitos, but sometimes they don't stop here. A couple of kilometers toward Tepic, La Peñita is a sure stop. *Colectivo* vans operate frequently between La Peñita and Guayabitos (US$0.50, 10 minutes) during daylight hours, or you can take a taxi (US$3).

AROUND RINCÓN DE GUAYABITOS

There are many pleasant little beach towns south of Rincón de Guayabitos that make good day trips from either Guayabitos or Puerto Vallarta; they all have places to stay and eat. The sleepy **Playa Los Ayala** (Km 96) beckons, about 2km south of Guayabitos, while the two pleasant beach towns of **Lo de Marcos** (Km 108) and **San Francisco** (Km 118), 13km and 9km south, respectively, make good day trips from either Rincón de Guayabitos or Puerto Vallarta. Be careful about swimming at these beaches: waves and currents are changeable, so ask locals if it's safe to enter the water during your time there.

First- and 2nd-class buses traveling along Hwy 200 will drop you at the *crucero* for Lo de Marcos or San Francisco, about 1km from the edge of each town.

Playa Los Ayala

Considerably earthier and more sedate than its neighbor Guayabitos, Playa Los Ayala is shared by sun worshipers and fishermen who spend much of the day sitting in a kind of manly sewing circle, mending their nets. Boats are for hire on the beach for snorkeling trips to Isla Islote and Boca del Naranjo. A 15-minute jungle hike over the headlands at the southern end of the beach will drop you down into a secluded cove and beach called **Playa del Beso** (Beach of the Kiss). You'll likely have it all to yourself.

Villas Minerva (☎ 274-11-10; Coral 42; r US$50-80, ste US$110; P ✄ ☜) Overlooking the beach, this well-run, recently completed hotel offers homey rooms sleeping up to six, and suites with kitchens and balconies. It has an appealing beachside pool and patio.

Playa Lo de Marcos

Playa Lo de Marcos, 13km south of Guayabitos and 49km north of the Puerto Vallarta airport, is a small village with a beautiful beach beloved by Mexican travelers and snowbirds from *el norte*. There are a couple of decent

---

DETOURS: PLAYA PUNTA RAZA

If you're lucky enough to be traveling in a high-clearance vehicle, or stalwart enough to consider making an arduous 5km hike from Hwy 200, the wild sands of Punta Raza offer glorious solitude, superlative bird- and wildlife-watching, and an exceptional place to set up a tent for a few relaxing days. The long, sloping beach is pummeled by crashing waves – making things dicey for swimmers – and ringed by near-virgin jungle. An elusive, edge-of-the-world charm means you'll want to stay at least as long as your sunscreen holds out.

If you prefer walls and a ceiling, you can spend the night at the seasonal **Hotel Rincón del Cielo** (☎ 274-70-70 in Monteón; d US$50), with six simple, personable rooms, including two at water's edge. You're well off the grid here and thus rooms are lit by lanterns or candles. A small restaurant with a short menu serves delicious fresh juices and seafood; from your table you can watch blue-footed boobies and magnificent frigate birds perform their singular acrobatics and crash headfirst into the sea.

To get there, look for El Monteón sign on Hwy 200, 5km south of Guayabitos. Turn to the west, pass through the village, then turn right at Calle Punta Raza. The rutted dirt road passes over a scenic ridge and through lush old-growth forest.

---

restaurants, and simple bungalows are available if you decide to spend the night. One simple choice is **Padre Nuestro** (☎ 275-00-24; bungalows US$20-30; ☒). A more upscale option is **Villas and Bungalows Tlaquepaque** (☎ 3-659-14-36 in Guadalajara; 44 Av Echeverría; d/q/bungalow $70/75/80; RV hookup US$20; ℗ ☒), with pleasant, spacious rooms decorated with religious iconography and an RV park well located by the beach.

Just 2km to 3km south from Lo de Marcos are two more beaches (**Playa Los Venados** and **Playa Miñitas**) with some restaurants. You'll also find a few trailer parks along the side road there.

Playa San Francisco
☎ 311 / pop 1800

You just might leave your heart in San Francisco (known locally as San Pancho). The big appeal here is the beach, of course – a wide, long expanse covered in thick sand and edged with crashing waves that attract surfers from miles around. Plenty of restaurants tend the more sedate tourists who'd rather lounge while sipping a margarita.

From September 26 to October 4 the town dresses up and takes part in the nine-day festival called San Pancho Days. There's a **casa de cambio** (exchange bureau; cnr Av Tercero Mundo & Av America Latino) with no set hours, and, at last count, two Internet cafés.

SLEEPING & EATING
Calandria Realty (☎ 258-42-85; www.calandriarealty .com; Av Tercero Mundo 50) manages several bungalow and villa rentals in San Pancho.

Hotel Cielo Rojo (☎ 258-41-55; hotelcielorojo@ yahoo.com; Asia 6; r US$58, ste US$68-73) Providing an exceptional value, this modern hotel offers substance and style with four colorful rooms and two well-appointed suites. The rooms are artfully furnished with handmade furniture and vibrant native touches. There's a small sitting pool, a hot tub, and a communal kitchen for steaming up that shrimp you bought on the beach.

Costa Azul Adventure Resort (☎ 258-41-20; www .costaazul.com; ste/villa US$140/160, all-inclusive d US$220-271; ℗ ☒ ☒) Perfect for a splurge, this eco-chic resort with a private beach is well suited to travelers too antsy to spend their vacations on the beach (although beach bums are also well taken care of). Surfing lessons and excursions take full advantage of the multiple point, reef and beach breaks nearby; there's also kayaking, mountain biking, horseback riding and snorkeling trips. Phew! Retire to your big, bright room or to Wahoo's Bar and Grill, the *palapa* restaurant. Activities are included in the all-inclusive rate. To get there, from the main village road, Av Tercero Mundo, take the signed right turn two blocks shy of the beach. From here it's a bumpy 2km ride.

Lydia Bungalows (☎ 258-43-37; bungalowslydia@ hotmail.com; apt/bungalow US$80/110) For delicious privacy, head 2km south of Costa Azul to this idyllic, exceedingly private retreat set on a secluded sandy beach and nestled beneath a grove of towering coconut palms. On offer are four small apartments with kitchenettes and a spacious one-bedroom bungalow. The suite sleeps up to six people. Discounts are available for longer stays.

Palapas Las Iguanas (☎ 258-40-15; genolamphiear@hotmail.com; Tercero Mundo s/n; palapa/apt US$60/90) With two flavors of accommodation, here you can choose between perpetually breezy, romantic open-air *palapa* units with kitchenettes and mosquito nets over the bed, and more traditional, fan-cooled kitchenette units. You'll find it on the main street, half a block from the beach and adjacent to Los Arcos Restaurant.

Casa Obelisco Bed & Breakfast (☎ 258-43-16; www.casaobelisco.com; d US$180-200; 🅿 🈂) Located 1km south of Costa Azul, this romantic, Mediterranean-style B&B offers four luxurious, richly decorated suites with ocean-view balconies overlooking a manicured jungle garden and pool. A generous breakfast, prepared by your American hosts, is included in the price. Children under six years are not allowed, and reservations are essential.

Restaurant Celia (☎ 258-40-16; Av Tercero Mundo; r US$26) On the interestingly named Av Tercero

Mundo, San Pancho's main street, this simple place offers a measure of decency and the cheapest accommodations in town in the form of fan-cooled rooms you probably won't write home about.

Gallo's Pizza (☎ 258-41-35; Av Tercero Mundo; mains US$5-14; 🕐 5-10pm Thu-Sun) An expat-favored hangout on the edge of town, Gallo's serves up good pizza and buckets of beer, with frequent live music.

Restaurante Las Palmas (☎ 258-40-35; mains US$6-12; 🕐 8am-9pm) A pleasant spot at sunset, this classic beachfront eatery celebrates shrimp in a big way. If you never care to eat another shrimp, try the spicy octopus (US$12).

GETTING THERE & AWAY

San Francisco is off Hwy 200, 22km south of Guayabitos and 8km north of Sayulita, at Km 118. Any 2nd-class bus heading north or south on Hwy 200 will drop you at the crossroads, 2km from the beach. From there, take a *combi* (US$2) or private taxi (US$4).

NAYARIT

TURTLE AID

Driven by primeval impulse and in the dark of night, thousands of olive ridley sea turtles arrive on the pristine beaches of Pacific Mexico for a few months each year to lay their leathery, ping-pong-ball–sized eggs in the sand. Six to 10 weeks later, turtle hatchlings emerge from the shell to scamper into the water, dodging numerous predators. Despite their numbers, the survival rate is less than one in 1000.

Playa San Francisco, which remained undeveloped well into the 1970s, once provided prime nesting grounds for marine turtles. The town's oldest inhabitants can still recall the nights when hundreds of the hulking turtles arrived en masse to lay their eggs. By 1992, however, their numbers suddenly started to plummet on a global scale. The pressures of coastal development, shrimp fishing and poaching had reduced the once thriving local population of nesting turtles from thousands to a scant 72. This was also the year that the **Grupo Ecológico de la Costa Verde** (☎ 258-41-35; www.project-tortuga.org; America Latina 102, Playa San Francisco) built their first marine nursery to provide large-scale protection of sea turtles and contribute to a worldwide effort to stave off the threat of their extinction. Today the group incubates and releases more than 25,000 hatchlings each year to the sea, and conducts outreach education in local schools in hopes of hatching young environmentalists.

During the summer and fall months, visitors are invited to tour the nursery, and in October and November they are invited to attend release events as turtle hatchlings scurry into the Pacific Ocean for the first time. On Wednesday nights at 7pm (in winter) or 8pm (in summer), Grupo Eco puts on a multimedia presentation about local efforts to protect marine turtles at the Costa Azul Adventure Resort (opposite), or sometimes at Gallo's Pizza (above) in the village.

The group depends on volunteers to, among other things, collect nests from six different beaches in the dark of night and relocate them to the nursery. The effort starts gathering momentum in June at the onset of the nesting season and ends in mid-November. To be accepted, volunteers must stay with the program for at least two months and pay their own expenses (about US$300 per month). No special skills or education are necessary – only the willingness to work in adverse weather at 3am! For more information, visit the website.

SAYULITA

☎ 329 / pop 1600

Sayulita is still low-key, but it has definitely been discovered and can feel crowded at times. The beautiful sandy beach, lined by homes and places to stay, is popular with surfers, especially novices. There are two surf shops, two campgrounds and many tasteful B&Bs. Meal options range from cheap fish tacos on the street to full gourmet Mediterranean dinners on white linen. In addition to playing in the waves, boat trips, horseback riding, trekking and kayaking are all possible. See the operators on the main street.

Sayulita (Nayarit) is one hour behind Puerto Vallarta (Jalisco). Sayulita has no banks or ATMs. Many businesses are closed from May through November.

Information

Sayulita has no tourist office, but the good folks at Sayulita Properties (right) can point you in the right direction – provided they're not too busy. The nearest full-service bank and ATM is in Bucerías.

Librería Sayulita (☎ 291-33-82; Navarrete 9; ♥ 9am-8pm Sun-Fri) A bookstore and de facto community center; pick up a tourist map (US$1.50) of the town.

Sayulita Caja de Cambio (☎ 291-30-05; Delfín 44; ♥ 8am-7pm Mon-Sat, 9am-2pm Sun) Near the *zócalo*; offers so-so rates.

Bre@kfast.net (per hr US$4; ♥ 7am to 8pm) Stop by here to get online; it's at the end of Delfín, on the beach. Customers ordering food get 15 minutes of free Internet time.

SayulitaNet Lounge (☎ 291-34-44; Marlín 12; per hr US$4; ♥ noon-midnight) Try this place to log on over a tipple. They have a wireless network, but it's also a chic bar serving well-made concoctions and imported beers.

Lava Zone (José Mariscal; wash/dry 6kg US$6; ♥ 8am-6pm Mon-Sat) The place to spin and tumble your washables.

Sayulita Properties (☎ 291-30-76; Delfín 9; www .sayulitaproperties.com; ♥ 8am-8pm) Has tourist and rental information as well as Internet service (per hour US$3.25).

Sights & Activities

Swimming in Sayulita is fairly calm in general, but if you have any doubts ask for local advice. You can arrange bicycle rental, boat trips, horseback riding, trekking or kayaking from operators on Delfín, the main street, including **Santa Crucecita Expediciones**

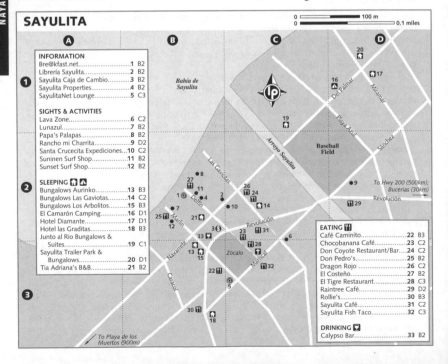

SAYULITA

0 —————— 100 m
0 —————— 0.1 miles

INFORMATION
Bre@kfast.net....................1 B2
Librería Sayulita................2 B2
Sayulita Caja de Cambio.......3 B2
Sayulita Properties..............4 B2
SayulitaNet Lounge.............5 C3

SIGHTS & ACTIVITIES
Lava Zone........................6 C2
Lunazul...........................7 B2
Papa's Palapas...................8 B2
Rancho mi Charrita.............9 D2
Santa Crucecita Expediciones..10 C2
Suninen Surf Shop.............11 B2
Sunset Surf Shop...............12 B2

SLEEPING
Bungalows Aurinko.............13 B3
Bungalows Las Gaviotas........14 C2
Bungalows Los Arbolitos.......15 B3
El Camarón Camping...........16 D1
Hotel Diamante..................17 D1
Hotel las Graditas..............18 B3
Junto al Rio Bungalows &
  Suites..........................19 C1
Sayulita Trailer Park &
  Bungalows.....................20 D1
Tia Adriana's B&B..............21 B2

Bahía de
Sayulita

Del Palmar

Miramar

Playa Azul

Sánchez

Baseball
Field

Arroyo Sayulita

Las Gaviotas

Delfín

Marlín

Navarrete

Caracol

Zócalo

Mariscal

Revolución

To Hwy 200 (500km);
Bucerías (30km)

EATING
Café Caminito...................22 B3
Chocobanana Café.............23 C2
Don Coyote Restaurant/Bar..24 C2
Don Pedro's.....................25 B2
Dragon Rojo.....................26 C2
El Costeño.......................27 B2
El Tigre Restaurant............28 C3
Raintree Café...................29 D2
Rollie's...........................30 B3
Sayulita Café....................31 C2
Sayulita Fish Taco.............32 C3

DRINKING
Calypso Bar.....................33 B2

To Playa de los
Muertos (900m)

NAYARIT

(☎ 291-01-91; Navarrete 14; bike rental per day US$17, snorkeling gear rental US$3; ☼ 9am-sunset), which also rents and repairs surfboards.

A popular nearby destination is **Playa de los Muertos**, where picnics and boogie-boarding top the action. It's a 15-minute walk south along the coast road, past the Villa Amor terraces. The road goes through a small cemetery; the first beach you come to is Los Muertos. Follow this dirt road to other, more isolated beaches.

You can also hire a boat to take your group out to the uninhabited **Islas Marietas** for picnicking, snorkeling and swimming.

Rancho mi Charrita (☎ 291-31-12; 14 Sánchez; ☼ 11am-sunset) offers horseback rides to Los Muertos and Carrisitos beaches (1½ hours; US$20), a zip-line canopy tour through the treetops (US$40), and boat trips to the Islas Marietas (three to four hours; US$150 for up to six people).

SURFING

Surfing is a way of life in Sayulita. With decent waves pouring into Bahía de Sayulita from both the left and the right, you can practice your well-honed moves with an audience, or even take up the sport for the first time. Try these full-service surf shops – all open from 8am until sundown:

Sunset Surf Shop (☎ 291-32-96; Marlín 10; sunset55@ hotmail.com; surfboard rental per day US$20-25, lessons per hr US$30) Also offers fishing and surfing trips to the Islas Marietas (four hours, up to six persons US$150).

Lunazul (☎ 291-20-09; Marlín 4; surfboard/body board rental per day US$20/12, lessons per 1½hr US$40)

Suninen Surf Shop (☎ 291-31-86; Delfín 4A; rentals per day/week US$20/150, lessons per 1½hr US$40)

Papa's Palapas (☎ 229-32-78; rentals per hr/day US$5/22, lessons per 2hr US$30; ☼ 8am-sundown) Next to El Costeño restaurant on the beach.

Sleeping

If you arrive during holiday periods, when everything's booked up, try the realtor **Sayulita Properties** (☎ 291-30-76; Delfín 9; www.sayulita properties.com; ☼ 8am-8pm), which can attempt to find you something. The following prices reflect the winter high season.

Bungalows Aurinko (☎ 291-31-50; www.sayulita -vacations.com; cnr Marlín & Revolución; 1-/2-bedroom bungalows US$68/106, ste US$88) Smooth riverstone floors, open-air kitchens, exposed raw beams and well-appointed decor make this a memorable place to stay. Huichol art adorns the walls while Oaxacan linen covers the beds. Free bike use and discounts on surfboard rentals are part of the deal.

Bungalows Los Arbolitos (☎ 291-31-46; sayulita bungalows@earthlink.net; Marlín 20; ste US$99) Harbors nine intimate and luxurious suites, two with kitchens. Craftsman touches, creative design and lush gardens add up to paradise. Add tax to prices.

El Camarón Camping (Del Palmar s/n; sites per person/ huts US$4/25) This grassy, kick-back spot, on the beach north of town, is the heart of the scene for young surfers and hippies, and its beach is the only place in town to enjoy both a left and a right break. Basic structures with *palapa* roofs and damp mattresses are available for those without a tent; the beachfront one is about as bodacious a party nook as one could ask for. Beware: many come for a day and end up staying for months.

Tía Adriana's B&B (☎ 291-30-29, 888-221-9247 in the US; www.tiaadrianas.com; cnr Delfín & Navarrete; ste US$65-120, incl breakfast) This B&B offers some vibrant suites with kitchenettes; top ones are open to breezes (no walls!) and have views. Other suites also have special touches. The large, hearty breakfasts are camaraderie-inducing.

Sayulita Trailer Park & Bungalows (☎ 390-27-50; sayupark@prodigy.net.mx; Miramar s/n; tent/trailer sites with hookup US$12/16, r/bungalow US$30/70, ste US$50-70) This place maintains an attractive, palm-shaded property beside the beach, with a restaurant and snack bar. Discounts are offered to those who choose to stick around for a while.

Bungalows Las Gavíotas (☎ 291-32-18; Las Gavíotas 12; r/bungalow for 6 US$25/50; ℗) Friendly, basic and family-run, Las Gavíotas shows its years, but it's only a few steps from the beach. At dusk you can expect a thunderous gaggle of boys to use the courtyard as a soccer field.

Hotel Diamante (☎ 291-31-91; Miramar 40; s/d/ q US$35/50/70; ✉) Diamante has downright small, basic and blah rooms – but there's a pool and outdoor covered kitchen area, which attracts thrifty backpackers.

Junto al Rio Bungalows & Suites (☎ 291-35-54; bungalow/suite US$40/60) By the edge of the arroyo on the beach, this place has hammocks, three simple bungalows and two suites with a kitchen. The owner can be hard to locate.

Hotel las Graditas (☎ 291-35-19; lasgraditas@ hotmail.com; Mariscal 12; s US$30-40, d US$60-70, house for 6-8 US$120; ✉ 🐾) With dark and musty rooms, this place is good only as a last resort. The small pool affords good views over the town.

The large house perched at the top of the epic flight of stairs is also for rent (but don't expect a porter to haul up your luggage).

Eating

The cheapest eats in town are Sayulita's wonderful taco stands: look for them in the *zócalo*. The most pleasant places, however, are the *palapas* on the beach, where a seafood dish, a cold beer and the salty sea breeze will cost you about US$8.

Sayulita Café (☎ 291-35-11; 37 Revolución; mains US$8-12; ☺ 5-11pm) With an atmospheric dining room and candle-lit sidewalk tables, this place serves hearty Mexican fare and splendid fresh seafood dishes. For a treat, try the *molcajete azteca* (US$12), a pre-Hispanic dish combining beef, chicken, chorizo, onions, *panela* (a mild fresh white cheese), grilled nopales (cactus) and... well, that's enough.

Sayulita Fish Taco (José Mariscal s/n; tacos from $0.50; ☺ 11am-9pm Mon-Sat) This place has perhaps the tastiest fish tacos in Mexico; American owner Albert spent years perfecting his recipe. There are only four outdoor tables and some stools.

Raintree Café (☎ 291-35-23; Revolución 21; mains US$6-20; ☺ 8am-11pm Mon-Sat) This brand-new bar and restaurant aims for swanky and hits the mark. The dinner menu proclaims itself to be '*fusión méxicana*,' with selections like Roquefort fettuccine with shrimp (US$7) and tequila shrimp fajitas (US$20). They also stage changing exhibitions of local art and employ a very talented bartender.

Café Caminito (☎ 291-3564; Marlín 12; mains US$4-7; ☺ 4:30-10pm Thu-Tue) Caminito has tables on the street facing the *zócalo*. Enjoy the flaky Argentine empanadas stuffed with fish (US$2), pizzas, pasta and big crunchy salads. For dessert, try the pear cooked in burgundy with English cream (US$4).

El Tigre Restaurant (mains US$6-18; ☺ 5-10pm Mon-Sat) On a small terrace upstairs overlooking the *zócalo*. Some locals think the town's best seafood is grilled here. Surf videos play while you wrestle with your lobster (US$18).

Chocobanana Café (☎ 291-30-51; cnr Revolución & Delfín; breakfast US$4-5; ☺ 6am-3pm) This small shack on the *zócalo* is a very popular patio for breakfast or the town's best burger. Vegetarians will find options here, and milkshake fanatics just might find heaven.

Rollie's (Revolución 58; breakfast US$4-6; ☺ 8am-noon) This is *the* place for breakfast. Rollie

and friends lovingly serve Western breakfasts with an occasional Mexican twist. Choose music from Rollie's collection, or sing along with him.

Don Pedro's (☎ 291-30-90; Marlín 2; meals US$11-22; ☺ restaurant 6-11pm, bar & grill noon-11pm) Overlooking the beach, this is two eateries in one: a fine restaurant upstairs offering elegant dining choices, and a bar and grill downstairs serving upscale pizza and salads. There's a generous veggie stir-fry on offer for US$8.

Other recommendations:

Dragon Rojo (☎ 291-32-01; cnr Las Gavíotas & Navarrete; mains US$5-8; ☺ 11am-10pm) Reasonably good Chinese fare under a shady *palapa*.

El Costeño (☎ 291-00-39; Delfín; mains US$8-12; ☺ 8am-8pm) Right on the beach; the tables on the sand get packed with gringos enjoying seafood.

Don Coyote Restaurant/Bar (cnr Las Gavíotas & Navarrete; mains US$8-12; ☺ 11am-10pm Tue-Sat) Serves good old Western favorites, including spaghetti, veggie dishes and grilled chicken on a *palapa* patio.

Drinking & Entertainment

Sayulita's not a place to paint the town red, but there are a few places where you can kick out the jams...or play chess. The local **chess club** (☺ Tue 6-8pm) meets at Librería Sayulita (p144); visitors are welcome (particularly those who bring their own chess set).

Calypso Bar (☎ 291-30-05; Revolución; mains US$8-20) Across from the *zócalo* and popular for its 5pm to 7pm happy hour. Surf videos liven up the TVs, and on Friday nights there's a DJ.

Don Pedro's (Marlín 2; ☺ restaurant 6-11pm, bar & grill noon-11pm) Don Pedro's has reggae and rock on Friday nights, DJs on Saturday nights and Cuban on Monday nights.

Don Coyote Restaurant/Bar (cnr Las Gavíotas & Navarrete; ☺ 11am-10pm Tue-Sat) This place offers music and dancing on its open patio several nights per week, and sports on satellite TV on weekends.

Getting There & Away

Sayulita is about 35km northwest of Puerto Vallarta, just west of Hwy 200. First-class buses leave daily from the long-distance terminal in Puerto Vallarta (US$4, one hour, 10 1st-class; US$2, 20 2nd-class). The bus stop is on Revolución by the bridge crossing the arroyo.

Buses headed for Puerto Vallarta leave every 30 minutes between 5:30am and 6:45pm (US$2 to US$4, one hour).

Jalisco, Colima & Michoacán Coasts

South of Puerto Vallarta, Hwy 200 continues into Jalisco state, skirting the Cabo Corrientes promontory and heading south to hug the coast again. Here begins the stretch of Mexico's Pacific shore known as the Costa Alegre (Happy Coast), a singularly beautiful territory of fine, isolated beaches and some of the most luxurious resorts in Mexico. It's prime territory for travelers seeking the quiet pleasures of unassuming towns, simple fishing villages and magnificent maritime landscapes. It extends all the way to the Melaque and Barra de Navidad region, and is a popular destination for Americans and Canadian 'snowbirds,' full-time retirees and short-term vacationers.

Continuing south, Hwy 200 hews to the coast of Colima, passing through the lovely city of Manzanillo before heading into Michoacán, one of Mexico's most beautiful states. The route passes dozens of untouched beaches – some with wide expanses of golden sand, some tucked into tiny rocky coves, some at river mouths where quiet estuaries harbor multitudes of birds. Several have gentle lapping waves that are good for swimming, while others have big breakers suitable for surfing. Many of the beaches are uninhabited, but some are home to small communities. Mango, coconut, papaya and banana plantations line the highway, while the green peaks of the Sierra Madre del Sur form a lush backdrop inland.

HIGHLIGHTS

■ Slurping oyster cocktails by the lagoon in the understated beach-resort town of **Barra de Navidad** (p158)

■ Scuba diving, sportfishing or just enjoying the sand around the bays of **Manzanillo** (p163)

■ Easing into the local tempo while brushing up your Spanish skills in **La Manzanilla** (p153)

■ Surfing awesome waves at the laid-back community of **Barra de Nexpa** (p174)

■ Watching sea turtles come ashore in summer and fall to lay precious eggs at **Playa Maruata** (p174)

La Manzanilla
★Barra de Navidad
★Manzanillo
Playa Maruata ★
★ Barra de Nexpa

■ MANZANILLO JANUARY DAILY HIGH: 27°C |80°F ■ MANZANILLO JULY DAILY HIGH: 30°C | 86°F

JALISCO, COLIMA & MICHOACÁN COASTS

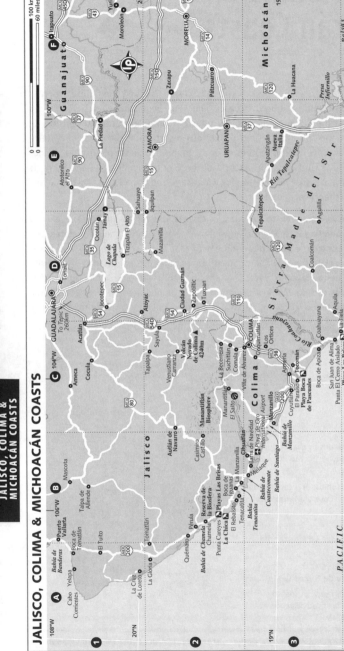

JALISCO

Along the untrammeled coastline between Puerto Vallarta and Barra de Navidad are a rewarding series of lightly developed beachside communities.

COSTA ALEGRE

Many remarkable beaches stretch along the coast south of Puerto Vallarta. The Km distances mentioned for destinations are measured on Hwy 200, heading northwest from the junction of Hwys 200 and 80 (the road to Guadalajara) at Melaque.

La Cruz de Loreto

☎ 322

The village of La Cruz de Loreto, west of Hwy 200 and 90km south of Puerto Vallarta, is next to a wetland estuary and nature reserve. It's also the closest village to one of Mexico's most attractive, ecofriendly and expensive all-inclusive hotels. Love for nature and luxury are in the air at **Hotelito Desconocido** (☎ 281-40-10, in the US 800-851-4130; www.hotelito .com; La Cruz de Loreto; r US$370, ste US$450-670; 🐾)), an unforgettable solar-powered resort. As the sun sets, the candles are lit and the evening orchestra of frogs, birds and cicadas begins, you'll find yourself drunk with relaxation.

COSTA ALEGRE BEACHES

South of Puerto Vallarta, somewhere on the Costa Alegre, is your beach, the one you've dreamed about. It may be an isolated, tricky-to-get-to stretch of creamy sand with no facilities, or perhaps it's dotted with beach-happy souls like yourself, quaffing beers and feasting on fresh seafood from a *palapa* (thatched-roof) restaurant. The following beaches, listed from north to south, are sure to satisfy even the pickiest beach connoisseur:

- **Playa Pérula** (Km 76; p150) This scenic stretch of honeyed sand, located at the northern end of 11km Bahía de Chamela, is known for its tranquil waters, which are ideal for swimming and fishing. There are a good selection of palapa restaurants, economical accommodations and *panga* (motorized skiff) captains looking for passengers intent on snorkeling and fishing excursions.

- **Playa Chamela** and **Playa La Negrita** (Km 64; p150) Barely touched by tourism, these two locally favored beaches at the south end of Bahía de Chamela have a smattering of seafood shacks, no accommodations, and a priceless quality called solitude.

- **Playa Careyes** (Km 52; p151) With verdant headlands rising from the sea and excellent bird- and wildlife-watching, this quiet beach provides the perfect setting for beach camping. Local fishermen are on hand, eager to take you fishing.

- **Playa Tecuán** (Km 33; p151) Located 10km off the highway near an abandoned resort, this deserted white-sand beach has no facilities but tremendous opportunities for camping, beach hiking and advanced surfing. A nearby lagoon is rife with birds, crocodiles and the occasional ocelot.

- **Playa Tenacatita** (Km 28; p152) Crystal-clear waters, terrific palapa restaurants, a fair selection of accommodations and a merry community of return visitors make this 3km white-sand beach on Bahía Tenacatita enduringly popular.

- **Playa Boca de Iguanas** (Km 19; p153) Also on Bahía Tenacatita, this 10km beach has mild surf and shallow waters ideal for swimming. The broad beach is a prime spot for hiking and beachcombing. A few good accommodation choices and a gorgeous palm-fringed bay make for a relaxing stay.

- **Playa La Manzanilla** (Km 13; p153) At the southern end of Bahía Tenacatita, this drowsy town is known for its long, gently sloping beach, friendly palapa restaurants, exceptional fishing and sizable population of crocodiles lazing away in the lagoon.

- **Playa Cuastecomate** (Km 3; p155) Located 3km west of San Patricio-Melaque, this tiny cove within Bahía de Cuastecomate is one of the most scenic beaches on the entire Pacific coast. Calm waters make for safe swimming and good snorkeling.

Take a dip in the saltwater pool before slipping into the ever-so-smooth sheets in your lagoon-side bungalow on stilts. In the morning simply raise a flag and the staff will bring you coffee in bed. There's 65km of beach, the bird-watching is excellent, and a sea-turtle protection project operates from June to February; guests can set baby turtles free from September to December. Rates include all meals and activities such as horseback riding, kayaking, windsurfing, yoga, and wildlife-watching excursions. Spa services will cost you extra.

Quémaro
☎ 322

At Km 83 is the sign for Quémaro, a small, dusty village of dirt roads and shabby housing. But just past this village, on a short gravel road toward the coast, is one of the fanciest and priciest resorts in all of Mexico. At **Las Alamandas** (☎ 285-55-00, in the US 888-882-96-16; www.alamandas.com; Hwy 200, Km 83.5; r US$460-910, ste US$910-1900; 🏊), luxurious and colorful suites nestle in six separate adobe buildings, all simply beautiful with private terraces or patios. Most have stunning sea views and are surrounded by spacious, well-manicured and palm-studded grounds. There's a nice pool, and the compact, golden-sand beach is deliciously private. Naturally the service is top-notch, as is the gourmet food – if you can afford to stay here, you may as well get the all-inclusive plan, as there aren't many restaurants in the area. Reservations are a must; without them you won't get past the security gate.

Playa Pérula
☎ 315

Down a side road from Km 76, toward the north end of tranquil 11km-long Bahía de Chamela, lies the rather bleak town of Pérula. Its beach, however, is long, flat and sheltered – great for swimming, boogie boarding and extended walks. There are only a few *palapa* restaurants, the sands aren't overrun with tourists, and islands offshore break the ocean's horizon. In winter, whales bask in the warm bay waters, and you can always hire a boat from the beach for fishing trips. For those who can deal with few luxuries and services in an unassuming Mexican beach town, this could end up being quite a pleasant stop.

Red Snapper RV Park & Restaurant (☎ 333-97-84; redsnapperrv@hotmail.com; tent/trailer US$6/12) occupies a prime stretch of beach. This well-run RV haven has 15 spaces, five of which front the beach. The casual restaurant is a good hangout. Monthly and weekly discounts are available. Get here by heading into town 3km from the highway; after the first *tope* (speed bump) turn left.

Although **Hotel y Bungalows Playa Dorada** (☎ 333-97-10; www.playa-dorada.com.mx; Tiburón 40; d/tr US$50/60, bungalow US$80-100; 🅿 🏊) won't win any architecture prizes, it's right on the beach overlooking a particularly glorious stretch of yellow sand. The rooms are basic, clean and freshly painted, and come with up-to-date fixtures. Bungalows up the ante with air-con, a full kitchen and a small living room. Also on offer are a dozen trailer spots with full hookups (US$12).

A stone's throw from the beach, the budget **Hotel Las Palmas** (☎ 333-98-77; Independencia 30; s US$15, d US$18-25, tr US$38) offers nine dark and cool rooms arranged around a shady courtyard. Meet like-minded souls in the communal kitchen.

Long-distance buses don't head straight into Pérula; they stop at the highway crossroads known as 'El Super'. From there, call a taxi – if you're lucky there will be cheaper *taxis colectivos* (shared taxis). It's about a 10-minute drive to Pérula.

Playas La Negrita & Chamela
☎ 315

Near the Km 64 highway marker, a dirt road leads to a couple of isolated and relaxing beaches nestled in at the south end of Bahía de Chamela and great for day trips. Chamela beach has a calm shore with small waves and is home to a handful of *palapa* restaurants and some fishing boats. The feel is small and local, so if you don't want to see any gringos this is a good shot. A five-minute walk from here and just past a rocky point is La Negrita, 50m of tiny cove beach with one small restaurant. Neither of these places is built up, so no accommodation is available (other than possibly camping – ask first).

To find these little havens, take the dirt road just 30m south of yellow 'Chamela principal' bridge. Go about 1km along this road – you'll pass a small village and then a lagoon. Don't follow the fork up to the left, unless you want to see some abandoned condominiums. Where it forks right is Chamela beach; at the stony end just past this fork is La Negrita.

Playa Careyes
☎ 315

Another small and beautiful beach is Careyes, sheltered in a dune cove and sloping steeply to the water. Here you'll find only friendly locals, a snack and beer shack and some fishing cooperative boats. A big pink *palapa* building sits as a landmark on the hillside above.

Careyes is 200m down a dirt road just south of the white Careyes bridge (*not* the nearby Careyitos bridge) at Km 52. Look for a bus-stop shed and an '*acceso publico*' (public access) sign signifying the turnoff.

At Km 53.5, taking full advantage of the amazing scenery, is the terrifically romantic **El Careyes Beach Resort & Spa** (☎ 800-508 79-23, in the US 800-728-9098; www.mexicoboutiquehotels.com/thecareyes; Hwy 200, Km 53.5; r US$365, ste US$455-1099; 🗶 🖭). A bottle of champagne and an overflowing fruit basket welcomes honeymooners and lovebirds to flower-filled suites with private, ocean-view plunge pools. You can relax to the sounds of the tranquil bay on sheltered, pillow-piled outdoor beds, or enjoy a massage before indulging in a sunset dinner at La Lantana, the on-site restaurant with a menu of 'food of the sea gods' as interpreted by renowned Mexican chef Patricia Quintana.

Playas Las Brisas & La Chica
☎ 315

These two beaches head off in opposite directions from the village of **Arroyo Seco**, about 4km down a dirt road from the highway at Km 36.

When you find the school yard with a mural of Snow White, turn right and go 1.5km past farmland and a red gate. A nice beach with latte-colored sand, no services and few people awaits between two headlands.

To get to Las Brisas, turn left at the schoolyard and right at the fork. Go past farmland about 1.5km and you'll reach the sea. Here too there are no services, though camping and RV parking are possible under the palm-tree-shaded area (someone may turn up to collect a small property-use fee). The long, flat beach has very surfable waves and little competition for them.

Playa Tecuán

About 10km off the highway at Km 33 lie the pristine shores of Playa Tecuán. High above the beach is the abandoned resort of Hotel Tucuán, a spooky skeleton of doorless rooms, broken windows and caved-in beamed hallways just waiting to be turned

---

COCOS FRIOS: 10 PESOS!

What says 'tropical' more than lying on a hammock at the beach, sipping through a straw the transparent and mildly sweet milk from a freshly opened coconut? *Cocos* are available at many beachside restaurants or road stalls; the dead giveaway is a shady pile of them near a chopping block (often a section of palm tree) cleaved by a large machete.

If you're very lucky, the *cocos* will be stored in big freezer-like compartments and come out cold, but sipping coconut milk straight out of a coconut is wonderfully refreshing even at air temperature. And, unlike some of Mexico's tap water, it's safe to drink. Some huge specimens can store up to 1L of liquid, though most probably hold about half that.

First the coconuteer selects a (hopefully) big green coconut, tender at the stalk end. This signifies the coconut is immature, has soft flesh and harbors plenty of milk. The coconuteer then chops off one end (enough to make it stand upright) and proceeds to chip away at the other end: once the outer shell is off, the tender white flesh begins to show. The trick is to avoid piercing this layer with a severe chop that would have liquid spraying everywhere, and instead to just expose and peel it back slowly without losing any milk. Most coconuteers have this down to an art, and we haven't seen any with missing fingers yet.

Prices vary from US$0.50 to US$1.50, but most cost around US$1. In tourist areas and fancier restaurants, expect to pay at least this. The price may include a final few whacks to split the fruit's hulk in half after you've finished the milk. Have the coconuteer add chili, lime juice and salt, grab a spoon, and enjoy scooping out the tender, meaty flesh…a great quick snack anytime!

into the snazziest youth hostel in existence. Horror film buffs might know this was the location for the slasher flick *I Still Know What You Did Last Summer*. You can still see steel kitchen freezers and bats in the pantries. It's a cool experience and worth getting to if you've got wheels – but remember to be respectful, as it's still considered private property.

The 2km road going south along Playa Tecuán is part of an old landing strip. It passes a private housing complex on the mountain and eventually peters out at the edge of a pretty lagoon.

Bahía Tenacatita

☎ 315 / pop 165

On the western promontory of **Bahía Tenacatita**, and a longtime favorite destination of snowbirds and escape artists, the town of Tenacatita is a sometimes crowded but always beguiling beach destination with a long, curving white-sand beach and safe conditions for extended camping. Take your pick from three separate beaches: as you drive the 8.5km into town from the highway, you pass **Playa Mar Abierto** on the right, which extends for kilometers back to the north toward **Playa Tecuán**. You then hit **Playa Tenacatita** itself, which is lined with *palapa* seafood restaurants but remains beautiful, wide and calm. And over to the right a bit, just over a small hill and tucked into some headlands in between these two larger beaches, are the tiny twin shores of **Playa Mora**. The snorkeling is great in the crystal-clear waters around the protected rocks here.

A mangrove lagoon backing onto Playa Tenacatita is home to scores of birds and sunning reptiles. Boat tours of **El Manglar** (the Mangrove) are available; ask at the Restaurant Fiesta Mexicana, which is on the main road in the center of town. Trips take one hour and cost US$30 per boatload for up to six; each extra person pays US$3 (boats can take a total of up to 10 people). Bring insect repellent.

For groceries or phone service, head to the village of El Rebalsito, 3km from the beach on the Hwy 200–Tenacatita road.

Sleeping & Eating

Stretching north from Punta Tenacatita along a particularly fine stretch of sand is a 3km-long sand dune where RVs set up camp for the winter. RV campers can try the unofficial free sites at Playa Mora – space is limited here, so be considerate. Camping is good on the main beach, though you may need to ask permission (check with the proprietors of the nearest beachfront restaurant).

Las Villetas Suites (☎ 355-53-54 in Barra de Navidad; d US$60; ▨) Overlooking the beach, Las Villetas has 10 very pleasant suites with kitchens, sofa areas, TVs with DVD players and beach views. It also has a pool and Jacuzzi, but the electricity and water supply don't always function properly here. Kayaks are available to borrow. You'll find Las Villetas 200m further south from Hotel Paraíso de Tenacatita.

Hotel Los Amigos (☎ 872-31-65; s US$45-50, d US$65-70; ▨) You can't miss this brand-new, bright-yellow small hotel 100m from the beach opposite the Restaurant Fiesta Mexicana. On offer are 18 modest and clean rooms, all with air-con and hot water. Prices drop precipitously during the low season, and discounts are offered for longer stays.

Hotel Paraíso de Tenacatita (☎ 355-59-15; dobie@prodigy.net.mx; d US$30; ▨ ▨) This hotel offers 23 adequate rooms on the beach, though there's no hot water. It's the orange building just beyond the last *palapa* restaurant toward the south. The restaurant here, open until 10pm, is the only place in town to get a meal after the sun goes down.

Hotel Costa Alegre (☎ 351-51-21; d US$28; ▨) If you can't find a room at any of the other places, try this one. It's on the main road in El Rebalsito, the service town between the highway and Tenacatita. It has air-con, hot water and large, modern rooms.

Seafood *palapas* provide most of the nourishment here. They cater to day-trippers and thus tend to close at 6pm or 7pm.

Restaurant Fiesta Mexicana (☎ 338-63-16; mains US$4-12; ☺ breakfast, lunch & dinner) is Tenacatita's most visible – and best – restaurant, serving delectable seafood dishes with a twist. Try their signature dish, *rollo del mar* (a fish fillet stuffed with shrimp, wrapped in bacon and smothered in an almond cream sauce; US$9). Also, if you've been curious to try *raicilla*, a fiery local distillate elicited from the maguey cactus, here they'll set you up.

Getting There & Away

Tenacatita is 8.5km from Hwy 200 (Km 28) via a good paved road. Bus service provided by Transportes Cihuatlán travels between El

Rebalsito and Manzanillo once a day; it departs at dawn (inquire for the hour, which varies) and returns from Manzanillo at around 3pm to arrive back in El Rebalsito at around 6pm. Taxis and *combis* (minibuses) operate between El Rebalsito and Tenacatita.

BOCA DE IGUANAS

Smack in the middle of Bahía Tenacatita lies the wide, long and very pleasant **Playa Boca de Iguanas** (Km 19). The surf is mild, the sand is hot and wonderful, and the beach is quite shallow for a long way out, making it good for a swim (just don't go past the rocky point, as a dangerous riptide kicks in). The palm-fringed bay curves uninterrupted all the way around to La Manzanilla, providing a tranquil one-hour walk along a firm waterline. An abandoned hotel nearby adds visual interest and curiosity (clue: propane explosion).

There's a couple of beachside RV parks, two 'hotels,' a restaurant and a small lagoon that's home to a very large crocodile.

To get there, take the paved road about 2.5km from the highway at Km 19. *Taxis colectivos* regularly pick up and drop off passengers at the highway turnoff; a ride into town will set you back US$1.

Sleeping & Eating

Coconuts by the Sea (☎ 351-52-32; www.coconutsby thesea.com; apt US$95;) Perched high on the bluff above the beach, Coconuts has grand views to the other side of the bay. The four extremely comfortable and charming apartments are very welcoming: all have full kitchens (bring food), wireless Internet, cable TV, air-con, king-size beds and patios. Plans are afoot for a third apartment. There's a small pool on a grassy cliff. Getting there is tricky: phone or email beforehand.

Boca de Iguana Camping & Trailer Park (camping per person US$5.50, trailer sites US$15) This campground sits on the beach, with pleasant sites under peaceful palms.

Boca Beach Campground (☎ 317-381-03-93; bocabeach@hotmail.com; trailer sites US$15, camping per person US$7) The biggest of all, Boca Beach has more than 60 palmy sites.

Entre Palmeras (☎ 33-36-13-67-35 in Guadalajara; camp sites per person US$3.50, r/bungalows US$25/45) With eight bungalows and 12 rooms with fans, Entre Palmeras offers unremarkable accommodation. Camp sites are cheap and OK but not right on the beach. The best thing here is the restaurant, which has views of the small lagoon and sometimes of Señor Cocodrilo. You'll find it just off the beach on the north side of the road.

LA MANZANILLA & AROUND

At the sheltered, southern end of Bahía Tenacatita basks the peaceful, dusty little town of La Manzanilla (Km 13). It's home to some decent restaurants, an agreeable beach, a few expat residents and many locals. Tourism still hasn't quite caught on here (there's no Internet café yet), but the town has grown mightily during the past few years.

Activities

Get out on the water or into the bush with **Immersion Adventures** (☎ 351-53-41; www.immersion adventures.com), an ecologically minded provider offering sea kayaking, snorkeling, birding and cultural tours to many corners of the Costa Alegre. Half-day tours cost US$60 to US$75 per person, while full-day tours cost US$110 to US$125. Prices include kayaks, snorkeling gear and a snack or lunch, all experience levels are accommodated. Custom tours are also possible. You can also just rent kayaks (US$10 to US$15 per hour). Dave, the manager, has his office at his home, on the road into town (look for the A-frame sign).

DON'T FEED THE CROCODILES!

At the northern end of the main road in La Manzanilla is a lagoon filled with…large crocodiles! They haul themselves up on the sandy beach to bask in the sun and lurk in the water like sinister logs. A recently built viewing platform over the lagoon, intended to prevent folks from getting too close to the crocs, has had the reverse effect. Now the crocs and the people gaze at each other through a chain-link fence at a *different* edge of the lagoon. An understated sign – *'Cuidado con los cocodrilos'* ('Take care with the crocodiles') – goes unheeded by some irresponsible souls who see fit to toss chicken bones over the fence to incite a water-churning ruckus. If you witness such a thing, use your burgeoning Spanish-language skills to chastise them roundly.

Courses

La Catalina Natural Language School (☎ 351-53-62; www.lacatalinaschool.com; Montana del Mar; per week US$135) offers one- to four-week courses for beginning to advanced-level students, and a Spanish camp for kids ages five to 12 (US$150 per week). In addition to daily classes, the school provides many opportunities to learn Spanish outside the classroom through volunteer work and cultural events, and they also arrange guided excursions to local areas of interest. Homestays with local families are available for US$95 to US$210 per week, depending on the number of meals. Courses start on Mondays year-round, except the week of Christmas.

Sleeping

With a slowly growing contingent of expats who've put down seasonal roots, La Manzanilla has a good selection of stylish, well-priced accommodation choices, in addition to one time-honored cheapie and ample space for camping.

Palapa Joe's Restaurant & Bungalows (☎ 351-52-67, 351-51-27; www.jjsantanavacationrentals.com; Asunción 163; bungalows d/tr US$65/70; ✖) For choice digs in the somnambulant heart of downtown La Manzanilla, commandeer one of these two big bungalows with kitchenettes in a peaceful backyard garden. The decor is refined, there's cable TV and you can hang out in the cool covered rooftop terrace with an unheated Jacuzzi.

La Casa de María (☎ 351-50-44; www.lacasamaria.com; cnr Los Angeles Locos & Conca Molida; apt US$70-90) This place has five peaceful, artistically decorated and very spacious apartments, all with private patios. María is the gracious host and opens her rooftop *palapa* terrace to community teaching projects such as art, yoga, meditation, cooking or dance (teachers with project ideas can contact her). Her house is one street south of the main road into town.

La Casa en la Playa (☎ 351-52-67; www.jjsantanavacationrentals.com; Asunción s/n; d/q US$50/65; ✖) Between the ocean and the main street, this little beach house offers three units with warm and unassuming decor, a kitchen and a spacious dining area well suited to dinner parties. A fully enclosed garden area has plenty of chairs and tables for seating and its own outdoor shower. Advance reservations are recommended.

Hotel Posada Tonalá (☎ 351-54-74; posadatonala@hotmail.com; Asunción 75; d US$30, q US$50-65) Tonalá comes modern and shiny-tile clean, with nice wood details and pleasing architecture. Spacious rooms include TV, fans and whimsically carved wooden furniture. Most face into a modern *palapa* patio area.

Casa Maguey (☎ 351-50-12; www.casamaguey.com; bungalows US$50-80) Perched above the beach and surrounded by a lush, hilly garden, Casa Maguey's three bungalows are all charmingly different. Each is like a home and is wonderfully decorated with Mexican tiles. Book early if you want to stay during high season (November through April).

Hotel Posada del Cazador (☎ 351-50-00; Asunción 183; s/d US$15/25) This posada may be barebones, budget and bleak, but it's basically bearable and won't break the bank.

El Tamarindo Golf Resort & Spa (☎ 800-508-79-23, in the US 800-728-9098; www.eltamarindoresort.com; Hwy 200, Km 7.5; villas US$479-835; P ✖ ♨ ♋) Bringing considerable luxury and panache to the southern tip of Bahía Tenacatita, this resort is the ultimate in romantic getaways, with three secluded beaches on 8 sq km of breathtaking wilderness. Visitors disappear into 28 warmly appointed, private bungalows with plunge pools and poolside beds. Oceanside massage *palapas* and double spa-treatment rooms make relaxing with your companion effortless. El Tamarindo also has a stunning golf course – think skinny dipping between birdies. El Tamarindo is 7km north of Melaque.

At the northern end of town, just past the crocodiles' lagoon, is **RV parking** (sites US$3); there are no hookups or services. Find a pleasant shady site that appeals, and pay the man snoozing under a palm. **Campamento Ecológico** (camp sites per person US$3.50) is a 10-minute walk further down the beach; rates include basic showers and toilets.

Eating

Activity in La Manzanilla winds down to the speed of molasses in the summer, and some of the restaurants close down altogether.

Martin's Restaurant (☎ 351-51-06; Playa Blanca; mains US$6-15; ☉ 8am-11pm) This rustic-chic restaurant, affording a pleasing view of the sea through swaying palms, prepares wonderful gourmet seafood, meats, soups, salads and fajitas. At breakfast, it's omelets, crepes and nicely arranged fruit platters. The 2nd-floor open *palapa* is romantically lit at night, and service is first-rate. Enjoy a Cuban cigar, if you must, but by all means save room for the flambéed bananas. The restaurant is on the main road at the south end of town.

Restaurant Rincón (☎ 351-71-97; Playa Blanca; mains US$4.50-11; ☼ 8am-6pm) This casual seafood *palapa* on the beach serves superlative shrimp seviche (US$6) and a delectable fish fillet *al mojo de ajo* (in a garlic sauce; US$5). Round it all out with coconut milk slurped straight from the shell (US$1).

Restaurant El Quetzal (☎ 351-52-76; Asunción 13; mains US$4-12, ☼ noon-11pm Mon-Sat) Though it sits underneath a rather gloomy indoor *palapa*, El Quetzal's Mexican and quasi-French menu is interesting – it ranges from *pozole* (a hearty soup of hominy, meat or seafood, vegetables and chilies) to duck in Dijon sauce.

Palapa Joe's Restaurant & Bungalows (Asunción 163; mains US$4-8; ☼ noon-10pm Tue-Sun) Joe's offers tasty food, such as roasted herb chicken or beer-battered shrimp, plus CNN on TV.

Chava's Café (Asunción s/n; ☼ 7am-4pm) This tiny but popular place near Hotel Posada Tonalá caters primarily to breakfasting gringos.

Getting There & Away
To get to La Manzanilla by bus, travel first to San Patricio-Melaque and then catch a local bus (US$1) at the depot. Local buses headed to San Patricio-Melaque (US$1) leave from the *zócalo* (main plaza). Local bus service between the two towns operates hourly from 8am to 5pm. A taxi costs about US$10. A taxi to/from Playa de Oro International Airport (64km from Manzanillo) costs US$30 to US$40, depending on your bargaining skills.

Playa Cuastecomate
You'll find this singular beach with mocha-colored sands and a full line-up of *palapa* restaurants about 3km west of Melaque. The little cove it inhabits is knockdown gorgeous: Bahía de Cuastecomate is nearly enclosed by the embrace of craggy mountains, and at its opening in the far distance strange rock formations rise from the sea in silhouette. Calm waters make for safe swimming and good snorkeling, and you can explore the village and surrounding hills. (A word to the wise: beware the mother of all speed bumps on the road as it descends into town.)

The only place to stay is at the resort wannabe **Royale Costa Azul** (☎ 315-355-5730; d US$45; ℗ ☒ ☒), a homely concrete hotel with rooms that are clean but clinical, with kitchens and rewarding views of the bay. The large pool overlooks the beach.

BAHÍA DE NAVIDAD
☎ 315
The tight arc of Bahía de Navidad is ringed by deep, honey-colored sand with two resort towns at either end, waving amiably at each other. Situated 5km apart, Barra de Navidad and San Patricio-Melaque are siblings with distinct personalities. Barra is beloved for its attractive cobbled streets and aura of good living, while Melaque, the scrappier of the two, draws budget-minded travelers seeking to get back to basics in a place that shuns pretension.

JALISCO, COLIMA & MICHOACÁN COASTS

PALM FRONDS, ANYONE?

One visit to any laid-back Mexican beach town and you will notice a peculiar commonality: almost all the open-air restaurants (called *enramadas* or *palapas*) on the sands are topped with layers and layers of dried palm-tree fronds. This ubiquitous, practical and extremely handy material literally grows on trees.

Each palm-tree frond produces its own sprig of coconuts and grows to about 4m in length. Fronds are 'harvested' and often dried on the ground before being layered onto rooftop support beams, where they'll last four to five years before needing to be replaced. Sit under one during a thunderstorm, and you will realize that they're a pretty efficient, inexpensive and protective covering – and they also provide vital shade under which to sip a refreshing margarita.

And if you ever drive your car onto the beach and get mired in sand, try this little trick: grab yourself a few fronds and stick them under the stuck tire, for traction. Often they're the only material on hand, and can save your ass surprisingly well.

Getting there & Away

Barra de Navidad and Melaque are served by Playa de Oro International Airport (ZLO), 26km southeast of Barra de Navidad on Hwy 200, which also serves Manzanillo. To get to each town from the airport, take a taxi (US$25, 30 minutes), or take a bus 15km to Cihuatlán and a cheaper taxi from there.

Both towns maintain separate bus terminals. See Getting There & Away in Melaque (p158) and Getting There & Around in Barra de Navidad (p162) for information on routes and pricing.

San Patricio-Melaque

pop 8000

Known by most as Melaque (meh-*lah*-keh), this kick-back beach resort on Bahía de Navidad hasn't lost its old-Mexico charm. Besides being a popular vacation destination for Mexican families and a low-key winter hangout for snowbirds (principally Canadians), the town is famous for its weeklong Fiesta de San Patricio in March.

The crumbling ruins of the Casa Grande Hotel are an imposing reminder of the destructive 1995 earthquake and subsequent *maremotos* (tidal waves) that severely damaged the region.

ORIENTATION

Melaque is compact and walkable. Most hotels, restaurants and public services are concentrated on or near east–west Farías, which runs parallel to the beach, and north–south López Mateos, the main Hwy 200 exit. Barra de Navidad is 5km southeast of Melaque via Hwy 200 or 2.5km by walking 30 to 45 minutes along the beach.

INFORMATION

The tourist office (p159) in Barra de Navidad has some basic information on Melaque.

Banamex (Farías s/n) Has an ATM but will not change US and Canadian dollars (unless you have an account there!); traveler's checks are changed from 9am to noon only.

Casa de Cambio Melaque (Pasaje Comercial 11, Farías s/n) Changes cash and traveler's checks at so-so rates.

Ciber@Net (Farías 27A; Internet per hr US$2; ☺ 9:30am-2:30pm & 4-8pm Mon-Sat) Air conditioned.

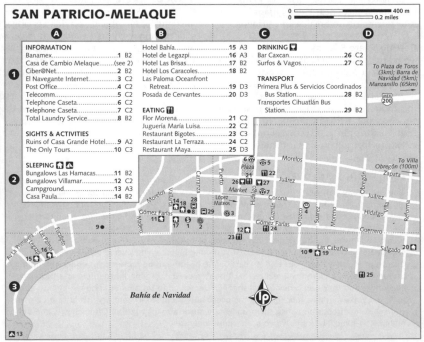

SAN PATRICIO-MELAQUE

INFORMATION	
Banamex	1 B2
Casa de Cambio Melaque	(see 2)
Ciber@Net	2 B2
El Navegante Internet	3 C2
Post Office	4 C2
Telecomm	5 C2
Telephone Caseta	6 C2
Telephone Caseta	7 C2
Total Laundry Service	8 B2

SIGHTS & ACTIVITIES	
Ruins of Casa Grande Hotel	9 A2
The Only Tours	10 C3

SLEEPING	
Bungalows Las Hamacas	11 B2
Bungalows Villamar	12 C2
Campground	13 A3
Casa Paula	14 B2

Hotel Bahía	15 A3
Hotel de Legazpi	16 A3
Hotel Las Brisas	17 B2
Hotel Los Caracoles	18 B2
Las Paloma Oceanfront Retreat	19 D3
Posada de Cervantes	20 D3

EATING	
Flor Morena	21 C2
Juguería María Luisa	22 C2
Restaurant Bigotes	23 C3
Restaurant La Terraza	24 C2
Restaurant Maya	25 D3

DRINKING	
Bar Caxcan	26 C2
Surfos & Vagos	27 C2

TRANSPORT	
Primera Plus & Servicios Coordinados Bus Station	28 B2
Transportes Cihuatlán Bus Station	29 B2

To Plaza de Toros (3km); Barra de Navidad (5km); Manzanillo (65km)

To Villa Obregón (100m)

Bahía de Navidad

El Navegante (Farías 48; Internet per hr US$2; ☺ 9am-2:30pm & 5-9pm Mon-Sat, 9am-2:30pm Sun) Air conditioned.

Post office (Orozco) Near Corona.

Telecomm (Morelos 53; ☺ 9am-2:30pm Mon-Fri) Offers the usual fax and phone services. See Map p156 for other *casetas telefónicas* (public telephone stations).

Total Laundry Service (Farías 26; per kg US$1)

SIGHTS & ACTIVITIES

Simply relax and take it easy. The main activities are swimming, lazing on the beach, watching pelicans fish at sunrise and sunset, climbing to the *mirador* (lookout) at the bay's west end, prowling the plaza and public market, or walking the beach to Barra de Navidad. A *tianguis* (indigenous people's market) is held every Wednesday starting around 8am; it's on Orozco two blocks east of the plaza.

The Only Tours (☎ 355-67-77; raystoursmelaque@yahoo.com; Las Cabañas 26) This small operation runs popular snorkeling tours (US$25) and tours to Colima (US$50). They also rent mountain bikes (half-/full-day US$6/10), snorkeling gear and body boards (each US$10 per day).

FESTIVALS & EVENTS

Melaque's biggest annual celebration is the **Fiesta de San Patricio** (St Patrick's Day Festival; March 17), honoring the town's patron saint. A week of festivities – including all-day parties, rodeos, a carnival, music, dances and nightly fireworks – leads up to the big day, which is marked with a Mass and the blessing of the fishing fleet. Take care when the *borrachos* (drunks) take over after dark.

SLEEPING

Rates vary greatly depending on the season; the following prices are for November through April. Discounts are common for longer stays.

Budget

Casa Paula (☎ 355-50-93; Vallarta 6; s/d US$15/30) Staying here is like staying with the sweetest grandma ever. In this simple home there are four basic rooms, with TVs and a fridge, set around a courtyard. It's very quiet and a family atmosphere pervades the place.

Hotel Los Caracoles (☎ 355-73-08; www.loscaracoles.com.mx; Farías 26; s/d/bungalow US$20/30/70) This fresh new hotel with 10 rooms and two

bungalows is not on the beach but makes amends with clean, modern rooms with hand-painted headboards and tiled desks.

Bungalows Villamar (☎ 355-50-05; Hidalgo 1; s/d US$20/28; ❄️) The Villamar has five spacious but worn garden bungalows, a pool and a beachfront terrace. It's owner Roberto speaks English.

The Ejidal beachfront **campground** (sites US$2), at the west end of town, has no facilities but inhabits an undeniably beautiful setting. Many of the nearby *enramadas* charge a nominal fee for showers and bathroom usage.

Midrange

Hotel Bahía (☎ 355-68-94; Legazpi 5; r US$30-35, bungalow US$30-50; ❄️) Just half a block from the beach, this family-run place is one of Melaque's best deals. It's clean, very well maintained and has a communal open-air kitchen. Four of the 23 units have private kitchens.

Posada de Cervantes (☎ 355-65-74; posadadecervantes@hotmail.com; Salgado 132; bungalows US$66-72; ❄️ ❄️) This well-decorated, gay-friendly inn has friendly management and charming sitting areas. The bungalows are a bit crammed, but some might call them cozy.

Hotel Las Brisas (☎ 355-51-08; Farías 9; s/d US$33/45, bungalows US$70-145; ❄️ ❄️) The beachfront Las Brisas has one of the nicest pools in the neighborhood, outdoor communal cooking facilities, friendly staff and a small library. All rooms have fridge, air-con and TV.

Hotel de Legazpi (☎ 355-83-97; hotel@delegazapi.com; Las Palmas 3; d/tr US$30/40, with kitchen US$50; P ❄️) Right on the beach, the Legazpi has bright, if slightly worn, rooms. It's very popular for the rooms with ocean views; they cost the same but are hard to get.

Bungalows Las Hámacas (☎ 355-51-13; Farías 13; d/q US$33/60; P ❄️) Ideal for larger groups, the beachfront Las Hámacas has chipping paint, and worn but big rooms with full kitchens.

Top End

Las Paloma Oceanfront Retreat (☎ 355-53-45; www.lapalomamexico.com; Las Cabañas 13; studios US$72-89; P ❄️ 💻 ❄️) Original art abounds at this unique boutique resort, which doubles as an art center. The singular, comfortable studios have kitchens and terraces with rewarding ocean views. Lush gardens, a 25m beachside swimming pool, complimentary breakfasts, a well-stocked library, and Internet access make an extended stay here extremely tempting. Reservations are a must, particularly if you are interested in the drawing, painting or mask-making classes held yearly from November to April.

EATING & DRINKING

From 6pm to midnight, food stands serve inexpensive Mexican fare a block east of the plaza along Juárez. A row of pleasant *palapa* restaurants (mains US$4 to US$11) stretches along the beach at the west end of town.

Flor Morena (Juárez s/n; mains $1.50-4; ☺ 6-11pm Tue-Sun) You may have to wait to get a seat in this tiny place run by women, but it's worth it. Everything is made fresh, there are plenty of vegetarian options and even the house specialty, shrimp *pozole,* costs less than US$4.

Restaurant Maya (Obregón 1; www.restaurantmaya .com; mains US$7-14; ☺ 6-11pm Wed-Sun & 10:30am-2pm Sun) The menu changes regularly but the quality at this Asian-fusion beachside hotspot is consistently excellent. Dinners include a range of gourmet salads, grilled meats and fish with exotic sauces, and there are appetizers like tequila lime prawns. Western favorites like eggs benedict and rich omelets with Brie rule the brunch menu.

Restaurant La Terraza (☎ 355-53-13; Guzmán 4; mains US$2.50-5; ☺ 7am-10pm) This warm, family-run spot serves organic coffee and a full breakfast menu in the morning and homemade bread, salads, salsa and traditional Mexican food for lunch and dinner. There's Internet access and a breezy 2nd-floor terrace, where on Friday nights there's a buffet (US$12 to US$15) and traditional dance performed by students from the local secondary school.

Restaurant Bigotes (☎ 355-69-34; López Mateos 2; mains US$5-10; ☺ 8am-9pm) Seafood is the specialty at this pleasant beachfront *palapa*; try the *guachinango a la naranja* (red snapper à l'orange) or *camarones al cilantro* (cilantro shrimp). The two-for-one happy hour (2pm to 8pm) is popular.

Juguería María Luisa (cnr López Mateos & Corona; snacks US$1-3) This place whips up fresh fruit and vegetable juices, *tortas* (Mexican-style sandwiches made with rolls) and good burgers.

Surfos & Vagos (☎ 355-64-13; cnr Juárez & Hidalgo; ☺ 8pm-2am) Rocking to an agreeable beat, this 2nd-floor open *palapa* has a pool table and board games.

Bar Caxcan (cnr López Mateos & Juárez) The new kid in town thumps out techno beats, has a pool table and an extended happy hour and attracts mostly young men.

ENTERTAINMENT

During the winter and spring, *corridas de toros* (bullfights) occasionally liven up the Plaza de Toros, 3km southeast of town off Hwy 200, near the Barra turnoff. Watch for flyers promoting *charreadas* (Mexican rodeos), and keep an ear out for cruising, megaphone-equipped cars scratchily announcing *béisbol* games and *fútbol* (soccer) matches.

GETTING THERE & AWAY
Bus

Melaque has three bus stations. Transportes Cihuatlán and Primera Plus/Servicios Coordinados are on opposite sides of Carranza at the corner of Farías. Both have 1st- and 2nd-class buses and ply similar routes for similar fares. The 1st-class Primera Plus bus station is a block east on Farías. Buses trundling daily out of these stations serve the following destinations:

Barra de Navidad (US$0.30, 10min, every 15min 6am-9pm) Or take any southbound long-distance bus.

Guadalajara (US$23, 5-7½hr, 6 1st-class; US$19, 5-7½hr, 10 2nd-class)

Manzanillo (US$5, 1-1½hr, 10 1st-class; US$4, 1-1½hr, 2nd-class at least hourly 3am-11:30pm)

Puerto Vallarta (US$17, 3½-5hr, 2 1st-class; US$14, 3½-5hr, 17 2nd-class)

Local buses for Villa Obregón (US$0.50, 1km) and Barra de Navidad (US$0.50, 15 to 20 minutes, 5km) stop near the plaza by the Paletería Michoacán every 15 minutes.

Taxi

A taxi between Melaque and Barra should cost no more than US$5, or as little as US$3, depending on how well *tu hablas espanglish.*

Barra de Navidad
☎ 315 / pop 4000

The charming town of Barra de Navidad (usually simply called 'Barra') is squeezed onto a sandbar between Bahía de Navidad and the Laguna de Navidad. Barra de Navidad first came to prominence in 1564 when its shipyards produced the galleons used by conquistador Miguel López de Legazpi and Father André de Urdaneta to deliver the Philippines to King Philip of Spain. By 1600, however, most of the conquests were being conducted from Acapulco, and Barra slipped into sleepy obscurity (a state from which it has yet to fully emerge).

ORIENTATION

Legazpi, the main drag, runs parallel to the beach. Veracruz, the town's other major artery and the highway feeder, runs parallel to Legazpi before merging with it at the southern end of town, which terminates in a finger-like sandbar. Buses drop passengers at offices on Legazpi.

INFORMATION

The regional **tourist office** (☎ 355-83-83; www .costaalegre.com; Jalisco 67; ☺ 9am-5pm Mon-Fri, 10am-6pm Sat & Sun) has free maps and information about more than just Barra; it also runs an information kiosk on the jetty during the high season.

Barra has an air-conditioned **Banamex ATM** (Veracruz s/n). You can change money at **Vinos y Licores Barra de Navidad** (Legazpi s/n; ☺ 8:30am-11pm), on the plaza, or at the more official **casa de cambio** (Veracruz 212).

Telecomm (Veracruz 212-B; ☺ 9am-3pm Mon-Fri) and **Mini-Market Hawaii** (Legazpi at Sonora; ☺ noon-10pm) both have telephone and fax services. See Map p159 for *caseta* locations. There's also a **post office** (cnr Sinaloa & Mazatlán).

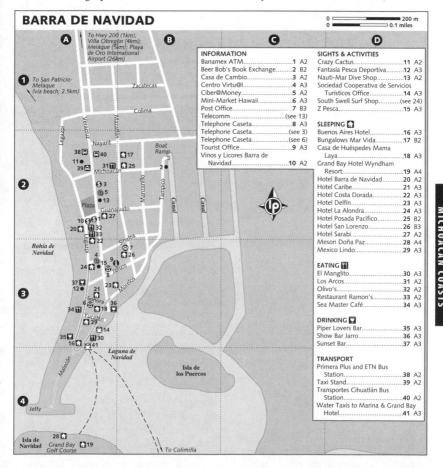

BARRA DE NAVIDAD

INFORMATION	
Banamex ATM	1 A2
Beer Bob's Book Exchange	2 B2
Casa de Cambio	3 A2
Centro Virtu@l	4 A3
Ciber@Money	5 A2
Mini-Market Hawaii	6 A3
Post Office	7 B3
Telecomm	(see 13)
Telephone Caseta	8 A3
Telephone Caseta	(see 3)
Telephone Caseta	(see 6)
Tourist Office	9 A3
Vinos y Licores Barra de Navidad	10 A2

SIGHTS & ACTIVITIES	
Crazy Cactus	11 A2
Fantasía Pesca Deportiva	12 A3
Nauti-Mar Dive Shop	13 A2
Sociedad Cooperativa de Servicios Turísticos Office	14 A3
South Swell Surf Shop	(see 24)
Z Pesca	15 A3

SLEEPING	
Buenos Aires Hotel	16 A3
Bungalows Mar Vida	17 B2
Casa de Huéspedes Mama Laya	18 A3
Grand Bay Hotel Wyndham Resort	19 A4
Hotel Barra de Navidad	20 A2
Hotel Caribe	21 A3
Hotel Costa Dorada	22 A3
Hotel Delfín	23 A3
Hotel La Alondra	24 A3
Hotel Posada Pacífico	25 B2
Hotel San Lorenzo	26 B3
Hotel Sarabi	27 A2
Meson Doña Paz	28 A4
Mexico Lindo	29 A3

EATING	
El Manglito	30 A3
Los Arcos	31 A2
Olivo's	32 A2
Restaurant Ramon's	33 A2
Sea Master Café	34 A3

DRINKING	
Piper Lovers Bar	35 A3
Show Bar Jarro	36 A3
Sunset Bar	37 A3

TRANSPORT	
Primera Plus and ETN Bus Station	38 A2
Taxi Stand	39 A2
Transportes Cihuatlán Bus Station	40 A2
Water Taxis to Marina & Grand Bay Hotel	41 A3

JALISCO, COLIMA & MICHOACÁN COASTS

Ciber@Money (Veracruz 212-C; per hr US$2.50; ⏱ 9am-2pm & 4-7pm Mon-Fri, 9am-6:30pm Sat) has a decent Internet connection, as does **Centro Virtu@l** (Veracruz s/n; per hr US$2; ⏱ noon-9pm Mon-Fri, 10am-3pm Sat).

You can exchange, but not buy, books at **Beer Bob's Book Exchange** (Tampico 8; ⏱ noon-3pm Mon-Fri).

ACTIVITIES

Barra's steep and narrow beach is lovely to behold, but with its steep slope waves crash close to shore. Conditions can get rough for swimming, with the gentlest waves arriving in the early mornings. Small but surfable right and left breaks are snatched up by determined souls at the southernmost end of the beach near the jetty.

South Swell Surf Shop (☎ 354-54-7; www.south swellmex.com; Sinaloa 16; rentals/lessons per day US$25/42), in the Hotel La Alondra, rents and sells body boards and surfboards and provides surfing lessons and information about surfing spots further afield.

Boards can also be rented from **Crazy Cactus** (☎ 355-60-99; Veracruz 165; ⏱ 9:30am-6pm Mon-Sat), as can snorkeling gear, kayaks and bicycles (not to mention cars and apartments). **Nauti-Mar dive shop** (☎ 355-57-91; Veracruz 204) rents out outfits for all manner of aquatic sports.

Boat Trips

Boat trips into the Laguna de Navidad are a Barra highlight. The boat operators' cooperative, **Sociedad Cooperativa de Servicios Turísticos** (Veracruz 40; ⏱ 7am-9pm), offers boat excursions, ranging from half-hour trips around the lagoon (US$20 per boat) to all-day jungle trips to Tenacatita (US$200 per boat). Prices (for up to eight people) are posted at the open-air lagoon-side office. The cooperative also offers fishing (from US$80 for four hours), snorkeling (from US$25) and diving trips.

For a short jaunt out on the water, you could also catch a **water taxi** from a nearby dock and head over to the Grand Bay Hotel on Isla de Navidad or to Colimilla (US$2 round-trip). At the latter, you can laze your afternoon away at one of the pleasant restaurants, all with rewarding views of the lagoon and super-fresh *mariscos* (seafood).

Walking

For a pleasant day of intensive beach strolling, you can pad the sands all the way to San Patricio-Melaque, 2.5km south on the other end of Bahía de Navidad. Start early in the morning with the sun at your back, and carry water and sun protection. At the far end of Melaque you'll find a trail leading beneath the cliff to a wonderfully craggy spot at the tip of the bay with splendid tide pools.

Sportfishing

The waters near Barra are rife with marlin, swordfish, albacore, *dorado* (dolphinfish), snapper and other more unusual catches. Fishing trips can be arranged at the boat operators' cooperative for about US$25 per hour, including gear. If a serious deep-sea fishing expedition is what you have in mind, pass on the *lanchas* (fast, open, outboard boats) and check out **Z Pesca** (☎ 355-60-99; Veracruz 204), or **Fantasía Pesca Deportiva** (☎ 355-68-24; Legazpi 213), both of which have better boats and equipment. A six-hour all-inclusive (except beer) trip costs US$180 to US$250, depending on the size of the boat and the number of fisher folk.

Golf

The Grand Bay Golf Course (☎ 355-50-50; Grand Bay Hotel Wyndham Resort, Isla de Navidad; green fees 18/27 holes US$216/240) is a celebrated 27-hole course with excellent vistas and greens carved into ocean dunes against a backdrop of mountains. Caddies and rental clubs are available.

FESTIVALS & EVENTS

Big-money international fishing tournaments are held annually for marlin, sailfish, tuna and *dorado*. The most important, the three-day **Torneo Internacional de Pesca**, is held around the third week in January. The two-day **Torneo Internacional de Marlin**, held during late May or early June, with another two-day tournament in mid-August.

SLEEPING

Barra has fewer beachfront rooms than its neighbor Melaque. The following prices are for the high season (between November and May). A bungalow is a room with a kitchen and sleeps at least three.

Budget

Hotel Caribe (☎ 355-59-52; Sonora 15; s US$15-20, d US$20-25) The popular Caribe is one of Barra's best budget deals. It has a rooftop terrace, hot water and 18 clean rooms, some of which are larger than others. Downstairs there's a pleasant garden offering respite on a hot afternoon. You'll be lucky to get a room here in the winter.

Hotel Posada Pacífico (☎ 355-53-59; Mazatlán 136 at Michoacán; s/d US$15/25, bungalow US$40; P) This friendly, comfortable posada has 25 large, clean rooms, plus four bungalows, each of which sleeps up to four people. Some English is spoken.

Casa de Huéspedes Mama Laya (☎ 355-50-88; Veracruz 69; r with/without bathroom US$20/15) On the lagoon side of town, the Mama Laya has stark, worn rooms with TV. Expect to get to know the family that runs the place. Prices appear to be negotiable.

Hotel San Lorenzo (☎ /fax 355-51-39; Sinaloa 7; s/d US$25/30) Try the less drab upstairs rooms at the bright-orange San Lorenzo (near Mazatlán) if all the other budget hotels in town are full.

Midrange

Hotel Delfín (☎ 355-50-68; www.hoteldelfinmx.com; Morelos 23; d/tr/ste US$50/60/120; P 🖳 🌫) With large, pleasant rooms that open onto shared balconies, a grassy pool area and exercise room, the Delfín is one of Barra's best hotels. Discounts are available for longer stays but repeat customers fill the place in winter.

Hotel Costa Dorada (☎ 355-64-10; Veracruz 174; bungalow s US$40-50, bungalow d US$60; P) This welcoming option offers 24 fastidious and whimsically tiled bungalows with diminutive TVs and good, firm mattresses. Grab an upstairs unit to benefit from the cross breeze.

Bungalows Mar Vida (☎ 355-59-11; www.tomzap .com/marvida.html; Mazatlán 168; apt US$55; 🌫 🌫) The fine little Mar Vida has five newly remodeled studio apartments, all with satellite TV, cheerful tile work and hand-carved doors. Some English is spoken.

Hotel La Alondra (☎ 355-83-73; www.alondrahotel .com; Sinaloa 16; s US$78-84, d US$106-117, ste US$182-264; P 🌫 🖳 🌫) Giving the town something of a skyline, this new five-story hotel tries to come off as a luxury hotel but falls short; the rooms have chintzy murals and balconies but are otherwise generic. The best reason to pay the prices asked is for the commanding views on the upper floors.

Hotel Barra de Navidad (☎ 355-51-22; www.hotel barradenavidad.com; Legazpi 250; s/d/tr US$62/72/78, bungalow US$144; 🌫 🌫) Providing Barra's best beach access, this modern, glowingly white

beachside hotel harbors a shaded, intimate courtyard and a small but inviting pool. The best rooms have ocean views and air-con.

Also recommended:

Buenos Aires Hotel (☎ 355-69-67; hotelbuenosaires mx@yahoo.com.mx; Veracruz 209; s/d US$50/60, ste US$85-90; 🌫 🌫 🌫) Crisp and efficient with no smoking and no children allowed.

Hotel Sarabi (☎ 355-64-10; www.hotelsarabi.com; Veracruz 196; bungalow US$50-80; P 🌫) Clean and efficiently run. Ask about the 'third night free' promotion.

Top End

Getting away from it all is a matter of considerable luxury on Isla de Navidad, a short water-taxi ride across the lagoon from Barra de Navidad.

Grand Bay Hotel Wyndham Resort (☎ 355-50-50; www.wyndham.com; Rinconada del Capitán s/n, Isla de Navidad; d US$350, ste US$550-680; 🌫 🖳 🌫) This superluxury resort is self-consciously magnificent and very large. The same adjectives apply to the rooms, which have marble floors, hand-carved furniture and bathrooms big enough to herd sheep in. If the weather's not hot enough for you, spend some time in your suite's steam bath or, better yet, at the pool's convenient swim-up bar. Justifying the hefty price tag are three grass tennis courts, golf packages, a 'kid's club' day-care center, and big fluffy bathrobes. Golf, tennis and other packages can be booked online.

Mesón Doña Paz (☎ 355-6441; www.mesondonapaz .com; Rinconada del Capitán s/n; Isla de Navidad; d US$350, ste US$460-575; 🌫 🖳 🌫) For something really special, check into this gorgeous colonial-style lodge where every room has a balcony facing the limpid lagoon. The grounds are graced by a tranquil private bay, lookout point and lush landscaping. All-inclusive plans and golf packages are available. Be sure to ask about low-season and promotional rates.

EATING

Several of Barra's many good restaurants are on the beachfront, offering beautiful sunset views, while others overlook the lagoon. Simple, inexpensive little indoor-outdoor places line Veracruz in the center of town. However, most are open only in the high season.

Sea Master Café (☎ 355-51-19; cnr Legazpi & Yucatán; mains US$6-15; 🕒 lunch & dinner) With a very pleasant environment perfect for tossing back cocktails, this place scores points by taking liberties with seafood. For instance, a dish called piña sea master fills a pineapple with shrimp, peppers, mushrooms and a buttery Kahlua sauce. Who needs desert?

Mexico Lindo (Legazpi 138; mains US$4-14; ☺ noon-10pm) With simple plastic tables under a corrugated tin roof, this place somehow manages to feel romantic and intimate at night. The menu features regional favorites like savory and sour tortilla soup, quesadillas, garlic fish tacos and shrimp seviche; a good selection of drinks and cocktails seals the deal.

El Manglito (☎ 355-85-90; Veracruz s/n; mains $7-10; ☺ 8am-7pm) An exuberantly decorated *palapa* overlooking the lagoon, El Manglito is a grand place to while away a hot afternoon watching the *lanchas* come and go. The service is slow but the seafood served is so good you'll soon forget about this minor inconvenience.

Los Arcos (cnr Mazatlán & Michoacán; mains US$3-5; ☺ 9am-11pm) One of the homiest place you'll eat at, Los Arcos has mom-and-pop cooking and serves homemade food in a tiny dining area.

Olivo's (cnr Legazpi & Guanajuato; mains US$9-14) Olivo's boasts artwork, a pleasant atmosphere and renowned Mediterranean food, including baked lamb and pork fillets.

Restaurant Ramon's (☎ 355-64-35; Legazpi 260; mains US$5-11; ☺ 7am-11pm) This casual and friendly *palapa* serves excellent fish tacos among other local and gringo favorites.

DRINKING

Sunset Bar (☎ 355-52-17; Jalisco 140; ☺ noon-2am) The waiter at this seaside saloon claims that 'the sunset' was named after the bar, and not the other way around. Humongous drink specials are served daily from 2pm to 10pm. A DJ spins nightly during the high season.

Piper Lovers Bar (☎ 355-67-47; Legazpi 154A; www.piperlover.com; ☺ 10am-2am) With its tough motorcycle-bar look and loud live music Wednesday through Saturday (from 9pm), this is the place to rock.

Show Bar Jarro (Veracruz near Yucatán; ☺ 9pm-4am) This down-to-earth, gay-friendly disco has pool tables and lagoon views.

GETTING THERE & AROUND
Bus

The long-distance buses stopping at San Patricio-Melaque (p158) also stop at Barra de Navidad (15 minutes before or after). Transportes Cihuatlán's station is at Veracruz 228; Primera Plus and ETN operate from small terminals nearby, on the opposite side of Veracruz.

In addition to the long-distance buses, colorful local buses connect Barra and Melaque (US$0.50, every 15 minutes, 6am to 9pm), stopping in Barra at the long-distance bus stations (buses stopping on the southbound side of the road loop round Legazpi and back to Melaque).

Boat

Water taxis operate on demand 24 hours a day from the dock at the southern end of Veracruz, offering service to the hotels on Isla de Navidad (US$1), the marina, the golf course and Colimilla. Also see p160 for information on boat tours.

Taxi

Catch taxis from the official **taxi stand** (cnr Veracruz & Michoacán) to ensure the best price.

COLIMA

Tiny Colima's coastline is dominated by the city of Manzanillo, home to one of Mexico's most important ports and a thriving tourism scene. South of town are the sleepy towns of Cuyutlán and El Paraíso, and Playa Boca de Pascuales, a legendary surf spot.

MANZANILLO
☎ 314 / pop 130,000

With a port that recently surpassed Veracruz to become the largest in Mexico, these are heady times in Manzanillo. Nowhere is the upbeat attitude more prevalent than downtown, where the waterfront has been enhanced with a 3km boardwalk along the ocean and a capacious seaside *zócalo*. Providing a dramatic setting for a promenade, at dusk swarms of starlings do their best to blot out the sunset, while the giant Swordfish Memorial creates an imposing silhouette. Away from the center, miles of pristine and unpopulated beaches ring nearby Bahía de Santiago and Bahía de Manzanillo, and the lagoons surrounding the town offer good bird-watching. And, befitting the city's deep-sea fishing reputation, fans call Manzanillo the 'World Capital of Sailfish,' and each year fishing tournaments draw hopeful anglers from all around.

Orientation

Manzanillo extends 16km from northwest to southeast. The resort hotels and finest beaches begin at Playa Azul, across the bay from Playa San Pedrito, the closest beach to the center. Further around the bay is the Península de Santiago, a rocky outcrop holding Las Hadas Resort and Playa La Audiencia. Just west of the peninsula, Bahía de Santiago is lined with excellent beaches.

Central Manzanillo is bound by Bahía de Manzanillo to the north, the Pacific Ocean to the west and Laguna de Cuyutlán to the south. Av Morelos, the main drag, runs along the north edge of town center, beside the sea. At its east end it meets Av Niños Héroes, which leads to Hwy 200.

Information

Banks Several banks with ATMs are scattered around the city center.

HSBC (Map p164; Av México s/n) Offers currency exchange.

Caseta Telefónica (Map p164; Av Morelos 144; ☾ 9am-10pm) Long-distance telephone and fax service. Public telephones are plentiful around the center.

Members.com (Map p164; Juárez 116; per hr US$2) Offers fast connections in a comfortable atmosphere.

Lavandería Lavimatic (Map p164; cnr Madero & Domínguez; per kg US$1.25; ☾ closed Sun) Within walking distance of the center.

Post office (Map p164; Galindo 30)

Tourist office (Map p163; ☎ 333-22-64; Blvd Miguel de la Madrid 4960, Km 8.5; www.visitacolima.com.mx; ☾ 9am-3pm & 5-7pm Mon-Thu, 9am-3pm Fri, 10am-2pm Sat) Dispenses information about Manzanillo and the state of Colima.

Tourist police (Map p164; ☎ 332-10-04) Stationed behind the Presidencia Municipal.

Sights & Activities

MUSEO UNIVERSITARIO DE ARQUEOLOGÍA

The University of Colima's **archaeological museum** (Map p164; ☎ 332-22-56; cnr Niños Héroes & Glorieta San Pedrito; admission US$1.50; ☾ 10am-2pm & 5-8pm Tue-Sat, 10am-1pm Sun) presents interesting objects from ancient Colima state and rotating exhibits of contemporary Mexican art. At the time of research the museum was undergoing renovation; it is scheduled to reopen in January 2007.

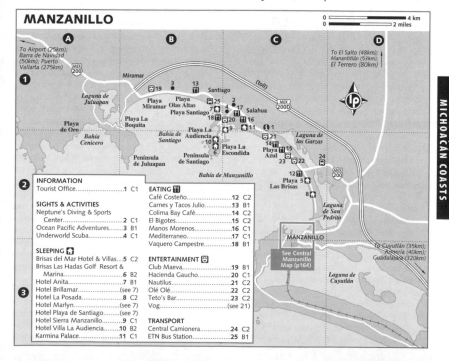

BEACHES

Playa San Pedrito, 1km northeast of the *zócalo*, is the closest beach to town. The next closest stretch of sand, spacious **Playa Las Brisas**, caters to a few hotels. **Playa Azul** stretches northwest from Las Brisas and curves around to Playa La Escondida and the best beaches in the area: **La Audiencia**, **Santiago**, **Olas Altas** and **Miramar**. Miramar and Olas Altas have the best surfing and bodysurfing waves in the area; surfboards can be rented at Miramar. Playa La Audiencia, lining a quiet cove on the west side of Península de Santiago, has more tranquil water and is popular for water-skiing and other noisy motorized water sports.

Getting to these beaches from the town center is easy: local buses marked 'Santiago,' 'Las Brisas' and 'Miramar' head around the bay to San Pedrito, Salahua, Santiago, Miramar and beaches along the way. 'Las Hadas' buses take a more circuitous, scenic route down Península de Santiago. These buses pick-up passengers from local bus stops, along the length of Calle 21 de Marzo, and from the main bus station, every 10 minutes from 6am to 11pm.

WATER SPORTS

Snorkeling, windsurfing, sailing, waterskiing and deep-sea fishing are all popular around the bay. The scuba diving in Manzanillo can be spectacular, and there are many sites to explore – either off one of the beaches or out on the bay.

The best diving operator is the well-established **Underworld Scuba** (Map p163; ☎ 333-06-42; www.divemanzanillo.com; Hwy 200, Km 15). This complete PADI dive center charges US$80 for two-tank dives, including equipment, or US$300 for PADI certification. Another good choice is **Neptune's Diving & Sports Center** (Map p163; ☎ 334-30-01; www.neptunesdiving.com; Hwy 200, Km 14.8), which offers similar dives, costs and services. They also do night dives and snorkeling trips.

SPORTFISHING

Sailfish and dorado are found in the waters off Manzanillo during every season of the year, while marlin and tuna are generally in the area from November to March.

Ocean Pacific Adventures (Map p163; ☎ 335-06-05, www.gomanzanillo.com/fishing) Supporting

CENTRAL MANZANILLO

INFORMATION		
ATM	1	A2
ATM	2	A2
ATM	3	A2
Caseta Telefónica	4	B2
HSBC	5	A2
Lavandería Lavimatic	6	A3
Members.com	7	A2
Post Office	8	A2
Presidencia Municipal	9	A2
Tourist Police	10	A2

SIGHTS & ACTIVITIES		
Museo Universitario de Arqueología	11	D1
Swordfish Memorial	12	A2

SLEEPING		
Hotel Colonial	13	A2
Hotel Emperador	14	A2
Hotel Flamingos	15	A2
Hotel San José	16	A3
Hotel San Pedrito	17	D1

EATING		
Los Candiles	(see 13)	
Market-Style Dining Hall	18	A2
Restaurant Emperador	(see 14)	
Restaurante Chantilly	19	A2

ENTERTAINMENT		
Bar Social	20	B2

TRANSPORT		
Local Bus Stop	21	B2
Local Bus Stop	22	A3
Local Bus Stop	23	D1
Local Bus Stop	24	D1

JALISCO, COLIMA & MICHOACÁN COASTS

DETOUR: EL SALTO FALLS & MANANTITLÁN BIOSPHERE

While it seems incredible, some people actually grow weary of gorgeous sandy beaches and crystalline ocean waters. For them, an excursion to the cool cascades of El Salto waterfall and to the highland cloud forests of Manantitlán Biosphere provides a lovely respite from the insufferable pressures of beach life.

The one-hour drive to El Salto takes you over meandering mountain roads through dense tropical deciduous forest and a few typical small villages. You'll pass by the Peña Colorada strip mine at the top of a mountain and the 27km blue pipeline used to move iron ore all the way back to the outskirts of Manzanillo.

One kilometer past the company town where the miners live is the entrance to **El Salto Park** (admission US$0.50). Beyond the gate, there's a new-fangled picnic area and water park with three spring-fed pools and an impressive water slide. Just down the road, across an iron bridge, is a nicer spot to lunch overlooking the falls, which cascade over two 10m steps into a series of inviting pools. Descend the stone steps and jump in! From the base of the falls, it's possible to float 100m downstream on your back beneath the canyon walls to where there's a beach of sorts. On weekends hungry masses devour tacos from a simple stand, but the rest of the week you'll likely have the place to yourself (and have to rely on the contents of your picnic basket). Overnight camping is allowed.

Back on the road, continue north 5km to the pleasant town of Manantitlán, which supports a good, traditional restaurant called La Herradura. Another 16km brings you to the entrance of **Manantitlán Biosphere** (☎ 317-381-01-54 in Spanish) an ecological reserve that gives refuge to more than 2900 plant species, half of which are endemic. A very bumpy but navigable road ascends 16km through exceptionally scenic territory to the 2700m summit and the small indigenous *ranchito* of **El Terrero**. Here you can spend the night in a rustic cabin shelter or at a shady campground with picnic tables, potable water and an outhouse. Even if there are no other people around, you may not be camping alone – the biosphere is home to a staggering 588 vertebrate animals including ocelots, pumas, boa constrictors, jaguars and lynxes. If this unnerves you, see if you can't get your hands on some locally brewed *pulque* (an ancient form of fermented agave) to calm your nerves.

If you've developed a taste for adventure, the road that brought you to El Terrero continues down the other side of the mountain into more unspoiled territory uncharted by this or any other guidebook. For more information about biospheres in Mexico visit www2.unesco.org/mab/bios 1-2.htm and access the interactive map.

Getting There & Away

Your journey begins in Manzanillo at the traffic circle near Km 4 on the main highway, where the highway to Manantitlán peels off to the north. From here it's 48km to El Salto and another 16km to the entrance of Manantitlán Biosphere (keep an eagle eye out for the sign reading 'Estación Biosfera'). You'll travel another slow 16km on bumpy roads to El Terrero. Departing from Manzanillo's Central Camionera (main bus station), 2nd-class buses bound for Manantitlán will drop you at El Salto, but you'll need a car to make it to El Terrero.

Manzanillo's only catch-and-release program, this well-run operation offers fishing trips on an 8m (26ft) and 12m (40ft) cruiser (US$200/US$260); prices are for the whole boat and include gear, drinks and having your fish cooked up for dinner.

Tours

Hectours (☎ 333-17-07; www.hectours.com) offers a half-day tour of Manzanillo (US$28) and a full-day excursion to Colima and the colonial town of Comala (US$70). The price includes transportation from your hotel.

Festivals & Events

The **Fiestas de Mayo** (May 1 to 10) celebrate the founding of Manzanillo in 1873 by holding sporting competitions and other events. The **Fiesta de Nuestra Señora de Guadalupe** is held from December 1 to 12 in honor of Mexico's revered manifestation of the Virgin Mary, here as elsewhere in Mexico.

Sailfish season runs November to March, with marlin, red snapper, sea bass and tuna also plentiful. The biggest international tournament is held in November, with a smaller national tournament in February.

Sleeping

Central Manzanillo has the town's best cheap options within a block or two of the *zócalo*. There are more places in the run-down area a few blocks south of the city center. Around the bay, where the better beaches are, hotels are more expensive; Playa Santiago, half an hour away by bus, is the exception.

BUDGET

Hotel San Pedrito (Map p164; ☎ 332-05-35; hotelsanpedrito@hotmail.com; Azueta 3; s/d US$30/40; P ☒) San Pedrito sits next to Playa San Pedrito, the beach nearest downtown. The old tiled rooms are generous in size, but worn and dank – see a few before deciding. From the *zócalo*, walk 15 leisurely minutes east along the *malecón* (waterfront street), or catch a local bus and get off at the archaeology museum and then walk from there.

Hotel Emperador (Map p164; ☎ 332-23-74; Dávalos 69; s US$15, d US$18-20) Half a block from the *zócalo*, this simple but clean refuge has some top-floor rooms that are marginally brighter than the rest. The hotel's restaurant is good and is one of the cheapest in town.

Hotel Flamingos (Map p164; ☎ 332-10-37; Madero 72; s US$14, d US$17-20) On a quiet side street, this old cheapie offers 30 clean, basic rooms. Some can be musty; ask for one with two beds and an outside window.

Hotel San José (Map p164; ☎ 332-51-05; Cuauhtémoc 138; s/d/tr US$15/25/35) This well-kept budget option near the market is a tad more pleasant than the cheapies near the waterfront.

AUTHOR'S CHOICE

Hotel Colonial (Map p164; ☎ 332-10-80, 332-06-68; Bocanegra 100; s US$25, d US$28-32; P ☒) This atmospheric, old-fashioned hotel in the heart of downtown retains the character of a bygone hacienda. Big rooms, blue-tiled outdoor hallways and a thick colonial ambience make it the best deal in town. There's limited underground parking and a quality restaurant-bar on the premises.

Hotel Anita (Map p163; ☎ 333-01-61; Balneario de Santiago s/n; r US$32) This is the cheapest place on Playa Santiago, with endless remodeling efforts and 36 large, faded rooms.

MIDRANGE

Brisas del Mar Hotel & Villas (Map p163; ☎ 334-11-97; www.brisasdelmarmanzanillo.com; Playa las Brisas; d/villa US$60/100; P ☒ ☒) The beautiful, generous suites and villas at Brisas del Mar are all modern and colorfully decorated. They're beachside and within walking distance of some action. The pool is large enough to do laps in. All-inclusive plans are available.

Hotel Villa La Audiencia (Map p163; ☎ 333-08-61; Península de Santiago; r/villas from US$76/92 P ☒ ☒) Near Playa Audiencia, but a bit far from the beach, this moderately priced hotel is good value, especially for families. All the villas come with a kitchen, air-con and satellite TV.

The following hotels overlooking Playa Santiago are a winding 15-minute walk (or five-minute bus ride) from Santiago town, down the road leading off Hwy 200 past the ETN bus station. The hotels perch on a bluff overlooking the beach, and all have beachfront swimming pools.

Hotel Playa de Santiago (Map p163; ☎ 333-02-70; hoplasan@prodigy.net.mx; Balneario de Santiago s/n; d/tr US$61/80, ste US$129-192; ☒) Perched at the end of the road, this hotel offers comfortable, semimodern rooms with balconies, sea views and decent – though ageing – baths.

Hotel Brillamar (Map p163; ☎ 334-11-88; Balneario de Santiago s/n; r/bungalows from US$32/73-100; ☒ ☒) Brillamar has air-con and TV, though some toilets may be missing their seats – unforgivable. Rooms are otherwise reasonable, but small. Large bungalows with kitchen are also available.

Hotel Marlyn (Map p163; ☎ 333-01-07; Balneario de Santiago s/n; d/ste from US$54/73; ☒ ☒) Marlyn hosts pleasant rooms with TV and fan. The ones you want have sea views and balconies, and consequently cost more. Six-person kitchen suites are available.

TOP END

Most of Manzanillo's upmarket hotels are on or near the beaches outside the city center. Many sprawl along the beach side of the main road near Playa Azul.

Hotel La Posada (Map p163; 333-18-99; www.hotel-la-posada.info; Cárdenas 201; s/d US$58/78; P ☒)

Right on the beach, this friendly, passionate-pink posada has spacious rooms with Mexican architectural touches. There's a breezy, well-appointed common area ideal for reading a book or chatting with the amiable staff.

Manzanillo also has plenty of all-inclusive resorts that are best booked in advance. The 'rack rate' listed here is easily improved by booking online.

Brisas Las Hadas Golf Resort & Marina (Map p163; ☎ 331-01-01; www.brisas.com.mx; Av Vista Hermosa s/n, Playa Audiencia; r US$292, ste US$540-652; P ⊠ ⊠ ⊡ ⊠) This resort sits like a Moroccan kingdom, so bright and white you'll need sunglasses just walking around. Las Hadas has a choice of 234 spacious rooms and suites with marble floors, all-white furnishings and plentiful amenities; some even have their own private pool. Hard-core film buffs may know this is where the Bo Derek film *10* was made. There's also a golf course.

Hotel Sierra Manzanillo (Map p163; ☎ 333-20-00; Av de la Audiencia 1, Playa Audiencia; all-inclusive d US$400, ste US$458-482; P ⊠ ⊠ ⊡ ⊠) This blindingly white, sterile hotel is beautifully situated above Playa Audiencia. It's not ultraluxurious, but pleasant enough for most vacationers – most of whom are package tourists from Canada.

Karmina Palace (Map p163; ☎ 334-13-00; www .karminapalace.com; Av Vista Hermosa 13; all-inclusive d ste US$425-449, q ste US$994-1170; P ⊠ ⊠ ⊡ ⊠) Conceived to evoke Mayan pyramids, the architecture of this posh 324-unit all-inclusive hotel is unintentionally silly, but after a day or two in your deluxe suite you may come to appreciate it. The amenities are extravagant, from the his and hers black-marble sinks in the swanky bathrooms to the eight connected swimming pools. Youngsters dig the Kid's Club so much that you may not see them for the rest of your vacation.

Eating

Several good, down-to-earth options are on the *zócalo*, while chain and chain-like spots line Hwy 200 around the bay.

Restaurant Emperador (Map p164; ☎ 332-23-74; Dávalos 69; mains US$2-5) Good, cheap and simple, this intimate ground-floor restaurant in the Hotel Emperador is popular with locals and budget travelers. Highlights here are the set breakfasts and the meat-and-seafood *comida corrida* (set-price lunch or dinner menu).

Restaurante Chantilly (Map p164; ☎ 332-01-94; Juárez 44; mains US$3-10) This crowded *cafetería* and *nievería* (ice creamery) has reasonably priced meals and snacks, plus a generous *comida corrida*, genuine espresso and good ice cream.

Los Candiles (Map p164; ☎ 332-10-80; Bocanegra 100; mains US$4-11) The Hotel Colonial's restaurant opens onto a pleasant patio, features surf-and-turf fare and has a full bar; sports dominates the satellite TV.

A **market-style dining hall** (Map p164; cnr Madero & Cuauhtémoc; mains US$2-5; ◷ 7am-6pm) has a number of inexpensive food stalls that you can choose from.

Many more restaurants are spread out around the bay all the way past the plaza in Santiago.

Café Costeño (Map p163; ☎ 333-94-60; Lázaro Cárdenas 1613, Playa Las Brisas; breakfast US$3-4.50; ◷ 9am-10:30pm Mon-Sat, 9am-1pm Sun) A good start to your day: French toast, hotcakes and omelets are cheerfully served along with espresso and cappuccino. Sit in the shady garden out back.

El Bigotes (Map p163; ☎ 334-08-31; Hwy 200, Km 8.4; mains US$9-22; ◷ 1-10pm) Popular for seafood like 'octopus drunken crazy' or 'snail garlic.' The beachside location is pretty fine.

Mediterraneo (Map p163; Hwy 200, Km 11; mains US$6-12; ◷ 8am-11pm) Boasts generous salads, good crepes, pasta and several versions of stuffed chicken breast. Have *tzatziki* (Greek yogurt and cucumber dip) for an appetizer while enjoying the view of the golf course.

Vaquero Campestre (Map p163; ☎ 334-14-48; Playa Audiencia; mains US$8-15; ◷ 2-10:30pm Tue-Sat) Near Las Palmas, this place serves pitchers of margaritas and sangria to help lubricate those servings of grilled beef and seafood. *Palapa* roofs and a few animal heads and skins surround diners.

Manos Morenos (Map p163; ☎ 333-03-20; Hwy 200, Km 11; mains US$6-13) Choose from fish with mango sauce or chicken with *huitlacoche* (corn truffle, a fungus that grows on maize) sauce or keep it simple with crepes or a generous salad at this *palapa* with a golf-course view.

Colima Bay Café (Map p163; ☎ 333-11-50; Hwy 200, Km 6.5, Playa Azul; mains US$7-16; ◷ 2pm-1am) This superfun Mexican restaurant keeps things lively. Service is professional, DJ music is thumpin' and portions are more than generous.

JALISCO, COLIMA &
MICHOACÁN COASTS

Carnes y Tacos Julio (Map p163; ☎ 334-00-36; Hwy 200, Km 14.3; Playa Olas Altas; mains US$4-11; ☺ 8am-midnight) Savory grilled meat is the specialty at this lively place, but breakfast, pasta and other tourist-friendly fare won't disappoint.

Entertainment

If you're in town on a Sunday evening, stop by the *zócalo*, where multiple generations come out to enjoy an ice cream and the warm evening air. On the most atmospheric of nights, a band belts out traditional music from the gazebo, and every night around sunset you can hear the cacophony of the resident *zanates* (blackbirds) – a regular bombing squad: don't stand under any electrical wire for too long. And be sure to check out the *golondrinas* (swallows) perching on the wires later in the evening; it's eerily reminiscent of the Hitchcock classic *The Birds*.

Behind the doors of **Bar Social** (Map p164; cnr Calle 21 de Marzo & Juárez; ☺ noon-midnight Mon-Sat) is a world frozen in the past; it's not scary, but it is odd.

Tourist nightlife starts in Playa Azul, with theme discos like **Vog** (Map p163; ☎ 333-18-75; Hwy 200, Km 9.2; women/men cover US$10/15; ☺ Fri & Sat nights) and **Nautilus** (Map p163; ☎ 334-33-31; Hwy 200, Km 9.5; cover US$15; ☺ Fri & Sat nights) and continues northwest around the bay. Near the Hotel Fiesta Mexicana, **Teto's Bar** (Map p163; ☎ 333-19-90; Hwy 200, Km 8.5) offers live music and dancing. **Olé Olé** (Map p163; Hwy 200, Km 7.5) is the place to dance to live salsa music.

Near Vaquero Campestre, **Hacienda Gaucho** (Map p163; ☎ 334-19-69; Playa Santiago) features *carne asada* (grilled beef) and dance music. On Playa Miramar, **Club Maeva** (Map p163; ☎ 335-05-96) houses the Disco Boom Boom and the casual Solarium Bar with a pool table; phone for reservations.

Getting There & Away

AIR

Playa de Oro International Airport lies between a long and secluded white-sand beach and tropical groves of bananas and coconut, 35km northwest of Manzanillo's Zona Hotelera on Hwy 200.

Alaska Airlines (☎ 334-22-11; Airport) Direct service to Los Angeles.

America West (☎ 800-235-9292 in the US) Direct service from Phoenix.

Continental (☎ 800-231-0856 in the US) Direct service to Houston.

The following carriers provide direct service to Mexico City:

Aero California (☎ 800-237-6225)

Aeroméxico (☎ 800-237-6639)

Mexicana (☎ 800-531-7921)

BUS

Manzanillo's new, airport-like, full-service Central Camionera (Map p163) is northwest of the center near Playa Las Brisas, just off Blvd Miguel de la Madrid (Hwy 200). It's an organized place with two tourist offices, phones, eateries and left luggage. There are several daily departures:

Armería (US$3, 45min, 2nd-class services at least hourly)

Barra de Navidad (US$6, 1-1½hr, 3 1st-class; US$5, 1-1½hr, 10 2nd-class)

Colima (US$6, 1½-2hr, 20 1st-class)

Guadalajara (US$19-21, 4½-8hr, frequent 1st-class services; US$14-18, 4½-8hr, 19 2nd-class)

Lázaro Cárdenas (US$21, 6hr, 1st-class at 2am & 6am; US$17, 6hr, 4 2nd-class)

Mexico City (US$59-62, 12hr, 4 1st-class; US$50, 4 2nd-class) To Terminal Norte.

Puerto Vallarta (US$21, 5-6½hr, 4 1st-class; US$18, 5-6½hr, 10 2nd-class)

San Patricio-Melaque (1-1½hr) Same services and fare as to Barra de Navidad.

ETN (☎ 334-10-50) offers deluxe and 1st-class service to Barra de Navidad (US$6, one to 1½ hours, three daily), Colima (US$8, 1½ to two hours, seven daily) and Guadalajara (US$28, seven daily) from its own bus station near Santiago at Hwy 200, Km 13.5. ETN also offers daily service to the international airport in Guadalajara (US$28).

Getting Around

There is no local or regional bus service to or from Playa de Oro airport. Most resorts have shuttle vans. **Transportes Turísticos Benito Juárez** (☎ 334-15-55) shuttles door-to-door to/from the airport. The fare is US$28 for private service (one or two people) or US$8 per person when three or more people share the ride. A taxi from the airport to Manzanillo's center or most resort hotels costs US$25.

Local buses heading around the bay to San Pedrito, Salahua, Santiago, Miramar and beaches along the way depart every 10 minutes from 6am to 11pm from the corner of Madero and Domínguez, the corner of Juárez and Calle 21 de Marzo near the *zócalo*, and from the Central Camionera. Fares (pay the

DETOUR: COLIMA CITY

If knocking around in the heart of Manzanillo has aroused in you a taste for the urban experience, consider a day trip or an overnighter to the pleasant inland capital city of Colima. Overshadowed by the imposing, actively puffing Volcán Nevado de Colima (4240m) – 30km to the north – this attractive (and growing) city is graced by lively plazas and several noteworthy examples of preserved colonial buildings. Standing proud over the heart of the city and Plaza Principal, the **cathedral** (Santa Iglesia), dates back to 1527 but was rebuilt in the original style after a cataclysmic 1941 earthquake. Next to the cathedral is the **Palacio de Gobierno**, built between 1884 and 1904. Local artist Jorge Chávez Carrillo painted the murals on the stairway to celebrate the 200th anniversary of the birth of independence hero Miguel Hidalgo y Costilla (p30), who was once parish priest of Colima. The murals depict Mexican history from the Spanish conquest to independence. There's also a **museum** (admission free; 🕑 10am-6pm Tue-Sun) with engrossing painting, currency and arms exhibits.

Equally edifying is the **Museo Regional de Historia de Colima** (☎ 312-312-92-28; Portal Morelos 1; admission US$3.25; 🕑 9am-6pm Tue-Sat, 5-8pm Sun), displaying an excellent collection of ceramic vessels and figurines and an impressive reconstruction of a shaft tomb, and the must-see **University Museum of Popular Arts** (☎ 312-312-68-69; cnr Barreda & Gallardo; admission US$1, free Sun; 🕑 10am-2pm & 5-8pm Tue-Sat, 10am-1pm Sun), about 1km north of Plaza Principal. On display are folk-art exhibits from Colima and other states, with a particularly grand collection of costumes and masks used in traditional Colima dances.

Spend the night in style at **Hotel Ceballos** (☎ 312-312-44-44; www.hotelceballos.com; Portal Medellín 12; r from US$77; 🅿 🕵 🖳 🍴), a stately five-star hotel on the north side of Plaza Principal, or more economically in one of the good, modern rooms at **Hospedajes del Rey** (☎ 313-36-83; Rey Colimán 125; s/d US$31, tw US$37; 🅿 🕵). Many small restaurants around Plaza Principal offer good simple fare – just pick one that appeals. For something special, try the Oaxacan delights served at **¡Ah Qué Nanishe!** (☎ 314-21-97; Calle 5 de Mayo 267; mains US$3.75-7.50; 🕑 1pm-midnight Wed-Mon), or perhaps the soy seviche at the all-natural **Centro de Nutrición Lakshmi** (☎ 312-64-33; Madero 265; meals under US$3; 🕑 8am-9:30pm Mon-Sat, 10am-2pm & 6-9:30pm Sun).

No visit to Colima is complete without visiting the volcano, which has erupted dozens of times in the past four centuries and as recently as June 2005. A visit to the **Parque Nacional Volcán Nevado de Colima**, 87km from Colima on roads of varying quality, will get you up close and personal. Bring your hiking boots to enjoy the well-tended trails. The easiest way to make the trip is with a tour operator such as **Colima Magic** (☎ 312-310-74-83 in Colima; www.colimamagic.com; tours US$75-120).

Getting There & Away

Colima is 45km from the coast, but quite a bit cooler and less humid. Getting there by car or bus from Manzanillo is a breeze. It's about an hour's drive on the four-lane Hwy 54; 20 1st-class buses make the journey daily from Manzanillo's Central Camionera.

driver as you board) are US$0.30 to US$0.60, depending on how far you're going.

Taxis are plentiful in Manzanillo. From the bus station buy a prepaid ticket for a *taxi colectivo* to ensure the best price. From the bus station, a cab fare is around US$2 to the *zócalo* or Playa Azul, US$6 to Playa Santiago and US$9 to Playa Miramar.

CUYUTLÁN & EL PARAÍSO
☎ 313

The laid-back black-sand-beach resort towns of Cuyutlán and El Paraíso are popular with Mexicans but see very few *norteamericanos*. Gentle waves and fun-in-the-

sun activities, such as swimming, people-watching and boogie boarding, can be savored on or about the charcoal-colored sands. Cuyutlán has a better selection of hotels, but the beach is less crowded and more tranquil in El Paraíso.

Orientation & Information

Cuyutlán is at the southeastern end of Laguna de Cuyutlán, 40km southeast of Manzanillo and 12km west of Armería. Sleepy El Paraíso is 6km southeast of Cuyutlán along the coast, but 12km by road.

Cuyutlán has a post office (El Paraíso does not), but neither town has a bank; for this you'll have to visit Armería. Both towns have public telephones and long-distance *casetas* near their *zócalos*.

The beachfront accommodations here are cheaper than they are at other coastal resorts. The high season is Christmas and Semana Santa (Holy Week), when Cuyutlán's hotels are booked solid by Mexican families.

Getting There & Away

Cuyutlán and Paraíso are connected to the rest of the world through Armería, a dusty but friendly little service center on Hwy 200, 46km southeast of Manzanillo and 55km southwest of Colima. From Armería a 12km paved road heads west to Cuyutlán; a similar road runs 8km southwest from Armería to El Paraíso.

To reach either place by bus involves a transfer in Armería. Two bus lines – Sociedad Cooperativa de Autotransportes Colima Manzanillo and Autotransportes Nuevo Horizonte – have offices and stops just off Armería's main street. They both operate 2nd-class buses to Manzanillo every 15 minutes from 6am to midnight (US$2.50, 45 minutes) and to Colima every half hour from 5:45am to 10:30pm (US$2.50, 45 minutes). Buses go every 20 minutes to Tecomán (US$0.70, 15 minutes), where you can connect with buses heading southeast on Hwy 200 to Lázaro Cárdenas and elsewhere.

Buses to Cuyutlán and El Paraíso depart from Armería's market, one block north and one block east of the long-distance bus depots. To Cuyutlán, they depart every half hour from 6am to 7:30pm (US$0.75, 20 minutes). To El Paraíso, they go every 45 minutes (US$0.65, 15 minutes).

No buses shuttle directly between Cuyutlán and El Paraíso. To go by bus, you must return to Armería and change buses again. However, you can take a boat from the Centro Tortuguero (right) between the hours of 9am and 4:30pm; the scenic 45-minute trip through the Palo Verde estuary costs US$3/6.50 per child/adult.

Cuyutlán

pop 1000

The long stretch of fine-grained, black-sand beach here attracts Mexican vacationers like bears to honey. Rickety wooden paths make walking the hot black sands tolerable, there are plenty of seaside restaurants, and

hundreds of colorful, rentable beach chairs and umbrellas keep the scorching sun off.

Cuyutlán is known for its **ola verde** (green wave), appearing just offshore in April and May. It's supposedly caused by little green phosphorescent critters, but it's the subject of much local debate.

Don't miss the **Centro Tortuguero** (☎ 328-86-76; admission US$2; ☺ 8:30am-5:30pm), about 4km toward Paraíso. This ecological center, founded in 1993, has incubated and released 500,000 baby sea turtles into the sea. On display are various small pools containing many of the endearing reptiles as well as some crocodile and iguana enclosures. Guides speak English, and there are educational talks almost hourly. Bring your swimsuit if you want to splash in the pool.

Lagoon trips lasting 45 minutes on the Palo Verde estuary – featuring passage through a mangrove 'tunnel' – leave from the Centro Tortuguero and cost US$2/US$4 per child/adult. You can also take a boat from here to El Paraíso (see opposite). Get there by car or taxi, or walk 4km along the beach.

SLEEPING & EATING

You can camp on the empty sands on either side of the hotels. Several of the beachfront *enramadas* rent showers.

Hotel Morelos (☎ 326-40-13; Hidalgo 185 at Veracruz; per person without/with meals US$13/25; ☑) Gets points for attractive, well-priced rooms with hot water. There's a whimsical swimming pool and an enthusiastically decorated restaurant (open 7am to 10pm) with a US$5 *comida corrida*.

Hotel María Victoria (☎ 326-40-04; Veracruz 10; per person US$21; P ☑) Has a giant mushroom-shaped structure in the airy lobby – see it for yourself. Cuyutlán's most luxurious hotel also sits next to the beach, and the spacious rooms have sitting areas. Get one with a view. The restaurant serves fresh typical Mexican fare at high-roller prices.

Hotel San Rafael (☎ 326-40-15; Veracruz 46; s US$20-30, d US$30-40; ☑ ☑) Just OK despite a remodel. Rooms are small and raggedy for the price, so unless you get a good sea view go somewhere else. At least there's a pleasant swimming pool and beachfront restaurant-bar.

Hotel El Bucanero (☎ 326-40-05; cnr Hidalgo & Malecón; interior/sea view r per person US$12) At last visit, major renovation was underway at

JALISCO, COLIMA & MICHOACÁN COASTS

this old beach favorite, but the owner swears he won't raise the price. Rooms are basic, some affording splendid views of the waves rolling in.

Hotel Posada del Sol (☎ 326-40-29; López Mateos 10; d US$20-30) Home to 17 good, plain rooms around a pleasant garden, this place is in a quiet neighborhood away from the center. Go one block past the radio towers at the south end of town (about five blocks from Hidalgo); it's a block from the beach on López Mateos.

Hotel Morelos and Hotel Posada del Sol both have good open-air restaurants. Beachfront restaurants and snack stands supply seafood and cold drinks. Or grab a snack at one of the simpler places near the *zócalo*.

El Paraíso
pop 300

As the crow flies, the small, rustic fishing village of El Paraíso is just 6km southeast of Cuyutlán, but by road it's more like 12km. Like its larger neighbor, it harbors a fine, charcoal-colored beach that attracts Mexican families. Unlike its larger neighbor, there are fewer decent places to stay, which makes for a less crowded and more tranquil beach. An unending line of seafood restaurants sits on the sands.

The nicest hotel in town, **Hotel Paraíso** (☎ 322-10-32; r US$29-35; **P** 🐝) has 60 decent rooms and is to the left of the T-junction at the entrance to town. Otherwise, you can camp on the beach or string up a hammock at one of El Paraíso's beachfront *palapas*. All the *palapas* serve basically the same food at similar prices; expect to spend US$5 to US$10 per person for a full, fresh meal.

PLAYA BOCA DE PASCUALES
☎ 313 / pop 50

Playa Boca de Pascuales, 3km south of El Paraíso, is a legendary surf spot where aggressive, surfable barrel swells ranging from 2m to 5m in height arrive in the summer season. There's a heavy beach break. If you're a neophyte surfer, don't try your luck. At last visit, three snapped surfboards were arranged to resemble headstones; fortunately there's a high-quality board-repair guy on hand.

Otherwise known as Edgar's Place, **Hotel Real de Pascuales** (☎ 329-42-29; www.pascualessurf .com.mx; r US$10-20) is the local surfing nexus. Proprietor Edgar Álvarez welcomes surfers

from all over the world and fixes their boards when they get munched. Everyone calls each other 'bro.' The rooms are Spartan to the extreme, but that's the way the 'bros' seem to like it.

To get to Pascuales, travel first to the town of Tecomán, 3km south of Cuyutlán. If driving, follow the sign from downtown about 10km to the beach. Taxis or *combis* provide transport from Tecomán to Pascuales.

MICHOACÁN

Travelers to the unspoiled coast of Michoacán may feel as if they have discovered the place. There are few tourists, only a smattering of accommodations but plenty of choice campsites.

BOCA DE APIZA
☎ 313 / pop 225

Near the Michoacán–Colima border, at the mouth of the Río Coahuayana, basks this dusty little fishing town lined with egret-filled mangrove lagoons. A 300m line of competing seafood *enramadas* crowd the beach, and on Sunday afternoons hordes of local kids bathe and splash in the river. Gentle waves, hot black sands and general fun-in-the-sun activities prevail here. To get there, turn off Hwy 200 at the town of Coahuayana (Km 228) and continue about 4km to the beach.

There's another side to Boca de Apiza, literally. Across the river (and across the Michoacán–Colima border) is where Mexican families have built many *palapa* shelters for Sunday picnics. Here a long beach heads northwards, with a sandy access road going inland 6.5km to meet back with the highway. There are no services here, so bring your own supplies.

Thinking about sticking around? Try **Hotel Sarahi** (☎ 327-05-64; 1/2 beds US$14/19, bungalows US$40), the most decent digs in town, with plain rooms that will do in a pinch. Management is hoping to add TV and aircon, so prices may rise.

SAN JUAN DE ALIMA
☎ 313

About 20km south of Boca de Apiza, near where the highway meets the coast, lie the concrete bumps of San Juan de Alima (Km 211).

BEACHES OF MICHOACÁN

Adventurers looking for desolate expanses of golden sand, tiny rocky beach coves, quiet estuaries harboring a multitude of birdlife, and mostly undeveloped coastal towns will discover them all here along the scenic 250km coast of Michoacán. Hwy 200 traces the shoreline and passes dozens of different beaches; some have gentle lapping waves and are good for swimming, while others have big breakers suitable for surfing. Many of the beaches are uninhabited; some have small communities. Overdeveloped megaresorts are few and far between, nightlife only comes calm and laid-back, and just a few towns attract large groups of gringos. Mango, coconut, papaya and banana plantations line the highway, while the Sierra Madre del Sur mountains form a verdant backdrop. Cattle pastures peek from between predominantly deciduous tree-covered hillsides, and the odd cactus or weaverbird nest adds visual curiosity.

At the Michoacán–Colima border, **Boca de Apiza**, deposited at the mouth of the Río Coahuayana, is a mangrove-lined beach with many competing seafood *enramadas*; turn off Hwy 200 at the town of Coahuayana. Kilometer markers begin counting down from Km 231 at the state border.

San Juan de Alima (Km 209), 20km south, after the highway meets the coast, is popular with surfers and has many beachfront restaurants and several modern hotels.

A short distance down the coast, **Las Brisas** (Km 207) is another beachside community with places to stay. Still further along, **Playa La Ticla** (Km 183) is a good surfing spot with beachfront cabanas for rent.

The next stop is **Faro de Bucerías** (Km 173), known for its clear, pale-blue waters, yellow sand and rocky islands. It's a good spot for camping, swimming and snorkeling, and the local Nahua community prepares fresh seafood.

Further along, white-sand **Playa Maruata** (Km 150) is one of Michoacán's most beautiful beaches, with clear turquoise waters. This is the principal Mexican beach where black sea turtles lay their eggs; these and other species of sea turtles are set free here each year by conservation programs. Camping and discreet nude bathing are possible, and services include rustic cabanas and some *palapas* serving fresh seafood.

Further south, **Pichilinguillo** (Km 95) is in a small bay, good for swimming. Further still are beautiful, unsigned **Barra de Nexpa** (Km 56), popular with surfers; **Caleta de Campos** (Km 50), on a lovely little bay; **La Soledad** (Solitude), a very beautiful, tranquil little beach; and **Las Peñas**, another good surfing beach. **Playa Azul**, 24km northwest of Lázaro Cárdenas, is another laid-back beach community that is easy to visit and has surfable waves.

Plenty of Michoacán's coves and beaches are not listed in this or any guidebook, and those places will be even more isolated and untouched. They are waiting to be discovered, so see them now.

It's a town still defining itself: half-finished constructions attest to continuing growth. A main road of cobbles and concrete keeps dust levels down and heat levels up. However, there are reasons to come: plenty of hotels, small stores and beachfront restaurants service the tourists and are spread out along the coast where creamy surfing breakers curl and fall. Be careful of swimming out too far, though, where heavier currents lurk.

Sleeping & Eating

The restaurants you want to eat at are on the beach, and they're just like the ones up and down the rest of the coast, so don't expect any surprises. There's a choice of well-priced hotels, ranging from dour to decent. *All* of them are blue.

Hotel Parador (☎ 327-90-38; s US$25-38, d US$29-58, tr US$59-65; 🛇 🛋) With the town's best ambience and a good variety of rooms, this is the best choice for groups and families. The smaller, cheaper rooms are fairly good but the more expensive ones with balconies with views are downright pleasant. The friendly atmosphere in the popular restaurant will make you linger over your lunch.

Hotel San Juan (☎ 327-90-11; r US$25-35, bungalow US$60; 🛇) It's new and light blue, with San Juan's only Internet café and an eagerness to please. Rooms are basic but immaculate; the more expensive ones have air-con. The *palapa* restaurant with well-made fare is watched over by rowdy parrots.

Hotel El Oceano (☎ 327-90-19; r/bungalow US$35/60; 🛇) El Oceano is sky blue with clean, well-kept lavender rooms and a serviceable restaurant. The fan-cooled bungalows have two bedrooms and full kitchen; the seven rooms have air-con and sleep two to four souls.

Hotel Villas de San Juan (☎ 327-90-64; r US$25, bungalows US$50) These centrally located villas are painted an indescribable shade of blue. Inside the high wing, sea-view rooms are decent but could use some balconies. The friendly, comfortable bungalows lining the driveway have kitchens and two bedrooms.

Hotel Coral (☎ 328-80-06; d/tr beds US$15/25) This dark-blue option has worn, comfortable rooms. The otherwise empty ground floor is marked by supporting pillars, giving a somewhat bleak, tidal-wave–ready feel to the whole place. Small pink rooms greet you up the concrete stairs, if that's where you want to go.

LAS BRISAS

The road south from San Juan de Alima affords one tremendous scenic overlook where visitors can survey desolate sandy beaches as far as the eye can see. The tiny community of Las Brisas, 1.5km down a dirt road from the highway (Km 204), is accented by just a few *palapa* restaurants and one big-ass, incongruous midrange hotel – the only solid building on the beach. It's very peaceful, with swaying palms and a long, wide, flat beach with fine, firm dark sand. The wind tends to kick up (as the name implies) and a nice bird-filled lagoon is nearby. Camping and RV parking (no hookups) are exceptionally pleasant here. To get there by bus, travel first to La Placita and then commandeer a taxi.

Unless you camp, you'll be staying at the moderately priced **Hotel Paraíso Las Brisas** (☎ 327-90-55; www.paraisolasbrisasmichoacan.com; r US$60-80, ste US$160-250; 🖳 🏊), where 30 large, modern and thoughtfully appointed rooms are on offer with cable TV and air-con.

LA PLACITA

Here's a cute little highway town (Km 199) with a leafy plaza and surrounding *comedores* (inexpensive restaurants) and, if you're going south, the last Pemex gas station until Caleta de Campos, about 150km away. Fill up here, and if you can't find a roof to sleep under in nearby Playa La Ticla (below), try

Hotel Reyna or Hotel de la Costa, two basic cheapies near the highway.

PLAYA LA TICLA

At Km 186 a bumpy dirt road peels off and leads over a hill and down to Playa La Ticla, another prime surfing destination. In the early morning, calm seas near the shore give birth to curving arcs of gorgeous, misty-edged waves, simply beautiful to watch – but even better to ride. The quaint pueblo of La Ticla, hiding behind a small coastal mountain, draws mostly foreign surfers with their own vehicles. They also bring their own boards and camping equipment, since beach services are fairly undeveloped and the quiet little town isn't yet geared toward tourism of any sort. A nearby palm-ringed lagoon provides bird-watching possibilities, salt-free swimming and a variation in landscape.

You can camp (per person US$1.50) under flimsy *palapa* shelters at the northern edge of town. Your other option is **Parador Turístico la Ticla** (☎ 313-88-665; camp sites per person US$3.50, r with shared bathroom US$13, cabanas US$66), offering well-kept, thatch-roofed cabanas on stilts. If you snag a tiny room, don't expect much privacy or peace: the ceiling is shared and your neighbors will be young surfers, dude, so bring earplugs. Perhaps the interesting burning smells in the air will aid entry into a dreamlike state.

HIGHWAY 200, MICHOACÁN STYLE

Be prepared for some slower driving along the stretch of coast from Km 74 to Km 134, somewhere between Barra de Nexpa and Faro de Bucerías. This area isn't the highest priority for Mexican highway funds, and the road is mostly curvy with some minor rough spots. Give yourself a couple more hours of daylight to cover this stretch, and make sure your vehicle is full of gas: there are no Pemex stations between La Placita (Km 199) and Caleta de Campos (Km 50), though you'll pass dinky little towns where signs may offer a few liters for sale. Also, don't expect much solid accommodation when the sun gets low: unless you're camping, you won't run across many places to stay, though there will be a few eateries along the way.

Restaurant Serrano (mains US$2.50-8), nearest the lagoon's mouth, is popular for breakfast and seafood. You can camp for free if you eat there often enough.

You have a choice of two dirt roads that lead to Playa La Ticla, at Km 183 or 186. Don't forget sunscreen and insect repellent.

FARO DE BUCERÍAS

About 2km down a beach dirt road, at Km 173, lies a calm cove, which has decent snorkeling and is wonderful for swimming. Known for its clear, pale-blue waters, soft yellow sand and rocky islands, Faro de Bucerías is also good for camping and having a spot of lunch with the Nahua community. A picturesque square red-and-white lighthouse sits high up on the hill, and there's some good tide-pooling behind the lofty restaurant Palapa Miramar – just be careful getting around the rocky point, and never turn your back on those ocean waves.

There are no hotels; either rumble in with your RV or camp (US$8) under one of the *palapa* shelters. There are a number of open-air seafood restaurants; lobsters are plentiful, well priced and beautifully prepared here.

PLAYA MARUATA

About 1km west of Km 150, past the town's bleak plaza, lies this paradise for beach lovers and rustic campers. Playa Maruata is three beaches in one; two climbable rocky heads, riddled with small caves and tunnels, separate the three sections of white-sand crescents. Each has a different size and character: the one on the right (northernmost) is about 1km long and has the roughest waters (don't try swimming here); the middle arc is more intimate and OK for strong swimmers; the one on the left is 3km long and decorated with fishing boats and is where most camping shelters and their snack sheds lie). There are also shallow, palm-ringed lagoons to explore, often visited by vultures looking for fish scraps (you can get mighty close to the birds on the ground). Two simple *palapa* restaurants and some camping shelters dot the varied landscape, but there are no real concrete structures or hotels. It's a pleasant and tranquil place to hang out with your sweetie or a large stack of paperbacks.

Playa Maruata is also the principal Mexican beach where black sea turtles lay their eggs –from June to December they come ashore nightly. Hatchlings of these and other species of sea turtles are set free here each year by conservation programs.

Camping shelters are pretty much all the same and most charge US$1.25 per person. You can also string up a hammock, or rent one at some shelters. Those who need four semisolid walls can try one of the few rustic, two-bed cabanas for US$11, and RV drivers have several discreet spots in which to park. For simple groceries such as fruit, ramen, cereal or beer, there's a small store at the end of the southernmost beach past all the *palapa* shelters.

BARRA DE NEXPA

☎ 753 / pop 50

At Km 55.5, just north of Puente Nexpa bridge and 1km from the highway down a cobbled road, lies Nexpa. The salt 'n' pepper bar of sand here, and a good number of healthy waves – which build up and curl sharply in the mornings – bring in surfers from around the world. Rustic cabanas, good campsites and some decent restaurants add comfort to the mix, and the very laid-back feel completes the recipe for a peaceful stay.

A long point break wave curls in from the left. The longest are about 150m, and 50m waves are common. As long as there's not an organized surfing tour in town, there are enough waves for everyone. Beginners hone their chops in winter but make way for more advanced surfers when the big swells hit, from March through October. With its rocky shoreline and strong surf, Nexpa is not ideal for swimming.

Twenty minutes by foot along the river and into the mountains, the fluorescent-blue **El Troncon** waterfall makes for a refreshing hike. Engage a local guide to lead the way for a small tip.

Jorge's Tienda (☎ 555-150-92-43; helennex@hotmail.com) rents surfboards (US$10/US$50 per day/week) and sells gear. It also has telephone service and Internet access (US$2 per hour), and sells groceries. Pablo's Palapa, near Restaurant Chichos, repairs and sells boards. There's a larger surf shop in the nearby Caleta de Campos (opposite); a taxi will take you there for about US$4.

Sleeping & Eating

Rio Nexpa Rooms (☎ 531-52-55 in Caleta de Campos; www.surf-mexico.com/sites/nexpa; r US$30; P) This beautifully crafted SE Asian-style *palapa* about 200m inland along the river has four comfortable rooms with three full-sized beds and a loft. It has a shared kitchen, lagoon-side garden area and tranquil communal sitting room.

Gilberto's Cabañas (cabanas per person US$10, tent/RV sites US$3/9; P) Gilberto's offers cabanas, some more rustic than others, some with kitchen, and most with hammocks. It has a communal kitchen and shower block for tent and RV campers, and Gilberto offers taxi service to Caleta. Look for Gilberto's sign on the right-hand side as you enter town.

Restaurant Chicho (cabanas US$14-23) Chico has tables perched just right for watching surfers cut waves nearby. The food (with mains costing US$3 to US$10) is good, and there are also grassy camp sites.

La Isla Restaurant (mains $3-12) This restaurant cooks up the best Western breakfasts around, with good cappuccinos and the largest fruit plate on the coast. A taxi service and a casual book exchange are available. Rooms (US$10 to US$35) are also available.

CALETA DE CAMPOS

☎ 753 / pop 2000

A friendly town on a bluff overlooking a lovely azure bay, 'Caleta' (Km 50) is a quiet place, but it has a pair of good, clean hotels and several satisfying places to eat. Caleta's paved main drag has all the essentials, including a telephone *caseta*, late-night *taquerías* (taco stalls) and *torta* shops, a pharmacy and grocery stores. The southern side of the bluff has perfect waves for novice surfers.

Just off the main drag, near Hotel Yuritzi, is **Surf y Espuma** (☎ 531-52-55; surfboard rental per day $10), which sells and rents surf gear. It also carries surfwear, does fishing charters and washes your laundry (US$1.25 per kg)

Modern, well maintained and comfortable, **Hotel Yuritzi** (☎ 531-53-53; www.hotelyuritzi .com; Corregidora 10; s US$35-45, d US$40-55, tr US$45-60; P ⚄ ⚑) counts as its customers business travelers, beach bums and families.

Hotel Los Arcos (☎ 531-50-38; s US$25, d US$30-35, with air-con & hot water US$35; P ⚄) affords dramatic sea views and bright rooms. It's toward the ocean, at the end of the main drag, and is a bit run-down, but the bird's-eye view of Bahía de Bufadero's blowhole is brilliant.

Large, well-appointed **Villa Tropical** (☎ 531-52-55; www.caletadecampos.com; villa US$235) can sleep

up to 12 and is thus a sweet deal. The owner, who also operates Surf y Espuma, is happy to negotiate, particularly when the house is empty. The breezy roof deck with views of the lighthouse is the ultimate party nook.

Hourly buses depart Caleta for Lázaro Cárdenas from 5am to 7pm (US$3.50, 1½ hours). A taxi between Caleta de Campos and Barra de Nexpa costs US$4.

LAS PEÑAS

A small cove at Km 18 is home to eight *enramadas* and one wide but cozy beach, punctuated by rocky headlands. Around the southern point is a much longer beach called **Playa Dorada**, dotted with a few rustic restaurants of its own and stretching as far as you can see. No accommodations are available, but camping may be possible – ask around at Playa Dorada or just pick an isolated spot.

PLAYA AZUL

☎ 753 / pop 3500

Playa Azul is a sleepy, dusty beach resort backed by lagoons fed by tributaries of the Río Balsas. It's usually quiet, with a trickle of foreign travelers enjoying the long beach and surfable waves. A strong undertow makes swimming touch-and-go; swimming is better (when it's not mosquito season) at Laguna Pichi, a couple of kilometers east along the beach, where boat trips take visitors to view the plants, birds and other animals that inhabit the surrounding mangrove forest.

You can string up a hammock at most of the beachfront *enramadas*; otherwise there are a couple of reasonable hotels, all with private bathrooms, in town.

The 42 large and comfortable balconied rooms at **Hotel María Teresa** (☎ 536-00-05; Independencia 626; s US$42-47, d US$57-68; ⚄ ⚑) are fresh and up-to-date. A poolside *palapa* restaurant-bar comes with an attractive patio area. Look for this place two blocks north of the plaza.

On the far (east) side of the plaza and a bit worn around the edges, **Hotel María Isabel** (☎ 536-00-16; Madero s/n; d US$25-40; P ⚄ ⚑), has impeccably clean and very peaceful rooms.

The upmarket, 73-room **Hotel Playa Azul** (☎ 536-00-24/91; Carranza s/n; r US$48-57, with air-con & TV US$72, RV sites US$18; P ⚄ ⚑) has a small trailer park and enjoyable rooms around a garden courtyard with an inviting pool. The poolside Las Gaviotas restaurant/bar (mains

US$7-15), open from 7:30am to 10:30pm, is a good bet for anything from pizza to *pozole*.

The *malecón* is lined by informal restaurants with beachside seating. One of the most laid-back is **Yupanky** (mains US$4-10; 8am-6pm), remarkable for its utter idleness. Hammocks are strung up throughout and the sound of the pounding surf often mixes with the melancholy music of Playa Azul's elderly mariachis. The menu features seafood, of course, and there's invariably a pile of coconuts waiting to be cracked open.

Locals recommend Restaurant Galdy and Restaurant Familiar Martita, both on the market street near Madero, around the corner from Hotel Playa Azul. Both serve fresh-squeezed juices and good cheap grub (*comida corrida* US$3.25).

Combis run every 10 minutes from 5am to 9pm between Playa Azul and Lázaro Cárdenas (US$1.25, 30 minutes, 24km). Taxis between Playa Azul and Lázaro Cárdenas cost around US$10.

LÁZARO CÁRDENAS
☎ 753 / pop 78,000

Industrial Lázaro isn't of interest to travelers, but since it's the terminus of several bus routes tourists do pass through. Once here, you can change buses, stock up on provisions and head 24km west to Playa Azul (p175). If you must spend the night, several adequate hotels are near the bus stations.

Hotel Reyna Pío (☎ 532-06-20; Corregidora 78; s/d US$20/25;) is a good, friendly budget hotel with clean, spacious rooms. It's on the corner of Av 8 de Mayo, a block west of Av Lázaro Cárdenas, near the bus terminals.

Hotel Viña del Mar (☎ 532-04-15; Javier Mina 352; s/d US$22/25;) has a leafy, inviting courtyard with pool, but most of the darkish rooms are not around it. Still, they're good-sized and come with air-con and TV. It's half a block west of Av Lázaro Cárdenas.

Hotel Casablanca (☎ 537-34-80; Nicolás Bravo 475; s/d US$36/48;) has air-con, TV, a pool with a Jacuzzi and secure parking. The 56 modern rooms with balconies and wide windows overlook the city or inland mountains. Look for this high-rise a block east of Av Lázaro Cárdenas.

Many cheap restaurants cluster around the bus terminals. Locals recommend **Restaurant El Tejado** (Lázaro Cárdenas s/n; mains $4.50-10), between Corregidora and Javier Mina,

for meats, seafood, six styles of frog legs and four pages of drinks. If you're tired of Mexican, **Restaurant Kame** (☎ 537-26-60; lunch US$4.50), one block south of the Estrella Blanca bus terminal, is a Japanese eatery with a variety of delicious meals.

Getting There & Away

Lázaro has four bus terminals, all a few blocks from each other. **Galeana** (☎ 532-02-62) and **Parhikuni** (☎ 532-30-06), with services northwest to Manzanillo and inland to Uruapan and Morelia, share a **terminal** (Lázaro Cárdenas 1810 at Constitución de 1814). Opposite, Autobuses de Jalisco, La Línea, Vía 2000 and Sur de Jalisco share another **terminal** (☎ 537-18-50; Lázaro Cárdenas 1791) and serve the same destinations, plus Colima, Guadalajara and Mexico City.

The terminal for **Estrella Blanca** (EB; ☎ 532-11-71; Francisco Villa 65) is also the home base for Cuauhtémoc and Elite. From here buses head southeast to Zihuatanejo and Acapulco; up the coast to Manzanillo, Mazatlán and Tijuana; and inland to Uruapan, Morelia and Mexico City. The **Estrella de Oro terminal** (☎ 532-02-75; Corregidora 318) serves Acapulco, Cuernavaca, Mexico City and Zihuatanejo.

Daily buses from Lázaro Cárdenas:

Acapulco EB (US$19, 6-7hr, 12 1st-class; US$16, 6-7hr, hourly 2nd-class); Estrella de Oro (US$19, 6-7hr, 3 1st-class; US$15, 6-7hr, 11 2nd-class)

Caleta de Campos Galeana (US$4.50, 1½hr, 10 2nd-class); Sur de Jalisco (US$4.50, 1½hr, 4 2nd-class)

Colima Autobuses de Jalisco (US$17, 4-6½hr) Same buses as to Guadalajara.

Guadalajara Autobuses de Jalisco (US$38, 9-11hr, 5 1st-class); Sur de Jalisco (US$28, 9-11hr, 4 2nd-class)

Manzanillo Elite (US$23, 7hr, 4 1st-class daily); Galeana (US$17.50, 6-7hr, 4 2nd-class); Autobuses de Jalisco (US$26, 6-7hr, 2nd-class at 2:30pm & 5:30pm)

Mexico City Vía Plus (US$45, 12hr, 5 1st-class); Futura (US$45, 5 1st-class); Estrella de Oro (US$44, 2 1st-class) To Terminal Sur.

Morelia Futura (US$29, 4-8hr, 5 1st-class); Parhikuni 'Plus' (US$36, 4-8hr, 1 executive; US$30, 14 2nd-class); Futura (US$29, 4-8hr, 5 1st-class)

Puerto Vallarta (US$34, 12hr, 4 1st-class *Elite*)

Uruapan (US$12-17, 3-6hr) Same buses as to Morelia.

Zihuatanejo (US$5-7, 2-3hr) Same buses as to Acapulco.

Combis to Playa Azul via La Mira trawl Av Lázaro Cárdenas every 10 minutes from 5am to 9pm (US$1.25, 30 minutes, 24km), stopping outside the Autobuses de Jalisco terminal, opposite Galeana. A taxi from Lázaro Cárdenas to Playa Azul is US$10 to US$12.

Ixtapa, Zihuatanejo & the Costa Grande

The Costa Grande, Guerrero state's 'Big Coast,' stretches 325km from the Río Balsas at the Michoacán border southeast to Acapulco. In the northwest, around Troncones and Majahua, low hills of tropical deciduous forest sit next to the sea. Around Ixtapa and Zihuatanejo and southeast to Acapulco, coconut plantations dominate the landscape. Just inland, the Sierra Madre del Sur, with its perpetually cloud-covered peaks, is the only reminder that temperatures cool down in other places.

Ixtapa and Zihuatanejo and, to an increasing extent, Troncones are the only serious blips on the Costa Grande tourist screen. Troncones is a growing stretch of hotels, B&Bs and guesthouses on a beautiful beach. Ixtapa is a planned resort development, with two golf courses and a raft of luxury mega-hotels lining a long, wave-pounded beach on the open sea. Its nearby 'sister city,' Zihuatanejo, about 8km away, is an overgrown fishing village set on a spectacular, tightly curved bay with four beaches that rarely receive a wave big enough to tip a toddler off an air mattress. It offers atmosphere, history, a more authentic taste of Mexico and many affordable restaurants and hotels. The beaches and fishing villages southeast of Zihuatanejo make great day trips or overnight stops en route to Acapulco (a four-hour drive from Zihuatanejo), as do the beaches to the north (all under two hours from Zihuatanejo).

HIGHLIGHTS

- Surfing the spectacular lefts of **La Saladita** (p182), goofy-footer's paradise
- Snorkeling, beachcombing and snoozing in sleepy **Troncones** (p179)
- Sailing out of **Zihuatanejo** (p190) to enjoy spinnaker rides, sunbathing and snorkeling
- Savoring fresh seafood and handmade tortillas after exploring the mangrove-fringed lagoon at **Barra de Potosí** (p196)
- Going after marlin, sailfish or other fierce fighters in a charter boat from **Zihuatanejo** (p190)

La Saladita

Troncones

Zihuatanejo Barra de Potosi

■ AVERAGE JANUARY HIGH/LOW: 29°C | 20°C   ■ AVERAGE JULY HIGH/LOW: 32°C | 25°C

IXTAPA, ZIHUATANEJO &
THE COSTA GRANDE

History

Archaeological sites near the Río Balsas, at Soledad de Maciel (near Petatlán), and at Puerto Marqués (near Acapulco) show human presence on the Costa Grande as far back as 2500–2000 BC. Ceramic pieces and architecture found on the Costa Grande, which are unlike those found on the coastal areas to the north, indicate the region had contact with the Olmecs and later with Teotihuacán. Still, settlements always remained small and widely dispersed.

Tourism, so to speak, goes back a long way. The Purépecha (aka Tarascos), who ruled what is now Michoacán from the early 15th century until the arrival of the Spanish, had an early king named Calzontzin who liked Bahía de Zihuatanejo enough to build a winter 'retreat' on the point at Playa Las Gatas. If tales are true, the retreat included an artificial reef (still there) constructed to form something of a swimming pool for Calzontzin and his many wives.

When the Spanish arrived in the early 16th century, the region was loosely controlled by the Aztecs. Following the conquest, Hernán Cortés set his sights on developing a maritime route between Mexico and Asia, and in 1523 he established the shipyard and port of Puerto Santiago (present-day Zacatula) on the Río Balsas. Álvaro Saavedra de Cerón sailed from Zihuatanejo in search of a trade route in 1527, never to return. When a return trade route from Asia was finally established in 1565 between Acapulco and Manila (Philippines), Zihuatanejo's importance fizzled out to all but a few English and Dutch pirates who occasionally used the bay as a hideout before they attacked treasure-filled galleons en route to Acapulco.

After independence, and the subsequent finish of the Acapulco–Manila maritime route, Zihuatanejo remained a sleepy fishing village – until the 1970s when Fonatur (p182) developed Ixtapa.

Information

Ixtapa and Zihuatanejo are now major tourist destinations; the latter receives cruise ships that anchor in the bay. Though they're right next door to each other, they still feel worlds apart. With its purpose-built

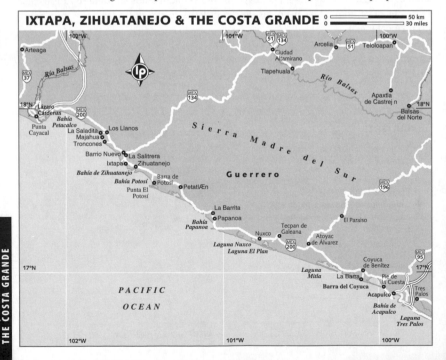

IXTAPA, ZIHUATANEJO & THE COSTA GRANDE

infrastructure, Ixtapa clearly exists only to accommodate tourists, while Zihuatanejo offers much more for locals and visitors alike.

Packed with useful information in Spanish and English are the **Ixtapa-Zihuatanejo municipal website** (www.ixtapa-zihuatanejo.com), **Zihua.net** (www.zihua.net) and **ZihuaRob's Travel Guide and Directory** (www.zihuatanejo.net). All three focus primarily on Zihuatanejo and Ixtapa, but also provide information on Troncones and other Costa Grande destinations.

Getting There & Away

See p195 for specifics. A few airlines fly direct to Zihuatanejo from US cities; most other flights involve transfers in Mexico City. Regular 1st-class buses connect Zihuatanejo with Mexico City, and there's even more frequent service to Lázaro Cárdenas and Acapulco, to the northwest and southeast respectively.

Getting Around

Regular 2nd-class buses run along the entire length of Hwy 200 through Guerrero state and will drop you either at your destination or at points where you can catch local transport. For car-rental agencies in Zihuatanejo and Ixtapa, see p196.

TRONCONES

☎ 755 / pop 400

About 35km northwest of Zihuatanejo, Troncones' coastline has several kilometers of vacation homes, B&Bs and guest inns, the majority gringo-owned. It also has some amazing surfing, good swimming and snorkeling, as well as various terrestrial activities such as bird-watching and mountain biking. Though accommodations are moderately expensive, the place is addictively relaxed and friendly.

Families generally fill Troncones' lodgings through the winter, but the place changes face in summer, when prices fall, the waves pick up and surfers roll in from all over.

Orientation

The village of Troncones is about 100m from the beach at the end of a 3km paved road from Hwy 200 – but most of what you'll be interested in is along the unpaved beachfront road. From its T-junction with the road from the highway, the dirt road

stretches along Playa Troncones in both directions. About 2km to the south (left) it ends, while to the north (right) from the T, it runs some 4km past Troncones Point to reach the calmer waters of Playa Manzanillo. The road continues a short way to the small village of Majahua, a 10-minute walk past Playa Manzanillo. From Majahua, the road (rough in wet season) continues about 6km to meet Hwy 200 near Km 32.

Information

Abarrotes Gaby (☉ 7:30am-9pm) Has long-distance telephone service. It's just off the coast road in Troncones village.

Inn at Manzanillo Bay (☎ 553-28-84) Charges a hefty US$10 per hour of Internet access.

Zihu@Rob's Troncones website (www.troncones.com.mx) Chock-full of useful information.

Activities
SURFING

With more than a dozen breaks within 20km of Troncones, short-boarders, long-boarders, rookies and rippers will all find something to ride. As usual, it's best to get out before the breeze picks up (usually around 11am), or around sunset when it gets glassy once again. The waves are biggest May to October.

Troncones itself has several world-class breaks. The beach breaks here can be excellent in summer, but the wave to chase is the left at **Troncones Point**. When it's small, the takeoff is right over the rocks (complete with sea urchins), but when it's big, it's beautiful, beefy and rolls halfway across the bay.

La Saladita (p182) has a blissfully long, rolling left, perfect for long-boarders. Yet another endless left and some rights can be had at the reef break of **El Rancho**. It's about 45 minutes northwest of La Saladita by car (standard drive OK in dry season), but it's easier (if pricier) by boat. **La Boca**, a river mouth just north of Majahua (via the beach and an easy-to-miss dirt track) and some 6km northwest of the Troncones T-junction, is best in summertime when the sandbar breaks and both rights and lefts are consistent.

The surf shop at the **Inn at Manzanillo Bay** (☎ 553-28-84; www.manzanillobay.com; Playa Manzanillo) rents an excellent selection of short- and long-boards (from US$18 per day) as well as boogie boards (US$5 per half day). They also offer surf lessons starting at

US$40 per, buy and sell boards and arrange guided boat trips (from US$100) to many of the best local surf spots. Troncosurfo, a couple of hundred meters inland from the T-junction, also offers lessons, as well as board rentals and repairs.

OTHER ACTIVITIES

There's good **snorkeling** at Troncones Point off Playa Manzanillo, and you can rent equipment for US$5 per half day at the Inn at Manzanillo Bay (p179), which also rents **mountain bikes** for about US$18 per day; a good ride heads north along the beach as far as La Saladita. **Costa Nativa Eco Tours** (☎ 044-755-556-3616) leads various bicycle tours around the Troncones area for US$20 per person (mountain bike and all equipment included).

Other activities include **fishing, hiking, bird-watching** and **sea-turtle spotting**; many hoteliers can help arrange these activities.

Sleeping

Reservations are necessary almost everywhere in Troncones during the high season (November through April); several places also require multiple-night stays. Prices at other times can be as much as 50% lower than those listed here, but be aware that many business owners aren't around in the low season. Two Troncones residents who between them manage several properties are Tina Morse at **Casa Ki** (☎ 553-28-15; casaki@ yahoo.com) and Anita LaPointe at the **Tropic of Cancer Beach Club** (☎ 553-28-00; casacanela@yahoo .com). With some advance notice, they can usually set you up with anything from an affordable room to a luxurious house.

BUDGET

The first listing here is not far south of the T-junction; the second and third are a bit inland from the T.

Quinta d'Liz (☎ 553-29-14; www.playatroncones .com; d with breakfast US$30) These six simple but stylish bungalows are just off the beach and come with fans and good beds, plus use of a communal kitchen. The combination of price, facilities, location and mellow management by the surfing owner make this one of the best deals in town.

Casa de la Amistad (d with fan/air-con US$24/38, q with fan US$34; 🐱) This place has two basic upstairs rooms with air-con and a shared bathroom. The two downstairs fan rooms have an OK bathroom and good screens, and their floors are covered with seashells and coral. A hammock area and a big fridge for guests' use increase the appeal.

Miscelánea Jasmín (r with fan/air-con US$24/47; 🐱) Behind the in-town *abarrotes* (small grocery), this place has a few OK rooms, most with tinted windows. The fan rooms are nicer overall; some share a large balcony.

MIDRANGE & TOP END

The following accommodations are spread out along the beachfront road. Going north from the T-junction you first reach Casa Ki, then the Delfín Sonriente, Casas Gregorio, the Inn at Manzanillo Bay, Posada de los Raqueros and Hacienda Edén. South from the T are Puesta del Sol and Casas Canela/ Canelita.

Hacienda Edén (☎ 553-28-02; www.edenmex.com; r US$85-110, bungalows US$85-95, air-con suites US$110, all with breakfast; **P** 🐱) On Playa Manzanillo, 4km north of the T-junction, this tranquil beachfront gem has lovingly decorated bungalows, rooms and suites, a gourmet restaurant and a full bar. Tropical hardwoods, Talavera (majolica) tile and other touches are used everywhere to great advantage, and screens are first rate, including over the otherwise roofless showers attached to the bungalows, which give bathers the sensation of showering under the open sky (without the bug bites).

Casa Delfín Sonriente (☎ 553-28-03, in the US 831-688-6578; www.casadelfinsonriente.com/delfin.htm; r US$65-119; 🐱 🐱) A striking Mediterranean-style seaside villa, this offers a variety of well-furnished B&B accommodation. Some have air-con available (for an additional US$15/day), while others are nearly open air, with hanging beds. All units have access to the gorgeous swimming pool, communal master kitchen and art supplies galore.

Casa Ki (☎ 553-28-15; www.casa-ki.com; 2-person bungalows US$95-110 with breakfast, house US$200) A charming retreat, Ki features a thoughtfully furnished main house sleeping up to six people (one-week minimum stay), and three colorful free-standing bungalows (three-night minimum) with access to a communal kitchen. All are set on a verdant beachside property.

Casas Gregorio (in US ☎ 425-228-2400; www.mex online.com/gregorio.htm; bungalows US$90-99, houses

US$188; 🏊) At the northern end of Playa Troncones, Gregorio has two spacious two-bedroom, two-bathroom houses beachside. Each has a fully equipped kitchen. The two bungalows are set back a bit and share a small kitchen. With cleverly constructed king-sized concrete 'bunkbeds,' each will accommodate four people.

Casas Canela & Canelita (☎ 553-28-00; www.tron conestropic.com/canela.html; r/house US$40/125) Across the road from the beach, this two-building garden property is an affordable, comfortable option. Casa Canela, the house in front, sleeps six and has a large kitchen and a hammock-strewn front porch. Casa Canelita is a much more modest duplex with rooms that can be rented individually and share a kitchen and terrace. All options require a three-night stay in high season.

Inn at Manzanillo Bay (☎ 553-28-84; www.man zanillobay.com; bungalows US$108; P 🖳 🏊) The inn has 10 well-appointed, thatched-roof bungalows with room safes, good mattresses, ceiling fans, mosquito nets and hammock-bedecked terraces. Other pluses are a popular restaurant, a full surf shop and easy access to the primo break at Troncones Point.

Posada de los Raqueros (☎ 553-28-70; www.ra queros.com; Playa Manzanillo; r US$105, bungalows US$120-170, house US$175; 🏊) This posada offers three split-level bungalows, each with beds above and a living room, kitchen and bathroom below. Two other private rooms have a shared kitchen, and the latest offering is a two-bedroom house with air-con. All are stylishly designed and open onto a sand and grass area leading to the beach. It's peaceful here; the name refers to beachcombers, not musicians.

La Puesta del Sol (☎ 557-05-03, in the US 818-553-3311; www.troncones.com.mx/puestadelsol; r US$40-65, ste US$95, penthouse US$175) This attractive four-room, three-story *palapa* (thatched-roof shelter) offers a simple 'surfers' room' on up to a superluxurious penthouse apartment.

Eating & Drinking

Be prepared to pay US$2 per beer in most places.

Huachinango's (mains US$8-10; 🕐 restaurant noon-10pm, bar till last person leaves, closed Tue) Just 100m south of the T-junction, Huachinango's serves good seafood, pasta, shrimp and octopus, all with a heaping helping of ocean view. The specialty here is *huachinango sarandeado* (red snapper marinated in red salsa and charcoal grilled).

La Cocina del Sol (mains $4-9) The renowned chef, Christian, turns out some sublime dishes here at Hacienda Edén's restaurant, wielding goat cheese, arugula and *jamón serrano* (cured ham) with equal dexterity. The kitchen is open for all meals (one dinner seating only, at 6:30pm, reservations recommended); on Sundays it puts on a rib barbecue.

Da Tiziano (☎ 559-2863; mains US$9-13; 🕐 5-10pm, closed Tue) Folks in Troncones are excited about this authentically Italian place (run by authentic Italians) a couple of hundred meters inland from the T-junction. They give it high marks for its bruschetta, salads, copious handmade pastas, and pizzas baked in the wood-fired oven.

Inn at Manzanillo Bay (mains US$7.50-13) At the inn's restaurant you can choose from Mexican dishes, American favorites (think cheeseburgers and hickory-smoked pork ribs), and such fusions as 'Thai-style' deep-fried shrimp tacos or a seared ahi-tuna sandwich with wasabi mayonnaise.

Café Sol (breakfasts US$2.50-3.75, sandwiches US$3.75-5.50; 🕐 8am-4pm, closed Tue) The breakfasts come with a view at this two-story open-air place run by the peripatetic chef from La Cocina del Sol. It's a short way north of the T-junction and serves great egg dishes, homemade bread, smoothies, good espresso drinks and gelato, plus sandwiches; at night it morphs into a taco bar. Bonus: the 2nd floor is one of the few places in Troncones where you can get cell-phone reception.

Troncones and Majahua proper each have a few taco stands where you can eat well for under US$3.25, as well as some beachfront *enramadas* (thatch-covered open-air restaurants) where US$12 goes a long way. Good beachfront restaurants include Costa Brava, north of the T-junction, and Doña Nica's Enramada, just south of the T-junction. A few steps south of Doña Nica's is the **Tropic of Cancer** (mains US$4-9; 🕐 closed Tue), a popular restaurant-bar-beach club with swimming pool.

In Majahua, Marta has an ideal bayside location and makes a *machaca* (dried seafood, often shark, made into a hash; $4) like no other in all of Mexico – it's a must for adventurous eaters.

Getting There & Away

Driving from Ixtapa or Zihuatanejo, head northwest on Hwy 200 toward Lázaro Cárdenas. Just north of Km 30 you'll see the marked turnoff for Troncones; follow this winding paved road 3km west to the beach.

Second-class buses heading northwest toward Lázaro Cárdenas or La Unión from Zihua's long-distance terminals will drop you at the turnoff for Troncones (US$2, 40 minutes) if you ask. You can also catch La Unión–bound buses from the lot a couple of blocks east of Zihua's market.

White *colectivo* (shared transport) vans and *microbuses* shuttle between Hwy 200 and Troncones roughly every half hour or so between 7am and 9am and from 2pm to 6pm (US$1). In a pinch you would probably have no problems hitching in either direction.

A taxi from Ixtapa or the Zihua airport to Troncones costs around US$57 to US$64, depending on where you're headed. It's cheaper to take a bus or even a cab from the airport to Zihua and then catch a cab to Troncones. These can be bargained down to around US$30, and taxis from Troncones back to Zihuatanejo may be even cheaper.

LA SALADITA

☎ 755 / pop 300

Around 7km northwest of Troncones, La Saladita has a long, gentle left, perfect for long-boarding. The beach itself stretches far to the northwest and makes for blissful walks. The area has become increasingly popular with surfers from the States, some of whom have bought land and built houses and rental units here.

Restaurant Jacqueline serves mind-blowing lobster (some swear it's the best on the coast; others make the same claim for the handmade tortillas), beer and other seafood dishes. One lodging option is the beach-front cabañas at **Saladita Surfing Resort Camp** (www.saladita.com; 1-/2-bedroom bungalow US$65/95). Each contains a bathroom, screens, fan, coffeemaker and a private deck with a hammock. Make reservations far in advance for May to October; you may get lucky simply showing up the rest of the year.

Some restaurants allow people to camp or sleep in a hammock and use bathrooms and showers for free, provided you eat regularly in the restaurant.

To get to La Saladita from Troncones, take Hwy 200 north and turn left at the town of Los Llanos (around Km 140); follow the road to the fork near the convenience stores, hang a right and follow the dirt road 5km to the beach. Any northbound 2nd-class bus will drop you at Los Llanos; busing is only feasible if you plan to stay more than a day.

IXTAPA

☎ 755 / pop 5000

Ixtapa (eeks-*tah*-pah), 240km northwest of Acapulco and next door to Zihuatanejo, is a glitzy, government-planned luxury resort with some fine beaches, a marina, golf courses, discos and several fairly expensive hotels.

Ixtapa was a coconut plantation and nearby Zihuatanejo a sleepy fishing village until 1970, when Fonatur – the Mexican government's tourism-development organization – decided that the Pacific coast needed a Cancún-like resort complex. Ixtapa was selected for its proximity to the USA, average temperature of 27°C, tropical vegetation and lovely beaches. Fonatur bought up the coconut plantation, laid down infrastructure and rolled out the red carpet for hotel chains and real-estate developers.

Orientation & Information

Most of the services or stores you'll need in Ixtapa are found in the outdoor *centros comerciales* (shopping centers), all within walking distance of each other on the main drag, Blvd Ixtapa. There are a few banks and *casas de cambio* (exchange houses, in the commercial malls) where you can change US dollars and traveler's checks; some hotel lobbies have ATMs. The banks give the best rate of exchange; the *casas de cambio* give a slightly less favorable rate but they're open longer. The town lacks a post office, but you can mail letters from any big hotel.

Bancomer (Centro Comercial La Puerta; ☽ 9am-5pm Mon-Fri) Behind Señor Frog's.

State tourist office (Sefotur; ☎ 553-19-67; Plaza Los Patios; ☽ 8am-8:30pm Mon-Fri, 8am-3pm Sat) Opposite the Hotel Presidente Inter-Continental. The many unofficial sidewalk kiosks offering tourist information are touting time-share schemes.

Telecomm office (Plaza Los Patios; ☽ 9am-3pm Mon-Fri) Behind the state tourist office.

Tourist police (☎ 553-20-08; Centro Comercial La Puerta)

Sights & Activities

BEACHES

Ixtapa's big hotels line **Playa del Palmar**, a long, broad stretch of white sand teeming with families, strolling beach vendors and sunburnt honeymooners. Be very careful if you swim here: the waves crash straight down and there's a powerful undertow. The western end of this beach, just before the entrance to the lagoon, is known as **Playa Escolleras** and is a favorite spot for surfing. Further west, past the marina, are three small beaches that are among the most beautiful in the area: **Playa San Juan**, **Playa Casa Blanca** and **Playa Cuatas**. Unfortunately, they've all been effectively privatized by new developments, so unless you can gain access by skiff or helicopter they are out of bounds – public access, required by Mexican law, appears to have been overlooked.

To the northwest, past Punta Ixtapa, are **Playa Quieta** and the long, wide **Playa Linda**. The latter has several decent seafood *enramadas* and a few shops selling souvenirs, snacks and beer, all at the beach's southern end, near the pier.

Isla Ixtapa

Just offshore, Isla Ixtapa is a small, wooded island with four pocket-sized beaches and several seafood *enramadas* that feed the island's steady stream of visitors. It's home to deer, raccoons, armadillos, iguanas and numerous species of birds, as well as the flipper-footed humans who migrate here daily for the excellent snorkeling. You can rent snorkeling gear there for about US$6 a day (US$11.50 if you add a life jacket).

Playa Cuachalalate, the main beach, has plenty of restaurants and the island's main pier, but, with fishing boats anchored along the beach and jet-skiers zipping around just offshore, it's the least appealing for swimming. No matter – the smaller but equally beautiful **Playa Varadero** is only a short walk away. The best snorkeling is at **Playa Coral**, directly behind Varadero, where you will see numerous species of tropical fish, including blowfish, butterfly fish, angelfish and, as the name suggests, lots of coral. **Playa Carey** is the most isolated beach of all and is accessible only by boat, usually from the pier at Cuachalalate.

Boats zip over to the island every few minutes (less frequently in the low season)

from the Playa Linda pier and drop visitors at Playa Cuachalalate or Playa Varadero. The return boat ride (five minutes each way) will set you back US$3; boats operate 9am to 5pm daily. A boat also goes to Isla Ixtapa from the Zihuatanejo pier, but only when there are eight passengers or more. It departs at 11am, and leaves the island at around 4pm. The trip (US$12 return) takes an hour each way. The ticket office is at the foot of the pier.

SURFING

The best bet for waves in the immediate area is the beach break at **Playa Linda**, directly in front of the parking lot at the end of the Playa Linda road. In winter, when it's pancake-flat everywhere else, it can be chest-high and fun. Further down the beach, the river mouth is good during the rainy season after the river breaks through the sandbar. For both spots, take a Playa Linda bus to the pier and walk up the road (or the beach) to the parking lot. Another local favorite for its proximity to town is **Playa Escolleras**, a jetty-side beach break in Ixtapa favoring rights and, on weekends, crowds. It's at the western end of Playa del Palmar next to (and thanks to) the marina; bring your short-board.

The best surf shop around is **Catcha L'Ola Surf Shop & Bar** (☎ 553-13-84; www.ixtapasurf.com; Centro Comercial Kiosko, Local 12, Ixtapa; ☺ 9am-9pm), owned by Masters Division national champ Leonel Pérez, who is a great source of information. Behind the movie theater in Ixtapa, it's well stocked and likely your best bet for board repairs. Leon rents short- and longboards by the day or week, and will drive you out to Playa Linda or up to Troncones or La Saladita. He also offers three-hour lessons. The shop is good for cheap beer and gossip.

OTHER ACTIVITIES

Bicycling is a breeze along the 15km *ciclopista* (bicycle path) that stretches from Playa Linda, north of Ixtapa, through the Aztlán Eco Park practically into Zihuatanejo. Mountain bikes can be rented at several places (see p186). If you'd prefer not to pedal, you can go **horseback riding** on Playa Linda (you can arrange this on the beach).

The **Ixtapa Club de Golf Palma Real** (☎ 553-10-62) and the **Club de Golf Marina Ixtapa**

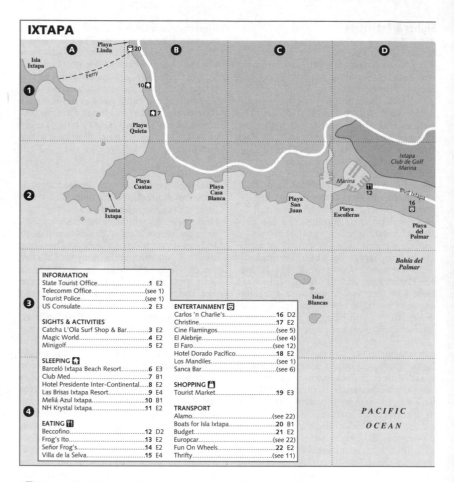

IXTAPA

INFORMATION
State Tourist Office................................1 E2
Telecomm Office.............................(see 1)
Tourist Police...............................(see 1)
US Consulate...2 E3

SIGHTS & ACTIVITIES
Catcha L'Ola Surf Shop & Bar...........3 E2
Magic World...4 E2
Minigolf..5 E2

SLEEPING
Barceló Ixtapa Beach Resort..............6 E3
Club Med..7 B1
Hotel Presidente Inter-Continental....8 E2
Las Brisas Ixtapa Resort......................9 E4
Meliá Azul Ixtapa...............................10 B1
NH Krystal Ixtapa...............................11 E2

EATING
Beccofino..12 D2
Frog's Ito...13 E2
Señor Frog's..14 E2
Villa de la Selva..................................15 E4

ENTERTAINMENT
Carlos 'n Charlie's..............................16 D2
Christine..17 E2
Cine Flamingos...............................(see 5)
El Alebrije.......................................(see 4)
El Faro..(see 12)
Hotel Dorado Pacífico........................18 E2
Los Mandiles..................................(see 1)
Sanca Bar.......................................(see 6)

SHOPPING
Tourist Market.....................................19 E3

TRANSPORT
Alamo...(see 22)
Boats for Isla Ixtapa...........................20 B1
Budget...21 E2
Europcar.......................................(see 22)
Fun On Wheels...................................22 E2
Thrifty...(see 11)

(☎ 553-14-10) both have 18-hole courses, tennis courts and swimming pools.

Brush up on your putting at the **minigolf** near Ixtapa's Cine Flamingos cinema, or get wet at **Magic World** (☎ 553-13-59; admission US$7.50; ⏱ 10:30am-5:30pm), an aquatic park beside the Hotel Ixtapa Palace. It has rides, water slides, toboggans and other amusements.

There are also snorkeling and scuba diving (p189) options, as well as sportfishing (p190).

Sleeping

Ixtapa's resorts are all top-end, with the cheapest running around US$125 a night in the winter high season (January to Easter). Some drop their rates by 25% or more at other times of year (at Christmas, Easter and outside of the holiday peaks). Try arranging a package deal through a travel agent, including airfare from your home country, or check online. Otherwise, Zihuatanejo's accommodations are generally cheaper.

Hotel Presidente Inter-Continental (☎ 553-00-18, in US 888-424-6835; http://ixtapa.interconti .com; Blvd Ixtapa s/n; d from US$260 with breakfast; P X X 🖥 🖼 🛗) One of the most popular hotels on the beach, the Presidente is first class all the way, with a gym, sauna, tennis courts, five restaurants and a kids' club that teaches the little ones basic Spanish on top of all the other activities.

NH Krystal Ixtapa (☎ 553-03-33; www.nh-hotels .com; Blvd Ixtapa s/n; d from US$125; P X X 🖼 🛗)

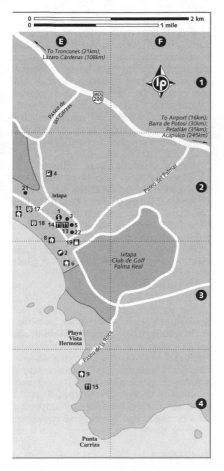

Krystal has some of the best-value rooms on the strip (all of them with ocean views), an excellent pool, one of the area's liveliest nightclubs and a highly regarded children's club, Krystalitos.

Barceló Ixtapa Beach Resort (☎ 555-20-00; www .barcelo.com; Blvd Ixtapa s/n; d from US$232, all-inclusive; 🅿 ⊠ ⊠ ⊠ 🅙) Another good family choice, the Barceló has especially fine pool and patio areas, as well as tennis courts and a gym. Its all-inclusive plan covers three meals, alcoholic beverages, gym use, tennis courts, room service and child care.

Las Brisas Ixtapa Resort (☎ 553-21-21; www.brisas .com.mx; Playa Vista Hermosa; d from US$197; 🅿 ⊠ ⊠ 🕮 ⊠ 🅙) Enormous Brisas (423 rooms) sits alone on the small, lovely Playa Vista

Hermosa, essentially laying claim to it. The main structure's design looks a bit dated, but gives all rooms a terrace with first-rate ocean views. The hotel has a great lobby bar, a plethora of pools and restaurants, a fitness center, kids' club and tennis courts.

Two resorts on Playa Linda, a bit removed from central Ixtapa, do business almost exclusively through all-inclusive packages: **Club Med** (☎ 555-10-00; www.clubmed .com; d US$246; closed Sept 15-Oct 31), and **Meliá Azul Ixtapa** (☎ 550-00-00; www.solmelia.com; d US$249).

Eating

Ixtapa has plenty of restaurants in addition to those in the big hotels.

Villa de la Selva (☎ 553-03-62; Paseo de la Roca Lote D; mains US$15-22; ⏰ 7pm-late) Reservations are a must at this elegant Italian/Mediterranean restaurant in the former home of Mexican president Luis Echeverría. Near Las Brisas resort (left), the cliffside villa overlooks the ocean (sunsets are superb). Offerings include glazed salmon with couscous, duck breast, several pastas with and without shellfish, and a good wine list.

Beccofino (☎ 553-17-70; Veleros Lote 6, Ixtapa Marina Plaza; mains US$16-23; ⏰ 9am-11pm) Indoor-outdoor Beccofino enjoys a good reputation for delicious (if pricey) northern Italian cuisine, especially seafood and pastas. Several other good restaurants ring the marina.

Frog's Ito (☎ 553-22-82; Blvd Ixtapa s/n; sushi per piece US$1.50-2.50, rolls US$2-8.50) This place serves sushi, noodle dishes and Asian salads.

Next door, **Señor Frog's** (☎ 553-22-82; Blvd Ixtapa s/n; mains US$9-12.50) serves large portions of zany antics along with familiar Mexican dishes, burgers and iguana. The same is true at **Carlos 'n' Charlie's** (p186; ☎ 553-00-85; Paseo del Palmar s/n; mains US$9-12.50).

Entertainment

All the big hotels have bars and nightclubs. Many also have discos; in low season most of these charge less and open fewer nights.

Christine (☎ 553-04-56; Blvd Ixtapa s/n; admission to US$25) Christine has the sizzling sound and light systems you'd expect from one of the most popular discos in town.

El Alebrije (☎ 553-27-10; Paseo de las Garzas s/n; admission for women/men US$24/19) A fog machine, banks of computerized lights, pop, rock, house, salsa and merengue, open bar – what more do you want?

Carlos 'n' Charlie's (☎ 553-00-85; Paseo del Palmar s/n) Things can get wild on this chain restaurant's dance floor right above the beach; on weekends it fills with hard-partying young tourists and locals alike.

Los Mandiles (Centro Comercial La Puerta) The upstairs bar-disco at this restaurant features a giant TV screen.

El Faro (☎ 553-10-27; Marina Ixtapa; ⏱ 5pm-1am) Slow things down at this piano bar at the top of a 25m-high lighthouse – a great spot for watching the sunset.

Also deserving mention are the Barceló Ixtapa Beach Resort's Sanca Bar, where you can shake it to Latin music, and the excellent lobby bar at Las Brisas resort.

Several of Ixtapa's big hotels hold evening 'Fiestas Mexicanas,' which typically include a Mexican buffet and open bar, entertainment (traditional dancing, mariachis and bloodless cockfighting demonstrations), door prizes and dancing; the total price is usually US$35 to US$42. The Barceló Ixtapa Beach Resort holds fiestas year-round; in the high season several other hotels, including the **Dorado Pacífico** (☎ 553-20-25), also present fiestas. Reservations can be made directly or through travel agents.

Cine Flamingos (☎ 553-24-90; admission US$4.50) Behind the tourist office and opposite Plaza Ixpamar and the minigolf, this shows two films nightly, usually in English with Spanish subtitles.

Shopping

Tourist Market (Blvd Ixtapa s/n; ⏱ 9am-10pm) Though this market is packed with everything from tacky T-shirts to silver jewelry and hand-painted pottery, shopping is much better in Zihuatanejo (see p195).

Getting There & Around

For information on car rental, and getting to Zihuatanejo, the essential stop for getting to Ixtapa, see p195. Private *colectivo* vans provide transportation from the airport to Ixtapa for US$9 per person, but not in the other direction. A taxi to the airport costs US$11 to US$13 from Ixtapa.

Mexicana (☎ 553-20-25), with an office in the Hotel Dorado Pacífico, flies to Mexico City.

Local 'Directo' and 'B Viejo' buses run frequently between Ixtapa and Zihua, a 15-minute ride. They depart every 15 minutes from 5:30am to 11pm (US$0.60). In Ixtapa,

buses stop all along the main street, in front of all the hotels. In Zihua, buses depart from the corner of Juárez and Morelos. Buses marked 'Zihua-Ixtapa-Playa Linda' continue through Ixtapa to Playa Linda (US$0.60), stopping near Playa Quieta on the way; they operate from 7am to 7pm.

Ixtapa has plenty of taxis. Always agree on the fare before climbing into the cab; between Zihua and Ixtapa it should be around US$4. For prearranged service call **Radio Taxi UTAAZ** (☎ 554-33-11).

Ixtapa has several places renting motorbikes (around US$19 per hour, US$85 per day), including **Fun On Wheels** (☎ 553-02-59; ⏱ 9am-8pm), in the Centro Comercial Los Patios, which also rents mountain bikes for US$5/US$19 per hour/day. You usually need a driver's license and credit card to rent; if you're not an experienced motorcycle rider, Mexico is *not* the place to learn.

ZIHUATANEJO

☎ 755 / pop 62,000
Like its sister city, Ixtapa, Zihuatanejo (see-wah-tah-*neh*-ho) is quite touristy. Nevertheless, it retains an easygoing coastal ambience, and its setting on a beautiful bay with several fine beaches makes it a gratifying place to visit. Small-scale fishing is still an economic mainstay; if you stroll down by the pier early in the morning, you can join the pelicans in greeting successful fisher folk and inspecting the morning's catch. Needless to say, seafood is superb here.

Orientation

Though Zihua's suburbs are extensive, spreading around Bahía de Zihuatanejo and climbing the hills behind town, in the city's center everything is compressed within a few blocks. It's difficult to get lost; there are only a few streets and they're clearly marked.

Information

EMERGENCY
General emergency (☎ 060; ⏱ 24hr)
Hospital (☎ 554-36-50; Av Morelos near Mar Egeo)
Tourist police (☎ 554-23-55)

INTERNET ACCESS
Zihuatanejo is crawling with Internet cafés; the following places charge US$1 per hour.
Infinitum Internet (Bravo 12)
El Navegante Internet (Bravo 41)

LAUNDRY
Lavandería del Centro (☎ 554-97-91; Guerrero 17; ☽ 8am-8pm Mon-Sat, 10am-4pm Sun) Charges US$4 for 3kg; self-service also available.

MONEY
Zihuatanejo has many banks and *casas de cambio* where you can change US dollars and traveler's checks. The following banks have air-conditioned ATMs:

Banamex (cnr Ejido & Guerrero)
Bancomer (cnr Juárez & Bravo; ☽ 8:30am-4pm Mon-Fri, 10am-2pm Sat)
Banorte (cnr Juárez & Ejido; ☽ 9am-4pm Mon-Fri, 10am-2pm Sat)

POST
Post office (☎ 8am-6pm Mon-Fri, 9am-1pm Sat) Located off Morelos, this is well signed but still hard to find. Several hotels and stores in town also sell stamps.

TELEPHONE & FAX
Long-distance telephone and fax services are available at several telephone *casetas*, including two on the corner of Galeana and Ascencio. Public Lada phones are all around town. **Telecomm** (☽ 8am-6pm Mon-Fri, 9am-1pm Sat), inside the post office, has a fax service.

TOURIST INFORMATION
Municipal tourist office (☎ 554-20-01; www.ixtapa -zihuatanejo.com; Zihuatanejo Pte s/n, Colonia La Deportiva; ☽ 8am-4pm Mon-Fri) Upstairs in the *ayuntamiento* (city hall), 2km northeast of the town center (local buses between Ixtapa and Zihuatanejo stop out front).
Tourist branch office (☽ 8am-4pm Mon-Fri) Near the southern end of Playa La Ropa.
Tourist kiosk (Álvarez s/n; ☽ 9am-8pm) Operates in high season in the heart of town and offers free information, maps and brochures.

TRAVEL AGENCIES
Various agencies provide travel services and arrange local tours.
América-Ixtamar Viajes (☎ 554-35-90; cnr Cuauhtémoc & Bravo)
Turismo Internacional del Pacífico (TIP; ☎ 554-75-10/11; cnr Juárez & Álvarez; ☽ 9am-2pm & 4-7pm Mon-Sat, 5-7pm Sun)

Dangers & Annoyances
A study published in 2003 by the Mexican government's environmental protection agency, Profepa, cited 16 of the country's beaches as having unacceptably high levels of bacterial contamination. At the top of the list were Playas La Ropa, Las Gatas and Municipal, all on Bahía Zihuatanejo. This is a result of insufficiently treated sewage flowing into the bay. Ocean currents in winter keep the bay flushed out, but at other times of year (particularly late summer and during periods of rain), you should use discretion (and your nose) when deciding whether to swim.

From late fall to early spring as many as four cruise ships a week anchor in the bay. When their passengers are in port, prices have a tendency to inflate, especially for things like cab rides and souvenirs.

Sights & Activities
See p183 for activities on offer in nearby Ixtapa.

MUSEO ARQUEOLÓGICO DE LA COSTA GRANDE
This small but recommended **archeology museum** (☎ 554-75-52; Paseo del Pescador at Plaza Olof Palme; admission US$1; ☽ 10am-6pm, closed Mon) houses exhibits on the history, archaeology and culture of the Guerrero coast, with Spanish captions; a free English-language brochure has translations.

BEACHES
Waves are gentle at all Bahía de Zihuatanejo's beaches. If you want big ocean waves, head west toward Ixtapa, only a few minutes away by local bus.

Fishing *pangas* (motorized skiffs) line the sands of the **Playa Municipal**, which buzzes with activity when the fishermen haul in their catch in the early morning. This beach is the least appealing for swimming, especially when the seasonal, polluted Agua de Correa Canal is flowing into the bay. Standing on this beach you can see several other beaches spread around the bay, starting with Playa Madera, just past the rocky point on your left, then the long white stretch of Playa La Ropa past that. Directly across the bay lies the enticing Playa Las Gatas.

Playa Madera was once isolated from Playa Municipal by two rocky points, but now a concrete pathway over the rocks makes it an easy five-minute walk from town. It's better for swimming than the municipal beach and has several decent seafood restaurants.

From Playa Madera, walk over the hill along the Camino a Playa La Ropa (about

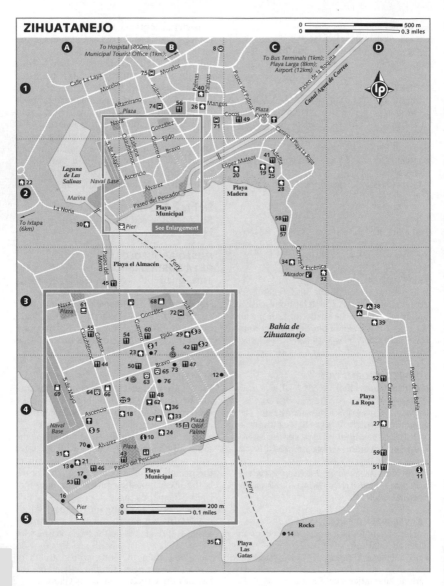

20 minutes) and you reach the broad expanse of **Playa La Ropa**, bordered by palm trees and lined with low-level hotels, seafood restaurants and sun beds. It's a pleasant walk, with the road rising up onto cliffs that offer a fine view over the bay. The first road to the beach is beside La Casa Que Canta hotel. Most restaurants along the beach require a minimum consumption of US$5 to US$7 of food or drink for use of their sun beds, but once you hit the minimum, you can stay all day – and feel pretty safe that someone is guarding your goodies while you swim. That said, La Ropa is hardly prone to theft. Arguably the most beautiful beach on the bay, La Ropa is great

INFORMATION
América-Ixtamar Viajes............(see 64)
Banamex..1 B3
Bancomer..2 B3
Banorte..3 B3
El Navegante Internet....................4 B4
HSBC ATM..5 A4
Infinitum Internet...........................6 B3
Lavandería del Centro..................7 B3
Post Office.......................................8 B1
Telecomm...................................(see 8)
Telephone Casetas.........................9 B4
Tourist Kiosk (high season only)..10 B4
Tourist Office Branch................ 11 D5
Turismo Internacional del Pacífico
  (TIP)..12 B4

SIGHTS & ACTIVITIES
Buceo Nautilus Divers................13 A5
Carlo Scuba...................................14 C5
Museo Arqueológico de la Costa
  Grande.......................................15 B4
Sportfishing Operators...........(see 46)
Ticket Office for Boats to Playa Las
  Gatas & Isla Ixtapa..................16 A5
Whisky Water World....................17 A5

SLEEPING 🏠 🏨
Angela's Hotel & Hostel.............18 B4
Bungalows Ley...............................19 C2
Bungalows Pacíficos....................20 C2
Casa de Huéspedes Elvira...........21 A4
Hostal del Viajero........................22 A2
Hotel Amueblados Valle.............23 B3

Hotel Ávila.....................................24 B4
Hotel Brisas del Mar...................25 C2
Hotel Bugambilias.......................26 B1
Hotel Casa del Mar.....................27 D4
Hotel Palacios...............................28 C2
Hotel Posada Michel...................29 B3
Hotel Raúl Tres Marías..............30 A2
Hotel Raúl Tres Marías Centro..31 A4
Hotel Royal Sotavento..............32 C3
Hotel Susy......................................33 B4
La Casa Que Canta......................34 C3
Las Gatas Beach Club.................35 B5
Posada Citlali................................36 B4
Trailer Park La Ropa....................37 D3
Trailer Park Los Cabañas...........38 D3
Villa del Sol...................................39 D3
Zihua Inn Hotel............................40 B1

EATING 🍴
Bad Bird Café.................................41 C2
Banana's...42 B3
Café Marina...................................43 B4
Cafetería Nueva Zelanda........... 44 A4
Casa Bahia.....................................45 A3
Casa Elvira.....................................46 A5
Cenaduría Antelia.......................47 B4
Coconuts...48 B4
Doña Licha.....................................49 C1
Il Paccolo.......................................50 B4
La Gaviota......................................51 D5
La Perla...52 D4
La Sirena Gorda............................53 A5
Los Braseros..................................54 B3
Mariscos El Acacio......................55 A3

Market...56 B1
Puerta del Sol................................57 C2
Restaurant Kau-Kan...................58 C2
Rossy's...59 D4
Tamales y Atoles Any.................60 B3

DRINKING 🍸 🍷
Café Zihuatanejo..........................61 A3
Jungle Bar......................................62 B4

ENTERTAINMENT 🎭
Black Bull Rodeo..........................63 B4
Cine Paraíso...................................64 A4
Ventaneando..................................65 B4

SHOPPING 🛍
Alberto's...66 A4
Coco's Cabaña...............................67 B4
El Jumil.....................................(see 43)
Mercado Municipal de las
  Artesanías.................................68 B3
Mercado Turístico La Marina....69 A4
Pancho's.....................................(see 64)

TRANSPORT
Aeroméxico....................................70 A4
Buses to Petatlán, La Unión......71 B1
Coacoyul Route Bus Stop (To Playa
  Larga & Airport).......................72 B3
Hertz..73 B4
La Correa Route Bus Stop (To
  Long-Distance Bus Stations).74 B1
Local Buses to Ixtapa.................75 B1
Mexicana Office............................76 B4

for swimming, parasailing, waterskiing, banana rides and sand-soccer. You can also rent sailboards and sailboats.

Opposite Zihuatanejo, **Playa Las Gatas** is a protected beach, crowded with sun beds and restaurants. It's good for snorkeling (there's some coral) and as a swimming spot for children, but beware of sea urchins. According to legend, Calzontzin, a Purépecha king, built a stone barrier here in pre-Hispanic times to keep the waves down and prevent sea creatures from entering, making it a sort of private swimming pool. Beach shacks and restaurants rent snorkeling gear for around US$5 per day.

Boats to Playa Las Gatas depart frequently from the Zihuatanejo pier from 9am to 5pm daily. Buy tickets (US$3 round-trip) at the booth at the foot of the pier; one-way tickets can be bought on board.

South of Zihuatanejo
About 10km south of Zihuatanejo, halfway between town and the airport, **Playa Larga** has big waves, beachfront restaurants and horseback riding. To reach Playa Larga, take a 'Coacoyul' combi (US$0.60) from

Juárez, opposite the market, and get off at the turnoff to Playa Larga. Another combi will take you from the turnoff to the beach, about 3km along a paved road through a coconut plantation.

SNORKELING & SCUBA DIVING
The ocean waters here enjoy an abundance of species because of a convergence of currents, and can offer great visibility, sometimes up to 35m. There are more than 30 dive sites nearby, offering conditions for beginners and advanced divers. Migrating humpback whales pass through from December to February, and manta rays can be seen all year, though there's greater likelihood of seeing them in summer, when the water is clearest, bluest and warmest.

A 40-minute boat ride southeast from Zihua, the granite rocks of **Los Morros del Potosí** offer some of the most fascinating diving along the coast, with submarine caves, walls, canals and tunnels; the high currents require experience. Isla Ixtapa offers numerous shallow- and deep-water dives for all skill levels. Experts can explore the nearby **Islas Blancas**, just off Playa del Palmar, with

IXTAPA, ZIHUATANEJO &
THE COSTA GRANDE

'IXTAPA' SOUNDS SO MUCH NICER

As in many in other parts of the world, several place-names around the Zihuatanejo area have colorful stories behind them. 'Zihuatanejo' itself comes from the Náhuatl *cihuatlán*, meaning 'place of women.' Depending on whose version you believe, this is derived from the fact that old Zihua was inhabited by a matriarchal society. Or that it was a ceremonial center which, like Isla Mujeres off the Yucatán Peninsula, was occupied solely by women. Or – least plausibly – that when the Spanish first arrived, the local menfolk had stashed their women here and gone off to hide. (Wouldn't it have a Spanish name, then?) In any case, the conquistadors added the diminutive suffix '-ejo,' supposedly to express their opinion of Zihua's insignificance. 'Ixtapa,' also from Náhuatl, means roughly 'covered in white,' and refers to the area's sands, or the white guano left by seabirds on the rocky islands just offshore. Coulda been worse.

The names of beaches lining Bahía de Zihuatanejo also tell stories. Playa Madera (Wood Beach) was so dubbed after the timber that was once milled on its shore, loaded aboard ships and carried to various parts of the world; at one time there was also a shipyard here. Playa Las Gatas does not have a history involving pussycats; it's named for the gentle nurse sharks that once inhabited the waters, called 'gatas' because of their whiskers. And finally, the name of Playa La Ropa (Clothing Beach) commemorates the occasion when a Spanish galleon coming from the Philippines was wrecked and its cargo of fine silks washed ashore.

---

coral-covered walls, caves, canals and abundant sea life.

Snorkeling is good at **Playa Las Gatas**, the home of **Carlo Scuba** (☎ 554-60-03; www.carloscuba .com; Playa Las Gatas), which offers a variety of PADI courses and dives (US$55/US$80 for one/two tanks). You're picked up at the Zihuatanejo pier, and dropped off there as well, or at Playa Las Gatas if you prefer.

Conveniently located in town, **Buceo Nautilus Divers** (☎ 554-91-91; www.nautilus-divers .com; Álvarez s/n; ☺ 8am-4pm Mon-Sat) does all of the usual dives and offers NAUI instruction and certification as well.

SPORTFISHING

Lugging a cooler full of beer onto a fishing boat and bringing it home full of fish (or empty of both) is one of Zihua's favorite tourist attractions. Sailfish are caught here year-round; seasonal fish include blue and black marlin (March to May), roosterfish (September to October), wahoo (October), mahimahi (November to December) and Spanish mackerel (December). Many captains now maintain a strict catch-and-release policy for billfish (especially sailfish and marlin). Deep-sea fishing trips for four people cost anywhere from US$150 to US$395 and up, depending on the size of the boat. Trips generally last six to eight hours and leave the Zihuatanejo pier no later than 7am.

Prices quoted by operators include equipment and usually include fishing license,

bait, beer and water – always ask. You can also walk along the pier and talk with the various fishermen, many of whom speak some English.

Among the fishing cooperatives near Zihuatanejo's pier are the **Sociedad Cooperativa José Azueta** (☎ 554-20-56) and **Sociedad de Servicios Turísticos** (☎ 554-37-58). English is spoken at privately run **Whisky Water World** (☎ 554-01-47; www.zihuatanejosportfishing.com; Paseo del Pescador 20).

SURFING

The only surf in Zihuatanejo is the point at **Playa Las Gatas**. Just inside the bay, it requires a big swell to break, but when it does, it's reportedly a perfect hollow left, rarely more than five feet; take a boat over from the Zihua pier. Ixtapa has more surf and better facilities; see p183.

CRUISES

A few sailboats offer cruises of local waters that often include snorkeling as part of the package. One of these is **Picante** (☎ 554-26-94, 554-82-70; www.picantecruises.com), a 23m catamaran based in Bahía de Zihuatanejo that offers a couple of different excursions. The 'Sail & Snorkel' trip (US$68, 10am to 2:30pm) goes outside the bay for brief snorkeling (gear rental US$5) at Playa Manzanillo, about an hour's cruise away. The trip includes lunch, an open bar, flying from the spinnaker and a great party. The 2½-hour sunset cruise (US$50, 5pm to 7:30pm) heads around the bay and out along the coast of Ixtapa. Reservations are required; private charters are also available.

Sleeping

The most reasonably priced hotels are in Zihuatanejo proper, with top-end hotels gravitating toward Playa La Ropa. Playa Madera is a good middle ground and has some excellent midrange hotels, many with kitchens, all with great views. If you like to stumble out of your hotel room into the ocean, try Playa La Ropa or Playa Madera; if you like to stumble home from the bar, go for Zihuatanejo.

During the December to April high season many hotels here fill up, so phone ahead to reserve a room; if you don't like what you get, you can always look for another room early the next day. The busiest times of year are Semana Santa (Holy Week) and the week between Christmas and New Year; at these peak times you *must* reserve a room and be prepared to pony up extra pesos. Tourism is much slower and rates are often negotiable from mid-April to mid-December; many high-end places offer lower rates during this time. Most places in Zihua will offer 10% to 20% (negotiable) off rack rates for longer stays, if asked. The following prices are for the high season.

BUDGET

The budget hotels listed here are in central Zihuatanejo and have rooms with fans.

Angela's Hotel & Hostel (☎ 554-50-84; www.zihuatanejo.com.mx/angelas; Ascencio 10; dm/d US$8.50/20; 🖳) Friendly, convenient and helpful, this hostel is hard to beat. Rooms are dark and crowded, but it's off a quiet street and offers a shared kitchen and Internet access (US$1 per hour).

AUTHOR'S CHOICE

La Casa Que Canta (☎ 554-70-30, in Mexico 800-710-93-45; www.lacasaquecanta.com; Carretera Escénica s/n; ste from US$486; P 🍴 🖳 🏊) Perched on the cliffs between Playa Madera and Playa La Ropa, this award-winning luxury hotel uses gorgeous Mexican handicrafts, furniture and textiles to great effect throughout. All rooms have terraces, full sea views and amenities galore, including free minibar drinks and fresh fruit daily.

Hotel Raúl Tres Marías (☎ 554-21-91; r3marias noria@yahoo.com; La Noria 4; s/d US$27/36) Across the lagoon footbridge, this popular budget option comes with clean, spacious rooms. Its best features, however, are the large terraced patios dotted with chairs and hammocks and boasting great views of the pier.

Casa de Huéspedes Elvira (☎ 554-20-61; Álvarez 32; s US$9.50 d US$15-19) This decent cheapie offers eight rooms on two floors surrounding an open courtyard. Upstairs rooms are much better, with more light and privacy, but they are accessible only via a rickety spiral staircase. No reservations are taken.

Hostal del Viajero (Salinas 50; camping US$3.75, dm US$7.50, r US$9.50-11; 🍴) Just getting going at the time of research and a bit rough around the edges, this hostel showed potential. It has an agreeable garden, and other common spaces include a terrace with hammocks, a laundry area and a kitchen with drinking water. For US$1.50 extra, guests can get a breakfast of fruit, bread and coffee. Shared baths for the two three-bed dorms are nicer than the private ones.

Two very small, basic trailer parks run by friendly families allow camping (tent or car) just off Playa La Ropa.

Trailer Park Los Cabañas (☎ 554-47-18; per person US$6) Six clean spaces in the Cabañas family's backyard, with bath, showers, a laundry sink and electricity. It's secure and usually full of return visitors.

Trailer Park La Ropa (☎ 554-60-30; per person US$5) Half a block beyond Los Cabañas, this is a bare-bones place with four showers (which *usually* work), four toilets, a small grocery and a restaurant.

MIDRANGE

Central Zihuatanejo has several midrange lodgings that provide easy access to banks, restaurants and other services. Other possibilities include the Playa Madera area, a five-minute walk east of the center on quiet López Mateos; Playa La Ropa, a bit further east; and the economical market area just east of Juárez from the center. If you're staying more than a few days, consider a place with a kitchen – the money you'll save cooking will offset the cost of the hotel.

Hotel Amueblados Valle (☎ 554-20-84; luisavall@ prodigy.net.mx; Guerrero 33; 1-/2-bed apt US$47/65) A great deal, especially for families or groups. A handful of large airy apartments come with full kitchens; some have balconies with partial mountain views. There's a wonderful sunny rooftop area, and three-bedroom apartments are also available. Ask the owner about other apartments in town and on Playa La Ropa, which may be cheaper, especially for longer stays.

Hotel Royal Sotavento (☎ 554-20-32; Carretera Escénica s/n; www.beachresortsotavento.com; s/d from US$58/71 with breakfast; ☒) Just above Playa La Ropa, at the northern end of the beach, the Sotavento is a well-maintained old favorite and has one of Zihuatanejo's most beautiful settings. Its white terraces are visible from all around the bay and offer incredible views; beds, baths and screens are all good, and the pool is large.

Bungalows Ley (☎ 554-45-63, 554-40-87; bunga lowsley@prodigy.net.mx; López Mateos s/n; 1-/2-bedroom bungalows US$85/170; ℗ ☒) Well-kept, spacious, with unbeatable views and beach access, these bungalows are only a short walk from the center. In short, a great value. They're not fancy, but all have terraces, room safes, air-con and kitchens or kitchenettes (some outdoors), and the biggest has a living room, dining room and two bathrooms.

Hotel Palacios (☎ 554-20-55; hotelpalacios@prodigy .net.mx; Adelita s/n; d US$71-75; ℗ ☒ ☒) Over-looking the eastern end of Playa Madera, pleasant Hotel Palacios is a family place with a swimming pool and beachfront terrace. Some rooms are on the smaller side, and not all have views, but they do all have air-con and good beds, baths and screens. Unlike other Playa Madera hotels, the Palacios is nearly at beach level, so you avoid the post-beach stair climbing.

Posada Citlali (☎ 554-20-43; Guerrero 4; s/d US$33/43) This pleasant older posada features small rooms that are basic but well kept and have good ventilation and light. It has a dark, leafy central courtyard.

Hotel Raúl Tres Marías Centro (☎ 554-67-06; www.ixtapa-zihuatanejo.net/r3marias; Álvarez 52; r US$64; ℗ ☒) Rooms at this spot are good and un-pretentious, and many come with a balcony. There's a popular downstairs restaurant, and in high season breakfast is included.

Hotel Posada Michel (☎ 554-74-23; www.zihua tanejo.net/hotels.html; Ejido 14; r with air-con US$52; ℗ ☒) The small but quality rooms here have interesting creative touches in the bathrooms, though exterior doors and windows are on the flimsy side.

Zihua Inn Hotel (☎ 554-38-68; Palapas 119; www .zihua-inn.com.mx; r with air-con US$56, with fan US$47;

℗ ☒ ☒) Near the market, the Zihua has four floors of bright, colorful, modern rooms, a decent pool with a kiddy section and a covered parking area.

Hotel Bugambilias (☎ 554-58-15; Mangos 28; s/d with air-con US$38/47, with fan US$29/38; ℗ ☒) The Boog has clean, bright decent-sized rooms next to the market, in a less touristy but quite lively part of town. It's a good value; balconied room 110 is the best of the lot.

Hotel Ávila (☎ 554-20-10; fax 554-20-10; Álvarez 8; r from US$70; ℗ ☒) Fronting Playa Munici-pal, the Ávila has 27 spacious but forget-table rooms with cable TV – get one with a balcony overlooking the bay if you want to remember something.

Hotel Susy (☎ 554-23-39; cnr Guerrero & Álvarez; s/d US$29/43; ℗ ☒) Just a block from Playa Mu-nicipal, this well-located place has good-sized but unremarkable and even cheerless rooms – avoid the ground-floor ones, which are dark and musty.

TOP END

Hotel Brisas del Mar (☎ 554-21-42; www.hotelbrisas delmar.com; López Mateos s/n; d from US$175; ☒ ▯ ☒) This attractive red adobe-style hotel has a large swimming pool, a beachfront restau-rant and a hilltop bar with fine views of the bay, as well as a spa with sauna and steam room and a small gym. All rooms have safes, minibars, coffeemakers and exquisite ocean-view terraces.

Bungalows Pacíficos (☎ 554-21-12; bungpaci@ prodigy.net.mx; López Mateos s/n; bungalows US$100) The six large bungalows have ample (some are enormous) sea-view terraces with green-ery, good bathrooms and fully equipped kitchens. The owner, a longtime Zihua resident, is a gracious and helpful hostess who speaks English, Spanish and German. Though maintenance is slipping a bit, clever construction maximizes breezes throughout all the rooms. From May to November the US$70 rate puts Pacíficos in the midrange category.

Villa del Sol (☎ 554-22-39, in the US & Canada 888-389-2645; www.hotelvilladelsol.com; d from US$596 with breakfast and dinner; ℗ ☒ ☒ ▯ ☒) Elegantly simple rooms, top-notch service and palm-studded beachside grounds have garnered this hotel (at northern end of Playa La Ropa) awards from travel magazines several years running. Most accommodations don't have bay views, but instead face the property's artificial lagoons. Meal plans are optional (and rates lower) from April to mid-December.

Las Gatas Beach Club (☎ 554-83-07; www.lasgatas beachclub.com; bungalows US$100) Four large free-standing bungalows sit on peaceful grounds at the edge of the bay, where at night you'll hear only the rhythmic sound of the surf and the sea breezes rustling through the palms. The unique, somewhat rustic bungalows are made of natural building materials and some sleep up to eight people. The last public-boat service from Zihuatanejo to Playa Las Gatas is at 5pm or 6pm (depending on the time of year), so you're under a bit of a curfew if you don't want to shell out bucks for private service.

Hotel Casa del Mar (☎ 554-38-73; www.zihua-casa delmar.com; r with fan US$100, with air-con US$120; P 🔀 🔝) This hideaway at the southern end of Calle Caracolito, on Playa La Ropa, has garden and beachfront rooms, the latter with good air-con, and all with OK beds and baths. Crocodiles, fed by the manager, inhabit the mangrove-lined waterway bordering the property. Good thing the small pool is above ground.

Eating

Guerrero is famous for its *pozole* (a hearty broth with hominy and pork, chicken, shrimp or other seafood), which is on most menus in town (especially on Thursday) and well worth a try.

Seafood in Zihuatanejo is excellent. *Tiritas* (slivers of raw fish quickly marinated in lemon juice, onion and green chili) are a local specialty. The dish originated with local fishermen: it was a quick snack requiring no cooking, easily prepared in the boat or on the beach after a morning at sea. *Tiritas* were just too damn good, however, to remain a treat for the fishermen alone. You can find them at seafood stands in the market, at carts near the bus stations and at some of the smaller seafood restaurants around town (ask – they're often not on the menu). They're served cold with soda crackers and *salsa picante* (hot chili sauce) on the side and make a great snack on a hot day.

PASEO DEL PESCADOR & NEARBY
Seafood here is fresh and delicious; many popular (if touristy) fish restaurants run parallel to Playa Municipal. The following are the best options.

La Sirena Gorda (☎ 554-26-87; Paseo del Pescador 90; mains US$5-17; ☽ 8:30am-10:30pm Thu-Tue) Close to the pier, the Fat Mermaid is a casual and popular open-air restaurant that's good for garlic shrimp, curry tuna and fish tacos, as well as burgers and traditional Mexican dishes.

Casa Elvira (☎ 554-20-61; Paseo del Pescador 8; mains US$6-16; ☽ 1-10:30pm) This old hand turns out some tasty food such as oysters Rockefeller, jumbo steamed shrimp and broiled octopus with garlic. Vegetarians will appreciate the soup, salad and spaghetti choices. Order the coconut custard for dessert.

Café Marina (☎ 554-24-62; Paseo del Pescador; mains US$5-12.50; ☽ 8am-9pm) This tiny place on the west side of the plaza bakes up some good pizzas, along with spaghettis and sandwiches. There's carrot cake and other goodies as well. Most tables are outside, taking advantage of the traffic-free area.

CENTRAL ZIHUATANEJO – INLAND
Many good inexpensive options lie a couple of blocks from the beach.

Doña Licha (☎ 554-39-33; Cocos 8; mains US$5-8.50; ☽ 8am-6pm) Licha is known up and down the coast for its down-home Mexican cooking, casual atmosphere and excellent prices. There are always several *comidas corridas* (set-price lunch menus) to choose from, including one delicious speciality, *pollo en cacahuate* (chicken in a peanut sauce). All come with rice, beans and handmade tortillas. Breakfasts are huge.

Cenaduría Antelia (☎ 554-30-91; Bravo 14 at Andador Pellicer; meals under US$3; ☽ 9am-2:30pm & 6pm-midnight) Antelia's popular and friendly eatery has been dishing out tasty *antojitos Mexicanos* (traditional Mexican snacks) and desserts since 1975. Tuck into a *tamal de chile verde* or a bursting bowl of daily *pozole*, and top it off with *calabaza con leche* (squash in milk) for dessert.

Cafetería Nueva Zelanda (☎ 554-23-40; Cuauhtémoc 23-30; mains US$3-5) Step back in time at this spotless diner, where you can order a banana split or chocolate malt with your shrimp taco and chicken fajitas. This place is great for breakfast, everything is available *para llevar* (to go) and it steams a decent cappuccino. There are entrances on both Cuauhtémoc and Galeana.

Los Braseros (☎ 554-87-36; Ejido 21; mains US$3-10; ☺ 9am-1am) The tacos *al pastor* (with sliced, rotisserie-cooked, marinated pork) are this open-fronted eatery's crowning glory. It specializes in grilled and skewered meat and veggie combinations, served in a festive, hangar-like space. Choose from 30 combinations or go for seafood, chicken mole, crepes or a plateful of US$0.40 tacos.

Mariscos El Acacio (Galeana 21; mains US$4-12; ☺ 11am-8pm Mon-Sat) A simple little seafood eatery, this place offers authentic *tiritas*, shrimp cocktails and fried fish, among other tasty treats. Prices are unbeatable and the shady sidewalk tables are fine. It's open on Sundays during the high season.

Il Paccolo (☎ 755-559-08-38; Bravo 38; mains US$6-10.50; ☺ 4pm-midnight) Aching for Italian? This is the place to come. Order delicious pizzas, pastas, meats and seafood dishes, and consider the caramel crepe for dessert. The atmosphere is dark and low-key, and the bar is friendly.

Banana's (☎ 554-47-21; Bravo 9; mains US$5-7; ☺ 8am-4pm Mon-Sat, 8am-1pm Sun) This small, airy restaurant offers a pretty fair selection of Mexican dishes, Western breakfasts and tasty *licuados* (fruit usually blended with milk, sometimes just with ice).

Hearty, cheap breakfasts and lunches can be had in the **market** (Juárez btwn Nava & González; ☺ 7am-6pm).

AROUND THE BAY

Casa Bahía (☎ 544-86-66; Paseo del Morro s/n; mains US$8-18; ☺ 3-11:30pm) The CB has an exquisite location overlooking the bay from Punta El Morro. To reach it, cross the footbridge over the lagoon, turn left (south) and head about 350m up the road. The food is well prepared

and leans to Italian, with several pastas on offer as well as carpaccio. The menu also has sashimi, burgers, steaks, seafood and some Mexican dishes. It's a romantic spot for dinner.

La Casa Que Canta (☎ 554-70-30; Carretera Escénica s/n; mains US$14-27; ☺ 6:30-10:30pm) The views and food are fab at this intimate, multilevel, open-air, hotel restaurant. Dishes range from Asian fusion and Mexican specialties to standards such as lobster and rack of lamb. Reservations are required, as is 'casual elegant' attire.

Coconuts (☎ 554-79-80; Ramirez 1; mains US$11-22; ☺ noon-11pm) For a romantic dinner this upscale place is hard to beat. Fairy lights fill the outdoor courtyard, service is attentive and dishes include garlic snapper, leg of duck, *chiles rellenos* (stuffed peppers), vegetable tart and herb chicken.

Restaurant Kau-Kan (☎ 554-84-46; Carretera Escénica 7; mains US$14-29; ☺ 5pm-midnight) High on the cliffs, this renowned gourmet restaurant enjoys stellar views. Making a selection is exhausting when faced with choices like stingray in black butter sauce, marinated abalone or grilled lamb chops with couscous.

Bad Bird Café (López Mateos s/n; breakfasts US$3.75-5; ☺ 8am-1pm Mon-Sat) Quite small and slightly discombobulated, the Bad Bird turns out some very good breakfasts: waffles, egg dishes, fruit and homemade yogurt, complemented by good imported coffee and free Internet access. All profits go to support a local free clinic, and the namesake macaw is a real cutup.

Puerta del Sol (☎ 554-83-42; Carretera Escénica s/n; mains US$7.50-18; ☺ 5pm-midnight) Reservations are recommended in high season at this romantic restaurant hanging on the cliffs between Playa Madera and Playa La Ropa. Spectacular bay and sunset views accompany the varied international menu, which features a lot of flambés. Ever seen a flaming saltimbocca?

On Playa La Ropa, **Rossy's** (☎ 554-40-04; mains US$7-12; ☺ 9am-9pm), **La Perla** (☎ 554-27-00; mains US$7.50-15) and **La Gaviota** (☎ 554-38-16; mains US$7.50-19; ☺ noon-9pm) are all good seafood restaurants. Playa Las Gatas has several restaurants offering fresh seafood as well.

SELF-CATERING
The enormous **Comercial Mexicana supermarket** is behind the Estrella Blanca bus station.

Drinking

In addition to these spots, many beachfront bars have an extended happy hour.

Jungle Bar (Ramírez s/n; ❤ 7pm-2am) Bob your head to the kick-back bass on the stereo at this street-side bar with a gregarious, English-speaking staff and cheap drinks. It's a good place to meet locals and other travelers and get the lowdown on town, though in the off-season its hours can be erratic.

Hotel Royal Sotavento (☎ 554-20-32; Carretera Escénica s/n; ❤ 3-11pm, happy hour 6-8pm) Tucked into the hillside over Playa La Ropa, the Sotavento is a great spot to watch the sunset. Its relaxed bar affords a magnificent view over the whole bay.

Café Zihuatanejo (Cuauhtémoc 48; coffees under US$2; ❤ 8am-7pm Mon-Sat) This tiny place brews up espressos and cappuccinos made from locally grown organic coffee beans; it also sells whole beans by the kilo. To find it look for the potted palms and sidewalk tables.

Entertainment

For big-time nightlife, head to Ixtapa. Zihuatanejo is all about being mellow.

Black Bull Rodeo (☎ 554-11-29; cnr Bravo & Guerrero; ❤ from 9pm) Zihuatanejo's only real discotheque, this corner joint claims to have the best *norteño* (one of Mexico's versions of country and western) band in town. There's also *cumbia*, merengue, salsa, electronica and reggae music on offer.

Ventaneando (☎ 554-108-38-36; Guerrero 24; ❤ 8pm-4am) Across the street from the club Black Bull Rodeo, this stuffy upstairs bar is a popular spot that attracts karaoke-loving crowds. It may not meet fire codes, however.

Cine Paraíso (☎ 554-23-18; Cuauhtémoc; admission US$2.25). Near Bravo, this cinema shows two films nightly, usually in English with Spanish subtitles.

Shopping

Zihua offers abundant Mexican handicrafts, including ceramics, *típica* (characteristic of the region) clothing, leatherwork, Taxco silver, wood carvings and masks from around the state of Guerrero.

El Jumil (☎ 554-61-91; Paseo del Pescador 9; ❤ 9am-2pm & 5-9pm Mon-Sat) This shop specializes in authentic guerrerense masks.

Guerrero is known for its variety of interesting masks, and El Jumil stocks museum-quality examples, many starting from around US$15, as well as cheaper but delightful coconut-shell masks.

Coco's Cabaña (☎ 554-25-18; cnr Guerrero & Álvarez) Coco's stocks an impressive selection of handicrafts from all over Mexico.

Mercado Turístico La Marina (5 de Mayo; ❤ 8am-9pm) This market has many stalls selling clothes, bags and knickknacks.

Mercado Municipal de las Artesanías (González near Juárez; ❤ 9am-8pm). Similar to La Marina, but smaller.

Several shops along Cuauhtémoc sell Taxco silver. **Alberto's** (☎ 554-21-61; Cuauhtémoc 12 & 15; ❤ 9am-10pm Mon-Sat, 10am-3pm Sun) and **Pancho's** (☎ 554-52-30; Cuauhtémoc 11; ❤ 9am-9pm Mon-Sat) have the best selection of quality pieces.

Keep your eyes peeled, especially in the central market, for *dulces de tamarindo* (gooey dark-brown sweets made from tamarind pulp) and *dulces de coco* (coconut sweets, sold in countless shapes and flavors, a speciality of this coconut-producing region).

Getting There & Away

AIR

The Ixtapa/Zihuatanejo **international airport** (☎ 554-20-70) is about 13km southeast of Zihuatanejo, a couple of kilometers off Hwy 200 heading toward Acapulco. Note that there are far fewer flights in the off-season. **Aeroméxico** (☎ 554-20-18, airport 554-22-37, 554-26-34; Álvarez 34) flies to Mexico City, with many onward connections. **Alaska** (☎ 554-84-57, 800-252-7522) flies to Los Angeles and San Francisco, **American** (☎ 800-904-60-00 in the US) flies to Dallas, **America West** (☎ 800-235-92-92 in the US) flies to Phoenix and Las Vegas, **Mexicana** (airport ☎ 554-22-27; Zihuatanejo ☎ 554-22-08/9; Guerrero 22) flies to Mexico City. **Continental** (☎ 554-42-19) flies to Houston and Minneapolis and **Northwest** (☎ 800-907-47-00 in the US) to Houston and Los Angeles.

BUS

Both long-distance bus terminals are on Hwy 200 about 2km south of the town center (toward the airport): the **Estrella Blanca terminal** (Central de Autobuses; ☎ 554-34-76/77) is a couple of hundred meters further from the center than the smaller **Estrella**

de Oro terminal (☎ 554-21-75). Bus services include the following:

Acapulco Estrella Blanca (US$11.50, 4hr, 1st-class hourly 5am-7:30pm; US$8.50, 4hr, 2nd-class hourly); Estrella de Oro (US$11.50, 4hr, 3 1st-class daily; US$8.50, 4hr, 13 2nd-class 5:30am-5pm)

Lázaro Cárdenas Estrella Blanca (US$6-8, 1½hr, 1st-class hourly 5am-7:30pm; US$5, 2hr, 2nd-class hourly 9am-10pm); Estrella de Oro (US$4.50, 2hr, 11 2nd-class daily)

Manzanillo Estrella Blanca (US$30, 8hr, 1st-class at 10am, 10:50am, 8pm)

Mexico City Norte Estrella Blanca (US$42, 9-10hr, 1st-class at 6:45pm, 8pm)

Mexico City Sur Estrella Blanca (US$50, 8-9hr, deluxe at 10:30pm; US$42, 8-9hr, 5 1st-class daily); Estrella de Oro (US$50, 8-9hr, deluxe at 10pm and 10:55pm; US$38, 8-9hr, 9 1st-class daily)

Petatlán Estrella Blanca (US$2, 30min, 1st-class every hour 3:45am-11:20pm); Estrella de Oro (US$1.50, 30min, 13 2nd-class buses 5:30am-6pm) Or take a local bus (US$1.25, 30min) from the bus lot a couple of blocks east of the market in Zihuatanejo.

Puerto Escondido Estrella Blanca (US$24, 12hr, 1 1st-class at 7:20pm)

Manzanillo-bound buses continue to Puerto Vallarta (US$50, 14 hours, 718km) and Mazatlán (US$72, 24 hours, 1177km).

CAR & MOTORCYCLE

There are several car-rental companies in Ixtapa and Zihuatanejo. Try to reserve ahead of time, but be warned that this won't always guarantee you a vehicle.

Alamo Ixtapa (☎ 553-02-06; Centro Comercial Los Patios); Airport (☎ 554-84-29)

Budget Ixtapa (☎ 553-03-97; Centro Comercial Ambiente, Local 10); Airport (☎ 554-48-37)

Europcar (☎ 553-10-32; Centro Comercial Los Patios, Ixtapa)

Hertz Zihuatanejo (☎ 554-22-55; Bravo 29); Airport (☎ 554-29-52)

Thrifty Ixtapa (☎ 553-30-19; Hotel NH Krystal, Ixtapa); Airport (☎ 553-70-20)

Getting Around

TO/FROM THE AIRPORT

The cheapest way to get to the airport is via a public 'Aeropuerto' *colectivo* (US$0.65) departing from Juárez near González between 6:20am and 10pm. Private *colectivo* vans provide transportation from the airport to Ixtapa or Zihua (US$9 per person), but they don't offer service to the airport. Taxis from Zihua to the airport cost US$8.

BUS

Ixtapa, 8km northwest, is easily reached by local bus. Local 'Directo' and 'B Viejo' buses run frequently between Ixtapa and Zihua, a 15-minute ride. They depart every 15 minutes from 5:30am to 11pm (US$0.60). In Ixtapa, buses stop all along the main street, in front of all the hotels. In Zihua, buses depart from the corner of Juárez and Morelos. Buses marked 'Zihua-Ixtapa-Playa Linda' continue through Ixtapa to Playa Linda (US$0.60), stopping near Playa Quieta on the way, and operate from 7am to 7pm.

The 'Correa' route goes to the Central de Autobuses from 5:30am to 9:30pm (US$0.40). Catch it on Juárez at the corner of Nava.

'Playa La Ropa' buses head south on Juárez and out to Playa La Ropa every half hour from 7am to 8pm (US$0.70).

'Coacoyul' *colectivos* heading toward Playa Larga depart from Juárez near the corner of González, every five minutes from 5am to 10pm (US$0.60).

TAXI

Cabs are plentiful in Zihuatanejo. Always agree on the fare before getting in. Approximate sample fares (from central Zihua) include US$3.75 to Ixtapa, US$2.50 to Playa La Ropa, US$5 to Playa Larga and US$1.50 to the Central de Autobuses. If you can't hail a taxi street-side, ring **Radio Taxi UTAAZ** (☎ 554-33-11).

BARRA DE POTOSÍ

☎ 755 / pop 400

About 34km (a 40-minute drive) southeast of Zihuatanejo, lovely Barra de Potosí has an endless fine-sand beach and a large lagoon teeming with birdlife (bring repellent; it teems with other flying things, too). You can swim, take boat trips, rent a canoe and paddle around the estuary or go horseback riding or hiking on local trails. In winter, when the waves are small, the ocean makes for sublime swimming outside the breakers, an almost divine experience as you gaze back at the dramatic backdrop of the cloud-capped Sierra Madre del Sur. The beach itself stretches north for miles, unbroken as far as Playa Larga, near Zihuatanejo. You can still see residents mending nets in the village, about 100m inland from the beach.

The area is beginning to change as outsiders buy up and develop land; the most notable example is 'Betseyville,' pricey lodgings built by American designer Betsey Johnson.

Exploring the lagoon is best in the cool of the morning, when bird-watching is good and the sun is gentle. Single and double kayaks and traditional wooden canoes can be rented at several restaurants. **Enramada Leticia** (8am-7pm), to the left as you approach the beach, has a good selection, charging US$5 and US$11.50 per hour for one-person and two-person kayaks respectively, and US$6 for three hours' use of canoes that hold up to three people. Boat tours aboard covered fishing *pangas* cost about US$5 per person for a 30-minute buzz around the lagoon.

By the time you read this, horses should once again be available for rent, at about US$15 per hour; check at Enramada Leticia, or with Laura at Casa del Encanto (below), who can give you information on bird-watching as well.

Low-season rates at the following places drop by between 20% and 40% from the prices listed here.

Casa del Encanto (044-755-100-14-46; www .casadelencanto.com; d US$80 with breakfast Nov-Apr) This is a knockout B&B three blocks inland from Tendejón Lupita. Private yet open-air rooms blend interior with exterior to keep things as cool and relaxed as possible, aided by numerous hammocks and fountains. The six spacious rooms have good baths and supercomfy beds; a separate bungalow (with full kitchen) holding up to four should be ready by the time you read this.

Bernie's Bed & Breakfast (Playa Calli; 044-755-556-63-33, www.zihuatanejo.net/playacalli; d US$110 with breakfast Dec-Apr;) A few kilometers toward Zihua from town, Bernie's has four first-rate rooms set back a bit in a well-constructed adobe building. The swimming pool is only a few steps from the beach, though. All rooms face the surf and have king-sized beds and ceiling fans. Bernie speaks excellent English, German, Spanish and French, and exudes a tranquility that settles over the place. Tips are included in the rates.

Several seafood *enramadas* line the beach and lagoon, and most are open between 8am or 9am and 7pm. The first in line, La Condesa, is one of the best. Try the *pescado a la talla* (broiled fish fillets) or *tiritas*, both local specialties, and don't pass up the

savory handmade tortillas. Tendejón Lupita is a small grocery store at the edge of town as you enter.

To reach the village, head southeast on Hwy 200 toward Acapulco; turn off at the town of Los Achotes, 25km from Zihua, and drive another 9km. Any bus heading to Petatlán (they depart frequently from both of Zihua's main terminals, and from the stop a couple of blocks east of Zihua's market; see Map pp188-9) will drop you at the turnoff. Tell the driver you're going to Barra de Potosí; you'll be let off where you can catch a *camioneta* (pickup truck) going the rest of the way. The total cost is about US$2.50 if you go by bus; a taxi from Zihua costs US$35/US$45 one way/round-trip (negotiable).

PETATLÁN

 758 / pop 18,000

An unprepossessing town 30 minutes southeast of Zihuatanejo, Petatlán is best known for its **Santuario Nacional del Padre Jesús de Petatlán**, a large, modern sanctuary attracting pilgrims from near and far, who leave votive offerings (often the tiny gold trinkets that are sold at shops across the street from the church's entrance) to the statue of Christ inside. Legend has it that the statue was found floating in a nearby stream shortly after Petatlán's congregation took up a collection to purchase a new one.

The archaeological site of **Soledad de Maciel**, known as **La Chole**, is about 5km up a signed road that takes you seaward from Hwy 200, about 6km north of Petatlán; you can visit on your own (ask for a guide in the village) or go as part of a tour from Zihuatanejo. The site contains some unexcavated mounds, a ball court, some large carved stones and a cave with carvings. The villagers of Soledad de Maciel display some artifacts at a modest museum; others are in Zihuatanejo's archaeological museum (p187).

During Semana Santa, Petatlán has a traditional fair with food, music and handicrafts exhibitions. Petatlán's religious festival is held on August 6.

Several restaurants flank the plaza, but the best deals are in the *fondas* (small restaurants) beside the church. They all charge around US$2.50 for the *comida corrida* and serve fresh, handmade tortillas to accompany the meal.

Petatlán is on Hwy 200, 32km southeast of Zihuatanejo. For bus information, see p195.

LA BARRITA

☎ 758 / pop 100

La Barrita (Km 187) is a shell-sized village on an attractive, rocky beach an hour southeast of Zihua off Hwy 200. Not many tourists stop here, but surfers might want to check the beach breaks here and 3km north at **Loma Bonita**. Several restaurants have very basic rooms for rent, the best probably being those at **Restaurant Las Peñitas** (d/q US$9.50/15); you can escape the evening heat of your room by dozing in the restaurants' hammocks.

Second-class buses heading south from Zihua or north from Acapulco will drop you at La Barrita.

One of the more dramatic stretches of highway in Guerrero starts about 4km south of La Barrita, running along clifftops above beaches and crashing surf. Several roadside restaurants offer opportunities to enjoy the view for a spell.

PLAYA CAYAQUITOS & OJO DE AGUA

At Km 160 (78km southeast of Zihuatanejo), Hwy 200 rolls through the nondescript town of **Papanoa**, where you can gas up and purchase basic provisions. At the southern outskirts of town, **Hotel Club Papanoa** (☎ 55-5648-36-89; www.hotelpapanoa.com; Hwy 200, Km 160; r from US$75; P ✂ ✆) overlooks the beautiful, and almost always deserted, Playa Cayaquitos. The hotel, built in 1963 and well worth a few days' stay, has a good restaurant, a lovely sundeck and a clean swimming pool; the rooms are spacious and clean.

Even if you don't plan to stay the night, Playa Cayaquitos is a beautiful place to spend the day. The main access is just north of the Hotel Club Papanoa sign. The beach is long and the swimming is good in winter when the waves are gentle. At the southern end of the beach, a tiny headland separates Cayaquitos from Ojo de Agua, a picture-perfect little cove with several beachfront seafood *enramadas*. Ojo de Agua is more sheltered and the restaurants will allow you to use their services if you eat their food.

Acapulco & the Costa Chica

The granddaddy of Mexican coastal resorts may be overweight, congested and incontinent – and it surely smokes too much – but Acapulco can still party all night long. Some of the old glamour lingers in sleek cliff divers, flash discos and glitzy hotels. A face-lift of sorts has improved the looks of the bay, once miserably polluted, and foreign visitors are coming back in growing numbers. It's not the jet set that used to come here in the '50s and '60s; the biggest boost is coming from American college students who drop in for spring break. This gets the old guy so feisty that he's promising to put that whippersnapper Cancún in its place any day now.

To escape the city and our overworked geriatric metaphor, head southeast, along Guerrero's Costa Chica, where the decadence and chaos of Acapulco fade like a summer sunset. Coastal Hwy 200 rolls through palm plantations, thorn forest, cattle land and villages, past turnoffs to some truly spectacular beaches. Many of the Costa Chica's inhabitants are Afro-mestizos, or *morenos*, as they refer to themselves – people of mixed African, indigenous and European descent. Cuajinicuilapa, the small-town de facto capital of the Costa Chica, is worth a stop for its museum of Afro-mestizo cultures. The beaches of Playa Ventura and Playa La Bocana make adventurous day trips from Acapulco, and offer basic accommodations for those who want to spend more time quietly relaxing.

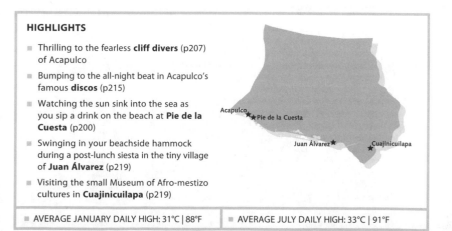

HIGHLIGHTS

- Thrilling to the fearless **cliff divers** (p207) of Acapulco
- Bumping to the all-night beat in Acapulco's famous **discos** (p215)
- Watching the sun sink into the sea as you sip a drink on the beach at **Pie de la Cuesta** (p200)
- Swinging in your beachside hammock during a post-lunch siesta in the tiny village of **Juan Álvarez** (p219)
- Visiting the small Museum of Afro-mestizo cultures in **Cuajinicuilapa** (p219)

Acapulco
★ ★ Pie de la Cuesta

Juan Álvarez ★   ★ Cuajinicuilapa

■ AVERAGE JANUARY DAILY HIGH: 31°C | 88°F   ■ AVERAGE JULY DAILY HIGH: 33°C | 91°F

Getting There & Around

Regular 1st-class buses and more frequent 2nd-class buses connect Acapulco with Zihuatanejo and points in between. Estrella Blanca (EB) has the most departures, and also offers frequent service to all points to the southeast on Hwy 200 along the Costa Chica. Several EB buses continue into Oaxaca state at least as far as Puerto Escondido.

PIE DE LA CUESTA

☎ 744 / pop 200

About 10km northwest of Acapulco, Pie de la Cuesta is a narrow 2km strip of land bordered by the beach and ocean on one side and the large, freshwater Laguna de Coyuca on the other (where Sylvester Stallone filmed *Rambo II*). Compared to Acapulco, it's quieter, cleaner, closer to nature and much more peaceful. Swimming in the ocean at Pie de la Cuesta can be dangerous due to a riptide. Laguna de Coyuca, three times larger than Bahía de Acapulco, is better for swimming; in the lagoon are the islands of Montosa, Presidio and Pájaros, which is a bird sanctuary.

Pie de la Cuesta has many beachside restaurants specializing in seafood, and it's a great place for watching the sunset. There's no nightlife, so if you're looking for excitement you may be better off staying in Acapulco.

There's one main road, with two names: Av de la Fuerza Aérea Mexicana or Calzada Pie de la Cuesta. **Netxcom** (per hr US$1; ⏲ 9am-10pm)

ACAPULCO & THE COSTA CHICA

PIE DE LA CUESTA

Activities

Pie de la Cuesta has been famous for water-skiing for decades. The glassy morning waters of the enormous Laguna de Coyuca are perfect for the sport, and several clubs, including **Club de Ski Chuy** (☎ 460-11-04; Calzada Pie de la Cuesta 74), will gladly pull you around the lagoon from their speedboats. They all charge approximately US$47 per hour, which includes boat, driver and ski equipment.

Wakeboarding is another possibility; try **Club Náutico Cadena X Ski** (☎ 460-22-83; cadenax@ yahoo.com; Calzada Pie de la Cuesta s/n).

Boat trips on the lagoon provide a glimpse of its attractions, though bird-watching is often reduced to a minimum because of speed-boats and jet skis. Still, if you can convince someone to take you early enough, chances are high you'll spot storks, herons, avocets, pelicans, ducks and other waterfowl. Stroll down to the boat launch along the southeast end of the lagoon and you'll be greeted by independent captains ready to take you for a tour. At the time of research, **Restaurant Coyuca 2000** (p202) was set to offer two-hour tours (US$40 per person) looking at bird habitat, flora of the region, fisher folk's homes and the like, finishing with a meal and drinks at the restaurant (included).

Finally, **horseback riding** on the beach runs at around US$15 an hour.

Sleeping

For accommodation, Pie de la Cuesta is a decent alternative to Acapulco, and every hotel provides safe car parking. High-season dates are approximately December 15 to around Easter. There are 15 or so hotels lining the single, 2km road along the lagoon; take a quick drive to check them out. More lie beyond to the northwest, one of which is listed here.

Quinta Erika (☎ /fax 444-41-31; www.quintaerika.de.vu; Playa Luces; r with breakfast US$52; 🅿 🏊) Located 6km northeast of Pie de la Cuesta at Playa Luces, on 2 hectares of lagoonside land, this quality seven-room lodging is one of the region's best places to relax for a few days.

Rooms come with many amenities. The owner, who speaks German, Spanish and a little English, rents kayaks and sailboats, and takes great pride in his place. Reservations are strongly suggested.

Villa Nirvana (☎ 460-16-31; www.lavillanirvana .com; rear Av Fuerza Aérea 302; d US$29-57, q US$94, additional person US$9.50; P 🖳 🏊) Villa Nirvana's friendly American owners have thoughtfully landscaped and expanded this cheerful property. It has a variety of accommodations, some with ocean views, all comfortable and decorated with local crafts. A beachside swimming pool, pleasant open-air bar and restaurant (breakfast only), and complimentary (but limited, please) Internet access round out the good-value offering.

Bungalows María Cristina (☎ 460-02-62; Av Fuerza Aérea s/n; s/d US$24/29, bungalows US$71; P) Run by English-speaking Enrique and his friendly family, this is a clean, well-tended, relaxing place with a barbecue and hammocks overlooking the beach. The large four- to five-person bungalows have kitchens and ocean-view balconies. A good budget choice. Rates double around Christmas and Easter.

Hotel Parador de los Reyes (☎ 460-01-31; Av Fuerza Aérea 305; s/d US$9.50/15; P 🏊) This clean, economical choice is right beside the road and has a small courtyard swimming pool. It has 11 large, no-frills rooms.

Hotel & Restaurant Casa Blanca (☎ 460-03-24; casablanca@prodigy.net.mx; Av Fuerza Aérea s/n; r with air-con US$47; P 🍴 🏊) This well-tended beachfront place aspires to be a resort without quite pulling it off. Happily, the restaurant retains a homey atmosphere. Rates can go much higher in the latter part of December.

Hotel Restaurante Rocío (☎ 460-10-08; Av Fuerza Aérea 9; s/d US$24/38; P) The beds at this beachfront hotel-restaurant-bar are a bit springy and the place could use some sprucing up, but newer oceanside rooms cost the same as the others.

Acapulco Trailer Park & Mini-Super (☎ 460-00-10; acatrailerpark@yahoo.com; campsites 1/2 people US$15/19; RV sites US$19-24; 🏊) Beachside with big spaces, clean facilities, friendly management and just enough shade, this is the nicest camping ground in the Acapulco area. You can usually negotiate discounts for long stays.

Eating & Drinking

Restaurants here are known for fresh seafood. Plenty of open-air places front the beach, though some close early in the evening. Most of the hotels and guesthouses have restaurants, as do many of the water-skiing clubs. Dining out tends to cost more here than in Acapulco, so it may be worth bringing some groceries and getting a room with kitchen access.

Coyuca 2000 (☎ 460-56-09; Playa Pie de la Cuesta; mains US$6-13, min consumption per person US$7; ☺ 9am-2am Dec-Apr, 8am-10pm Mar-Nov;) Pull up a chair on the sand, watch the waves and enjoy good fish *al mojo de ajo* (with garlic sauce) or in fajitas, plus other tasty seafood and meat dishes in a casual atmosphere. The owner is known for concocting new cocktails and offers several margaritas and numerous tropical drinks.

Club de Ski Tres Marías (☎ 460-00-13; Calzada Pie de la Cuesta 375; mains US$8-20; ☺ 8am-7pm) Said to have the best food on the strip, though service can be lax. It's a comfy lagoonside restaurant and the closest you'll come to upscale dining in town.

Restaurante Rocío (☎ 460-10-08; Av Fuerza Aérea 9; mains US$6-8.50) Serves a limited menu of a few seafood dishes and simple Mexican fare such as quesadillas, under *palapas* (thatched-roof shelters) on the beach.

Steve's Hideaway/El Escondite (☺ 9am-11pm) Esteban, the owner, serves drinks, steaks and seafood at a bar on stilts over the water; the view up the lagoon is great. On the southeast side of the lake.

Getting There & Away

From Acapulco, catch a 'Pie de la Cuesta' bus on La Costera across the street from the Sanborns near the *zócalo* (main plaza). Buses go every 15 minutes from 6am until around 8pm; the bumpy, roundabout 35- to 50-minute ride costs US$0.40. Buses marked 'Pie de la Cuesta – San Isidro' or 'Pie de la Cuesta – Pedregoso' stop on Hwy 200 at Pie de la Cuesta's arched entrance; those marked 'Pie de la Cuesta – Playa Luces' continue all the way along to Playa Luces, 6km further along toward Barra de Coyuca. *Colectivo* (shared) vans (US$0.50) continue on from Barra de Coyuca back out to Hwy 200.

Colectivo taxis to Pie de la Cuesta operate 24 hours along La Costera, and elsewhere in Acapulco's old town, and charge US$1.25 one way. A private taxi from Acapulco costs anywhere from US$7 to US$11 one way (more after dark).

ACAPULCO

☎ 744 / pop 912,000

Acapulco's golden beaches, death-defying cliff divers, endless nightlife and towering resort hotels have been attracting more and more visitors in recent years, reversing a decline that began in the late 1970s. New touristic life is being breathed into the city, in part by American university students who come to spend their spring break in a more welcoming and economical environment than Cancún has become.

A bustling city, Acapulco offers pockets of calm, from romantic cliffside bars and restaurants to the old town's charming, shady zócalo and impressively sited 16th-century fort. The arc of beach that sweeps around many kilometers of Bahía de Acapulco (Bay of Acapulco) can be a good place to relax as well – if you take the beach vendors in your stride – but step off it and you'll find much of the rest of the city a bedlam of clogged traffic, crowded sidewalks and smoggy fumes (which at least make for a nice sunset).

Afternoon showers are common from June to September but rare the rest of the year.

History

The name 'Acapulco' is derived from ancient Náhuatl words meaning 'where the reeds stood' or 'place of giant reeds.' Archaeological finds show that when the Spanish discovered Bahía de Acapulco in 1512 people had already been living in the area for some 2000 years.

The Spanish quickly established port and shipbuilding facilities in the substantial natural harbor, and in 1523 Hernán Cortés and two partners financed a road between Mexico City and Acapulco. This 'Camino de Asia' became the principal trade route between Mexico City and the Pacific; the 'Camino de Europa,' from Mexico City to Veracruz on the Gulf Coast, completed the overland leg of the route between Asia and Spain.

Acapulco became the only port in the New World authorized to receive naos (Spanish trading galleons) from China and the Philippines. By the 17th century trade with Asia was flourishing, and English and Dutch privateers were busily looting ships and settlements along the Pacific coast. To fend off these pirates, the Fuerte de San Diego was built atop a low hill overlooking Bahía de Acapulco. It was not until the end of the 18th century that Spain permitted its American colonies to engage in free trade, ending the monopoly of the naos.

Upon gaining independence Mexico severed most of its trade links with Spain and Spanish colonies, and Acapulco declined as a port city. It became relatively isolated from the rest of the world until a paved road linked it with Mexico City in 1927. As Mexico City flourished, its citizens began vacationing on the Pacific coast. A new international airport was built, Hollywood filmed a few flicks here, and by the '50s Acapulco was becoming a glitzy jet-set resort.

Over the next few decades Acapulco's population climbed and development soared, the bay became polluted, and by the '80s foreign tourists were looking elsewhere to spend their cash. Vacationers continued to come from Mexico City and Guadalajara, and cruise ships brought in cargoes of American tourists, but thousands of hotel rooms stayed empty.

The city has poured millions into cleanup efforts since the 1990s, and the bay has benefited greatly, but many locals and visitors still refuse to swim there (the state and local governments have declared the waters to be acceptably clean; federal authorities do not always agree). Spring-breakers, attracted by discounted rooms and a welcoming hotel industry, began coming to Acapulco in droves in 2002, and don't show signs of letting up.

Orientation

Acapulco is on a narrow coastal plain along the 11km shore of Bahía de Acapulco. Reached by Hwy 200 from the east and west and by Hwys 95 and 95D from the north, it is 400km south of Mexico City and 240km southeast of Zihuatanejo and Ixtapa.

Acapulco's tourist industry divides the city into three parts: Acapulco Viejo (Old Acapulco, more commonly called 'el centro'), Acapulco Dorado (Golden Acapulco) and Acapulco Diamante (Diamond Acapulco). Acapulco Viejo is the old part of town on the west side of the bay. Acapulco Dorado, usually called the Zona Dorada, wraps around the bay from Playa Hornos to the Icacos naval base. Acapulco Diamante is the relatively new, luxury resort area that stretches 10km from the peninsula on the

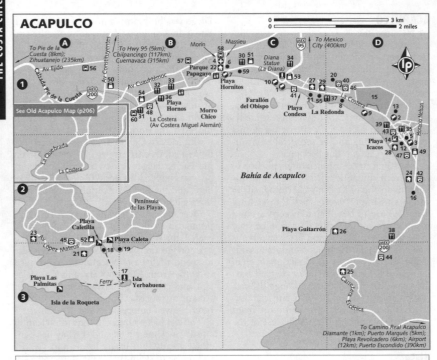

ACAPULCO

southern tip of Puerto Marqués – a bay situated about 18km southeast of Acapulco proper – down Playa Revolcadero to the international airport.

At the west end of Bahía de Acapulco, the Peninsula de las Playas juts south from central Acapulco. South of the peninsula is the popular Isla de la Roqueta. From Playa Caleta on the southern edge of the peninsula, Av López Mateos climbs west and then north to Playa La Angosta and Playa La Quebrada before curling east back toward the city center.

Playa Caleta also marks the beginning of Av Costera Miguel Alemán. Known simply as 'La Costera' or as 'Miguel Alemán,' it's Acapulco's principal bayside avenue. Addresses along La Costera don't follow an entirely sequential numbering scheme. From Playa Caleta, La Costera cuts north-northwest across the Península de las Playas and then hugs the shore all the way around the bay to the Icacos naval base at the east end of the city. Most of Acapulco's major hotels, restaurants, discos and other points of interest are along or just off La Costera. After the naval base, La Costera becomes La Carretera Escénica (the Scenic Highway) and, 9km further on, intersects the road to Hwy 200 on the left and the road to Puerto Marqués on the right. The airport is about 3km past this intersection.

Information
BOOKSTORES
For its size, Acapulco is woefully lacking good bookstores. The shop in the Fuerte de San Diego (p207) maintains a good supply of art, architecture and history books, though most are in Spanish.

Sanborns La Costera 1260 (Map p204; ☎ 481-24-80; La Costera 1260; ⏱ 7am-1am); La Costera 209 (Map p206; ☎ 482-61-67; La Costera 209; ⏱ 7am-11pm) You can almost always find a small selection of books and magazines in English at these department stores, as well as good road and city maps for all of Mexico.

EMERGENCY
Locatel (☎ 481-11-00) Operated by Sefotur, 24-hour hot line for all types of emergencies.
Tourist police (☎ 440-70-22)

IMMIGRATION
Instituto Nacional de Migración (Immigration Office; Map p204; ☎ 484-90-14; cnr La Costera & Elcano; ⏱ 9am-1pm Mon-Fri)

INTERNET ACCESS
It's impossible to walk more than a few blocks without passing a cybercafé in Acapulco's major hotel districts; most have quick connections and charge just under US$1 per hour.
Big M@sternet (Hidalgo 6; Map p206; ⏱ 9am-midnight) Family-run with air-con.
Vig@net (Hidalgo 8; Map p206; ⏱ 8am-midnight) Keeps more reliable hours than some.
Internet (Galeana 13; Map p206; ⏱ 10am-11pm) Fifteen computers and loud music.

INTERNET RESOURCES
www.allaboutacapulco.com Good source of general information.

LAUNDRY
Lavandería Lavadín (Map p206; ☎ 482-28-90; cnr La Paz & Iglesias, 3kg min, per kg wash & dry US$1.25; ⏱ 8am-10pm Mon-Sat)
Lavandería Azueta (Map p206; Azueta 14-A; per kg wash & dry US$1.25; ⏱ 9am-7pm Mon-Fri) Below Hotel Paola.

LEFT LUGGAGE
The three 1st-class bus stations have luggage storage facilities. See p217.

MEDICAL SERVICES
Hospital Magallanes (Map p204; ☎ 485-61-94; Massieu 2)

MONEY
Omnipresent banks (many with ATMs) give the best exchange rates, and many will change US-dollar traveler's checks and euro banknotes. Conspicuous *casas de cambio* (exchange bureaus) pay a slightly lower rate, but are open longer hours and are less busy than banks; shop around, as rates vary. Banks and *casas de cambio* cluster around the *zócalo* and line La Costera. Hotels will also change money, but their rates are usually painful.

POST
Post office (Map p204; ☎ 483-53-63; La Costera 125, Palacio Federal; ⏱ 8am-5:30pm Mon-Fri, 9am-1pm Sat)

TELEPHONE
You can make long-distance calls from the many Telmex card phones throughout the city, or from private telephone *casetas* (with signs saying *'larga distancia'*). These abound near the *zócalo* and along La Costera.
Caseta Alameda (Map p206) Telephone and fax services. West side of the *zócalo*.

OLD ACAPULCO

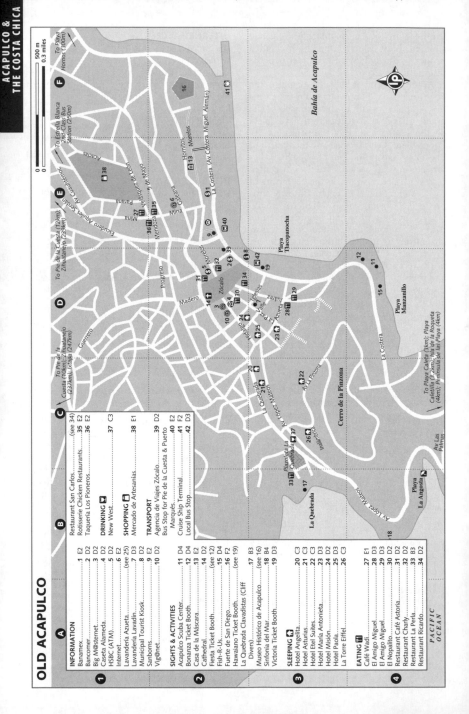

INFORMATION
Banamex..1 E2
Bancomer...2 D2
Big M@sternet.....................................3 D2
Caseta Alameda...................................4 D2
HSBC (ATM)..5 D2
Internet..6 E2
Lavandería Azueta..........................(see 25)
Lavandería Lavadín.............................7 D3
Municipal Tourist Kiosk.......................8 D2
Sanborns..9 E2
Vig@net...10 D2

SIGHTS & ACTIVITIES
Acapulco Scuba Center.......................11 D4
Bonanza Ticket Booth.........................12 D4
Casa de la Máscara............................13 E2
Cathedral..14 D2
Fiesta Ticket Booth.......................(see 12)
Fish-R-Us..15 D4
Fuerte de San Diego..........................16 F2
Hawaiano Ticket Booth..................(see 19)
La Quebrada Clavadistas (Cliff
  Divers)...17 B3
Museo Histórico de Acapulco........(see 16)
Sinfonía del Mar................................18 B4
Victoria Ticket Booth.........................19 D3

SLEEPING
Hotel Angélita...................................20 C3
Hotel Asturias....................................21 C3
Hotel Etel Suites................................22 D3
Hotel María Antonieta........................23 D3
Hotel Misión.....................................24 D2
Hotel Paola.......................................25 D3
La Torre Eiffel....................................26 C3

EATING
Café Wadi...27 E1
El Amigo Miguel................................28 D3
El Amigo Miguel................................29 D3
El Nopalito.......................................30 D2
Restaurant Café Astoria......................31 D2
Restaurant Charly..............................32 D2
Restaurant La Perla............................33 B3
Restaurant Ricardo............................34 D2

Restaurant San Carlos...................(see 34)
Rotisserie Chicken Restaurants...........35 E2
Taquería Los Pioneros........................36 E2

DRINKING
New West...37 C3

SHOPPING
Mercado de Artesanías.......................38 E1

TRANSPORT
Agencia de Viajes Zócalo....................39 D2
Bus Stop for Pie de la Cuesta & Puerto
  Marqués...40 E2
Cruise Ship Terminal..........................41 F2
Local Bus Stop...................................42 D3

PACIFIC
OCEAN

Telecomm (Map p204; ☎ 484-69-76; La Costera 125) Fax, telephone and limited Internet service. At main post office.

TOURIST INFORMATION

The city maintains an **information kiosk** (Map p206; ☯ 8:30am-10pm) on the waterfront sidewalk across from the *zócalo*, mostly dispensing brochures. The following offices on the grounds of the Centro de Convenciones all provide tourist information and assistance. The first two are in the yellow building out front.

Procuraduría del Turista (Map p204; ☎ 484-45-83; La Costera 4455; ☯ 8am-11pm) This government dispenser of visitor information will also try to resolve complaints and problems with documents.

Casa Consular (Map p204; ☎ 481-25-33; La Costera 4455; ☯ 9am-3pm Mon-Fri) Provides consular assistance to visitors of all nationalities.

State tourist office (Sefotur; Map p204; ☎ 484-24-23; sefotur@yahoo.com; La Costera 4455; ☯ 9am-9pm Mon-Fri) Inside the Centro de Convenciones; provides basic information on Acapulco and the state of Guerrero.

Dangers & Annoyances

A 2006 report ranked Acapulco fifth among Mexican cities for the number of crimes committed per capita, which surpasses Mexico City. Smugglers use the Guerrero coast as a drop point for shipments of cocaine from Colombia, much of which then passes through Acapulco on its way to the United States. A significant portion is sold for use within the city itself, mostly in the form of crack. Violence between rival drug cartels has escalated greatly, and in late 2005 it may have spilled over into a touristed area when four city residents were killed in a hail of bullets in the parking lot of La Quebrada for reasons as yet unexplained. At least 13 people died in drug-related violence in early 2006, including four killed in a dramatic shootout between police and suspected traffickers on a downtown street a couple of kilometers inland from the beach.

All that said, to date at least, as far as physical harm goes, tourists who avoid Acapulco's inland neighborhoods probably have more to fear from the rough surf at Playa Revolcadero (which does claim lives), the raw sewage that flows into the bay following rains and the traffic on La Costera.

Regarding crimes against property, the Casa Consular receives many reports from visitors who have suffered thefts from their hotel rooms in the area around the *zócalo*. Secure your valuables!

Sights

Acapulco may not have a wealth of colonial architecture, but it does have an interesting history and culture off the beach. The history museum at the Fuerte de San Diego (San Diego fort), the mask museum and the cliff divers are country highlights, not just highlights for the city.

LA QUEBRADA CLIFF DIVERS

The famous *clavadistas* of **La Quebrada** (the Ravine; Map p206; admission US$3, children under 9yr free; ☯ shows at 1pm, 7:30pm, 8:30pm, 9:30pm & 10:30pm) have been dazzling audiences since 1934, diving with fearless finesse from heights of 25m to 35m into the rising and falling swells of the narrow ocean cove below. Understandably, the divers pray at small clifftop shrines before leaping over the edge. The last show usually features divers making the plunge with a torch in either hand. For a view from below the jump-off point, walk up Calle La Quebrada from the *zócalo* or catch a cab; either way, you climb down about 60 steps to the viewing platform. Get there at least 30 minutes early to get a spot on the edge. La Quebrada is also an excellent place to watch the sunset.

La Perla restaurant-bar (p215) provides a great view of the divers from above, plus two drinks, for US$18. Dinner costs US$33.

FUERTE DE SAN DIEGO

This handsomely restored, five-sided fort (Map p204) was built in 1616 atop a hill just east of the *zócalo* to protect the *naos* that conducted trade between the Philippines and Mexico from marauding Dutch and English buccaneers. Thanks in no small part to the fort's effectiveness, the trade route – which was a crucial link between Europe, Nueva España and Asia – lasted until the early 19th century. It was also strong enough to forestall independence leader Morelos' takeover of the city in 1812 for four months. The fort had to be rebuilt after a 1776 earthquake damaged most of Acapulco, fort included. It remains basically unchanged today, except for having been restored to top condition by the Instituto Nacional de Antropología e Historia (INAH). The panorama of Acapulco you get from the fort's surroundings is free and it alone is worth the trip.

The fort is home to the **Museo Histórico de Acapulco** (Map p206; ☎ 482-38-28; Morelos s/n; admission US$3.25; ☷ 9:30am-6pm Tue-Sun). It explains the story of the Yopes and Tepuztecos, the native inhabitants at the time of the Spanish arrival in the early 16th century. Most of the museum recounts Acapulco's historical importance as a port, with exhibits explaining the *tornavuelta* (the fastest return route from Manila to Nueva España), the galleons and the treasure they carried, and the famous buccaneers who tried to capture that treasure and take it home to England or the Netherlands. On fine days during high season, the museum puts on an evening sound-and-light show (8pm Friday and Saturday).

CASA DE LA MÁSCARA

This lovely **mask museum** (Map p206; Morelos s/n; admission by donation; ☷ 10am-4pm Tue-Sun) is near the Fuerte de San Diego, on the pedestrian portion of Morelos. It has an amazing collection of masks from around Mexico – including some by Afro-mestizos on the Costa Chica – as well as masks from Cuba, Italy and Africa. A central room displays modern creations. The scant signage is in Spanish.

CENTRO CULTURAL ACAPULCO

Set around a garden just southeast of CICI down La Costera, this **complex** (Casa de la Cultura; Map p204; ☎ 484-23-90, for schedules 484-40-04; La Costera 4834; ☷ 9am-9pm) houses a groovy café-art gallery, a handicrafts shop, an open-air theater and an indoor auditorium, as well as the **Salon de Fama de los Deportistas de Guerrero** (Guerrero Sports Hall of Fame; admission free).

CENTRO DE CONVENCIONES

Acapulco's **convention center** (Map p204; ☎ 484-71-52, 484-70-98; La Costera 4455) is a huge complex with a permanent crafts gallery (Galería de Artesanías), temporary special exhibitions, a large plaza, theaters and concert halls. The grounds have reproductions of statuary from archaeological sites throughout Mexico. Also on site are the tourist offices, Casa Consular and Locatel. Phone the center to ask about current offerings.

BEACHES

Visiting Acapulco's beaches tops most visitors' lists of things to do here. During the December–April high season, you can bank on the beaches being Speedo-to-Speedo, with rental chairs, umbrellas, vendors, sunsoakers, jet skis and parasailers dominating the view. But that's Acapulco.

Zona Dorada

The beaches heading east around the bay from the *zócalo* are the most popular (Map p204). If you jump on a bus in the old town and head east, the first beach you'll pass is **Playa Hornos**, a narrow strip of sand crowded with fishing boats and families. In the morning it's abuzz with activity as the fishers haul in their catch, but the Costera sits right on its shoulder, making it noisy in the afternoon. At **Playa Hornitos** the beach widens, and from here east it's flanked by high-rise hotels and restaurants. The beach narrows in front of Parque Papagayo before opening up again at **Playa Condesa**, the trendiest of Acapulco's beaches, where you go to show it all off – and watch others do the same. It's also home to Acapulco's most outwardly gay beach. **Playa Icacos** is the easternmost stretch of sand on the bay, backed by more hotels and restaurants. Nearly all the beaches east of Playa Hornos are good for swimming and great for sunbathing, and various entrepreneurs set up stands to rent chaise longues and umbrellas. These are also the beaches where you can parasail, ride banana boats and water-ski; mobile outfitters set up shop all down the beach. City buses constantly ply La Costera, the beachside avenue, making it easy to get up and down this long arc of beaches.

Península de las Playas

The beaches on the southwestern shores of Bahía de Acapulco (Map p204) have a markedly different feel than those to the east; they're smaller, more sheltered, lack the glitz of the Zona Dorada, and are often even more crowded due to their smaller size. They're well worth a visit for their old-time feel. Playas **Caleta** and **Caletilla** are two small, protected beaches beside one another in a cove on the south side of the Península de las Playas. They're lined end-to-end with cheap seafood *enramadas* (thatch-covered open-air restaurants). During Sunday afternoons they're a spectacle of family fun, the shallow water chaotic with splashing children, anchored fishing *pangas* (small motorized skiffs) and paddling vendors selling trinkets. Music blares over it all from Mágico Mundo Marino, an aquarium on the spit of land separating the two beaches. Boats leave frequently from near the aquarium to Isla de la Roqueta.

All buses marked 'Caleta' heading down La Costera stop here, though it's a pleasant 30-minute walk; take the *malecón* (waterfront street) from the *zócalo* and then follow the Costera and the signs from there.

Playa La Angosta ('Narrow Beach,' Map p206) is in a thin, protected cove nestled between two high cliffs on the west side of the peninsula. It has a few seafood *enramadas* and the only stretch of sand in Acapulco with a view of the sunset on the water. From the *zócalo* it takes about 30 minutes to walk there, either along the Costera (turn right on Av Las Palmas and walk another block), or along the cliffside walkway heading downhill from La Quebrada, a more strenuous but also more scenic route. The latter takes you past the **Sinfonía del Mar**, perhaps the best spot in Acapulco for sunsets.

Outer Beaches

Other good beaches are further afield, but can be easily reached by bus or taxi and make good day trips from Acapulco proper.

Laden with seafood restaurants, the beach at **Puerto Marqués** lies on a striking little bay of the same name about 18km southeast of old Acapulco. It's a madhouse on weekends when families pour in to devour seafood prepared in the countless restaurants that have come to be Puerto Marqués' main attraction. Midweek it can be quiet. Beyond Puerto Marqués lies the long, wide **Playa Revolcadero**, home to Acapulco's grandest luxury resorts. They're spread out, however, so you rarely feel crowded here. It has the only surf in Acapulco; though it's best as a big-wave break, there are people out chasing waves all year. Swimming can be very dangerous here: mind the warning flags. Horseback riding along the beach is popular.

If you're going to Puerto Marqués from La Costera, take an eastbound 'Puerto Marqués' bus (US$0.50) from the west end of Playa Hornos; they pass every 30 minutes or so, less frequently on weekends. The other option is a 'Colosio' bus (from anywhere along La Costera) to La Glorieta, the junction east of town where you turn right to Puerto Marqués (or left to Hwy 200). From La Glorieta, take a *colectivo* (US$0.60) to the beach or walk (20 minutes). To Playa Revolcadero, take a private taxi (about US$1.50).

Your best chance of finding a relatively quiet beach is to head to Pie de la Cuesta (p200), about 10km northwest of Acapulco. There are plenty of places to stay, though it's great to head over for a day on the beach, catch the spectacular sunset from one of the beachside restaurants, and head back to Acapulco for a night on the town.

ISLA DE LA ROQUETA

This island (p204) offers a popular (crowded) beach and snorkeling and diving possibilities. You can rent snorkeling gear, kayaks and other water-sports equipment on the beach.

From Playas Caleta and Caletilla, boats make the eight-minute one-way trip every 20 minutes or so (US$3 round-trip). The alternative is a glass-bottomed boat that

---

CHASING SUNSETS

All those beaches stretching around Bahía de Acapulco, and not a single sunset – over the water, anyway. If you're aching to watch the sun sink slowly into the sea, you'll have to pick your spot carefully. First off, think Old Acapulco. The only place you can sit on the sand (within the city limits) and watch the sun set on the water is Playa La Angosta (above), a sliver of a beach on the Península de las Playas. The bar at Hotel Los Flamingos (p213), perched high on the peninsula's western cliffs, has an almost dizzying perspective of the event, always aided by hoisting a few to the fading sun. Plazoleta La Quebrada, near where the divers perform, is another great spot; the parking lot fills with people around sunset. One of the finest views of all is at the small Sinfonía del Mar (Symphony of the Sea), a stepped plaza built on the edge of the cliffs just south of La Quebrada. Its sole purpose is to give folks a magical view. If you really feel like chasing the sunset, you should head over to Pie de la Cuesta (p200), about a half hour's ride northwest of Acapulco. Its long, wide beach and hammock-clad restaurants are famous for spectacular sunsets.

makes a circuitous trip to the island, departing from the same beaches but traveling via **La Virgen de los Mares** (the Virgin of the Seas), a submerged bronze statue of the Virgen de Guadalupe; visibility varies with water conditions. The round-trip fare is US$5; the trip takes about 45 minutes, depending on how many times floating vendors accost your boat. You can alight on the island and take a later boat back, but find out when the last boat leaves, usually around 5pm.

Activities

As one might expect, Acapulco's activities are largely beach-based. There are nonbeach things to do, but generally everything is in the mega-vacation spirit, with once-in-a-lifetime adventure and/or adrenaline rush promised.

WATER SPORTS

Just about everything that can be done on, or below, the water is done in Acapulco. On Bahía de Acapulco, water-skiing, boating, 'banana-boating' and parasailing *(paracaída)* are all popular activities. To partake in any of these, walk along the Zona Dorada beaches and look for the usually orange kiosks. They charge about US$7 for snorkel gear, US$23 for a five-minute parasailing flight, US$29 for a jet-ski ride and US$52 for one hour of water-skiing. The smaller Playas Caleta and Caletilla have sailboats, fishing boats, motorboats, pedal boats, canoes, snorkel gear, inner tubes and water bicycles for rent.

Though Acapulco isn't quite a scuba destination in itself, there are some decent dive sites nearby. At least two outfitters offer quality services. **Acapulco Scuba Center** (☎ 482-94-74; www.acapulcoscuba.com; Paseo del Pescador 13 & 14) has PADI- and NAUI-certified instructors and offers several certification courses and guided day trips. All prices include a guide, gear, a boat and refreshments. They range from US$70 for a beginning-level dive to US$350 for a five-day PADI open-water certification. A guided two-tank dive for experienced divers costs US$70.

Swiss Divers Association (SDA; Map p204; ☎ 482-13-57; www.swissdivers.com; La Costera 100) is a first-rate shop at the Hotel Caleta that also offers PADI and NAUI instruction – in Spanish, English and German – with a variety and prices similar to those of Acapulco Scuba's.

The best **snorkeling** is off small Playa Las Palmitas on Isla de la Roqueta (p209). Unless you pony up for an organized snorkeling trip, you'll need to scramble over rocks to reach it. You can rent gear on the Isla or on Playas Caleta and Caletilla, which also have some decent spots. Both scuba operations mentioned above do half-day snorkeling trips for around US$35 per person, including boat, guide, gear, food and drink, and hotel transport.

Sportfishing is very popular in Acapulco and many companies offer six- to seven-hour fishing trips; book at least a day in advance and figure on a 6am or 7am departure time. **Acapulco Scuba Center** (left) and **Fish-R-Us** (Map p206; ☎ 487-87-87, 482-82-82; www.fish-r-us.com; La Costera 100) both offer fishing trips starting at around US$250 (for the entire eight-person boat, gear and bait). If you don't have a group large enough to cover the boat, the captain can often add one or two people to an existing group for US$70 to US$80 per person.

CRUISES

Various boats and yachts offer cruises, most of which depart from near Playa Tlacopanocha or Playa Manzanillo near the *zócalo*. Cruises (from US$12 for 90 minutes to US$25 and up for four hours) are available day and night. They range from glass-bottomed boats to multilevel craft with blaring salsa music and open bars to yachts offering quiet sunset cruises around the bay. Most offer a lunchtime cruise (around 11am to 3:30pm) and a sunset cruise (around 4:30pm to 7pm, later in winter). Some offer moonlight cruises (10:30pm to 2am), complete with dancing. A typical trip heads from Tlacopanocha around Península de las Playas to Isla de la Roqueta, passes by to see the cliff divers at La Quebrada, crosses over to Puerto Marqués and then returns around Bahía de Acapulco.

The **Victoria** (Map p206; ☎ 044-744-516-24-94), **Hawaiano** (☎ 482-21-99), **Fiesta** (Map p206) and **Bonanza** (Map p206; ☎ 482-20-55) cruise operations are all popular; you can make reservations directly or through travel agencies and most hotels.

OTHER ACTIVITIES

Acapulco has squash courts, tennis courts, public swimming pools, gymnasiums, tracks and facilities for other sports. The tourist office stays abreast of most sport-related opportunities and events and is a good source of information.

For tennis, try **Club de Golf Acapulco** (Map p204; ☎ 484-12-25; La Costera s/n), Club de Tenis Hyatt at the Hyatt Regency Acapulco (p214), **Villa Vera Racquet Club** (☎ 484-03-33; Lomas del Mar 35) or Fairmont Acapulco Princess Hotel (p213).

Acapulco has many 18-hole golf courses, among them the **Club de Golf Acapulco** (Map p204; ☎ 484-65-83; La Costera s/n) next to the convention center on La Costera; **Tres Vidas** (☎ 444-51-26) in Acapulco Diamante near the airport; and the **Fairmont Acapulco Princess Hotel** (p213), also in Diamante. Those in Diamante front Playa Revolcadero and have spectacular views.

The 50m-high bungee tower at **AJ Hackett Bungy** (☎ 484-75-29; La Costera 107; ☽ noon-midnight Mon-Thu, noon-2am Fri-Sun) is easy to spot on La Costera, and for US$60 you can throw yourself (bungee included) from its platform.

Acapulco for Children

Acapulco is very family friendly (if not wallet friendly), with many amusement options designed for children, but fun for adults too.

PARQUE PAPAGAYO

This large **amusement park** (Map p204; La Costera; admission free; ☽ 8am-8pm, rides operate 3-10pm) is full of tropical trees and provides access to Playas Hornos and Hornitos. Its attractions include a go-kart track, a lake with paddle-boats, a children's train, mechanical rides, animal enclosures with deer, rabbits, crocodiles and turtles, an aviary, a restaurant-bar and a hill affording an excellent view. A 1.2km 'interior circuit' pathway is good for jogging. The park is between Morín and El Cano and has entrances on all four sides.

CICI

The **Centro Internacional de Convivencia Infantil** (CICI; Map p204; ☎ 484-19-60; La Costera 101; admission US$9.50; ☽ 10am-6pm) is a family water-sports park on the east side of Acapulco. Dolphins perform several shows daily, and humans occasionally give diving exhibitions. You can also enjoy an 80m-long water toboggan, a pool with artificial waves and the Sky Coaster ride (US$15 per person), which simulates the La Quebrada cliff-diving

experience, as well as ascending 100m in a tethered balloon (US$10 per person). Children who are two years and up pay full price, plus you'll need to rent a locker (US$2), and an inflatable ring (US$2.50) to use the toboggan.

Any local bus marked 'CICI,' 'Base' or 'Puerto Marqués' will take you there.

MÁGICO MUNDO MARINO

This **aquarium** (Map p204; ☎ 483-12-15; admission adult/child 3-12yr US$3.75/2; ☽ 9am-6pm) stands on a small islet just off Playas Caleta and Caletilla. Highlights include a sea lion show, swimming pools, water toboggans and the feeding of crocodiles, turtles and piranhas.

Festivals & Events

Acapulco hits its height of merry-making during the three weeks around **Semana Santa** (Holy Week), when the city fills with tourists, the discos stay packed every night of the week and the beaches are crammed.

The **Festival Francés** (French Festival), celebrating French food, cinema, music and literature, began in 2004 and is held in March. More long-standing is the **Tianguis Turístico** (www.tianguisturistico.com), Mexico's major annual tourism trade fair, held the second or third week in April. The **Festivales de Acapulco**, held for one week in May, feature Mexican and international music at venues around town.

Flight fans shouldn't miss the **Acapulco Air Show**, which takes place over three days around the beginning of November. It features everything from biplanes to F-16s, plus wing-walking, parachute teams, precision aerobatics and high-speed fighter maneuvers over the bay and between the hotels. The USAF Thunderbirds team appeared at the show for the first time in 2005.

The festival for Mexico's favorite figure, the **Virgen de Guadalupe**, is celebrated all night on December 11 and all the following day; it's marked by fireworks, folk dances and street processions accompanied by small marching bands. The processions converge at the cathedral in the zócalo, where children dressed in costumes congregate.

Sleeping

Acapulco has a plethora of hotels (more than 30,000 rooms) in every category imaginable. What part of town you choose to stay in will depend on your budget and your interests.

THE AUTHOR'S CHOICE

Las Brisas (☎ 469-69-00, in the US 800-223-6800; www.brisas.com.mx; Carretera Escénica 5255; casitas with continental breakfast from US$330; P ⊠ 🖳 🕾) Classic Las Brisas commands some amazing views from its vantage point high above the bay. Built in the late '50s, the place has great bones, including a lot of lovely stonework and tile floors. Each of 236 'casitas' has a private terrace or balcony and either a private swimming pool or one shared with at most two other casitas. Service gets high ratings (room rates include US$20 in lieu of tips). The hotel's beach club is nestled far below in a rocky cove.

The cheapest hotels are near the *zócalo* and uphill along La Quebrada. This also happens to be the part of town with the most historical character, cheaper restaurants and easily accessible services and bus lines. The Zona Dorada hotels are more expensive, but are on or near the beaches and closer to the clubs and bars. Some of the hotels on the Península de las Playas are extremely relaxing and offer a romantic, old-time Acapulco feel, but they are a fair distance from other restaurants and services.

Rooms are priciest from mid-December until a week or so after Semana Santa, and through the July and August school holidays. Reservations are recommended between Christmas and New Year's Day and around Semana Santa. Unless specified, the following prices are high season; they can drop 10% to 40% when business is slow.

BUDGET

Most of Acapulco's budget hotels are concentrated around the *zócalo* and on La Quebrada; the latter catch more breezes.

La Torre Eiffel (Map p206; ☎ 482-16-83; Inalámbrica 110; hoteltorreeiffel@hotmail.com; s US$11.50, d from US$23; P 🕾) Perched on a hill above Plazoleta La Quebrada, the popular Eiffel has a small swimming pool, huge shared balconies and some spectacular sunset views. It's a bit out of the way, but the friendly, helpful management, good baths and comfortable beds help make the climb worth it.

Hotel Angelita (Map p206; ☎ 483-57-34; La Quebrada 37; r per person US$10) Clean, spacious rooms – each with at least one fan, a hot-water

bathroom and good screens – are set back along a narrow, plant-filled courtyard. A paperback library augments the small TV room in front, where a friendly group of grandmotherly types sometimes gathers.

Hotel Asturias (Map p206; ☎ 483-65-48; gerardomancera@aol.com; La Quebrada 45; s/d US$17/29, with air-con & TV US$22/43; P 🕾 🕾) This friendly, family-run hotel is clean and well tended, with mostly pleasant rooms on a courtyard, cable TV in the lobby, a small swimming pool and a book exchange.

Hotel Misión (Map p206; ☎ 482-36-43; hotelmision@hotmail.com; Valle 12; per person US$19; P) Acapulco's oldest hotel certainly looks it from the outside, but step into the colonial compound's leafy, relaxing courtyard and things get nicer (one happy reader described the Misión as 'a diamond in the rough'). Basic rooms feature colorful tiles, heavy Spanish-style furniture and comfortable beds in a variety of configurations. Some of the toilets lack seats.

Hotel María Antonieta (Map p206; ☎ 482-50-24; Azueta 17; s/d US$11.50/19) The 'Ma Antonieta' has 38 decent budget rooms with fans. They're very plain, but clean and good-sized, and guests have use of a communal kitchen.

Hotel Paola (Map p206; ☎ 482-62-43; Azueta 16; per person US$15) The positively pink Paola is clean and family-run. Outside rooms have small private balconies; the interior rooms are quieter, and all are outfitted in pastels.

MIDRANGE

Most of the high-rise hotels along La Costera tend to be expensive. But there are some good deals in older places around town. A few places offer rooms with fully equipped kitchens.

Hotel Etel Suites (Map p206; ☎ 482-22-40/41; etelsuites@terra.com.mx; Av La Pinzona 92; d/ste/apt from US$45/57/99; P 🕾 🕾 🖢) High atop the hill overlooking Old Acapulco, the Etel is run by a delightful mother and daughter. The good value, spotless suites and apartments all sleep at least three people, and most have expansive terraces with views of La Quebrada and the Pacific to one side and the bay to the other. Amenities include full kitchens, well-manicured gardens, a children's play area and at least one swimming pool.

Suites Selene (Map p204; ☎ 484-36-43; suitesselene@hotmail.com; Colón 175; d/q with kitchen US$66/77 without kitchen US$55/66; P 🕾 🕾) One door from the sands of Playa Icacos, Selene is a great option, especially for long-stay self-caterers. Though a little worn, it has fine, firm beds, good air-con (though only fans in the dining room/kitchens), good baths, a nice deep pool and cable TV throughout.

Hotel Los Flamingos (Map p204; ☎ 482-06-90; www .flamingosacapulco.com; López Mateos s/n; r from US$76; P ☒ ☒) Perched 135m over the ocean on the highest cliffs in Acapulco, this single-story classic boasts one of the finest sunset views in town, as well as a bar and restaurant. Rooms themselves are modest and comfortable, with great baths, good screens and a long shared lounging terrace. John Wayne, Johnny Weissmuller (best movie Tarzan ever!) and some of their Hollywood pals once owned the place. The 'Round House' is a two-room circular house surrounded by trees with its own small pool, private entry and a stone walkway down to a tiny parapet on the cliff's edge. Weissmuller died here in 1984, of natural causes. You can rent it out, if you dare.

Romano Palace Hotel (Map p204; ☎ 484-77-30, 800-090-15-00; www.romanopalace.com.mx; La Costera 130; r US$71; P ☒ ☒) This 22-story hotel offers very good accommodations for the price: rooms have private balconies, air-con and floor-to-ceiling windows with great bay-front views (ask for an upper-story room). The faintly Asian decor is dated, whereas the marble bathrooms still look good, and the Romano has multiple restaurants and a beach club.

Youth Hostel K3 (Map p204; ☎ 481-31-11; La Costera 116; www.k3acapulco.com; dm/r with continental breakfast US$20/57; ☒ ☐) It's shared baths only, and the rooms have almost a Japanese capsule-hotel feel. But both dorms and private rooms have air-con, there's a shared kitchen and the terrace, bar and game room provide ample space for socializing. Most importantly, it's right across La Costera from the beach.

Hotel del Valle (Map p204; ☎ 485-83-36/88; cnr Morín & Espinoza; r with fan/air-con US$57/71; P ☒ ☒) On the east side of Parque Papagayo, near La Costera and popular Playa Hornitos, the del Valle has reasonably comfortable rooms, a small swimming pool and communal kitchens (US$9.50 surcharge per day).

TOP END

The original high-rise zone begins at the eastern end of Parque Papagayo and curves

east around the bay; new luxury hotels have been springing up on Playa Revolcadero, east of Puerto Marqués. Most of the establishments listed here offer at least a couple of rooms set up for disabled guests, and recreation programs for children (though these may be available only on weekends and at school vacation times).

Off-season package rates and special promotions can be less than half the standard rack rates – ask reservation agents for special deals, or travel agents for air/lodging packages. Even during the high season, simply reserving through a hotel's website can sometimes save a lot off walk-in rates. All prices given here are high-season rack rates.

Camino Real Acapulco Diamante (☎ 435-10-10/ 20, in the US 800-722-6466; www.caminoreal.com/aca pulco; Carretera Escénica, Km 14; r from US$280; P ☒ ☒ ☐ ☒ ☒) The CR lies down a steep, gated 1km access road off the Carretera Escénica, directly above its own small, rocky stretch of Playa Pichilingue on the calm bay of Puerto Marqués. Each of the 157 luxuriously appointed rooms has a terrace or balcony looking out on the bay, and their showers put out enough filtered water to drown a hippo in no time flat. The well-designed, multilevel hotel has a spa, a gym, three shallow swimming pools and the usual multiplicity of bars and restaurants.

Hotel Boca Chica (Map p204; ☎ 483-67-41; www .bocachicahotel.com; Playa Caletilla; r from US$130; P ☒ ☒) The family-run Boca Chica preserves the best elements of Acapulco's heyday as a resort town. Tucked into the rocks at the end of Playa Caletilla, it has a virtually private ocean cove for snorkeling, diving and boating. Comfortable, air-conditioned rooms have views of Isla de la Roqueta, Playa Caletilla or the garden, and the seaside Marina Club Sushi & Oyster Bar (p214) is a real treat.

Fairmont Acapulco Princess (☎ 469-10-00, in the US 800-441-1414; www.fairmont.com; Playa Revolcadero s/n; r from US$300; P ☒ ☒ ☐ ☒ ☒) This Aztec-themed place on Playa Revolcadero is BIG. Its core 'pyramid' has a towering, 15-story atrium lobby and is one of three huge structures that hold a total of 1015 guestrooms and suites. The 194 hectares of lush landscaped grounds also contain a golf course, nine tennis courts, five swimming pools, two fitness centers and a dozen bars and restaurants. Rooms come with varying views, but all have a high standard of comfort and lots of nice touches like ironing boards, hairdryers, dual sinks and digital room safes.

Hyatt Regency Acapulco (Map p204; ☎ 469-12-34, 800-005-00-00, in the US 800-233-1234; www .acapulco.hyatt.com; La Costera 1; r from US$175; P ✗ ✗ ⊡ ⚟ ⚜) The Hyatt is right on the beach and at the middle of La Costera's action. Its 638 plush rooms and suites have marble bathrooms, and most have private balconies. Two inviting swimming pools, a passel of palm trees, a bevy of bars and restaurants (one serving kosher food from December to February) and an on-site synagogue round things out.

Park Royal (Map p204; ☎ 440-65-65; www.park royalhotels.com.mx; Costera Guitarrón 110; r per person all-inclusive from US$200; P ✗ ✗ ⊡ ⚟) The Park Royal opened for business in its present incarnation in 2003, and remodeling continues on the former Radisson resort. Its 218 rooms are spread out on various levels and floors, but only about 40 of them have sea views. Most standards have two beds, a really big TV, great air-con and a bathroom done up in lovely subdued brown marble. A tram carries guests down to a large swimming pool sitting just above the hotel's relatively secluded stretch of beach, and a gym was going in at the time of research. Rack rates cover three meals a day and all the drinks you want.

Eating

For inexpensive, down-home Mexican cooking, the eateries around the *zócalo* offer the best pop for your peso. For finer dining and a more celebratory atmosphere, try something on La Costera – many serve outstanding food.

THE AUTHOR'S CHOICE

Marina Club Sushi & Oyster Bar (Map p204; ☎ 482-78-79; Hotel Boca Chica, Playa Caletilla; mains US$6-16; sushi rolls US$4.50-8, nigiri per piece US$1.50-3.50; ☿ 1-10:30pm) Only ultra-fresh seafood hits the plates at this intimate bayside spot. Live chocolate clams are flown in weekly from Baja, and the fish is limited to what's being caught locally at the moment. Have a drink under the high thatched roof and enjoy the views of Isla de la Roqueta and the bay.

OLD ACAPULCO

Taquería Los Pioneros (Map p206; ☎ 482-23-45; cnr Mendoza & Mina; five tacos for US$2, mains US$3.75-5; ☿ 9am-3am) The tacos are tiny but their various fillings are tasty, plus you can load up on accompaniments: jalapeños, pickled carrots, onions, cilantro and so forth. The food comes with plenty of open-air atmosphere, too, at the sweaty, busy, noisy intersection. Hang with locals and watch the elaborately painted buses go by (with luck you'll spot the vomiting scene from *The Exorcist*).

El Amigo Miguel (Map p206; ☎ 483-69-81; Juárez 31 & Juárez 16, La Costera s/n; ☿ 10am-9pm; mains US$4-8.50) This cheery open-air restaurant is one of the busiest, featuring cheap and delicious seafood. Miguel has two restaurants opposite one another, on the same corner, with other branches around town (the branch on La Costera is open from 11am to 8pm). Several other good seafood places are nearby.

Restaurant San Carlos (Map p206; Juárez 5; mains US$3-6) An open-air patio, good traditional Mexican fare and a US$3 *comida corrida* (set menu). Want more? OK: the menu has an endless list of Mexican standards, including green and white *pozole* (a hearty pork and hominy soup).

Restaurant Ricardo (Map p206; Juárez 9; set lunch US$3) A couple of doors further from the *zócalo*, Ricardo's is another good choice for cheap *comidas corridas* and tasty house specials like *camarones en ajo* (shrimp with garlic) or *pollo en salsa de cacahuete* (chicken in peanut sauce), all served under bright fluorescent light shining onto white tile.

Restaurant Café Astoria (Map p206; zócalo, Edificio Pintos 4C; snacks US$1.50-4, mains US$3.75) This friendly café has indoor and outdoor tables in a shady, semiquiet spot just east of the cathedral. It serves some OK espresso drinks, including a massive *tarro* (cup) of *capuchino* for US$2.

El Nopalito (☎ 483-84-76; cnr La Paz & Ramírez; mains US$3-3.50, set lunch US$3; ☿ 7am-8pm) Reader-recommended, the 'Little Cactus' serves inexpensive and filling fish and meat dishes (*pozole* on Thursday) and a good *menú del día* (lunch special).

Restaurant Charly (Map p206; Carranza s/n; four tacos US$2) Just steps east of the *zócalo*, on the pedestrian alley of Carranza, economical Charly has shady sidewalk tables and offers up *barbacoa de chivo* (goat) as both a main dish and taco.

Café Wadi (Map p206; ☎ 482-09-14; cnr Mina & Velásquez; coffee US$1-2; ⏰ 8am-8pm Mon-Sat) This is a great morning stop for good fresh-roasted espresso drinks before hitting the nearby artisan market.

For eat-in or takeout rotisserie-roasted chicken, head to the corner of Mina and 5 de Mayo, where there are five places side by side, each serving quarter/half/whole fowls for about US$2/3.50/7. There's nothing like tearing a hot bird limb from limb, dumping on the salt and chowing down.

LA COSTERA
Dozens of restaurants line La Costera heading east toward the high-rise hotels; most specialize in fresh seafood or flashy gimmicks.

Fersato's (Map p204; ☎ 484-39-49; La Costera 44; mains US$5.50-14) Opposite the Centro Cultural, this long-standing family establishment features good Mexican food.

Mariscos Pipo's (Map p204; ☎ 484-17-00; cnr La Costera & Nao Victoria; mains US$7-19; ⏰ 1-9pm) Pipo's has a varied menu that includes baby shark quesadillas, freshwater bass, grilled crawfish and scallop cocktail, all served in a large dining area with a simple, nautical theme.

El Gaucho (Map p204; ☎ 484-17-00; La Costera 8, Hotel Presidente; mains US$7.50-22.50; ⏰ 5pm-midnight) The Gaucho is upscale but not stuffy, and one of the top spots in town for a steak (though you pay dearly for it). All the meat is grilled in the true Argentine style. Less carnivorous or extravagant folk can choose from an assortment of pasta dishes. The short but decent wine list includes Mexican, Chilean, Spanish, and of course Argentine selections.

Many other open-air beachfront restaurant/bars line the Costera opposite the Romano Palace Hotel. Stroll along, browse the posted menus, and take your pick.

100% Natural (Map p204; ☎ 485-52-79; La Costera 200, 34 & 112; mains US$4-7; Ⓥ) This health-conscious chain has several branches along La Costera and elsewhere in town, all with a mellow ambience and good, friendly service. The food is consistently good, mostly vegetarian fare, including whole-grain breads and rolls and a large variety of fruit and veggie juice blends, *licuados* (smoothies) and shakes. The restaurant at La Costera 200 is open 24 hours.

El Fogón (Map p204; ☎ 484-50-79; La Costera 10; mains US$4.50-9.50) Another chain, El Fogón

serves its traditional Mexican dishes at several La Costera branches. Many fast-food chains also litter La Costera, especially near the east end.

OUTSKIRTS
Madeiras (☎ 446-56-36; Carretera Escénica 33; prix-fixe dinner US$40; ⏰ 7-9:30pm Mon-Fri, 7-10:30pm Sat & Sun) A great spot for a romantic meal, Madeiras has been in operation for more than 25 years. You construct a four-course meal from the fairly wide menu of offerings that blend Old World favorites with Mexican flourishes, such as tournedos with Roquefort and *huitlacoche* (corn truffle, a fungus that grows on maize), accompanied by a sauce made with *guajillo* chilies and madeira. Decor is appealingly simple, but it can't compete with the spectacular views over Bahía de Acapulco from the terrace.

Restaurant La Perla (Map p206; ☎ 483-11-55; Hotel El Mirador, Plazoleta La Quebrada 74; dinner US$33; ⏰ 7-11pm) First-rate views of the death-defying *clavadistas* (see La Quebrada Cliff Divers, p207) justify the high price of a meal here; candlelit terraces and sea breezes are a bonus. The three-course menu is meat-heavy but includes several fish choices and a couple each of chicken and pasta dishes.

SELF-CATERING
The huge air-conditioned Comercial Mexicana, Bodega Aurrera and Bodega Gigante combination supermarkets and big-box discount department stores are along La Costera between the *zócalo* and Parque Papagayo, among other places. Aside from the fresh produce and all manner of groceries, you can find some pretty high-quality, ready-to-eat stuff in the bakery and deli departments.

Entertainment
Acapulco's active nightlife probably outdoes its beaches as the city's main attraction. Much of the entertainment revolves around discos and nightclubs.

DISCOS
Most of the discos open around 10:30pm (but don't get rolling till midnight or later). Cover charges vary seasonally and nightly; when they include an open bar, you still usually need to tip your server. Dress codes prohibit shorts, sneakers and the like.

Palladium (Map p204; ☎ 446-54-90; Carretera Escénica s/n; cover & open bar women/men US$33/43) Hailed by many as the best disco in town, Palladium attracts a 20s-to-30s crowd with its fabulous views from giant windows and a range of hip-hop, house, trance, techno and other bass-heavy beats emanating from an ultraluxe sound system. Dress up, and expect to wait in line.

Baby'O (Map p204; ☎ 484-74-74; La Costera 22; cover US$10-38) Very popular with the upscale crowd, Baby'O has a laser-light show, Wednesday theme nights and spins rock, pop, house and 'everything but electronica.' Drinks are not included in the cover charge.

Los Alebrijes (Map p204; ☎ 484-59-02; La Costera 3308; cover & open bar women/men US$26/36) This disco-concert hall bills itself as 'one of the largest and most spectacular discos in the world.' Less spectacular than big, it's usually packed with a young Mexican crowd. The music is middle-of-the-road Latin rock and pop; open bar between 1am and 5am.

Disco Beach (Map p204; ☎ 484-8230; La Costera s/n, Playa Condesa; cover & open bar women/men US$25/27; � Wed-Sat) This popular spot is in the line of beachfront restaurant-bars, right on Playa Condesa (the beach forms part of the dance floor). Dress policy is more relaxed here than at most other clubs, and the place draws a fairly young crowd. Music is house, disco, techno, hip-hop, '70s and '80s; women get in (and drink) free Wednesday, and the Friday foam parties can be wild. Check out Ibiza Lounge next door, too.

LIVE MUSIC & BARS

Most of the big hotels along La Costera have bars with entertainment, be it quiet piano music or live bands; head to the following for something different.

Nina's (Map p204; ☎ 484-24-00; La Costera 41; cover & open bar US$24) Nina's is one of the best places in town for live *música tropical* (salsa, *cumbia*, cha-cha, merengue etc); it has a smokin' dance floor, variety acts and impersonators.

Salon Q (Map p204; ☎ 484-32-52, 481-01-14; La Costera 3117; cover US$11.50, with open bar US$23) This *'catedral de la salsa'* gives Nina's a run for its money, with first-rate salsa singers and bands, celebrity impersonators and a Carnaval atmosphere. Reservations are recommended; discounts for groups are available.

Tropicana (Map p204; Playa Hornos; cover US$4.50) Like Nina's, Tropicana has a full spectrum of live *música tropical*, only without the bells and whistles.

Hotel Los Flamingos (Map p204; ☎ 482-06-90; López Mateos s/n) The one quiet spot in this rowdy bunch, Los Flamingos' clifftop bar has the hands-down best sunset-viewing/drinking spot in Acapulco. Not a car or hustler in sight, and you can sip *cocos locos* to your heart's content.

New West (Map p206; ☎ 483-10-82; La Quebrada 81) This popular local bar has cheap beer, rodeo videos and a jukebox blaring *música ranchera: norteño, banda, tejano* and a smattering of US country and western hits. You WILL see cowboy hats and big belt buckles.

Hard Rock Cafe (Map p204; ☎ 484-00-47; La Costera 37; � noon-2am) It's hard to miss the Hard Rock. Just west of CICI, the chain's Acapulco branch has live music from 10pm to 2am.

GAY VENUES

Acapulco has an active gay scene with several gay bars and clubs.

Demas (Map p204; ☎ 484-13-70; Piedra Picuda 17) Men only; weekend shows.

Picante (Map p204; Piedra Picuda 16) Behind Demas.

Relax (Map p204; ☎ 484-04-21; Lomas del Mar No 4; � Thu-Sat nights) Men and women welcome.

DANCE, MUSIC & THEATER

The city's not all booze and boogying. The **Centro de Convenciones** (Map p204; ☎ 484-71-52; La Costera s/n) presents plays, concerts (by the Acapulco Philharmonic, among others), dance and other performances, as does the **Centro Cultural** (Map p204; ☎ 484-40-04; La Costera 4834). **Parque Papagayo** (Map p206; La Costera btwn Morín & El Cano) sometimes hosts alfresco events.

BULLFIGHTS

Bullfights take place at the Plaza de Toros (Map p204), southeast of La Quebrada and west of Playas Caleta and Caletilla, every Sunday at 5:30pm from January to March; for tickets, try your hotel, a travel agency or the **bullring box office** (☎ 482-11-81) between 10am and 2pm. The 'Caleta' bus passes near the bullring.

Shopping

100% Mexico (Map p204; ☎ 486-28-45; www.100mexico .com; La Costera 127, Local 17; � 10am-2pm & 4-10pm) For high-quality crafts from around Mexico, visit this Fonart shop.

Mercado de Artesanías (Map p206; btwn Cuauhtémoc & Vicente de León at Parana) Bargaining is the rule at this 400-stall *mercado*, Acapulco's main craft market, especially as the sellers often find soft touches among the many cruise-ship passengers. It's paved and pleasant, and is an OK place to get better deals on everything that you see in the hotel shops – serapes, hammocks, jewelry, huaraches, clothing and T-shirts. Other artisan markets include the Mercados de Artesanías Papagayo, Noa Noa, Dalia and La Diana (near the statue of the same name), all on La Costera, and Mercados de Artesanías La Caletilla at the west end of Playa Caletilla (Map p204).

Mercado Central (Map p204; Diego H de Mendoza s/n) A truly local market, this sprawling indoor-outdoor bazaar has everything from *atole* to *zapatos* (not to mention produce, hot food and souvenirs). Any eastbound 'Pie de la Cuesta' or 'Pedregoso' bus will drop you there; get off where the sidewalk turns to tarp-covered stalls.

Getting There & Away

AIR

Acapulco has a busy **airport** (☎ 466-94-34) with many international flights, most connecting through Mexico City or Guadalajara – both short hops from Acapulco. All flights mentioned here are direct; some are seasonal. **Aeroméxico/Aerolitoral** (Map p204; ☎ 485-16-25/00; La Costera 286) flies to Guadalajara, Mexico City and Tijuana, and **America West** (☎ 466-92-75; Airport) to Los Angeles and Phoenix. **American Airlines** (Map p204; ☎ 481-01-61; La Costera 116, Plaza Condesa, Local 109) flies to Dallas and Chicago. **Aviacsa** (☎ 466-92-09; Airport) flies regularly to Oaxaca, Mexico City and Tijuana. **Azteca** (☎ 466-90-29; Airport) serves Ciudad Juárez, Guadalajara and Tijuana. **Continental Airlines** (☎ 466-90-46; Airport) flies to and from Houston, Minneapolis and Newark, while **Mexicana/Click Mexicana** (Map p204; ☎ 486-75-70; La Costera 1632, La Gran Plaza) serves Mexico City, and **Northwest** (☎ 800-900-08-00; Airport) travels between Acapulco and Houston.

BUS

There are two major 1st-class long-distance bus companies in Acapulco: Estrella de Oro and Estrella Blanca. The modern, air-conditioned **Estrella de Oro terminal** (Map p204; ☎ 01-800-900-01-05; Av Cuauhtémoc 1490), just east of Massieu, has free toilets, a Banamex ATM and a ticket machine that accepts bank debit

cards (left luggage US$0.20 per hour per piece). Estrella Blanca has two 1st-class terminals: **Central Papagayo** (Map p204; ☎ 469-20-80; Av Cuauhtémoc 1605) just north of Parque Papagayo (left luggage US$0.35 per hour per piece); and **Central Ejido** (☎ 469-20-28/30; Av Ejido 47). Estrella Blanca also has a **2nd-class terminal** (☎ 482-21-84; Av Cuauhtémoc 97) that sells tickets for all buses, but only has departures to relatively nearby towns. Estrella Blanca tickets are also sold at several agencies around town, including **Agencia de Viajes Zócalo** (Map p206; ☎ 482-49-76; La Costera 207, Local 2).

Both companies offer frequent services to Mexico City, with various levels of luxury; journey durations depend on whether they use the faster *autopista* (Hwy 95D) or the old federal Hwy 95.

The following destinations are among those served from Acapulco:

Chilpancingo Frequent 1st-class services to Estrella de Oro (US$7, 1¾hr). Several 1st-class services (US$7, 1¾hr) and 2nd-class services every half hour from the 2nd-class terminal, from 5am to 7pm (US$5.50, 3hr), from Central Ejido to Estrella Blanca.

Cuernavaca Seven daily 1st-class services (US$22, 4-5hr) and frequent *semi-directo* services (US$19, 5hr) to Estrella de Oro. Three daily 1st-class services to Estrella Blanca Central Papagayo (US$24, 4-5hr).

Iguala Has 18 daily 1st-class services (US$12.50, 3hr) and frequent *semi-directo* services (US$11.50, 3½hr) to Estrella de Oro. Hourly 1st-class services to Estrella Blanca Central Ejido (US$12.50, 4hr).

Mexico City (Norte) Seven daily 1st-class services to Estrella de Oro (US$29, 6hr). Also has one deluxe daily service (US$43, 6hr) and several daily 1st-class services (US$29, 6hr) to Estrella Blanca from Central Papagayo, and two daily 1st-class services from Central Ejido.

Mexico City (Sur) Many daily 1st-class services (US$29, 5hr) and six deluxe services daily (US$43, 5hr) to Estrella de Oro. Four daily deluxe services (US$43, 5hr) and frequent daily 1st-class services (US$29, 5hr) to Estrella Blanca from Central Papagayo, and eight daily 1st-class services (US$29, 5hr) from Central Ejido.

Puerto Escondido Five daily 1st-class services (US$22, 7hr) and five 2nd-class services ($18, 9½hr) to Estrella Blanca Central Ejido.

Taxco Two daily 1st-class services to Estrella de Oro (US$15, 4hr). Three daily 1st-class services to Estrella Blanca Central Ejido (US$15, 4hr).

Zihuatanejo Has 16 daily 1st-class services (US$11.50, 4-5hr) and 13 daily Primera Plus services (US$12.50, 4-5hr) to Estrella Blanca Central Ejido. Has three 1st-class daily services (US$11.50, 4-5hr) and 12 2nd-class services, hourly from 5am to 5:30pm (US$8.50, 4-5hr), to Estrella de Oro.

The 2nd-class Estrella Blanca buses depart Central Ejido roughly half-hourly to Costa Chica destinations southeast of Acapulco along Hwy 200, including Copala (US$6, 2½ hours, 120km), Marquelia (US$6.75, three hours, 133km) and Cuajinicuilapa (US$7, 3½ hours, 200km).

CAR & MOTORCYCLE
Many car-rental companies rent Jeeps as well as cars; several have offices at the airport as well as in town, and some offer free delivery to you. Note that rental rates are more expensive at the airport. Shop around to compare prices, or find good deals via the Internet ahead of time. Consider waiting until you're finished with Acapulco before you pick up your vehicle; it's not very practical to try to get around town by car. Rental companies include the following.

Alamo (Map p204; ☎ 484-33-05, 466-94-44; La Costera 2148)

Avis (Map p204; ☎ 466-91-90; La Costera 97, Fiestamericana Hotel)

Budget (Map p204; ☎ 481-24-33, 466-90-03; La Costera 93, Local 2)

Hertz (Map p204; ☎ 485-89-47; La Costera 137)

Saad (Map p204; ☎ 484-34-45; www.acapulcorentacar .com; La Costera 28) Local rentals only.

Thrifty (Map p204; ☎ 486-19-40; La Costera 139; ☎ 466-92-86 airport)

Drivers heading inland on Hwy 95D need to have some cash handy. The tolls to Chilpancingo, about 117km north, total US$25, including US$6.50 just to get through the 'Maxi Túnel' beyond the edge of town. If you've been driving in Acapulco much, it may seem a small price to pay for being on the open road again.

Getting Around
TO/FROM THE AIRPORT
Acapulco's airport is 23km southeast of the zócalo, beyond the junction for Puerto Marqués. Arriving by air, you can buy a ticket for transportation into town from the colectivo desk at the end of the domestic terminal; it's about US$7.50 per person for a lift to your hotel (a bit more if it's west of the zócalo).

Leaving Acapulco, phone **Móvil Aca** (☎ 462-10-95) 24 hours in advance to reserve transportation back to the airport; the cost varies, depending on where your pickup is, from

US$15 to US$19 per person or US$28 to US$38 for the whole vehicle, holding up to five passengers. Taxis from the center to the airport cost from around US$17 to US$22, depending on the amount of luggage.

BUS
Acapulco has a good bus system (especially good when you get an airbrushed beauty with a bumping sound system). Buses operate from 5am to 11pm daily and cost US$0.50 with air-con, US$0.40 without. From the centro, a good place to catch buses is the stop opposite Sanborns department store on La Costera, two blocks east of the zócalo – it's the beginning of several bus routes (including to Pie de la Cuesta), so you can usually get a seat. There are several useful city routes:

Base–Caleta From the Icacos naval base at the southeast end of Acapulco, along La Costera, past the zócalo to Playa Caleta.

Base–Cine Río–Caleta From the Icacos naval base, cuts inland from La Costera on Av Wilfrido Massieu to Av Cuauhtémoc, heads down Av Cuauhtémoc through the business district, turning back to La Costera just before reaching the zócalo, continuing west to Playa Caleta.

Puerto Marqués–Centro From opposite Sanborns, along La Costera to Puerto Marqués.

Zócalo–Playa Pie de la Cuesta From opposite Sanborns, to Pie de la Cuesta (see p202 for details).

TAXI & CAR
Hundreds of blue and white VW cabs scurry around Acapulco like cockroaches, maneuvering with an audacity that borders on the comical. Drivers sometimes quote fares higher than the going rate, so ask locals what a fair price for your ride is, and agree on the fare with the cabby before you climb in.

If you can possibly avoid driving in Acapulco, do so. The streets are in poor shape and the anarchic traffic is often horridly snarled.

COSTA CHICA
When Guerrero state tourist brochures refer to the Costa Chica ('small coast'), they're usually referring to the coast of Guerrero from Acapulco southeast to the border of Oaxaca. The Costa Chica actually stretches as far south as Puerto Ángel in Oaxaca, though even that boundary varies depending on whom you talk to, what you read, or what radio station you're tuned to. This

section covers the Costa Chica as far as the Oaxacan border. The coast south of there is described in the Oaxaca chapter.

Guerrero's Costa Chica is far less traveled than its Costa Grande (the stretch of coast from Acapulco northwest to the border of Michoacán), though it has some spectacular beaches. Afro-mestizos – people of mixed African, indigenous and European decent – make up a large portion of the population; the region was a safe-haven for Africans who escaped slavery, some from the interior, others (it's believed) from a slave ship that sank just off the coast.

San Marcos & Cruz Grande

San Marcos (pop 12,000), 65km east of Acapulco, and Cruz Grande (pop 10,000), about 40km past that, are both unremarkable towns, but they provide basic services including banks, gas and simple hotels. They're the only two towns of significant size before Cuajinicuilapa near the Oaxacan border.

Playa Ventura

☎ 744

About 2½ hours southeast of Acapulco, Playa Ventura is a long, beautiful beach with soft white and gold sand, decent swimming and a number of simple beachfront fish restaurants and places to stay. From Playa Ventura you can walk or drive about 1.5km southeast through the tiny village of **Juan Álvarez** (population 600) to an even more spectacular beach, **Playa La Piedra** (stone beach), so named for the golden, wave-sculpted rock formations at its north end and the jagged rocks that accent its long, sandy shoreline as it disappears from sight to the south. The rock formations are known as La Casa de Piedra ('house of stone'). On weekdays it's possible to have both beaches all to yourself, a blissful condition that makes leaving extremely difficult.

Most restaurants will allow you to camp beneath their beach *ramadas* (palm-frond shelters) and use their toilet and shower (if they have one), provided you patronize the restaurant. If you plan to cook your own food, bring it with you; the several little *mini-supers* (convenience stores) stock little beyond snacks, cold drinks and, on a good day, fruit.

There are several good places to stay, all of them cheaper in the May-to-November

low season and midweek during high season. All of them offer clean rooms with private baths and cold showers.

It's worth walking into the village to have a cold beer at the outdoor, standing-only bar simply because it's there.

You won't find Playa Ventura on most maps, which only show Juan Álvarez. To get there from Acapulco, take a bus heading southeast on Hwy 200 to Copala (US$6, 2½ hours, 120km; see p217), a small town on Hwy 200. Ask the driver to drop you there or at *el crucero*, the turnoff to Playa Ventura just southeast of town. In Copala, *combis* (microbuses) and *camionetas* (pickups) depart for Playa Ventura about every half hour (US$1.50, 30 minutes, 13km) from just east of the bus stop.

If you're driving, the signed turnoff to Playa Ventura is at Km 124, about 3km past Copala, to the southeast.

Playas La Bocana & Las Peñitas

The same buses that depart from Acapulco for Copala continue 13km east on Hwy 200 to **Marquelia** (population 6600; US$6.75, three hours). It's a market town with travelers' services, including several inexpensive hotels, and offers access to an immense stretch of beach backed by coco palms, which follows the coastline's contours for many kilometers in either direction.

From Marquelia's center you can take a *camioneta* (US$0.50 shared; US$2.75 private; 3km) to a section of the beach known as **Playa La Bocana**, where the Río Marquelia meets the sea and forms a lagoon. The lagoon has rich birdlife and makes for great morning exploration and bird-watching. Except during large swells, ocean swimming is excellent outside the breakers. La Bocana has some cabañas, as well as *comedores* (simple, inexpensive eateries) with hammocks that diners can spend the night in. Another portion of the beach, **Playa Las Peñitas**, is reached by a 5km road heading seaward from the east end of Marquelia. Las Peñitas has two small hotels and some cabañas that also offer camping spaces.

Cuajinicuilapa

☎ 741 / pop 9000

Cuajinicuilapa (kwah-hee-nee-kwee-*lah*-pah, usually shortened to Cuaji (*kwah*-hee), is the nucleus of Afro-mestizo culture on the Costa Chica and well worth a stop if you're at all interested in the mixed African-indigenous heritage that is unique to this region. Hwy 200 is the main drag in Cuaji, and gas, food and lodging are all available right off its dusty shoulders.

If you're only stopping for a few hours, be sure to visit the interesting **Museo de las Culturas Afromestizas** (Museum of Afro-mestizo Cultures; ☎ 414-03-10; cnr Manuel Zárate & Cuauhtémoc; admission US$0.50; ◱ 10am-2pm & 4-7pm Tue-Sun), a tribute to the history of African slaves in Mexico and, specifically, to local Afro-mestizo culture. Behind the museum are three examples of *casas redondas,* the round houses typical of West Africa that were built around Cuaji until as late as the 1960s. The museum is a block inland from the Banamex just west of the main plaza.

Hotel Lozano (☎ 414-07-08; Ignacio Zaragoza 19A; r US$17-34) is the best hotel in town, owned by the amiable Dr Enrique, the local dentist. It's half a block inland from Hwy 200, and the bathroom in its deluxe suite features a Jacuzzi and steam cabinet!

Las Siete Flores, near the bus terminal on the inland side of the highway, is a great, rickety *palapa* restaurant serving inexpensive daily specials for breakfast, lunch and dinner. The Thursday bowls of *pozole* are huge and delicious.

Coming from Acapulco, 2nd-class buses to Cuaji depart hourly, 3:30am to 6:30pm (US$7, 3½ hours, 200km), from Estrella Blanca's Central Ejido terminal.

Punta Maldonado

☎ 741 / pop 1100

The last beach worth checking out before crossing the Oaxacan border is at Punta Maldonado (also known as El Faro), a remote fishing village about 31km down a partially paved road from Hwy 200. It's a ramshackle little place, almost eerie in its isolation, at the base of dramatic cliffs on a small bay. The swimming is good, and the surfing, on occasion, is excellent; the break is a reef/point favoring lefts. Punta Maldonado has a few seafood restaurants on the beach. Its small hotel has suffered storm damage but may be open by the time you read this.

To reach Punta Maldonado by bus, you first must get to Cuajinicuilapa. Then take one of the *camionetas* that leave Cuaji every half hour or so (US$2, 45 minutes) from just off the main plaza. A taxi from Cuaji is also possible. If you're driving, the turnoff from Hwy 200 is just east of Cuaji. Unless the washed-out bridge a couple of kilometers in on this road is rebuilt, don't attempt the drive immediately following rains.

Oaxaca

The southern state of Oaxaca (wah-*hah*-kah) offers a delightful variety of physical and cultural landscapes. The state capital, Oaxaca city, lies inland at an altitude that gives it a relatively temperate climate. The city boasts marvelous colonial architecture and is the focal point for the region's renowned culinary tradition. Here art and artisanship reach heights seen in few other places in the country. Adding to the city's allure are the nearby ruins of Monte Albán, with their impressive temples and magnificent hilltop vistas.

An immensely scenic bus ride over the mountains connects Oaxaca city with the sultry, sybaritic coast, which has a beach for every budget and a wave for every level of surfing and swimming skill. Long-established beach spots such as Puerto Escondido, Puerto Ángel and Zipolite offer visitors a relaxed beach scene, with plenty of shady hammocks to laze in. For the more actively inclined, opportunities abound for spotting sea turtles, whales, dolphins, crocodiles and scads of bird species.

The eastern third of Oaxaca state is occupied by the hot, low-lying Isthmus of Tehuantepec. Of the areas covered in this chapter, this is where you'll see the greatest numbers of indigenous people (mostly Zapotecs), who make up a large percentage of the state's population. Inhabitants of the isthmus, known as *istmeños*, are fiercely independent (though utterly friendly), and have preserved many of their customs. Visitors to the region can catch glimpses of a Mexico that has all but vanished from many other parts of the country.

HIGHLIGHTS

- Watching the exhilarating spectacle of surfers tackle the Mexican Pipeline's perfect break in mellow **Puerto Escondido** (p244)
- Chilling on the beach at **Mazunte** (p263), between rounds of turtle- and dolphin-spotting
- Feasting your senses on the incomparable artistic and culinary delights of colonial **Oaxaca city** (p224)
- Bird-watching on tropical **Laguna de Manialtepec** (p253)
- Exploring the superb hilltop ruins and tombs of **Monte Albán** (p240), the ancient Zapotec capital
- Discovering the **Parque Nacional Lagunas de Chacahua** (p243), a coast studded with lagoons, pristine beaches and prolific bird and plant life

- AVERAGE JANUARY DAILY HIGH: OAXACA CITY: 25°C | 77°F, PUERTO ESCONDIDO: 32°C | 90°F
- AVERAGE JULY DAILY HIGH: OAXACA CITY: 28°C | 82°F, PUERTO ESCONDIDO: 35°C | 95°F

History

The Valles Centrales (Central Valleys) have always been the hub of Oaxacan life, and the pre-Hispanic cultures reached heights rivaling those of central Mexico. The hilltop city of Monte Albán became the center of the Zapotec culture, which extended its control over much of Oaxaca by conquest, peaking between AD 300 and AD 700. Monte Albán declined suddenly, for reasons still unknown; by about AD 750 it was deserted, as were many other Zapotec sites in the Valles Centrales. From about 1200, the surviving Zapotecs came under the growing power of the Mixtecs, renowned potters and metalsmiths from Oaxaca's northwest uplands. Mixtec and Zapotec cultures became entangled in the Valles Centrales before the Aztecs conquered them in the 15th and early 16th centuries.

The Spaniards had to send at least four expeditions before they felt safe enough to found the city of Oaxaca in 1529. Cortés donated large parts of the Valles Centrales to himself and was officially named Marqués del Valle de Oaxaca. In colonial times, the indigenous population dropped disastrously as a result of introduced diseases and mistreatment by the Spanish. The population of the Mixteca (the mountainous western region) is thought to have fallen from 700,000 at the time of the Spanish arrival to about 25,000 in 1700. Rebellions continued into the 20th century, but the indigenous peoples rarely formed a serious threat.

Benito Juárez, the great reforming leader of mid-19th-century Mexico, was a Zapotec. He served two terms as Oaxaca state governor before being elected Mexico's president in 1861.

Through the close of the 19th century, tobacco planters set up virtual slave plantations in northern Oaxaca, and indigenous communal lands were commandeered by foreign and mestizo (of mixed European and American Indian ancestry) coffee planters. After the Mexican Revolution, plantations were dissolved and about 300 *ejidos* (peasant land-holding cooperatives) were set up, effectively returning lands to the people who worked them. However, land ownership remains a source of conflict even today. With little industry,

OAXACA

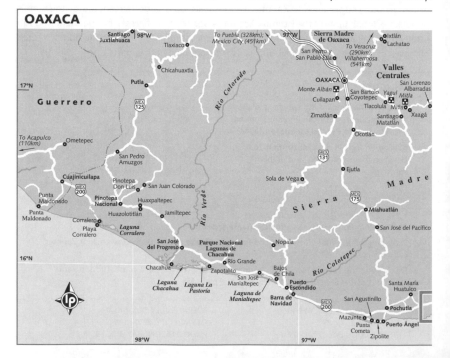

Oaxaca is one of Mexico's poorest states, and many of its residents leave to work in the cities or the USA. The situation is made worse in some areas, notably the Mixteca, by deforestation and erosion. Tourism is thriving in Oaxaca city and nearby villages and in a few places on the coast, but the backcountry remains largely underdeveloped.

The Land

The Sierra Madre del Sur (average height 2000m) runs parallel to the Pacific coast. It meets the Sierra Madre de Oaxaca (average height 2500m), which runs down from Mexico's central volcanic belt, roughly in the center of the state. Between them lie the three Valles Centrales, which converge at the city of Oaxaca. In Oaxaca city December and January are the coldest months, with average lows between 8°C and 9°C and highs around 25°C; March through May are the hottest months, with average highs around 30°C. The valleys are warm and dry, with most rain falling between June and September. The coast and low-lying areas are hotter and a bit wetter.

Situated in a region where temperate and tropical climatic zones and several mountain ranges meet, Oaxaca has spectacularly varied landscapes and a biodiversity greater than any other Mexican state. The inland highlands still have cloud forests and big stands of oak and pine, while lower-lying areas and Pacific-facing slopes support deciduous tropical forest.

Internet Resources

Oaxaca's Tourist Guide (oaxaca-travel.com) is an excellent photo-filled website with everything from information pertaining to beaches and hotels to regional recipes and biographies of famous Oaxacans. **Oaxaca's Forum** (bbs.oaxaca .com) is a bulletin board where you can look for rented accommodation or shared transport or ask any old question.

Dangers & Annoyances

Buses and other vehicles traveling along isolated stretches of highway, including the coastal Hwy 200 and Hwy 175 from Oaxaca city to Pochutla, are occasionally stopped and robbed. Though incidents have decreased in

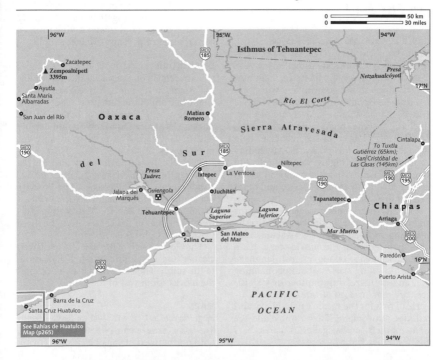

recent years, it's still advisable not to travel at night. Robberies aside, this is a good rule of thumb in all of Mexico, particularly on the winding mountain roads connecting the coast to Oaxaca city.

Getting There & Around

Oaxaca city has good bus links with Mexico City and Puebla to the north, and a few daily services to/from Veracruz, Villahermosa, Tuxtla Gutiérrez and San Cristóbal de Las Casas. Services between the city and the state's main coastal destinations are fairly frequent though mostly 2nd-class. Plenty of buses (again mostly 2nd-class) also travel the length of the Oaxacan coast along Hwy 200 from Acapulco and Chiapas.

Several daily flights link Oaxaca city with Mexico City. Further flights go east to Tuxtla Gutiérrez, Tapachula, Villahermosa and beyond. Small planes hop over the mountains between Oaxaca city and the coastal resorts Puerto Escondido and Bahías de Huatulco, which you can also reach direct from Mexico City.

OAXACA CITY

☎ 951 / pop 263,000 / elevation 1550m

Large numbers of foreigners, particularly Americans, visit the state capital every year. Oaxaca takes them all in its stride, maintaining its cosmopolitan atmosphere with a relaxed grace. Dry mountain heat, the colonial center's manageable scale, lovely architecture (including some phenomenal churches), broad shady plazas and leisurely cafés help slow the pace of life. The arts – including gastronomy – are highly valued here, and supremely talented locals are joined by others attracted from around Mexico and other parts of the world.

The city has some first-class museums and galleries, arguably the best handicrafts shopping in Mexico, and a vivacious cultural, culinary, bar and music scene. It's a popular venue for taking Spanish-language courses, cooking classes or simply hanging out, and an increasing number of US citizens are making a go of retiring here.

Head first for the zócalo (main plaza) and taste the atmosphere. Then ramble and see what markets, crafts, galleries, cafés, bars and festivities you run across.

History

The Aztec settlement here was called Huaxyácac (meaning 'In the Nose of the Squash'), from which 'Oaxaca' is derived. The Spanish laid out a new town around the existing zócalo in 1529. It quickly became the most important place in southern Mexico.

Eighteenth-century Oaxaca grew rich from exports of cochineal, a highly prized red dye made from tiny insects living on the prickly pear cactus in the Mixteca Alta, and from textile weaving. By 1796 it was probably the third biggest city in Nueva España, with about 20,000 people (including 600 clergy) and 800 cotton looms.

In 1854 an earthquake destroyed much of Oaxaca city. It wasn't until decades later, under the presidency of Porfirio Díaz, that Oaxaca began to grow again; in the 1890s its population exceeded 30,000. Then in 1931 another earthquake left 70% of the city uninhabitable.

Oaxaca's major expansion has come in the past 25 years, with tourism, new industries and rural poverty all encouraging migration from the countryside. The population of the city proper has almost doubled in this time, and together with formerly separate villages and towns it now forms a conurbation of perhaps 450,000 people.

Orientation

Oaxaca centers on the zócalo and the adjoining Alameda de León, a tree-lined promenade in front of the cathedral. Calle Alcalá, running north from the cathedral to the Iglesia de Santo Domingo (a universally known landmark), is pedestrian-only for three blocks.

The road from Mexico City and Puebla traverses the northern part of Oaxaca as Calz Niños Héroes de Chapultepec. The 1st-class bus station is on this road, 1.75km northeast of the zócalo. The 2nd-class bus station is almost 1km west of the center, near the main market, the Central de Abastos.

The blocks north of the zócalo are smarter, cleaner and less traffic-infested than those to the south. The commercial area occupies the blocks southwest of the zócalo.

MAPS

Inegi (Map pp226-7; ☎ 512-48-00; cnr Zapata & Escuela Naval Militar, Colonia Reforma; ☉ 8:30am-8:30pm Mon-Fri) On a northern extension of Netzahualcóyotl,

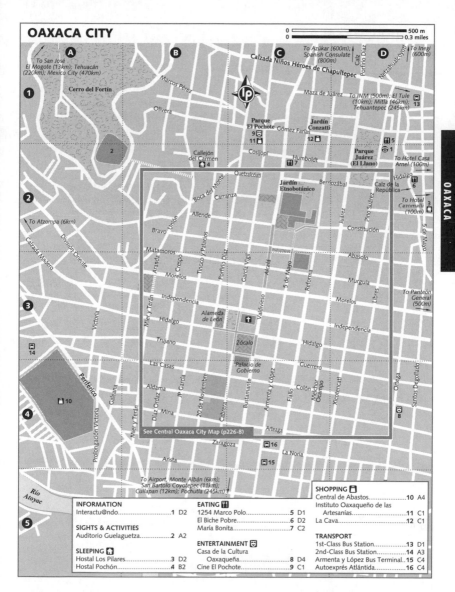

OAXACA CITY

Inegi sells a great range of topographical maps covering Oaxaca; you can also consult maps and census statistics for free.

Information
BOOKSTORES

Amate (Map pp226-7; ☎ 516-69-60; www.amatebooks .com; Plaza Alcalá, Alcalá 307-2; �•️ 10:30am-2:30pm & 3:30-7:30pm Mon-Sat) Probably the best English-language bookstore in all Mexico, stocking almost every Mexico-related title (in print) in English.

Librería Universitaria (Map pp226-7; ☎ 516-42-43; Guerrero 108; �•️ 9:30am-2pm & 4:30-8pm Mon-Sat) Located just off the *zócalo*, long-standing LU sells some English-language books about Oaxaca and Mexico, as well as maps and secondhand paperbacks.

CENTRAL OAXACA CITY

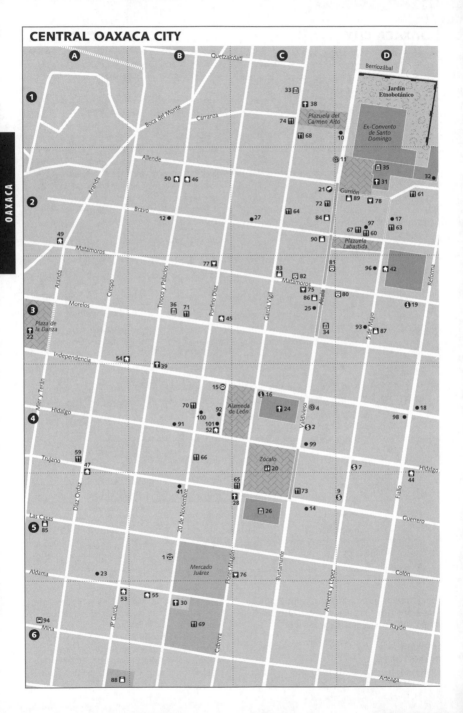

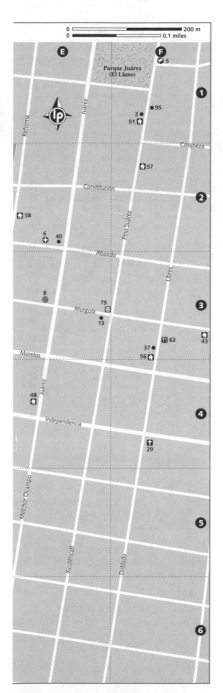

Notice boards (Map pp226-7; Plaza Gonzalo Lucero, Calle 5 de Mayo 412) Check these for ads for rental apartments, classes in everything from Spanish to yoga, and other interesting stuff. You'll also find useful notice boards in the language schools.

Oaxaca Times (www.oaxacatimes.com) Available at various places around town. Similar to Go-Oaxaca but in English only.

MEDICAL SERVICES

Clínica Hospital Carmen (Map pp226-7; ☎ 516-26-12; Abasolo 215; ⏰ 24hr) One of the town's best private hospitals, with emergency facilities and English-speaking doctors.

MONEY

There are plenty of banks and ATMs around the center. Banks with reasonable exchange rates include those listed.

Banamex (Map pp226-7; ☎ 514-57-47; Valdivieso 116; ⏰ 11am-6pm Mon-Fri)

HSBC (Map pp226-7; ☎ 516-19-67; cnr Armenta y López & Guerrero; ⏰ 8am-7pm Mon-Sat)

Consultoria Internacional (Map pp226-7; ☎ 514-91-92; Armenta y López 203C; ⏰ 8:30am-7pm Mon-Fri, 9am-2pm Sat) Changes cash euros, yen, sterling, Canadian dollars and Swiss francs too.

POST

Main post office (Map pp226-7; Alameda de León; ⏰ 8am-7pm Mon-Fri, 9am-1pm Sat)

TELEPHONE & FAX

There are many *casetas teléfonicas* (public telephone call stations) scattered about; those on Independencia and Trujano (Map pp226–7) offer fax service too.

ATSI (Map pp226-7; Calle 20 de Noviembre 402) Cheaper than pay phones for national long-distance calls and calls to Europe; offers fax service as well.

dspot (Map pp226-7; García Vigil 512D; ⏰ 9am-10pm) Behind La Biznaga restaurant; offers probably the cheapest foreign calls in town, via the Internet.

Interactu@ndo (Map p225; Pino Suárez 804) Calls to the USA are around US$0.40 per minute, US$0.80 to the rest of world.

TOILETS

Clean facilities (Map pp226–7) under the bandstand in the middle of the *zócalo* cost US$0.20.

TOURIST INFORMATION

Sectur (Map pp226-7; ☎ 576-48-28; www.aoaxaca.com; Murguía 206; ⏰ 8am-8pm) The state tourism department usually has someone who can speak English, but workers are often student volunteers with limited knowledge.

Municipal tourist kiosk (Map pp226-7; cnr García Vigil & Independencia; 10am-7pm)

TRAVEL AGENCIES

Turismo Joven (Map pp226-7; 514-22-20; www
.turismojoven.com; Alcalá 407, Local 19; 9am-7pm Mon-Sat) Books tours, issues ISIC cards and sells student air fares and trips to Cuba and elsewhere.

Dangers & Annoyances

It's best not to go up on Cerro del Fortín, the hill with the Auditorio Guelaguetza (Guelaguetza auditorium; Map p225), except for special events such as the Guelaguetza (p230). It's a well-known haunt of robbers.

Traffic can be horrendously slow during the morning and evening rush hours; the Periférico (Map p225) near the 2nd-class bus terminal is particularly bad.

Those traveling by bus (especially 2nd-class) between Oaxaca city and coastal destinations should keep a close eye on their personal possessions.

Sights
ZÓCALO, ALAMEDA & AROUND

Traffic-free, shaded by trees and surrounded by *portales* (arcades) with many cafés and eateries, the *zócalo* (Map pp226–7) is the perfect place to soak up the Oaxaca atmosphere. The adjacent Alameda, also traffic-free but without the cafés, is popular too.

The south side of the *zócalo* is occupied by the former **Palacio de Gobierno** (Map pp226-7), whose stairway mural by Arturo García Bustos depicts famous Oaxacans and Oaxacan history; the building was being converted to a museum at the time of research. The city's **cathedral** (Map pp226-7), begun in 1553 and finished (after several earthquakes) in the 18th century, stands just north of the *zócalo.*

Fine carved facades adorn two nearby colonial churches: **Iglesia de La Compañía** (Map pp226-7), just off the southwest corner of the *zócalo,* and the popular **Iglesia de San Juan de Dios** (Map pp226-7; Aldama at Calle 20 de Noviembre), whose first incarnation was finished in 1526, making it the oldest church site in Oaxaca.

Many colonial-era stone buildings have been cleaned up or restored on **Calle Alcalá** (Map pp226-7); its three pedestrian-only blocks make it a good route north from the *zócalo* to the Iglesia de Santo Domingo.

IGLESIA DE SANTO DOMINGO

Four blocks north of the cathedral, **Santo Domingo** (Map pp226-7; cnr Alcalá & Gurrión; 7am-1pm & 4-8pm) is the most splendid of Oaxaca's churches. It was built mainly between 1570 and 1608 as the city's Dominican monastery. The finest artisans from Puebla and elsewhere helped with its construction. Excluding the transept, nearly every square inch of the church's interior above floor level is decorated in 3-D relief: a base of white stucco bursts into elaborate gilt and colored designs that swirl around a profusion of painted figures. It all takes on a magically warm glow during candlelit evening Masses.

MUSEUMS

The excellent **Museo de las Culturas de Oaxaca** (Map pp226-7; 516-29-91; cnr Alcalá & Gurrión; admission US$3.75, over 60 & under 13 free; 10am-7pm Tue-Sun) occupies the beautifully restored ex-Convento de Santo Domingo, adjoining the Iglesia de Santo Domingo. These old monastery buildings were used as military barracks for more than 100 years until 1994, when they were handed over to the city of Oaxaca. The comprehensive museum takes you through the history and cultures of Oaxaca state up to the present day. One of its big draws is a priceless treasure trove discovered at Monte Albán in 1932, featuring beautifully worked silver, precious stones, pearls, crystal goblets, a skull covered in turquoise, and gold. Wrapping around the back of the museum is the **Jardín Etnobotánico** (Map pp226-7; 516-79-15; cnr Constitución & Reforma; admission free; tours in English 11am Sat, in Spanish 10am & 5pm Tue-Sat), a fascinating landscaped display of Oaxaca state plants, most of them cacti. Sign up at the entrance in advance (the day before or earlier).

The **Museo de Arte Contemporáneo de Oaxaca** (Map pp226-7; 514-22-28; Alcalá 202; admission US$1; 10:30am-8pm Wed-Mon) occupies a handsome colonial house built around 1700. Its changing exhibits feature recent art from around the world and work by leading modern Oaxacan artists such as Rufino Tamayo, Francisco Toledo, Rodolfo Morales, Rodolfo Nieto and Francisco Gutiérrez.

Museo Casa de Juárez (Juárez House Museum; Map pp226-7; 516-18-60; García Vigil 609; admission US$2.75; 10am-7pm Tue-Sun), opposite the Templo del Carmen Alto, is where Benito Juárez found work as a boy with a bookbinder. The orphaned Zapotec Indian went on to become president of Mexico in 1861. The renovated house shows how the early-19th-century Oaxacan middle class lived.

Museo Rufino Tamayo (Map pp226-7; 516-47-50; Morelos 503; admission US$3; 10am-2pm & 4-7pm Mon & Wed-Sat, 10am-3pm Sun), an excellent museum of Mexican pre-Hispanic artifacts, was donated to Oaxaca by its most famous artist, the Zapotec Rufino Tamayo (1899–1991).

BASÍLICA DE LA SOLEDAD

The image of Oaxaca's patron saint, the Virgen de la Soledad (Virgin of Solitude), resides in this 17th-century church (Map p225), about four blocks west of the Alameda along Independencia. The church, with a rich carved stone baroque facade, stands where the image is said to have miraculously appeared in a donkey pack a few centuries ago. In the mid-1990s, the Virgin's 2kg gold crown was stolen, along with the huge pearl and many of the 600 diamonds with which she was adorned.

Courses

Oaxaca is a terrific place to study, and the following schools have received complimentary reviews from some of our readers. The language schools can arrange accommodation.

LANGUAGE

Becari Language School (Map pp226-7; ☎ 514-60-76; www.becari.com.mx; Bravo 210; 15/20/30hr per week US$105/140/210) A medium-sized school with maximum class size of five. Start any Monday morning. There's a US$70 registration fee.

Oaxaca International (Map pp226-7; ☎ 514-72-24; www.oaxacainternational.com; Libres 207; US$80/113/175 a week or per hr $15/20/30) Includes a wide range of workshops with its lessons, from cooking and crafts to dance. Its offerings are tailored to student interest. Special programs for professionals are also offered.

COOKING

The following well-received classes are (or can be) held in English, and include market visits to buy ingredients.

La Casa de los Sabores (Map pp226-7; ☎ 516-57-04; www.lasbugambilias.com; Libres 205; 4hr class per person US$60) Pilar Cabrera, owner of La Olla restaurant, gives classes from 9:30am to 2pm on Wednesday and Friday at her guesthouse (p232) in central Oaxaca. Participants prepare and eat a five-course meal, usually including some vegetarian dishes. The price is reduced if you attend more than one class, or if more than 10 people attend.

La Casa de Mis Recuerdos (Map pp226-7; ☎ 515-56-45; www.misrecuerdos.net; Pino Suárez 508; classes from US$65) Nora Gutiérrez, from a family of celebrated Oaxacan cooks, conducts classes for groups of up to 10 at her family's charming B&B (p233). You prepare a Oaxacan lunch (planned a couple of days ahead), then sit down to eat it. The price depends on the number of participants and what they want to cook. Vegetarian classes are available.

Tours

A variety of tours foster closer contact with Mexican nature or Mexican communities; most reach destinations that few other visitors get to.

Bicicletas Pedro Martínez (Map pp226-7; ☎ 514-59-35; www.bicicletaspedromartinez.com; Aldama 418; ☺ 9am-7pm Mon-Sat) Offers a variety of rides, including four-hour jaunts (US$43) to the northern fringe of the city and two-day, all-inclusive bike-and-hike trips in outlying areas for US$188.

Expediciones Sierra Norte (Map pp226-7; ☎ 514-82-71; www.sierranorte.org.mx in Spanish; Bravo 210; ☺ 9am-3pm & 4-7pm Mon-Fri, 9am-2pm Sat) This very well-run rural community organization offers walking, mountain biking and accommodations in the beautiful Sierra Norte, northeast of the city.

Tierraventura (Map pp226-7; ☎ 501-13-63; www.tierraventura.com; Abasolo 217; ☺ 10am-3pm Mon-Sat) Run by a multilingual Swiss and German couple who take groups to some fairly remote destinations in Oaxaca state; there's a focus on hiking, nature, crafts, traditional

---

GUELAGUETZA GALA

In its full-scale form, the Guelaguetza (geh-la-*gets*-ah) is a brilliant feast of Oaxacan folk dance. It's held from 10am to 1pm on the first two Mondays after July 16, in the open-air Auditorio Guelaguetza (Map p225) on Cerro del Fortín. Thousands of people flock into Oaxaca for it and associated events, turning the city into a feast of celebration and regional culture (and a rich hunting ground for visiting pickpockets, so stay alert). On the appointed Mondays, known as Los Lunes del Cerro (Mondays on the Hill), magnificently costumed dancers from the seven regions of Oaxaca state perform a succession of dignified, lively or comical traditional dances, tossing offerings of produce to the crowd as they finish. The excitement climaxes with the incredibly colorful pineapple dance by women of the Papaloapan region, and the stately Zapotec Danza de las Plumas (Feather Dance), which reenacts, symbolically, the Spanish conquest.

Seats in the amphitheater (which holds perhaps 10,000) are divided into four areas called *palcos*. For Palcos A and B, the two nearest the stage, tickets (around US$38) go on sale online about three months beforehand (see www.aoaxaca.com/guelaguetza/en.htm for more information). Tickets guarantee a seat, but you should arrive before 8am if you want one of the better ones. The two much bigger rear *palcos*, C and D, are free and fill up early – if you get in by 8am you'll get a seat, but by 10am you'll be lucky to get even standing room. Wherever you sit, you'll be in the open air for hours, with no shelter, so equip yourself accordingly.

Many other events have grown up around the Guelaguetza. Highlights include the **Desfile de Delegaciones** (on Saturday afternoons preceding Guelaguetza Mondays), a parade of the regional delegations through the city center; and the **Bani Stui Gulal** (on Sunday evenings preceding Guelaguetza Mondays), a vibrant show of music, fireworks and dance telling the history of the Guelaguetza, in Plaza de la Danza by the Basílica de la Soledad. There are lots of concerts, exhibitions, sports events and a mezcal fair.

medicine and meeting locals, wherever possible working with local community tourism projects.

Several companies offer less adventurous day trips to outlying attractions. A typical three- or four-hour trip to Monte Albán costs around US$17. There are also agencies with a wide choice of itineraries:

Continental-Istmo Tours (Map pp226-7; ☎ 516-96-25; Alcalá 201)

Viajes Turísticos Mitla Hotel Rivera del Ángel (Map pp226-7; ☎ 516-61-75; Mina 518); Hostal Santa Rosa (Map pp226-7; ☎ 514-78-00; Trujano 201)

Festivals & Events

All major national festivals are celebrated here, and Oaxaca has some unique fiestas of its own, the biggest and most spectacular being the **Guelaguetza** (opposite).

There are many other festivities throughout the year.

Fiesta de la Virgen del Carmen (a week or more before July 16) The streets around the Templo del Carmen Alto on García Vigil become a fairground and the nights are lit by processions and fireworks.

Blessing of Animals (about 5pm, August 31) Pets are dressed up and taken to the Iglesia de La Merced (Map pp226–7), on Independencia.

Día de Muertos (November 2) Day of the Dead is a big happening here, with associated events starting several days in advance. These include music and dance at the main cemetery, the Panteón General (Map p225), on Calz del Panteón about 1.25km east of the *zócalo*.

Posadas (December 16-24) Nine night-time neighborhood processions symbolizing Mary and Joseph's journey to Bethlehem.

Día de la Virgen de la Soledad (December 18) Processions and traditional dances, including the Danza de las Plumas, at the Basílica de la Soledad (Map pp226–7).

Noche de los Rábanos (Night of the Radishes; December 23) Amazing figures carved from radishes are displayed in the *zócalo* (Map pp226–7). Sounds silly, but it's really neat.

Calendas (December 24) These Christmas Eve processions from local churches converge on the *zócalo* (Map pp226–7) about 10pm, bringing music, floats and fireworks.

Sleeping

Prices given here are for Oaxaca's high seasons, generally mid-December to mid-January, a week each side of Easter and Día de Muertos, and from mid-July to mid-August (dates vary from one establishment to another). Outside of these periods many places drop their prices by between 15% and 30%. Those in the hard-core budget bracket

---

AUTHOR'S CHOICE

Camino Real Oaxaca (Map pp226-7; ☎ 501-61-00, in the US & Canada 800-722-6466; www .caminoreal.com/oaxaca; Calle 5 de Mayo 300; r US$328-412; P ✗ ✗ ☎) Built in the 16th century as a convent, the majestic Camino Real served time as a prison, and was converted to a hotel in the 1970s. It has been designated a national treasure by the Mexican government and a historic monument by Unesco. The old chapel is a banquet hall, one of the five lovely courtyards contains an enticing swimming pool, and the bar is lined with books on otherworldly devotion. Beautiful thick stone walls help keep the place cool and add to the considerable atmosphere. The 91 rooms are well decorated in colonial styles, and have marble sinks, air-con, safes and good bathrooms.

---

tend to hold prices steady throughout the year. Street-side rooms everywhere tend to be noisy.

BUDGET

Oaxaca has more backpacker hostels than any other city in Mexico, and many budget hotels. Hostels in the following listings all have shared bathrooms.

Hostal Paulina (Map pp226-7; ☎ 516-20-05; www .paulinahostel.com; Trujano 321; dm US$12, s/d/tr/q US$27/29/43/57, all incl breakfast) Impeccably clean and efficiently run, this splendid 92-bed hostel provides bunk dorms for up to 11 people, and rooms with one double bed and a pair of bunks, all with lockers. There's a 4% discount if you have an HI or ISIC card. A neat little interior garden and a roof terrace add to the appeal. They should have free Internet for guests by the time you read this.

Hostal Luz de Luna Nuyoo (Map pp226-7; ☎ 516-95-76; mayoraljchotmail.com; Juárez 101; dm US$7, hammock or tent per person US$5) Readers continue to praise this friendly, medium-sized hostel run by a pair of Oaxacan musician brothers. Separate bunk rooms for women, men and couples (eight beds each) open on to a wide patio; you can hang a hammock or stay in the rooftop cabana. A few self-contained dogs add to the tranquil atmosphere, and there's a good shared kitchen.

Hostal Pochón (Map p225; ☎ 516-13-22; www.hostal pochon.com; Callejón del Carmen 102; dm US$7, d/tw

US$16/22; ☐) This hostel gets high marks from guests. It has six four-bed dorms and a couple of private rooms, a full kitchen, good common areas and no curfew, and offers bike rental, luggage storage, cheap phone calls and free Internet access. Beds are comfortable and the common areas brightly painted.

Hotel Posada El Chapulín (Map pp226-7; ☎ 516-16-46; hotelchapulin@hotmail.com; Aldama 317; s/d/tr/q US$24/27/29/38; ☐) This good, eight-room family-run hotel, perennially full of international backpackers, has a roof terrace, TV and fans in rooms. The owners are opening an overflow facility in nearby Zaachila (Map p225), where they'll take guests by van.

MIDRANGE
Oaxaca boasts some delightful midrange hotels and B&Bs, many of them in colonial or colonial-style buildings.

Las Bugambilias (Map pp226-7; ☎ 516-11-65, in the US 321-249-9422; www.lasbugambilias.com; Reforma 402; s US$70-85, d US$75-100, all with breakfast; ✂ ✗ ☐) This delightful B&B has nine rooms decorated with inspired combinations of folk and contemporary art. Some have air-con and/or a balcony; all have tiled bathrooms and fans. A big treat here is the gourmet two-course Oaxacan breakfast. Further attractions include a high-speed Internet connection, cheap international phone calls and an inviting roof terrace with fantastic views.

Hostal Casa del Sótano (Map pp226-7; ☎ 516-24-67; www.hoteldelsotano.net; Tinoco y Palacios 414; r US$71-92; ☐) This small, modern, quality hotel is very well done up in colonial style. The good-sized rooms are arranged along two elegant patios with fountains, little water gardens and pools, and have solid wooden furnishings, cable TV, phone and fan; some have balconies. The Sótano also has a restaurant and a high terrace with amazing views.

Hotel Las Golondrinas (Map pp226-7; ☎ 514-32-98; lasgolon@prodigy.net.mx; Tinoco y Palacios 411; s/d/tr US$39/43/52; ✗ ☐) Lovingly tended by friendly owners and staff, this fine small hotel has about 30 rooms that open out onto three beautiful, leafy labyrinthine patios. It's often full, so you should try to book ahead. None of the rooms is huge but all are tastefully decorated and immaculate. Good breakfasts (not included in room rates) are served in one of the patios. A very good value!

Hotel Posada Catarina (Map pp226-7; ☎ 516-42-70; Aldama 325; s US$34, d US$43-58; ☐) Posada Catarina is on a busy street southwest of the *zócalo*, but inside it's spacious and elegant with lush garden patios and a dramatic rooftop terrace. Rooms are clean and comfortable, if poorly ventilated. Readers love it.

Hotel Las Mariposas (Map pp226-7; ☎ 515-58-54; www.lasmariposas.com.mx; Pino Suárez 517; s/d US$35/40, studio apt s/d US$40/45, all with breakfast; ☐) Las Mariposas offers six studio apartments (with a small kitchen) and seven rooms. All are large, spotlessly clean and simply but prettily decorated. It's a tranquil, friendly and very secure place. Free wireless Internet access, a library, a kitchen for use by all guests, luggage storage and a good breakfast are among the many extras that make this a great deal.

Hotel Posada del Centro (Map pp226-7; ☎ 516-18-74; www.mexonline.com/posada.htm; Independencia 403; s/d US$46/50, with shared bathroom US$24/29; ℗) Attractive, centrally situated Posada del Centro has two large, verdant patios where breakfast is available. The 22 rooms have fans and pleasing Oaxacan artisanry; there's an ample roof terrace, and the staff are young, bright and helpful.

Hotel Azucenas (Map pp226-7; ☎ 514-79-18, 800-717-25-40, in US & Canada 800-882-6089; www.hotel azucenas.com; Aranda 203; s/d US$47/52) This small, welcoming, Canadian-owned hotel is in a beautifully restored colonial house. The 10 cool, white, tile-floored rooms are prettily designed, and a delicious buffet breakfast (US$3.75) is served on the lovely roof terrace. Street-side rooms may get early-morning noise.

Hotel Cazomalli (Map p225; ☎ 513-86-05; www.hotel cazomalli.com; El Salto 104; d/tr/q US$61/66/80; ☐) The welcoming, family-run Cazomalli, decked with tasteful Oaxacan artwork, is five minutes' walk from the 1st-class bus station, in quiet Colonia Jalatlaco. The 18 rooms all have safe, fan and hair dryer, and the roof terrace has lovely views. Breakfast is available.

La Casa de los Sabores (Map pp226-7; ☎ 516-57-04; www.lasbugambilias.com; Libres 205; s/d incl breakfast US$59/72; ✗ ☐) Sabores offers five individually decorated, high-ceilinged rooms with ultra-comfortable beds. Four of them are around the quiet patio in which owner Pilar Cabrera gives her twice-weekly cooking classes (see above). The breakfasts are large and gourmet, and the service attentive. A roof terrace provides a change of scene and the venue for the fifth room.

Hotel Casa Arnel (Map p225; ☎ 515-28-56; www .casaarnel.com.mx; Aldama 404, Colonia Jalatlaco; s/d from US$40/50, with shared bathroom US$12.50/25; ☐) Family-run Casa Arnel is 20 minutes northeast of the city center and five minutes' walk from the 1st-class bus station (head to the right on Calz Niños Héroes de Chapultepec, turn immediately right on Calle 5 de Mayo and watch for the signs). The clean, smallish rooms surround a big, leafy courtyard; many have very nice touches. The common areas – including hammock spots, a sundeck, and many semiprivate spaces – outshine the rooms themselves and have some great views. Arnel offers many travelers' services, including car rental.

Casa de la Tía Tere (Map pp226-7; ☎ 501-18-45; www.mexonline.com/tiatere.htm; Murguía 612; r incl continental breakfast US$71-92; P ☐ ☎) Tere has 12 large, uncluttered rooms with tiled floors, most around a vine-draped patio, some with balconies, all with good showers. There's a small gym, and this is one of few accommodations in central Oaxaca with a swimming pool. Tere also offers a large, clean kitchen and dining room for guests, laundry service and low-cost phone calls, plus free Internet and coffee.

Hotel Monte Albán (Map pp226-7; ☎ 516-27-77; hotelmontealban@prodigy.net.mx; Alameda de León 1; s interior/exterior US$43/52, d US$52/57) In a grand old high-ceilinged building smack on the Alameda de León, the MA is an atmospheric place all in all, though the fluorescent lighting and somewhat threadbare rooms diminish the romance. The cheaper, interior rooms are no great shakes, but the exterior rooms are large and have balconies or views of the cathedral. The hotel restaurant serves three meals and has nightly Guelaguetza shows.

TOP END
Top-end accommodations range from a converted convent to modern resort hotels.

La Casa de Mis Recuerdos (Map pp226-7; ☎ 515-56-45; www.misrecuerdos.net; Pino Suárez 508; s incl breakfast US$53-66, d incl breakfast US$83-96; ☒) A marvelous decorative aesthetic prevails throughout this guesthouse. Old-style tiles, mirrors, *milagros* (votives), masks, tinwork and all sorts of other Mexican crafts adorn the walls and halls. The best rooms overlook a fragrant central garden; two are air-conditioned and two have a shared bathroom. A large breakfast in the beautiful dining room is included in the price. Street-side room windows are double-glazed against noise, but you may still get some. There's a minimum stay of three nights.

Hostal Los Pilares (Map p225; ☎ 518-70-00; www .lospilareshostal.com; Curtidurías 721, Colonia Jalatlaco; s/d/ tr US$85/113/131; ☐ ☎) Opened in mid-2005, Pilares is a very well equipped, faux-colonial hotel. Rooms have plasma TVs (with SKY satellite reception), minibars, nice beds and attractive furniture. The hotel has garden-terrace dining, a bar, pool and Jacuzzi.

Casa de Sierra Azul (Map pp226-7; ☎ 514-84-12; www.mexonline.com/sierrazul.htm; Hidalgo 1002; r US$117-139) The Sierra Azul is a 200-year-old house converted to a beautiful small hotel, centered on a broad courtyard with a fountain and stone pillars. The 14 good-sized, tasteful rooms have high ceilings, old-fashioned furnishings and good tiled bathrooms.

Hostal Casa Antica (Map pp226-7; ☎ 51-26-73; www.hotelcasantica.com; Morelos 601; r US$97-121; ☒ ☐ ☎) The remodel and furnishings of this 200-year-old former convent sometimes work and sometimes don't. It's comfortable enough, with lots of exposed stone or brick in rooms, most of which have safes.

Eating
The menus at many of Oaxaca's restaurants, especially the higher-end places, have good English descriptions of the dishes.

ON & NEAR THE ZÓCALO
All the cafés and restaurants beneath the *zócalo* arches are great spots for watching Oaxaca life, but quality and service vary.

Terranova Café (Map pp226-7; ☎ 514-05-33; Portal Juárez 116, Bustamente; mains US$4.50-7.50) Terranova serves good breakfasts until 1pm (with a US$9 unlimited buffet on Sunday) and a variety of mostly Oaxacan and Mexican standards for lunch and dinner. Children's plates are on offer also.

El Asador Vasco (Map pp226-7; ☎ 514-47-55; Portal de Flores 10A; mains US$8-15; ☺ 1-11:30pm) Upstairs at the southwest corner of the *zócalo*, the Asador Vasco serves up good Oaxacan, Spanish and international food. It's strong on meat and seafood. For a table overlooking the plaza on a warm evening, book earlier in the day.

AUTHOR'S CHOICE

Restaurante Los Danzantes (Map pp226-7; ☎ 501-11-84; Alcalá 403; mains US$11-15; ❤ 1:30-11:30pm) Innovative Mexican food and a dramatic architect-designed setting make Los Danzantes one of the most exciting places to eat in Oaxaca. A formerly derelict colonial patio now sports high patterned walls of adobe brick, tall wooden columns and cool pools of water in an impeccably contemporary configuration, half open to the sky. Efficient and welcoming young staff serve up a short but first-class selection of food: you might start with a delicious salad or a *sopa de nopales con camarón* (prawn and prickly pear cactus soup) and follow it with pork ribs in plum sauce. Wine selections and desserts are very good, and the restaurant has its own lines of cigars and mezcal.

Mercado 20 de Noviembre (Map pp226-7; btwn Calle 20 de Noviembre & Cabrera; mains US$1.75-3) Cheap *oaxaqueño* meals can be had in this market south of the *zócalo*. Most of the many small *comedores* (inexpensive eateries) here serve up local specialties such as chicken in mole negro (cooked in a dark sauce of chilies, fruits, nuts, spices and chocolate). Pick one that's busy – they're worth the wait. Many *comedores* stay open until early evening, but their food is freshest earlier in the day.

WEST OF THE ZÓCALO

Café Alex (Map pp226-7; ☎ 514-07-15; Díaz Ordaz 218; mains US$3.25-4.50; ❤ 7am-10pm Mon-Sat, 7am-1pm Sun) Airy, full of people, clean and comfortable, Alex is a great place to fill up on good cheap food. Breakfast combinations are only part of the larger menu of traditional Oaxacan dishes.

Restaurant Colonial (Map pp226-7; ☎ 516-5193; Calle 20 de Noviembre 112; lunch US$3.50; ❤ 8am-5:30pm Mon-Sat) The Colonial's 10 or so tables fill up with locals for the good-value four-course *comida corrida* (set-price lunch menu), which includes soup, rice, a main course such as *pollo a la naranja* (chicken *à l'orange*), dessert and *aguas frescas* ('fresh waters' – pulped fruits and cornmeal or rice blended with water).

Fidel Pan Integral (Map pp226-7; Calle 20 de Noviembre 211; baked goods around US$0.30 to US$0.50; ❤ 9am-9:30pm Mon-Sat) Fidel is a brown-bread-lover's dream, serving whole-wheat cookies, *pandulces* (sweet breads) and even croissants.

NORTH OF THE ZÓCALO

Casa Oaxaca (Map pp226-7; ☎ 516-88-89; Constitución 104A; mains US$6-15; ❤ 1-11pm Mon-Sat) This is Oaxacan fusion at its finest. The chef here works magic by combining ingredients and flavors: witness the chayote and banana puree, or the 'cannelloni,' with thinly sliced jicama in place of pasta tube, surrounding a filling of grasshoppers and *huitlacoche* (corn truffle, a fungus that grows on maize). Presentation is outstanding as well, and all is enhanced by the courtyard setting and a good selection of wines. The only negative is that waiters will sometimes do a hard sell on food and wine.

La Olla (Map pp226-7; ☎ 516-66-68; Reforma 402; dishes US$2.50-9, menú del día US$7.50; ❤ 8am-10pm Tue-Sat, 9am-10pm Sun; ⓥ) This restaurant produces marvelous Oaxacan specialties, good whole-wheat *tortas* (Mexican-style sandwiches made with rolls), juices and salads made with organic lettuce. There are plenty of vegetarian choices, fine breakfasts (US$2.50 to US$4.50) and the *menú del día* (aka *menú*; lunch special) is a multicourse gourmet treat.

La Biznaga (Map pp226-7; ☎ 516-80-00; García Vigil 512; mains US$7-9.50; ❤ 1-10pm Mon-Sat, 2-8pm Sun) La Biznaga's cutting-edge ambience is the work of two brothers from the Distrito Federal (Federal District, which includes half of Mexico City). The courtyard is ringed with slick art, an eclectic music mix plays, and someone will take your order, eventually (for best results, sit close to the full bar). People rave about the *cocina mestiza* (mestizo cuisine) dishes here, including great salads made with organic produce, and fish, fowl and meat cleverly prepared and presented.

Zandunga (Map pp226-7; ☎ 044-951-156-27-02; cnr García Vigil & Carranza; mains US$5.50-6; ❤ 2-11pm Mon-Sat) Give *istmeño* (isthmian) cooking a preview here before you head off to Tehuantepec. The *cochito horneado* (baked pork) goes down easily, as do the *tamales de cambray* (stuffed with beef and chicken and cooked in a banana leaf) and other dishes. The corner location's warm decor includes grade-A artwork on the walls and low light. Service is friendly and low-key.

Café Los Cuiles (Map pp226-7; ☎ 514-82-59; Plaza de las Vírgenes, Plazuela Labastida 115-1; breakfast US$2.50-3.50, salad, soup & snacks US$1.50-3; ☺ 8am-10pm) With a handy central location and spacious lounge-gallery feel, Los Cuiles is an excellent spot for breakfast, outstanding organically grown, fair-traded coffee or light eats at any time of day. Sit inside and make use of the wi-fi Internet access, or enjoy the courtyard and its fountain.

María Bonita (Map p225; ☎ 516-72-33; cnr Alcalá & Humboldt; breakfast US$3-5, mains US$5.50-9; ☺ 8:30am-9pm Tue-Sat, 8:30-5pm Sun) Readers love the economical and tasty variety of traditional Oaxacan food here. Precede your mole (a dish with a chili-based sauce) with one of a good range of appetizers (US$3 to US$5.50) and soups, such as the *sopa xóchitl* (squash, squash blossom and sweet corn). The old building is on a noisy traffic corner, but the tasteful art on the walls and relaxed, unhurried service make it all OK.

Gaia (Map pp226-7; ☎ 516-70-79; Plaza de las Vírgenes, Plazuela Labastida 115-3; breakfast US$3.75-6, panini US$3.75, salads US$3; Ⓥ) Behind Café Los Cuiles, and sharing courtyard space with it, Gaia is a mellow café–juice bar serving many vegetarian dishes. Choose from breakfast combinations, panini, omelets, frittatas, excellent organic salads, pastas, and good cold veggie soups with yogurt. Plus a wide range of healthful and delicious juice blends, *licuados* (fruit blended usually with milk, sometimes just with ice) and smoothies (mostly US$2.75).

1254 Marco Polo (Map p225; ☎ 513-43-08; Pino Suárez 806; breakfast US$2.50-3, mains US$5-9.50; ☺ 8am-6pm Wed-Mon) Popular Marco Polo has a large garden dining area, attentive waiters and great food. The large breakfasts come with bottomless cups of coffee; from noon until closing, *antojitos* (snacks), seviches and oven-baked seafood are the main draws.

Coffee Beans (Map pp226-7; Calle 5 de Mayo 500C; coffee drinks US$1.25-2; ☺ 8am-midnight) This place roasts and brews some of the best coffee in town; it's strong, tasty and available in several forms, including a good variety of espresso drinks. It also serves an assortment of teas and some good desserts, cookies and the like in a relaxed atmosphere.

Comala (Map pp226-7; García Vigil 406; sandwiches US$3-5; ☺ 9am-11pm Mon-Sat) Comala's sandwiches are made with excellent bread (rolls or ciabatta) and contain ingredients like prosciutto, olives and mozzarella. The *hamburguesa de res* (US$5) is a big, juicy, filling burger, which probably won't leave you with any room for the salads and soups.

El Biche Pobre (Map p225; ☎ 513-46-36; cnr Calz de la República & Hidalgo; mains US$3-6.50; ☺ 8am-9pm Wed-Mon) El Biche Pobre, 1.5km northeast of the *zócalo*, is an informal place serving a range of Oaxacan food at about a dozen tables, some long enough to stage lunch for a whole extended Mexican family. For an introduction to local cuisine, you can't beat the US$6.50 *botana surtida*, a dozen assorted little items that add up to a tasty meal.

Restaurant Flor de Loto (Map pp226-7; ☎ 514-39-44; Morelos 509; mains US$3.25-5; Ⓥ) Flor de Loto makes a pretty good stab at pleasing a range of palates from vegan to carnivore. The chicken brochette (US$4.50) is a large and very tasty choice. Vegetarian options include spinach and soy burgers, and *vegetales al gratín* (vegetables with melted cheese). The US$4.50 *comida corrida* is quite a meal.

Cenaduría Tlayudas Libres (Map pp226-7; Libres 212; servings around US$3; ☺ 9 or 10pm-4:30am) Drivers double park along the entire block to eat here. Enormous tortillas *(tlayudas)* are folded over frijoles, *quesillo* (Oaxacan goat's cheese) and your choice of salsa, and crisped directly atop hot coals; you can add tough *tasajo* (strips of marinated beef) or spicy *salchicha* (pork

---

CHO-CO-*LA*-TE

Oaxacans love their chocolate. A bowl of the steaming hot liquid, served with porous sweet bread to dunk, is the perfect warmer when winter sets in 1500m above sea level. Hot milk or water is added to a blend of cinnamon, almonds, sugar and, of course, ground cacao beans. The area around the south end of Oaxaca's Mercado 20 de Noviembre has several shops specializing in this time-honored treat – and not just chocolate for drinking but also chocolate for moles, hard chocolate for eating, and more. You can sample chocolate with or without cinnamon, light or dark chocolate with varying quantities of sugar, and many other varieties at any of these places. And most of them have vats where you can watch the mixing.

sausage). It's a filling, tasty meal, but half the fun is taking in the great local, late-night scene as the cooks fan the street-side charcoal grills, raising showers of sparks.

Drinking

Tapas y Pisto (Map pp226-7; ☎ 514-40-93; Alcalá 403; ⏰ 5pm-2am Tue-Sun) Upstairs from Restaurante Los Danzantes and in keeping with its ultrasensual theme, T&P has a black light in the bar, and a rooftop terrace (well removed from the bar) with fabulous views.

Bar del Borgo (Map pp226-7; Matamoros 100-B; ⏰ 10am-1am) A very small but neatly arranged, semisubterranean space, the Borgo offers some unique street views and a jazzy, arty atmosphere. Check it out!

La Casa del Mezcal (Map pp226-7; Flores Magón 209; ⏰ 10am-1am) Open since 1935, this is one of Oaxaca's oldest bars, 1½ blocks south of the zócalo. It's a cantina, but a safe one. One room has a large stand-up bar and shelves full of mezcal (US$2 to US$3 a shot); the other room has tables where botanas are served. Most but not all patrons are men.

La Cucaracha (Map pp226-7; ☎ 501-16-36; Porfirio Díaz 301A; ⏰ 7pm-2am Mon-Sat) A good place to make acquaintance with some classic Mexican beverages, this specialist bar pours 40 varieties of mezcal, including fruit-flavored types and shots from jugs holding scorpions awash in the stuff. A six-flavor sampler runs US$9.50, while shots are US$2 and US$4. Various tequilas are on offer also. Everyone's welcome here, food is available, and on Friday and Saturday a small disco operates in one corner, with live Latin music (trova, rancheras and boleros) in another.

Entertainment

Live Music

Candela (Map pp226-7; ☎ 514-20-10; Murguía 413; admission US$2-3 Tue & Wed, US$5 Thu-Sat; ⏰ 1pm-2am Tue-Sat) Candela's writhing salsa band and beautiful colonial-house setting have kept it at the top of Oaxaca nightlife for over a decade. Arrive fairly early (9:30pm to 10:30pm) to get a good table, and either learn to dance or learn to watch. Candela is a restaurant too, with a good lunchtime menú (US$4). Tuesday and Wednesday are mellow trova (folk music) nights, but salsa, merengue and cumbia (a style of music and dance that originated in Colombia) take over Thursday through Saturday.

La Tentación (Map pp226-7; ☎ 514-95-21; Matamoros 101; admission US$4; ⏰ 9pm-2am Tue-Sun) This venue can be erratic, but when it gets up a good head of steam, everyone has a great time. This is most likely to happen on Friday and Saturday, when you can move to live salsa, merengue and cumbia. The DJ'd weeknights tend to be lame.

Other places with regular live music include **La Cucaracha** (left) and **Azúkar** (Map p225; ☎ 513-11-70; cnr Calz Porfirio Díaz & Escuela Naval Militar; ⏰ Thu-Sat), about six blocks north of Calz Niños Héroes de Chapultepec in Colonia Reforma. It alternates between live salsa and other música tropical and DJs spinning house, techno and electronica. The banda (Mexican big-band music) club next door, La Mata, provides large doses of quintessentially Mexican music.

Free **concerts** in the zócalo are given several evenings each week at 7pm, and at 12:30pm on Wednesday and Sunday, by the state marimba (wooden xylophone) ensemble or state band.

Bars & Clubs

La Divina (Map pp226-7; ☎ 582-05-08; Gurrión 104; ⏰ 5pm-1am Tue-Sun) Loud, busy La Divina has a disco-esque interior and music from Spanish-language rock and house to English pop. A mixed-nationality crowd generates a warm atmosphere that spills out on to the street if you're lucky. Drinks start at around US$2.

The bar at **La Biznaga** (p234) is an utterly cool spot for drinks.

Cinema, Theatre & Dance

Cine El Pochote (Map p225; ☎ 514-11-94, 516-69-80; García Vigil 817; admission free, donations accepted; ⏰ screenings 6pm & 8pm Tue-Sun) El Pochote shows independent, art-house and classic Mexican and international movies (the latter in their original language with Spanish subtitles). There's usually a different theme each month. To reach it, duck under the old aqueduct into Parque El Pochote.

Casa de Cantera (Map pp226-7; ☎ 514-75-85; Murguía 102; admission US$14; ⏰ 8:30pm) A lively mini-Guelaguetza is staged here nightly in colorful costume with live music. To make a reservation, phone or stop by during the afternoon. Food and drinks are available.

The **Centro Cultural Ricardo Flores Magón** (Map pp226-7; ☎ 514-62-93; Alcalá 302) and the **Casa de la**

Cultura Oaxaqueña (Map p225; ☎ 516-24-83; Ortega 403) both stage musical, dance, theater and art events several evenings and a few mornings a week. These are largely nontouristic events and many of them are free; drop by to see the programs.

Shopping

The state of Oaxaca has the richest, most inventive folk-art scene in Mexico, and the city is its chief marketplace. You'll find the highest-quality crafts mostly in the smart stores on and near Calle Alcalá, Calle 5 de Mayo and García Vigil, but prices are lower in the markets. Some artisans have grouped together to market their own products directly (see right).

Special crafts to look out for include the distinctive black pottery from San Bartolo Coyotepec; blankets, rugs and tapestries from Teotitlán del Valle; *huipiles* (indigenous women's tunics) and other Oaxacan indigenous clothing; pottery figures from Ocotlán; and stamped and colored Oaxacan tin. Jewelry is also made and sold here, and you'll find pieces using gold, silver or precious stones, but prices are a bit higher than in Mexico City or Taxco. Many shops can mail things home for you.

Just as fascinating as the fancy craft stores is Oaxaca's commercial area, which stretches over several blocks southwest of the *zócalo*. Oaxacans flock here, and to the big Central de Abastos market, for all their everyday needs.

MARKETS

Mercado de Artesanías (Crafts Market; Map pp226-7; cnr JP García & Zaragoza) This sizable indoor crafts market is strong on pottery, rugs and textiles. As you walk through, you're likely to see many of the vendors passing the time

by plying their crafts, such as weaving or embroidering.

Central de Abastos (Supplies Center; Map p225; Periférico) The enormous main market, on the western edge of the city center, is a hive of activity every day, though Saturday is the biggest day. If you look long enough, you can find almost anything here. Each type of product has a section to itself, and you can easily get lost in the profusion of household goods, CDs, *artesanía* (handicrafts) and overwhelming quantities of every sort of produce grown from the coast to the mountaintops.

CRAFT SHOPS

MARO (Map pp226-7; ☎ 516-06-70; Calle 5 de Mayo 204; �ّ 9am-8pm) This is a sprawling store with a big range of good work (such as woven-to-order rugs) at good prices, all made by the hundreds of members of the MARO women artisans' cooperative around Oaxaca state.

Instituto Oaxaqueño de las Artesanías (Map p225; ☎ 514-40-30; www.oaxaca.gob.mx/ioa; García Vigil 809; ☙ 9am-8pm Mon-Fri, 10am-5pm Sat, 10am-1pm Sun) Government-run IOA offers a large variety of beautiful craft items, including some gorgeous textiles.

La Mano Mágica (Map pp226-7; ☎ 516-42-75; www.lamanomagica.com; Alcalá 203; ☙ 10:30am-3pm & 4-8pm Mon-Sat) They sell some wonderfully original and sophisticated craft products here, including work by master weaver Arnulfo Mendoza.

Casa de las Artesanías de Oaxaca (Map pp226-7; ☎ 516-50-62; Matamoros 105; ☙ 9am-9pm Mon-Sat, 10am-6pm Sun) This store sells the work of 80 family workshops and crafts organizations from around Oaxaca state. Its patio is surrounded by several rooms full of varied crafts.

Oro de Monte Albán (Map pp226-7; ☎ 516-45-28; www.orodemontealban.com); Plaza Alcalá (Alcalá 307);

GOOD TO THE LAST DROP

Central Oaxaca state – especially around Santiago Matatlán and the Albarradas group of villages, south and east of Mitla – produces probably the best mezcal in Mexico (and therefore the world). Just like its cousin tequila, mezcal is made from the maguey plant and is usually better when *reposado* or *añejo* (aged). There are also some delicious *crema* varieties with fruit or other flavors.

Several Oaxaca shops southwest of the *zócalo* specialize in mezcal. Try **El Rey de los Mezcales** (Map pp226-7; Las Casas 509) or look along Aldama, JP García or Trujano. Around US$11 will buy you a decent bottle but some US$4 mezcals are also fine. For some export-quality mezcals from Santiago Matatlán (up to US$55), head to **La Cava** (Map p225; ☎ 515-23-35; Gómez Farías 212B; ☙ 10am-3pm & 5-8pm Mon-Sat), north of the center. It has a good selection of wines, too.

Taller (workshop, Gurrión C) This firm's goldsmiths produce high-class jewelry in gold, silver and semiprecious stones, including copies of pre-Hispanic jewelry and pieces inspired by colonial-era designs. It has multiple locations on Calle Alcalá and one at Monte Albán itself. The workshop tour (in Spanish) is very interesting and includes a demonstration of lost-wax casting.

Getting There & Away

AIR

Most international flights to Oaxaca city (airport code OAX) connect through Mexico City. Direct flights to/from Mexico City (one hour) are operated by Mexicana at least four times daily and Aviacsa once, while Azteca flies once a day except Thursday. Continental has daily flights to/from Houston, Texas.

For the spectacular half-hour hop over the Sierra Madre del Sur to Puerto Escondido and Bahías de Huatulco on the Oaxaca coast, Aerotucán (with a 13-seat Cessna) flies daily to/from both destinations, with fares to either around US$100 one way. Aerovega flies a seven-seater daily to/from Puerto Escondido (US$90 one-way) and to/from Bahías de Huatulco (US$100).

AIRLINE OFFICES

Aeroméxico (Map pp226-7; ☎ 516-10-66; Hidalgo 513; ✆ 9am-7pm Mon-Fri, 9am-5:30pm Sat)

Aerotucán (Map pp226-7; ☎ 501-05-30; Alcalá 201, Interior 204)

Aerovega (Map pp226-7; ☎ 516-49-82; aerovega@ prodigy.net.mx; Alameda de León 1; ✆ 9am-8pm Mon-Fri, 9am-5pm Sat)

Aviacsa Centro (Map pp226-7; ☎ 513-72-14; Pino Suárez 604); Airport (☎ 511-50-39)

Azteca (☎ 01-800-229-83-22)

Mexicana Centro (Map pp226-7; ☎ 516-73-52; Fiallo 102); Airport (☎ 511-52-29)

BUS

The **1st-class bus station** (Terminal de Autobuses de Primera Clase or Terminal ADO; Map p225; ☎ 515-12-48; Calz Niños Héroes de Chapultepec 1036) is 2km northeast of the *zócalo*. It's used by, among others, UNO and ADO GL (deluxe lines); the 1st-class lines ADO and Cristóbal Colón (OCC); and 2nd-class Sur buses. The **2nd-class bus station** (Terminal de Autobuses de Segunda Clase; Map p225; Trujano) is 1km west of the *zócalo*; the main companies serving the coast and Isthmus of Tehuantepec from it are **Estrella del Valle/ Oaxaca Pacífico** (EV/OP; ☎ 516-54-29); **Fletes y Pasajes** (Fypsa; ☎ 516-22-70); **Estrella Roja** (ER; ☎ 516-06-94) and **Transportes Oaxaca-Istmo** (TOI; ☎ 516-36-64). Some of EV/OP's services stop at the **Armenta y López terminal** (Map p225; ☎ 501-02-88; Armenta y López 721), 500m south of the *zócalo*, after leaving the 2nd-class terminal.

It's advisable to buy your ticket a day or two in advance for some of the less frequent

---

THE LONG & WINDING ROAD

Three main paved routes connect Oaxaca city and the Pacific coast:

■ **Hwy 175** A spectacular, winding road passing through Miahuatlán to Pochutla (about seven hours by 2nd-class bus, 245km), the jumping-off point for Puerto Ángel, Zipolite and other nearby beaches. Mind your wallet and carry-on luggage, as thieves work this route.

■ **Hwy 190** First-class buses use this, the longest, smoothest route. They take about five hours to reach Hwy 200 at the coast near Salina Cruz, then head west to Bahías de Huatulco (eight hours total), Pochutla (nine to 10 hours, 450km) and on to Puerto Escondido (10 to 12 hours).

■ **Hwy 131** A few decent 2nd-class buses travel directly to Puerto Escondido (six to eight hours, 250km) via this road, which is scenic but poorly maintained in parts, with many potholes.

The most picturesque route is Hwy 175, climbing high into mountainous pine forests then dropping precipitously to the coast. All in all, it's the happy, quick and affordable medium; however, some bus and van drivers take its many curves nauseatingly fast. Many seasoned travelers tell tales of fear and barfing; others report having no problems. When choosing among the routes, consider your destination, budget, schedule and intestinal fortitude (literally and figuratively). Traveling by day is recommended, for general road safety, sightseeing value, security and to avoid motion sickness. Be aware that Hwys 131 and 175 are particularly susceptible to landslides in periods of heavy rain (most likely from June through October).

services, especially in high season. **Ticket Bus** (Calle 20 de Noviembre Map pp226-7; ☎ 514-66-55; Calle 20 de Noviembre 103D; ◷ 8am-10pm Mon-Sat, 8am-9pm Sun; Valdivieso Map pp226-7; ☎ 516-38-20; Valdivieso 2A; ◷ same), in the city center, sells tickets for many 1st-class lines. See the boxed text on opposite for information on bus routes to the coast.

Other daily bus departures from Oaxaca: **Mexico City** (US$32-42, 6hr, 47 daily from 1st-class terminal); Fypsa (US$19, 6hr, 3 daily) Most go to Terminal Oriente (TAPO), and a few to Terminal Sur or Terminal Norte. **Pochutla** OCC (US$20, 9-10hr, 5 daily, via Hwys 190 & 200); EV/OP (US$7.50, 7hr, 10 *ordinarios*; US$8.50-9, 6hr, 3 *directos* at 9:45am, 2:45pm and 10:30pm, all via Hwy 175) **Puebla** ADO/ADO GL (US$25-29, 4½hr, 12 daily from 1st-class terminal) **Puerto Ángel** EV/OP (US$7, 7½hr, 1 nightly at 11:15pm) **Puerto Escondido** OCC (US$21, 10hr, 5 daily, via Hwys 190 & 200); EV/OP (US$8.50, 8½hr, 10 *ordinario*; US$10-10.50, 7½hr, 3 *directo* at 9:45am, 2:45pm, and 10:30pm; all via Hwys 175 & 200); ER (US$9.50, 6½-7hr, 5 daily, via Hwy 131) **Santa Cruz Huatulco** OCC/ADO-GL (US$19/25, 8hr, 6 daily, via Hwys 190 & 200); EV/OP (US$10.50, 8hr, 1 nightly at 10pm, via Hwys 175 & 200) **Tehuantepec** (US$12, 4½hr, 16 1st-class daily from 1st-class terminal; Sur (US$11, 4½hr, 7 daily); TOI (US$7.50, 5½hr, 13 daily)

CAR & MOTORCYCLE

See the boxed text on opposite for information on roads to the coast.

Car tolls from Mexico City to Oaxaca on Hwys 150D and 135D total US$30; the trip takes about six hours. Highway 135D is signed as 131D for some stretches. The main toll-free alternative, via Huajuapan de León on Hwy 190, takes several hours longer.

There are several rental-car agencies in Oaxaca. Prices can start as low as US$35 a day, including tax and insurance, for an old-style VW Beetle without air-con. **Alamo** Centro (Map pp226-7; ☎ 514-85-34; Calle 5 de Mayo 203); Airport (☎ 511-62-20) **Budget** (Map pp226-7; ☎ 516-44-45; Calle 5 de Mayo 315A); Airport (☎ 511-52-52) **Hertz** Centro (Map pp226-7; ☎ 516-24-34; Plaza de las Vírgenes, Plazuela Labastida 115); Airport (☎ 511-54-78)

VAN

Autoexprés Atlántida (Map p225; ☎ 514-70-77; La Noria 101) runs 14-seat, air-conditioned vans nine times daily via Hwy 175 to Pochutla (US$11.50, 6½ hours); try to reserve a seat up front.

Getting Around

TO/FROM THE AIRPORT

Oaxaca airport is 6km south of the city, 500m off Hwy 175. Transporte Terrestre *combis* (minibuses) from the airport will take you to anywhere in the city center for US$2.75. Catching a cab outside the terminal should cost between US$9.50 and US$11.50, depending on your destination. A ticket taxi desk at the south end of the terminal charges US$12 if you want to avoid possible hassles.

You can book a *combi* seat from the city to the airport (US$2.75), a day or more ahead, at **Transportes Aeropuerto** (Map pp226-7; ☎ 514-43-50; Alameda de León 1G; ◷ 9am-2pm & 5-8pm Mon-Sat).

BICYCLE

Two full-service establishments rent excellent mountain bikes: **Bicicletas Pedro Martínez** (Map pp226-7; ☎ 514-59-35; Aldama 418; per day US$11.50) and **Zona Bici** (Map pp226-7; ☎ 516-09-53; García Vigil 406; US$12 per day, per hr US$2.50). Rentals at both incorporate helmet, lock and tools.

BUS & TAXI

Most points of importance in the city are within walking distance of each other, but you might want to use city buses (US$0.30) to/from the bus stations.

From the 1st-class bus station, a westbound 'Juárez' bus will take you down Juárez and Melchor Ocampo, which are three blocks east of the *zócalo*; a 'Tinoco y Palacios' bus will take you down Tinoco y Palacios, which is two blocks west of the *zócalo*. To return to the bus station, take an 'ADO' bus north up Xicoténcatl (which becomes Pino Suárez), four blocks east of the *zócalo*, or up Díaz Ordaz (which becomes Crespo), three blocks west of the *zócalo*.

Buses between the 2nd-class bus station and the center make their way slowly along congested streets. 'Centro' buses head toward the center along Trujano, then turn north up Díaz Ordaz. Going out to the 2nd-class bus station, 'Central' buses head south on Tinoco y Palacios, then west on Las Casas.

A taxi anywhere within the central area, including the bus and train stations, costs about US$2.75.

OAXACA

DETOUR: MONTE ALBÁN

The ancient Zapotec capital of **Monte Albán** (☎ 951-516-12-15; admission US$3.75; 8am-6pm) stands on a flattened hilltop 400m above the valley floor, just a few kilometers southwest of Oaxaca. It's one of the most impressive ancient sites to be found in Mexico, and it has the most spectacular 360-degree views. Its name, pronounced 'mohn-teh ahl-*bahn*,' means White Mountain.

At the site's entrance are a very good museum (with artifacts from the site, including several skulls and a re-created burial; explanations in Spanish only), a café, a bookstore and an Oro de Monte Albán (p237) jewelry store. Official guides offer their services, in Spanish, English, French and Italian, outside the ticket office (about US$20 for a small group). Parts of the site are wheelchair-accessible. A good scale model of the site, with a handy north point, lies just past the entrance turnstiles.

HISTORY

Monte Albán was first occupied around 500 BC, probably by Zapotecs. It probably had early cultural connections with the Olmecs to the northeast.

Archaeologists divide Monte Albán's history into five phases. The years up to about 200 BC (phase Monte Albán I) saw the leveling of the hilltop, the building of temples and probably palaces, and the growth of a town of 10,000 or more people on the hillsides. Hieroglyphs and dates in a dot-and-bar system carved during this era may well mean that the elite of Monte Albán were the first to use writing and a written calendar in Mexico. Between 200 BC and about AD 300 (Monte Albán II) the city came to dominate more and more of Oaxaca. Buildings of this period were typically made of huge stone blocks and had steep walls.

The city was at its peak from about AD 300 to 700 (Monte Albán III), when the main and surrounding hills were terraced for dwellings, and the population reached about 25,000. Most of what we see now dates from this time. Monte Albán was the center of a highly organized, priest-dominated society, controlling the extensively irrigated Valles Centrales, which held at least 200 other settlements and ceremonial centers. Many Monte Albán buildings were plastered and painted red, and *talud-tablero* (a stepped building style with alternating vertical and sloping sections) architecture indicates influence from Teotihuacán. Nearly 170 underground tombs from this period have been found. Skulls with holes drilled, cut or scraped into them have been found in more than 20 burials here – thought to be evidence of medical treatments unique in ancient Mexico.

Between about AD 700 and 950 (Monte Albán IV), the place was abandoned and fell into ruin. Monte Albán V (AD 950–1521) saw minimal activity, except that Mixtecs arriving from northwestern Oaxaca reused old tombs here to bury their own dignitaries.

SIGHTS

Gran Plaza

About 300m long and 200m wide, the **Gran Plaza**, was the center of Monte Albán. Its visible structures are mostly from the peak Monte Albán III period. Some were temples, others residential. The following description takes you clockwise around the plaza. Many of the structures in and around the plaza are cordoned off to prevent damage by too many visitors' feet.

The stone terraces of the deep, I-shaped **Juego de Pelota** (Ball Court), constructed about 100 BC, were probably part of the playing area, not stands for spectators. The **Pirámide** (Edificio P) was topped by a small pillared temple and was probably an observatory of some sort. At the bottom of its staircase a very low tunnel leads into a tomb. The **Palacio** (Palace) bears atop it a patio surrounded by the remains of typical Monte Albán III residential rooms.

The big **Plataforma Sur** (South Platform), with its wide staircase, is still good for a panorama of the plaza and the surrounding mountains, and has some carvings at the corner of its eastern base. **Edificio J**, an arrowhead-shaped building constructed about 100 BC and riddled with tunnels and staircases (unfortunately you can't go inside), stands at an angle of 45° to the other Gran Plaza structures and was an observatory. Figures and hieroglyphs carved on its walls record Monte Albán's military conquests of other towns.

Edificio O, at the front of **Sistema M** (a patio-temple-altar complex from the Monte Albán III phase), was added to an earlier structure in an apparent attempt to conceal the plaza's lack of symmetry. (The rock mounds supporting the Plataforma Sur and Plataforma Norte are not directly opposite each other.)

Edificio L is an amalgam of the Monte Albán I building that contained the famous Danzante carvings and a later structure built over it. The **Danzantes** (Dancers), some of which are seen around the lower part of the building, are thought to depict leaders of conquered neighboring people. Carved between 500 and 100 BC, they generally have open mouths (sometimes downturned in Olmec style) and closed eyes. Some have blood flowing where their genitals have been cut off. Hieroglyphs accompanying them are the earliest known examples of true writing in Mexico.

Sistema IV, the twin to Sistema M, combines typical Monte Albán II construction with overlays from Monte Albán III and IV.

Plataforma Norte

The **North Platform**, over a rock outcrop, is almost as big as the Gran Plaza, and offers the best views overall. It was rebuilt several times over the centuries. Chambers on either side of the main staircase contained tombs, and columns at the top of the stairs supported the roof of a hall. Atop the platform is a ceremonial complex built between AD 500 and 800; points of interest here include the **Patio Hundido** (Sunken Patio), with an altar at its center, **Edificios D, VG** and **E** (which were topped with adobe temples) and the **Templo de Dos Columnas**. Stele **VGE-2**, on the southern side of Edificio E, shows members of Monte Albán's ruling class around AD 800 – four women and a fifth figure represented by a jaguar.

Tombs

Most of Monte Albán's ancient tombs are usually closed to visitors to help their preservation. But if you're lucky you might be able to peer into one of the following.

Behind Plataforma Norte, **Tumba 104** dates from AD 500 to AD 700. Above the tomb's underground entrance is an urn in the form of Pitao Cozobi, the Zapotec maize god, wearing a mask of Cocijo, the rain god whose forked tongue represents lightning. The walls are covered with colorful Teotihuacán-style frescoes. The figure on the left wall is probably the Zapotec flayed god and god of spring, Xipe Tótec; on the right wall, wearing a big snake-and-feather headdress, is Pitao Cozobi again.

Tumba 7, just off the main parking lot, was built around AD 800, beneath a dwelling. In the 14th or 15th century it was reused by Mixtecs to bury a dignitary, two sacrificed servants and one of the richest ancient treasure hoards in the Americas, the famed Mixtec treasure, now in the Museo de las Culturas de Oaxaca (p229).

Behind the Juego de Pelota Chica (Small Ball Court), **Tumba 105** features decaying Teotihuacán-influenced murals showing a procession of figures that may represent nine gods of death or night and their female consorts. It lies beneath one of Monte Albán's biggest palace-residences, built between AD 500 and AD 800.

Getting There & Away

Autobuses Turísticos (Map pp226-7; ☎ 951-516-53-27) runs buses to the site from Hotel Rivera del Ángel, at Mina 518 in Oaxaca, six blocks (a 10- to 15-minute walk) southwest of the *zócalo*. The buses leave every hour from 8:30am to 3:30pm (details of the schedule change from time to time). The ride up takes 20 minutes. The US$3 fare includes a return trip at a designated time, giving you about two hours at the site. If you want to stay longer, you must hope for a spare place on a later return bus and pay a further US$1.50. The last bus back leaves Monte Albán at 6pm.

A taxi from Oaxaca to Monte Albán costs about US$8, but coming down you may have to pay more. Walking up from the city center takes about 1½ hours.

OAXACA

OAXACA COAST

The once-remote Oaxaca coast has seen tourism rise as connections with the outside world improve. The fishing villages and former coffee ports of Puerto Escondido and Puerto Ángel have turned into minor resorts, but they remain relatively small and relaxed – Puerto Ángel especially so. Puerto Escondido has famous surf, while Puerto Ángel is at the center of a series of wonderful beaches with plenty of low-cost accommodations. Some of these – including the fabled backpackers' hangout, Zipolite – are gradually turning into resorts of sorts themselves. To the east, a new tourist complex on Bahías de Huatulco is being developed with *some* respect for the area's lovely surroundings. West of Puerto Escondido, nature lovers can visit the lagoons of Manialtepec and Chacahua, which teem with birdlife.

The coast is hotter and much more humid than the highlands. Most of the year's rain falls between June and September, turning everything green. From October the landscape starts to dry out, and by March many of the trees – which are mostly deciduous – are leafless. May is the hottest month.

The coast is described from west to east, except for the towns around Pochutla (including Puerto Ángel, Zipolite and Mazunte), which are described in the order you reach them when coming from that transport hub.

Internet Resources

Pacific Coast of Oaxaca (www.tomzap.com) This site is a mine of information about the coast.

Sleeping

The peak tourism seasons on this coast are from mid-December to mid-January, Semana Santa (Holy Week), and the months of July and August. At other times hotel prices may come down anywhere between 10% and 50% from the prices we list.

Dangers & Annoyances

Though incidents have decreased greatly in recent years, there have been cases of highway robbery along Hwy 200 from Pochutla north to Acapulco, as well as on Hwy 175 between Oaxaca and the coast.

Much of coastal Oaxaca is cattle country, and the numbers of cows (and burros and horses) wandering loose on the highway at all hours give new meaning to the term 'free range.' Both robbery and roadkill occur with greater frequency at night, so try to do your traveling in the daytime.

Getting There & Away

If you're coming from Guerrero state (Acapulco usually), Pinotepa Nacional will be the first major town you'll pass on Hwy 200. From Oaxaca, you'll either hit Pochutla from Hwy 175, Puerto Escondido from Hwy 131 or Bahías de Huatulco from Hwy 190/200. See p238 for routes from Oaxaca city.

PINOTEPA NACIONAL

☎ 954 / pop 23,000

Pinotepa is the biggest town between Puerto Escondido (145km) and Acapulco (260km). It's an important market town and urban center for indigenous Mixtecs and Amuzgos who live here and in outlying villages. Though there's little to do *in* Pinotepa, there is lots to do *around* the town, and many of the nearby villages, most of them Mixtec, make good day trips.

Pino's bus terminal is about 2km west of the central plaza. Two banks on the main drag, Bancomer and Bancrecer, change traveler's checks and have ATMs.

The following hotels are friendly and clean and have private bathrooms with hot water.

The semimodern **Hotel Las Gaviotas** (☎ 543-24-02; Carretera a Acapulco s/n; s/d US$14/17, with air-con US$19/24; P ✷), about 600m east of the bus station, has decent rooms with good bathrooms and OK beds.

Hotel Carmona (☎ 543-23-22; Porfirio Díaz 401; s/d US$17/24, with air-con US$25/34; ✷ ✷), on the main road about 500m west of the main plaza, is clean, well run and fairly quiet. Rooms have hot-water bathroom and TV.

All Estrella Blanca buses between Puerto Escondido and Acapulco stop here. It's three hours to Puerto Escondido (1st-class/*ordinario* US$7.50/6.50), 1½ hours to Cuajinicuilapa (US$2.75), and five to 6½ hours to Acapulco (1st-class/*ordinario* US$13/12). First-class OCC buses and 2nd-class Fypsa buses go north on Hwy 125 through the Mixteca, some reaching Oaxaca (US$20, 10 hours, 1st-class) that way. Estrella Roja has two buses nightly to Oaxaca via Hwy 131 (US$14, nine to 10 hours).

AROUND PINOTEPA NACIONAL
Playa Corralero
Southwest of Pinotepa, Playa Corralero is a fine beach near the mouth of **Laguna Corralero**. You can stay in *palapas* (thatched-roof shelters) at Corralero village. To get there from Pinotepa by car go about 25km west on Hwy 200, then some 15km southeast. Ten *camionetas* (pickups) run there daily from Pinotepa (US$1.75, one hour).

East of Pinotepa Nacional
About 20km (a 20-minute drive) east of Pinotepa, the village of **Huazolotitlán** is famous for its colorful wooden Carnaval masks; the village maestro is José Luna López, and anyone will point you to his home. Another long-time carver to ask for is Florencio Gallardo Sánchez. There are many others.

The mainly Mixtec town of **Jamiltepec** (pop 19,000), 30km east of Pinotepa Nacional on Hwy 200, holds a colorful Sunday market below the *plaza central*. Many Mixtec women here wear their colorful *pozahuancos*: horizontally striped, purple wraparound skirts traditionally dyed with *púrpura* (a purple dye made from the shells of sea snails from near Bahías de Huatulco) and cochineal. Mixtec women traditionally wear nothing above the waist, but now often don a small white cloth draped loosely over their shoulders as a nod to the mestizo culture. Mixteca men dress mostly in white.

Buses to both places leave from a small terminal on Pinotepa's main drag just east of the *zócalo*.

PARQUE NACIONAL LAGUNAS DE CHACAHUA
The area around the coastal lagoons of Chacahua and La Pastoría forms the beautiful Parque Nacional Lagunas de Chacahua. Birds from Alaska and Canada migrate here in winter. Mangrove-fringed islands with stands of mahogany trees harbor cormorants, wood storks, herons, egrets, ibis and roseate spoonbills, as well as crocodiles and turtles. El Corral, a mangrove-lined waterway filled with countless birds, connects the two lagoons. Among the Puerto Escondido agencies offering good day trips is **Hidden**

Voyages Ecotours (p253, US$52 per person, minimum 6; ☼ Thu, Dec-Mar only).

Zapotalito
About 60km west of Puerto Escondido, a 5km road leads south from Hwy 200 to Zapotalito, a small fishing village with a few simple restaurants on the eastern edge of Laguna La Pastoría. A cooperative here runs three- to four-hour boat tours of the lagoons (US$75 per boat for up to 10 people). The trips visit islands, channels to the ocean, and the fishing village of Chacahua, at the western end of the park.

You can travel straight to Chacahua village by a *colectivo* (shared) boat and truck combination (see p244).

Chacahua
Chacahua village straddles the channel that connects the western end of Laguna Chacahua to the ocean. The ocean side of the village, fronting a wonderful beach, is a perfect place to bliss out. The waves here (a right-hand point break) can be excellent for surfers, including beginners, but there are some strong currents: check with locals on where it's safe to swim. The inland half of the village contains a **crocodile-breeding center** (admission free) with a sorry collection of about 320 creatures kept for protection and reproduction. They range from 15cm to 3.5m in length; Chacahua's wild croc population (not human-eating) has been decimated by hunting.

SLEEPING & EATING
Several places along the beach at Chacahua village offer basic cabanas. You can sleep in a hammock or camp for free if you eat at a particular establishment. However, this arrangement is not exactly secure, and some readers have complained of theft.

Restaurante Siete Mares (mains US$5.50-7.50) At the west end of the beach, the Siete Mares prepares phenomenal fish and seafood meals. It has some of Chacahua's better cabanas (cabanas d US$19), 300m away along the beach, with two beds, fans, nets and clean bathrooms. The señora here will lock up your valuables.

Cabañas Los Almendros (r or cabanas US$12-31) The waters of the lagoon lap against this place, just two minutes' walk from the beach. It's run by a friendly young couple, and although it's not luxury it's fine. There are three caba-nas and a couple of other rooms – the up-stairs cabana is the pick of the bunch. The shared bathroom is acceptable.

GETTING THERE & AWAY
From Puerto Escondido, you first have to get to the town of Río Grande, 50km west on Hwy 200. Río Grande–bound minibuses (US$1.50, one hour) leave 2 Norte just east of the Carretera Costera, in the upper part of Puerto Escondido, about every half hour. All Estrella Blanca buses between Puerto Es-condido and Acapulco stop at Río Grande too. From the minibus stop in Río Grande, cross the dirt road and get a *colectivo* taxi (US$1) to Zapotalito, 14km southwest.

The simplest one-way route from Za-potalito to Chacahua village is by a com-bination of shared *lancha regular* and *camioneta*, for US$3. You travel half an hour across the lagoon from Zapotalito to meet with a *camioneta* that will make the half-hour trip along the spit to Chacahua. *Lanchas* leave Zapotalito every two hours from 7:20am to 5:20pm (schedule is sub-ject to change); the last return is at 5pm. Their departure point is 300m further along the main road beyond the tours departure point. This route is adventurous but misses out on the delights of the Lagunas de Chaca-hua. Shared *directo* boats to Chacahua vil-lage (US$5 per person, 45 minutes, 25km), which take you the full length of the lagoons, also leave from 300m beyond the *lancha* tours departure point. They have no sched-ule, however, and only leave when US$50 worth of fares are aboard, so you may have a long wait. You should be able to return to Zapotalito by direct boat, but you need to allow for waiting time. If this fails, take the last afternoon *camioneta/lancha regular* service. Check its departure time before you settle in for the day!

Chacahua village is linked to San José del Progreso, 29km north on Hwy 200, by a sandy track that is impassable in the wet season. A very few *camionetas* travel this route daily (US$2.75) when possible.

PUERTO ESCONDIDO
☎ 954 / pop 20,000
Don't be fooled by the few multistory buildings dotting the landscape: Puerto Escondido (Hidden Port) has held on to

its relaxed atmosphere, and boasts a lively travelers' scene. The big draw from day one has been Puerto's astounding waves, which attract an amazing number of tanned, buff and good-looking surfer dudes and dudettes. The rest of the visitors settle for watching the surfers and enjoying any of several beaches, a broad range of accom-modations, some excellent restaurants and cafés and a spot of nightlife. When that gets old, several nearby ecotourist destinations provide a change of pace.

Orientation
The town rises above the small, south-facing Bahía Principal. Highway 200, here called the Carretera Costera, runs across the hill halfway up, dividing the upper town – where buses arrive and most of the locals live and work – from the lower, tourism-dominated part. The heart of the lower town is referred to by all as El Adoquín (*adoquín* is Spanish for paving stone). This is the pedestrianized section (from 5pm until late) of Pérez Gasga. The west end of Pérez Gasga winds up the slope to meet Hwy 200 at an intersection with traffic sig-nals, known as El Crucero.

Bahía Principal curves around at its east end to the long Playa Zicatela, the hub of the surf scene, with loads more places to stay and eat. About 1km west of El Crucero, the area above Playa Carrizalillo has a few places to stay, restaurants and services.

Information
BOOKSTORES
PJ's Book Bodega (☎ 044-954-100-36-56; Calle del Morro s/n) A large collection of new and used books in English, Spanish and other languages.

EMERGENCY
Tourist police (☎ 582-34-39, 24hr; Pérez Gasga s/n) Assistance in English or Spanish.

INTERNET ACCESS
Cofee Net (Calle del Morro 310; per hr US$1.50, ⏱ 24 hours) In Hotel Surf Olas Altas; free coffee.
Internet Acuario (Calle del Morro s/n; per hr US$1.50) Located in Hotel Acuario building.
Copacabana (Pérez Gasga 705; per hr US$1)

LAUNDRY
Lava-Max (☎ 540-16-17; Pérez Gasga 405A; ⏱ 8am-8pm) Self-service. Wash up to 3.5kg of clothes for US$1.30

(plus US$0.70 for detergent, US$1.25 for dryer); complete wash and dry service costs US$1.20 per kg.

MEDIA

The free monthly paper **El Sol de la Costa** (www .elsoldelacosta.com), in Spanish and English, is full of information about what's on and what to do.

MEDICAL SERVICES

In a medical emergency, your best bet is to call the tourist police. The **IMSS clinic** (☎ 582-01-42; Calle 2 Pte s/n) may accept walk-ins.

MONEY

Many hotels give a fair rate for dollars. The town's *casas de cambio*, named Money Exchange, open longer hours than the banks, and most change US dollar traveler's checks, cash US dollars and euros. A handy **HSBC ATM** (El Adoquín) stands next door to Restaurant Los Crotos. The following banks in the upper part of town all have ATMs and will change US dollar traveler's checks and cash US dollars:

Bancomer (cnr 3 Poniente & 2 Norte; ⏱ 9am-2pm Mon-Sat)

Banorte (Hidalgo 4; ⏱ 9am-4pm Mon-Fri, 10am-4pm Sat)

HSBC (1 Norte btwn 2 & 3 Poniente; ⏱ 8am-7pm Mon-Sat) Changes cash euros.

POST

Post office (cnr Av Oaxaca & 7 Norte; ⏱ 8am-3pm Mon-Fri) A 20- to 30-minute uphill walk (about 2km) from El Adoquín, but you can take a 'Mercado' bus or *colectivo* taxi up Av Oaxaca.

TELEPHONE

You'll find Telmex card phones and a couple of *casetas telefónicas* on El Adoquín, and more card phones along Calle del Morro on Zicatela and in other parts of town.

TOURIST INFORMATION

Sectur (☎ 582-01-75; www.aoaxaca.com; cnr Carretera Costera & Juárez; ⏱ 9am-2pm & 4-7pm Mon-Fri, 10am-2pm Sat) This state tourist office (the sign probably still reads Sedetur) is about 2.5km northwest of the center on the road to the airport.

Tourist information kiosk (ginainpuerto@yahoo.com; cnr Pérez Gasga & Marina Nacional; ⏱ 9am-2pm & 4-6pm Mon-Fri, 10am-2pm Sat) This very helpful place is at the west end of El Adoquín. Gina Machorro, the energetic, multilingual information officer usually found here, happily answers your every question.

TRAVEL AGENCIES

Viajes Dimar (☎ 582-15-51; Pérez Gasga 905B) You can buy air tickets as well as book excursions and rental cars here.

Dangers & Annoyances

Puerto's safety record is improving, but to minimize any risks, avoid isolated or empty places, and stick to well-lit areas at night (or use taxis). Some residents say the greatest danger on the beach at night is the local cops: if you are discovered drinking, peeing or even making out beachside, you could end up paying an on-the-spot fine.

Sights

BAHÍA PRINCIPAL

The main town beach, **Playa Principal**, is long enough to accommodate restaurants at its west end, the local fishing fleet in its center and sun worshipers and young bodyboarders at its eastern end (called Playa Marinero). Occasional flocks of pelicans wing in inches above the waves. Boats bob on the swell, and a few hawkers wander up and down. The smelly water entering the bay at times from the inaptly named Laguna Agua Dulce will put you off dipping away from Playa Marinero.

PLAYA ZICATELA

Long, straight **Zicatela** is Puerto's happening beach, with enticing cafés, restaurants and accommodations as well as the waves of the legendary 'Mexican Pipeline' just offshore, which test the mettle of experienced surfers from far and wide.

Nonsurfers beware: the Zicatela waters have a lethal undertow and are definitely not safe for the boardless. Lifeguards rescue several careless people most months (their base, the Cuartel Salvavidas, is in front of Restaurante El Jardín).

BAHÍA PUERTO ANGELITO

The sheltered bay of **Puerto Angelito**, about 1km west of Bahía Principal, has two small beaches separated by a few rocks. Playa Manzanillo, the eastern one, is quieter because vehicles can't reach it. Puerto Angelito is a 20- to 30-minute walk or a US$2 taxi ride west of El Adoquín.

PLAYAS CARRIZALILLO & BACOCHO

Just west of Puerto Angelito, small **Playa Carrizalillo** is in a rockier cove reached by

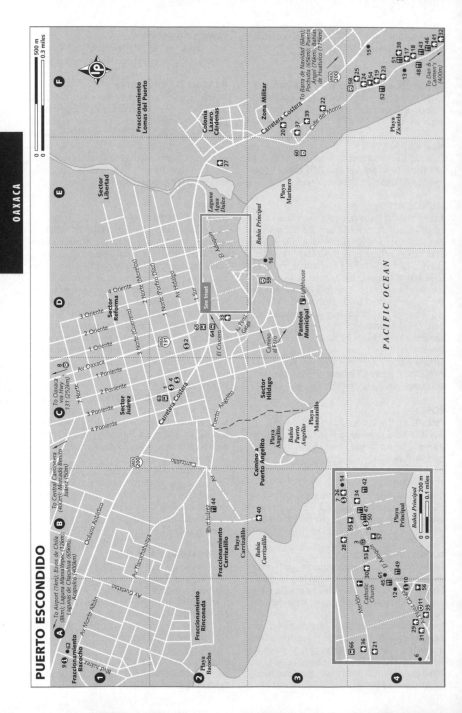

PUERTO ESCONDIDO

a stairway of about 170 steps. It's OK for swimming, snorkeling, body-boarding and surfing, and has a bar with a few *palapas*.

Playa Bacocho is a long, straight beach on the open ocean west of Carrizalillo; it has a dangerous undertow.

Activities

More than anything, Puerto is known for surfing. The main break is Zicatela, and it's at its biggest from late April to August. When it's big, it's unforgiving, offering serious punishment to all but the most experienced surfers. If you're a beginner, try **La Punta**, a rolling left point at the far end of Playa Zicatela. When swells are really pumping, Carrizalillo shapes up with some soft lefts and fast rights out over the reef.

You can rent boards for surfing and body-boarding in a few places on Playa Zicatela. One is **Central Surf** (☎ 582-22-85; www.centralsurf shop.com; Calle del Morro s/n; short board/body-board & fins per hr/day US$3.75/9.50, long-board per hr/day US$3.75/14), in the Hotel Acuario building. Central Surf also offers surfing lessons (in English or Spanish) for US$29 per hour. Other places offering rental and lessons, for about the same prices, include **PJ's Book Bodega** (p244), which also buys and sells boards, and the

Instituto de Lenguajes (☎ 582-20-55; www.puerto school.com; Carretera Costera, Zicatela).

Lanchas from the west end of Bahía Principal will take groups of four out for about an hour's **turtle-spotting** for around US$30, with a dropoff at Puerto Angelito or Playa Carrizalillo afterwards. You can sometimes see other marine life, such as loggerhead turtles, manta rays, dolphins and whales. **Omar's Sportfishing** (☎ 044-954-544-57-90) at Puerto Angelito offers a unique twist to this activity with an underwater microphone that lets you eavesdrop on marine mammals.

Local marlin and sailfish anglers will take two to four people **fishing** with them for three hours for US$84. Ask at the *lancha* kiosk at the west end of Bahía Principal. The price includes cooking some of the catch for you at one of the town's seafood restaurants.

Diving is another possibility. PADI-certified **Aventura Submarina** (☎ 582-23-53; asubmarina@hot mail.com; Pérez Gasga 601A; one-/two-tank dive trips per person US$38/57, Discover Scuba Diving US$71, 4-day open-water certification course US$328) teaches diving courses and leads dive trips for all levels. **Deep Blue Dive School** (☎ 582-07-92; lorenzo2escondido .com; Calle del Morro s/n; 1-/2-tank dive trips per person US$40/60, minimum two people), in Beach Hotel

OAXACA

Inés (opposite), also offers a variety of trips, as well as PADI courses and certificates.

Horseback riding on Playa Zicatela looks fab. Ask the guys on the beach or arrange your rides through Beach Hotel Inés.

Festivals & Events

Semana Santa is a big week for local partying; a local surf carnival is held at this time. At least two international **surf contests** are held on Zicatela each year, usually in August or September, and the **national surfing championships** happen on the last weekend of November.

November is a big month in other ways too: the **Festival Costeña de la Danza** (a fiesta of Oaxaca coastal dance), a sailfishing contest and art exhibitions all take place over the second and/or third weekends of the month. Puerto has begun putting on a February **Carnaval** celebration, but it's still pretty low-key.

Sleeping

The two main accommodation zones are the central Pérez Gasga area and the surf beach Playa Zicatela. In the peak seasons the most popular places will probably be full, especially on Zicatela. Your best chance of getting into a place you like, if you haven't booked ahead, is to ask early in the day, about 9am or 10am. Many places drop prices drastically in low season from those listed here, and some offer discounts for longer stays.

Several apartments and houses are available for short and long stays. Apartments start at US$400/US$800 a month in low/high season; houses overlooking the beach start at around US$1500. Ask at the tourist information kiosk on Pérez Gasga.

BUDGET

Playa Zicatela is about the only beach with decent budget accommodations, and the supply is limited.

Dan & Carmen's (☎ 582-27-60; www.casadanycar men.com; Jacaranda 14, Colonia Santa María; cabanas US$19, r with garden/sea/big sea view US$26/33/38; **P** **ጬ**) This excellent place offers 13 self-contained units with fully equipped kitchens and lovely Talavera-tiled bathrooms. Units vary in size from small cabanas for one or two people to larger family rooms for three to four people, with terrace and views. There's a terrific extra-long lap pool. Reservations are essential, and all the units are available weekly and monthly. It's up the paved road just south of Hotel Papaya Surf, then right across a small bridge.

Hotel Papaya Surf Beach (☎ 582-11-68; www.pa payasurf.com; Calle del Morro s/n; d with air-con US$36, with fan US$28; **ጬ** **ጬ**) Italian-run Papaya has at least 19 rooms with good bathrooms and mosquito screens. Upstairs rooms have shared balconies with hammocks. A restaurant-bar, rooftop *palapa* and pool round out the scene; the combination of beachfront location and facilities make the place a good value.

Hotel Buena Vista (☎ 582-14-74; www.prodigyweb .net.mx/buenavista101; Calle del Morro s/n; d/tr US$24/33, with kitchen US$29/38) Another good value is the well-built Buena Vista, set above Playa Zicatela and reached by a steep flight of steps from Calle del Morro. Its good-sized, spotless rooms all have one double bed and one single, mosquito screens or nets, and a hot-water bathroom. Many have breezy balconies, some with great views.

Cabañas Edda (☎ 582-23-22; Carretera Costera; s/d cabanas US$6/12, with shared bathroom US$4/8, camping US$3 per person) Though it's not really a beach place, Edda's extensive grounds and basic lodgings above Zicatela are well kept, and all guests can use the common kitchen and laundry facilities. All rooms have screens or nets and ceiling or floor fans; many of the private-bathroom 'cabanas' have tile floors. Some units are rather close to the highway.

There are a number of budget spots in the area around Pérez Gasga.

Hotel Rubi (☎ 582-36-84; Pérez Gasga 309; d/tr/q US$19/27/34; **P** **ጬ** **ጬ**) Opened in 2003, the Rubi is one of the only hotels in the budget category offering air-con. All rooms have two double beds and OK bathrooms. None has a sea view, but the small pool and proximity to the bay round it into an attractive package.

Cabañas Pepe (☎ 582-20-37; Merklin 101; d US$18-30) Close to El Crucero, friendly, family-run Pepe's is geared to backpackers and offers 12 simple, well-maintained rooms with two good double beds, fan, nets and hot-water bathroom. Five have superb views and a shared balcony; the others have hammocks slung outside for relaxing in the shade.

Hotel Mayflower (☎ 582-03-67; minnemay7@hot mail.com; Andador Libertad s/n; dm US$7.50, s/d/tr US$21/26/30) The attractive, popular Mayflower, beside the steps leading down to

El Adoquín from the east end of Merklin, has five fan-cooled dormitories (the largest has seven beds; none have bunkbeds) with more than 40 places in all. Rates include filtered water and the use of a kitchen with fridge and microwave. The 16 pleasing private rooms have fan and bathroom. There are semi-open sitting areas, a billiard table, board games, a safety box and luggage storage facilities. An HI card gets you a 10% discount.

MIDRANGE

There's plenty of choice near the beaches. Zicatela is sublime but it can get hectic in high seasons. There's also a good range of places around Pérez Gasga.

Beach Hotel Inés (☎ 582-07-92; www.hotelines .com; Calle del Morro s/n; r US$18-75; P ✖ 🖳 🖳) German-run Inés has a wide range of bright, cheerful cabanas, rooms, bungalows and suites. All have safes, good mosquito screens and fans; most have wireless Internet access, and some come with kitchens, some with air-con. Tasteful art and *artesanía* abound, and other pluses include a sauna, sundeck and spa, and a relaxed, shaded pool area with a café serving good food. You can arrange horseback riding and scuba here as well.

Hotel Flor de María (☎ 582-05-36; www.mexonline .com/flordemaria.htm; 1a Entrada a Playa Marinero; d US$48-55, extra person US$10; 🖳 🖳) A friendly Canadian couple run this good hotel on a lane behind Playa Marinero. The 24 ample rooms are set around a columned patio; all have two double beds; safes; good, large bathrooms; and very well rendered painted murals and door panels. Two rooms have sea views. Extras include a rooftop pool and bar with fabulous views, and a good international restaurant.

Hotel Arco Iris (☎ 582-04-32; www.oaxaca-mio.com /arcoiris.htm; Calle del Morro s/n; d/tr/q from US$57/61/66; P 🖳) The attractive, colonial-style Arco Iris has 32 big, clean rooms with balconies or terraces, most looking straight out to the surf, plus a large pool and a good upstairs restaurant-bar open to the breeze. All rooms have two double beds and ceiling fans, and some have a kitchen. You can also park a camper in the sizable grounds.

Tabachín del Puerto (☎ 582-11-79; www.tabachin .com.mx; d incl breakfast US$65-85, extra person US$15, children under 12 free; P ✖) At the end of a

short lane behind Hotel Santa Fe, Tabachín has a gracious and erudite owner and six studio rooms of various sizes (including an enormous one), in varying states of maintenance. All have kitchen, air-con, TV and phone; most have balcony access, some have sea views. The good breakfasts, which include vegetarian choices and organically grown coffee and fruits from the owner's farm in Nopala, draw nonguests as well and are always lively occasions.

Hotel Acuario (☎ 582-03-57; fax 582-10-27; Calle del Morro s/n; r US$70-120; P ✖ 🖳 🖳) The 30 or so accommodations here range from cramped rooms and wooden cabanas to spacious upstairs rooms with terrace and beach view. The more substantial bungalows have kitchens and the most appealing interiors. Acuario's complex includes a surf shop, Internet café and an inviting pool area. Prices drop by half out of season.

Bungalows Zicatela (☎ 582-07-98; www.bungalow szicatela.com.mx; Calle del Morro s/n; s/d US$19/38, bungalow with fan US$47, with air-con & view US$66; ✖ 🖳) The straightforward Zicatela has a sociable pool and restaurant and all its 40-odd accommodations are a good size, solidly built and have mosquito-netted windows. Though squeezed a little tightly together, they have good beds and bathrooms, and most bungalows have kitchens.

Bungalows Puerta del Sol (☎ 582-29-22; Calle del Morro s/n; r US$49; 🖳) This place has a small pool, a communal kitchen and 16 spacious, well-constructed rooms with fan, balcony and hammock (and beds of course!).

Casas de Playa Acali (☎ 582-07-54; arnulfodiaz59@ hotmail.com; Calle del Morro s/n; cabanas US$37, bungalows US$50, r US$68; ✖ 🖳) Acali's fenced property holds a fair bit of greenery. The varnished-wood cabanas are fairly rustic but ample, each with one double and one single bed. The bungalows have decent bathrooms, screens and beds (two doubles in each), as well as kitchens. The more expensive rooms climb up the hillside in blocks, and have air-con, large upstairs kitchens and decks for relaxing on.

Hotel Hacienda Revolución (☎ 582-18-18; www .haciendarevolucion.com; Andador Revolución 21; d/tr/q US$33/38/43, d/tr casita US$43/47) On a flight of steps leading up from El Adoquín, this Revolution-themed place has 11 attractive and spacious rooms around a garden-courtyard with a beautiful central fountain.

OAXACA

Rooms have colorful paintwork and Talavera-tiled hot-water bathrooms; most have a patio and hammock. Set apart under a shared roof, the casitas are even nicer than the rooms; each has a hammock on the patio. A restaurant in the shady area below opens from December to March.

Hotel Nayar (☎ 582-01-13; www.oaxaca-mio.com /hotelnayar.htm; Pérez Gasga 407; s/d with air-con US$41/ 47; **P** ✖ 🖭 🐾) The Nayar was built in a '60s-modern style that looks much better once you get inside. Its 41 rooms have good beds, OK bathrooms with hot water, and small balconies. Fifteen rooms have sea views, and the view from the terrace is excellent. The pool is in a big garden by the entrance.

Hotel San Juan (☎ 582-05-18; www.hotelsanjuan .cjb.net; Merklin 503; d from US$27, r with air-con US$45; **P** ✖ 🐾) The friendly San Juan, just below El Crucero, has 31 good, straightforward rooms. All have hot water, mosquito screens, cable TV and a security box; some have terraces and excellent views. The hotel also boasts a pool and a rooftop sitting area.

Hotel Rincón del Pacífico (☎ 582-00-56; Pérez Gasga 900; s/d/tr/q US$30/38/45/54 with fan, with air-con US$53/66/79/94; ✖) This hotel on El Adoquín has 30 spacious, big-windowed rooms (half with air-con, some with sea views) with good beds and hot-water bathrooms around a palm-filled courtyard. Staff are helpful and the hotel has a beachside café-restaurant.

Hotel Casablanca (☎ 582-01-68; www.ptohcasa blanca.com; Pérez Gasga 905; s/d/tr/q US$33/47/57/66; 🐾) The friendly Casablanca is right at the heart of things on the inland side of El Adoquín, and it fills up with guests quickly. It has a small pool and 21 large, clean tile-floored rooms with fan. Some have fridges; the best are street-side with balconies.

Hotel Loren (☎ 582-00-57; fax 582-05-91; Pérez Gasga 507; d/tr/q with fan US$24/33/43, with air-con US$33/43/52; **P** ✖ 🐾) A minute uphill from El Adoquín, this friendly, sky-blue-and-lobster-colored hotel has bare, dimly lit but spacious rooms. All have two or three (somewhat springy) double beds, cable TV and balconies; some catch a sea view. It's a good place for the price.

Zicatela Dorada Resort (☎ 582-37-27; www.oaxaca -mio.com/zicateladorada.htm; Calle del Morro s/n; r US$55 with fan, with air-con US$71; **P** ✖ 🐾) New in 2003, and still being decorated at the time of research, the semi-Mediterranean-style ZD features 60 rooms with hot water and cable TV set around a courtyard with swimming pool, bar and restaurant. Most have two double beds; the upper ones have small balconies and air-con.

TOP END

Hotel Santa Fe (☎ 582-01-70; in the US 888-649-6407; www.hotelsantafe.com.mx; cnr Blvd Zicatela & Calle del Morro; r US$120, bungalow US$155, junior ste US$155, master ste US$260; **P** ✖ 🖭 🐾) The well-landscaped, neocolonial Santa Fe has more than 60 rooms attractively set around small terraces and three pools (a fourth, smaller pool is shared by the master suites). Rooms vary in size and view, but all are well designed and decorated, and have air-con and room safes. Also available are eight appealing bungalows with kitchens, and two impressive master suites furnished with colonial antiques and fabulous modern art. The views are spectacular from the suites and their wraparound terraces.

Villas Carrizalillo (☎ 582-17-35; www.villascarri zalillo.com; Av Carrizalillo 125, Carrizalillo; apt US$80-125) Sublimely perched on the cliffs above the small Bahía Carrizalillo, Villas Carrizalillo has apartments for two to six people, with fully equipped kitchens and private terraces. Some have stunning sea views. A path goes directly down to Playa Carrizalillo.

Hotel Surf Olas Altas (☎ 582-23-15, 582-00-94; www.surfolasaltas.com.mx; Calle del Morro 310; d/tr/q US$117/131/145; **P** ✖ 🖭 🐾) This modern, three-story 61-room hotel has less character than some of the smaller places, but the rooms are spotless and ample, and set well back from the street. Most have two double beds, room safe, air-con and satellite TV. Some rooms catch a sea view, some look over the pool, some do neither.

Hotel Paraíso Escondido (☎ 582-04-44; Unión 10; d US$99, tr or q US$141; ✖ 🖭 🐾) The rambling neocolonial Paraíso is decorated with tiles, pottery, stained glass and stone sculpture. Its 20 clean, fair-sized rooms have air-con, good bathrooms, old-fashioned red-tile floors and small terraces. The hotel also has a library and an attractive restaurant, bar and pool area.

Eating

Puerto has some excellent eateries, a large proportion of them Italian thanks to the tide of Italian travelers drawn here by the movie

Puerto Escondido. Most places are at least partly open-air. You'll eat some of the freshest fish and seafood you've ever had. Tofu products and a mind-boggling range of fruit and vegetable juices and milk and yogurt combos, make this a vegetarian's paradise.

UPPER TOWN

Mercado Benito Juárez (cnr 8 Norte & 3 Poniente; fish/vegetarian dishes US$4/3) Several clean stalls in the market prepare good fare, and the sights and smells of the produce section make it worth a wander as well, even if you're not hungry.

PLAYAS ZICATELA & MARINERO

Sakura (Calle del Morro s/n; mains US$3.75-15, sushi per pair US$2.50-3.75, rolls US$3.50-5, noodle dishes US$3.75-7.50) Eating raw fish with your toes in the sand (or on cement, if you prefer), watching the Pipeline's curl – does it get any better than this? The Japanese chefs put out some excellent, tight, super-fresh nigiri, or you can choose from tempura, tofu and teriyaki dishes, curries and spring rolls. Heighten your sense of geocultural displacement by ordering a *michelada* (an iced 'cocktail' made with beer, lime juice, salt and spicy seasoning).

La Hostería (☎ 582-00-05; Calle del Morro s/n; mains US$3-9; 🕒 8am-12:30am; V) The Hostería is a labor of love, from its gleaming, super-pro kitchen (with computerized, wood-fired pizza oven) down to the excellent Talavera-tiled bathrooms. A broad selection of delicious Italian, Mexican and international dishes – including many veggie selections – is paired with a great wine list, and the espresso is some of the best in town.

Restaurant Flor de María (☎ 582-05-36; 1a Entrada a Playa Marinero; mains US$3.75-11.50, breakfast US$2.50-3; V) In the hotel of the same name, the dinner menu here changes daily depending on what's fresh, and includes fish, grilled meats and Italian dishes. There's always a vegetarian option.

Restaurante El Jardín (☎ 582-23-15; Calle del Morro s/n; dishes US$3.50-7; 🕒 8am-11pm) This *palapa* restaurant in front of the Hotel Surf Olas Altas serves very good vegetarian dishes, including good gado gado, tempeh dishes, hummus, many salad varieties and, of course, tofu offerings. The menu also includes some seafood dishes and an extensive beverage and juice list.

El Cafecito (☎ 582-05-16; Calle del Morro s/n; breakfast US$2.50-3.75, lunch & dinner mains US$2.75-6.50)

The cinnamon rolls alone are worth a visit, but the Cafecito also serves good breakfasts, whole-wheat *tortas*, espresso drinks and excellent, inexpensive pastries, croissants and cakes. A second El Cafecito at Carrizalillo on Juárez features the same great food and the same sullen service.

Restaurante Bar Los Tíos (Calle del Morro s/n; mains US$3-5.50; 🕒 9am-10pm Wed-Mon) Right on the beach rather than across from it, as most other Zicatela restaurants are, the Uncles serve great *licuados* and several fresh fruit juices to go with their tasty egg dishes, *antojitos*, burgers, salads, and seafood. It's wonderfully relaxed and very popular with locals.

Hotel Santa Fe (☎ 582-01-70; cnr Zicatela & Calle del Morro; pasta US$6.50-9, seafood dishes US$13-17, vegetarian & vegan dishes US$5-6.50) The airy and romantically sited restaurant here looks down on the west end of the Pipeline. Sink into a comfy leather chair and choose from the list of inspired vegetarian and vegan meals. Seafood choices are average, but service is excellent.

La Galera (☎ 582-04-32; Hotel Arco Iris, Calle del Morro s/n; menu del día US$5.75, mains US$4.9-9.50) This restaurant has a good, open-air, upstairs setting and tasty mixed Mexican and international fare. Main dishes focus on fish and meat, but the *menú del día* is usually a three-course (plus drink) vegetarian meal.

Zicatela also has two or three small convenience stores.

PÉREZ GASGA

La Galería (☎ 582-20-39; mains US$4.50-11.25) At the west end of El Adoquín, La Galería is one of Puerto's more agreeable Italian spots, with art on the walls and good fare on the tables. The pasta dishes and pizza are original and tasty, and the jumbo mixed green salad is a real treat. You can breakfast here, too.

Restaurant Junto al Mar (☎ 582-12-72; mains US$5.75-13) On the bay side of El Adoquín, the JaM has a terrace overlooking the beach. Attentive waitstaff serve up excellent fresh seafood here; the squid dishes and the fish fillet *a la veracruzana* (tomato, onion and pepper sauce) get the thumbs up.

Restaurant Los Crotos (☎ 582-00-25; mains US$6-11.25; 🕒 7am-11pm) With romantic night lighting and an attractive setting almost on the sands of Playa Principal, Los Crotos is a good choice for seafood.

OAXACA

Danny's Terrace (☎ 582-02-57; mains US$6-8.50) Reader-recommended Danny's is beachside at the Rincón del Pacifico Hotel. In addition to the usual seafood, chicken and meat dishes, they serve up…vichyssoise! A decent selection of desserts and wines ties up the package.

Restaurant Alicia (dishes US$3-8.50) Economical little Alicia offers multiple spaghetti variations, seafood cocktails and good fish dishes. Breakfasts and beer are cheap, too – why not try them together?

Drinking

Casa Babylon (Calle del Morro s/n; ☽ 10am-late) This cool little travelers' bar has board games and a big selection of secondhand books to sell or exchange. The owner prides herself on her Cuban and Brazilian specialty drinks: *mojitos* and *caipirinhas*.

Barfly (Pérez Gasga) The 2nd-story balcony, music and drink mixes draw a lively crowd most nights.

Rival drinking dens with loud music on El Adoquín include Terraza Bar, Wipeout Bar and Los 3 Diablos. **Tarros** (Marina Nacional), around the corner, is in the same league. Most of these hold two-for-one happy hours from 9pm to 10pm but don't expect much action before 11pm.

A few bars and restaurants overlooking the sea, including Danny's Terrace (above) off the Adoquín and the bar at Hotel Arco Iris (p249) on Zicatela, have happy hours from about 5pm to 7pm to help you enjoy Puerto's spectacular sunsets.

Entertainment

El Son y La Rumba (☎ 582-10-30; Calle del Morro s/n; ☽ 7pm-late Tue-Sun) Tucked against the rocks at the Zicatela end of Playa Marinero, this friendly place usually features the acoustic guitar and vocals of Mayca, who performed the music for the film *Puerto Escondido*. She performs mostly bolero, Mexican *son* and *trova*. Guest artists playing a wide variety of music pass through as well.

Club Tribal (Marina Nacional; admission US$5; ☽ 10pm-4am Fri off-season, Fri & Sat high season) One of a cluster of discos a block or so southwest of El Adoquín.

La Hostería (Calle del Morro s/n) La Hostería (p251) shows the 1993 Italian travel-and-crime film *Puerto Escondido* nightly at 6pm. This film (directed by Gabriele Salvatores,

who also did *Mediterraneo*) has attracted thousands of Italians and others to Puerto and is worth seeing, even if it makes the place seem more remote than it really is.

Cinemar (Calle del Morro s/n; film showings at 5pm, 7pm & 9pm; admission with popcorn & drink US$4.25) Air-conditioned Cinemar, sharing the building with PJ's Book Bodega, shows films ranging from classics to latest general releases, in Spanish and English.

Shopping

The Adoquín is great for a browse – shops and stalls sell fashions from surf designers and from Bali. You'll also find New Age and silver jewelry, souvenirs and classy crafts that are works of art.

Getting There & Away

AIR

Aerotucán (☎ 582-17-25; Puerto Escondido airport) and **Aerovega** (☎ 582-01-51; Pérez Gasga 113) fly to/from Oaxaca. See Getting There & Away (p238) for details. **Click Mexicana** (☎ 01-800-122-54-25) flies nonstop to/from Mexico City twice daily. Continental Express flies from Houston to Bahías de Huatulco (p272) from one to four times a week in winter; from there it's an easy bus ride to Puerto Escondido.

BUS

Puerto Escondido's main bus terminal, the Central Turística de Autobuses (generally known as the *central camionera*), is between 3 and 4 Poniente, north of 10 Norte. All long-distance lines use it except **OCC** (Cristóbal Colón; ☎ 582-10-73), which at the time of research was breaking ground on a new facility on the Carretera Costera just west of Av Oaxaca. Bus companies include **Estrella Blanca** (EB; ☎ 582-00-86), Estrella del Valle/Oaxaca Pacífico (EV/OP) and **Estrella Roja** (ER; ☎ 582-38-99). The only true 1st-class bus services are OCC's and a couple of the Estrella Blanca Mexico City runs.

It's advisable to book ahead for all OCC buses and the better services to Oaxaca. Keep a particularly close eye on your belongings when going to/from Acapulco or Oaxaca, and be sure to get a ticket for any bags placed in the baggage hold.

Oaxaca City

See the boxed text on p238 for an explanation of the three possible routes between

Oaxaca and Puerto Escondido. There are various daily departures from Puerto:

Via Hwy 131 ER (US$9.50, 6-8hr, 5 daily)
Via Hwys 200 & 175 EV/OP (US$8/8.50-9.50 *ordinario/ directo*, 8½/7½hr, 14 daily)
Via Hwys 200 & 190 OCC (Salina Cruz route; US$20, 10-11hr, 3 daily)

Other Destinations

There are also daily departures to other destinations:

Acapulco EB (US$22 *semi-directo*, 8hr, 3 daily; US$18 *ordinario*, 9½hr, 9 daily)
Bahías de Huatulco OCC (US$6, 2½hr, 11 daily); EB (US$6.50, 2½hr, 8 daily)
Juchitán (US$15, 6hr, 3 OCC)
Mexico City EB (US$42 12-13hr, 870km, 2 1st-class); OCC (US$48, 18hr, via Hwys 200 and 190, 1 nightly)
Pinotepa Nacional EB (US$7.50 *semi directo*, 3hr, 151km, 3 daily; US$6.50 *ordinario*, 3½hr, 9 daily)
Pochutla OCC (US$3.50, 1½hr, 7 daily); EB (US$4, 1½hr, 8 daily); Servicio Mixto de Río Grande (US$2.25, 1½hr, from El Crucero every 20min from 5am-7pm)
Tehuantepec OCC (US$14, 5½hr, 3 daily)
Zihuatanejo EB (US$33, 12 hours, 640km, 1 1st-class at 8pm)

EB 2nd-class *económicos* leave every hour to Acapulco and will drop you anywhere you want to get off along coastal Hwy 200.

CAR

Budget (☎ 582-03-12; Juárez), opposite the tourist office, charges walk-ins US$90 a day for its cheapest cars, including unlimited kilometers and insurance.

Getting Around

The **airport** (☎ 582-04-92) is 4km west of the center on the north side of Hwy 200. A taxi costs around US$3.50, if you can find one (look on the main road outside the airport). Otherwise, *colectivo combis* (US$4 per person) will drop you anywhere in town. You should have no problem finding a taxi from town to the airport for about US$3.50. A taxi from the bus station to most parts of town should cost no more than US$3.

Taxis are the only available transportation between the central Pérez Gasga/Bahía Principal area and the outlying beaches if you don't want to walk. Taxis wait at each end of El Adoquín. The standard fare to Playa Zicatela is US$2.

AROUND PUERTO ESCONDIDO
Laguna de Manialtepec

This lagoon, 6km long, begins about 14km west of Puerto Escondido along Hwy 200. It's home to ibis, roseate spoonbills, parrots and several species of hawks, falcons, ospreys, egrets, herons, kingfishers and iguanas. December to March is the best time to observe birds, and they're most often seen in the early morning. The lagoon is mainly surrounded by mangroves, but tropical flowers and palms accent the oceanside. It makes an excellent day trip from Puerto Escondido.

The best (and practically only) way to see the lagoon is by boat. Several early-morning or sunset tours (from four to five hours, including road time) can be booked from Puerto Escondido. Not all of them include English-speaking guides.

Hidden Voyages Ecotours (☎ 954-582-15-51; www .wincom.net/~pelewing; Pérez Gasga 905B, Puerto Escondido; tours for 4-10 people Dec 1-Apr 1 per person US$37-40) offers highly recommended trips; morning tours are led by a knowledgeable Canadian ornithologist. Hidden Voyages' office is in the Viajes Dimar travel agency.

Lalo's Ecotours (☎ 954-588-91-64; www.lalo-ecotours .com, Las Negras Mixtepec; tours per person US$29) is run by a lagoon local who has worked as a boatman for Hidden Voyages and knows his birds. Tours are year-round. Lalo also rents kayaks, leads nature hikes and offers night time visits to the lagoon when it contains phosphorescent plankton, a magnificent occasional occurrence.

A handful of restaurants along the lagoon's north shore (just off Hwy 200) run boat trips.

At the eastern end of lake, **Las Hamacas** (☎ 954-588-85-52; 9am-8pm; 2½hr trip for up to 5 people US$56) is a Spanish-Mexican operation renting single- and double-seat kayaks for US$5 per hour. Boat tours (one to five passengers) start at US$43. The food's good, too, and you can go water-skiing for US$56 an hour.

Restaurant Isla del Gallo (2hr trip for up to 6 people US$56), halfway along the lake, offers shaded boat trips, and the boatmen are knowledgeable about birds. Good grilled fish and seafood are available at the restaurant for US$6 to US$9.50.

Restaurán Puesta del Sol (☎ 954-588-38-67; Km 24; 2½hr trip for up to 5 people US$47), toward the west end of the lake, is another recommended embarkation point. One- or two-person kayaks run US$5 per hour; fish and shrimp dishes cost US$6 to US$7.50.

GETTING THERE & AWAY
From Puerto Escondido, take a Río Grande–bound minibus from 2 Norte just east of the Carretera Costera, in the upper part of town. They leave every half hour from 6am to 7pm (US$0.90). These and westbound 2nd-class EB buses stop along the lagoon.

Bajos de Chila
Pelota mixteca (a Mixtec ball game), a five-a-side team sport descended from the pre-Hispanic ritual ball game, is played at 3pm every Saturday in the village of Bajos de Chila, 10km west of Puerto Escondido along Hwy 200 (5pm if weather is hot). This is a living relic of Mexico's ancient culture, played for the enjoyment of the participants. The field, called the *patio* or *pasador*, is easy to find in the village.

Colectivos leave Puerto Escondido's bus station every 30 minutes, stopping at 2 Norte, just east of the Carretera Costera, on their way to Bajos de Chila (US$0.50, 15 minutes).

Lagunas Los Naranjos & Palmazola
These coastal lagoons, near the village of **Barra de Navidad** (6km southeast of Puerto Escondido and just off Hwy 200), offer another chance to get close to the abundant birdlife of the Oaxaca coast – and to the local crocodile population. Villagers have formed a society to protect the lagoons and offer guided visits (US$15) lasting about 1¼ hours, including a 30-minute boat ride. It's best to go in the early morning or late afternoon. Unaccompanied visits are not permitted.

Barra de Navidad is a short walk south from Hwy 200 on the east side of the Río Colotepec bridge; catch a 'La Barra' *colectivo* from the highway west of El Crucero in Puerto Escondido.

POCHUTLA
☎ 958 / pop 13,000
This bustling, sweaty market town is the starting point for transportation to the nearby beach spots of Puerto Ángel, Zipolite, San Agustinillo and Mazunte. It also has the nearest banks to those places.

Orientation
Highway 175 from Oaxaca runs through Pochutla as Cárdenas, the narrow north–south (uphill–downhill) main street, and meets coastal Hwy 200 about 1.5km south of town. Everything described in this section is on Cárdenas, with the approximate midpoint for sites being Hotel Izala. The long-distance bus stations cluster around 300m to 400m downhill from the Izala.

Information
HSBC (Cárdenas 48; ☉ 8am-7pm Mon-Fri, 8am-3pm Sat) One block uphill from Hotel Izala. Changes traveler's checks and cash US dollars, and has an ATM. There are several other banks on this street with exchange services and ATMs.
Post office (Cárdenas s/n, ☉ 8am-3pm Mon-Fri) About 150m downhill from Hotel Izala.
Telnet (Cárdenas 94; Internet access per hr US$1; ☉ 8am-10pm Mon-Sat) Opposite the EV/OP bus terminal, has fast Internet connections plus long-distance telephone service.

Sleeping & Eating
Hotel Costa del Sol (☎ /fax 584-03-18; Cárdenas 47; 1-bed/tw r US$20/22 with fan, with air-con US$24/29; P ⊠) Probably Pochutla's best central hotel, 1½ blocks uphill from the Izala, this hotel has a few artistic touches and some greenery. Rooms have good bathrooms, erratic hot water, and cable TV.

Hotel Izala (☎ 584-01-15; Cárdenas 59; s/d with fan US$15/24, with air-con US$24/33; P ⊠) The Izala offers plain, clean rooms, with bathroom and cable TV, on two levels around a leafy courtyard.

Hotel Santa Cruz (☎ /fax 584-01-16; Cárdenas s/n; s/d with shared bathroom & fan US$10/12, with private bathroom US$12/15, with private bathroom & air-con US$20/25; ⊠) About 150m north of the main cluster of bus stations, the Santa Cruz has simple, good-sized, adequate rooms. Some private bathrooms lack toilet seats; the air-con is good in those rooms that have it.

Restaurant y Marisquería Los Ángeles (Cárdenas s/n; mains US$4-9; ☉ 10am-9pm Mon-Sat) This breezy little upstairs place, downhill from the OCC bus station serves a good octopus cocktail.

Getting There & Away
The three main bus stations, in north–south order along Cárdenas, are **EV/OP** (☎ 584-01-38), on the left side of the street; **OCC/Sur** (☎ 584-02-74), on the right side; and

---

TRANSPORT BETWEEN POCHUTLA & BEACH TOWNS

Transportation services to the nearby coast change frequently. When all is in harmony, frequent *camionetas* and *taxis colectivos* (painted two-tone, either dark-red and white, or cream and blue) run from Pochutla to the coastal towns between 7am and 7pm, usually picking up passengers in Pochutla in front of Mueblería García, a furniture store about five doors uphill from Hotel Santa Cruz, on the same side of Cárdenas.

At the time of writing, plenty of *taxis colectivos* were running to Puerto Ángel (US$0.70, 20 minutes, 13km), Zipolite (US$1.50, 30 minutes, 16km), San Agustinillo (US$2, 40 minutes, 20km) and Mazunte (US$2, 45 minutes, 21km). *Camioneta* service, though even cheaper (US$0.50 to Puerto Ángel, US$0.80 to either Zipolite or Mazunte), was much less frequent.

Be aware that some vehicles reach the coast by heading west on Hwy 200 from Pochutla, stopping first in Mazunte, then San Augustinillo, and so on; this gives quicker service to Mazunte and San Agustinillo, but longer to Zipolite and Puerto Ángel.

Private *(servicio especial)* cabs during the day should cost around US$6 to Puerto Ángel, US$9 to Zipolite and US$11 to San Agustinillo or Mazunte, but you may have to negotiate hard to even get close to these prices; at night they are the only game in town and charge even more.

OAXACA

EB (☎ 584-03-80), also on the right side. See the boxed text (p238) for information on routes to Oaxaca city.

There are daily bus departures to various destinations:

Acapulco EB (US$27 *semi-directo*, 8-9hr, 7 daily)
Bahías de Huatulco OCC (US$2.25, 1hr, 8 daily); EB (US$2.25, 1hr, 5 daily); Sur (US$1.50, 1hr, every 40min); Transportes Rápidos de Pochutla (US$1.25, 1hr, every 15min 5:30am-8pm, from terminal just uphill from EV/OP)
Juchitán OCC (US$12, 5hr, 5 daily)
Mexico City OCC (US$50, 15-16hr, 1 daily 7:20pm); EB (US$45, 14-15hr, 2 daily)
Oaxaca OCC (US$20, 9-10hr, 5 daily, via Hwys 200 & 190); EV/OP (US$7.50, 7hr, 10 *ordinarios*; US$8.50-9, 6hr, 3 *directos* at 9:45am, 2:45pm & 10:30pm; all via Hwy 175)
Pinotepa Nacional EB (US$12, 4hr, 7 daily); EB (US$4 *semi-directo*, 1hr, 7 daily); Sur (US$2.50, 1½hr, hourly 7:30am-7:30pm)
Puerto Escondido OCC (US$3.75, 1½hr, 5 daily); EB (US$4 *semi-directo*, 1hr, 7 daily); Sur (US$2.50, 1½hr, hourly 7:30am-7:30pm)
Tehuantepec OCC (US$11, 4½hr, 5 daily)
Zihuatanejo EB (US$38, 12hr, 7 daily)

Autoexprés Atlántida (☎ 584-01-16; Hotel Santa Cruz, Cárdenas s/n) runs nine daily air-conditioned vans, taking up to 14 people, by Hwy 175 (US$12, 6½ hours) between 4am and 11pm. Two other companies, Eclipse 7 (across the street from Atlántida) and Delfines (just uphill from Atlántida) offer similar service. Drivers will usually stop when you need a bathroom break or want to take photos (or vomit, as not a few people tend to do on this route).

PUERTO ÁNGEL
☎ 958 / pop 3000

The small fishing town, naval base and travelers' hangout of Puerto Ángel (pwerr-toh *ahn*-hel) straggles around a picturesque bay between two rocky headlands, 13km south of Pochutla. Many travelers prefer to stay out on the beaches a few kilometers west at Zipolite, San Agustinillo or Mazunte, but the marginally more urban Puerto Ángel is a good base too. It offers its own little beaches, some good places to stay and eat, and easy transportation to/from Zipolite.

Orientation

The road from Pochutla emerges at the east end of the small Bahía de Puerto Ángel. The road winds around the back of the bay, over an often-dry arroyo and up a hill. It then forks – right to Zipolite and Mazunte, left to Playa del Panteón. It's called Blvd Uribe through most of town, though after it crosses the arroyo it's also referred to as Carretera a Zipolite.

Information

Banks The nearest banks are in Pochutla, but several accommodations and restaurants will change cash or traveler's checks at their own rates.
Caseta Telefónica Lila (Blvd Uribe) Has Internet, phone and fax service.
Farmacia El Ángel (☎ 584-30-58; Vasconcelos) Dr Constancio Aparicio's practice is here (☒ 9am-2pm & 4pm-8pm Mon-Sat).
G@l@p@gos (Blvd Uribe s/n; Internet access per hr US$1.50) Does phone calls also.

PUERTO ÁNGEL

INFORMATION
Caseta Telefónica Lila...............1 B2
Farmacia El Ángel.....................2 C2
G@l@p@gos............................3 B2
Gel@net................................4 C3
Post Office..............................5 C3
Tourist Office..........................6 C3

SIGHTS & ACTIVITIES
Azul Profundo.........................7 A2
Byron Luna............................8 A3

SLEEPING
Casa Arnel.............................9 B2
Casa de Huéspedes Gundi y
  Tomás...............................10 B2
El Almendro..........................11 C2
Hotel Cordelia's.....................12 A2
Hotel Puesta del Sol...............13 A2

Hotel Soraya.........................14 C3
La Buena Vista.......................15 B1
La Posada Cañón Devata........16 A2
Penelope's............................17 A2
Villa Serena Florencia.............18 C2

EATING
Beto's..................................19 A2
Other Beach Restaurants........(see 20)
Restaurante Susy...................20 A3

TRANSPORT
Buses to Oaxaca....................21 C3
Taxi Stand............................22 C3

To Zipolite (2.5km);
Mazunte (8km);
San Agustinillo (7km);
Puerto Escondido (64km)

Carretera a Zipolite
Arroyo
Azueta

Naval Base

Blvd Uribe

Cemetery

Playa Principal

Calle Sáenz de Baranda

Playa del Panteón

Bahía de Puerto Ángel

Pier

Beach Restaurants

Vasconcelos

Av Principal

Calle del Tajo

To Playa Estacahuite (700m);
Playa La Boquilla (7.5km);
Bahía de la Luna (7.5km);
Pochutla (12.5km);

La Playita

Gel@net (Vasconcelos 3; ☉ 9am-10pm) Has telephone, fax and Internet (per hr US$1.50).

Post office (Av Principal; ☉ 9am-2pm Mon-Fri) East end of town.

Municipal tourist office (Blvd Uribe; ☉ 9am-4pm & 5:30-8pm Mon-Fri) In a *palapa*-roofed building at the entrance to the pier; useful for transportation details.

Sights & Activities

Snorkeling and **fishing** are popular around Puerto Ángel, and **diving** is also an option. The drops and canyons out to sea from Puerto Ángel are suitable for very deep dives; a nearby shipwreck, dated 1870, is a popular site.

Some of the café-restaurants on Playa del Panteón rent snorkel gear (US$2.75/ US$6.75 per hour/day). **Azul Profundo** (☎ 584-31-09; azul_profundomx@hotmail.com; Playa del Panteón; 4hr snorkeling trips per person US$9.50; fishing trips per person per hr US$31), run by friendly Chepe, offers snorkeling, fishing and dives at all levels. Dives run US$38. Instruction offered includes a five-day SSI certification course for US$337. Ask at Hotel Cordelia's if you can't find him.

BEACHES

On the west side of Bahía de Puerto Ángel, **Playa del Panteón** is shallow and calm, and its waters are cleaner than those near the pier across the bay.

About 500m north along the road to Pochutla, a sign points right along a path to **Playa Estacahuite** 700m away. The three tiny, sandy bays here are all great for snorkeling, but watch out for jellyfish. A couple of shack restaurants serve good, reasonably priced seafood or spaghetti, and may rent snorkel gear.

The coast northeast of Estacahuite is dotted with more good beaches, none of them very busy. A good one is **Playa La Boquilla**, on a small bay about 5km (by boat) from town; it's the site of the Bahía de la Luna bungalows and restaurant (opposite). To get to the beach, take a turnoff 4km out of Puerto Ángel on the road toward Pochutla and then follow the road for 3.5km. A taxi from Puerto Ángel costs around US$4.50 each way, but it's more fun to go by boat – you can arrange one for a few people from Playa del Panteón or from the pier for around

US$11 per person, including a return trip at an agreed time.

Sleeping

Accommodations with an elevated location are more likely to catch any breeze, and mosquito screens are a big plus too. Some places develop a water shortage now and then.

La Buena Vista (☎ 584-31-04; www.labuenavista .com; La Buena Compañía s/n; d US$35-48; extra person US$6; 🏊) The 19 big rooms and five excellent mud-brick bungalows on this verdant property are kept scrupulously clean. All have private bathrooms with pretty Talavera tiles, fans, mosquito screens and comfortable beds. Many have breezy balconies with hammocks, and some have excellent views. Wood, stone and brick are cleverly used throughout. There's a good restaurant on an expansive terrace, and a truly lovely pool area.

Bahía de la Luna (☎ 589-50-20; www.bahiadela luna.com; Playa La Boquilla; s/d/tr from US$61/72/111; 🅿) This tropical hideaway out at gorgeous Playa La Boquilla (opposite) has attractive adobe bungalows set on a tree-filled hillside overlooking the beach. Two two-bedroom bungalows can each hold up to five people, and a house holds up to eight (US$205 for four, plus US$11 per extra person). It also has a good beachside restaurant-café with moderate prices, and offers snorkeling gear, sea kayaks and yoga and meditation instruction.

La Posada Cañón Devata (☎ 584-31-37; www .posadapacifico.com; off Sáenz de Baranda; s/d with fan US$29/33, bungalows for 2 US$66, extra adult US$19; all rates include breakfast; 🌣 closed June; 🅿) On a woodsy hillside behind Playa del Panteón, the friendly Cañón Devata has a variety of attractive accommodations scattered about its sprawling property. It's run by the artistic and ecologically minded López family, and is a good place for those seeking a quiet retreat. Yoga courses are on offer, and the super-clean kitchen turns out fine food (vegetarian and fish dishes only).

Hotel Puesta del Sol (☎ 584-30-96; www.puerto angel.net; Blvd Uribe s/n; s with shared bathroom US$11.50, d with shared bathroom US$15-18, d with private bathroom US$25-32; 🖳) The friendly German/Mexican-owned Puesta del Sol offers sizable, clean rooms with fans and screens. Some sleep up to six people. The more expensive ones have their own terraces and hot-water bath-

room. The sitting room has a small library and satellite TV. Hammocks on a breezy terrace invite relaxation, and breakfast is available.

Penelope's (☎ 584-30-73; Cerrada de la Luna s/n; r US$14-24 with shared bathroom, with private bathroom US$29, all with continental breakfast) Penelope's, with just four rooms, is set in a quiet, leafy neighborhood high above Playa del Panteón. It's just off the Zipolite road, clearly signposted about 200m beyond the fork to Playa del Panteón. The rooms are clean, with good beds and screens, decent bathrooms and ceiling fans; three are spacious. An attractive terrace restaurant serves economical meals, and hammocks provide lounging opportunities. Ownership was changing at the time of research; the new management may start offering yoga classes.

Casa de Huéspedes Gundi y Tomás (☎ 584-30-68; www.puertoangel-hotel.com; off Blvd Uribe; r with shared/private bathroom US$24/29) This tranquil guesthouse has a variety of brightly decorated, basic rooms, all with fans, mosquito nets and/or screens, and some offbeat artistic touches. Good food is available, including homemade bread, mainly vegetarian snacks, fruit drinks and a nightly US$6.50 *menú*. The main dining area and one clutch of rooms have outstanding views. Gundi, the friendly German owner, speaks good English and Spanish and provides a safe for valuables, a book exchange, bus and plane tickets and an exchange service for cash or traveler's checks.

El Almendro (☎ 584-30-68; www.puertoangel-hotel .com; off Blvd Uribe; r US$29, bungalow US$57) Set in a shady garden up a little lane, El Almendro has six clean, brightly painted, basic rooms with OK beds and bathrooms, plus a bungalow for up to six people. From November to April, the 6pm to 7pm happy hour is followed by a barbecue dinner of marinated meats or fish, salad from the salad bar and baked potatoes (US$7).

Villa Serena Florencia (☎ 584-30-44; villa serena oax@hotmail.com; Blvd Uribe s/n; s/d/tr US$24/33/38, air-con US$3 extra; 🌣) The well-established Florencia has 13 agreeable, smallish rooms with fans and screens, all set off a couple of walkways. It also offers a shady sitting area and a good Italian restaurant.

Hotel Soraya (☎ 584-30-09; Vasconcelos s/n; with fan d US$29-38, tr US$33-43, q US$38-47, with air-con d/ tr/q US$47/52/57; 🅿 🌣) Overlooking the bay, the Soraya has 32 clean, tiled-floor rooms with fairly good beds and good bathrooms. All have balconies and some have very good views and a hot-water bathroom.

Hotel Cordelia's (☎ 584-31-09; Playa del Panteón; d with/without ocean view US$33/19, tr US$38/57; P ⚡) Cordelia's is a newer hotel right in the middle of this lovely beach. Run by the same family as the Azul Profundo dive shop, it has at least eight rooms, four of which are spacious with good-sized Talavera-tiled bathrooms, and terraces overlooking the sea. Construction was ongoing at the time of research, and Cordelia was about to install air-con and hot water in all rooms as well as good mosquito screens.

Casa Arnel (☎ 584-30-51; arnelpto.angel@huatulco .net.mx; Azueta 666; s/d US$24/29; 🖳) Casa Arnel, up the lane past the market, has five clean, ample tile-floored rooms with fans, and OK beds and bathrooms. *Refrescos* (soft drinks), coffee and tea are available, and there's an upstairs hammock area as well as a small library and a place to wash and dry clothes.

Eating & Drinking

La Buena Vista (☎ /fax 584-31-04; La Buena Compañía s/n; breakfast US$2.50-4, dinner mains US$5-8; ⏲ 7-11am & 6-10pm, Mon-Sat) Be sure to pre-book dinner out of the high seasons or you may find they're not serving food. On an airy terrace overlooking the bay, La Buena Vista's restaurant offers well-prepared Mexican and Italian fare, from hotcakes to *chiles rellenos* with a *quesillo* filling.

La Posada Cañón Devata (☎ 584-31-37; off Sáenz de Barandas; breakfast US$3-4, dinner US$15; ⏲ breakfast 8:30am-noon, dinner from 7:30pm) Outsiders are welcome here. A good three-course dinner is served at long tables in a lovely palm-roofed, open-sided dining room. Fare is whole-food vegetarian and fish dishes. Book early in the day.

Villa Serena Florencia (☎ 584-30-44; Blvd Uribe s/n; dishes US$3-7) A reliable standby, this Italian restaurant turns out good pasta dishes, salads, Mexican fare and pizzas, all at very good prices. Breakfasts (served in high season only) are inexpensive.

Beto's (Carretera a Zipolite s/n; fish fillets US$3.75, seviche US$3, chicken & beef dishes US$4.25-5; ⏲ 4pm-midnight) On the uphill stretch of Blvd Uribe, Beto's is a relaxed, economical, friendly and clean little place with a large terrace.

The restaurants on Playa del Panteón offer fish and seafood for US$5 to US$11, plus cheaper fare such as *entomatadas* (a variation on enchiladas, made with corn tortillas, tomato sauce, spices and various fillings, such as chicken or cheese) and eggs. Be careful about the freshness of seafood in the low season. The setting is very pretty after dark. **Restaurante Susy** (☎ 584-30-19) is one of the better beachside establishments.

You'll also find several economical places to eat on the main town beach, though none is very well frequented.

Getting There & Away

See the boxed text on p255 for details of transportation from Pochutla. An EV/OP bus to Oaxaca (US$7.50, seven hours) departs at 10pm nightly from near the foot of Vasconcelos. A taxi to/from Zipolite costs US$0.50 *colectivo*, or US$3 for the whole cab (US$5 after dark and even more after 10pm or 11pm). You can find cabs on Blvd Uribe; there's a stand at the foot of Vasconcelos.

A taxi to Bahías de Huatulco airport costs US$35, to Puerto Escondido airport US$45.

ZIPOLITE

☎ 958 / pop 1200

The beautiful 1.5km stretch of pale sand called Zipolite, beginning about 2.5km west of Puerto Ángel, is fabled as southern Mexico's perfect budget chill-out spot. Inexpensive places to stay and eat line nearly the whole beach, and the combination of pounding sea and sun, open-air sleeping, eating and drinking, unique scenery and a lively travelers' scene make Zipolite a great place to indulge yourself for a few days. Or overindulge, if you follow the lead of some visitors.

Orientation

The eastern end of Zipolite (nearest Puerto Ángel) is called Colonia Playa del Amor, the middle part is Centro, and the western end (divided from Centro by a narrow creek or lagoon, often called *el arroyo*) is Colonia Roca Blanca. The few streets behind the beach are mostly nameless; Av Roca Blanca, a block back from the beach in Colonia Roca Blanca, is the most prominent and is more commonly known as the Adoquín, for its paving blocks.

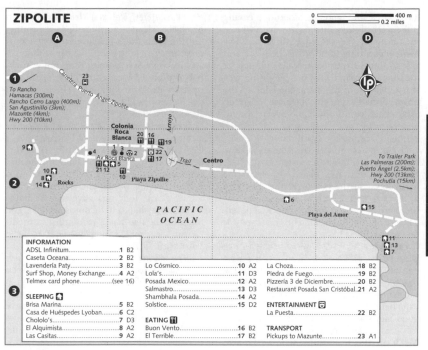

ZIPOLITE

INFORMATION		
ADSL Infinitum	..1	B2
Caseta Oceana	..2	B2
Lavendería Paty	..3	B2
Surf Shop, Money Exchange	..4	A2
Telmex card phone	(see 16)	

SLEEPING 🏠		
Brisa Marina	..5	B2
Casa de Huéspedes Lyoban	..6	C2
Chololo's	..7	D3
El Alquimista	..8	A2
Las Casitas	..9	A2
Lo Cósmico	.10	A2
Lola's	.11	D3
Posada Mexico	.12	A2
Salmastro	.13	D3
Shambhala Posada	.14	A2
Solstice	.15	D2

EATING 🍴		
Buon Vento	.16	B2
El Terrible	.17	B2
La Choza	.18	B2
Piedra de Fuego	.19	B2
Pizzería 3 de Diciembre	.20	B2
Restaurant Posada San Cristóbal	.21	A2

ENTERTAINMENT 🎭		
La Puesta	.22	B2

TRANSPORT		
Pickups to Mazunte	.23	A1

Information

Banks The nearest banks are in Pochutla, but some accommodations may accept US dollars or euros. A combination surf shop and money exchange lies at the west end of the Adoquín.

Caseta Oceana (Av Roca Blanca) Has long-distance phone service.

Lavandería Paty (Av Roca Blanca; same-day laundry service per kilo US$1.25; 🕑 8am-5pm Mon-Sat)

ADSL Infinitum (Av Roca Blanca; Internet per hr US$1.50; 🕑 9am-9pm) Has Internet service and long-distance phone service.

There's a Telmex card phone outside the Buon Vento restaurant.

Dangers & Annoyances

By most reports, security in Zipolite has improved, but theft can be a problem, and it's not advisable to walk along the Puerto Ángel–Zipolite road or the beach after dark.

Sleeping

Most accommodation is right on the beach, where nearly every business rents small rooms, cabanas or hammocks. Unless otherwise stated, rooms here have shared bathrooms and beds have mosquito nets. Rates here are for the high season (roughly mid-November to mid-April, as well as August for many places).

Posada México (☎ 584-31-94; www.posadamexico .com; Av Roca Blanca; r US$15-20) Opened in 2004, the latest arrival on the Zipolite beachfront injects some welcome freshness. All rooms

---

DEADLY SURF

The Zipolite surf is deadly, literally. It's fraught with riptides, changing currents and a strong undertow. Locals don't swim here, and going in deeper than your knees can mean risking your life. Most years several people drown here. Local voluntary *sal-vavidas* (lifeguards) have rescued many, but they don't maintain a permanent watch. If you do get swept out to sea, swim calmly parallel to the shore to get clear of the current pulling you outward. *Surfistas* take note: the beach break here is one only experienced surfers should attempt.

have safes and good beds, and pleasing Italian-sensibility touches are everywhere, including in the shared bathrooms. The owners continue to improve the place and are adding private bathrooms, though at the time of research only the delightful two-story, two-room cabana at the back of the property had them. By the time you read this, a chef from Italy's Cinquerre should be serving up meals in the restaurant (which is open December to April only).

El Alquimista (www.el-alquimista.com; bungalow US$50) One of Zipolite's most luxurious accommodations, this place has eight fine bungalows on the beach (at the west end of Playa Zipolite), each with homespun textiles, fan, bathroom and hammocked porch. They're often full. The attached restaurant is one of Zipolite's best.

Las Casitas (☎ 585-72-63; www.las-casitas.net; bungalows s US$17, d US$24-43, tr US$29-38) At the west end of Playa Zipolite and set back from the beach on a hill, Las Casitas has seven tasteful, semi–open-air bungalows (six with private bathrooms and kitchens). Most have good views as well, at least in the dry, leafless season, and some have swinging beds. Meals in the beautifully sited restaurant start at US$20.

Lo Cósmico (www.locosmico.com; d cabanas US$10-25, extra person US$5, hammocks US$5) Very relaxed Lo Cósmico has conical-roofed cabanas dotted around a tall rock outcrop at the west end of Playa Zipolite. Each has a double bed, hammock and fan; the cheaper ones are a bit enclosed, while the pricier ones have two stories and views. The hammock area is on a clifftop overlooking the beach, and has lockers; a security box is available to cabana guests. Some private bathrooms are going in to supplement the mediocre common ones, and there's a good on-site restaurant.

Solstice (www.solstice-mexico.com; Colonia Playa del Amor; dm US$11, studio US$27-32, bungalow US$39) This excellent, friendly, Dutch-owned retreat, set back from the beach, specializes in yoga courses. Thatched bungalows, studios and dorm accommodations, all fan-cooled, are set around a central space; decor is bright and homey. Bathrooms have a barrel and bucket in lieu of showers. The yoga room is large and inviting, with a full inventory of props. Book ahead, as group retreats fill the place up.

Casa de Huéspedes Lyoban (☎ 584-31-77; www .lyoban.com.mx; Colonia Playa del Amor; hammock US$6,

s/d/tr US$13/16/21) Relaxed, friendly Lyoban has basic, clean rooms: the beds are comfy, but the walls don't reach the ceiling. Common areas include a sociable bar-restaurant space with board games; ping-pong, foosball and pool tables; a small library; and an upstairs deck for lounging. The hammock price includes a blanket, a sturdy locker and shower usage.

Shambhala Posada (Casa Gloria; www.advantage mexico.com/shambhala; hammock US$4, dm US$6, s US$7-8, d US$8-9, cabanas from US$25; **P**) This ecologically (if somewhat shambhalically) run guesthouse climbs the hill at the west end of Playa Zipolite, and has some great views. Some lodgings have private bathrooms; the shared bathrooms are all right. Shambhala also has a restaurant, a meditation area, and a luggage room to keep your stuff safe.

Brisa Marina (☎ 584-31-93; brisamarinaca@yahoo .com; Colonia Roca Blanca; r with/without bathroom US$30/15; **P**) The more expensive rooms at American-owned Brisa occupy a concrete building fronting the beach. They have bathroom, fan and safe; some have views and balconies. There is also a common safe. A rear wooden section has cheaper rooms.

Lola's (☎ 584-32-01; s/d US$15/30; **P** **▢**) Third from the east end of Playa del Amor, Lola's has 25 reasonable rooms on two levels of a brick building. They come with good beds, tiled floors, OK private bathrooms, fans and mosquito screens.

Chololo's (☎ 584-31-59; r US$20, with private bathroom US$25; **P**) With five simple rooms at the easternmost spot on Playa del Amor, this very friendly place also serves good Mexican and Italian food.

Salmastro (☎ 584-31-61; r US$12-32; **P**) At the east end of Playa del Amor, Salmastro's eight basic rooms (some upstairs, some with sea views) have good beds and thatched roofs.

Trailer Park Las Palmeras (Fernando's Camp Ground; Carretera Puerto Ángel-Zipolite; tent space US$2 plus US$2 per person; **P**) This small park, beside the road from Puerto Ángel as you enter Zipolite, has a grassy plot edged with trees. Rates include showers and toilets, water for washing and 24-hour caretaking.

Eating

Eating and drinking in the open air a few steps from the surf is an inimitable Zipolite experience. Most accommodations have a restaurant of some kind, and some good independent places serve food as well.

El Alquimista (mains US$3.50-9.50; 3pm-midnight) One of Zipolite's classiest, the Alchemist is delightfully sited in a sandy cove at the west end of Playa Zipolite. Its very wide-ranging fare runs from falafel *tortas* to good meat and chicken dishes, complemented by a full bar and good espresso.

Buon Vento (Colonia Roca Blanca; pastas US$3.50-5; 6pm-midnight Thu-Tue) On the street between Av Roca Blanca and the main road, this excellent Italian restaurant has good music and subtle vibes. The huge pasta list includes some delicious baked options, and the wine list is decent for Mexico.

Piedra de Fuego (Colonia Roca Blanca; mains US$3.50-5; 3-11pm) At this superbly simple, relaxed and family-run place, you'll get a generous serving of fish fillet or prawns, accompanied by rice, salad and tortillas. They have four rooms for rent also, smelling pleasantly of wood.

El Terrible (Colonia Roca Blanca; pizzas US$5.50-7.25, crepes US$2.25-4.75; 6am-midnight Fri-Wed) The Francophone couple here make a variety of damn good pizzas large enough to feed two moderate people or one gluttonous travel writer. Fresh anchovies, anyone? They do sweet and savory crepes as well.

Lo Cósmico (dishes US$3-5; 8pm-4am; V) Mellow out on the rocks above the beach, at the west end of Playa Zipolite, at this open-air restaurant with good food from an impeccably clean kitchen. Especially tasty are the crepes (sweet and savory) and salads.

Pizzería 3 de Diciembre (Colonia Roca Blanca; prices US$3.75-6; 7pm-2am Wed-Sun) The 3 de Diciembre serves not only excellent pizzas but also good pastry pies with fillings such as cauliflower and Parmesan or baked spinach. It's just the place for late-night munchies.

La Choza (☎ 584-31-90; Colonia Roca Blanca; mains US$5-8) La Choza's beachside restaurant has a wide-ranging menu including many Mexican favorites, such as *pescado al mojo de ajo* (grilled fish with garlic sauce), most done well, with generous servings.

Restaurant Posada San Cristóbal (☎ 584-31-91; Colonia Roca Blanca; mains US$3.50-11.50) St Chris' wide variety of food runs from several breakfast items to *antojitos*, salads, whole fish, prawns, octopus and chicken.

Drinking & Entertainment

Zipolite's beachfront restaurant-bars have unbeatable locations for drinks around sunset and after dark. Those toward the west end of the beach are generally the most popular – especially **El Alquimista**, which plays cool music and serves cocktails as well as the usual beer, mezcal and so forth. The swing seats at the bar can get tricky after a few. The open-air *discoteca* **La Puesta** (Colonia Roca Blanca; 9pm-late Tue-Sat) provides slightly more active nightlife than the bars, cranking tunes out through the ether into the wee hours. Nothing much happens before midnight.

Getting There & Away

See the boxed text on p255 for details on transportation from Pochutla and Puerto Ángel. The *camionetas* between Pochutla and San Agustinillo, via Mazunte, terminate on the main road at the far west end of Zipolite (about 2km from the east end of the beach). *Colectivo* taxis from Puerto Ángel will go to the same spot too, but pass along the length of Av Roca Blanca en route so are a better bet if you're heading for the east end of the beach.

After dark, an *especial* taxi is your only option for getting to Puerto Ángel or San Agustinillo (about US$5 from 6pm until about 10pm, more after that).

SAN AGUSTINILLO

☎ 958 / pop 250

Long, straight and nearly empty Playa Aragón stretches west from the headland at the west end of Zipolite to the growing village of San Agustinillo. Footpaths behind Shambhala Posada cross the headland from Zipolite; by the main coast road, it's a 4km drive. Most tourist facilities are right on or just off the main road.

Sights & Activities

San Agustinillo's small curved bay has waves that are perfect for **boogie-boarding** and often good for **bodysurfing**. The **swimming** is very good as well, but don't get near the rocks. Several relaxed little places to stay and a line of open-air beach *comedores* round out the picture. San Agustinillo has much more of a family atmosphere than its sometimes hedonistic neighbors, Zipolite and Mazunte, and generally higher standards of sanitation.

You can rent surfboards and boogie boards at **México Lindo y qué Rico!** (below) for US$5 and US$3 an hour respectively; snorkel gear costs US$2/US$4 per hour/day. They will also hook you up with surfing lessons, snorkeling trips, guided hikes, coffee *finca* tours and other activities. **Palapa Olas Altas** (right) offers 1½-hour *lancha* trips at US$15 per person for turtle-viewing (and occasionally dolphin-viewing). Internet access at **Hotel Malex**, on the east side of town, is US$1.50 per hour.

The coast between Zipolite and Puerto Escondido is a major sea-turtle nesting ground. Until hunting and killing sea turtles was banned in Mexico in 1990, San Agustinillo was the site of a slaughterhouse where some 50,000 turtles were killed per year for their meat and shells.

Sleeping & Eating

As with most places along the coast, unscreened rooms (and sometimes screened rooms) come with mosquito nets over the beds.

Un Sueño (www.unsueno.com; d/tr/q US$55/70/90; P) At the east end of Playa San Agustinillo, Sueño boasts four large, freestanding beachfront cabanas. Each has its own terrace with hammock, table and chairs, and artistic touches throughout, especially in the bathrooms. Fans augment the breeze coming through slatted-shutter windows. More cabanas were being built at the time of research.

México Lindo y qué Rico! (fafinyleila@latinmail .com; r US$30; closed Oct) Fourth along from the western end of Playa San Agustinillo, México Lindo's seven large rooms feature slat windows, fans and some bright touches such as tiled bathrooms. Especially good are the pair of breezy upstairs rooms under the tall *palapa* roof. The young, friendly owners serve good food (mains cost US$4 to US$7), including pizzas cooked in a brick oven.

Paraíso del Pescador (in the US & Canada 705-266-7771; www.paraiso-del-pescador.com; d/q US$35/50; P) In the center of town, uphill from the road, Pescador's spacious, modern rooms all have tile floors and good bathrooms, beds, air-con and screens, plus delicious views. The Canadian co-owner does sportfishing trips, and you can get decent coffee in the friendly restaurant.

Casamar (589-24-01; http://home1.stofanet .dk/casamar; r US$35 & US$45, ste US$65) Casamar, at the west end of Playa San Agustinillo, has two serviceable downstairs rooms with good hot-water bathrooms and two springy double beds each. The star here is the upstairs suite, with its large salon, ample balcony with shady hammock area, and kitchen (fridge and microwave). Beachside there's a small garden area with soaking pool.

Palapa Olas Altas (r with shared/private bathroom US$15/30; hammock/camping per person US$4/5) At the west end of Playa San Agustinillo, Olas Altas has 16 palatable fan rooms, one with sea views. The beachside restaurant serves decent food (mains US$5 to US$7).

Palapa de Evelia (breakfast US$2.50-3.50, mains US$6-7.50; 8am-5pm) Evelia's, third along from the west end of Playa San Agustinillo, does some of the best food on the beach, with straightforward but well-prepared fish and seafood, and great guacamole.

Two places have stunning positions atop the steep slope backing Playa Aragón (between Zipolite and San Agustinillo). Both can be reached by drivable tracks from the road or by paths up from the beach.

Rancho Cerro Largo (ranchocerrolargomx@yahoo .com.mx; Playa Aragón; s US$45-75, d US$45-85, extra person US$20, all incl breakfast & dinner; P) The RCL offers a variety of excellent accommodation in some half-dozen fan-cooled cabanas (both individual and shared, some with private bathrooms and some with tiny fridges). The beds and meals are top-notch, and the views from the shared toilets are superb.

Rancho Hamacas (589-85-48; hamacasilva@hot mail.com; Playa Aragón; cabanas with/without kitchen US$25/20; P) Further west on the hilltop from Rancho Cerro Largo, Rancho Hamacas has six cabanas with double beds. Half have fridges and gas burners. The owners make beautiful, strong hammocks (around US$60 to US$170 depending on size), and serve food at their restaurant from December to March.

Getting There & Away

See p255 for information about transportation from Pochutla. *Colectivo* taxis to/from Zipolite or Mazunte cost US$0.50, and *camionetas* between Roca Blanca and Mazunte run US$0.30.

MAZUNTE
☎ 958 / pop 450

A kilometer west of San Agustinillo, Mazunte has a fine, curving, sandy beach, an interesting turtle research center and a variety of places to places to stay and eat, many of them inexpensive and right on the sand. It's well known as a travelers' hangout and in recent years has seen an increase in foreign residents, attracted by either the area's beauty or, as one person put it, the 'old-time hippie vibe.' After 1990, when the turtle industry was banned, several attempts at replacing Mazunte's former mainstay were made. Among those that stuck are the research center, a natural cosmetics factory and, obviously, tourism. The waters here are generally safe, though the waves can be quite big.

Orientation & Information

The paved road running west from Zipolite to Hwy 200 passes through the middle of Mazunte. Three sandy lanes run from the road to the beach (about 500m). The western one is called Camino al Rinconcito, as the west end of the beach is known as El Rinconcito, while the middle one is Camino a la Barrita. The eastern one shall remain nameless. **Mazunet** (Camino al Rinconcito; per hr US$1.50), near the main road, offers Internet access.

Sights & Activities

The **Centro Méxicano de la Tortuga** (Mexican Turtle Center; ☎ 584-30-55; admission US$2.25; ⊗ 10am-4:30pm Tue-Sat) is a turtle aquarium and research center with specimens of all seven of Mexico's marine turtle species on view in large tanks. It's enthralling to get a close-up view of these creatures, some of which are *big*. Visits are guided (in Spanish) and run every 10 to 15 minutes.

Mazunte's natural cosmetics workshop and store, **Cosméticos Naturales** (⊗ 9am-4pm Mon-Sat, 9am-2pm Sun), is on the Pacific side of the main road toward the west end of the village. It's a small cooperative making excellent shampoo and cosmetics from natural sources such as maize, coconut, avocado and sesame seeds. They also sell organic coffee, peanut butter and natural mosquito repellents, and rent out clean, affordable rooms that share bathrooms.

Aromatherapy massage is available at **Cabañas Balamjuyuc** (www.balamjuyuc.com; Camino a Punta Cometa), where a full-body massage costs US$22 per hour.

PUNTA COMETA

This rocky cape, jutting out from the west end of Mazunte beach, is the southernmost point in the state of Oaxaca and a fabulous place to be at sunset, with great long-distance views in both directions along the coast. You can walk there in 30 minutes over the rocks from the end of Mazunte beach, or start up the path that leads from the beach to Cabañas Balamjuyuc and make the first left.

PLAYA VENTANILLA

Some 2.5km along the road west from Mazunte, a sign points left to Playa Ventanilla, 1.2km down a dirt track. The settlement here includes a handful of simple homes, a couple of *comedores* and the *palapa* of **Servicios Ecoturísticos La Ventanilla** (☎ 589-92-77; laventanillamx@yahoo.com.mx; 1½hr lagoon tours adult/child US$5/2.50, under 6 free; ⊗ 8:30am-5pm). This local cooperative provides interesting 10-passenger canoe trips on a mangrove-fringed lagoon, the Estero de la Ventanilla, 400m along the beach. You'll see river crocodiles (there are about 380 in the lagoon), lots of water birds (most prolific from April to July) and, in an enclosure on an island in the lagoon, a few white-tailed deer. For the best fauna-spotting, make your trip in the early morning. Servicios Ecoturísticos also offers three-hour horseback rides (US$20; by reservation only) to another lagoon further west.

Frequent *camionetas* pass the turnoff, leaving you with the 1.2km walk. A taxi from Mazunte costs upwards of US$3.

Sleeping

Most places along Playa Mazunte (including restaurants) have basic rooms or cabanas, hammocks to rent and often tent space. Bathrooms are shared unless otherwise stated. Security can be a problem here.

Cabañas Ziga (☎ 583-92-95; d with shared/private bathroom US$20/38; ℗) Friendly Ziga, at the far east end of Playa Mazunte, is near the end of the easternmost access road, on a breezy beachside promontory that gives up some marvelous views after a very short climb. It has a good restaurant, a little flower garden and 17 fan rooms, all with good mosquito nets. The more expensive rooms have tile floors, good bathrooms and beds, as well as hammocks and terraces. Some of the best views are from the shared-bathroom quarters, which are in a wooden section at the front of the hotel.

Posada Arigalan (www.arigalan.com; d US$50-65, tr US$65; P ⊠ ⊠) Up a steep dirt track (above Playa Mazunte) from the main road, between Mazunte and San Agustinillo, Arigalan has commanding views of the Pacific and Punta Cometa, lovely landscaping and nine simply but tastefully furnished air-con rooms with private bathrooms. Its restaurant is open mid-November to mid-January (room rates outside of this time are 30% lower). A trail from the beach provides access as well.

The following two properties are perched next to each other on a hilltop above the west end of the beach, with some superb views. Their entrances are about 400m along a road that leads uphill from Camino al Rinconcito, and they're also reachable by steps up from the beach (it can be a hot climb).

Alta Mira (☎ 584-31-04; www.labuenavista.com /alta_mira; Camino a Punta Cometa; d with private bathroom US$35-40; P) The Alta Mira is run by the people from La Buena Vista at Puerto Ángel (p257), and its 10 electricity-free rooms are among Mazunte's classiest and comfiest, all with beautiful Talavera-tiled bathrooms, mosquito nets and terrace with hammock. They're strung beside steps leading down the hillside, and most catch some breeze and excellent views. The restaurant serves breakfast and dinner, and there's also a safety box.

Cabañas Balamjuyuc (www.balamjuyuc.com; Camino a Punta Cometa; s US$11, d US$16-40, extra person US$5; hammock US$4.50, tent s/d US$7/11.50; P) This quiet, tree-covered property has about seven cabana rooms, some of which are large and airy with good sea views. The shared showers are prettily tiled, and for true budget travelers there's a *palapa* with hammocks and tents (with mattresses). A safety box is available for storing valuables. Breakfast at the restaurant here costs US$2.50 to US$3, while mains are US$2 to US$7.

Palapa El Pescador (camping per person US$5, r US$15) This popular restaurant in the middle of Playa Mazunte has a small tent/hammock area on the sand and good, clean upstairs rooms with power.

Restaurante Tania (☎ 583-95-94; d US$20) Near the end of 2005, Tania completed a few simple rooms on the hill at the western edge

of town about 600m from the beach, above her restaurant. They're solid if not cheerful, with ceiling fans, private bathrooms and a removed sea view.

La Nueva Luna (Camino a La Barrita; r US$7.50 per person) A couple of hundred meters off the beach, the Luna is an exception among low-end Mazunte lodgings in that it has plenty of good (shared) bathrooms, as well as a shared kitchen. The three rooms are adjacent to a bar that was about to open at the time of research; how well the two would coexist was uncertain.

El Agujón (elagujonmazunte@yahoo.com.mx; Camino al Rinconcito; s/d cabana US$6.50/11; P) Friendly El Agujón has 10 small, very rustic, clean cabanas on the hillside just above its restaurant.

Estrella Fugaz (☎ 583-92-97; estrellafugazmazunte@ hotmail.com; Camino al Rinconcito; r per person US$15-20) The nine rooms here tend toward the gloomy and some are a bit malodorous, but all have, fans, mosquito nets, and sleep up to four people. Six have private bathrooms, and the restaurant upstairs has a good selection of Mexican and international dishes (mains US$3.50 to US$7), as well as veggie and fruit drinks and coffees.

Palapa Yuri (hammock per person US$5; tr with shared bathroom US$15, d with private bathroom US$29) Near the east end of Playa Mazunte, Yuri has adequate rooms that are plain but clean and have fans. Those with shared bathroom have OK views; a thatched roof blocks the view from those with private bathroom. There's a safety deposit box.

Palapa Omar (hammock or camping per person US$2.50, r US$10 per person) Omar is beside the end of the middle lane (Camino a La Barrita) to Playa Mazunte. The eight rooms in brick buildings have mosquito nets, fans and one or two double beds.

Eating

Most places to stay are also places to eat, or vice versa.

Palapa El Pescador (dishes US$2.50-7) One of the best and most popular places, El Pescador offers fish, seafood and lighter eats such as quesadillas, tacos, fruit salad, eggs and *tortas*. It's on Playa Mazunte, east of the lagoon.

El Agujón (Camino al Rinconcito; dishes US$2.25-7) Another good restaurant, with a very wide range from large and excellent French-bread *tortas* to crepes, fish and, in the evening, pizzas.

Restaurante Bar Bella Vista (fish fillets US$4.50, spaghetti US$3.50) With its elevated position at the east end of Playa Mazunte, this restaurant, which belongs to Cabañas Ziga, catches a breeze.

La Dolce Vita (mains US$5-8; ☙ closed October) This Italian restaurant, on the main road (east of Cosméticos Naturales), is well known for its excellent food.

La Empanada (sushi US$3-4, rice dishes US$1-5; ☙ from 5pm low seasons, 9am-late high seasons) Choose from a Mexican-Asian mix of delectable items including vegetable and fish sushi, all lovingly prepared. You'll find La Empanada on the main road, at the west edge of town.

Restaurante Tania (comida corrida US$3.50, fish fillets US$4.50-5, vegetarian dishes US$2-3) At the western edge of town, on the main road, Tania's scores high marks for both its good-value food and hospitality.

Entertainment

La Nueva Luna (Camino a La Barrita; ☙ 6pm-late; closed October) Adjacent to the lodgings of the same name, this bar was nearly ready to open at the time of research. It has a ping-pong table and a pleasantly shady ambience. The Argentine operator hopes to have live music from December to April, and to serve mixed drinks made with natural fruit juices.

Getting There & Away

See p255 for information about transportation from Pochutla. *Camionetas* between Mazunte and San Agustinillo or Zipolite cost US$0.40.

BAHÍAS DE HUATULCO

☎ 958 / pop 18,000

Mexico's newest big coastal resort is strung along a series of beautiful sandy bays, the Bahías de Huatulco (wah-*tool*-koh), 45km east of Pochutla. This stretch of coast had just one small fishing village until the 1980s. The Mexican government has trod more gently here than at other resort projects: pockets of development are separated by tracts of unspoiled shoreline, the maximum building height is six stories, and water-processing plants supposedly assure that no sewage goes into the sea. (Testing by Mexico's

environmental agency has shown that there is in fact some contamination of the waters.) Lower than expected occupancy rates have slowed development, and for now at least, Huatulco is still a relatively uncrowded resort with a succession of scenic beaches lapped by beautiful water and backed by forest. You can have an active time here – agencies offer all sorts of energetic pursuits from rafting and horseback riding to diving and kayaking. Huatulco is not a place to stay long on a tight budget, however.

The Parque Nacional Huatulco, declared in 1998, protects 119 sq km of land, sea and shoreline west of Santa Cruz Huatulco. Balancing this, a cruise ship pier has gone in at Bahía de Santa Cruz, and between October and May an average of two ships a week dock there, discharging thousands of passengers for brief visits to the area.

Orientation

A divided road leads about 4km down from Hwy 200 to La Crucecita, the service town for the resort. La Crucecita has the bus stations, market, most of the shops and virtually the only cheap accommodations. One kilometer south, on Bahía de Santa Cruz, is Santa Cruz Huatulco (often just called Santa Cruz), with somewhat plush hotels and a harbor. The other main developments so far are at Bahía Chahué, with mainly midrange hotels, 1km east of Santa Cruz; Tangolunda, 4km further east with most of the luxury hotels; and El

LA CRUCECITA

0 — 200 m
0 — 0.1 miles

INFORMATION
Bahías Plus	1 B3
Banamex (ATM)	2 B3
Casa de la Cultura	(see 7)
El Telefonito	3 B3
HSBC	4 A2
HSBC (ATM)	(see 16)
Information Kiosk	5 B3
Lavado Express	6 B4
Municipal Tourist Office	7 B4
Post Office	8 C3
Surf Conejo (Internet)	(see 16)
Turismo Conejo	(see 16)

SIGHTS & ACTIVITIES
Centro de Buceo Sotaveno	9 B4
Parroquia de Nuestra Señora de Guadalupe	10 A3

SLEEPING
Hotel Arrecife	11 A4
Hotel Busanvi I	12 B3
Hotel Flamboyant	13 A3
Hotel Jaroje	14 B4
Hotel María Mixteca	15 B3
Hotel Plaza Conejo	16 B3
Hotel Suites Begonias	17 B4
Misión de los Arcos	18 A3
Posada Michelle	19 A2

EATING
Comedores	20 B3
Don Wilo	21 B3
El Patio	22 B3
Paletería Zamora	23 B3
Restaurant La Crucecita	24 B4
Restaurant-Bar Oasis	25 B3
Terra-Cotta	26 A3
Tostado's Grill	27 B4

DRINKING
La Crema	28 B3

ENTERTAINMENT
Cinemas Huatulco	29 B3
La Peña	30 B3

TRANSPORT
Budget	31 A3
Bus Stop	32 B3
Colectivo Taxi & Microbus Stop	33 B3
Estrella Blanca Bus Station	34 A2
OCC & Sur Bus Station	35 A2
Transportes Rápidos de Pochutla Bus Stop	36 A1

Faro, near Playa La Entrega, 2.5km south of Santa Cruz.

The Huatulco bays are strung along the coast about 10km in each direction from Santa Cruz. From southwest to northeast, the main ones are San Agustín, Chachacual, Cacaluta, Maguey, El Órgano, Santa Cruz, Chahué, Tangolunda and Conejos.

Bahías de Huatulco airport is 400m north of Hwy 200, 12km west of the turnoff to La Crucecita.

Information

INTERNET ACCESS

The two La Crucecita facilities listed here have swift connections and allow laptops to jack in for the same price as regular browsing (US$1 per hour).

El Telefonito (Map p266; Flamboyán 208; ⏱ 24hr)
Surf Conejo (Map p266; Guamuchil 208)

LAUNDRY

Lavado Express (Map p266; ☎ 587-27-37; Bugambilia 402, La Crucecita; ⏱ 9am-9pm Mon-Sat, 10am-3pm Sun) Washes and dries 3kg for US$4.50. Ask for it *sin suavizante* to avoid the perfumey fabric softener.

MEDICAL SERVICES

Dr Andrés González Ayvar (☎ 587-06-00, 044-958-587-60-65) Provides 24-hour medical assistance.

The big hotels have English-speaking doctors on call.
Hospital IMSS (☎ 587-11-84; Blvd Chahué) Halfway between La Crucecita and Bahía Chahué; some doctors speak English.

MONEY

La Crucecita has several ATMs and banks, including the following:
Banamex ATM (Map p266; cnr Carrizal & Guamuchil)
HSBC (Map p266; cnr Bugambilia & Sabalí; ⏱ 9am-7pm Mon-Sat) Changes cash and traveler's checks, and has two ATMs, with another in Hotel Plaza Conejo.

There are more facilities in Santa Cruz Huatulco and Tangolunda:
Banamex (Map p268; Blvd Santa Cruz, Santa Cruz) Changes cash and traveler's checks and has an ATM.
Bancomer (Map p268; Blvd Santa Cruz, Santa Cruz)
HSBC ATM (Blvd Juárez, Tangolunda) In Hotel Gala.

POST

Post office (Map p266; Blvd Chahué, La Crucecita) About 300m east of Plaza Principal.

TOURIST INFORMATION

Information kiosk (Map p266; Plaza Principal, La Crucecita; ⏱ 9am-2pm & 4-7pm Mon-Fri, 9am-1pm Sat, closed in off-season)
Municipal tourist office (Map p266; ☎ 587-18-71; turismohuatulco@hotmail.com; cnr Bugambilia & Ceiba, La Crucecita; ⏱ 9am-5pm Mon-Fri, 9am-1pm Sat, closed in off-season) Upstairs in the Casa de la Cultura.
Parque Nacional Huatulco Office (Map p268; ☎ 587-08-49; Santa Cruz; ⏱ 9am-noon, 2-6pm Mon-Fri) Upstairs in the port.
State tourist office (☎ 581-01-77; sedetur@oaxaca.gob .mx; Blvd Juárez s/n; ⏱ 8am-4pm Mon-Fri, 9am-2pm Sat) In Tangolunda, on the left as you arrive from the west.

TRAVEL AGENCIES

Bahías Plus (Map p266; ☎ 587-02-16; Carrizal 704, upstairs, La Crucecita) Can help with air tickets; also books rafting tours, coffee *finca* visits etc.

Sights & Activities

La Crucecita's modern church, the **Parroquia de Nuestra Señora de Guadalupe** (Plaza Principal), has an impressively large image of the Virgin painted on its ceiling. The rest of the area's attractions are on the water, at the beaches or in jungle hinterland. You can sail, snorkel, dive, kayak, surf, fish, raft, canoe, walk in the jungle, watch birds, ride horses, rappel, canyon, cycle, visit a coffee plantation and waterfalls and more. Most outings cost US$23 to US$33. **Bahías Plus** travel agency, **Turismo Conejo** (Map p266; ☎ 587-00-09; turismoconejo@hotmail.com; Guamuchil 208, La Crucecita) and several hotels will book many of the activities listed here.

BEACHES

Huatulco's beaches are sandy with clear waters (though boats and jet skis leave an oily film here and there). Like the rest of Mexico, all beaches are under federal control, and anyone can use them – even when hotels appear to treat them as private property. Some have coral offshore and excellent snorkeling, though visibility can be poor in the rainy season.

Lanchas will whisk you out to most of the beaches from Santa Cruz Huatulco harbor any time between 8am and 5pm or 6pm, and they'll return to collect you by dusk. Taxis can get you to most beaches for less money, but a boat ride is more fun. Hire and board the *lanchas* (Map p268) beside the harbor. Round-trip rates for up to 10 people

SANTA CRUZ HUATULCO

0 _____ 200 m
0 _____ 0.1 miles

INFORMATION
Banamex.................................1 B2
Bancomer..............................2 B2
HSBC......................................3 C2
Parque Nacional Huatulco
    Office.................................4 D2

SIGHTS & ACTIVITIES
Hurricane Divers.....................5 C3

SLEEPING
Hotel Castillo Huatulco.............6 C1
Hotel Marina Resort..................7 D2
Hotel Sol y Mar.......................8 B3

EATING
Café Huatulco.........................9 C2
Jardín del Arte.......................10 B3
Restaurant Ve El Mar..............11 D3

SHOPPING
Mercado de Artesanías...........12 C2

To Chahué Hotels (500m);
Bahía Chahué (500m);
Plaza Chahué (700m);
La Crucecita (1km);
Tangolunda (3km)

Blvd Santa Cruz
Tehuantepec
Harbor
Coyula
Pochutla
Ortlán
Monte Albán
Plaza Santa Cruz
Mitla
Huatulco
To Playa La Entrega (2km);
Bahía Maguey (5km)
Cruise Ship Pier
Playa Santa Cruz
Bahía de Santa Cruz

TRANSPORT
Aerotucán Huatulco..............13 C1
Colectivo Taxi & Microbus
    Stop................................14 C2
Lancha Tickets & Embarkation.15 C2
Private Taxi Stand..................16 C2

include Playa La Entrega (US$18), Bahía Maguey and Bahía El Órgano (US$46) and La India (US$73). Another possibility for a fun day is a 6½-hour, **seven-bay boat cruise** (per person US$20; ☉ 11am-5:30pm) with an open bar. A *lancha* will make the same excursion (less the booze) for US$120 for up to 10 people.

At Santa Cruz Huatulco, the small, accessible **Playa Santa Cruz** is rather pretty, though its looks are somewhat marred by the cruise-ship pier. **Playa La Entrega** lies toward the outer edge of Bahía de Santa Cruz, a five-minute *lancha* trip or 2.5km by paved road from Santa Cruz. The 300m-long beach, backed by a line of seafood *palapas*, can get crowded, but it has calm water and good snorkeling in a large area from which boats are cordoned off. 'La Entrega' means 'the Handover': it was here in 1831 that Mexican independence hero Vicente Guerrero was betrayed to his enemies by a Genoese sea captain. Guerrero was taken to Cuilapan near Oaxaca and shot.

Some of the western bays are accessible by road; at times groups of young men congregate in their parking lots, offering to

'watch your car,' and touting for the beach restaurants. A 1.5km paved road diverges to **Bahía Maguey** from the road to La Entrega, about half a kilometer out of Santa Cruz. Maguey's fine 400m beach curves around a calm bay between forested headlands. It has a line of seafood *palapas*. There's good snorkeling around the rocks at the left (east) side of the bay. **Bahía El Órgano**, just east of Maguey, has a 250m beach. You can reach it by a narrow 10-minute footpath that heads into the trees halfway along the Santa Cruz–Maguey road. El Órgano has calm waters good for snorkeling, but it lacks *comedores*.

The beach at **Bahía Cacaluta** is about 1km long and protected by an island, though there can be undertow. Snorkeling is best around the island. Behind the beach is a lagoon with bird life. The road to Cacaluta (which branches off just above the parking lot for Maguey) is paved except for the last 1.5km, but it can be a long, hot walk, and there are no services at the beach itself. You probably wouldn't want to leave a car at pavement's end, either, as it's quite isolated.

Cacaluta has a research station for the study of turtles and sea snails.

Bahía Chachacual, inaccessible by land, has a headland at each end and two beaches. The easterly **Playa La India** is one of Huatulco's most beautiful and one of the area's best places for snorkeling.

Thirteen kilometers down a dirt road from a crossroads on Hwy 200, 1.7km west of the airport, is **Bahía San Agustín**. After 6km the road fords a river. The beach is long and sandy, with a long line of *palapa comedores*, some with hammocks for rent overnight. It's popular with Mexicans on Saturdays, Sundays and holidays, but quiet at other times. Usually the waters are calm and the snorkeling is good (some of the *comedores* rent equipment).

A paved road runs to the eastern bays from La Crucecita and Santa Cruz, continuing eventually to Hwy 200. **Bahía Chahué** has a good beach and a new marina at its east end. Further northeast, **Bahía Tangolunda** is the site of the major top-end hotel developments to date. The sea is sometimes rough here, so be wary of currents and be sure to heed the colored-flag safety system. Tangolunda has an 18-hole golf course too. Three kilometers further east is the long sweep of **Playa Punta Arena**, on Bahía Conejos. Around a headland at the east end of Bahía Conejos is the more sheltered **Playa Conejos**, unreachable by road.

PARQUE ECOLÓGICO RUFINO TAMAYO

This park (Map p266) on the edge of La Crucecita is composed mainly of natural vegetation, with some paved paths and tile-roofed shelters with benches.

SNORKELING & DIVING

You can rent snorkeling gear beside the *lancha* kiosk at Santa Cruz harbor for about US$5.75 a day. At Playa Maguey you can rent a snorkel, mask and fins for US$5.50 a day. Tour guides will take you snorkeling for US$20 to US$45, or you can arrange a trip with one of the dive outfits listed here.

Huatulco has around 13 dive sites, with a wide variety of fish and corals, as well as dolphins and sea turtles. At least two companies will take you diving and offer instruction from beginner's sessions through to full certification courses.

Centro de Buceo Sotavento La Crucecita (Map p266; ☎ 587-21-66; www.tomzap.com/sotavento.html; Local 18

Interior, Plaza Oaxaca, Flamboyán); Tangolunda (☎ 581-00-51; Plaza Las Conchas, Local 12) This excellent local company offers a range of options from a four-hour introduction (US$65) to full certification (five days; US$320) or specialty night dives (US$65); they also do two-hour fishing trips for one to six people (US$45 to US$80, depending on vessel), as well as snorkeling trips for US$15 per person.

Hurricane Divers (Map p268; ☎ 587-11-07; www .hurricanedivers.com; Playa Santa Cruz) The professional international crew here speak English, Spanish, Dutch and German, and offer a variety of courses and dives. One-tank dives are US$50; PADI programs (with ocean dive) start at US$95. They do half- and full-day snorkeling trips as well (US$50/100).

RAFTING

The Copalita and Zimatán Rivers near Bahías de Huatulco have waters ranging from class 1 to class 4/5 in rafting terms. They're at their biggest in the rainy season, between July and November. **Turismo Conejo** (p267) books rafting and kayaking trips for US$61 to US$66 per person, or contact **Pablo Nárvaez** (☎ 044-958-585-03-03; pablo_rafting@ yahoo.com).

HORSEBACK RIDING

Rancho Caballo de Mar (☎ 587-03-66; Playa Punta Arena, Bahía de Conejos; 3½hr rides US$47) This company runs a beach and forest tour (reservations necessary); the staff speak English and French.

Sleeping

All midrange and top-end rooms listed here are air-conditioned. Rates quoted in those categories are for the high seasons (roughly December to April and July to mid-August). Peak periods around Christmas and Easter see considerably higher rates.

BUDGET

With the exception of holiday peak periods (when their rates roughly double), these hotels maintain their prices year-round.

Hotel Jaroje (Map p266; ☎ 583-48-01; http://jaroje .tripod.com.mx; Bugambilia 304, La Crucecita; s/d US$29/38 with continental breakfast; ✕ 🖳) Bright, fresh, three-story Jaroje has good-sized, pleasantly decorated rooms with air-con, cable TV and fine bathrooms. Prices include 15 minutes of email checking.

Hotel Arrecife (Map p266; ☎ 587-17-07; hotel arrecife@hotmail.com; Colorín 510, La Crucecita; s with fan US$26-32, d with fan US$30-35, with air-con US$39; P ✗ 🖳 🖳) In a quiet, leafy neighborhood, the Arrecife has a small pool and a good little restaurant. Of the 24 rooms, the best are sizable, with two double beds, aircon (some old units) and balcony; others are small and open straight onto the street.

Hotel Busanvi I (Map p266; ☎ 587-00-56; Carrizal 601, La Crucecita; s/d with air-con US$14/28; ✗) The plain, largeish rooms here are a deal. Comfy beds, modern air-con and a small common area are all good, and the showers excellent. Six of the rooms have balconies, and prices stay low year-round.

Posada Michelle (Map p266; ☎ 587-05-35; Gardenia 8, La Crucecita; d US$29, tr or q US$47; ✗) The Michelle is next to the Estrella Blanca bus station and can be noisy until 9pm. Beds are springy and bathrooms poor, but the dozen or so rooms are brightly decorated and have decent air-con and cable TV. A little sitting area with hammocks adds some appeal as well.

Hotel Sol y Mar (Map p268; ☎ 587-16-61; Mitla s/n, Santa Cruz Huatulco; r US$30) This small hotel, whose good-sized rooms have fans and decent bathrooms, was still coming together at the time of research. Prices may rise as hot water and air-con are installed.

MIDRANGE

Santa Cruz' and Bahía Chahué's midrange options are generally more luxurious than those in La Crucecita.

María Mixteca (Map p266; ☎ 587-23-36; www.travel bymexico.com/oaxa/mariamixteca; Guamuchil 204, La Crucecita; s/d/tr US$50/55/60; ✗ 🖳) Small and a good value, the MM opened in 2004. It has 14 modern, very well equipped rooms on two upper floors, with super-comfy beds, great bathrooms, and room safes.

Misión de los Arcos (Map p266; ☎ 587-01-65; www .misiondelosarcos.com; Gardenia 902, La Crucecita; r/ste US$57/61; P ✗ 🖳) This 13-room American-owned hotel is embellished by a touch of interior greenery. It has big, bright comfortable rooms (all decorated in simple white and beige), a gym and a good restaurant.

Hotel Suites Begonias (Map p266; ☎ 587-03-90; getosa@prodigy.net.mx; Bugambilia 503, La Crucecita; d/tr US$57/66) Most of the lodgings here are comfortable two-room suites with two double beds and attractive bathrooms.

Hotel Posada Edén Costa (Map p266; ☎ 587-24-80; www.edencosta.com; Calle Zapoteco s/n, Chahué; r US$77, ste with salon & kitchen US$137; P ✗ 🖳) Swiss- and Laotian-owned Eden Costa, a block inland from Blvd Juárez, has quiet rooms with nice touches. Most overlook the small pool. The attached restaurant, L'échalote (p272), is a big bonus.

Hotel Flamboyant (Map p266; ☎ 587-01-13; flamboyhuatulco@prodigy.net.mx; Plaza Principal, La Crucecita; r incl breakfast US$89; P ✗) This pink hotel has a pleasant courtyard, an attractive pool, its own restaurant and 70 rooms. Decor is Oaxacan folksy.

Hotel Plaza Conejo (Map p266; ☎ 587-00-09; turis moconejo@hotmail.com; Guamuchil 208, La Crucecita; s US$29, d from US$47; ✗ 🖳) This friendly hotel has 10 tidy, bright, clean rooms off an interior patio; air-con is good, bathrooms so-so.

TOP END

Air and lodging packages are your best bet for an affordable holiday in a top-end Huatulco hotel. Another way to save is to look for promotions at hotel websites; you can often find prices well below the rack rates given here.

Quinta Real (☎ 581-04-28; www.quintareal.com; Paseo Juárez 2, Tangolunda; ste from US$346; P ✗ ✗ 🖳 🖳) The utterly gorgeous Quinta Real has a hilltop position at the west end of Tangolunda. Its 27 suites have Jacuzzi and ocean view; some have fountain-fed private pools that threaten to spill down the hillside to the beach and main swimming pool area.

Casa del Mar (☎ 581-02-03; Balcones de Tangolunda 13, Tangolunda; ste from US$120; P ✗ 🖳) Elegant and sensationally sited Casa del Mar, east of Tangolunda's main hotel cluster, has 25 well-appointed suites with great views, as well as a beautiful pool and restaurant. Reservations recommended.

Las Brisas (☎ 583-02-00; www.brisas.com.mx; Bahía de Tangolunda Lote 1, Tangolunda; r from US$188; ste from US$204; P ✗ ✗ 🖳 ⚓) Sprawling across more than 22 hectares, with its own four beaches, this former Club Med boasts 484 rooms, most with ocean views. It also offers 12 tennis courts; volleyball, squash and basketball courts; a children's club (babysitting available); and a full range of aquatic activities.

Camino Real Zaashila (☎ 581-04-60; www.camino real.com/zaashila; Blvd Juárez 5, Tangolunda; r from US$205 with breakfast; P ☒ ☒ ☐ ☒) Toward the east end of Tangolunda, this tranquil, attractive, Mediterranean-style property has a big pool in lovely gardens. There are 120 rooms; of these, 41 come with their own small pool and, of course, a higher price!

Hotel Marina Resort (Map p268; ☎ 587-09-63; www.hotelmarinaresort.com; Tehuantepec 112, Santa Cruz; r/ste US$142/177 with buffet breakfast; P ☒ ☒) The 50-room Marina Resort, on the east side of Santa Cruz harbor, has three pools, a nearby *temazcal* (a traditional-style steambath where mud is rubbed on you) and beach club, and lots of pastel green. Rooms have balconies, while suites have kitchenettes and private terraces with marina views.

Hotel Castillo Huatulco (Map p268; ☎ 587-01-44; www.boyce.com.mx; Blvd Santa Cruz 303, Santa Cruz; r US$153; P ☒ ☒) Colonial-style Castillo Huatulco has an attractive pool, a restaurant and 112 good-sized, brightly decorated rooms with safes. Transportation to the Castillo's beach club on Bahía Chahué is free. The hotel also offers packages with the third night for free.

Eating

LA CRUCECITA

Restaurant-Bar Oasis (Map p266; ☎ 587-13-00; Flamboyán 211, Plaza Principal; mains US$5.50-11.50) The Oasis has good, moderately priced fare, including *tortas,* fish fillets, steaks and Oaxacan specialties, sushi and other Japanese food. It's a popular breakfast spot but the execrable pop music can be hard to take in the morning.

Tostado's Grill (Map p266; ☎ 587-02-19; Flamboyán 306; mains US$5.50-12) Much of the menu is Italian food here, but they also serve a mean spinach salad with bacon. It's found in front of Hotel Posada del Parque.

Don Wilo (Map p266; ☎ 587-06-23; Guanacastle, Plaza Principal; mains US$5-15; closed Tue) The don's Oaxacan dishes, including tamales and *tlayudas*, are very popular. He also does fish, steaks and pizza.

Restaurant La Crucecita (Map p266; ☎ 587-09-06; cnr Bugambilia & Chacah; mains US$5-9; 7am-11pm) This inexpensive spot is a block south of the plaza. Its *sincronizadas a la mexicana* (multiple flour tortillas layered with ham and cheese then lightly fried; US$4) make a good *antojito*. Tasty *licuados* with yogurt or milk are a specialty (US$2). Early in the day, watch the chef prepare serious quantities

guacamole

of *salsa roja* (a red sauce of plum tomatoes, onions, garlic and salt).

El Patio (Map p266; ☎ 587-02-11; Flamboyán 214; breakfast US$3.50-5.50, mains US$5.50-9) An appealing garden patio with tables out back welcomes you here. The breakfasts are good deals; the rest of the day they offer the usual range of fish, seafood, chicken dishes and Oaxacan specialties, as well as a full selection of alcoholic drinks.

Terra-Cotta (Map p266; ☎ 587-12-28; cnr Gardenia & Priv Tamarindo; breakfast dishes US$3-4.50, sandwiches US$6.50; 8am-11:30pm) Soothing air-con and a garden view complement the good food at popular, American-run Terra-Cotta. Egg dishes, waffles, baguettes, fine espresso and ice cream go down easy, as do the several Mexican dishes on the menu.

Paletería Zamora (Map p266; cnr Flamboyán & Bugambilia) Don't let the name fool you; in addition to the wide variety of popsicles and ice cream, Zamora blends up a full range of fresh fruit drinks, *licuados* and *aguas frescas* (literally, 'cool waters' – fruit blended with water and sweetener).

Mercado (Map p266; cnr Bugambilia & Guanacastle; fish or shrimp platters US$5.50-6.50) The market's very clean *comedores* serve up good food, including *enfrijoladas* (corn tortillas smothered in beans, with a sprinkling of cheese) or *entomatadas* for US$3.25 each.

SANTA CRUZ HUATULCO

Restaurant Ve El Mar (Map p268; ☎ 587-03-64; Playa Santa Cruz; mains US$8.50-10; 8am-10pm) Food at the eateries on Playa Santa Cruz is mostly average, but this place at the east end is an exception. The seafood is fine and the margaritas mighty. Try a whole fish, an octopus or shrimp dish or, if you prefer, lobster (US$24).

Jardín del Arte (Map p268; ☎ 587-00-55; Hotel Marlin, Mitla 28; mains US$6-13) This restaurant features international cuisine with a French touch, and homemade bread. You can enjoy crepes, fish dishes, and occasionally *codorniz* (quail), or a sociable breakfast on the terrace.

Café Huatulco (Map p268; ☎ 587-12-28; Plaza Santa Cruz; breakfast US$4.50-6, coffee US$1.50-3.50, cake US$3; 8am-10:30pm) Mid-plaza near the harbor, Huatulco serves good Pluma coffee in many different ways – the *capuchino paraíso* (cold cappuccino with a dollop of ice cream) is well worth a try.

OAXACA

BAHÍA CHAHUÉ & TANGOLUNDA

L'échalote (☎ 587-24-80; Calle Zapoteco s/n, Chahué; mains US$7.50-14, desserts US$4-7; ⏰ 2-11pm Tue-Sun) This restaurant is attached to the Hotel Posada Edén Costa in Chahué (p270). The Swiss-French chef here prepares French, Thai, Vietnamese, Oaxacan and other dishes. The Thai salad with prawns and bean sprouts is delicious. Quiche lorraine, *nem* (spring rolls) and the chicken-liver salad are also quite good, and the desserts aren't too shabby either.

Casa del Mar (☎ 581-02-03; Balcones de Tangolunda 13, Tangolunda; starters US$4-8, mains US$7-13.50) A great view and romantic setting make it worth the trouble to get here. Try the *tamal de pescado* (steamed corn dough stuffed with fish). Flambéed bananas to finish? Why not?

Tangolunda's big hotels offer a choice of expensive bars, coffee shops and restaurants.

BEACHES

There are decent seafood *palapas* at Playas La Entrega, Maguey, and San Agustín. A whole grilled *huachinango* (red snapper) will cost US$6 to US$9.

Drinking

La Crema (Map p266; ☎ 587-07-02; cnr Flamboyán & Carrizal, La Crucecita; ⏰ 7pm-3am) This dark, moody bar has a good music mix and delicious wood-oven pizza.

Entertainment

La Peña (Map p266; Carrizal s/n, La Crucecita; ⏰ 7pm-3am) Head across the street from La Crema for a great Latin party vibe, with good live music, Cuban-style, from Tuesday to Saturday.

La Papaya (☎ 583-94-11; Blvd Juárez, Chahué; admission US$11; ⏰ 11pm-5am Thu-Sat) This long-standing disco above Plaza del Mezcal appeals to the 18 to 25 age group.

Noches Oaxaqueñas (☎ 581-00-01; Blvd Juárez s/n, Tangolunda; admission US$19; ⏰ 8:30pm Tue, Thu & Sat off-season, daily high season) Catch a Guelaguetza regional dance show here, by the Tangolunda traffic circle. Drinks and/or dinner (US$7 to US$17) are extra.

La Crucecita's **Cinemas Huatulco** (Map p266; Guamuchil s/n) is in Plaza Madero, a shopping mall at the corner of Guamuchil and Carrizal.

Shopping

Mercado de Artesanías (Map p268; Plaza Santa Cruz) Santa Cruz' market has a wide range of beach gear and handicrafts, including some good jewelry and textiles, but with the cruise ships arriving constantly you're not likely to find many bargains.

Getting There & Away

AIR

Mexicana and its subsidiary, Click Mexicana, offer three to five flights daily to/from Mexico City. Aerotucán (with a 13-seat Cessna) flies daily to/from Oaxaca, as does Aerovega, with a seven-seater. **Continental Express** (☎ 01-800-900-50-00) flies from Houston from one to four times a week in winter, and cheap charters from Canada, the US and the UK are sometimes available. Airline offices: **Aerotucán Huatulco** Santa Cruz (Map p268; ☎ 587-24-27; Blvd Santa Cruz).

BUS

The main bus stations are on Gardenia in La Crucecita. Some buses coming to Huatulco are marked 'Santa Cruz Huatulco,' but they still terminate in La Crucecita. Make sure your bus is not headed to Santa María Huatulco, which is a long way inland. See the boxed text on p238 for information on bus routes to Oaxaca city.

First-class **OCC** (Map p266; ☎ 587-02-61; cnr Gardenia & Ocotillo) is four blocks north of the plaza. Most of its buses are *de paso* (buses that start their journeys elsewhere but stop to drop off and pick up passengers; scheduled times are often very approximate). **Sur** buses pull up here too. **Estrella Blanca** (EB; Map p266; ☎ 587-03-90; cnr Gardenia & Palma Real) has *primera* services that are quick and fairly comfortable, and *ordinario* buses, which are typical *ordinario*. Daily departures include the following:

Acapulco EB (US$28, 10hr, 7 daily)

Oaxaca OCC (US$19, 8hr via Salina Cruz, 3 daily)

Pochutla OCC (US$2.25, 1hr, 6 daily); EB (US$2.50, 1hr, 7 daily); Transportes Rápidos de Pochutla (US$1.25, every 15min 6am-8pm) From Blvd Chahué, opposite the north end of Bugambilia in La Crucecita.

Puerto Escondido OCC (US$6, 2½hr, 6 daily); Sur (US$3, 2½hr, 12 daily); EB (US$6.50, 2½hr, 7 daily)

Tehuantepec OCC (US$8, 3½hr, 8 daily); Sur (US$7, 3½hr, 2 daily)

For coastal destinations west of Huatulco, take an Acapulco-bound EB bus; the 2nd-class buses will stop just about anywhere along Hwy 200. OCC also runs a few buses to Juchitán (US$9, four hours); OCC and

EB go to Mexico City (US$43 to US$50, 15 hours); and EB has one daily bus to Zihuatanejo (US$43, 14 hours).

CAR

Budget (Map p266; ☎ 587-00-10; cnr Ocotillo & Jazmín, La Crucecita)
Hertz (☎ 581-90-92; Airport)

Getting Around

TO/FROM THE AIRPORT

Transportación Terrestre (☎ 581-90-14) provides *colectivo combis* for US$8 per person from the airport to La Crucecita, Santa Cruz or Bahía Chahué and for US$9 to Tangolunda. Get tickets at the company's airport kiosk. For a whole cab at a reasonable price, walk just outside the airport gate, where you can pick one up for about US$13 to La Crucecita, Santa Cruz or Tangolunda, or US$14 to Pochutla. Even cheaper, walk 400m down to Hwy 200 and catch a microbus for US$0.70 to La Crucecita or US$1.50 to Pochutla. Those buses heading to La Crucecita may be marked 'Santa Cruz' or 'Bahías Huatulco' or something similar.

BUS & COLECTIVO

Colectivo taxis and a few microbuses provide transportation between La Crucecita, Santa Cruz Huatulco and Tangolunda. In La Crucecita catch them just east of the corner of Guamuchil and Carrizal, one block east of Plaza Principal. In Santa Cruz they stop by the harbor, and in Tangolunda at the traffic circle outside the Hotel Gala. Fares are the same in either type of vehicle: from La Crucecita to Santa Cruz US$0.30, and to Tangolunda US$0.50.

TAXI

Official taxi rates are posted on the east side of Plaza Principal in La Crucecita, from where you pay around US$1.50 to Santa Cruz, US$2.50 to Tangolunda, US$4.50 to Bahía Maguey and US$9.50 to the airport. There's a private taxi stand in Santa Cruz Huatulco, on the east side of the main plaza. By the hour, cabs run US$15.

BARRA DE LA CRUZ

☎ 958 / pop 700
This tranquil fishing village is reached via a good 1.5km road that heads coastward from Hwy 200 about 20km east of Santa Cruz. At the mouth of the Río Zimatán, Barra is known for its excellent surfing. At its peak, the right-hand point break gets up to a double overhead. A lack of undertow makes for good swimming as well. Barra's beach has showers and toilets, and a *comedor* offering food, drinks and plenty of hammocks and shade. The municipality charges US$1 per person to pass along the last stretch of road to the beach, and imposes a 7:30pm curfew; after sunset it's off *la playa*, baby.

You can rent surfboards just outside the toll gate for US$9.50 per day. Villagers will rent rooms in their houses for around US$5 a night, but conditions are very rustic. Go more upscale and stay at **Barradise** (☎ 044-958-585-03-03; pablo_rafting@yahoo.com; r US$14-19), which consists of two fan-cooled, rooms with private bathrooms above the surf shop. It's run by the very able Pablo Nárvaez, who in addition to doing surf guiding can also take you rafting, mountain biking and birding, and has the certificates to prove it.

Taxis from La Crucecita to Barra cost about US$9.50, or US$15 all the way to the beach. Eastbound 2nd-class buses will drop you at the turnoff on Hwy 200; the total distance from there to the beach is just under 4km.

From Barra to the east, Hwy 200 provides almost no views of the Pacific until you begin to approach Salina Cruz, and then it's mostly tantalizing glimpses of sea and beaches with enormous dunes piled against rocks, testament to the force of the winds that blow across the isthmus.

ISTHMUS OF TEHUANTEPEC

Eastern Oaxaca comprises the southern half of the 200km-wide Isthmus of Tehuantepec (teh-wahn-teh-*pek*), Mexico's narrowest point. Though dramatic mountains are seldom out of view, this is sweaty, flat country. Zapotec culture is strong here, and foreign visitors few. Spend some time and you're bound to encounter some lively, friendly people; you may even get an impromptu tour from schoolkids curious to see a foreign face in their midst.

OAXACA

DIFFERENT STROKES

Coming from a matrilineal society, Zapotec Isthmus women are noticeably open and confident and take a leading role in business and government. Many older women still wear embroidered *huipiles* and voluminous printed skirts. For the numerous *velas* (fiestas), Tehuantepec and Juchitán women turn out in velvet or sateen *huipiles*, gold and silver jewelry (a sign of wealth), skirts embroidered with fantastically colorful silk flowers and a variety of headgear. An unusual feature of many *velas* is the *tirada de frutas*, in which women climb onto rooftops and throw fruit at the men below!

TEHUANTEPEC

☎ 971 / pop 38,000

Tehuantepec is a friendly town, often with a fiesta going on in one of its barrios.

Orientation

The Oaxaca–Tuxtla Gutiérrez highway (190) meets Hwy 185 from Salina Cruz about 1km west of Tehuantepec. The combined highways then skirt the west edge of the town center and turn east to form the northern edge of town. It's here where Tehuantepec's bus stations – collectively known as La Terminal – cluster just south of the highway (1.5km northeast of the town center via the highway, considerably closer in a straight line on foot). To walk to the plaza from La Terminal, follow Av Héroes until it ends at a T-junction, then turn right along Guerrero for four blocks to another T-junction. Then go one block left along Hidalgo – the Palacio Municipal (town hall) stands on the south side of the plaza.

Information

Café Internet La Frontera (Calle 5 de Mayo; per hr US$1; ☼ open 9am-9pm), next door to Banorte, is one of several Internet places in town.
Cruz Roja (☎ 715-02015) Call in a medical emergency.
Santander Serfin (Calle 22 de Mayo; ☼ 9am-4pm Mon-Sat) North side of the plaza; will change traveler's checks and cash US dollars.

Bancomer and Banorte banks, both on Calle 5 de Mayo, are a few steps west of the Palacio Municipal. Both have ATMs; Banorte changes US dollars.

Sights

EX-CONVENTO REY COSIJOPÍ

This former Dominican monastery, north and west of the plaza on a short street off Guerrero, is Tehuantepec's **Casa de la Cultura** (Callejón Rey Cosijopí; admission free; ☼ 9am-2pm & 5-8pm Mon-Fri, 9am-2pm Sat). It bears traces of old religious frescoes and has modest but interesting exhibits of traditional dress, archaeological finds, historical photos and the like. King Cosijopí, the local Zapotec leader at the time, provided the funds for its construction in the 16th century, at the urging of Cortés.

MARKET

Tehuantepec's dark, almost medieval indoor **market** (☼ daily) is on the west side of the plaza. It spills out into the surrounding streets, where you can often see flowers for sale.

Sleeping

Hotel Donají (☎ 715-00-64; hoteldonaji@hotmail.com; Juárez 10; s/d/tr/q with fan US$16/23/31/38, with air-con US$23/30/40/43; P ✗ ⬚) The bright Donají is two blocks south of the east side of the central plaza, and has clean rooms with TV on two upper floors around a shady, colorful patio. Bonuses include a small gym and a small pool.

Guiexhoba (☎ 715-17-10; guiexhoba@prodigy.net .mx; Carretera Panamericana Km 250.5; s/d/tr US$40/50/60; P ✗ ⬚) This motel sits at the junction of Hwys 185 and 190, a kilometer southwest of the center. The rooms are large, as is the covered swimming pool, but rooms on the Hwy 190 side can get quite a bit of traffic noise. Not to worry: some of the air-con units will drown it out entirely. The hotel's restaurant is on the expensive side, but serves enormous salads and good espresso.

Hotel Oasis (☎ 715-00-08; Ocampo 8; r with fan US$15-18, with air-con US$25; P ✗) A block south of the plaza, the Oasis has 26 basic rooms, with warm showers.

Eating

The **market** has the usual eateries, and at night the entire east sidewalk of the plaza is lined with plastic tables and chairs beside carts serving inexpensive tacos and other delights.

Bar Restaurante Scarú (☎ 715-06-46; Callejón Leona Vicario 4; dishes US$4-11) Two short blocks east and 50m north of Hotel Donají, the relaxed, friendly Scarú occupies an 18th-century house with a courtyard and colorful modern murals of Tehuantepec life. Sit beneath a fan, quaff a *limonada* or a mixed drink and sample one of the many fish, seafood, meat and chicken dishes on offer. On Saturday and Sunday old-timers plunk out marimba tunes.

Getting There & Away

At La Terminal, OCC and ADO (1st-class) and Sur and AU (2nd-class) share one building. Some 1st-class buses are *de paso*. Transportes Oaxaca-Istmo (TOI, 2nd-class) is next door, nearer to the highway.

Local buses to Juchitán (US$1.50, 30 minutes) depart across the street from OCC at least every half hour during daylight hours. Other services:

Bahías de Huatulco OCC (US$8, 3½hr, 3 1st-class); Sur (US$6.50, 3½hr, 2 2nd-class)

Mexico City (TAPO) OCC & ADO (US$46-54, 11½hr, 6 1st-class & deluxe); AU (US$41, 13hr, 3 2nd-class)

Oaxaca OCC & ADO (US$12, 4½hr, 15 1st-class); Sur (US$11, 4½hr, 7 2nd-class); TOI (US$7.50, 5½hr, 13)

Pochutla OCC (US$10, 4½hr, 3 1st-class)

Puerto Escondido OCC (US$14, 6½ hr, 3 1st-class)

Getting Around

Taxis between La Terminal and the plaza charge around US$1.75. A delightful local variation on the common Mexican theme of three-wheeled transportation is the *motocarro*, whose passengers sit – or stand, to better catch the breeze – on a platform behind the driver. The sight of colorfully garbed women riding tall is one that lingers in memory. Motocarros congregate by the railway track west of the market.

JUCHITÁN

☎ 971 / pop 68,000

Istmeño culture is strong in this friendly town, which is visited by few gringos.

Orientation & Information

Prolongación 16 de Septiembre leads into Juchitán from a busy intersection with traffic signals on Hwy 190, on the north edge of town. The main bus terminal is about 100m toward town from the intersection. The street curves left, then right, then divides into Calle 5 de Septiembre (the right fork) and Av 16 de Septiembre (left). These emerge as opposite sides of the central plaza, Jardín Juárez, after seven blocks. The Palacio Municipal, painted yellow with green and white trim, forms the Jardín's eastern boundary.

At least two banks with ATMs are on the Jardín; at its southwest corner, **Scotiabank** (9am-5pm Mon-Fri) changes traveler's checks and cash US dollars. Internet places abound, particularly on Prolongación 16 de Septiembre. Most charge US$1 an hour, including **La-Net@.com** (noon-midnight), opposite Hotel Lopez Lena Palace. Try **Hospital Fuentes** (☎ 711-14-41; Efraín R Gómez s/n) in a medical emergency.

Sights

Jardín Juárez is a lively central square. A thriving market on its east side spills into the surrounding streets. Here you can find traditional Isthmus women's costumes, and

---

DETOUR: GUIENGOLA

In 1496 the isthmus Zapotecs successfully defended the hillside fortress of Guiengola from Aztec invaders, and the isthmus never became part of the Aztec empire. The stronghold's ruins lie north of Hwy 190 and are reached via a turnoff just past the Km 240 marker, about 11km out of Tehuantepec (signed 'Ruinas Guiengola'; at the time of research there was a military checkpoint directly at the turnoff). A guide (recommended) may be waiting here or nearer the site. The unpaved 7km stretch of road is passable in dry weather, though the last kilometer or so (heading uphill) requires a high-clearance vehicle. The road ends at a signed trailhead, and about an hour's sweaty walk up the trail gets you to the remains of two pyramids, a ball court, a 64-room complex and a thick defensive wall. You'll also see interesting limestone formations and some fine views over the isthmus.

If you lack a vehicle, catch a bus bound for Jalapa del Marqués from La Terminal. From the turnoff on Hwy 190 it's about a 2½-hour walk. Take plenty of water, and start early (6am or before) to take advantage of the morning cool.

sometimes iguana on the menus of the market *comedores*.

Juchitán's **Lidxi Guendabiaani** (Casa de la Cultura; Belisario Domínguez; admission free; ☾ 10am-3pm & 5-8pm Mon-Fri, 10am-2pm Sat), one block south and one block west of Jardín Juárez, has an interesting archaeological collection and an art collection with works by leading 20th-century Mexican artists, including Rufino Tamayo and the prolific *juchiteco* Francisco Toledo. It's beside the church, and set around a big patio that often buzzes with children.

Sleeping & Eating

Hotel López Lena Palace (☎ 711-13-88; Prolongación 16 de Septiembre 70; s US$24-31, tw US$42; **P** ☒) Look for the mock Arabic exterior about halfway between the bus station and town center. The Lena has reasonable rooms with comfy beds; the best value are the cheerful but windowless 'minis,' with excellent aircon and showers. The attached **Restaurant El Califa** (mains US$3-13) prepares some excellent dishes, including fresh salads and stuffed fish, though the breakfasts leave something to be desired.

Hotel Santo Domingo del Sur (☎ 711-10-50; hsto@ prodigy.net.mx; Carretera Juchitán-Tehuantepec; s/d/tr with air-con US$36/48/59; **P** ☒ ☒) Situated by the Hwy 190 crossroads, the popular Santo Domingo has decent rooms (though some have poor bathrooms for the price), a large swimming pool surrounded by a garden, and a good restaurant (meals US$3 to US$14).

Casagrande Restaurant (☎ 711-34-60; mains US$4.50-14) This is the flashest eatery in town, in a pleasant covered courtyard with ceiling fans and tall plants. All the goodies, from regional dishes and pasta to seafood, get 15%

tax added. It's on the south side of Jardín Juárez; the Casagrande cinema sign makes it easier to find.

Café Santa Fe (☎ 711-15-45; Cruce de Carretera Transístmica; dishes US$4-8; ☾ 24hr) For cool air and good food, try this restaurant, handily wedged between the main bus stations and the highway. It does excellent breakfasts and good espresso, served briskly by white-coated waiters.

Getting There & Away

OCC and ADO (1st-class) and Sur and AU (2nd-class) use the main bus terminal on Prolongación 16 de Septiembre; they're housed in separate structures. Frequent 2nd-class Istmeño buses to Tehuantepec (US$1.25, 30 minutes) and Salina Cruz (US$2, 1 hour) stop at the next corner south on Prolongación 16 de Septiembre during daylight hours. Fletes y Pasajes (Fypsa; 2nd-class) has its own terminal, separated from the main one by a Pemex station and the Café Santa Fe.

Some buses are *de paso* and leave in the middle of the night; many others originate in nearby Salina Cruz and stop at Juchitán not long after.

Bahías de Huatulco (US$9, 4hr, 5 1st-class); Sur (US$6.50, 3½hr, 2 2nd-class)

Mexico City (TAPO) OCC/ADO/UNO (US$46-67, 10hr, 7 1st-class & deluxe); AU (US$42, 12hr, 3 2nd-class)

Oaxaca OCC & ADO (US$12.50, 5hr, 20 1st-class & deluxe); Sur & Fypsa (US$9, 6hr, many 2nd-class)

Pochutla (US$12, 5hr, 5 1st-class)

Puerto Escondido (US$16, 7hr, 5 1st-class)

Getting Around

'Terminal-Centro' buses run between the bus station and Jardín Juárez. A taxi costs US$1.50.

Directory

CONTENTS

ACCOMMODATIONS

Accommodations on the Pacific coast range from hammocks, palm-thatched huts and camping grounds to hostels, *casas de huéspedes* (guesthouses) and budget hotels, to world-class luxury resorts. This book divides accommodations into three price ranges: budget (where a typical room for two people costs under US$35), midrange (US$35 to US$85) and top end (above US$85).

The normal tourist high season is November to April, when many North Americans and Europeans travel to Mexico for the winter. Reservations are advisable for popular places during this time. Tourism peaks during the Christmas–New Year holidays, Semana Santa (the week before Easter and up to a week after it) and the July/August summer holidays. During these periods, reservations are a must. The low season lasts from May to October, with the exception of the holiday jolt in July and August.

Prices quoted throughout this book, unless specified, are for the November to April winter high season. Rates for peak season – which usually runs from December 20 through January 2 and also the week of Semana Santa – may rise 10% to 20% above the high season rate. Low-season rates are

---

PRACTICALITIES

- Mexicans use the metric system for weights and measures.

- Most prerecorded videotapes on sale in Mexico (like the rest of the Americas and Japan) use the NTSC image registration system, incompatible with the PAL system common to most of Western Europe and Australia.

- If buying DVDs, look for the numbered globe motif indicating which regions of the world it can be played back in. Region 1 is the US and Canada; Europe and Japan are in region 2; and Australia and New Zealand join Mexico in region 4.

- Electrical current is 110V, 60Hz, and most plugs have two flat prongs, as in the US and Canada.

- Mexico's only English-language daily newspaper is *The Herald*, which is the *Miami Herald* with an eight-page Mexico insert, available in Mexico City and some other cities.

- For the online editions of about 300 Mexican newspapers and magazines, and links to hundreds of Mexican radio and TV stations and other media sites, visit www.zonalatina.com.

- Free-to-air TV is dominated by Televisa, which runs four of the six main national channels; TV Azteca has two (Azteca 7 and Azteca 13).

often 10% to 40% lower than those we quote. Rates at budget accommodations tend to fluctuate the least.

Accommodation prices are subject to two taxes: IVA (value-added tax; 15%) and ISH (lodging tax; 2% in most states). Generally IVA and ISH are included in quoted prices. In top-end hotels a price may often be given as, say, 'US$100 *más impuestos*' (US$100 plus taxes), in which case you must add 17% to the figure. When in doubt, you can ask '*¿Están incluidos los impuestos?*' ('Are taxes included?'). Prices given in this book are those you are most likely to be charged at each place, with or without the taxes according to the establishment's policy.

Camping Grounds & Trailer Parks

Camping grounds are common on Mexico's Pacific coast. Most organized camping grounds are trailer parks set up for RVs (camper vans) and trailers (caravans), but they accept tent campers at lower rates. Expect to pay about US$5 to pitch a tent for two, and US$10 to US$20 for two people with a vehicle, using full facilities. Some restaurants and guesthouses in beach spots or country areas will let you pitch a tent on their patch for a couple of dollars per person.

All Mexican beaches are public property. You can camp for nothing on most of them, but always assess the safety of the beach before spending the night on it.

Casas de Huéspedes & Posadas

Inexpensive and congenial accommodations are often to be found at a *casa de huéspedes,* a home converted into simple guest lodgings. Good *casas de huéspedes* are usually family-run, with a relaxed, friendly atmosphere.

A double typically costs US$15 to US$20, though a few places are more comfy and more expensive. Some *posadas* (inns) are like *casas de huéspedes;* others are small hotels.

Hammocks & Cabañas

You'll find hammocks and *cabañas* available mainly in low-key beach spots. A hammock can be a very comfortable place to sleep (but mosquito repellent often comes in handy). You can rent one and a place to hang it – usually under a palm roof outside a small guesthouse or beach restaurant – for US$3 or US$4 in some places. With your own hammock, the cost comes down a bit.

It's easy enough to buy hammocks in Pacific Mexico, especially in Oaxaca.

Cabañas are usually huts with a palm-thatched roof. Some have dirt floors and nothing inside but a bed; others are deluxe, with electric light, mosquito nets, fans, fridge, bar and decor. Prices for simple *cabañas* range from US$10 to US$35; luxury *cabañas* can set you back as much as US$100.

Hotels

Mexico specializes in good midrange hotels where two people can get a comfortable room with private bathroom, TV and often air-conditioning for US$35 to US$60. Often there's a restaurant and bar.

Among the most charming lodgings, in both the midrange and the top end, are the many old mansions, inns, and even convents, turned into hotels. These can be wonderfully atmospheric, with fountains gurgling in flower-bedecked stone courtyards. Some are a bit Spartan (but relatively low in price); others have modern comforts and are more expensive. These are probably the lodgings you will remember most fondly after your trip.

Every Mexican town also has its cheap hotels. There are clean, friendly, secure ones, and there are dark, dirty, smelly ones where you may not feel your belongings are safe. Decent rooms with private hot shower are available for under US$25 a double in most of the country.

Mexico has plenty of large, modern luxury hotels too, particularly in the coastal resorts and largest cities. They offer the expected levels of luxury – with pools, gyms, bars, restaurants and so on – at prices that are sometimes agreeably modest (and sometimes not!).

Fortunately for families and small groups of travelers, many hotels in all price ranges have rooms for three, four or five people that cost not much more than a double.

Rental Accommodations

Those planning to stick around for a while in one spot have a lot to gain by moving into an apartment, condominium or villa vacation rental. Prices fluctuate according to amenities, season and proximity to a beach, from as little as US$400 per month for a simple bungalow to many times that for a lavish villa.

BOOK ACCOMMODATION ONLINE

For more accommodation reviews and recommendations by Lonely Planet authors, check out the online booking service at www.lonelyplanet.com. You'll find the true, insider lowdown on the best places to stay. Reviews are thorough and independent. Best of all, you can book online.

The Internet is your friend in finding listings; start your search at sites like **Choice1** (www.choice1.com/mexico) or on the rentals page maintained by **MexOnline** (www.mexonline.com/rentals.htm).

Resorts

An abundance of sea, sun and sand usually means resort hotels, and Mexico's Pacific coast is no exception. These properties offer deluxe amenities, manicured grounds and often private beaches, and they offer a full range of activities, excursions, multiple pools and sports facilities. All-inclusive meal, activity and beverage plans are increasingly the norm.

Rates for all-inclusive resorts presented in this book are guidelines based on each resort's unpublicized 'rack' or 'standard' rate. This is to say that you will likely spend considerably less depending on the source of booking, season and current specials. Most resorts perpetually publicize special rates, and further discounts can be found either on their websites or on booking sites like **Expedia** (www.expedia.com) and **Travelocity** (www.travelocity.com).

ACTIVITIES

Mexico's Pacific coast has a panoply of sports and special-interest activities for those to whom bumming out on the beach spells eventual boredom. Diving and snorkeling (p47) devotees are spoiled for choice with loads of dazzling sites up and down the coast and plenty of operators waiting to take you to them. These are also world-class waters for deep-sea fishing (p48), with opportunities ranging from deluxe guided charters leaving from the resort towns to pared-down excursions in a *panga* (motorized skiff) with local fishermen. Surfing (p48) is also celebrated in a big way, with several famous spots including the country's

most famous surfing beach – Puerto Escondido's 'Mexican Pipeline.' The coastal lagoons and sheltered bays of the Pacific coast are magnificent waters for kayaking (p51) and also provide superlative spots for wildlife and bird-watching (p51). If all this makes you feel a bit seasick, then stretch your legs with some splendid hiking (p53) along scenic beaches or through a tropical forest to a waterfall. Mountain biking (p53) and horseback riding (p53) offer a different pace and perspective, and everything you need to enjoy these activities is available in the major tourist towns.

BUSINESS HOURS

On the coast, shops are generally open from 9am or 10am to around 9pm Monday to Saturday. They close for siesta between 2pm and 4pm. Inland, shops will generally skip the siesta and close around 7pm. Shops in malls and tourist resorts often open on Sunday.

Offices have similar Monday to Friday hours, often with the 2pm to 4pm lunch break. Those with tourist-related business might open for a few hours on Saturday.

Typical restaurant hours are from 7am to between 10pm and midnight. Cafés typically open from 8am to 10pm daily. Bars, too, are normally open daily, but each seems to have its own special pattern of hours.

Museums are usually closed on Monday; on Sunday nearly all museums are free.

In this book we only spell out opening hours where they do not fit these parameters. See inside the front cover for further typical opening hours.

CHILDREN

Mexicans love children, and children are welcome at all kinds of hotels and in virtually every café and restaurant. The sights, sounds and colors of Mexico excite and stimulate most children, but few kids like traveling all the time; they're happier if they can settle into a place for a while and make friends. Try to give them time to get on with some of what they like doing back home. Children are also more easily affected than adults by heat, disrupted sleeping patterns and strange food. They need time to acclimatize and you should take extra care to avoid sunburn. Ensure you replace fluids if a child gets diarrhea (p307).

DIRECTORY

Lonely Planet's *Travel with Children* has lots of practical advice on the subject, drawn from firsthand experience.

Practicalities

Cots for hotel rooms and high chairs for restaurants are available mainly in mid-range and top-end establishments. If you want a rental car with a child safety seat, the major international rental firms are the most reliable providers. You will probably have to pay a few dollars extra per day.

It's usually easy to find a cheap baby-sitter if parents want to go out on their own – ask at your hotel. Diapers are widely available, but if you depend on some particular cream, lotion, baby food or medicine, bring it with you. Public breast-feeding is not common and, when done, is done discreetly.

DOCUMENTS FOR UNDER-18 TRAVELERS

To conform with regulations aimed at preventing international child abduction, minors (under 18s) traveling to Mexico without one or both of their parents may need to carry a notarized consent form signed by the absent parent or parents, giving permission for the young traveler to make the international journey. Mexico does not specifically require this documentation, but airlines flying to Mexico may refuse to board passengers without it. In the case of divorced parents, a custody document may be required. If one or both parents are dead, or the traveler has only one legal parent, a death certificate or notarized statement may be required.

These rules are aimed primarily at visitors from the USA and Canada but may also apply to people from elsewhere. Procedures vary from country to country; contact your country's foreign affairs department and/or a Mexican consulate to find out exactly what you need to do. The required forms are usually available from these authorities.

Sights & Activities

In larger resort towns, apart from the obvious beaches and swimming pools, you'll find excellent attractions such as water parks, including **Parque Papagayo** (p211) in Acapulco, **Splash Parque Acuático** (p77) in Puerto Vallarta and **MazAgua** (p116) in Mazatlán.

Kids don't have to be very old to enjoy activities such as snorkeling, boating, riding bicycles and horses, watching wildlife (p279),

and even – for some! – shopping and visiting markets. Many kids will stay happy for under US$1 an hour at Mexico's myriad Internet cafés, and archaeological sites (eg Monte Albán, p240) can be fun if the kids are into climbing pyramids and exploring tunnels.

CLIMATE CHARTS

June to October are the hottest and wettest months across most of Mexico. For tips on the best seasons to travel, see p17.

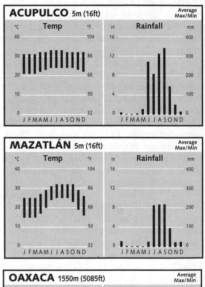

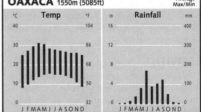

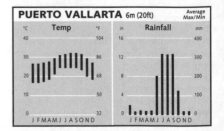

COURSES

Taking classes in Mexico can be a great way to meet people and get an inside angle on local life as well as study the language or culture. The country specializes in short courses in the Spanish language. In addition, Mexican universities and colleges often offer tuition to complement college courses you may be taking back home. For long-term study in Mexico you'll need a student visa; contact a Mexican consulate.

Hit the Internet to learn about study possibilities in Mexico from sites such as the **Council on International Educational Exchange** (CIEE; www.ciee.org), the **National Registration Center for Study Abroad** (www.nrcsa.com) and **AmeriSpan** (www.amerispan.com).

Cooking Courses

See p230 for two of Mexico's great little cooking schools for foreigners, and see p60 for other general information about cooking courses.

Language Courses

Mexico's best, most popular language schools are inland. Oaxaca (p229) is an excellent place to study Spanish and get an inside angle on local life and culture. Multiweek courses can also be taken in Puerto Vallarta (p76), Mazatlán (p116) and La Manzanilla (p154).

Course lengths range from a few days to a year. In many places you can enroll on the spot and start any Monday. You may be offered accommodations with a local family as part of the deal – which can help your language skills as much as the formal tuition. In a growing number of schools, extra or alternative courses in art, crafts, dance, indigenous languages or in-depth study of Mexico are also available.

Costs per week, with accommodations and meals included, can range from around US$180 to over US$400, depending on the city, the school and how intensively you study.

CUSTOMS

Things that visitors are allowed to bring into Mexico duty-free include items for personal use such as clothing; a camera and video camera; up to 12 rolls of film or videotapes; a cellular phone; a laptop computer; a portable radio or CD player; medicine for personal use, with prescription in the case of psychotropic drugs; 3L of wine, beer or liquor (adults only); 400 cigarettes (adults); and US$300 worth of other goods (US$50 if arriving by land).

The normal routine when you enter Mexico is to complete a customs declaration form (which lists duty-free allowances), and then place it in a machine. If the machine shows a green light, you pass without inspection. If a red light shows, your baggage will be searched.

On leaving Mexico, you may be subjected to an exit inspection. Certain cultural and religious artifacts require exit permits, and most pre-Hispanic objects cannot legally be removed from the country.

Returnees to the US are allowed a fixed value of duty-free goods, including no more than 1L of alcoholic spirits, 200 cigarettes and 100 cigars. At the time of research, the allowance was US$400 per person.

DANGERS & ANNOYANCES

Official information can make Mexico sound more alarming than it really is, but for a variety of useful information on travel to Mexico consult your country's foreign-affairs department:

Australia (☎ 1300-139-281; www.dfat.gov.au)
Canada (☎ 800-267-6788; www.dfait-maeci.gc.ca)
UK (☎ 0845-850-2829; www.fco.gov.uk)
USA (☎ 888-407-4747; www.travel.state.gov)

If you're already in Mexico, you can contact your embassy (p283). Keep an ear to the ground as you travel.

Theft & Robbery

Tourism on the Pacific coast is a *major* source of income, both locally and nationally, and Mexico has a vested interest in keeping it safe for visitors. Major coastal resorts have a large and visible police presence, so violent crimes are rare. Remote beach spots and dark streets are the places where muggings are most likely to occur.

Purse- or bag-snatching and pickpocketing can occur in crowded buses, bus stops, bus stations, airports, markets, thronged streets and plazas.

HIGHWAY ROBBERY

Bandits occasionally hold up buses, cars and other vehicles on intercity routes, especially at night, taking luggage or valuables. Sometimes buses are robbed by people who board as passengers. The best ways to avoid highway robbery are to travel by day and to travel on toll highways as much as possible. Deluxe and 1st-class buses use toll highways, where they exist; 2nd-class buses do not.

Hwy 200 along the Pacific coast through Michoacán and Guerrero states and as far south as Pochutla in Oaxaca has been the scene of many highway robberies over the years but is now mostly safe for travel. Hwys 134 and 51 between Ixtapa and Iguala and Hwy 175 between Oaxaca city and Pochutla are also known to be robbery-prone.

IN THE CITY

To avoid being robbed in cities, steer clear of lonely places like empty streets or little-used pedestrian underpasses where there are few other people. Use ATMs only in secure locations and not those that open to the street.

Pickpockets often work in teams; the operative principle is to distract you and get you off balance. If your valuables are *underneath* your clothing (in a money belt, a shoulder wallet or a pouch on a string around your neck), the chances of losing them are greatly reduced. Visible round-the-waist money belts are an invitation to thieves. Carry a small amount of ready-money in a pocket.

DISABLED TRAVELERS

Mexico is not yet very disabled-friendly, though some hotels and restaurants (mostly towards the top end of the market) and some public buildings and archaeological sites now provide wheelchair access. Mobility is easiest in the major tourist resorts and the more expensive hotels. Bus transportation can be difficult; flying or taking a taxi is easier.

Mobility International USA (☎ 541-343-1284; www.miusa.org) advises disabled travelers on mobility issues and runs exchange programs (including in Mexico). Its website includes international databases of exchange programs and disability organizations, with several Mexican organizations listed.

In the UK, **Radar** (☎ 020-7250-3222; www.radar.org.uk) is run by and for disabled people. Its excellent website has links to good travel and holiday sites.

DISCOUNT CARDS

The ISIC student card, the IYTC card for travelers under 26 and the ITIC card for teachers can help you obtain reduced-price air tickets to or from Mexico at student- and youth-oriented travel agencies. Reduced prices on Mexican buses and at museums, archaeological sites and so on are usually only for those with Mexican education credentials, but the ISIC, IYTC and ITIC will sometimes get you a reduction. The ISIC card is the most recognized.

All these cards can be obtained in Mexico. One outlet is the youth/student travel agency **Mundo Joven** (www.mundojoven.com in Spanish), with six offices in Mexico City and others in Guadalajara, Puebla, Toluca and León. You need proof of your student/teacher/youth status to obtain the ISIC/ITIC/IYTC card.

EMBASSIES & CONSULATES
Mexican Embassies & Consulates

The following are embassies unless otherwise noted. Updated details can be found at www.sre.gob.mx. Some Mexican embassy and consulate websites are very useful information sources on visas and similar matters.

Australia (☎ 02-6273-3963; www.mexico.org.au; 14 Perth Ave, Yarralumla, ACT 2600)

Canada Ottawa (☎ 613-233-8988; www.embamexcan.com; 45 O'Connor St, Suite 1000, ON K1P 1A4); consulate in Montreal (☎ 514-288-2502; www.consulmex.qc.ca; 2055 rue Peel, Bureau 1000, QC H3A 1V4); consulate in Toronto (☎ 416-368-2875; www.consulmex.com; 199 Bay St, Suite 4440 Commerce Court West, ON M5L 1E9); consulate in Vancouver (☎ 604-684-3547; www.consulmexvan.com; 710-1177 West Hastings St, BC V6E 2K3)

France Paris (☎ 01-53-70-27-70; www.sre.gob.mx/francia; 9 rue de Longchamp, 75116); consulate in Paris (☎ 01 42 86 56 20; 4 rue Notre Dame des Victoires, 75002)

Germany Berlin (☎ 030-269-323; www.embamex.de in Spanish & German; Klingelhöferstrasse 3, 10785); consulate in Frankfurt-am-Main (☎ 069-299-8750; www.consulmexfrankfurt.org in Spanish & German; Taunusanlage 21, 60325)

Ireland (☎ 01-260-0699; www.sre.gob.mx/irlanda; 43 Ailesbury Rd, Ballsbridge, Dublin 4)

Netherlands (☎ 070-360-2900; www.embamex-nl.com; Nassauplein 28, The Hague 2585EC)

New Zealand (☎ 04-472-0555; Level 8, 111 Customhouse Quay, Wellington)

UK (☎ 020-7235-6393; www.embamex.co.uk; 8 Halkin St, London SW1X 7DW)

USA (☎ 202-728-1600; www.sre.gob.mx/eua; 1911 Pennsylvania Ave NW, Washington, DC 20006)

Embassies & Consulates in Mexico

Mexico City entries in the following selective list are for embassies or their consular sections; other entries are consulates. Embassy websites are often useful sources of information about Mexico.

Australia Guadalajara (☎ 33-3615-7418; López Cotilla 2018, Colonia Arcos Vallarta); Mexico City (☎ 55-1101-2200; www.mexico.embassy.gov.au; Rubén Darío 55, Polanco)

Canada Acapulco (☎ 744-484-13-05; Centro Comercial Marbella, Local 23); Guadalajara (☎ 33-3615-6215; Hotel Fiesta Americana, Local 31, Aceves 225, Colonia Vallarta Poniente); Mazatlán (☎ 669-913-73-20; Hotel Playa Mazatlán, Av Las Gaviotas 202, Zona Dorada); Mexico City (☎ 55-5724-7900; www.canada.org.mx; Schiller 529, Polanco); Oaxaca (☎ 951-513-37-77; Pino Suárez 700, Local 11B); Puerto Vallarta (☎ 322-293-00-98; Edificio Obelisco Local 108, Av Francisco Medina Ascencio 1951, Zona Hotelera Las Glorias)

France Acapulco (☎ 744-484-45-80; Local 205, La Costera 91, Fraccionamiento Club Deportiva); Guadalajara (☎ 33-3616-5516; López Mateos Nte 484); Mazatlán (☎ 669-985-12-28; Belisario Domínguez 1008 Sur, Colonia Centro); Mexico City (☎ 55-9171-9700; www.francia.org.mx in Spanish & French; Campos Elíseos 339, Polanco); consulate in Mexico City (☎ 55-9171-9840; Lafontaine 32, Polanco)

Germany Acapulco (☎ 744-484-18-60; Alaminos 26, Casa Tres Fuentes, Colonia Costa Azul); Guadalajara (☎ 33-3613-9623; Casa Wagner de Guadalajara, Madero 215); Mazatlán (☎ 669-914-93-10; Av Playa Gaviotas 212, Zona Dorada); Mexico City (☎ 55-5283-2200; www.mexiko .diplo.de in Spanish & German; Lord Byron 737, Polanco)

Ireland (☎ 55-5520-5803; embajada@irlanda.org.mx; Cerrada Blvd Ávila Camacho 76, piso 3, Lomas de Chapultepec, Mexico City)

Netherlands Acapulco (☎ 486-83-59; Hotel Ritz, La Costera 159); Guadalajara (☎ 33-3673-2211; 2nd fl, Av Vallarta 5500, Colonia Lomas Universidad, Zapopan); Mexico City (☎ 55-5258-9921; www.paisesbajos.com.mx in Spanish & Dutch; Edificio Calakmul, Av Vasco de Quiroga 3000, 7th fl, Santa Fe)

New Zealand (☎ 55-5283-9460; kiwimexico@compuserve.com.mx; Balmes 8, Level 4, Los Morales, Mexico City)

UK Acapulco (☎ 744-484-17-35; Casa Consular, Centro Internacional Acapulco, La Costera); Guadalajara (☎ 33-3343-2296; Jesús de Rojas 20, Colonia Los Pinos, Zapopan); Mexico City (☎ 55-5242-8500; www.embajadabritanica .com.mx; Río Lerma 71, Colonia Cuauhtémoc); consulate in Mexico City (☎ 55-5242-8500; Río Usumacinta 26)

USA Acapulco (☎ 744-469-05-56; Hotel Continental Plaza, La Costera 121, Local 14); Guadalajara (☎ 33-3268-2100; Progreso 175); Mazatlán (☎ 669-916-58-89; Hotel Playa Mazatlán, Av Las Gaviotas 202, Zona Dorada); Mexico City (☎ 55-5080-2000; mexico.usembassy.gov; Paseo de la Reforma 305); Oaxaca (☎ 951-514-30-54; Plaza Santo Domingo, Alcalá 407, Interior 20); Puerto Vallarta (☎ 322-222-00-69; Zaragoza 160)

FESTIVALS & EVENTS

Mexico's many fiestas are full-blooded, highly colorful affairs that often go on for several days. In addition to the major national festivals listed below, each town has many local saint's days, regional fairs, arts festivals and so on (see destination chapters for information on these). There's also a national public holiday just about every month (see p284), often the occasion for further partying.

January

Día de los Reyes Magos (Three Kings' Day or Epiphany; Jan 6) This is the day when Mexican children traditionally receive gifts, rather than at Christmas.

February/March

Día de la Candelaría (Candlemas; Feb 2) Commemorates the presentation of Jesus in the temple 40 days after his birth; celebrated with processions, bullfights and dancing in many towns.

Carnaval (late Feb/early Mar) A big bash preceding the 40-day penance of Lent, Carnaval takes place during the week or so before Ash Wednesday (which falls 46 days before Easter Sunday). It's celebrated wildly in Mazatlán with parades and masses of music, food, drink, dancing, fireworks and fun.

March/April

Semana Santa Holy Week starts on Palm Sunday (Domingo de Ramos); most of Mexico seems to be on the move at this time.

September

Día de la Independencia (Independence Day; Sep 16) The anniversary of the 1810 start of Mexico's independence war provokes an upsurge of patriotic feeling every year: on the evening of the 15th, the words of Padre Miguel Hidalgo's famous call to rebellion, the Grito de Dolores, are repeated from the balcony of every town hall in the land, usually followed by fireworks. The biggest celebrations are in Mexico City, where the Grito is issued by the national president from the Palacio Nacional.

November

Día de Todos los Santos (All Saints' Day; Nov 1) The souls of dead children (*angelitos*, little angels) are celebrated on All Saints' Day.

Día de Muertos (Day of the Dead; Nov 2) Every cemetery in the country comes alive as families visit graveyards to commune with their dead on the night of November 1 and the day of November 2, when the souls of the dead are believed to return to earth.

December

Día de Nuestra Señora de Guadalupe (Dec 12) A week or more of celebrations throughout Mexico leads up to the Day of Our Lady of Guadalupe, the Virgin who appeared to an indigenous Mexican, Juan Diego, in 1531, and has since become Mexico's religious patron. The biggest festivities are at the Basílica de Guadalupe in Mexico City.

Día de Navidad (Dec 25) Christmas is traditionally celebrated with a feast in the early hours of December 25, after midnight mass.

FOOD

Some Eating sections in chapters of this book are divided into budget, midrange and top-end categories. We define a midrange restaurant as one where a main dish at lunch or dinner costs between US$6 and US$11. Budget and top-end places are, respectively, less than US$6 and over US$11. If a restaurant has a closing day, it's usually Sunday, Monday or Tuesday. For a full introduction to Mexico's fabulously piquant cuisine, see the Food & Drink chapter (p55).

GAY & LESBIAN TRAVELERS

Mexico is more broad-minded about sexuality than you might expect. Gays and lesbians don't generally maintain a high profile, but rarely attract open discrimination or violence. There are large, lively gay communities and/or gay tourism scenes in Puerto Vallarta and Guadalajara (especially), and also in Mexico City, Mazatlán, and Acapulco. Gay men have a more public profile than lesbians, however. Discrimination based on sexual orientation has been illegal since 1999, and can be punished with up to three years in prison.

The **International Gay and Lesbian Travel Association** (www.iglta.org) provides information on the major travel providers in the gay sector. San Diego–based **Arco Iris Tours** (☎ 800-765-4370; www.arcoiristours.com) specializes in gay travel to Mexico and organizes an annual International Gay Festival in Cancún.

The **Out&About** (www.gay.com/travel/outandabout) website has a detailed Mexico gay-travel guide and articles. Another good source of information is the **Gay Mexico Network** (www.gaymexico.net). It offers information on gay-friendly hotels and tours in Mexico, and publishes a newsletter offering discounted rooms in gay-friendly accommodations.

HOLIDAYS

The chief holiday periods are Christmas to New Year, Semana Santa (the week leading up to Easter and a couple of days afterwards), and mid-July to mid-August. Transportation and tourist accommodations are heavily booked at these times. Banks, post offices, government offices and many shops throughout Mexico are closed on the following national holidays:

Año Nuevo (New Year's Day) January 1
Día de la Constitución (Constitution Day) February 5
Día de la Bandera (Day of the National Flag) February 24
Día de Nacimiento de Benito Juárez (anniversary of Benito Juárez' birth) March 21
Día del Trabajo (Labor Day) May 1
Cinco de Mayo (anniversary of Mexico's victory over the French at Puebla) May 5
Día de la Independencia (Independence Day) September 16
Día de la Raza (commemoration of Columbus' discovery of the New World) October 12
Día de la Revolución (Revolution Day) November 20
Día de Navidad (Christmas Day) December 25

At Easter, businesses usually close from Good Friday (Viernes Santo) to Easter Sunday (Domingo de Resurrección). Many offices and businesses close during major national festivals (see p283).

INSURANCE

A travel-insurance policy to cover theft, loss and medical problems is a good idea. Some policies specifically exclude dangerous activities such as scuba diving, motorcycling and even trekking.

You may prefer a policy that pays doctors or hospitals directly rather than you having to pay on the spot and claim later. If you have to claim later, ensure you keep all documentation. Check that the policy covers ambulances or an emergency flight home. For further information on medical insurance, see p302.

Worldwide cover to travelers from over 44 countries is available online at www.lonelyplanet.com/travel_services.

For information on motor insurance see p295.

INTERNET ACCESS

Most travelers make constant use of Internet cafés (which cost US$0.50 to US$2 per hour) and free Web-based email such as Yahoo (www.yahoo.com) and Hotmail (www.hotmail.com). A number of Mexican Internet cafés are equipped with CD burners, webcams, headphones and so on. But a lot don't have card readers, so bring your own or the camera-to-USB cable if you plan on burning photos to CD along the way.

Quite a few accommodations provide Internet access of some kind (they receive an 🖳 icon in this book). Facilities vary from a couple of computers in the lobby, for which you may or may not have to pay, to well-equipped business centers or wi-fi access *(internet inalámbrico)* in rooms. You may also be able to connect your own laptop or hand-held to the Internet through the telephone socket in your room. Be aware that your modem may not work once you leave your home country. The safest option is to buy a reputable 'global' modem before you leave home. A second issue is the plug: Mexico uses 110V plugs with two flat prongs, like those found in the US.

See p20 for some useful websites.

LEGAL MATTERS
Mexican Law

Mexican law is based on the Roman and Napoleonic codes, presuming an accused person is guilty until proven innocent.

The minimum jail sentence for possession of more than a token amount of any narcotic, including marijuana and amphetamines, is 10 months. As in most other countries, the purchase of controlled medication requires a doctor's prescription.

Road travelers should expect occasional police or military checkpoints. They are normally looking for drugs, weapons or illegal migrants. Drivers found with drugs or weapons on board may have their vehicle confiscated and may be detained for months while their cases are investigated.

See p295 for information on road rules and the legal aspects of road accidents.

Useful warnings on Mexican law are found in website of the **US Department of State** (www.travel.state.gov).

Getting Legal Help

If arrested, you have the right to contact your embassy or consulate. Consular officials can tell you your rights, provide lists of local lawyers, monitor your case, make sure you are

---

LEGAL AGE

- Voting: 18
- Drinking: 18
- Driving: 18
- Sex: Illegal with someone under 18 if their consent was obtained by deception, such as a false promise of marriage
- Marriage: 12

---

treated humanely, and notify your relatives or friends – but they can't get you out of jail. More Americans are in jail in Mexico than in any other country except the USA – about 800 at any one time. By Mexican law the longest a person can be detained by police without a specific accusation is 72 hours.

Tourist offices in Mexico, especially those run by state governments, can often help you with legal problems such as complaints or reporting crimes or lost articles. The national tourism ministry, **Sectur** (☎ 55-5250-0123, 800-903-92-00), offers 24-hour telephone advice.

If you are the victim of a crime, your embassy or consulate, or Sectur or state tourist offices, can give advice. In some cases, you may feel there is little to gain by going to the police, unless you need a statement to present to your insurance company. If you go to the police and your Spanish is poor, take a more fluent speaker. Also take your passport and tourist card, if you still have them. If you just want to report a theft for the purposes of an insurance claim, say you want to *'poner una acta de un robo'* (make a record of a robbery). This should make it clear that you merely want a piece of paper and you should get it without too much trouble.

If Mexican police wrongfully accuse you of an infraction, you can ask for the officer's identification, to speak to a superior or to be shown documentation about the law you have supposedly broken. You can also note the officer's name, badge number, vehicle number and department (federal, state or municipal). Pay any traffic fines at a police station and get a receipt, then make your complaint at Sectur or a state tourist office.

MAPS

GeoCenter, Nelles, ITM and the AAA (American Automobile Association) all produce good country maps of Mexico, available internationally for between US$6 and US$15. The map scales vary between 1:2,500,000 (1cm:25km) and 1:3,700,000 (1cm:37km). ITM also publishes good 1:1 million (1cm:10km) maps of some Mexican regions including the Pacific coast.

City, town and regional maps of varying quality are often available free from local tourist offices in Mexico, or for about US$3 at bookstores, newsstands and department stores like Sanborn's.

Inegi (Instituto Nacional de Estadística, Geografía e Informática; ☎ 800-490-42-00; www.inegi.gob.mx in Spanish) publishes a large-scale map series covering all of Mexico at 1:50,000 (1cm:500m) and 1:250,000 (1cm:2.5km), plus state maps at 1:700,000 (1cm:7km).

US-based **Maplink** (www.maplink.com) is an excellent source for mail-order maps; it stocks nearly all the above maps, including Inegi topo maps. Another good source is **Maps of Mexico** (www.maps-of-mexico.com), with detailed maps of all the states and of 90 cities.

MONEY

Mexico's currency is the peso, usually denoted by the '$' sign. Any prices quoted in US dollars will normally be written 'US$5' or '5 USD' to avoid misunderstanding. The peso is divided into 100 centavos. Coins come in denominations of five, 10, 20 and 50 centavos and one, two, five, 10, 20 and 100 pesos. There are notes of 20, 50, 100, 200, 500 and 1000 pesos.

Since the peso's exchange value is sometimes unstable, in this book we give prices in US dollar equivalents. For exchange rates, see inside the front cover. For information on costs, see p19.

The most convenient form of money in Mexico is a major international credit card or debit card. Visa, MasterCard and American Express cards can be used to obtain cash easily from ATMs in Mexico. Making a purchase by credit card normally gives you a more favorable exchange rate than exchanging money at a bank, and isn't subject to commission, but you'll normally have to pay your card issuer a 'foreign exchange' transaction fee of around 2.5%. Note that Visa, Amex or MasterCard stickers on a door or window in Mexico do *not* necessarily mean that these cards will be accepted for payment there.

US dollars are by far the most easily exchangeable foreign currency in Mexico. In tourist areas you can even pay for some things in US dollars, though the exchange rate used will probably not be in your favor. Euros, British pounds and Canadian dollars, in cash or as traveler's checks, are accepted by most banks and some *casas de cambio* (exchange houses).

For tips on keeping your money safe, see p281.

ATMs

ATMs (*caja permanente* or *cajero automático* in Spanish) are plentiful in Mexico, and are the easiest source of cash. You can use major credit cards and some bank cards, such as those on the Cirrus and Plus systems, to withdraw pesos from ATMs. The exchange rate that banks use for ATM withdrawals is normally more in your favor than the 'tourist rate' for currency exchange.

Banks & Casas de Cambio

You can exchange cash and traveler's checks in banks or at *casas de cambio*. Banks are more time-consuming than *casas de cambio*, and usually have shorter exchange hours (typically 9am to 5pm Monday to Friday and 9am to 1pm Saturday). *Casas de cambio* can be found easily in just about every large or medium-size town and in many smaller ones. These places are quick and often open evenings or weekends, but some don't accept traveler's checks, whereas banks usually do.

Exchange rates vary a little from one bank or *cambio* to another. There is often a better rate for *efectivo* (cash) than for *documento* (traveler's checks).

If you have trouble finding a place to change money, particularly on a weekend, try a hotel, though the exchange rate won't be the best.

International Transfers

Should you need money wired to you in Mexico, an easy and quick method is the 'Dinero en Minutos' (Money in Minutes) service of **Western Union** (☎ in the US 800-325-6000; www.westernunion.com). It's offered by thousands of bank branches and other businesses around Mexico, identified by black-and-yellow signs proclaiming 'Western Union Dinero en Minutos.'

US post offices (☎ 888-368-4669; www.usps.com) offer reasonably cheap money transfers to branches of Bancomer bank in Mexico. The service is called Dinero Seguro.

Taxes

Mexico's *impuesto de valor agregado* (IVA, value-added tax) is levied at 15%. By law the tax must be included in virtually any price quoted to you and should not be added afterward. Signs in stores and notices on restaurant menus often state '*IVA incluido.*' Occasionally they state instead that IVA must be added to the quoted prices.

Hotel rooms are also subject to the *Im puesto sobre hospedaje* (ISH, lodging tax). Each Mexican state sets its own rate, but in most it's 2%. See p277 for further information on taxes on hotel rooms.

Tipping

In general, workers in small, cheap restaurants don't expect much in the way of tips, while those in expensive resorts expect you to be lavish in your largesse. Workers in the tourism and hospitality industries often depend on tips to supplement miserable basic wages. In resorts frequented by foreigners (such as Acapulco, Puerto Vallarta and Mazatlán) tipping is up to US levels of 15%; elsewhere 10% is usually plenty. If you stay a few days in one place, you should leave up to 10% of your room costs for the people who have kept your room clean (assuming they have). A porter in a midrange hotel will be happy with US$1 a bag. Taxi drivers don't generally expect tips unless they provide some special service. Car-parking attendants expect a tip of US$0.20 to US$0.50, and the same is standard for gas-station attendants.

Traveler's Checks

Whether or not you have a credit card or bank card, you should also take some traveler's checks (denominated in US dollars) and a little US cash. Traveler's checks should be a major brand such as American Express or Visa. American Express traveler's checks are recognized everywhere, and are a good choice. The **AmEx 24-hour hotline** (☎ 800-828-0366, collect to US 801-964-6665) in Mexico City can help if you have lost traveler's checks or cards.

POST

Post offices (*oficinas de correos*) are typically open along the Pacific coast from 8am to 6pm Monday to Friday, and 9am to 1pm Saturday. An airmail letter or postcard weighing up to 20g costs US$1 to the US or Canada, US$1.25 to Europe or South America, and US$1.40 to the rest of the world. Mark airmail items 'Vía Aérea.' Delivery times (outbound and inbound) are elastic. An airmail letter from Mexico to the USA or Canada (or vice versa) should take somewhere between four and 14 days to arrive. Mail to or from Europe may take between one and two weeks; for Australasia, two to three weeks.

If you are sending a package internationally from Mexico, be prepared to open it for customs inspection at the post office. In light of this, it is better to take packing materials with you, or not seal it until you get there. For assured and speedy delivery, you can always use one of the more expensive international courier services, such as **UPS** (☎ 800-902-92-00; www.ups.com), **Federal Express** (☎ 800-900-11-00; www.fedex.com) or Mexico's **Estafeta** (☎ 800-903-35-00; www.esta feta.com).

SHOPPING

Mexico is so richly endowed with appealing *artesanías* (handicrafts) that few visitors can make it home without at least one pair of earrings or a little wooden animal. Because the Pacific coast is a popular tourist destination, you'll find all sorts of shops and *mercados de artesanías* (artisans' markets) selling handicrafts from all over the country, often at very reasonable prices. If you buy crafts from individual vendors on the streets, then a greater proportion of the profit will go to the (usually poor) people who make them, instead of to entrepreneurs. If you're traveling throughout the states of Guerrero, Michoacán, Nayarit and Oaxaca – which produce some of the country's finest handicrafts – you can even purchase *artesanías* in the villages where they are made, often directly from the artisans themselves. Always inspect for quality.

Don't be afraid to bargain. In markets bargaining is the rule, and you may pay much more than the going rate if you accept the first price quoted.

DIRECTORY

SERENDIPITOUS TREASURES

From around Mexico, here are just a few of the many crafts to keep an eye out for:

- **Animalitos & Alebrijes** *Animalitos* are tiny, light-brown and rust-colored ceramic animals from Chiapas. *Alebrijes* are little multicolored figurines from Oaxaca.
- **Baskets & Hats** Colorful, homemade baskets of multifarious sizes are great for carrying other souvenirs home. The Mexican straw sombrero (literally 'shade maker') is a classic souvenir.
- **Ceramics** The Guadalajara suburbs of Tonalá and Tlaquepaque are renowned pottery centers. Watch for the distinctive black pottery from San Bartolo Coyotepec, Oaxaca.
- **Hammocks** The best are the tightly woven, cotton, thin-string ones from the Yucatán and Oaxaca.
- **Huaraches** Sandals! Can't spend any time on the coast without a pair of these. Guadalajara is known for good *huaraches*.
- **Huipiles** Sleeveless tunics for women, mostly made in the southern states. They're often embroidered and wonderfully colorful. Coastal Mixtec and Amuzgos of Oaxaca are famous for them.
- **Jewelry** Silverwork from the central Mexican town of Taxco is sold everywhere.
- **Masks** Guerrero is famous for its masks, as are the villages of San Juan Colorado and Huazolotitlán, Oaxaca.
- **Rug weavings** Those from Teotitlán del Valle, Oaxaca, are most famous.
- **Serapes** An indigenous men's garment worn over the shoulders – essentially a blanket with an opening for the head.
- **Skulls & Skeletons** These crafty creations come in all shapes, sizes and materials, and have their origin in the November 2 Día de los Muertos (Day of the Dead) festival.

SOLO TRAVELERS

Lone travelers don't generally need to remain alone when traveling in Mexico unless they choose to. It's very easy to pair up with others, as there's a steady stream of people following similar routes around the country. In well-touristed places, notice boards advertise for traveling companions, flatmates, volunteer workers and so on. Local tours are a good way to meet people and get more out of a place.

Solo travelers should be especially watchful of their luggage when on the road and should stay in places with good security for their valuables, so that they don't have to be burdened with them when out and about.

Traveling alone can be a very good way of getting into the local culture and it definitely improves your Spanish skills. You can also get a kick out of doing what you want, when you want. Eating by yourself night after night can get a bit tiresome, but you'll only be left alone if you want it that way, as Mexicans are very sociable.

See p291 for information regarding women traveling solo.

TELEPHONE

Local calls are cheap; international calls can be expensive, but needn't be if you call from the right place at the right time. Mexico is well provided with fairly easy-to-use public card phones. *Casetas de teléfono* (call offices where an on-the-spot operator connects the call for you) are quite widespread and can be cheaper than the card phones. A third option is to call from your hotel, but hotels charge what they like for this service. It's nearly always cheaper to go elsewhere.

Calling Cards

Some calling cards from other countries can be used for calls from Mexico by dialing special access numbers:

AT&T (☎ 01-800-288-2872, 01-80-462-4240)
Bell Canada (☎ 01-800-123-0200, 01-800-021-1994)
BT Chargecard (☎ 01-800-123-02-44, 01-800-021-6644)
MCI (☎ 01-800-674-7000)
Sprint (☎ 01-800-877-8000)

Warning: if you get an operator who asks for your credit card instead of your calling-card number, or says the service is unavailable, hang up. There have been scams in which calls are rerouted to super-expensive credit-card phone services.

Cell Phones

If you want to use a cell phone in Mexico, one option for short visits is to get an international plan for your own phone, which will enable you to call home. You can also buy a Mexican cell phone for as little as US$30 to US$60 including some air time. The most widespread cellular phone system in Mexico is **Telcel** (www.telcel.com in Spanish), which has coverage almost everywhere that has a significant population, and roaming partnerships with systems from many other countries. Amigo cards, for recharging Telcel phones, are widely available from newsstands and minimarts.

Collect Calls

If you need to make a *llamada por cobrar* (collect call), you can do so from card phones without a card. Call an operator on ☎ 020 for domestic calls, or ☎ 090 for international calls, or use a 'home country direct' service, through which you make an international collect call via an operator in the country you're calling. The Mexican term for 'home country direct' is *país directo;* be prepared to provide the access numbers for the country you're trying to call.

Some telephone *casetas* and hotels will make collect calls for you, but they usually charge for the service.

Casetas de Teléfono

Costs in *casetas* are often lower than those for Telmex card phones (see right), and their advantages are that they eliminate street noise and you don't need a phone card to use them. They often have a telephone symbol outside, or signs saying '*teléfono*,' 'Lada' or 'Larga Distancia.'

Dialing Codes

If you're calling a number in the town or city you're in, simply dial the local number (eight digits in Mexico City, Guadalajara and Monterrey; seven digits everywhere else).

To call another town or city in Mexico, you need to dial the long-distance prefix ☎ 01, followed by the area code (two digits for Mexico City, Guadalajara and Monterrey; three digits for everywhere else) and then the local number. You'll find area codes listed under city and town headings through this book.

To make international calls, you need to dial the international prefix ☎ 00, followed by the country code, area code and local number.

To call a number in Mexico from another country, dial your international access code, then the Mexico country code ☎ 52, then the area code and number.

Phone Cards

These are common in towns and cities: you'll usually find some at airports, bus stations and around the main plaza. Easily the most common, and most consistent on costs, are those marked with the name of the country's biggest phone company, Telmex. To use a Telmex card phone you need a phone card known as a *tarjeta Ladatel*. These are sold at kiosks and shops everywhere – look for the blue-and-yellow signs that read *'De venta aquí Ladatel.'* The cards come in denominations of 30 pesos (about US$3), 50 pesos (US$5) and 100 pesos (US$10).

Calls from Telmex card phones cost US$0.10 per minute for local calls; US$0.40 per minute long-distance within Mexico; US$0.50 per minute to the USA or Canada; US$1 per minute to Central America; US$2 per minute to Europe, Alaska or South America; and US$2.50 per minute to Hawaii, Australia, New Zealand or Asia.

In some parts of Mexico frequented by foreign tourists, you may notice a variety of phones advertising that they accept credit cards, or that you can make easy collect calls to the USA on them. While some of these phones may be of fair value, there are others on which very high rates are charged.

TIME

Most of the country, including Jalisco, Michoacan, Guerrero and Oaxaca, are on Hora del Centro, the same as US Central Time (GMT minus six hours in winter, and GMT minus five hours during daylight saving). Five western states, including Nayarit and Sinaloa, are on Hora de las Montañas, the same as US Mountain Time (GMT minus seven hours in winter, GMT minus six hours during daylight saving). *Horario*

DIRECTORY

de verano (daylight saving time) runs from the first Sunday in April to the last Sunday in October.

TOILETS

Public toilets are rare, so take advantage of facilities in places such as hotels, restaurants, bus stations and museums. When out and about, carry some toilet paper with you if you think you're going to need it because it often won't be provided. If there's a bin beside the toilet, put paper in it because the drains can't cope otherwise.

TOURIST INFORMATION

For general information about travel in Mexico consult the **Mexico Tourism Board** (USA & Canada ☎ 800-446-3942, 800-44-MEXICO; Europe ☎ 00-800-11-11-22-66; www.visitmexico.com). Alternatively, you can call the Mexico City office of the national tourism ministry **Sectur** (☎ 55-5250-0123/51, 800-903-92-00; in the US & Canada 800-446-3942, 800-482-9832; in Europe 00-800-1111-2266) at any time – 24 hours a day, seven days a week – for information or help in English or Spanish.

Just about every town of touristic interest in Mexico has a state or municipal tourist office. They are generally helpful with maps, brochures and questions, and usually some staff members speak English. Here are the contact details for the head tourism offices for the states covered in this book:

Colima (☎ 312-316-20-21; www.visitacolima.com.mx)
Guerrero (☎ 744-484-24-23; www.sectur.guerrero.gob.mx)
Jalisco (☎ 33-3668-1600, 800-363-22-00; visita.jalisco.gob.mx in Spanish)
Michoacán (☎ 443-312-80-81, 800-450-23-00; www.turismomichoacan.gob.mx in Spanish)
Nayarit (☎ 311-216-56-61; www.turismonayarit.gob.mx)
Oaxaca (☎ 951-576-48-28; www.aoaxaca.com in Spanish)

TOURS

For travelers seeking an activity-based holiday – and particularly for those who are short on time – organized tours are a good way to get to the most popular places and partake in hassle-free outdoor activities such as mountain biking, diving or horseback riding. More and more providers are adding cultural excursions to hard-to-get-to places to attract travelers who might not otherwise consider an organized tour. The biggest and best-regarded operator in the region is Vallarta Adventures (p77).

VISAS

Every tourist must have an easily obtainable Mexican government tourist card. Some nationalities must also have visas. Because the regulations sometimes change, it's wise to confirm them with a Mexican embassy or consulate before you go (see p282).

Citizens of the USA, Canada, EU countries, Australia, New Zealand, Iceland, Israel, Japan, Norway and Switzerland are among those who do not require visas to enter Mexico as tourists. Again, check with your local Mexican embassy or consulate well ahead of travel in case the list has changed. Visa procedures, for those who need them, can take weeks and you may be required to apply in your country of residence or citizenship.

For information on passport requirements, see p292). Non-US citizens passing (even in transit) through the USA on the way to or from Mexico, or visiting Mexico from the USA, should also check the passport and visa requirements for the USA.

Tourist Card & Tourist Fee

The Mexican tourist card – the *forma migratoria para turista* (FMT) – is a document that you must fill out and get stamped by Mexican immigration when you enter Mexico and keep till you leave. It's available at official border crossings, international airports and ports, and often at airlines, travel agencies and Mexican consulates. At the US–Mexico border you won't usually be given one automatically – you have to ask for it.

At many US–Mexico border crossings you don't have to get the card stamped at the border itself, as Mexico's Instituto Nacional de Migración (INM, National Immigration Institute) has control points on the highways into the interior where it's also possible to do it. But it's better to get it done at the border in case there are complications elsewhere.

One section of the card deals with the length of your stay in Mexico, and this section is filled out by the immigration officer. The maximum possible stay is 180 days for most nationalities (90 days for Australians, Austrians, Israelis and Italians, among others), but immigration officers will often put a much lower number (as little as 15 or 30 days) unless you tell them otherwise. It's advisable to ask for more days than you think you'll need in case you are delayed or change your plans.

Though the tourist card is free, it brings with it the obligation to pay the tourist fee of about US$20, called the *derecho para no inmigrante* (DNI, nonimmigrant fee). If you enter Mexico by air, the fee is included in your airfare. If you enter by land, you must pay the fee at a bank in Mexico before you reenter the frontier zone on your way out of Mexico (or before you check in at an airport to fly out of Mexico). The frontier zone is the territory between the border and the INM's control points on the highways leading into the Mexican interior (usually 20km to 30km from the border). Most Mexican border posts have on-the-spot bank offices where you can pay the DNI fee immediately. When you pay at a bank, your tourist card will be stamped to prove that you have paid.

Look after your tourist card because it may be checked when you leave the country. You can be fined US$42 for not having it.

EXTENSIONS & LOST CARDS

If the number of days given on your tourist card is less than the maximum for your nationality (90 or 180 days in most cases), its validity may be extended one or more times, up to the maximum. To get a card extended, apply to the INM, which has offices in many towns and cities: they're listed on the **INM website** (www.inm.gob.mx), under 'Servicios Migratorios.' The procedure costs about US$20 and should take between half an hour and three hours, depending on the office. You'll need your passport, tourist card, photocopies of the important pages of these documents and, at some offices, evidence of 'sufficient funds.' Most INM offices will not extend a card until a few days before it expires.

If you lose your card or need further information, contact a tourist office, the **Sectur tourist office** (☎ 55-5250-0123, 800-903-92-00) in Mexico City, or your embassy or consulate. Any of these should be able to give you an official note to take to an INM office, which will issue a duplicate for US$42.

See right for information on the documentation required to work in Mexico.

WOMEN TRAVELERS

Women can have a great time in Mexico, traveling with companions or solo, but in this land that invented machismo, some concessions have to be made to local custom. Gender equalization has come a long way in a few decades, and Mexicans are generally a very polite people, but they remain, by and large, great believers in the difference (rather than the equality) between the sexes.

Lone women must expect a few catcalls and attempts to chat them up. Often these men only want to talk to you, but you can discourage unwanted attention by avoiding eye contact (wear sunglasses), dressing modestly, moving confidently and speaking coolly but politely if you are addressed and must respond. Wearing a wedding ring can prove helpful. Don't put yourself in peril by doing things that Mexican women would not do, such as challenging a man's masculinity, drinking alone in a cantina, hitchhiking or going alone to remote places.

On local transportation it's best to don long or mid-calf-length trousers and a top that meets the top of your pants, with sleeves of some sort. That way you can keep your valuables out of sight with ease.

Most of all, appear self-assured.

WORK

Mexicans need jobs, so people who enter Mexico as tourists aren't legally allowed to take employment. The many expats working in Mexico have usually been posted there by their companies or organizations with all the necessary papers. Permits are issued to people sponsored by companies in Mexico (or foreign companies with Mexican operations/subsidiaries), or to people with specific skills required in Mexico. English-speakers (and a few German- or French-speakers) may find teaching jobs in language schools, *preparatorias* (high schools) or universities, or can offer personal tutoring. The pay is low, but you can live on it. Press ads, especially in the various local English-language papers and magazines, and the Yellow Pages are sources of job opportunities.

Schools will often pay a foreign teacher in the form of a *beca* (scholarship), and thus circumvent the laws precluding foreigners from working in Mexico without a permit. In some cases, the school's administration will procure the appropriate papers. Apart from teaching, you might find a little bar or restaurant work in tourist areas.

Jobs Abroad (www.jobsabroad.com) posts paid and unpaid job openings in Mexico. The **Lonely Planet** website (www.lonelyplanet.com) has several useful links.

Transportation

CONTENTS

> **THINGS CHANGE...**
>
> The information in this chapter is particularly vulnerable to change. Check directly with the airline or a travel agent to make sure you understand how a fare (and ticket you may buy) works, and be aware of the security requirements for international travel. Shop carefully. The details given in this chapter should be regarded as pointers and are not a substitute for your own careful, up-to-date research.

GETTING THERE & AWAY

ENTERING THE COUNTRY

Immigration officers won't usually keep you waiting any longer than it takes to flick through your passport and enter your length of stay on your tourist card (p290). Anyone traveling to Mexico via the USA should be sure to check the current US visa and passport requirements. Flights, tours and rail tickets can be booked online at www.lonelyplanet.com/travel_services.

Passport

Though it's not recommended, US and Canadian tourists can still, at the time of writing, enter Mexico without a passport if they have official photo identification such as a driver's license, plus some proof of their citizenship, for example an original birth certificate. But this is likely to change soon, including for Canadians passing through the USA, due to new US regulations called the Western Hemisphere Travel Initiative. These regulations, which come into effect from December 31, 2006 (for air and sea travelers), and from December 31, 2007 (for land travelers), are expected to require all travelers entering the USA from Mexico or Canada to carry passports. In theory, travelers will still be able to enter Mexico from the US with just proof of citizenship and photo ID, but they won't be able to return to the US (or to enter the US from Canada) without a passport. For more information on the regulations, visit the **US State Department website** (travel.state.gov).

In any case it's much better to have a passport. In Mexico you will often need your passport to change money or when you check into a hotel.

All citizens of countries other than the US and Canada should have a passport that's valid for at least six months after they arrive in Mexico.

Travelers under 18 who are not accompanied by both parents may need special documentation (see p280).

For information on Mexican visa requirements and the tourist card, see p290. Flights, tours and rail tickets can be booked online at www.lonelyplanet.com/travel_services.

AIR

Most visitors to Mexico's Pacific coast arrive by air. You can fly direct to Mexico's Pacific coast from at least a dozen US cities and from Toronto. From anywhere else you'll have to either fly first to Mexico City or to the cities with direct connections. Airports in the region are shown in the boxed text, opposite.

Airports & Airlines

Mexico's two flag airlines are Mexicana and Aeroméxico. Formerly state-controlled, Mexicana was bought by Grupo Posadas, Mexico's biggest hotel company, in 2005, and the government hoped to sell off

---

PACIFIC COAST AIRPORTS

Acapulco (ACA; ☎ 744-466-94-34)
Guadalajara (GDL; ☎ 33-3688-5504)
Huatulco (Bahías de Huatulco) (HUX; www
.asur.com.mx)
Ixtapa-Zihuatanejo (ZIH; ☎ 755-554-20-70)
Manzanillo (Playa de Oro) (ZLO; ☎ 314-
333-25-25)
Mazatlán (MZT; ☎ 669-928-04-38)
Oaxaca (OAX; ☎ 951-511-50-78; www.asur
.com.mx)
Puerto Vallarta (PVR; ☎ 322-221-28-48)

Aeroméxico in 2006. Their safety records are comparable to major US and European airlines: Mexicana has had one fatal crash in about two million flights since 1970, while Aeroméxico has suffered no fatal events since 1986.

The following airlines service Mexico's Pacific coast. The phone numbers are those in Mexico.

Aero California (code JR; ☎ 800-237-62-25; hub Tijuana)
Aeroméxico (code AM; ☎ 800-021-40-00; www.aero mexico.com; hub Mexico City)
Air Canada (code AC; ☎ 800-719-28-27; www.air canada .ca; hub Toronto)
Alaska Airlines (code AS; ☎ 800-252-75-22; www .alaska-air.com; hub Seattle)
America West (code HP; ☎ 800-235-92-92; www.america west.com; hub Phoenix)
American Airlines (code AA; ☎ 800-904-60-00; www .aa.com; hub Dallas)
Continental Airlines (code CO; ☎ 800-900-50-00; www .continental.com; hub Houston)
Delta Air Lines (code DL; ☎ 800-123-47-78; www.delta .com; hub Atlanta)
Mexicana (code MX; ☎ 800-502-20-00; www.mexicana .com; hub Mexico City)

Tickets

The cost of flying to Mexico's Pacific coast is usually higher around Christmas and New Year, and during July and August. In addition to online and other ticket agents such as those recommended in the following sections, it's often worth checking the airlines' own websites for special deals. Newspapers, magazines and websites serving Mexican communities outside of Mexico are also good sources.

Try international online booking agencies such as **CheapTickets** (www.cheaptickets.com)

and, for students and travelers under the age of 26, **STA Travel** (www.statravel.com).

A departure tax equivalent to about US$25 is levied on international flights from Mexico. It's usually included in the cost of your ticket, but if it isn't you must pay in cash at check-in. Ask your travel agent in advance.

Asia

You normally have to make a connection in the US or Canada (often Los Angeles, San Francisco or Vancouver), and maybe one in Asia as well. From more westerly Asian points such as Bangkok, routes via Europe are also an option. There are numerous branches in Asia of **STA Travel** Bangkok (☎ 02-2237-9400; www.statravel.co.th); Singapore (☎ 6737-7188; www.statravel.com.sg); Hong Kong (☎ 2736-1618; www .statravel.com.hk); Japan (☎ 03-5391-2922; www.statravel .co.jp). Another resource in Japan is **No 1 Travel** (☎ 03-3205-6073; www.no1-travel.com).

Australia & New Zealand

The cheapest routes are usually via the USA (normally Los Angeles). You're normally looking at A$2300 or NZ$2300 or more, round-trip (several hundred dollars extra during high season).

The following agents are well-known for cheap fares and have branches throughout both countries:

Flight Centre Australia (☎ 133-133; www.flightcentre .com.au); New Zealand (☎ 0800-243-544; www.flight centre.co.nz)
STA Travel Australia (☎ 1300 733 035; www.statravel .com.au); New Zealand (☎ 0508-782-872; www.statravel .co.nz)

For online fares try www.travel.com.au or www.zuji.com from Australia, and www .travel.co.nz or www.zuji.co.nz from New Zealand.

Canada

Montreal, Toronto and Vancouver all have direct flights to Mexico, though better deals are often available with a change of flight in the USA. Round-trip fares from Toronto start around C$900 to Mexico City, Cancún or Puerto Vallarta. **Travel Cuts** (☎ 800-667-2887; www.travelcuts.com) is Canada's national student-travel agency. For online bookings try www.kayak.com, www.expedia.ca and www.travelocity.ca.

TRANSPORTATION

Europe

Airlines with direct flights to Mexico City include Aeroméxico, Air Europa, Air France, Air Madrid, British Airways, Iberia, Jetair, KLM and Lufthansa. An alternative is to fly with a US or Canadian airline or alliance partner, changing planes in North America.

For online bookings throughout Europe, try **Opodo** (www.opodo.com) or **Ebookers** (www.ebookers.com).

THE UK

Round-trip fares to Mexico City or Cancún start around UK£500 to UK£600 from London. Flight ads appear in the travel pages of the weekend broadsheet newspapers, in *Time Out*, the *Evening Standard* and the free online magazine *TNT* (www.tntmagazine.com).

An excellent place to start your inquiries is **Journey Latin America** (☎ 020-8747-3108; www.journeylatinamerica.co.uk), which offers a variety of tours as well as flights. Other recommended agencies include the following:

Travelbag (☎ 0800-082-5000; www.travelbag.com)
Flight Centre (☎ 0800-587-700-58; flightcentre.co.uk)
Flightbookers (☎ 0800-082-3000; www.ebookers.com)
STA Travel (☎ 08701-630-026; www.statravel.co.uk) For travelers under the age of 26.
Trailfinders (☎ 0845-058-5858; www.trailfinders.co.uk)

CONTINENTAL EUROPE

Flights to Mexico City or Cancún cost €600 to €700 from Frankfurt, Paris or Madrid. The two budget airlines currently operating between Europe and Mexico (Air Madrid from Madrid to Mexico City, and Jetair from Brussels to Cancún) can save you a couple of hundred euros if you fly on certain dates. Recommended ticket agencies include the following:

France
Nouvelles Frontières (☎ 0825-00-07-47; www.nouvelles-frontieres.fr)
Voyageurs du Monde (☎ 0892-68-83-63; www.vdm.com)
OTU Voyages (☎ 01-55-82-32-32; www.otu.fr) A student and youth travel specialist.

Germany
Expedia (www.expedia.de)
Just Travel (☎ 089-747-3330; www.justtravel.de)
STA Travel (☎ 069-743-032-92; www.statravel.de) For travelers aged under 26.

Other European Countries

Airfair (☎ 070-307-6110; www.airfair.nl) Dutch company.
CTS Viaggi (☎ 199-501150; www.cts.it) Italian specialist in student and youth travel.
eDreams (☎ 902-887-107; www.edreams.es) Spanish company.
Kilroy Travels (www.kilroytravels.com) Scandinavian company.
Rumbo (☎ 902-123-999; www.rumbo.es) Spanish company.

South America

You can fly direct to Mexico City from at least eight cities in South America. Round-trip fares start around US$800 to US$1000. Recommended ticket agencies include the following:

ASATEJ (☎ 011-4114-7595; www.asatej.com) In Argentina.
IVI Tours (☎ 0212-993-6082; www.ividiomas.com) In Venezuela.
Student Travel Bureau (☎ 3038-1555; www.stb.com.br) In Brazil.

USA

You can fly to Mexico without changing planes from around 30 US cities. A number of these cities have direct flights to Mexico's Pacific coast. There are one-stop connecting flights from many other cities. Continental (from Houston), Aeroméxico and Mexicana offer the most Mexican destinations.

US budget airlines including ATA, Spirit Air, America West, Frontier Airlines, and Ted have entered the USA–Mexico market, and economical fares are also available on Mexico's Aero California, Aviacsa and Líneas Aéreas Azteca. If you're lucky, you can get round-trip fares from the USA to Mexico for US$250. If you're not lucky, 'budget' operators can cost as much as other airlines. For current bargain offers, check **Airfare Watchdog** (www.airfarewatchdog.com).

Here are some typical return-trip, midseason fares for trips booked two weeks in advance:

From	To Acapulco	To Puerto Vallarta	To Mazatlán
Chicago	US$520	US$400	US$580
Dallas/ Fort Worth	US$600	US$500	US$570
Los Angeles	US$460	US$350	US$320
Miami	US$500	US$400	US$740
New York	US$740	US$530	US$650

In high season you may have to pay US$100 to US$200 more, though competitive fares are offered by some of the major booking websites, such as Expedia or Travelocity, year-round if you book ahead.

Another possibility is a package-tour flight. Check newspaper travel ads and call a package-tour agency, asking if you can buy 'air only' (just the return air ticket, not the hotel or other features). This often works out cheaper than buying a discounted return ticket.

LAND
Border Crossings
There are about 40 crossings on the USA–Mexico border, including the following:

Arizona Douglas–Agua Prieta, Nogales–Nogales, San Luis–San Luis, Río Colorado and Naco–Naco (all open 24 hours); Sasabe–El Sásabe (open 8am to 10pm); Lukeville–Sonoita (open 8am to midnight).

California Calexico–Mexicali (two crossings, one open 24 hours); San Ysidro–Tijuana (open 24 hours); Otay Mesa–Mesa de Otay (near Tijuana airport; open 6am to 10pm); Tecate–Tecate (open 6am to midnight).

New Mexico Columbus–General Rodrigo M Quevedo (also called Palomas; open 24 hours).

Texas Brownsville–Matamoros, McAllen–Reynosa, Laredo–Nuevo Laredo, Del Rio–Ciudad Acuña, Eagle Pass–Piedras Negras, Presidio–Ojinaga and El Paso–Ciudad Juárez (all open 24 hours).

There are also 10 border crossings between Guatemala and Mexico and two crossings between Belize and Mexico.

See below for more information on entering Mexico with a car.

Car & Motorcycle
The regulations for taking a vehicle into Mexico change from time to time. See p297 if you're bringing in a vehicle from the US or Canada. For information on driving and motorcycling once you're inside Mexico, see p299.

INSURANCE
It is very foolish to drive in Mexico without Mexican liability insurance. If you are involved in an accident, you can be jailed and have your vehicle impounded while responsibility is assessed. If you are to blame for an accident causing injury or death, you may be detained until you guarantee restitution to the victims and payment of any

fines. This could take weeks or months to arrange. Adequate Mexican insurance coverage is the only real protection.

Mexican law recognizes only Mexican motor *seguro* (insurance), so a US or Canadian policy, even if it provides coverage, is not acceptable to Mexican officialdom. Sanborn's and the AAA are both well worth looking into for motor insurance in Mexico. Mexican insurance is also sold in US border towns; as you approach the border from the USA you will see billboards advertising offices selling Mexican policies. Some deals are better than others.

Short-term insurance costs about US$15 a day for full coverage on a car worth under US$10,000; for periods longer than two weeks it's often cheaper to get an annual policy. Liability-only insurance costs around half the full coverage cost.

DRIVER'S LICENSE
To drive a motor vehicle in Mexico, you need a valid driver's license from your home country.

VEHICLE PERMIT
You will need a *permiso de importación temporal de vehículos* (temporary vehicle import permit) if you want to take a vehicle to Mexico's Pacific coast. The permits are issued at offices at border crossings or (for some border crossings) at posts a few kilometers into Mexico. Information on their locations and application forms for the vehicle permit are available online at www.banjercito.com.mx (mostly in Spanish). The person importing the vehicle will need the original and one or two photocopies (people at the office may make photocopies for a small fee) of each of the following documents, which as a rule must all be in their own name (except that they can bring in a spouse's, parent's or child's vehicle if they can show a marriage or birth certificate proving a relationship):

- tourist card (FMT): go to *migración* before you get your vehicle permit
- certificate of title or registration certificate for the vehicle (note: you should have both of these if you plan to drive through Mexico into Guatemala or Belize)
- a Visa, MasterCard or American Express credit card issued by a non-Mexican institution; if you don't have one, you

must pay a returnable deposit of between US$200 and US$400 (depending on how old the car is) at the border. Your card details or deposit serve as a guarantee that you'll take the car out of Mexico before your tourist card (FMT) expires.

■ proof of citizenship or residency such as a passport, birth certificate or voter's registration card accompanied by official photo ID such as a driver's license

■ driver's license

■ if the vehicle is not fully paid for, a partial invoice and/or letter of authorization from the financing institution

■ for a leased or rented vehicle (though few US rental firms allow their vehicles to be taken into Mexico), the contract, which must be in the name of the person importing the vehicle

■ for a company car, proof of employment by the company and proof of the company's ownership of the vehicle

At the border there will be a building with a parking area for vehicles awaiting permits. After some signing and stamping of papers, you sign a promise to take the car out of the country, pay a processing fee of about US$29 to the Banco del Ejército (also called Banjército; it's the army bank), and go and wait with your vehicle. Make sure you get back the originals of all documents. Eventually someone will come out and give you your vehicle permit and a sticker to be displayed on your windshield.

While in Mexico, other persons are allowed to drive the car only if the permit holder is in the car with them.

You have the option to take the vehicle in and out of Mexico for the period shown on your tourist card. Ask for a *tarjetón de internación*, a document that you exchange for a *comprobante de retorno* each time you leave Mexico; when you return to Mexico, you swap the *comprobante* for another *tarjetón*. When you leave Mexico the last time, you must have the import permit canceled by the Mexican authorities. An official may do this as you enter the border zone, usually 20km to 30km before the border itself. If not, you'll have to find the right official at the border crossing. If you leave Mexico without having the permit canceled, the authorities may assume you've left the vehicle in the country illegally and decide either to keep your

deposit, charge a fine to your credit card, or deny you permission to bring a vehicle into the country on your next trip.

Only the owner may take the vehicle out of Mexico. If the vehicle is wrecked completely during your visit, you must contact your consulate or a Mexican customs office to make arrangements to leave without it.

Belize

Novelo's Bus Line (☎ 227-2025 in Belize City) runs around 20 buses a day between Belize City and Chetumal, Mexico (US$5 to US$7, four hours), calling at the Belizean towns of Orange Walk and Corozal en route. From Chetumal you can hop on a long-distance bus to the Pacific coast.

Guatemala

The road borders at La Mesilla–Ciudad Cuauhtémoc, Ciudad Tecún Umán–Ciudad Hidalgo and El Carmen–Talismán are all linked to Guatemala City, and nearby cities within Guatemala and Mexico, by plentiful buses and/or combis. **Transportes Galgos** (☎ 2232-3661 in Guatemala City; www.transgalgosinter .com.gt), **Línea Dorada** (☎ 2232-5506 in Guatemala City; www.tikalmayanworld.com) and **Tica Bus** (☎ 2331-4279 in Guatemala City; www.ticabus.com) run a few buses daily from Guatemala City to Tapachula, Chiapas (US$14 to US$22, six hours) via Escuintla and Mazatenango.

There are a few daily buses from Flores, Guatemala, to Chetumal, Mexico (US$25, seven to eight hours), via Belize City, run by **Línea Dorada** (☎ 7926-0070 in Flores) and **San Juan Travel** (☎ 7926-0041 in Flores).

USA
BUS

Cross-border bus services, mainly used by Mexicans working in the US, link many US cities with northern Mexican cities. They're not very well publicized: Spanish-language newspapers in the US have the most ads. The major companies include **Autobuses Americanos** (www.autobusesamericanos.com.mx in Spanish; ☎ 512-928-9237 in Austin, ☎ 303-292-0333 in Denver, ☎ 713-928-8832 in Houston, ☎ 213-627-5405 in Los Angeles, ☎ 602-258-4331 in Phoenix), operating to northeast Mexico, central north Mexico and central Mexico from Los Angeles, Denver, Albuquerque, Chicago, Phoenix and Tucson and several Texan cities; **Autobuses Crucero** (☎ 602-258-4331 in Phoenix), operating from California, Nevada and Arizona to northwest Mexico; and **Transportes Baldomero Corral** (TBC; ☎ 602-258-2445 in Phoenix), operating between Arizona and northwest Mexico. **Greyhound** (☎ 800-231-2222; www.greyhound.com) also has some cross-border routes.

You can also, often in little or no extra time, make your way to the border on one bus (or train), cross it on foot or by local bus, and then catch an onward bus on the other side. Greyhound serves many US border cities; to reach others, transfer from Greyhound to a smaller bus line.

For train travel to the border, **Amtrak** (☎ 800-872-72-45; www.amtrak.com) serves four US cities from which access to Mexico is easy: San Diego, El Paso, Del Rio and San Antonio, which is linked by bus to Eagle Pass and Laredo.

CAR & MOTORCYCLE
For information on the procedures for taking a vehicle into Mexico, check with the **American Automobile Association** (AAA; www.aaa.com), **Sanborn's** (☎ 800-222-0158; www.sanborns insurance.com), a Mexican consulate or the Mexican tourist information numbers in the USA and Canada (☎ 800-446-3942, 800-482-9832). If you're traveling from Mexico into the USA at a busy time of year, have a look at the website of **US Customs & Border Protection** (apps.cbp.gov), which posts waiting times at entry points.

SEA
If you'd like to combine snatches of Mexico with a life of ease on the high seas, take a cruise! Ever more popular, cruises from the USA now bring over 7 million passengers a year to Mexican ports, enabling people to enjoy activities and attractions on and near Mexico's coasts. On the Pacific route (the Mexican Riviera in cruise parlance), the main ports of call are Ensenada, Cabo San Lucas, Mazatlán, Puerto Vallarta and Acapulco, each with more than 100 cruises a year (over 200 at Puerto Vallarta); some cruises also call at Manzanillo, Zihuatanejo and Bahías de Huatulco, and a new cruise port is opening at Puerto Chiapas, near Tapachula.

Following are some of the cruise lines visiting Mexico, with US phone numbers:
Carnival Cruise Lines (☎ 888-227-6482; www.carni val.com)

Celebrity Cruises (☎ 800-722-5941; www.celebrity .com)
Crystal Cruises (☎ 800-804-1500; www.crystalcruises .com)
Holland America Line (☎ 877-724-5425; www.holland america.com)
Norwegian Cruise Lines (☎ 800-327-7030; www.ncl .com)
P&O Cruises (☎ 415-382-8900; www.pocruises.com)
Princess Cruises (☎ 800-774-6237; www.princess .com)
Royal Caribbean International (☎ 800-398-9813; www.royalcaribbean.com)

GETTING AROUND
AIR
Flying is considerably cheaper between an inland city (Mexico City, Guadalajara or Oaxaca) and a coastal destination, than from one coastal destination to another. This is because nearly all flights head to/ from Mexico City and Guadalajara, making it necessary to purchase two fares to get from coastal-point A to coastal-point B (via the inland city). Mazatlán, Tepic, Puerto Vallarta, Manzanillo, Colima, Lázaro Cárdenas, Acapulco, Puerto Escondido, Ixtapa-Zihuatanejo, Oaxaca, and Bahías de Huatulco all have passenger airports.

Aeroméxico and Mexicana are the country's two largest airlines. There are also smaller ones, often flying to/from smaller cities on the coast that the big two companies don't bother with (see the boxed text on p298 for websites and telephone numbers in Mexico). Information on specific flights can be found within the Getting There & Away sections of individual city sections.

Aerolitoral and Aeromar are feeder airlines for Aeroméxico and normally share its ticket offices and booking networks.

Tickets
Fares can depend on whether you fly at a busy or quiet time of day, week or year, and how far ahead you book and pay. High season generally corresponds to the Mexican holiday seasons (see p284). Round-trip fares are usually simply twice the price of one-way tickets, though some advance-payment cheaper deals do exist.

TRANSPORTATION

MEXICAN DOMESTIC AIRLINES

Airline	Phone	Website	Areas served
Aero California	☎ 800-237-62-25	–	Mexico City, Baja California, north, west
Aero Tucán	☎ 800-640-41-48, 951-501-05-30	www.aero-tucan.com	Oaxaca city, Puerto Escondido, Puebla
Aerolitoral	☎ 800-800-23-76	www.aerolitoral.com	Central Mexico, Baja California, north, west, Gulf coast
Aeromar	☎ 800-237-66-27	www.aeromar.com.mx	Central Mexico, west, northeast, Gulf coast, southeast
Aeroméxico	☎ 800-021-40-00	www.aeromexico.com	Mexico City & more than 50 cities nationwide
Aviacsa	☎ 800-006-22-00	www.aviacsa.com	Mexico City & 19 other cities around the country
Avolar	☎ 800-021-90-00	www.avolar.com.mx	Puebla, Acapulco, Tijuana, Hermosillo, Uruapan
Click Mexicana	☎ 800-122-54-25	www.clickmx.com	Mexico City & 16 other cities around the country
Interjet	☎ 800-011-23-45	www.interjet.com.mx	Guadalajara, Toluca, Cancún, Monterrey
Líneas Aéreas Azteca	☎ 800-229-83-22	www.aazteca.com.mx	Mexico City, Oaxaca, Acapulco, Cancún, north, west
Magnicharters	☎ 55-5566-8199	www.magnicharters .com.mx	Mexico City, Guadalajara, Toluca, Aguascalientes, Monterrey, Bajío, Torreón, San Luis Potosí, Morelia, Mérida
Méxicana	☎ 800-502-20-00	www.mexicana.com	Mexico City and more than 50 cities nationwide

Here are examples of one-way fares to/from Mexico City for trips booked two weeks in advance:

To/from	Fare
Acapulco	US$152
Bahías de Huatulco	US$129
Guadalajara	US$157
Ixtapa-Zihuatanejo	US$173
Manzanillo	US$315
Mazatlán	US$260
Oaxaca	US$135
Puerto Vallarta	US$217

BICYCLE

Cycling is not a common way to tour Mexico's Pacific coast, but some people do it. Reports of highway robbery, poor road surfaces and road hazards are deterrents. However, this method of moving up or down the coast is not impossible if you're prepared for the challenges. You should be very fit, use the best equipment you can muster and be able to handle your own repairs. Take the mountainous topography and hot climate into account when planning your route.

It's possible to rent bikes in many resort towns for short excursions, and the same places often offer guided rides.

BOAT

Vehicle and passenger ferries connecting Baja California with the Mexican mainland travel between La Paz and Mazatlán, and La Paz and Topolobampo, Sinaloa. For more information, see p124.

BUS

Mexico has a good road and bus network, and comfortable, frequent, reasonably priced bus services connect all cities. Most cities and towns have one main bus terminal where all long-distance buses arrive and depart. If there is no main terminal, different bus companies will have separate terminals scattered around town.

Baggage is safe if stowed in the bus's baggage hold, but get a receipt for it when you hand it over. Keep your most valuable documents (passport, money etc) on you, and keep them closely protected.

Classes
DELUXE

De lujo (deluxe) services, sometimes termed *ejecutivo* (executive), run mainly on the busy routes. They are swift, modern and comfortable, with reclining seats, adequate legroom, air-conditioning, few or no stops, toilets on board (but not necessarily toilet paper), and sometimes drinks or snacks.

1ST-CLASS

Primera (1a) clase buses have a comfortable numbered seat for each passenger. All sizable towns have 1st-class bus services. Standards of comfort are adequate at the very least. The buses usually have air-conditioning and a toilet and they stop infrequently. They always show movies (often bad ones) for most of the trip: too bad if you don't want to watch, as all seats face a video screen. As with deluxe buses, buy your ticket in the bus station before boarding.

2ND-CLASS

Segunda (2a) clase buses serve small towns and villages, and provide cheaper, slower travel on some intercity routes. Many 2nd-class services have no ticket office; you just pay your fare to the conductor. These buses tend to take slow, nontoll roads in and out of big cities and will stop anywhere to pick up passengers: if you board midroute you might make some of the trip standing. The small amount of money you save by traveling 2nd-class is not usually worth the discomfort or extra journey time entailed.

Second-class buses can also be less safe than 1st-class or deluxe buses, due to lower maintenance or driver standards or because they are more vulnerable to being boarded by bandits on some roads. Out in the remoter areas, however, you'll often find that 2nd-class buses are the only buses available.

You may also encounter various other types of buses in your travels:

- *directo*: very few stops
- *semi-directo*: a few more stops than a *directo*
- *ordinario*: stops wherever passengers want to get on or off the bus

Costs

First-class buses typically cost roughly US$4 per hour of travel (70km to 80km). Deluxe buses may cost just 10% or 20% more than 1st-class, or about 60% more for super-deluxe services such as ETN, UNO and Turistar Ejecutivo. Second-class buses cost 10% or 20% less than 1st-class.

Reservations

For trips of up to four or five hours on busy routes, you can usually just go to the bus terminal, buy a ticket and head out without much delay. For longer trips, or routes with infrequent services, buy a ticket a day or more in advance. Deluxe and 1st-class bus companies have computerized ticket systems that allow you to select your seat when you buy your ticket. Try to avoid the back of the bus, which is where the toilets are and also tends to give a bumpier ride.

CAR & MOTORCYCLE

Driving in Mexico is not as easy as it is in North America and Europe (much of Europe anyway), but few experiences can replace dodging donkeys and homemade speed bumps as you buzz along coastal Hwy 200 or chug up mountain roads in a VW Beetle. It's often the only way to reach those isolated beaches and tiny villages.

See p281 for a warning about risks of highway robbery in some areas, and p295 and p297 for information on the paperwork required for bringing a vehicle into Mexico.

Automobile Associations

Sectur, the Mexican tourism ministry, maintains a network of *Ángeles Verdes* (Green Angels) – bilingual mechanics in green uniforms and green trucks, who patrol 60,000km of major highways throughout the country daily during daylight hours looking for tourists in trouble. They make minor repairs, change tires, provide fuel and oil, and arrange towing and other assistance if necessary. Service is free; parts, gasoline and oil are provided at cost. If you are near a phone when your car has problems, you can call their **24-hour hotline** (☎ 078). There's a map of the roads they patrol at www.sectur.gob.mx/wb2/sectur /sect_9454_rutas_carreteras.

Bring Your Own Vehicle

Drivers should know some Spanish and have basic mechanical knowledge, reserves of patience and access to extra cash for emergencies. Good makes of car to take to Mexico are Volkswagen, Nissan, General Motors and Ford, which have plants in Mexico and dealers in most big towns. A sedan with a trunk (boot) provides safer storage than a station wagon or hatchback. For security, have something to immobilize the steering wheel, and consider getting a kill switch installed.

Motorcycling in Mexico is not for the fainthearted. Roads and traffic can be rough, and parts and mechanics hard to come by. The parts you'll most easily find will be for Kawasaki, Honda and Suzuki bikes.

Driver's License

To drive a motor vehicle in Mexico, you need a valid driver's license from your home country.

Fuel & Spare Parts

All *gasolina* (gasoline) and diesel fuel in Mexico is sold by the government's monopoly, Pémex (Petróleos Mexicanos). Most towns, even small ones, have a Pémex station, and the stations are pretty common on most major roads. Nevertheless, in remote areas you should fill up whenever you can.

The gasoline on sale is all *sin plomo* (unleaded). At the time of research, a liter cost about US$0.60 (US$2.40 a US gallon). Gas stations have pump attendants (who appreciate a tip of US$0.20 to US$0.50).

Mexican mechanics are resourceful, and most repairs can be done quickly and inexpensively, but it still pays to take as many spare parts as you can manage (spare fuel filters are very useful). Tires (including spare), shock absorbers and suspension should be in good condition.

Hire

Auto rental in Mexico is expensive by US or European standards but not hard to organize. You can book by Internet, phone or in person and pick up cars at city offices, at airports, at many big hotels and sometimes at bus terminals.

Renters must provide a valid driver's license (your home license is OK), passport and major credit card, and are usually required to be aged at least 21 (or sometimes 25; otherwise, if you're aged 21 to 24 you may have to pay a surcharge). Be sure to read the small print of the rental agreement. In addition to the basic rental rate, you pay tax and insurance costs to the rental company, and the full insurance that rental companies encourage can almost double the basic cost. You'll usually have the option of taking liability-only insurance at a lower rate. Ask exactly what the insurance options cover: theft and damage insurance may only cover a percentage of costs. It's best to have plenty of liability

coverage: Mexican law permits the jailing of drivers after an accident until they have met their obligations to third parties. The complimentary car-rental insurance offered with some US credit cards does not usually cover Mexico.

Local firms may or may not be cheaper than the big international ones. In most places the cheapest car available (often a Volkswagen Beetle) costs US$50 to US$60 a day including unlimited kilometers, insurance and tax. If you rent by the week or month or during the low season the per-day cost can come down by 20% to 40%.

Here is contact information (with Mexican phone numbers) for some major firms:

Alamo (☎ 800-849-8001; www.alamo.com)
Avis (☎ 800-288-88-88; www.avis.com.mx)
Budget (☎ 55-5705-5061; www.budget.com.mx)
Dollar (☎ 998-886-23-00; www.dollar.com)
Hertz (☎ 800-709-50-00; www.hertz.com)
National (☎ 800-716-6625; www.nationalcar.com.mx)
Thrifty (☎ 55-5207-1100; www.thrifty.com.mx)

Insurance

For information about motor insurance in Mexico, see p295.

Road Conditions

Many Mexican highways, even some toll highways, are not up to the standards of US, Canadian or European ones. Still, the main roads are serviceable and fairly fast when traffic is not heavy. Mexicans on the whole drive cautiously, and traffic density, poor surfaces and frequent hazards (potholes, speed bumps, animals, bicycles, children) all help to keep speeds down.

Road Hazards

Driving on a dark night is best avoided since unlit vehicles, rocks, pedestrians and animals on the roads are common. Hijacks and robberies do occur, most often after dark.

In towns and cities and on rural roads, be especially wary of *Alto* (Stop) signs, *topes* (speed bumps) and holes in the road. They are often not where you'd expect, and missing one can cost you a traffic fine or car damage. Speed bumps are also used to slow traffic on highways that pass through built-up areas: they are not always signed, and some of them are severe!

Road Rules

Drive on the right-hand side of the road. Speed limits range between 80km/h and 120km/h on open highways (less when highways pass through built-up areas), and between 30km/h and 50km/h in towns and cities. Seat belts are obligatory for all occupants of a car, and children under five must be strapped into safety seats in the rear.

One-way streets are the rule in cities. Priority at street intersections is indicated by thin black and red rectangles containing white arrows. A black rectangle facing you means you have priority; a red one means you don't. The white arrows indicate the direction of traffic on the cross street; if the arrow points both ways, it's a two-way street.

HITCHHIKING

Hitchhiking is never entirely safe in any country in the world, and is not recommended. Travelers who decide to hitch should understand that they are taking a small but potentially serious risk. People who do choose to hitch will be safer if they travel in pairs and let someone know where they are planning to go. A woman traveling alone certainly should not hitchhike in Mexico, and even two women together is not advisable.

LOCAL TRANSPORTATION
Bicycle

Most Mexican towns and cities are flat enough to make cycling an option. Seek out the less traffic-infested routes and you should enjoy the experience. Even Mexico City has its biking enthusiasts. You can rent bikes in several towns and cities for US$10 to US$15 a day.

Boat

Here and there you may find yourself traveling by boat to an outlying beach, along a river or across a lake or lagoon. The craft are usually *lanchas* (fast, open outboard boats). Fares vary widely: on average costs are about US$1 a minute if you have to charter the whole boat (haggle!), or around US$1 for five to 10 minutes if it's a public service.

Bus

Generally known as *camiones,* local buses are often the cheapest way to get around cities and out to nearby towns and villages. They run everywhere frequently and are cheap. Fares in cities are rarely more than US$0.50. In many cities, fleets of small, modern *microbuses* have replaced the noisy, dirty and crowded older buses.

Buses usually halt only at fixed *paradas* (bus stops), though in some places you can hold your hand out to stop one at any street corner.

Colectivo, Combi, Minibus & Pesero

These are all names for vehicles that function as something between a shared taxi and a bus, running along fixed urban routes usually displayed on the windshield. They're cheaper than taxis and quicker than buses. They will pick you up or drop you off on any corner along their route: to stop one, go to the curb and wave your hand. Tell the driver where you want to go. Usually, you pay at the end of the trip and the fare (a little higher than a bus fare) depends on how far you go. In some northern border towns, *pesero* is used to mean a city bus.

Taxi

Taxis are common in towns and cities, and surprisingly economical. City rides cost around US$1 per kilometer, and in some cities there's a posted fixed rate for journeys within defined central areas. If a taxi has a meter, you can ask the driver if it's working (*'¿Funciona el taxímetro?'*). If it's not, or if the taxi doesn't have a meter, establish the price of the ride before getting in (this may involve a bit of haggling.)

Some airports and big bus terminals have a system of authorized ticket-taxis: you buy a fixed-price ticket to your destination from a special *taquilla* (ticket window) and then hand it to the driver instead of paying cash. This saves haggling and major rip-offs, but fares are usually higher than you could get on the street.

In some (usually rural) areas, some taxis operate on a *colectivo* basis, following set routes, often from one town or village to another, and picking up or dropping off passengers anywhere along that route. Fares per person are around one-quarter of the normal cab fare.

Health Dr David Goldberg

Travelers to Pacific Mexico need to be concerned chiefly about food-borne diseases, though mosquito-borne infections can also be a problem. Most of these illnesses are not life threatening, but they can certainly have an impact on your trip or even ruin it. Besides getting the proper vaccinations, it's important that you bring along a good insect repellent and exercise great care in what you eat and drink.

BEFORE YOU GO

Bring medications in their original containers, clearly labeled. A signed, dated letter from your physician describing all medical conditions and medications, including generic names, is also a good idea. If carrying syringes or needles, be sure to have a physician's letter documenting their medical necessity.

INSURANCE

Mexican medical treatment is generally inexpensive for common diseases and minor treatment, but if you suffer from a serious medical problem, you may want to find a private hospital or fly out for treatment. Travel insurance can typically cover the costs. Some US health insurance policies stay in effect (at least for a limited time) if you travel abroad, but it's worth checking exactly what you'll be covered for in Mexico. For people whose medical insurance or national health systems don't extend to Mexico – which includes most non-Americans – a travel policy is advisable. Check the Travel Links section of the **Lonely Planet website** (www.lonelyplanet.com.au/travel_links/) for more information.

You may prefer a policy that pays doctors or hospitals directly rather than requiring you to pay on the spot and claim later. If you have to claim later, keep all documentation. Some policies ask you to call collect to a center in your home country, where an immediate assessment of your problem is made. Check that the policy covers ambulances or an emergency flight home. Some policies offer lower and higher medical-expense options; the higher ones are chiefly for countries such as the USA, which have extremely high medical costs. There is a wide variety of policies available, so check the small print.

RECOMMENDED VACCINATIONS

Since most vaccines don't produce immunity until at least two weeks after they're given, visit a physician four to eight weeks before departure. Ask your doctor for an International Certificate of Vaccination (otherwise known as the yellow booklet), which will list all the vaccinations you've received. This is mandatory for countries that require proof of yellow fever vaccination upon entry, but it's a good idea to carry it wherever you travel.

The only required vaccine for entry into Mexico is yellow fever, and that's only if you're arriving from a yellow fever-infected country in Africa or South America. However, a number of vaccines are recommended (see table following). Note that some of these are not approved for use by children and pregnant women – check with your physician.

MEDICAL CHECKLIST

It is a very good idea to carry a medical and first-aid kit with you, to help yourself in

Vaccine	Recommended for	Dosage	Side effects
hepatitis A	all travelers	1 dose before trip; booster 6-12 months later	soreness at injection site; headaches; body aches
typhoid	all travelers	4 capsules by mouth, 1 taken every other day	abdominal pain; nausea; rash
yellow fever	travelers arriving from a yellow fever–infected area in Africa or the Americas	1 dose lasts 10 years	headaches; body aches; severe reactions are rare
hepatitis B	long-term travelers in close contact with the local population	3 doses over 6-month period	soreness at injection site; low-grade fever
rabies	travelers who may have contact with animals and may not have access to medical care	3 doses over 3-4 week period	soreness at injection site; headaches; body aches
tetanus-diphtheria	all travelers who haven't had booster within 10 years	1 dose lasts 10 years	soreness at injection site
measles	travelers born after 1956 who've had only 1 measles vaccination	1 dose	fever; rash; joint pains; allergic reactions
chickenpox	travelers who've never had chickenpox	2 doses 1 month apart	fever; mild case of chickenpox

HEALTH

the case of minor illness or injury. Following is a list of items you should consider packing.

- acetaminophen/paracetamol (eg Tylenol) or aspirin
- adhesive or paper tape
- antibacterial ointment (eg Bactroban) for cuts and abrasions
- antibiotics
- antidiarrheal drugs (eg loperamide)
- antihistamines (for hay fever and allergic reactions)
- anti-inflammatory drugs (eg ibuprofen)
- bandages, gauze, gauze rolls
- DEET-containing insect repellent for the skin
- iodine tablets (for water purification)
- oral rehydration salts
- permethrin-containing insect spray for clothing, tents and bed nets
- pocket knife
- scissors, safety pins, tweezers
- steroid cream or cortisone (for poison ivy and other allergic rashes)
- sun block
- syringes and sterile needles
- thermometer

INTERNET RESOURCES

There is a wealth of travel health advice on the Internet. For further information, the **Lonely Planet website** (www.lonelyplanet.com) is a good place to start. The **World Health Organization** (www.who.int/ith) publishes a superb book called *International Travel and Health*, which is revised annually and is available online at no cost. Another website of general interest is **MD Travel Health** (www.mdtravelhealth.com), which provides complete travel health recommendations for every country, updated daily, also at no cost.

It's usually a good idea to consult your government's travel health website before departure, if one is available.

Australia www.dfat.gov.au/travel/
Canada http://www.hc-sc.gc.ca/english/index.html
New Zealand (www.mfat.govt.nz/travel)
UK (www.dh.gov.uk/PolicyAndGuidance/HealthAdviceFor Travellers/fs/en)
United States www.cdc.gov/travel/

FURTHER READING

For further information, see *Healthy Travel Central & South America,* also from Lonely Planet. If you're traveling with children,

Lonely Planet's *Travel with Children* may be useful. The *ABC of Healthy Travel*, by E Walker et al, and *Medicine for the Outdoors*, by Paul S Auerbach, are other valuable resources.

IN TRANSIT

DEEP VEIN THROMBOSIS (DVT)

Blood clots may form in the legs (deep vein thrombosis) during plane flights, chiefly because of prolonged immobility. The longer the flight, the greater the risk. Though most blood clots are reabsorbed uneventfully, some may break off and travel through the blood vessels to the lungs, where they could cause life-threatening complications.

The chief symptom of DVT is swelling or pain of the foot, ankle, or calf, usually but not always on just one side. When a blood clot travels to the lungs, it may cause chest pain and breathing difficulties. Travelers with any of these symptoms should immediately seek medical attention.

To prevent the development of DVT on long flights you should walk about the cabin, perform isometric compressions of the leg muscles (ie contract the leg muscles while sitting), drink plenty of fluids, and avoid alcohol and tobacco.

JET LAG & MOTION SICKNESS

Jet lag is common when crossing more than five time zones, resulting in insomnia, fatigue, malaise or nausea. To avoid jet lag try drinking plenty of fluids (nonalcoholic) and eating light meals. Upon arrival, get exposure to natural sunlight and readjust your schedule (for meals, sleep etc) as soon as possible.

Antihistamines such as dimenhydrinate (Dramamine) and meclizine (Antivert, Bonine) are usually the first choice for treating motion sickness. Their main side effect is drowsiness. An herbal alternative is ginger, which works like a charm for some people.

IN MEXICO

AVAILABILITY & COST OF HEALTH CARE

There are a number of first-rate hospitals in Puerto Vallarta. In general, private facilities offer better care, though at greater cost, than public hospitals.

Adequate medical care is available in other major cities, but facilities in rural areas may be limited. The **US embassy** (www.usembassy-mexico.gov/guadalajara/GePVhospitals.htm) provides an online directory to local physicians and hospitals in Puerto Vallarta.

Many doctors and hospitals expect payment in cash, regardless of whether you have travel health insurance. If you develop a life-threatening medical problem, you'll probably want to be evacuated to a country with state-of-the-art medical care. Since this may cost tens of thousands of dollars, be sure you have insurance to cover this before you depart.

Mexican pharmacies are identified by a green cross and a 'Farmacia' sign. Most are well supplied and the pharmacists well trained. Reliable pharmacy chains include Sanborns, Farmacia Guadalajara, Benavides and Farmacia Fenix. Some medications requiring a prescription in the US may be dispensed in Mexico without a prescription. To find an after-hours pharmacy, ask your hotel concierge or check the front door of a local pharmacy, which will often post the name of a nearby pharmacy that is open for the night.

INFECTIOUS DISEASES
Cholera

Cholera is an intestinal infection acquired through ingestion of contaminated food or water. The main symptom is profuse, watery diarrhea, which may be so severe that it causes life-threatening dehydration. The key treatment is drinking oral rehydration solution. Antibiotics are also given, usually tetracycline or doxycycline, though quinolone antibiotics such as ciprofloxacin and levofloxacin are also effective.

Only a handful of cases have been reported in Mexico over the last few years. Cholera vaccine is no longer recommended.

Hepatitis A

Hepatitis A occurs throughout Central America. It's a viral infection of the liver usually acquired by ingestion of contaminated water, food or ice, though it may also be acquired by direct contact with infected persons. The illness occurs worldwide, but the incidence is higher in developing nations. Symptoms may include fever, malaise, jaundice, nausea, vomiting and abdominal pain. Most cases resolve uneventfully, though hepatitis A occasionally causes severe liver damage. There is no treatment.

The vaccine for hepatitis A is extremely safe and highly effective. If you get a booster six to 12 months later, it lasts for at least 10 years. You really should get it before you go to Mexico or any other developing nation. Because the safety of hepatitis A vaccine has not been established for pregnant women or children under age two, they should instead be given a gammaglobulin injection.

Hepatitis B

Like hepatitis A, hepatitis B is a liver infection that occurs worldwide but is more common in developing nations. Unlike hepatitis A, the disease is usually acquired by sexual contact or by exposure to infected blood, generally through blood transfusions or contaminated needles. The vaccine is recommended only for long-term travelers (on the road more than six months) who expect to live in rural areas or have close physical contact with the local population. Additionally, the vaccine is recommended for anyone who anticipates sexual contact with the local inhabitants or a possible need for medical, dental or other treatments while abroad, especially if a need for transfusions or injections is expected.

The hepatitis B vaccine is safe and highly effective. However, a total of three injections are necessary to establish full immunity. Several countries added hepatitis B vaccine to the list of routine childhood immunizations in the 1980s, so many young adults are already protected.

Malaria

Malaria occurs in every country in Central America, including parts of Mexico. It's transmitted by mosquito bites, usually between dusk and dawn. The main symptom is high spiking fevers, which may be accompanied by chills, sweats, headaches, body aches, weakness, vomiting, or diarrhea. Severe cases may involve the central nervous system and lead to seizures, confusion, coma and death.

Taking malaria pills is strongly recommended when visiting rural areas in the states of Oaxaca, Chiapas, Sinaloa, Michoacán, Nayarit, Guerrero, Tabasco, Quintana Roo and Campeche; for the mountainous northern areas in Jalisco; and for an area between 24° and 28° north latitude, and 106° and 110° west longitude, which includes parts of the states of Sonora, Chihuahua and Durango.

For Mexico, the first choice malaria pill is chloroquine, taken once weekly in a dosage of 500mg, starting one to two weeks before arrival and continuing through the trip and for four weeks after departure. Chloroquine is safe, inexpensive and highly effective. Side effects are typically mild and may include nausea, abdominal discomfort, headache, dizziness, blurred vision or itching. Severe reactions are uncommon.

Protecting yourself against mosquito bites is just as important as taking malaria pills (see p307), since no pills are 100% effective.

If you may not have access to medical care while traveling, bring along additional pills for emergency self-treatment, which you should take if you can't reach a doctor and develop symptoms that suggest malaria, such as high spiking fevers. One option is to take four tablets of Malarone once daily for three days. If you start self-medication, you should try to see a doctor at the earliest possible opportunity.

If you develop a fever after returning home, see a physician, as malaria symptoms may not occur for months.

Malaria pills are not recommended for the major resorts along the Pacific Coast.

Rabies

Rabies is a viral infection of the brain and spinal cord that is almost always fatal. The rabies virus is carried in the saliva of infected animals and is typically transmitted through an animal bite, though contamination of any break in the skin with infected saliva may result in rabies. Rabies occurs in all Central American countries. Most cases in Mexico are related to dog bites, but bats and other wild species remain important sources of infection.

Rabies vaccine is safe, but a full series requires three injections and is quite expensive. Those at high risk for rabies, such as animal handlers and spelunkers (cave explorers), should certainly get the vaccine. In addition, those at lower risk for animal bites should consider asking for the vaccine if

HEALTH

they are traveling to remote areas and might not have access to appropriate medical care if needed. The treatment for a possibly rabid bite consists of rabies vaccine with rabies immune globulin. It's effective, but must be given promptly. Most travelers don't need rabies vaccine.

All animal bites and scratches must be promptly and thoroughly cleansed, and local health authorities contacted to determine whether or not further treatment is necessary (see opposite).

Typhoid Fever

Typhoid fever is caused by ingestion of food or water contaminated by a species of *Salmonella* known as *Salmonella typhi*. Fever occurs in virtually all cases. Other symptoms may include headache, malaise, muscle aches, dizziness, loss of appetite, nausea and abdominal pain. Either diarrhea or constipation may occur. Possible complications include intestinal perforation, intestinal bleeding, confusion, delirium or (rarely) coma.

Unless you expect to take all your meals in major hotels and restaurants, typhoid vaccine is a good idea. It's usually given orally, but is also available as an injection. Neither vaccine is approved for use in children under age two.

The drug of choice for typhoid fever is usually a quinolone antibiotic such as ciprofloxacin (Cipro) or levofloxacin (Levaquin), which many travelers carry for treatment of travelers' diarrhea. However, if you self-treat for typhoid fever, you may also need to self-treat for malaria, since the symptoms of the two diseases can be indistinguishable.

Yellow Fever

Yellow fever no longer occurs in Central America. Even so, many Central American countries, including Mexico, require yellow fever vaccine before entry if you're arriving from a country in Africa or South America where yellow fever occurs. If you're not arriving from a country with yellow fever, the vaccine is neither required nor recommended. Yellow fever vaccine is given only in approved yellow fever vaccination centers, which provide validated International Certificates of Vaccination (yellow booklets). The vaccine should be given at least 10 days before departure and remains effective for approximately 10 years. Reactions to the vaccine are generally mild and may include headaches, muscle aches, low-grade fevers or discomfort at the injection site. Severe, life-threatening reactions have been described but are extremely rare.

Other Infections
BRUCELLOSIS

This is an infection occurring in domestic and wild animals that may be transmitted to humans through direct animal contact or by consumption of unpasteurized dairy products from infected animals. Symptoms may include fever, malaise, depression, loss of appetite, headache, muscle aches and back pain. Complications can include arthritis, hepatitis, meningitis and endocarditis (heart valve infection).

CHAGAS' DISEASE

This is a parasitic infection transmitted by triatomine insects (reduviid bugs), which inhabit crevices in the walls and roofs of substandard housing in South and Central America. In Mexico, most cases occur in southern and coastal areas. The triatomine insect lays its feces on human skin as it bites, usually at night. A person becomes infected when he or she unknowingly rubs the feces into the bite wound or any other open sore. Chagas' disease is extremely rare in travelers. However, if you sleep in a poorly constructed house, especially one made of mud, adobe or thatch, you should be sure to protect yourself with a bed net and good insecticide.

GNATHOSTOMIASIS

This is a parasite acquired by eating raw or undercooked freshwater fish, including seviche, a popular lime-marinated fish salad. Cases have been reported from Acapulco and other parts of Mexico. The chief symptom is intermittent, migratory swellings under the skin, sometimes associated with joint pains, muscle pains or gastrointestinal problems. The symptoms may not begin until many months after exposure.

HISTOPLASMOSIS

This is caused by a soil-based fungus and acquired by inhalation, often when soil has been disrupted. Initial symptoms may include fever, chills, dry cough, chest pain and headache, sometimes leading to pneumonia. An outbreak was recently described among visitors to an Acapulco hotel.

HIV/AIDS
This has been reported from all Central American countries. Be sure to use condoms for all sexual encounters.

LEISHMANIASIS
This occurs in the mountains and jungles of all Central American countries. The infection is transmitted by sand flies, which arc about one third the size of mosquitoes. Leishmaniasis may be limited to the skin, causing slowly-growing ulcers over exposed parts of the body, or (less commonly) disseminate to the bone marrow, liver and splccn. The disease may be particularly severe in those with HIV. The disseminated form is rare in Mexico and is limited chiefly to the Balsas River basin in the southern states of Guerrero and Pueblas. There is no vaccine for leishmaniasis. To protect yourself from sand flies, follow the same precautions as for mosquitoes (right), except that netting must be finer mesh (at least 18 holes to the linear inch).

TULAREMIA
Also known as 'rabbit fever,' this is a bacterial infection that primarily affects rodents, rabbits and hares. Humans generally become infected through tick or deerfly bites or by handling the carcass of an infected animal. Occasional cases are caused by inhalation of an infectious aerosol. In Mexico, most cases occur in rural areas in the northern part of the country. Tularemia may develop as a flu-like illness, pneumonia or skin ulcers with swollen glands, depending upon how the infection is acquired. It usually responds well to antibiotics.

TYPHUS
This may be transmitted by lice in scattered pockets of the country.

TRAVELERS' DIARRHEA
To prevent diarrhea, avoid tap water unless it has been boiled, filtered or chemically disinfected (iodine tablets); only eat fresh fruits or vegetables if cooked or peeled; be wary of dairy products that might contain unpasteurized milk; and be highly selective when eating food from street vendors.

If you develop diarrhea, be sure to drink plenty of fluids, preferably an oral rehydration solution containing lots of salt and sugar. A few loose stools don't require treatment, but if you start having more than four or five stools a day you should start taking an antibiotic (usually a quinolone drug) and an antidiarrheal agent (such as Loperamide). If diarrhea is bloody or persists for more than 72 hours or is accompanied by fever, shaking chills or severe abdominal pain you should seek medical attention.

ENVIRONMENTAL HAZARDS
Animal Bites
Do not attempt to pet, handle or feed any animal, with the exception of domestic animals known to be free of any infectious disease. Most animal injuries are directly related to a person's attempt to touch or feed the animal.

Any bite or scratch by a mammal, including bats, should be promptly and thoroughly cleansed with large amounts of soap and water, followed by application of an antiseptic such as iodine or alcohol. Contact the local health authorities immediately for possible postexposure treatment, whether or not you've been immunized against rabies. It may also be advisable to start an antibiotic, since wounds caused by animal bites and scratches frequently become infected. One of the newer quinolones, such as levofloxacin (Levaquin), which many travelers carry in case of diarrhea, would be an appropriate choice.

Air Pollution
Air pollution may be a significant problem. Pollution is typically most severe from December to May. Travelers with respiratory or cardiac conditions and those who are elderly or extremely young are at greatest risk for complications from air pollution, which may include cough, difficulty breathing, wheezing or chest pain. Minimize the risk by staying indoors, avoiding outdoor exercise and drinking plenty of fluids.

Mosquito Bites
To prevent mosquito bites, wear long sleeves, long pants, hats and shoes (rather than sandals). Bring along a good insect

HEALTH

repellent, preferably one containing DEET, which should be applied to exposed skin and clothing, but not to eyes, mouth, cuts, wounds or irritated skin. Products containing lower concentrations of DEET are as effective, but for shorter periods of time. In general, adults and children over 12 should use preparations containing 25% to 35% DEET, which usually lasts about six hours. Children between two and 12 years of age should use preparations containing no more than 10% DEET, applied sparingly, which will usually last about three hours. Neurological toxicity has been reported from DEET, especially in children, but appears to be extremely uncommon and generally related to overuse. Don't use DEET-containing compounds on children under the age of two.

Insect repellents containing certain botanical products, including oil of eucalyptus and soybean oil, are effective but last only 1½ to 2 hours. Where there is a high risk of malaria or yellow fever, use DEET-containing repellents. Products based on citronella are not effective.

For additional protection, apply permethrin to clothing, shoes, tents and bed nets. Permethrin treatments are safe and remain effective for at least two weeks, even when items are laundered. Permethrin should not be applied directly to skin.

Don't sleep with the window open unless there is a screen. If sleeping outdoors or in accommodation that allows entry of mosquitoes, use a bed net treated with permethrin, with edges tucked in under the mattress. The mesh size should be less than 1.5mm. Alternatively, use a mosquito coil, which will fill the room with insecticide through the night. Repellent-impregnated wristbands are not effective.

Snake & Scorpion Bites

Venomous snakes in the region include the bushmaster, fer-de-lance, coral snake and various species of rattlesnakes. The fer-de-lance is the most lethal. It generally does not attack without provocation, but may bite humans who accidentally come too close as its lies camouflaged on the forest floor. The bushmaster is the world's largest pit viper, measuring up to 4m in length. Like other pit vipers, the bushmaster has a heat-sensing pit between the eye and nostril

on each side of its head, which it uses to detect the presence of warm-blooded prey.

Coral snakes are somewhat retiring and tend not to bite humans. North of Mexico City, all coral snakes have a red, yellow, black, yellow, red banding pattern, with red and yellow touching, in contrast to non-venomous snakes, where the red and yellow bands are separated by black. South of Mexico City, the banding patterns become more complex and this distinction is not useful.

In the event of a venomous snake bite, place the victim at rest, keep the bitten area immobilized, and move them immediately to the nearest medical facility. Avoid tourniquets, which are no longer recommended.

Scorpions are a problem in much of Mexico. If stung, you should immediately apply ice or cold packs, immobilize the affected body part and go to the nearest emergency room. To prevent scorpion stings, be sure to inspect and shake out clothing, shoes and sleeping bags before use, and wear gloves and protective clothing when working around piles of wood or leaves.

Sun

To protect yourself from excessive sun exposure, you should stay out of the midday sun, wear sunglasses and a wide-brimmed hat, and apply sunscreen with SPF 15 or higher, providing both UVA and UVB protection. Sunscreen should be generously applied to all exposed parts of the body approximately 30 minutes before sun exposure and be reapplied after swimming or vigorous activity. Drink plenty of fluids and avoid strenuous exercise when the temperature is high.

Tick Bites

To protect yourself from tick bites, follow the same precautions as for mosquitoes, except that boots are preferable to shoes, with pants tucked in. Be sure to perform a thorough tick check at the end of each day. You'll generally need the assistance of a friend or mirror for a full examination. Remove ticks with tweezers, grasping them firmly by the head. Insect repellents based on botanical products, described above, have not been adequately studied for insects other than mosquitoes and cannot be recommended to prevent tick bites.

Water

Tap water in Mexico is generally not safe to drink. Vigorous boiling for one minute is the most effective means of water purification. At altitudes greater than 2000m, boil for three minutes.

Another option is to disinfect water with iodine pills. Instructions are usually enclosed and should be carefully followed. Or you can add 2% tincture of iodine to one quart or liter of water (five drops to clear water, 10 drops to cloudy water) and let stand for 30 minutes. If the water is cold, a longer time may be required. The taste of iodinated water can be improved by adding vitamin C (ascorbic acid). Don't consume iodinated water for more than a few weeks. Pregnant women, those with a history of thyroid disease and those allergic to iodine should not drink iodinated water.

A number of water filters are on the market. Those with smaller pores (reverse osmosis filters) provide the broadest protection, but they are relatively large and are readily plugged by debris. Those with somewhat larger pores (microstrainer filters) are ineffective against viruses, although they remove other organisms. Manufacturers' instructions must be carefully followed.

TRAVELING WITH CHILDREN & WOMEN'S HEALTH

In general, it's safe for children and pregnant women to go to Mexico. However, because some of the vaccines listed previously are not approved for use in children and pregnancy, these travelers should be particularly careful not to drink tap water or consume any questionable food or beverage. Also, when traveling with children, make sure they're up to date on all routine immunizations. It's sometimes appropriate to give children some of their vaccines a little early before visiting a developing nation. You should discuss this with your pediatrician. If pregnant, bear in mind that should a complication such as premature labor develop while abroad, the quality of medical care may not be comparable to that in your home country.

Since yellow fever vaccine is not recommended for pregnant women or children less than nine months old, if you are arriving from a country with yellow fever, obtain a waiver letter, preferably written on letterhead stationery and bearing the stamp used by official immunization centers to validate the International Certificate of Vaccination.

HEALTH

Language

CONTENTS

The predominant language of Mexico is Spanish. Mexican Spanish is unlike Castilian Spanish (the language of much of Spain) in two main respects: in Mexico the Castilian lisp has more or less disappeared and numerous indigenous words have been adopted. About 50 indigenous languages are spoken as a first language by more than seven million people, and about 15% of these don't speak Spanish.

Travelers in cities, towns and larger villages can almost always find someone who speaks at least some English. All the same, it is advantageous and courteous to know at least a few words and phrases in Spanish. Mexicans will generally respond much more positively if you attempt to speak to them in their own language.

It's easy enough to pick up some basic Spanish, and for those who want to learn the language in greater depth, courses are available in several cities in Mexico (see Language Courses, p281). You can also study using books, records and tapes before you leave home. These resources are often available for loan from public libraries. Evening or college courses are also an excellent way to get started.

For a more comprehensive guide to the Spanish of Mexico, get a copy of Lonely Planet's *Mexican Spanish Phrasebook*. For words and phrases that will come in handy when dining, see p55.

PRONUNCIATION

Spanish spelling is phonetically consistent, meaning that there's a clear and consistent relationship between what you see in writing and how it's pronounced. In addition, most Spanish sounds have English equivalents, so English speakers shouldn't have too much trouble being understood.

Vowels

a	as in 'father'
e	as in 'met'
i	as in 'marine'
o	as in 'or' (without the 'r' sound)
u	as in 'rule'; the 'u' is not pronounced after **q** and in the letter combinations **gue** and **gui**, unless it's marked with a diaeresis (eg *argüir*), in which case it's pronounced as English 'w'
y	at the end of a word or when it stands alone, it's pronounced as the Spanish **i** (eg *ley*); between vowels within a word it's as the 'y' in 'yonder'

Consonants

As a rule, Spanish consonants resemble their English counterparts. The exceptions are listed below.

While the consonants **ch**, **ll** and **ñ** are generally considered distinct letters, **ch** and **ll** are now often listed alphabetically under **c** and **l** respectively. The letter **ñ** is still treated as a separate letter and comes after **n** in dictionaries.

b	similar to English 'b,' but softer; referred to as 'b larga'
c	as in 'celery' before **e** and **i**; otherwise as English 'k'
ch	as in 'church'
d	as in 'dog,' but between vowels and after **l** or **n**, the sound is closer to the 'th' in 'this'
g	as the 'ch' in the Scottish *loch* before **e** and **i** ('kh' in our guides to pronunciation); elsewhere, as in 'go'

h	invariably silent. If your name begins with this letter, listen carefully if you're waiting for public officials to call you.
j	as the 'ch' in Scottish *loch* (written as 'kh' in our guides to pronunciation)
ll	varies between the 'y' in 'yes' and the 'lli' in 'million'
ñ	as the 'ni' in 'onion'
r	a short **r** except at the beginning of a word, and after **l**, **n** or **s**, when it's often rolled
rr	very strongly rolled (not reflected in the pronunciation guides)
v	similar to English 'b,' but softer; referred to as 'b corta'
x	usually pronounced as **j** above; in some indigenous place names it's pronounced as an 's'; as in 'taxi' in other instances
z	as the 's' in 'sun'

Word Stress

In general, words ending in vowels or the letters **n** or **s** have stress on the next-to-last syllable, while those with other endings have stress on the last syllable. Thus *vaca* (cow) and *caballos* (horses) both carry stress on the next-to-last syllable, while *ciudad* (city) and *infeliz* (unhappy) are both stressed on the last syllable.

Written accents will almost always appear in words that don't follow the rules above, eg *sótano* (basement), *porción* (portion), *América*.

GENDER & PLURALS

In Spanish, nouns are either masculine or feminine, and there are rules to help determine gender (there are of course some exceptions). Feminine nouns generally end with -**a** or with the groups -**ción**, -**sión** or -**dad**. Other endings typically signify a masculine noun. Endings for adjectives also change to agree with the gender of the noun they modify (masculine/feminine -**o**/-**a**). Where both masculine and feminine forms are included in this language guide, they are separated by a slash, with the masculine form first, eg *perdido/a*.

If a noun or adjective ends in a vowel, the plural is formed by adding **s** to the end. If it ends in a consonant, the plural is formed by adding **es** to the end.

ACCOMMODATIONS

I'm looking for ...
Estoy buscando ...	e·*stoy* boos·*kan*·do ...

Where is ...?
¿Dónde hay ...?	*don*·de ai ...

  a cabin/cabana
una cabaña	*oo*·na ca·*ba*·nya

  a camping ground
un área para acampar	oon *a*·re·a *pa*·ra a·kam·*par*

  a guesthouse
una pensión	*oo*·na pen·*syon*

  a hotel
un hotel	oon o·*tel*

  a lodging house
una casa de huéspedes	*oo*·na *ka*·sa de wes·pe·des

  a posada
una posada	*oo*·na po·*sa*·da

  a youth hostel
un albergue juvenil	oon al·*ber*·ge khoo·ve·*neel*

MAKING A RESERVATION

(for phone or written requests)

To ...	A ...
From ...	De ...
Date	Fecha
I'd like to book ...	Quisiera reservar ... (see under 'Accommodations' for bed and room options)
in the name of ...	en nombre de ...
for the nights of ...	para las noches del ...
credit card ...	tarjeta de crédito ...
number	número
expiry date	fecha de vencimiento
Please confirm ...	Puede confirmar ...
availability	la disponibilidad
price	el precio

Are there any rooms available?
  ¿Hay habitaciones libres?
  ay a·bee·ta·*syon*·es *lee*·bres

I'd like a ... room.	Quisiera una habitación ...	kee·*sye*·ra *oo*·na a·bee·ta·*syon* ...
double	doble	*do*·ble
single	individual	een·dee·vee·*dwal*
twin	con dos camas	kon dos *ka*·mas

How much is it per ...?	¿Cuánto cuesta por ...?	*kwan*·to *kwes*·ta por ...
night	noche	*no*·che
person	persona	per·*so*·na
week	semana	se·*ma*·na

LANGUAGE

full board	pensión completa	pen·*syon* kom·*ple*·ta
private/shared bathroom	baño privado/ compartido	ba·nyo pree·*va*·do/ kom·par·*tee*·do
too expensive	demasiado caro	de·ma·*sya*·do *ka*·ro
cheaper	más económico	mas e·ko·no·*mee*·ko
discount	descuento	des·*kwen*·to

Does it include breakfast?
¿Incluye el desayuno?   een·*kloo*·ye el de·sa·*yoo*·no

May I see the room?
¿Puedo ver la   *pwe*·do ver la
habitación?   a·bee·ta·*syon*

I don't like it.
No me gusta.   no me *goos*·ta

It's fine. I'll take it.
Está bien. La tomo.   es·ta byen la *to*·mo

I'm leaving now.
Me voy ahora.   me *voy* a·o·ra

CONVERSATION & ESSENTIALS

When approaching a stranger for information you should always extend a greeting, and use only the polite form of address, especially with the police and public officials. Young people may be less likely to expect this, but it's best to stick to the polite form unless you're quite sure you won't offend by using the informal mode. The polite form is used in all cases in this guide; where options are given, the form is indicated by the abbreviations 'pol' and 'inf.'

Saying *por favor* (please) and *gracias* (thank you) are second nature to most Mexicans and a recommended tool in your travel kit.

Hi.	Hola.	o·la (inf)
Hello.	Buen día.	bwe·n *dee*·a
Good morning.	Buenos días.	bwe·nos *dee*·as
Good afternoon.	Buenas tardes.	bwe·nas *tar*·des
Good evening/ night.	Buenas noches.	bwe·nas *no*·ches
Goodbye.	Adiós.	a·*dyos*
See you soon.	Hasta luego.	as·ta *lwe*·go
Yes.	Sí.	see
No.	No.	no
Please.	Por favor.	por fa·*vor*
Thank you.	Gracias.	*gra*·syas
Many thanks.	Muchas gracias.	moo·chas *gra*·syas
You're welcome.	De nada.	de *na*·da
Apologies.	Perdón.	per·*don*
May I?	Permiso.	per·*mee*·so
Excuse me.	Disculpe.	dees·*kool*·pe

(used before a request or when apologizing)

How are things?
¿Qué tal?   ke tal

What's your name?
¿Cómo se llama usted?   ko·mo se *ya*·ma oo·*sted* (pol)
¿Cómo te llamas?   ko·mo te *ya*·mas (inf)

My name is ...
Me llamo ...   me *ya*·mo ...

It's a pleasure to meet you.
Mucho gusto.   moo·cho *goos*·to

The pleasure is mine.
El gusto es mío.   el *goos*·to es *mee*·o

Where are you from?
¿De dónde es/eres?   de *don*·de es/*er*·es (pol/inf)

I'm from ...
Soy de ...   soy de ...

Where are you staying?
¿Dónde está alojado?   don·de es·ta a·lo·*kha*·do (pol)
¿Dónde estás alojado?   don·de es·tas a·lo·*kha*·do (inf)

May I take a photo?
¿Puedo sacar una foto?   pwe·do sa·*kar* oo·na *fo*·to

DIRECTIONS

How do I get to ...?
¿Cómo llego a ...?   ko·mo *ye*·go a ...

Is it far?
¿Está lejos?   es·*ta le*·khos

Go straight ahead.
Siga/Vaya derecho.   see·ga/va·ya de·*re*·cho

Turn left.
Voltée a la izquierda.   vol·*te*·e a la ees·*kyer*·da

Turn right.
Voltée a la derecha.   vol·*te*·e a la de·*re*·cha

Can you show me (on the map)?
¿Me lo podría señalar   me lo po·*dree*·a se·nya·*lar*
(en el mapa)?   (en el *ma*·pa)

north	norte	*nor*·te
south	sur	soor
east	este	*es*·te
west	oeste	o·*es*·te
here	aquí	a·*kee*

SIGNS	
Entrada	Entrance
Salida	Exit
Información	Information
Abierto	Open
Cerrado	Closed
Prohibido	Prohibited
Comisaria	Police Station
Servicios/Baños	Toilets
Hombres/Varones	Men
Mujeres/Damas	Women

LANGUAGE

there	*ahí*	a·*ee*
avenue	*avenida*	a·ve·*nee*·da
block	*cuadra*	*kwa*·dra
street	*calle/paseo*	*ka*·lye/pa·*se*·o

EMERGENCIES

Help!	*¡Socorro!*	so·*ko*·ro
Fire!	*¡Fuego!*	*fwe*·go
I've been robbed.	*Me han robado.*	me an ro·*ba*·do
Go away!	*¡Déjeme!*	*de*·khe·me
Get lost!	*¡Váyase!*	*va*·ya·se
Call ...!	*¡Llame a ...!*	*ya*·me a
the pollce	*la policía*	la po·*lee see*·a
a doctor	*un médico*	oon *me*·dee·ko
an ambulance	*una ambulancia*	oo·na am·boo·*lan*·sya

It's an emergency.
Es una emergencia.   es *oo*·na e·mer·*khen*·sya
Could you help me, please?
¿Me puede ayudar,   me *pwe*·de a·yoo·*dar*
por favor?   por fa·*vor*
I'm lost.
Estoy perdido/a.   es·*toy* per·*dee*·do/a
Where are the toilets?
¿Dónde están los baños?   *don*·de stan los *ba*·nyos

HEALTH

I'm sick.
Estoy enfermo/a.   es·*toy* en·*fer*·mo/a
I need a doctor.
Necesito un doctor.   ne·se·*see*·to oon dok·*tor*
Where's the hospital?
¿Dónde está el hospital?   *don*·de es·*ta* el os·pee·*tal*
I'm pregnant.
Estoy embarazada.   es·*toy* em·ba·ra·*sa*·da
I've been vaccinated.
Estoy vacunado/a.   es·*toy* va·koo·*na*·do/a

I have ...	*Tengo ...*	*ten*·go ...
diarrhea	*diarrea*	dya·*re*·a
nausea	*náusea*	*now*·se·a
a headache	*un dolor de cabeza*	oon do·*lor* de ka·*be*·sa
a cough	*tos*	tos

I'm allergic to ...	*Soy alérgico/a a ...*	soy a·*ler*·khee·ko/a a ...
antibiotics	*los antibióticos*	los an·tee·*byo*·tee·kos
penicillin	*la penicilina*	la pe·nee·see·*lee*·na
nuts	*las fruta secas*	las *froo*·tas *se*·kas

I'm ...	*Soy ...*	soy ...
asthmatic	*asmático/a*	as·*ma*·tee·ko/a
diabetic	*diabético/a*	dya·*be*·tee·ko/a
epileptic	*epiléptico/a*	e·pee·*lep*·tee·ko/a

LANGUAGE DIFFICULTIES

Do you speak (English)?
¿Habla/Hablas (inglés)?   *a*·bla/*a*·blas (een·*gles*) (pol/inf)
Does anyone here speak English?
¿Hay alguien que hable   ai *al*·gyen ke *a*·ble
inglés?   een·*gles*
I (don't) understand.
(No) Entiendo.   (no) en·*tyen*·do
How do you say ...?
¿Cómo se dice ...?   *ko*·mo se *dee*·se ...
What does ...mean?
¿Qué significa ...?   ke seeg·nee·*fee*·ka ...

Could you please ...?	*¿Puede ..., por favor?*	*pwe*·de ... por fa·*vor*
repeat that	*repetirlo*	re·pe·*teer*·lo
speak more slowly	*hablar más despacio*	a·*blar* mas des·*pa*·syo
write it down	*escribirlo*	es·kree·*beer*·lo

NUMBERS

1	*uno*	*oo*·no
2	*dos*	dos
3	*tres*	tres
4	*cuatro*	*kwa*·tro
5	*cinco*	*seen*·ko
6	*seis*	says
7	*siete*	*sye*·te
8	*ocho*	*o*·cho
9	*nueve*	*nwe*·ve
10	*diez*	dyes
11	*once*	*on*·se
12	*doce*	*do*·se
13	*trece*	*tre*·se
14	*catorce*	ka·*tor*·se
15	*quince*	*keen*·se
16	*dieciséis*	dye·see·*says*
17	*diecisiete*	dye·see·*sye*·te
18	*dieciocho*	dye·see·*o*·cho
19	*diecinueve*	dye·see·*nwe*·ve
20	*veinte*	*vayn*·te
21	*veintiuno*	vayn·tee·*oo*·no
30	*treinta*	*trayn*·ta
31	*treinta y uno*	*trayn*·ta ee *oo*·no
40	*cuarenta*	kwa·*ren*·ta
50	*cincuenta*	seen·*kwen*·ta
60	*sesenta*	se·*sen*·ta
70	*setenta*	se·*ten*·ta
80	*ochenta*	o·*chen*·ta

LANGUAGE

90	noventa	no·ven·ta
100	cien	syen
101	ciento uno	syen·to oo·no
200	doscientos	do·syen·tos
1000	mil	meel
5000	cinco mil	seen·ko meel

PAPERWORK

birth certificate	certificado de nacimiento
border (frontier)	la frontera
car-owner's title	título de propiedad
car registration	registración
customs	aduana
driver's license	licencia de manejar
identification	identificación
immigration	migración
insurance	seguro
passport	pasaporte
temporary vehicle import permit	permiso de importación temporal de vehículo
tourist card	tarjeta de turista
visa	visado

SHOPPING & SERVICES

I'd like to buy ...
Quisiera comprar ... kee·sye·ra kom·prar ...
I'm just looking.
Sólo estoy mirando. so·lo es·toy mee·ran·do
May I look at it?
¿Puedo verlo/la? pwe·do ver·lo/la
How much is it?
¿Cuánto cuesta? kwan·to kwes·ta
That's too expensive for me.
Es demasiado caro es de·ma·sya·do ka·ro
para mí. pa·ra mee
Could you lower the price?
¿Podría bajar un poco po·dree·a ba·khar oon po·ko
el precio? el pre·syo
I don't like it.
No me gusta. no me goos·ta
I'll take it.
Lo llevo. lo ye·vo

Do you accept ...?
¿Aceptan ...? a·sep·tan ...
  American dollars
  dólares americanos do·la·res a·me·ree·ka·nos
  credit cards
  tarjetas de crédito tar·khe·tas de kre·dee·to
  traveler's checks
  cheques de viajero che·kes de vya·khe·ro

| less | menos | me·nos |
| more | más | mas |

| large | grande | gran·de |
| small | pequeño/a | pe·ke·nyo/a |

I'm looking for (the) ... *Estoy buscando ...* es·toy boos·kan·do

ATM	el cajero automático	el ka·khe·ro ow·to·ma·tee·ko
bank	el banco	el ban·ko
bookstore	la librería	la lee·bre·ree·a
exchange house	la casa de cambio	la ka·sa de kam·byo
general store	la tienda	la tyen·da
laundry	la lavandería	la la·van·de·ree·a
market	el mercado	el mer·ka·do
pharmacy/ chemist	la farmacia	la far·ma·sya
post office	la oficina de correos	la o·fee·see·na de ko·re·os
supermarket	el supermercado	el soo·per·mer·ka·do
tourist office	la oficina de turismo	la o·fee·see·na de too·rees·mo

What time does it open/close?
¿A qué hora abre/cierra?
a ke o·ra a·bre/sye·ra
I want to change some money/traveler's checks.
Quisiera cambiar dinero/cheques de viajero.
kee·sye·ra kam·byar dee·ne·ro/che·kes de vya·khe·ro
What is the exchange rate?
¿Cuál es el tipo de cambio?
kwal es el tee·po de kam·byo
I want to call ...
Quisiera llamar a ...
kee·sye·ra lya·mar a ...

airmail	correo aéreo	ko·re·o a·e·re·o
letter	carta	kar·ta
registered (mail)	certificado	ser·tee·fee·ka·do
stamps	timbres	teem·bres

TIME & DATES

What time is it?
¿Qué hora es? ke o·ra es
It's one o'clock.
Es la una. es la oo·na
It's seven o'clock.
Son las siete. son las sye·te
Half past two.
Dos y media. dos ee me·dya

midnight	medianoche	me·dya·no·che
noon	mediodía	me·dyo·dee·a
now	ahora	a·o·ra

today	hoy	oy
tonight	esta noche	es·ta no·che
tomorrow	mañana	ma·nya·na
yesterday	ayer	a·yer

Monday	lunes	loo·nes
Tuesday	martes	mar·tes
Wednesday	miércoles	myer·ko·les
Thursday	jueves	khwe·ves
Friday	viernes	vyer·nes
Saturday	sábado	sa·ba·do
Sunday	domingo	do·meen·go

January	enero	e·ne·ro
February	febrero	fe·bre·ro
March	marzo	mar·so
April	abril	a·breel
May	mayo	ma·yo
June	junio	khoo·nyo
July	julio	khoo·lyo
August	agosto	a·gos·to
September	septiembre	sep·tyem·bre
October	octubre	ok·too·bre
November	noviembre	no·vyem·bre
December	diciembre	dee·syem·bre

TRANSPORT
Public Transport

What time does	¿A qué hora ...	a ke o·ra ...
... leave/arrive?	sale/llega?	sa·le/ye·ga
the boat	el barco	el bar·ko
the bus (city)	el camión	el ka·myon
the bus (intercity)	el autobús	el ow·to·boos
the minibus	el pesero	el pe·se·ro
the plane	el avión	el a·vyon

the airport	el aeropuerto	el a·e·ro·pwer·to
the bus station	la estación de	la es·ta·syon de
	autobuses	ow·to·boo·ses
the bus stop	la parada de	la pa·ra·da de
	autobuses	ow·to·boo·ses
a luggage locker	un casillero	oon ka·see·ye·ro
the ticket office	la taquilla	la ta·kee·ya

A ticket to ..., please.
  Un boleto a ..., por favor.   oon bo·le·to a ... por fa·vor
What's the fare to ...?
  ¿Cuánto cuesta hasta ...?   kwan·to kwes·ta a·sta ...

student's	de estudiante	de es·too·dyan·te
1st class	primera clase	pree·me·ra kla·se
2nd class	segunda clase	se·goon·da kla·se
single/one-way	viaje sencillo	vee·a·khe sen·see·yo
round trip	redondo	re·don·do
taxi	taxi	tak·see

Private Transport

I'd like to	Quisiera	kee·sye·ra
hire a/an ...	rentar ...	ren·tar ...
4WD	un cuator por	oon kwa·tro por
	cuatro	kwa·tro
car	un coche	oon ko·che
motorbike	una moto	oo·na mo·to

bicycle	bicicleta	bee·see·kle·ta
hitchhike	pedir aventón	pe·deer a·ven·ton
pickup (ute)	pickup	pee·kop
truck	camión	ka·myon

Where's a petrol station?
  ¿Dónde hay una   don·de ai oo·na
  gasolinera?   ga·so·lee·ne·ra
How much is a liter of gasoline?
  ¿Cuánto cuesta el litro   kwan·to kwes·ta el lee·tro
  de gasolina?   de ga·so·lee·na

ROAD SIGNS

Though Mexico mostly uses the familiar international road signs, you should be prepared to encounter these other signs as well:

Acceso	Entrance
Estacionamiento	Parking
Camino en Reparación	Road Repairs
Ceda el Paso	Give way
Conserve Su Derecha	Keep to the Right
Curva Peligrosa	Dangerous Curve
Derrumbes	Landslides
Despacio	Slow
Desviación	Detour
Dirección Única	One-way
Escuela (Zona Escolar)	School (zone)
Hombres Trabajando	Men at Work
Mantenga Su Derecha	Keep to the Right
No Adelantar	No Overtaking
No Hay Paso	Road Closed
Pare/Stop	Stop
Peaje	Toll
Peligro	Danger
Prepare Su Cuota	Have Toll Ready
Prohibido Aparcar/	No Parking
No Estacionar	
Prohibido el Paso	No Entry
Puente Angosto	Narrow Bridge
Salida de Autopista	Freeway/Highway Exit
Topes/Vibradores	Speed Bumps
Tramo en Reparación	Road Under Repair
Vía Corta	Short Route (often
	a toll road)
Vía Cuota	Toll Highway

LANGUAGE

Please fill it up.
Lleno, por favor.   ye·no por fa·*vor*
I'd like (100) pesos worth.
Quiero (cien) pesos.   kye·ro (syen) pe·sos

diesel	diesel	dee·sel
gas (petrol)	gasolina	ga·so·lee·na
unleaded	gasolina sin	ga·so·lee·na seen
	plomo	plo·mo
oil	aceite	a·say·te
tire	llanta	yan·ta
puncture	agujero	a·goo·khe·ro

Is this the road to (...)?
¿Por aquí se va a (...)?
por a·kee se va a (...)
(How long) Can I park here?
¿(Por cuánto tiempo) Puedo estacionarme aquí?
(por kwan·to tyem·po) pwe·do ess·ta·syo·nar·me a·kee
Where do I pay?
¿Dónde se paga?
don·de se pa·ga
I need a mechanic/tow truck.
Necesito un mecánico/remolque.
ne·se·see·to oon me·ka·nee·ko/re·mol·ke
Is there a garage near here?
¿Hay un garaje cerca de aquí?
ai oon ga·ra·khe ser·ka de a·kee
The car has broken down (in ...).
El coche se se descompuso (en ...).
el ko·che se des·kom·poo·so (en ...)
The motorbike won't start.
La moto no arranca.
la mo·to no a·ran·ka
I have a flat tire.
Tengo una llanta ponchada.
ten·go oo·na yan·ta pon·cha·da
I've run out of petrol.
Me quedé sin gasolina.
me ke·de seen ga·so·lee·na

I've had an accident.
Tuve un accidente.
too·ve oon ak·see·den·te

TRAVEL WITH CHILDREN
I need ...
Necesito ...
ne·se·see·to ...
Do you have ...?
¿Hay ...?
ai ...
  a car baby seat
  un asiento de seguridad para bebés
  oon a·syen·to de se·goo·ree·dad pa·ra be·bes
  a child-minding service
  oon club para niños
  oon kloob pa·ra nee·nyos
  a children's menu
  un menú infantil
  oon me·noo een·fan·teel
  a daycare
  una guardería
  oo·na gwar·de·ree·a
  (disposable) diapers/nappies
  pañales (de usar y tirar)
  pa·nya·les de oo·sar ee tee·rar
  an (English-speaking) babysitter
  una niñera (que habla inglés)
  oo·na nee·nye·ra (ke a·bla een·gles)
  formula (milk)
  leche en polvo
  le·che en pol·vo
  a highchair
  una silla para bebé
  oo·na see·ya pa·ra be·be
  a potty
  una bacinica
  oo·na ba·see·nee·ka
  a stroller
  una carreola
  oona ka·re·o·la

Do you mind if I breast-feed here?
¿Le molesta que dé el pecho aquí?
le mo·les·ta ke de el pe·cho a·kee
Are children allowed?
¿Se admiten niños?
se ad·mee·ten nee·nyos

Also available from Lonely Planet:
Mexican Spanish Phrasebook

Glossary

For general information on Spanish, see p310. For food and drink terms, see p60; for transportation terms, see p315.

abarrotería – small grocery
agave – family of plants, including *maguey*
alfarería – potter's workshop
amate – paper made from tree bark
antojitos – appetizers; literally 'little whims'
Apdo – abbreviation for Apartado (Box) in addresses; hence Apdo Postal means Post Office Box
artesanías – handicrafts
arroyo – brook, stream
artesanías – handicrafts, folk arts
auriga – transport pickup

bahía – bay
balneario – bathing place, often a natural hot spring
banda – (Mexican brass-based big-band music)
barrio – district, neighborhood, often a poor neighborhood
béisbol – baseball
billete – bank note
boleto – ticket
brujo, -a – witch doctor, shaman; similar to *curandero, -a*

caballeros – literally 'horsemen,' but corresponds to 'gentlemen' in English; look for it on toilet doors
cabana – cabin, simple shelter
calle – street
callejón – alley
camión – truck or bus
camioneta – pickup truck
campesino, -a – country or rural person, peasant
casa de cambio – exchange bureau; place where currency is exchanged
**caseta de larga distancia, caseta de teléfono,
caseta telefónica** – public telephone call station
cazuela – clay cooking pot; usually sold in a nested set
cerro – hill
charreada – Mexican rodeo
charro – Mexican cowboy
chingar – literally 'to fornicate'; has numerous colloquial usages in Mexican Spanish equivalent to those in English
Churrigueresque – Spanish late-baroque architectural style; found on many Mexican churches
cigarro – cigarette
clavadistas – the cliff divers of Acapulco and Mazatlán
colectivo – minibus or car that picks up and drops off passengers along a predetermined route; can also refer to other types of transport, such as boats

colonia – neighborhood of a city, often a wealthy residential area
combis – minibuses
comedor – simple, inexpensive eateries
comida corrida – set-price lunch or dinner menu
completo – no vacancy, literally 'full up'; a sign you may see at hotel desks
conquistador – early Spanish explorer-conqueror
cordillera – mountain range
correos – post office
criollo – Mexican-born person of Spanish parentage; in colonial times considered inferior by peninsular Spaniards
crucero – crossroads or turnoff
crudo – hangover
cuota – toll; a vía cuota is a toll road
curandero, -a – literally 'curer'; a medicine man or woman who uses herbal and/or magical methods and often emphasizes spiritual aspects of disease

damas – ladies; the sign on toilet doors
dársena – pier, dock
Día de los Muertos – a celebration of the memory of the deceased, observed on November 1
Distrito Federal – the official name for Mexico City, often shortened to DF

edificio – building
ejido – communal landholding
embarcadero – jetty, boat landing
encomienda – a grant made to a *conquistador* of labor by or tribute from a group of indigenous people; the conquistador was supposed to protect and convert them, but usually treated them as little more than slaves
enramada – literally a bower or shelter, but it generally refers to a palm-frond–covered, open-air restaurant
enredo – wraparound skirt
escuela – school
esq – abbreviation of esquina (corner) in addresses
ex-convento – former convent or monastery

faja – waist sash used in traditional indigenous costume
feria – fair or carnival, typically occurring during a religious holiday
ficha – locker token available at bus terminals
fútbol – football (soccer)

gringo, -a – US or Canadian (and sometimes European, Australasian etc) visitor to Latin America; can be used derogatorily
gruta – cave, grotto

guarache – also *huarache*; woven leather sandal, often with tire tread as the sole
guardería de equipaje – room for storing luggage, eg in a bus station
güero, -a – fair-haired, fair-complexioned person; a more polite alternative to *gringo*

hacienda – estate; Hacienda (capitalized) is the Treasury Department
hombres – men; sign on toilet doors
huarache – see *guarache*
huipil, -es – indigenous woman's sleeveless tunic, usually highly decorated; can be thigh-length or reach the ankles
huitlacoche – a black fungus that grows on young corn; considered a delicacy

iglesia – church
INAH – Instituto Nacional de Antropología e Historia; the body in charge of most ancient sites and some museums
indígeno, -a – indigenous, pertaining to the original inhabitants of Latin America; can also refer to the people themselves
INI – Instituto Nacional Indígenista; set up in 1948 to improve the lot of indigenous Mexicans and to integrate them into society
ISH – *impuesto sobre hospedaje*; lodging tax on the price of hotel rooms
isla – island
IVA – *impuesto de valor agregado*, or 'ee-bah'; a 15% sales tax added to the price of many items

jai alai – the Basque game *pelota*, brought to Mexico by the Spanish; a bit like squash, played on a long court with curved baskets attached to the arm
jefe – boss or leader, especially political

lancha – fast, open, outboard boat
latifundio – large landholding; these sprang up after Mexico's independence from Spain
latifundista – powerful landowner who usurped communally owned land to form a *latifundio*
lleno – full, as with a car's fuel tank

machismo – Mexican masculine bravura
maguey – a type of agave; tequila and *mezcal* are made from its sap
malecón – waterfront street, boulevard or promenade
mariachi – ensemble of street musicians playing traditional ballads on guitars and trumpets
marimba – wooden xylophone-type instrument, popular in the south
menú del día – lunch special, also called *comida corrida*
mercado – market
Mesoamerica – the region inhabited by the ancient Mexican and Mayan cultures

mestizo – person of mixed (usually indigenous and Spanish) ancestry, ie most Mexicans
metate – shallow stone bowl with legs; for grinding maize and other foods
mezcal – an aolcoholic drink made from the sap of the *maguey* plant
mirador, -es – lookout point(s)
Montezuma's revenge – Mexican version of Delhi-belly or travelers' diarrhea
mordida – literally 'little bite,' a small bribe to keep the wheels of bureaucracy turning
mota – marijuana
mujeres – women; seen on toilet doors
municipio – small local-government area; Mexico is divided into 2394 of them

Nafta – North American Free Trade Agreement; see *TLC*
Nahuatl – language of the Nahua people, descendants of the Aztecs
nievería – frozen-dessert shop
Nte – abbreviation for *norte* (north), used in street names

Ote – abbreviation for *oriente* (east), used in street names

pachanga – party
palacio municipal – town or city hall, headquarters of the municipal corporation
palapa – thatched-roof shelter
paleta – frozen fruit on a stick
pandulces – sweet breads
panga – motorized skiff for fishing, excursions and transport
para llevar – (to go) in reference to food
parada – bus stop, usually for city buses
parque nacional – national park
paseo – boulevard, walkway or pedestrian street; also the tradition of strolling in a circle around the plaza in the evening
Pemex – government-owned petroleum extraction, refining and retailing monopoly
periférico – ring road
petate – mat, usually made of palm or reed
peyote – a hallucinogenic cactus
piñata – clay pot or papier-mâché mold decorated to resemble an animal, pineapple, star etc; filled with sweets and gifts and smashed open at fiestas
playa – beach
plaza de toros – bullring
plazuela – small plaza
Porfiriato – Porfirio Díaz's reign as president-dictator of Mexico for 30 years, until the 1910 revolution
portales – arcades
presidio – fort or fort's garrison
PRI – Partido Revolucionario Institucional (Institutional Revolutionary Party); the political party that ruled Mexico for most of the 20th century

propina – tip; different from a *mordida*, which is closer to a bribe
Pte – abbreviation for *poniente* (west), used in street names
puerto – port
pulmonía – special type of open-air taxi similar to a golf cart

Quetzalcóatl – plumed serpent god of pre-Hispanic Mexico

raicilla – rare agave distillage that may or may not have slightly psychedelic properties
ramada – thatched shelter
rebozo – long woolen or linen shawl covering the head or shoulders
reserva de la biósfera – biosphere reserve; an environmentally protected area where human exploitation is steered towards ecologically unharmful activities
retablo – altarpiece; or painting in a church to give thanks for miracles, answered prayers etc
río – river

s/n – sin número (without number); used in street addresses
sanitario – toilet, literally 'sanitary place'
sarape – blanket with opening for the head, worn as a cloak
Semana Santa – Holy Week, the week from Palm Sunday to Easter Sunday; Mexico's major holiday period, when accommodations and transport get very busy
servicios – toilets
sierra – mountain range
sitio – taxi stand; place
supermercado – supermarket
Sur – south; often seen in street names

taller – shop or workshop; a taller mecánico is a mechanic's shop, usually for cars; a taller de llantas is a tire-repair shop
tapatío, -a – person born in Jalisco state
taquilla – ticket window
telar de cintura – backstrap loom
templo – church; anything from a wayside chapel to a cathedral
tianguis – indigenous people's market
tienda – store
típico, -a – characteristic of a region; particularly used to describe food
TLC – Tratado de Libre Comercio; the North American Free Trade Agreement *(Nafta)*
topes – speed bumps; found on the outskirts of many towns and villages
torta – Mexican-style sandwich made with a roll
trova – folk music, ballad

UNAM – Universidad Nacional Autónoma de México (National Autonomous University of Mexico)

viajero, -a – traveler

zócalo – main plaza or square; a term used in some (but not all) Mexican towns
Zona Dorada – literally 'Pink Zone'; an area of expensive shops, hotels and restaurants in Mazatlán and Acapulco frequented most by the wealthy and tourists; by extension, a similar area in another city

Behind the Scenes

THIS BOOK

Puerto Vallarta & Pacific Mexico 2 was researched and written by Michael Read and Ben Greensfelder. Carolina Miranda wrote the Culture chapter, James Peyton wrote the Food & Drink chapter, and the Health chapter was adapted from text by Dr David Goldberg. Danny Palmerlee and Sandra Bao wrote the first edition. This guidebook was commissioned in Lonely Planet's Oakland office, and produced by the following:

Commissioning Editors Suki Gear, Greg Benchwick, Emily Wolman
Coordinating Editors Adrienne Costanzo, Simon Williamson
Coordinating Cartographer Damien Demaj
Coordinating Layout Designer Margie Jung
Managing Editor Jennifer Garrett
Managing Cartographers Julie Sheridan, Alison Lyall, Adrian Persoglia
Assisting Editors Brooke Clark, Evan Jones, Jeanette Wall
Cover Designer James Hardy
Project Managers Brigitte Ellemor, Sarah Sloane
Language Content Coordinator Quentin Frayne

Thanks to Sally Darmody, Matt Kelly, Kate McDonald, , Stephanie Pearson, Paige Penland, Wibowo Rusli, Meagan Williams, Celia Wood

THANKS
MICHAEL READ

Thanks to the many tourist offices, taxi drivers and random passersby who helped me find the hidden gems and cast out the stones. Thanks to co-author Ben Greensfelder for his superb work and congenial camaraderie. To Sandra Bao and Danny Palmerlee, the authors of this book's first edition, thank you for giving us a solid foundation to work from. Thanks also to commissioning editor Suki Gear for giving me the nod for this engrossing project, and to Adrienne Costanzo, Emily Wolman and Greg Benchwick for toiling over my manuscript. Los Tigres del Norte deserve special mention for helping me stay awake during the marathon drive from Mazatlán to Lázaro Cárdenas. Most of all, thanks to my wife, Irene Constanze Rietschel, and baby Malena Wilder Read for teaching me how to travel without leaving the house.

BEN GREENSFELDER

Gracias to everyone in Mexico who gave freely of their time, knowledge and kindness, including Gina Machorro and Paul Cleaver in Puerto Escondido, and Eva and Jim in Troncones. Warmest thanks to Cheryl Koehler for all her help around Oaxaca. On the Lonely Planet US side, many thanks to Suki Gear for signing me up, Greg Benchwick for staying on the case, Michael Read for suffering through the coordinating and Danny Palmerlee for blazing the trail in the first edition. In Oz, much gratitude to Alison Lyall and cartographer Damien Demaj for sorting out the maps, and editor Adrienne Costanzo for giving coherence to my fevered babbling. Finally, a world of thanks to my wife, Sandra, for navigating Acapulco and Mexico City, and for everything else.

THE LONELY PLANET STORY

The story begins with a classic travel adventure: Tony and Maureen Wheeler's 1972 journey across Europe and Asia to Australia. There was no useful information about the overland trail then, so Tony and Maureen published the first Lonely Planet guidebook to meet a growing need.

From a kitchen table, Lonely Planet has grown to become the largest independent travel publisher in the world, with offices in Melbourne (Australia), Oakland (USA) and London (UK). Today Lonely Planet guidebooks cover the globe. There is an ever-growing list of books and information in a variety of media. Some things haven't changed. The main aim is still to make it possible for adventurous travelers to get out there – to explore and better understand the world.

At Lonely Planet we believe travelers can make a positive contribution to the countries they visit – if they respect their host communities and spend their money wisely. Every year 5% of company profit is donated to charities around the world.

SEND US YOUR FEEDBACK

We love to hear from travelers – your comments keep us on our toes and help make our books better. Our well-traveled team reads every word on what you loved or loathed about this book. Although we cannot reply individually to postal submissions, we always guarantee that your feedback goes straight to the appropriate authors, in time for the next edition. Each person who sends us information is thanked in the next edition – and the most useful submissions are rewarded with a free book. See the Behind the Scenes section.

To send us your updates – and find out about Lonely Planet events, newsletters and travel news – visit our award-winning website: **www.lonelyplanet.com/feedback**.

Note: We may edit, reproduce and incorporate your comments in Lonely Planet products such as guidebooks, websites and digital products, so let us know if you don't want your comments reproduced or your name acknowledged. For a copy of our privacy policy, go to www.lonelyplanet .com/privacy.

OUR READERS

Many thanks to the travelers who used the last edition and wrote to us with helpful hints, useful advice and interesting anecdotes:

Tulio Aarun, Emily Achtenberg, Federico Arrizabalaga, David Authers, Rebecca Banyas, Jay Bautista, Noreen Beg, Ger Bekink, Jenny Campbell, Marianna Campbell, Claire Cappel, Marianne Casto, Daniel Delministro, Kristel Dempster, Louisa Dow, Nathalie Dupraz, Rob Erickson, Peter Eskow, Michael Evoy, Marc & Lisy Fairon, Kim Felmingham, Jiri Frybert, Tina Furnari, Diane Garmo, Gaelen Gates, Lucia Gayon, Enrico Halix, Daniel Hansen, Juan Havas, Judith Hendin, Nancy Heuman, Maarten Hustinx, Jan Hutta, Kara Hyne, Leandro Irigoyen, Leeann Jorgensen, James Kellum, Michael Kerr, Linda Kersey, Steve Keul, Peter Krebs, Lindy Laing, Stefan Landman, Jessa Lewis, John Lewis, Susan Lightfoot, Nora McCarthy, M McCusker, Sara Miller, Natalie Moore, Gustavo Morales, Eva Niepagenkemper, Antonio Orozco, Lucy Owen, Luca Pagani, Alena Parizkova, Nora Pyne, Jamie Reynolds, Peter Robinson, Dorna Sakurai, Laura Sawyer, Susi Schuegraf, Joann Elizabeth Seibert, Eric Stephen Singer, Ajay Skolka, Brian Taylor, Jim Tendick, Mark Terry, Kirstine Therkelsn, Evi Watt, Kat West, Brendan White, Liz Wittmann-Todd, Paul Yacht, Ginger Yaunt

Index

INDEX

INDEX

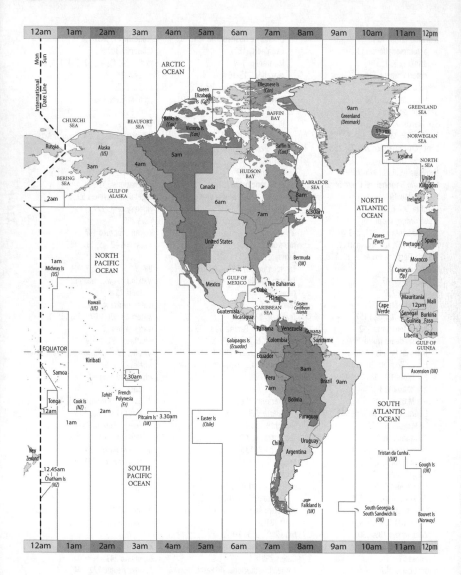

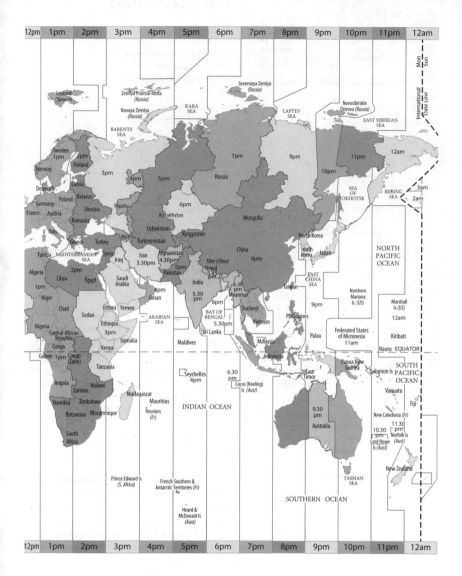

MAP LEGEND

ROUTES

Tollway	Unsealed Road
Freeway	One-Way Street
Primary Road	Street Mall/Steps
Secondary Road	Tunnel
Tertiary Road	Walking Trail
Lane	Walking Path
Under Construction	Pedestrian Overpass

TRANSPORT

Ferry — Rail

HYDROGRAPHY

River, Creek — Water
Mudflats

BOUNDARIES

State, Provincial — Cliff
Marine Park

AREA FEATURES

Airport	Land
Area of Interest	Mall
Beach, Desert	Market
Building	Park
Cemetery, Christian	Sports

POPULATION

○ CAPITAL (NATIONAL)	◉ CAPITAL (STATE)
● Large City	● Medium City
○ Small City	○ Town, Village

SYMBOLS

Sights/Activities
- Beach
- Christian
- Monument
- Museum, Gallery
- Point of Interest
- Pool
- Ruin

Eating
- Eating

Drinking
- Drinking
- Café

Entertainment
- Entertainment

Shopping
- Shopping

Sleeping
- Sleeping
- Camping

Transport
- Airport, Airfield
- Bus Station
- Parking Area
- Petrol Station
- Taxi Rank

Information
- Bank, ATM
- Embassy/Consulate
- Hospital, Medical
- Information
- Internet Facilities
- Police Station
- Post Office, GPO
- Telephone
- Toilets

Geographic
- Lighthouse
- Lookout
- Mountain, Volcano
- National Park

LONELY PLANET OFFICES

Australia
Head Office
Locked Bag 1, Footscray, Victoria 3011
☎ 03 8379 8000, fax 03 8379 8111
talk2us@lonelyplanet.com.au

USA
150 Linden St, Oakland, CA 94607
☎ 510 893 8555, toll free 800 275 8555
fax 510 893 8572
info@lonelyplanet.com

UK
72–82 Rosebery Ave,
Clerkenwell, London EC1R 4RW
☎ 020 7841 9000, fax 020 7841 9001
go@lonelyplanet.co.uk

Published by Lonely Planet Publications Pty Ltd
ABN 36 005 607 983

© Lonely Planet Publications Pty Ltd 2006

© photographers as indicated 2006

Cover photographs: cliff diver in Acapulco, World Travel Images/Alamy
(front); Two boys holding a ray fish, Pascale Beroujon/Lonely Planet
Images (back). Many of the images in this guide are available for
licensing from Lonely Planet Images: www.lonelyplanetimages.com.

Printed through Colorcraft Ltd, Hong Kong.
Printed in China